Racial and Ethnic Groups

Racial and Ethnic Groups

SIXTH EDITION

Richard T. Schaefer
Western Illinois University

HarperCollins*CollegePublishers*

Acquisitions Editor: Alan McClare
Project Coordination and Text Design: York Production Services
Supervising Production Editor: Lois Lombardo
Cover Design: John Callahan
Art Coordination: York Production Services
Photo Researcher: Karen Koblik
Electronic Page Makeup: York Production Services
Printer and Binder: R. R. Donnelley and Sons Company
Cover Printer: The Lehigh Press, Inc.

Racial and Ethnic Groups, Sixth Edition

Library of Congress Cataloging-in-Publication Data

Schaefer, Richard T.
    Racial and ethnic groups / Richard T. Schaefer. — 6th ed.
        p. cm.
    Includes bibliographical references and index.
    ISBN 0–673–52363–2
        1. Minorities—United States.   2. United States—Race relations.
    3. United States—Ethnic relations.   4. Prejudices—Unites States.
    I. Title.
    E184.A1S3   1996
    305.8'00973—dc20   95–47150
                                                                                    CIP

96 97 98 99 9 8 7 6 5 4 3 2 1

To my wife, Sandy

Contents

Chapter 5
ETHNICITY AND RELIGION 120

Part Three
MAJOR RACIAL AND ETHNIC MINORITY GROUPS IN THE UNITED STATES 151

Chapter 6
THE FIRST NATIVE AMERICANS 153

Chapter 7

THE MAKING OF AFRICAN AMERICANS IN A WHITE AMERICA　　189

Chapter 8

AFRICAN AMERICANS TODAY　　220

Preface

Race and ethnicity remain firmly a part of the national agenda. Immigration, affirmative action, inner-city economic development, race-based districting in elections, poverty, and the reform of welfare, to name a few, are issues that are debated. Terms like *underclass, glass ceiling,* and *angry white men* may be new, but they reflect the latest manifestations of intergroup conflict and the failure to address past problems adequately.

The very issue of national identity is also a part of the agenda. The public and politicians alike question, "How many immigrants can we accept?" and "How much should be done to make up for past discrimination?" We are also witnessing the emergence of race, ethnicity, and national identity as global issues. Nations throughout the world find themselves confronting similar issues, often with no more success than in the United States.

This book, like the earlier editions, reflects the changes accompanying recent events and displays how useful theoretical orientations and social science concepts can be in unraveling social relationships in a culturally diverse nation like the United States.

The information in this edition has been thoroughly updated. Relevant scholarly findings in a variety of disciplines have been incorporated. The feature "Listen to Their Voices" appears in every chapter. These selections include excerpts from the writings or speeches of noted members of racial and ethnic groups such as Martin Luther King, Jr., Nikki Giovanni, David Henry Hwang, and Nelson Mandela. Their writings will help students appreciate both the emotional and the intellectual energies felt by subordinate groups.

The changing social fabric of race and ethnic relation is apparent in the revisions since the fifth edition. Some examples are the following:

- Application of the concept *racial formation* (Chapter 1 and elsewhere)
- The latest evidence of ethnic and racial residential segregation (Chapter 1)
- The growing discussion of panethnic identity (Chapter 1 and elsewhere)
- Data on prejudice among subordinate racial and ethnic groups (Chapter 2)
- A section on Arab Americans and American Muslims (Chapter 2)
- Empirical evidence of the glass ceiling (Chapters 3, 8, 16)
- Attacks, political and legal, on affirmative action (Chapter 3)
- Political debates in the wake of the passage of Proposition 187 (Chapter 4)
- Evidence concerning whether immigration is an economic benefit or liability (Chapter 4)
- Religious and spiritual expression among Native Americans (Chapter 6)
- Religion as a significant social force among African Americans (Chapter 7)

- A provocative "Listen to Their Voices" entitled "Racism 101" (Chapter 8)
- The latest evidence on migrant farm workers in light of the legacy Cesar Chávez (Chapter 10)
- A case study on a Hmong community (Chapter 12)
- Sweatshop conditions in U.S. Chinatowns (Chapter 13)
- The double jeopardy experienced by women of color (Chapter 16)
- The Aboriginal Peoples, the Quebecois, and immigration in Canada (Chapter 17)
- The new tentative peace accords in Northern Ireland and in Israel (Chapter 17)

There are a total of 28 new tables and figures; 17 glossary terms have been added; and 78 of the readings listed in "For Your Information" are also new. In addition photographs, maps, and political cartoons have been updated.

Any constructive discussion of racial and ethnic minorities must do more than merely describe events. Part One, "Perspectives on Racial and Ethnic Groups," includes the relevant theories and operational definitions that ground the study of race and ethnic relations in the social sciences. We specifically present the functionalist, conflict, and labeling theories of sociology in their relation to the study of race and ethnicity. We show the relationship between subordinate groups and the study of stratification. You will find sociology such as the concept of racial formation and the conflict perspective. You will also be introduced to the dual labor market theory and the irregular economy from economics and reference group theory from psychology. The extensive treatment of prejudice and discrimination covers anti-White prejudice as well as the more familiar topic of bigotry aimed at subordinate groups. Discrimination is analyzed from an economic perspective, the discussion including the latest efforts to measure discrimination empirically and the continuing legal saga of attempts to define affirmative action's role.

In Part Two, "Ethnic and Religious Sources of Conflict," we examine some often-ignored sources of intergroup conflict in the United States: White ethnic groups and religious minorities. Diversity in the United States is readily apparent when we look at the ethnic and religious groups that have been formed primarily by immigration. Even refugees, now primarily from Haiti and Central America, continue to be a major issue.

Any student needs to be familiar with the past to understand present forms of discrimination and subordination. Part Three, "Major Racial and Ethnic Minority Groups in the United States," brings into sharper focus the history and contemporary status of Native Americans, African Americans, Hispanics, Asian Americans, and Jews in the United States. Social institutions such as family, education, politics, and the economy receive special attention for each group. It is only appropriate that institutions are given special notice because the author contends that institutional discrimination, rather than individual action, is the source of conflict between the subordinate and dominant elements in the United States.

Part Four, "Other Patterns of Dominance," includes topics definitely related to American racial and ethnic relations. The author recognizes, as have Gunnar Myrdal and Helen Mayer Hacker before, that relations between women and men resemble those between Blacks and Whites. Therefore, in this book, we consider the position of women as a subordinate group. Since the first edition of *Racial and Ethnic Groups,* published 17 years ago, debates over equal rights and abortion have shown no sign of resolution. For women of color, we document the double jeopardy suffered because of subordinate status twice over: race and gender. Perhaps we can best comprehend intergroup conflict in the United States by comparing it to the ethnic hostilities in other nations. The similarities and differences between the United States and other societies treated in this book are striking. Again, as in the fifth edition, we examine the tensions in Brazil, Israel, Northern Ireland, and South Africa to document further the diversity of intergroup conflict. In addition, we now also consider Canada from a perspective of ethnic relations.

Several features are included in the text to facilitate student learning. A "Chapter Outline" appears at the beginning of each chapter and is followed by "Highlights," a short section alerting students to important issues and topics to be addressed. To help students review, each chapter ends with a summary, "Conclusion." A bibliography, "For Further Information," provides references for additional research. The "Key Terms" are highlighted in italics when they are first introduced in the text and are listed with definitions at the conclusion of each chapter. In addition there is an end-of-book "Glossary" with full definitions referenced to chapter numbers. Added to each chapter in this edition are "Critical Thinking Questions," which allow the reader to reconsider some of the major issues raised in the chapter. An extensive illustration program, which includes maps and political cartoons, expands the text discussion and provokes thought. For the instructor, an "Instructor's Resource Manual," written by the author, serves as an effective reference and teaching aid. The manual includes a chapter overview, identification terms with page references, multiple-choice questions, essay questions, discussion questions and class topics, and a listing of audiovisual material.

Changes in race and ethnic relations will continue, because these relations are a part of our constantly changing behavior. *Racial and Ethnic Groups* gives the reader a firm knowledge of the past and the present, as well as a sufficient conceptual understanding to prepare for the future.

Acknowledgments

This revision creating a sixth edition benefited from the thoughtful reaction of my students at Western Illinois University, where special programs enabled me to teach the course in race and ethnicity to older students through independent home study and to inmates at a maximum-security prison, as well as to undergraduates. This edition benefits from my past collaborative writing experiences on other projects with Robert P. Lamm. The manuscript for the sixth edition was improved by the suggestions of Nancy Terjesen, Kent State University; Michael Collins, University of Wisconsin; Cynthia Chan Imanaka, Seattle Central Community College; Gail Gehrig, Lewis University; Pat Burton, Delaware Technical and Community College; William Egelman, Iona College; and Beverly M. John, Hampton University. I would also like to thank Christine Cardone for editorial assistance, Karen Koblik for photographic research, Susan Free and York Production Services for production assistance, Karen Nelson for manuscript preparation, and Scott Miner (Department of Geography, Western Illinois University) for cartographic work. My relationship with the publisher has been particularly gratifying because of the professional assistance I received from Alan McClare.

The task of writing and researching is often a lonely one. I have always found it an enriching experience, mostly because of the supportive home I share with my wife, Sandy, and our son, Peter. They know my appreciation and gratitude now as in the past and the future.

Richard T. Schaefer

PART One

PERSPECTIVES ON RACIAL AND ETHNIC GROUPS

Chapter
1

Understanding
Race and Ethnicity

Chapter Outline

Highlights

Minority groups are subordinated in terms of power and privilege to the *majority,* or dominant group. A minority is defined not by being outnumbered but by having five characteristics: distinguishing physical or cultural traits, involuntary membership, in-group marriage, awareness of subordination, and unequal treatment. Subordinate groups are classified in terms of *race, ethnicity, religion,* and *gender.* The *social* importance of race is significant through a process of *racial formation;* its *biological* significance is uncertain. The theoretical perspectives of *functionalism, conflict theory,* and *labeling* offer insights into the sociology of intergroup relations.

Social processes such as *immigration* can be identified as bringing about the existence of subordinate groups. Other processes such as *expulsion* may remove the presence of a subordinate group. Especially significant for race and ethnic relations in the United States today is the distinction between *assimilation* and *pluralism.* The former demands subordinate-group conformity to the dominant group, and the latter implies mutual respect among diverse groups.

The United States is a nation of widespread diversity. For example, in the West, shops catering to Indonesians flourish on famed Sunset Boulevard in Los Angeles, where it is not uncommon to hear the Indonesian language of Bahasa. In the East, in Lowell, Massachusetts, originally settled by Irish immigrants, 40 percent of the immigrant population is Cambodian, Hispanic, Laotian, and Vietnamese.

Such cultural diversity does not always come peacefully. For example, a White superintendent in a rural Georgia district angered local residents when he charged in 1995 that African-American students were being assigned to the lowest class grouping based on race, not on academic performance. In mid-1994, by a 3–2 vote, the school board of Lake County, Florida (north of Orlando), adopted a policy under which teachers are required to tell students that the culture, values, and political institutions of the United States are inherently "superior to other foreign or historic cultures." The board added that students should be instilled with an appreciation of the nation's heritage, including "strong family values, freedom of religion, and other basic values that are superior to other foreign or historic cultures" (D. Sharp, 1994; also see S. Brown, 1994; *New York Times,* 1995a; M. Puente, 1994).

Issues of race and ethnicity appear in all aspects of life. For example, baseball star Henry Aaron passed Babe Ruth's career record for home runs in 1969. Despite this achievement, he received racially linked death threats and hate mail because he had usurped a white man's place in history. Moreover, Aaron received few invitations for commercial endorsements, which instead went to white players who had more modest playing careers. Issues of race also exist in the music industry. The lyrics of some rap and rock music have recently promoted racism emphasizing violence against other groups. The college campus is not exempt from issues of race, ethnicity, and gender. Many universities with diverse populations, such as Stanford University and the University of Wisconsin, have instituted codes prohibiting discrimination or victimization of students on the basis of race, ethnicity, gender, or sexual preference.

People battle over language, culture, and ethnicity across the globe. In 1994, about 10,000 Russian troops were posted in Latvia, supposedly to protect the rights of Latvia's Russian minority. Despite this effort, Latvia maintains legislation that restricts residency to Latvian-speaking people. Ethnic Albanians make up 90 percent of the population of Kosovo, now a Serbian territory. However, Serbian rulers forbid the use of the native Albanian language. Further, beginning in 1993 we witnessed "ethnic cleansing" in Bosnia and Herzegovina and other parts of the former Yugoslavia with ethnic rivalries continuing into 1996. And perhaps the most devastating of all in recent years has been the brutal battle between the Tutsi and Hutu peoples of Burundi and Rwanda, leaving millions dead or as refugees (J. Fox, 1995; A. Neier, 1994).

Tensions in the United States arise in an extremely diverse nation, as shown in Table 1.1 At present, 15 percent of the population are members of racial minorities and another 9 percent are Hispanic. These percentages represent 1 out of 4, without counting White ethnic groups. Already, in 15 of the 28 largest U.S. cities, Whites are outnumbered by African Americans, Hispanics, and Asian Americans. The trend is toward even greater diversity. Between 1993 and 2050, as shown in Figure 1.1 on p. 7, the population in the United States is expected to go from 24 percent Black-Hispanic-Asian to 47 percent people of color.

Dealing with intergroup hostility is becoming increasingly complex. By 1990, people in the United States were speaking out against racial hatred, and laws were passed imposing special penalties for actions reflecting racial or ethnic bias. Critics of these efforts created the label *politically correct* (PC) to refer to many of the efforts on behalf of racial, ethnic, and religious minorities, as well as women. The controversy emerged especially on college campuses, where courses were introduced and sometimes required on issues of racial diversity. Opponents said these "PC" moves were watering down the curriculum. In some instances, students and even faculty were punished for offensive racist and sexist comments or actions raising serious concerns about freedom of expression. Where does the First Amendment protecting the freedom of speech end and unacceptable bigotry begin?

WHAT IS A SUBORDINATE GROUP?

Identifying a subordinate group or a minority in a society would seem to be a simple enough task: Single out the group with fewer members. In the United States, those groups readily identified as minorities—Blacks and Native Americans, for example—are outnumbered by non-Blacks and non-Native Americans. But minority status is not necessarily the result of being outnumbered. A social minority need not be a mathematical one. A *minority group* is a subordinate group whose members have significantly less control or power over their own lives than

Table 1.1   RACIAL AND ETHNIC GROUPS IN THE UNITED STATES, 1990

Classification	Number in Thousands	Percentage of Total Population
Racial Groups		
Whites	199,686	80.3
Blacks/African Americans	29,986	12.1
Native Americans, Eskimos, Aleuts	1,959	0.8
Chinese	1,645	0.7
Filipinos	1,407	0.6
Japanese	848	0.3
Asian Indians	815	0.3
Koreans	799	0.3
Vietnamese	615	0.2
Laotians	149	0.1
Cambodians	147	0.1
Ethnic Groups		
White ancestry (single or mixed)		
Germans	57,986	23.3
Irish	38,740	15.6
English	32,656	13.1
Italians	14,715	5.9
French	10,321	4.1
Poles	9,366	3.8
Jews	5,935	2.6
Hispanics (or Latinos)	22,354	9.0
Mexican Americans	13,496	5.4
Puerto Ricans	2,728	1.0
Cubans	1,044	0.4
Other	5,086	2.2
Total (all groups)	248,710	

Note: Percentages do not total 100 percent, and subheads do not add up to figures in major heads, since overlap between groups exists (e.g., Polish-American Jews or people of mixed ancestry, such as Irish and Italian). Therefore, numbers and percentages should be considered approximations. Data on Jews are for 1989.

Source: Bureau of the Census (1992, pp. 24–25; 1993a, pp. 18, 51).

the members of a dominant or majority group. *Minority* should be taken as synonymous with *subordinate,* and *dominant* will be used interchangeably with *majority.*

Confronted with evidence that a particular minority in the United States is subordinate to the will and whim of the majority, some individuals will respond, "Why not? After all, this is a democracy, and so the majority rules." The subordination of a minority, however, is more than its inability to rule over society. A member of a subordinate or minority group experiences a narrowing of life's opportunities—for success, education, wealth, the pursuit of happiness—that goes beyond any personal shortcoming he or she may have. A minority group does not share in

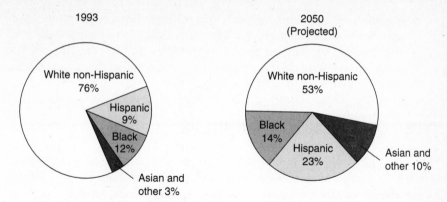

Figure 1.1 **Population of the United States by Race and Ethnicity, 1993 and 2050 (Projected)**
According to projections by the Bureau of the Census, the proportion of residents of the United States
who are White and non-Hispanic will decrease significantly by the year 2050. By contrast, there will be
a striking rise in the proportion of both Hispanic Americans and Asian Americans.

proportion to its numbers in what a given society, such as the United States,
defines as valuable.

Being superior in numbers does not guarantee a group control over its destiny
and assure it of majority status. In 1920, the majority of people in Mississippi and
South Carolina were African American, but in no way did African Americans have
as much significant control over their lives as Whites, let alone have control of the
states of Mississippi and South Carolina. Throughout the United States are counties or neighborhoods today in which the majority of people are African American
or Native American or Hispanic, but White Americans are the dominant force.
Nationally, 51.2 percent of the population is female, but males still dominate the
positions of authority and wealth well in excess of their numbers.

A minority or subordinate group has five characteristics: distinguishing physical or cultural traits, unequal treatment, involuntary membership, awareness of
subordination, and in-group marriage (Wagley and Harris, 1958).

1. Members of a minority group share physical or cultural characteristics that
   distinguish them from the dominant group, such as skin color or language.
   Each society has its own arbitrary standard for determining which characteristics are most important in defining dominant and minority groups.
2. Members of a minority experience unequal treatment and have less power
   over their lives than members of a dominant group have over theirs. Social
   inequality may be created or maintained by prejudice, discrimination, segregation, or even extermination.
3. Membership in a dominant or minority group is not voluntary: people are born
   into the group. A person does not choose to be an African American or a White.
4. Minority-group members have a strong sense of group solidarity. William
   Graham Sumner, writing in 1906, noted that individuals make distinctions
   between members of their own group (the *in-group*) and everyone else
   (the *out-group*). When a group is the object of long-term prejudice and discrimination, the feeling of "us versus them" can and often does become
   extremely intense.

5. Members of a minority generally marry others from the same group. A member of a dominant group is often unwilling to join a supposedly inferior minority by marrying one of its members. In addition, the minority group's sense of solidarity encourages marriages within the group and discourages marriages to outsiders.

TYPES OF SUBORDINATE GROUPS

There are four types of minority or subordinate groups. All four, except where noted, have the five properties outlined in the previous section. The four criteria for classifying minority groups are race, ethnicity, religion, and gender.

Racial Groups

The term *racial groups* is reserved for those minorities, and the corresponding majorities, that are classified according to obvious physical differences. Notice the two crucial words in the definition: *obvious* and *physical*. What is obvious? Hair color? Shape of an earlobe? Presence of body hair? Each society defines what is obvious. In the United States, skin color is one obvious difference. On a cold winter day with clothing covering all but one's head, however, skin color may be less obvious than hair color, but people in the United States have learned informally that skin color is important and hair color is unimportant. We need to say more than that. In the United States, a person is classified and classifies himself or herself as either Black or White; there is no in-between except for people readily identified as Native Americans or Asians.

Other societies use skin color as a standard but may have a more elaborate system of classification. In Brazil, where hostility among races is less than in the United States, numerous categories identify people on the basis of skin color. In the United States, a person is Black or White; in Brazil, a variety of terms, such as *cafuso, mazombo, preto,* and *escuro,* are applied to describe various combinations of skin color, facial features, and hair texture. What makes differences obvious is subject to a society's definition.

The designation of a racial group emphasizes physical differences as opposed to cultural distinctions. For the next type of minority group, culture is the primary distinguishing feature. In the United States, minority races include Blacks, Native Americans (or American Indians), Japanese Americans, Chinese Americans, Arab Americans, Filipinos, Hawaiians, and other Asian peoples. The issue of race and racial differences has been an important one, not only in the United States but also throughout the sphere of European influence. Later in this chapter, we will examine race and its significance more closely.

Ethnic Groups

Minority groups that are designated by their ethnicity are differentiated from the dominant group on the basis of cultural differences such as language, attitudes toward marriage and parenting, and food habits. *Ethnic groups,* therefore, are groups set apart from others because of their national origin or distinctive cultural patterns.

Ethnic groups in the United States include a grouping that we refer to collectively as Hispanics or Latinos, including Chicanos (Mexican Americans), Puerto Ricans, Cubans, and other Latin Americans in the United States. White ethnics are also included in this category, such as Irish Americans, Polish Americans, and Norwegian Americans.

The cultural traits that make groups distinctive usually originate from the "homeland" or, for Jews, from a long history of being segregated and prohibited from becoming a part of the host society. Once in the United States, an ethnic group may maintain distinctive cultural practices through associations and clubs. Ethnic enclaves such as a Little Italy or a Greektown in urban areas also perpetuate cultural distinctiveness.

Some of the racial groups discussed in the preceding section may also have distinctive cultural traditions, as we can readily see in the many Chinatowns throughout the United States. For racial groups, however, the physical distinctiveness and not the cultural differences generally prove to be the barrier to acceptance by the host society. For example, Chinese Americans who are faithful Protestants and know the names of all the members of the Baseball Hall of Fame may well be bearers of American culture, but they are still a minority because they are seen as physically different.

Ethnicity has proved to be less significant than race in contemporary societies. Almost a century ago, African-American sociologist W. E. B. DuBois, addressing an audience in London, called attention to the overwhelming importance of the color line throughout the world. In "Listen to Their Voices," we read the remarks of the first Black person to receive a doctorate from Harvard, who later helped to organize the National Association for the Advancement of Colored People (NAACP). DuBois's observations give us a historical perspective on the struggle for equality. In the chapters to come, we will learn more about this struggle, and from this vantage point, we can look ahead—knowing how far we have come and speculating on how much further we have to go.

Religious Groups

The third basis for minority-group status is associated with a religion other than the dominant faith. In the United States, Protestants outnumber members of all other religions, although Protestantism is divided into numerous denominations and splinter groups. Roman Catholics form the largest minority religion, and it may seem inappropriate to consider them a minority. Chapter 5, focusing on Roman Catholics and other minority faiths, details how all five properties of a minority group apply to such faiths in the United States. Other religious minorities include such groups as the Church of Jesus Christ of Latter-day Saints (the Mormons), the Hutterites, the Amish, the Muslims, Buddhists, and cults or sects associated with such things as doomsday prophecy, demon worship, or the use of snakes in a ritualistic fashion. Jews are excluded from this category and placed among ethnic groups because, in their case, culture is a more important defining trait than religious dogma. Jewish Americans share a cultural tradition that goes beyond theology. In this sense, it is appropriate to view them as an ethnic group rather than as members of a religious faith.

Listen to Their Voices
Problem of the Color-Line
W. E. B. DuBois

W. E. B. DuBois

In the metropolis of the modern world, in this the closing year of the nineteenth century, there has been assembled a congress of men and women of African blood, to deliberate solemnly upon the present situation and outlook of the darker races of mankind. The problem of the twentieth century is the problem of the color-line, the question as to how far differences of race—which show themselves chiefly in the color of the skin and the texture of the hair—will hereafter be made the basis of denying to over half the world the right of sharing to their utmost ability the opportunities and privileges of modern civilization. . . .

Let the world take no backward step in that slow but sure progress which has successively refused to let the spirit of class, of caste, of privilege, or of birth, debar from life, liberty and the pursuit of happiness a striving human soul.

Let not color or race be a feature of distinction between white and black men, regardless of worth or ability. . . .

Thus we appeal with boldness and confidence to the Great Powers of the civilized world, trusting in the wide spirit of humanity, and the deep sense of justice of our age, for a generous recognition of the righteousness of our cause.

From *An ABC of Color*, pp. 20–21, 23, by W. E. B. DuBois. Copyright 1969 by International Publishers. Reprinted by permission.

Gender Groups

Another attribute that divides dominant and subordinate groups is gender: males are the social majority; females, although more numerous, are relegated to the position of the social minority. Women are a minority even though they do not exhibit all the characteristics outlined earlier (there is, for example, little in-group marriage). Women encounter prejudice and discrimination and are physically visible. Group membership is involuntary, and many women have developed a sense of sisterhood.

Women who are members of racial and ethnic minorities face a special challenge to achieving equality. They suffer from "double jeopardy" because they belong to two separate minority groups: a racial or ethnic group plus a subordinate gender group. The 1991 U.S. Senate confirmation hearings for Clarence Thomas as a justice of the U.S. Supreme Court are a noteworthy example. When African American Anita Hill charged Thomas (also an African American) with sexual harassment, she faced an all-White, all-male panel of U.S. Senators—reaffirming the interconnectedness of race and gender in contemporary society.

Given the diversity in the nation, the workplace is increasingly the place at which intergroup tensions develop.

Other Subordinate Groups

The focus of this book is on groups that meet a set of criteria for subordinate status. But this focus does not include all the reasons that people encounter prejudice or are excluded from full participation in society. Racial, ethnic, religious, and gender barriers are the main ones, but there are others. Age discrimination, for instance, can automatically exclude a person from an activity in which he or she is actually qualified to engage.

People with physical disabilities, individuals with AIDS, and gays and lesbians all experience prejudice and discrimination. It is little surprise that social movements seeking greater recognition of the rights of these subordinate groups have surfaced in recent years. The legal reforms, protests, and occasional violence parallel those in the history of racial and ethnic groups. Similarly, the accusations of "asking too much" or "pushing where not wanted" rise in response to these "outsiders'" desire to be a part of the "American dream" with everyone else.

As with the other sources of subordination and even oppression, unexpected issues emerge. In 1995, a federal commission unveiled a monument to be constructed in Washington, D.C., honoring Franklin D. Roosevelt. Immediately, the National Organization on Disability expressed concern that the sculptures did not show him in a wheelchair or the leg braces that were a constant aid to the president, who had contracted polio and was unable to walk. The monument designers said that they were not trying to hide this significant aspect of Roosevelt's life, but that they wished to focus on his presidency. Even tributes to long-dead leaders can become the basis for contemporary conflict (D. Moss, 1995).

RACE

Race has many meanings for many people. Probably, the only thing about race that is clear is that most people are confused about the origins and proper use of the term. As we will see, race is a socially constructed concept.

Biological Significance

The way *race* is used lacks scientific meaning. A *biological race* is a genetically isolated group characterized by a high degree of inbreeding that leads to distinctive gene frequencies. This distinctiveness is made most apparent by the presence of hereditary physical characteristics that differentiate the members of one group from those of other human groups. This definition corresponds closely to that adopted in the 1950 UNESCO Statement on Race (A. Montagu, 1972, p. 40)

It is very difficult to consider race in a strictly biological sense. Even among proponents in the past, there were endless debates over what were the races of the world. Given people's frequent migration, exploration, and invasions, pure genetic types have not existed for some time, if they ever did. There are no mutually exclusive races. Skin color among African Americans varies tremendously, as it does among White Americans. There is even an overlapping of dark-skinned Whites and light-skinned African Americans. If we grouped people by genetic resistance to malaria and by fingerprint patterns, Norwegians and many African groups would be of the same race. If we grouped people by some digestive traits, some Africans, Asians, and southern Europeans would be of one group and West Africans and northern Europeans of another (R. Leehotz, 1995).

Biologically there are no pure, distinct races. For example, blood type cannot determine racial groups with any accuracy. Furthermore, applying pure racial types to humans is problematic because of interbreeding. Despite continuing prejudice about Black-White marriages, a large number of Whites have African-American ancestry. Scientists, using various techniques, maintain that the proportion of African Americans with White ancestry is between 20 and 75 percent. Despite the wide range of these estimates, the mixed ancestry of today's Blacks and Whites is part of the biological reality of race (M. Herskovits, 1930, p. 15; D. Roberts, 1955).

Research has been conducted to determine whether personality characteristics such as temperament and nervous habits are inherited. Clearly, the most explosive conclusions have consistently been those that ask whether intelligence is inherited and then try to generalize that races have different innate levels of intelligence.

While the questions about inherited intelligence may seem simple, the issues raised are actually complex. First, what is intelligence? The effort to measure intelligence has a long history in the United States and Europe. Today, intelligence is usually measured by a test that is designed to tap intelligence. Intelligence is, by operational definition, what intelligence tests measure (H. Gans, 1994; S. Gould, 1981; R. Hofstadter, 1992).

Typical intelligence is summarized in an *intelligence quotient*, or IQ, where 100 represents the average intelligence, and higher scores represent greater intelligence. Intelligence tests are adjusted to a person's age, so that 10-year-olds take a very different test from someone aged 20. While research does show that certain learning strategies can improve a person's IQ, generally the IQ remains stable as one ages.

There is a great deal of debate over the accuracy of these tests. Are they biased toward people who come to the tests with knowledge similar to that of the test writers? Consider the following two questions used on standard tests:

1. RUNNER:MARATHON (A) envoy:embassy, (B) oarsman:regatta, (C) martyr:massacre, (D) referee:tournament.
2. Your mother sends you to a store to get a loaf of bread. The store is closed. What should you do? (A) return home, (B) go to the next store, (C) wait until it opens, (D) ask a stranger for advice.

Both correct answers are "B." But is a lower-class youth likely to know, in the first question, what a "regatta" is? Skeptics argue that such test questions do not truly measure intellectual potential. Inner-city youth have been shown often to respond with "A" to the second question, as that may be the only store with which the family has credit. Rural youth, where the next store may be miles away, are also unlikely to respond with the "correct answer." The issue of culture bias in tests remains an unresolved concern (J. Kagan, 1971; Herrnstein and Murray, 1994, p. 30).

The second issue, trying to associate these results with certain subpopulations such as races, also has a long history. Some researchers contend that, as a group, Whites have more intelligence on the average than Blacks. All researchers agree that within-group differences are much greater than any speculated differences between groups. That is, the range of intelligence among, for example, Korean Americans is much greater than any average difference between them as a group and Japanese Americans.

The third issue relates to the subpopulations themselves. If Blacks or Whites are not mutually exclusive biologically, how can there be measurable differences? Many Whites and most Blacks have a mixed ancestry that complicates the heritability issue. Both groups reflect a rich heritage of very dissimilar populations from Swedes to Slovaks and Zulus to Tutus. The latest research effort of *The Bell Curve* by Richard J. Herrnstein and Charles Murray (1994) even made generalizations about IQ levels among Asians and Hispanics in the United States—groups subject to even more intermarriage (A. Hacker, 1994; Murray and Herrnstein, 1994).

All these issues and controversial research have led to the basic question of what difference it would make. No researcher believes that race can be used to predict one's intelligence. Also, there is a general agreement that certain intervention strategies can improve scholastic achievement and even intelligence. Should we mount efforts to upgrade the abilities of those alleged to be below average? Rather than leading to rethinking or expanding positive intervention efforts, these debates tend to contribute to a sense of hopelessness among some policymakers who think biology is destiny and who ignore even the IQ proponents' calls to improve opportunities for all (E. Dionne, 1994).

Why does such IQ research reemerge if the data are subject to different interpretations? The argument that "we" are superior to "them" is very appealing to the dominant group. It justifies receiving opportunities that are denied to others. For example, *The Bell Curve* argues that intelligence significantly determines the poverty problem in the United States. We can anticipate that the debate over IQ and the allegations of significant group differences will continue. Yet policymakers need to acknowledge the difficulty in using race in any biologically significant manner.

Social Significance

Whatever significance race has biologically is overwhelmed by the effect that membership in a certain race has on the interaction of people. The 1950 UNESCO Statement on Race maintains that "for all practical social purposes 'race' is not so much a biological phenomenon as a social myth" (A. Montagu, 1972, p. 118). Adolf Hitler expressed concern over the "Jewish race" and translated this concern into Nazi death camps. Winston Churchill spoke proudly of the "British race" and used that pride to spur a nation to fight. Evidently race was a useful political tool for two rather different leaders in the 1930s and 1940s.

People speculate that if human groups have obvious physical differences, then they must have corresponding mental or personality differences. No one disagrees that people differ in temperament, potential to learn, sense of humor, and so on. But in its social sense, race implies that groups that differ physically also bear distinctive emotional and mental abilities or disabilities. Such beliefs are based on the notion that humankind can be divided into distinct groups, and we have already seen the difficulties associated with pigeonholing people into racial categories. Despite these difficulties, belief in the inheritance of behavior patterns and in an association between physical and cultural traits is widespread. When this belief is coupled with the feeling that certain groups or races are inherently superior to others, it is called *racism*. Racism is a doctrine of racial supremacy, stating that one race is superior.

We questioned the biological significance of race in the previous section. In modern complex industrial societies, we find little adaptive utility in the presence or absence of prominent chins, epicanthic folds of the eyelids, or the comparative amount of melanin in the skin. What is important is not that people are genetically different but that they approach one another with dissimilar perspectives. It is in the social setting that race is decisive. Race is significant because people have given it significance.

Race definitions are crystallized through what Michael Omi and Howard Winant (1994) called *racial formation*. Racial formation is a sociohistorical process by which racial categories are created, inhibited, transformed, and destroyed. People come to be defined, usually by those in power, in a certain way that depends on a racist social structure as with Native Americans and the creation of the reservation system in the latter 1800s. While we vary in the extent and frequency to which we are subjected to racial formation, no one—absolutely no one—escapes it.

Breaking both racial and gender barriers, Mae C. Jemison, who has degrees in chemical engineering and medicine, is a NASA astronaut.

A particularly sobering aspect of racial formation is that the United States is exporting this development. Just as this nation promotes tastes in music and television, the racial identities in the United States are being internationalized. While the United States is certainly not responsible for racial, ethnic, and religious tensions, we have been contributing to the defining of racial awareness. This globalization of race is also reciprocal, as we witness a variety of cultural imports from the samba and reggae to Islamic fundamentalism, taking root in North America (H. Winant, 1994, p. 20).

SOCIOLOGY AND THE STUDY OF RACE AND ETHNICITY

Before proceeding further with our study of racial and ethnic groups, let us consider several sociological perspectives that provide insight into dominant-subordinate relationships.

Stratification

All societies are characterized by members' having unequal amounts of wealth, prestige, or power. Sociologists observe that entire groups may be assigned to have less or more of what a society values. The hierarchy that emerges is *stratification*. Stratification, therefore, is the structured ranking of entire groups of people that perpetuates unequal rewards and power in a society.

Much discussion of stratification identifies the *class*, or social ranking, of people who share similar wealth, according to sociologist Max Weber's classic definition. While boundaries between classes may not be clearly defined, mobility from one class to another is not necessarily easy. Movement into classes of greater wealth may be particularly difficult for subordinate group members faced with life-long prejudice and discrimination.

Recall that the second property of subordinate group standing is unequal treatment by the dominant group in the form of prejudice, discrimination, and segregation. Stratification is intertwined with the subordination of racial, ethnic, religious, and gender groups. Sociologist Thomas Pettigrew (1981) refers to the *interactive effect* of race and class. Race has implications for the way people are treated; so does class, but one also has to add the two together. For example, being poor *and* Black is not the same as being either one. Similarly, a wealthy Chicano is not the same as an affluent Anglo or as Chicanos in general. The most accurate explanation of how race and class operate today lies in the *interactive effect* of race and class acting together, not considering them separate.

The monumental 1993 South-Central Los Angeles riots following the acquittal of four police officers charged with the beating of Rodney King illustrated both race and class. The most visible issue was White brutality against Blacks, yet the concentrated attack on Korean American merchants whose economic role placed them in a very vulnerable social position underscored the role of race. The multiracial—that is, not just African-Americans—character of the looting was a response not only to the judicial system but also to poverty. Indeed, Hispanic citizens were the most likely group to be arrested during the riot period.

Frequently, public discussions of issues such as housing or public assistance are disguised as class issues when, in fact, they are primarily based on race. Similarly, some topics such as the "underclass" are addressed in terms of race when the class component should be explicit. The link between race and class in society should become abundantly clear (H. Winant, 1994, pp. 32–36, 76–84).

Theoretical Perspectives

Sociologists view society in different ways. Some see the world basically as a stable and ongoing entity. They are impressed by the endurance of a Chinatown, the relative sameness of male-female roles over time, and other aspects of intergroup relations. Some sociologists see society as composed of many groups in conflict, competing for scarce resources.

Within this conflict, some people or even entire groups may be labeled or stigmatized in a way that blocks access to obtaining what a society values. We will examine three theoretical perspectives that are widely used by sociologists today: the functionalist, conflict, and labeling perspectives.

Functionalist Perspective   In the view of a functionalist, a society is like a living organism in which each part contributes to the survival of the whole. Therefore, the *functionalist perspective* emphasizes how the parts of society are structured to maintain its stability. According to this approach, if an aspect of social life does not contribute to a society's stability or survival—if it does not serve some identifiably useful function—it will not be passed on from one generation to the next.

It would seem reasonable to assume that bigotry between races offers no such positive function, and so why, we ask, does it persist? The functionalist, although agreeing that racial hostility is hardly to be admired, would point out that it does serve some positive functions from the perspective of racists. Manning Nash (1962) describes four functions that racial beliefs have for the dominant group:

1. Racist ideologies provide a moral justification for maintaining a society that routinely deprives a group of its rights and privileges. Southern Whites justified slavery by believing that Africans were physically and spiritually subhuman and devoid of souls.
2. Racist beliefs discourage subordinate people from attempting to question their lowly status, for to do so is to question the very foundations of the society.
3. Racial beliefs provide a cause for political action and focus social uncertainty on a specific threat. Racial ideologies not only justify existing practices but serve as a rallying points for social movements, as seen in the rise of the Nazi Party.
4. Racial myths encourage support for the existing order by introducing the argument that, if there were any major societal change, the subordinate group would suffer even greater poverty and the dominant group would suffer lower living standards.

As a result, Nash feels, racial ideology grows when a value system (for example, that underlying a colonial empire or slavery) is being threatened.

There are also definite dysfunctions caused by prejudice and discrimination. *Dysfunctions* are an element of society that may disrupt a social system or may tend to decrease its stability. Arnold Rose (1951, pp. 19–24) outlined seven ways in which racism is dysfunctional to a society and even its dominant group:

1. A society that practices discrimination fails to use the resources of all individuals. Discrimination limits the search for talent and leadership to the dominant group.
2. Discrimination aggravates social problems such as poverty, delinquency, and crime and places the financial burden of alleviating these problems on the dominant group.

3. Society must invest a good deal of time and money to defend its barriers to the full participation of all members.
4. Goodwill and friendly diplomatic relations between nations are often undercut by racial prejudice and discrimination.
5. Communication between groups is restricted. Little accurate knowledge of the minority and its culture is available to the society at large.
6. Social change is inhibited since it may contribute to assisting the minority.
7. Discrimination promotes disrespect for law enforcement and the peaceful settlement of disputes.

These costs may seem small compared to the price paid for subordinate group membership. They do, however, remind us that intergroup conflict is exceedingly complex.

Conflict Perspective   In contrast to the functionalists' emphasis on stability, conflict sociologists see the social world as in continual struggle. The *conflict perspective* assumes that social behavior is best understood in terms of conflict or tension among competing groups. Specifically, society is a struggle between the privileged (the dominant group) and the exploited (the subordinate groups). Such conflicts need not be physically violent and may take the form of immigration restrictions, real estate practices, or disputes over cuts in the federal budget.

The conflict model is often selected today when one is examining race and ethnicity, because it readily accounts for the presence of tension between competing groups. The competition, according to the conflict perspective, takes place between groups with unequal amounts of economic and political power. The minorities are exploited by the dominant group or, at the very best, ignored. The conflict perspective also tends to be viewed as more radical and activist than functionalism, because conflict theorists emphasize social change and the redistribution of resources. Functionalists are not necessarily in favor of such inequality; rather, their approach, as in Nash's analysis of racial beliefs, helps us to understand why such systems persist.

Those who follow the conflict approach to race and ethnicity have repeatedly remarked that the subordinate group is criticized for its low status, whereas the responsibilities of the dominant group for the subordination are often ignored. William Ryan (1976) calls this an instance of "blaming the victim": portraying the problems of racial and ethnic minorities as their fault rather than recognizing society's responsibility. This idea is not new. Gunnar Myrdal, a Swedish social economist of international reputation, headed a project that produced the classic 1944 work on Blacks in the United States, *The American Dilemma*. Myrdal concluded that the plight of the subordinate group is the responsibility of the dominant majority. It is not a Black problem, but a White problem. Similarly, it is not a Hispanic problem or a Haitian refugee problem, but a White problem. He and others since then have reminded the public and policymakers alike that the ultimate responsibility for society's problems must rest with those who possess the most authority and the most economic resources (D. Southern, 1987).

Labeling Approach   Related to the conflict perspective and its concern over the victim's taking the blame is labeling theory. *Labeling theory*, introduced by sociologist Howard Becker, is an attempt to explain why certain people are viewed as different or less worthy and others are not. Students of crime and deviance have relied heavily on labeling theory. A youth who misbehaves, according to labeling theory, may be considered a delinquent if she or he comes from the "wrong kind of family," whereas another youth, this time one from a middle-class family, who commits the same sort of misbehavior will be given another chance.

The labeling perspective directs our attention to the role that stereotypes play in race and ethnicity. The image that prejudiced people maintain of a group toward which they hold ill feelings is called a *stereotype*. Stereotypes are exaggerated images of the characteristics of a particular group. The term *stereotype* was coined by columnist Walter Lippmann (1922, pp. 95–156), who called stereotypes pictures in our heads. In Chapter 2, we will review some of the research on the stereotyping of minorities. This labeling is not limited to racial and ethnic groups, however. Age, for instance, can be used to exclude a person from an activity in which he or she is actually qualified to engage. Groups are subjected to stereotypes and discrimination in such a way that they resemble social minorities. Social prejudice exists toward ex-convicts, gamblers, alcoholics, lesbians, gays, prostitutes, people with AIDS, and people with disabilities to name a few.

Individuals who deviate physically or mentally from a society's standards are also seen as different and are generally subjected to second-class treatment, such as being labeled unemployable. The physically handicapped, the blind, the deformed, the epileptic, the diabetic, the deaf, the mentally ill, and the mentally retarded are cast out from the mainstream of society. It is important to remember that racial and ethnic minority groups are not the only ones that encounter prejudice and discrimination. Although we here limit ourselves to discussing dominant and subordinate groups, we must, in our daily lives, be mindful of other groups that suffer from arbitrary placement in our social hierarchy.

The labeling approach points out that stereotypes, when applied by people in power, can have very negative consequences for people or groups falsely identified. A crucial aspect of the relationship between dominant and subordinate groups is the prerogative of the dominant group to define society's values. American sociologist William I. Thomas (1923, pp. 41–44), an early critic of racial and sexual differences, saw that the "definition of the situation" could mold the personality of the individual. In other words, Thomas observed that people respond not only to the objective features of a situation (or person) but also to the meaning these features have for them. In this manner, we can create false images or stereotypes that become real in their consequences.

In certain situations, we may respond to stereotypes and act on them, with the result that false definitions become accurate. This is known as a *self-fulfilling prophecy*. A person or group described as having particular characteristics begins to display the very traits that were said to exist. Thus, a child who is praised for

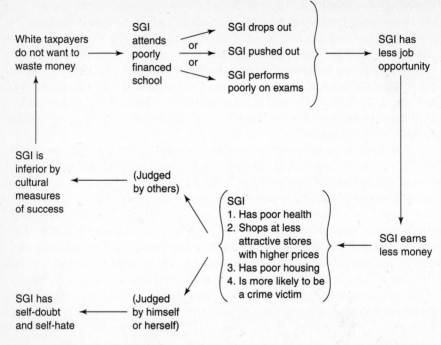

Figure 1.2 Self-Fulfilling Prophecy
The self-validating effects of dominant-group definitions are shown in this figure. The subordinate group individual (SGI) attends a poorly financed school and is left unequipped to perform jobs that offer high status and pay. He or she then gets a low-paying job and must settle for a standard of living far short of society's standards. Since the person shares these standards, he or she may begin to feel self-doubt and self-hatred.

Source: Bureau of the Census (1993c).

being a "natural comic" may focus on learning to become funny in order to gain approval and attention.

Self-fulfilling prophecies can be especially devastating for minority groups (see Figure 1.2). Such groups often find that they are allowed to hold only low-paying jobs with little prestige or opportunity for advancement. The rationale of the dominant society is that these minority individuals lack the ability to perform in more important and lucrative positions. Subordinate-group individuals are then denied the training needed to become scientists, executives, or physicians and are locked into society's inferior jobs. As a result, the false definition becomes real; in terms of employment, the subordinate group has become inferior because it was defined at the start as inferior and was therefore prevented from achieving equality.

Because of this vicious circle, a talented subordinate-group individual may come to see the worlds of entertainment and professional sports as his or her only hope for achieving wealth and fame. Thus, it is no accident that successive waves of Irish, Jewish, Italian, African American, and Hispanic performers and athletes have made their mark on culture in the United States. Unfortunately, these very successes may convince the dominant group that its original stereotypes were valid—that these are the only areas of society in which subordinate-group members can excel. Furthermore, athletics and the arts are well known in our society as highly competitive areas. For every Michael Jordan and Oprah Winfrey who makes it, many, many more will end up disappointed.

In the 1960s and 1970s, many subordinate minorities in the United States rejected traditional definitions and replaced them with feelings of pride, power, and strength. "Black is beautiful" and "Red power" movements were efforts by African Americans and Native Americans to take control of their own lives and self-images. Although a minority can make a determined effort to redefine a situation and resist stereotypes, the definition or label that remains most important is the one used by society's most powerful groups. In this case, the traditional White, Anglo-Saxon, Protestant norms of the United States still shape American definitions and stereotypes of racial and ethnic minorities (G. Allport, 1979; R. Merton, 1968; G. Myrdal, 1944).

THE CREATION OF SUBORDINATE-GROUP STATUS

Four situations are likely to lead to the formation of a subordinate-group–dominant-group relationship. A subordinate group emerges through (1) voluntary migration, (2) involuntary migration, (3) annexation, and (4) colonialism.

Voluntary Migration

People who immigrate to a new country often find themselves a minority in that new country. The immigrant is set apart from the dominant group by cultural or physical traits or by religious affiliation. Immigration from Europe, Asia, and Latin America has been a powerful force in shaping the fabric of life in the United States. *Migration* is the general term used to describe any transfer of population. *Emigration* (by emigrants) describes leaving a country to settle in another; *immigration* (by immigrants) denotes coming into the new country. From Vietnam's perspective, the boat people were emigrants from Vietnam to the United States, where they were counted among this nation's immigrants.

Although people may come voluntarily, leaving the home country is not always voluntary. Throughout human history, people have been displaced by conflict or war. In the twentieth century, we have seen huge population movements caused by two world wars; revolutions in Spain, Hungary, and Cuba; the partition of British India; conflicts in Southeast Asia, Korea, and Central America; and the confrontation between Arabs and Israelis.

In all types of movement, even the movement of an American family from Ohio to Florida, two sets of forces operate: *push* factors and *pull* factors. Push factors discourage a person from remaining where he or she lives. Religious persecution and economic factors such as dissatisfaction with employment opportunities are possible push factors. Pull factors, such as a better standard of living, friends and relatives who have already emigrated, and a promised job, attract an immigrant to a particular country.

Involuntary Migration

The forced movement of people into another society guarantees a subordinate role. Because they have been brought as slaves or indentured servants, their position as subordinate is understood from the beginning. Involuntary migration is no longer common; although enslavement has a long history, all industrial societies today prohibit such practices. Of course, many contemporary societies, including the United States, bear today the legacy of enforced labor.

In some instances, we might include contract laborers and indentured servants among involuntary migrants. Such workers generally participate in the transfer freely, but coercion is at times involved. Unlike slaves, contract laborers and indentured servants may return home at the end of a specified period, but historically, many have remained, forming the beginnings of a new group with minority status. Despite the possibility of freedom, life for these people has hardly been ideal. Importation of laborers from India to British Guiana and Trinidad and from China, Japan, Portugal, and the Philippines to Hawaii often involved conditions little better than those that afflicted people in bondage.

Annexation

Nations, particularly during wars or as a result of war, incorporate or attach land. This new land is *contiguous* to the nation, as in the German occupation of Europe in the 1940s and in the Louisiana Purchase of 1803. The Treaty of Guadalupe Hidalgo that ended the Mexican-American War in 1848 gave the United States California, Utah, Nevada, most of New Mexico, and parts of Arizona, Wyoming, and Colorado. The indigenous peoples in some of this huge territory were dominant in their society one day, only to become minority-group members the next.

When annexation occurs, the dominant power generally suppresses the language and culture of the minority. Such was the practice of Russia with the Ukrainians and Poles, and of Prussia with the Poles. Minorities try to maintain their cultural integrity despite annexation. The area inhabited by the Poles was divided into territories ruled by three countries, but the Poles maintained their own culture across political boundaries.

Colonialism

Colonialism has been the most frequent way for one people to dominate another. *Colonialism* is the maintenance of political, social, economic, and cultural domination over a people by a foreign power for an extended period (W. Bell, 1991). In simple terms, it is rule by outsiders, but unlike annexation, it does not involve actu-

Symbolic of lingering racism is the state flag of Georgia, shown on the left, into which the Confederate flag was incorporated in 1965. On the right is the earlier state flag.

al incorporation into the dominant people's nation. The long control exercised by the British Empire over much of North America, parts of Africa, and India is an example of colonial domination.

Societies gain power over a foreign land through military strength, sophisticated political organization, and the massive use of investment capital. The extent of power may also vary according to the extent of settlement by the dominant group in the colonial land. Relations between the colonial nation and the colonized people are similar to those between a dominant group and exploited subordinate groups. The colonial subjects are generally limited to menial jobs, and the profits from their labor and from the natural resources of their land benefit the members of the ruling class.

By the 1980s, colonialism worldwide had largely become a phenomenon of the past. A significant exception is Puerto Rico, whose territorial or commonwealth status with the United States is basically that of a colony. The more than 2 million people on the island are United States citizens but are unable to vote in presidential elections unless they migrate to the mainland. In 1993, 48 percent of Puerto

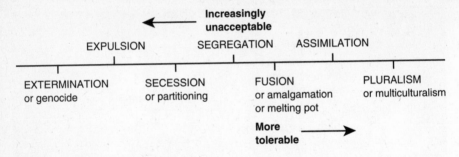

Figure 1.3 Subordinate-Group Status
The social consequences of being in a subordinate group can be viewed along a continuum ranging from extermination to forms of mutual acceptance such as pluralism.

Ricans on the island voted in a nonbinding referendum to remain a common-wealth, 46 percent favored statehood, and less than 5 percent voted for independence. Despite their poor showing, proindependence forces are very vocal and enjoy the sympathies of others concerned about the cultural and economic dominance of the United States mainland.

Colonialism is domination by outsiders. Relations between the colonizer and the colony are similar to those between the dominant and subordinate peoples within the same country. This distinctive pattern of oppression is called *internal colonialism.* Among other cases, it has been applied to the plight of Blacks in the United States and tribal Indians in Mexico, who are colonial peoples in their own country. Internal colonialism covers more than just economic oppression. Just as nationalist movements in African colonies struggled to achieve political as well as economic independence from Europeans, African Americans, who have suffered internal colonialism, also call themselves nationalists in trying to gain more autonomy over their lives (R. Blauner, 1969, 1972).

THE CONSEQUENCES OF SUBORDINATE-GROUP STATUS

There are several consequences for a group of subordinate status. These differ in their degree of harshness, ranging from physical annihilation to absorption into the dominant group. In this section, we will examine six consequences of subordinate-group status: extermination, expulsion, secession, segregation, fusion, and assimilation. Figure 1.3 illustrates how these consequences can be defined.

Extermination

The most extreme way of dealing with a subordinate group is eliminating the group itself. One historical example is the British destruction of the people of Tasmania, an island off the coast of Australia. There were five thousand Tasmanians in 1800, but because they were attacked by settlers and forced to live on less habitable islands, the last full-blooded Tasmanian died in 1876. A human group had become extinct, totally eliminated.

Today the term *genocide* is used to describe the deliberate, systematic killing of an entire people or nation. This term is frequently used in reference to the Holocaust—Nazi Germany's extermination of 12 million European Jews and other ethnic minorities during World War II. More recently the term *ethnic cleansing* was introduced into the world's vocabulary as, within the former Yugoslavia, ethnic Serbs instituted a policy intended to "cleanse" Muslims from parts of Bosnia.

Genocide, however, also appropriately describes White policies toward Native Americans in the nineteenth century. In 1800, the American Indian population in the United States was about 600,000; by 1850 it had been reduced to 250,000 through warfare with the U.S. cavalry, disease, and forced relocation to inhospitable environments.

Expulsion

Dominant groups may choose to force a specific subordinate group to leave certain areas or even vacate the country. Expulsion is therefore another extreme consequence of minority-group status. European colonial powers in North America and eventually the U.S. government itself drove Native Americans out of their tribal lands into territory unfamiliar to the tribes.

More recently, Vietnam in 1979 expelled nearly 1 million ethnic Chinese from the country, partly as a result of centuries of hostility between the two Asian neighbors. These "boat people" were abruptly eliminated as a minority within Vietnamese society. This expulsion meant, though, that they were now uprooted and became a new minority group in many nations, from Australia to France, the United States, and Canada. Thus, expulsion may remove a minority group from one society; however, the expelled people merely go to another nation, where they are again a minority group.

Secession

A group ceases to be a subordinate group when it secedes to form a new nation or moves to an already established nation where it becomes dominant. After Great Britain withdrew from Palestine, Jewish people achieved a dominant position in 1948, attracting Jews from throughout the world to the new state of Israel. In a similar fashion, Pakistan was created in 1947 when India was partitioned. The predominantly Muslim areas in the north became Pakistan, making India predominantly Hindu. Throughout this century, minorities have repudiated dominant customs. In this spirit, the Estonian, Latvian, Lithuanian, and Armenian peoples, for example, not content with mere toleration by the majority, all seceded to form independent states following the demise of the Soviet Union in 1991.

Some African Americans have called for secession. Suggestions dating back to the early 1700s supported the recolonization of Blacks in Africa as a solution to racial problems. The target for colonization of the American Colonization Society was Liberia, but proposals were also advanced to establish settlements of freed slaves in Canada, Haiti, South America, and the western United States. Territorial separatism and the emigrationist ideology were recurrent and interrelated themes among African Americans from the late nineteenth century well into the 1980s. The Black Muslims, or Nation of Islam, once expressed the desire for complete separation in their own state or territory within the present borders of the United States. Although a secession of Blacks from the United States has not taken place, it has been considered and even attempted in many ways (Bracey, Meier, and Rudwick, 1970; F. Butterfield, 1986).

Segregation

Segregation refers to the physical separation of two groups of people in residence, workplace, and social functions. Generally, it is imposed by a dominant group on a subordinate group. Segregation is rarely complete, however; intergroup contact inevitably occurs even in the most segregated societies.

Racial isolation has been a continuing theme in the United States. The Native Americans were forced onto isolated reservations—many of them located some distance from their tribal homelands. African Americans, Asian Americans, and Hispanics are isolated into separate neighborhoods or communities.

The extent of racial and ethnic isolation in the United States is staggering. Two-thirds of all Blacks attend schools in which more than half of the students are either Black or Hispanic. Almost three-fourths of all Hispanics attend predominantly Hispanic and Black schools (G. Orfield, 1993).

Residential segregation is also pervasive in the United States. In Table 1.2, using an index value, we present the most segregated metropolitan areas. The segregation index is a measure of how closely the racial and ethnic makeup of each neighborhood resembles the population mix of the entire metropolitan area. For instance, Chicago has a segregation index of 66 between Hispanics and non-Hispanics, which means that 66 percent of either Hispanic or non-Hispanic residents would have to move from segregated neighborhoods to achieve integration.

Data from the 1976 and 1992 Detroit Area Study shed some light on the attitudes of Whites and African Americans toward residential segregation. Metropolitan Detroit, like many American urban areas, resembles what sociologists call "chocolate city, vanilla suburbs." Would Whites and Blacks change if they could? The responses of Whites were discouraging, especially because they were only asked their opinions and knew they were not committed to any action. Figure 1.4 represents the responses of Whites about their willingness to move into or out of a neighborhood. About one-sixth of Whites in 1992 would not have wanted to move into a neighborhood of 15 homes even where only one was occupied by a Black family. Half of the Whites responding said they would try to move out of a neighborhood if there were as many as five Black families.

African Americans in both the 1976 and 1992 surveys, on the other hand, showed a preference for a racially mixed neighborhood, but few were willing to be the first Black family to move into a previously all-White neighborhood. Black respondents may have looked upon a mixed neighborhood as better in housing and

Table 1.2   MOST SEGREGATED METROPOLITAN AREAS

	Segregation Index
Blacks from Non-Whites	
1. Gary	89
2. Detroit	88
3. Chicago	86
3. Cleveland	86
5. Milwaukee	83
5. Buffalo	83
7. St. Louis	81
8. Philadelphia	80
9. Cincinnati	79
9. Birmingham, AL	79
Hispanics from Non-Hispanics	
1. Chicago	66
2. Miami	56
2. Bergen-Passaic, NJ	56
4. Los Angeles	53
4. San Antonio	53
4. Oxnard, CA	53
4. El Paso	53
4. Bakersfield, CA	53
Asians from Non-Asians	
1. Stockton, CA	52
2. San Francisco	47
3. Los Angeles	45
4. Vallejo, CA	45
5. Honolulu	41

The most segregated metropolitan areas in the United States. Ranked are areas with at least 480,000 people with a 10 percent minority population. The segregation index indicates the percentage of dominant or subordinate residents who would have to move to achieve integration.

Note: Areas with index ties are arranged in order by population, the largest first.

Source: Frey and Farley (1993).

social class, apart from the race of their would-be neighbors. This study supports the proposition that White opposition to integration, rather than Black preference for segregation, is the key to explaining the residential separation of the races in America. The Blacks worried that they would not be welcomed, or, as one respondent said, that they "might get burned or never wake up" (Farley et al., 1978; Frey and Farley, 1993).

This focus on metropolitan areas should not let us ignore the continuing legally sanctioned segregation of Native Americans on reservations. Although the majority of our nation's first inhabitants do live outside these tribal areas, the reservations play a prominent role in the identity of Native Americans. They are faced

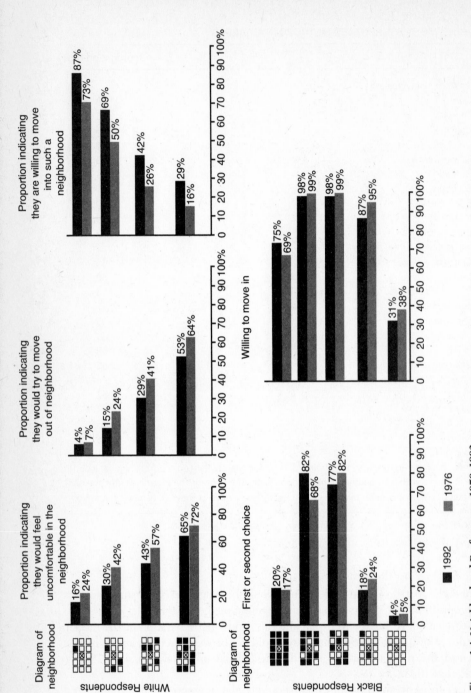

Figure 1.4 Neighborhood Preferences, 1976–1992
White people, as shown in the top figure, were more likely, both in 1976 and 1992, to indicate a desire to avoid integrated neighborhoods than Black people, as shown in the bottom figure. Respondents were shown diagrams representing neighborhoods of different racial mixes (Black houses and White houses). The house in the center of the neighborhood was designated "your house." Responses to these diagrams are shown in the right-hand columns.

While the word segregation usually evokes images of urban neighborhoods and schools, the desolation of reservations is yet another illustration of the legacy of past segregation. Shown here is part of the Hopi reservation in Arizona.

with the difficult choice that, while it is easier to maintain tribal identity on the reservation, economic and educational opportunities are more limited in these areas segregated from the rest of society.

Residential segregation patterns are not unique to the United States. In Germany today, they speak of *Ghettoisierung* (or "ghettoization") as concentrations of Turkish immigrants are emerging. Social scientists in Sweden have used the segregation index to document the isolation of Greek, Chilean, and Turkish immigrants from the rest of the population. Segregation is present in virtually all multiracial societies.

Fusion

Fusion describes the result when a minority and a majority group combine to form a new group. This combining can be expressed as $A + B + C = D$, where A, B, and C represent the groups present in a society and D signifies the result, a cultural-racial group unlike any of the initial groups. Theoretically, fusion does not require intermarriage, but it is very similar to *amalgamation,* or the cultural and physical synthesis of various groups into a new people. In everyday speech, the words fusion and amalgamation are rarely used, but the concept is expressed in the notion of a human *melting pot,* in which diverse groups form a new creation (W. Newman, 1973).

The analogy of an alchemist's cauldron, the "melting pot," is appropriate and was first used to describe the United States by the French observer Crèvecoeur in 1782 (see P. Gleason, 1980, p. 33). The phrase refers to the Middle Ages, when the alchemist attempted to change less costly metals into gold and silver. Similarly, the idea of the human melting pot implied that the new group would represent only the best qualities and attributes of the different cultures contributing to it. The belief in the United States as a melting pot became widespread in the first part of the twentieth century, particularly because it suggested that America had an almost divinely inspired mission to destroy artificial divisions and create a single humankind. The dominant group, however, had indicated its unwillingness to welcome such groups as Native Americans, Blacks, Hispanics, Jews, Asians, and Irish Roman Catholics into the melting pot. It is a mistake to think of the United States as an ethnic mixing bowl. While there are superficial signs of fusion, as in a cuisine that includes sauerkraut and spaghetti, virtually all contributions of subordinate groups are ignored.

Marriage patterns indicate the resistance to fusion. People are unwilling, in varying degrees, to marry out of their own ethnic, religious, and racial groups. Surveys still show that 20–50 percent of various White ethnic groups report single ancestry. When White ethnics do cross boundaries, they tend to marry within their religion and social class. For example, Italians are more likely to marry Irish who are still Roman Catholic than Protestant Swedes.

There is only modest evidence in the United States of a fusion of races. Racial intermarriage has been increasing, and the number of interracial couples immigrating to the United States has also increased. While in 1970 there were 310,000 such unions, by 1993 there were over 1,195,000 interracial married couples. Spike Lee's 1991 movie *Jungle Fever* was influenced by his own father's marrying a White woman after his mother died. Yet intermarriage is still the exception, involving only a fraction of married couples in the United States—less than 2 percent (M. Kalmijn, 1994; C. Leslie, 1995).

Assimilation

Assimilation is the process by which a subordinate individual or group takes on the characteristics of the dominant group and is eventually accepted as part of that group. Assimilation is a majority ideology in which $A + B + C = A$. The majority (A) dominates in such a way that the minorities (B and C) become indistinguishable from the dominant group. Regardless of how many racial, ethnic, or religious groups are involved, assimilation dictates conformity to the dominant group (H. Bash, 1979; C. Hirschman, 1983; W. Newman, 1973, p. 53).

To be complete, assimilation must entail not only an active effort by the minority group individual to shed all distinguishing actions and beliefs, but also the complete, unqualified acceptance of that individual by the dominant society. In the United States, assimilation is encouraged by dominant White society. The assimilationist perspective tends to devalue alien culture and to treasure the dominant. For example, an assimilationist assumes that whatever is admirable among Blacks was adapted from Whites, and that whatever is bad is inherently Black. The assimilationist's solution to Black–White conflict is the development of a consensus around White American values (L. Broom, 1965, p. 23).

Assimilation is difficult. The individual must forsake his or her cultural tradition to become part of a different, often antagonistic, culture. Members of the subordinate group who choose not to assimilate look on those who do as deserters. Many Hindus in India complained of their compatriots who copied the traditions and customs of the British. Those who assimilate must totally break with the past. Australian Aborigines who become part of dominant society conceal their origin by ignoring darker-skinned relatives, including their immediate family. As one assimilated Aborigine explained, "Why should I have anything to do with them? I haven't anything in common with them, and I don't even like most of them." These conflicting demands leave an individual torn between two value systems (Berndt and Berndt, 1951; B. McCully, 1940).

Assimilation does not occur at the same pace for all groups or for all individuals in the same group. Assimilation tends to take longer when the following are true:

1. The differences between the minority and the majority are large.
2. The majority is not receptive, or the minority retains its own culture.
3. The arrival of the minority group occurs in a short period of time.
4. The minority-group residents are concentrated rather than dispersed.
5. The arrival is recent, and the homeland is accessible.

Assimilation is not a smooth process (Warner and Srole, 1945).

Assimilation is also a process that is not regarded favorably in intellectual life today. It is viewed as "unfair" or even "dictatorial." In public discussions today, assimilation has practically become an ideology of the dominant group as to how to force people to act. Consequently, the social institutions in the United States, such as education, economy, government, religion, and medicine, all push toward assimilation, with occasional references to the pluralist approach.

THE PLURALIST PERSPECTIVE

Thus far, we have concentrated on how subordinate groups cease to exist (removal) or take on the characteristics of the dominant group (assimilation). The alternative to these relationships between the majority and the minority is pluralism. *Pluralism* implies mutual respect between the various groups in a society for one another's culture, a respect that allows minorities to express their own culture without suffering prejudice or hostility. Whereas the assimilationist or integrationist seeks the elimination of ethnic boundaries, the pluralist believes in maintaining many of them.

There are limits to cultural freedom. A Romanian immigrant to the United States could not expect to avoid learning English and still move up the occupational ladder. In order to survive, a society must have a consensus among its members on basic ideals, values, and beliefs. Nevertheless, there is still plenty of room for variety. Earlier, fusion was described as $A + B + C = D$ and assimilation as $A +$

$B + C = A$. Using this same scheme, we can think of pluralism as $A + B + C = A + B + C$, where groups coexist in one society (W. Newman, 1973; J. Simpson, 1995.)

In the United States, cultural pluralism is more an ideal than a reality. Though there are vestiges of cultural pluralism—in the various ethnic neighborhoods in major cities, for instance—the general rule has been for subordinate groups to assimilate. The cost of cultural integrity has been high. The various Native American tribes have succeeded to a large extent in maintaining their heritage, but in exchange for bare subsistence on reservations dominated by federal control.

Horace Kallen, seeing evidence of pluralism in the persistence of cultural identity in the settlements of Norwegians in Minnesota, Germans in Wisconsin, and Irish in Massachusetts, called attention to how Americanization threatened his goal, a federation or commonwealth of national cultures. A multiracial, multicultural society of people getting along with one another and learning from each other is an attractive notion. But the maintenance of largely separate cultural identities may only increase their visibility and encourage discrimination and other socially disabling mechanisms. Pluralism may also detour minorities from challenging their subordinate position because they are satisfied with their distinctive cultures (H. Kallen, 1915a, 1915b, 1924; P. Rose, 1981).

Today, 80 years after Kallen drew attention to cultural pluralism, Americans see a reemergence of ethnic identification by groups that had long since expressed little interest in their heritage. In fact, groups that make up the dominant majority are also reasserting their ethnic heritage. Various nationality groups are rekindling interest in almost forgotten languages, customs, festivals, and traditions. In some instances, this expression of the past has taken the form of a protest against exclusion from the dominant society. Chinese youths, for example, chastise their elders for forgetting the old ways and accepting White American influence and control.

The most visible controversy about pluralism is the debate surrounding bilingualism. *Bilingualism* is the use of two or more languages in places of work or education and the treatment of each language as equally legitimate.

According to a report released by the U.S. Bureau of the Census (1993), almost 32 million residents of the United States—or about 1 of every 7 people—speak as their native language something other than English. Indeed, 50 different languages are spoken by at least 30,000 residents of this country. Over the period 1980–1990, there was a 38 percent increase in the number of people in the United States who spoke a foreign language as their native language (M. Usdansky, 1993).

These data are frequently cited as part of the passionate debate under way in the United States over bilingualism. In education, bilingualism has seemed one way of assisting millions of people who do not speak English as their first language, but who may want to *learn* English in order to function more efficiently within the United States. Bilingualism has been a particularly sensitive matter for millions of immigrants from Spanish-speaking nations.

In the 1990s, bilingualism has become an increasingly controversial political issue. For example, a proposed constitutional amendment was introduced in the U.S. Senate in the mid-1980s to designate English as the "official language of the nation." A major force behind the proposed constitutional amendment and other efforts to restrict bilingualism is "U.S. English," a nationwide organization that views the English language as the "social glue" that keeps the nation together. This organization supports assimilation. By contrast, Hispanic leaders see the U.S. English campaign as a veiled expression of racism (M. Perez, 1986, 1989).

Representative of the reassertion of one's cultural heritage is the *Afrocentric perspective*. African-American studies scholar Molefi Kete Asante (1992) has called for an Afrocentric perspective that emphasizes the customs of African cultures and how they have penetrated the history, culture, and behavior of Blacks in the United States and around the world. The Afrocentric approach could begin in our school curriculum, which has not adequately acknowledged the importance of this heritage. In a very real sense, Afrocentrism is meant to counter Eurocentrism and to work toward a multiculturalist or pluralist orientation where no viewpoint is suppressed.

The Afrocentric perspective has attracted considerable attention in colleges. Opponents view it as a separatist view of history and culture that distorts the past and present. Its supporters counter that African peoples everywhere can come to full self-determination only when they are able to overthrow "White" or Eurocentric intellectual interpretations (G. Early, 1994).

Spike Lee's motion picture *Do the Right Thing* highlights aspects of prejudice and discrimination between small-business owners and neighborhood residents.

WHO AM I?

The diversity of the United States today has made it more difficult for any people to view themselves clearly on the racial and ethnic landscape. Obviously, the reason is that this "landscape," as we have seen, is not naturally but socially constructed and is therefore subject to change and to different interpretations. While our focus is on the United States, every nation faces the same dilemmas.

Within little more than a generation, we have witnessed changes in labeling subordinate groups from Negroes to Blacks to African Americans, from American Indians to Native Americans or Native Peoples. However, more Native Americans prefer the use of their tribal name, such as Seminole, instead of a collective label. The old 1950s statistical term of "people with a Spanish surname" has long been discarded, yet there is disagreement over a new term: Latino or Hispanic. As with Native Americans, Hispanic Americans avoid such global terms and prefer the use of their native names, such as Puerto Ricans or Cubans. People of Mexican ancestry indicate preferences for a variety of names, such as Chicano, Mexican American, or simply Mexican.

Some advocates for racial and ethnic groups consider names a very important issue with great social significance. If nothing else, others argue, changes in names reflect people taking over the power to name themselves. Still others see this as a nonissue, or as editor Anna Maria Arias of *Hispanic* magazine termed the debate, "It's stupid. There are more important issues we should be talking about" (P. Bennett, 1993, p. A10).

In the United States and other multiracial, multiethnic societies, *panethnicity* has emerged. *Panethnicity* is the development of solidarity among ethnic subgroups. The coalition of tribal groups as Native Americans or American Indians to confront outside forces, notably the federal government, is one example of panethnicity. Hispanic/Latinos and Asian Americans are other examples of panethnicity (Lopez and Espiritu, 1990).

Is panethnicity a convenient label for "outsiders" or a term that reflects a mutual identity? Certainly, many people are unable or unwilling to recognize ethnic differences and prefer "umbrella" terms like *Asian Americans*. For some small groups, combining with others is emerging as a useful way to make themselves heard, but there is always a fear that their own distinctive culture will become submerged. While many Hispanics share the Spanish language and many are united by Roman Catholicism, only 1 in 4 native-born people of Mexican, Puerto Rican, or Cuban descent prefers a panethnic label over nationality or ethnic identity. Yet the growth of a variety of panethnic associations among many groups, including Hispanics, continues in the 1990s (de la Garza et al., 1992; Y. Espirito, 1992).

There is even less agreement about how to identify oneself in racially conscious America if one is of "mixed ancestry." Roberto Chong, who immigrated to the United States, has a Chinese father and a Peruvian mother. He considers himself "Hispanic," but others view him as "Asian" or "Latino-Asian-American." Few intermarriages exist in America, and social attitudes discourage them, but such unions are on the increase. Interracial births doubled from 63,700 in 1978 to 133,200 in 1992. In a race-conscious society, how are we going to respond to these multiracial children? As the mother of one such child, Hannah Spangler, noted, how is she to complete the school form as Hannah starts first grade in Washington, D.C.? Hannah's father is White and her mother is half Black and half Japanese. We may be slowly recognizing that the United States is a multiracial society, but we are not prepared to respond to such a society (S. Kalish, 1995).

Add to this cultural mix the many peoples with clear social identities who are not yet generally recognized in the United States. Arabs are a rapidly growing segment whose identity is heavily subject to stereotypes or, at best, is still ambiguous. Haitians and Jamaicans affirm they are Black but rarely accept the identity of African American. Brazilians, who speak Portuguese, often object to being called Hispanic because of that term's association with Spain. Similarly, there are White Hispanics and non-White Hispanics, some of the latter being Black, and others, like Roberto Chong, Asian (P. Bennett, 1994; Omi and Winant, 1994, p. 162).

Another challenge to identity is *marginality*, which refers to the status of being between two cultures, as in the case of an individual whose mother is a Jew and whose father is a Christian. Incomplete assimilation, as in a Korean woman's migrating to the United States, also results in marginality. While she may take on the characteristics of her new host society, she may not be fully accepted and may therefore feel neither Korean nor American. The marginal person finds himself or herself being perceived differently in different environments, with varying expectations. In the family circle, the marginal person's ethnic heritage is clear, but in the workplace, a different label may be used to identify this person (J. Billson, 1988; R. Park, 1928; E. Stonequist, 1937).

As we seek to better understand diversity in the United States, we must be mindful that ethnic and racial labels are just that, labels that have been socially constructed. Yet these social constructs can have a powerful impact, whether self-applied or applied by others.

CONCLUSION

In the first chapter, we have attempted to organize our approach to subordinate-dominant relations in the United States. We observed that subordinate groups do not necessarily have fewer people than the dominant group. Subordinate groups can be classified into racial, ethnic, religious, and gender groups. Racial classification has been of interest, but scientific findings do not explain contemporary race relations. Biological differences of race are relatively unimportant. Yet continuing debates demonstrate that attempts to establish a *biological* basis of race have not been entirely swept into the dustbin of history. The *social* meaning given to physical differences, however, is very significant. People have defined racial differences in such a way as to encourage or discourage the progress of certain groups.

The confinement of certain people to subordinate groups may function to serve *some* people's vested interests. This denial of opportunities or privileges to an entire group, however, only leads to conflict between dominant and subordinate groups.

Societies, such as the United States, develop ideologies to justify privileges given to some and opportunities denied to others. These ideologies may be subtle, such as assimilation (that is, "You should be like us"), or overt, such as racist thought and behavior.

Subordinate groups generally emerge in one of four ways: voluntary migration, involuntary migration, annexation, or colonialism. Once a group is given subordinate status, it does not necessarily keep it indefinitely. Extermination, expulsion, secession, segregation, fusion, and assimilation remove the status of subordination, although inequality may persist.

Subordinate-group members' reactions include an alternate avenue to acceptance and success: "Why should we forsake what we are to be accepted by them?" In response to this question, there is a resurgence of ethnic identification. *Pluralism* describes a society in which several different groups coexist, with no dominant or subordinate groups. The hope for such a society remains unfulfilled, except perhaps for isolated exceptions, like Switzerland. But even Switzerland has not entirely lived up to the ideal of mutual respect and cultural diversity.

The two significant forces that are absent in a truly pluralistic society are prejudice and discrimination. In an assimilationist society, prejudice disparages outgroup differences, and discrimination financially rewards those who shed their past. In the next two chapters, we will explore the nature of prejudice and discrimination in the United States.

KEY TERMS

Afrocentric perspective An emphasis on the customs of African cultures and how they have penetrated the history, culture, and behavior of Blacks in the United States and around the world.

amalgamation The process by which a dominant group and a subordinate group combine through intermarriage to form a new group.

assimilation The process by which an individual forsakes his or her own cultural tradition to become part of a different culture.

bilingualism The use of two or more languages in places of work or education and the treatment of each language as legitimate.

biological race The mistaken notion of a genetically isolated human group.

class As defined by Max Weber, persons who share similar levels of wealth.

colonialism A foreign power's maintenance of political, social, economic, and cultural dominance over a people for an extended period.

conflict perspective A sociological approach that assumes that social behavior is best understood in terms of conflict or tension among competing groups.

dysfunction An element of society that may disrupt a social system or lead to a decrease in its stability.

emigration Leaving a country to settle in another.

ethnic group A group set apart from others because of its national origin or distinctive cultural patterns.

functionalist perspective A sociological approach emphasizing how parts of a society are structured in the interest of maintaining the system as a whole.

fusion A minority and a majority group combining to form a new group.

genocide The deliberate, systematic killing of an entire people or nation.

immigration Coming into a new country as a permanent resident.

intelligence quotient (IQ) The ratio of an individual's mental age (as computed by an IQ test) divided by his or her chronological age and multiplied by 100.

interactive effect Pettigrew's view that race and class act together to place an individual in a stratification system.

internal colonialism The treatment of subordinate peoples like colonial subjects by those in power.

labeling theory An approach introduced by Howard Becker that attempts to explain why certain people are viewed as deviants and others engaging in the same behavior are not.

marginality The status of being between two cultures at the same time, such as the status of Jewish immigrants in the United States.

melting pot Diverse racial or ethnic groups or both forming a new creation, a new cultural entity.

migration A general term that describes any transfer of population.

minority group A subordinate group whose members have significantly less control or power over their own lives than that held by the members of a dominant or majority group.

panethnicity The development of solidarity among ethnic subgroups as reflected in "Hispanic" or "Asian American."

pluralism Mutual respect between the various groups in a society for one another's cultures, allowing minorities to express their own culture without experiencing prejudice or hostility.

politically correct A description of efforts on behalf of racial, ethnic, and religious minorities as well as women. The phrase is often used negatively, in criticism of such measures.

racial formation A sociohistorical process by which racial categories are created, inhibited, transformed, and destroyed.

racial group A group that is socially set apart from others because of obvious physical differences.

racism A doctrine that one race is superior.

relative deprivation The conscious experience of a negative discrepancy between legitimate expectations and present actualities.

segregation The act of physically separating two groups; often imposed on a subordinate group by the dominant group.

self-fulfilling prophecy The tendency of individuals to respond to and act on the basis of stereotypes, a predisposition that can lead to the validation of false definitions.

stereotypes Unreliable generalizations about all members of a group that do not take into account individual differences within the group.

stratification A structured ranking of entire groups of people that perpetuates unequal rewards and power in a society.

FOR FURTHER INFORMATION

Steven Gregory and Roger Sanjek, eds. *Race*. New Brunswick, NJ: Rutgers University Press, 1994.

The shifting role of race is viewed in a variety of disciplines and contexts, as well as from differing ethnic and gender views.

James B. McKee. *Sociology and the Race Problem*. Urbana: University of Illinois Press, 1993.

A historical analysis of how sociology from the 1920s to the 1960s often failed to effectively understand race relations in the United States.

Michael Newton and Judy Ann Newton. *Racial and Religious Violence in America.* New York: Garland, 1991.

> Starting with the 1501 Portuguese enslavement of East Coast Native Americans, this 728-page chronology offers a concise description of riots, vandalism, supremacist actions, assassinations, and so forth through 1989.

Michael Omi and Howard Winant. *Racial Formation in the United States,* 2d ed. New York: Routledge, 1994.

> Presentation of the authors' concept of "racial formation" in light of political development in the United States.

Gregory D. Squires. *Capital and Communities in Black and White.* Albany: State University of New York Press, 1994.

> The author considers how the decline of inner-city neighborhoods is related to economic restructuring in a global context.

Margaret Wetherell and Jonathan Potter. *Mapping the Language of Racism: Discourse and the Legitimation of Exploitation.* New York: Columbia University Press, 1992.

> Considers the emergence of racist thinking by using the relationship between White New Zealanders and the Maori as a case study.

CRITICAL THINKING QUESTIONS

1. In what ways have you seen issues of race and ethnicity emerge unexpectedly?
2. How diverse is your community? What evidence can you see that some group is being subordinated?
3. Identify groups that have been subordinated for reasons other than race, ethnicity, or gender.
4. How can a significant political or social issue be viewed in assimilationist and pluralistic terms?
5. How does the concept *racial formation* relate to the concluding issue of "Who Am I?"

Chapter
2

Prejudice

Chapter Outline

Highlights

*P*rejudice is a negative attitude rejecting an entire group; *discrimination* is behavior depriving a group of certain rights or opportunities. Prejudice does not necessarily coincide with discrimination, as made apparent by a typology developed by Robert Merton. Several theories have been advanced to explain prejudice. The explanations are *exploitation, scapegoating, authoritarian personality,* and *normative.* These explanations examine prejudice in terms of content (stereotypes) and its extent. Prejudice is not limited to the dominant group; subordinate groups often dislike one another. It has been argued that the subordinate people may suffer low self-esteem because of their low status, but the evidence does not support this belief. The mass media seem to be of limited value in reducing prejudice and may even intensify ill feeling. Equal-status contact and the shared-coping approach may reduce hostility among groups.

Courts in the state capitals of Columbus, Ohio, and Springfield, Illinois, consider requests for Ku Klux Klan demonstrations. Janesville, Wisconsin, a community of less than 60,000 people, is the site of a Klan-recruiting rally complete with a burning cross in a town park. These communities are outside the Old South and distant from the violence of inner cities; yet, symbolically, this evidence of intolerance shows that prejudice has no boundaries in either time or space.

© Dan Wasserman, *Boston Globe.* Distributed by Los Angeles Times Syndicate. Reprinted with permission.

In 1993, looking for a night's entertainment in the movie *Falling Down,* people cheered the Michael Douglas character of Bill "D-Fens" Foster as he went over the edge, assaulting a convenience store owned by a Korean immigrant over his English and the price of a soda. We accept the brooding portrayal of Japanese businessmen in *Rising Sun* (1993). We applaud the appearance of mascots dressed as Native Americans or deliver a "tomahawk chop" to signal the demise of the opponent. It takes the combined effort of Native Americans and several large church groups to block the sale of a malt liquor named "Crazy Horse." They argued that the alcoholic beverage was offensive to the honored position Crazy Horse has as a political and religious leader in Oglala Lakota history. And for those too young for liquor, but not too old for video games, one finds that the only time Asian characters appear are in martial arts games such as E. Honda in Street Fighter or Liu Kang in Mortal Kombat II.

Prejudice is so prevalent that it is tempting to consider it inevitable or, even more loosely, "just part of human nature." Such a view ignores its variability from individual to individual and from society to society. Children must learn prejudice before they exhibit it as adults. Therefore, prejudice is a *social* phenomenon, an acquired characteristic. Only a truly pluralistic society would lack unfavorable distinctions made through prejudicial attitudes among racial and ethnic groups.

Ill feeling among groups may result from ethnocentrism. *Ethnocentrism* is the tendency to assume that one's culture and way of life are superior to all others. The ethnocentric person judges other groups or even other cultures by the standards of his or her own group. This attitude leads people quite easily into prejudice against cultures they view as inferior.

Hostility toward groups different from one's own is not unusual. A 1991 study asked a nationwide sample what they thought was the "social standing" of a variety of racial and ethnic groups. Whites did well, and racial and ethnic minorities were shown to be held in low social standing. However, fully 39 percent were willing to evaluate the "Wisian Americans," a nonexistent group made up by the researchers. Not only was this fictitious group rated, but it received one of the lowest evaluations. Obviously, fear of those who are different extends to imaginary groups that sound strange (T. Smith, 1991).

While prejudice is certainly not new in the United States, it is receiving renewed attention as it occurs in neighborhoods, at meetings, and on college campuses. In 1990, President George Bush signed into law the Hate Crime Statistics Act, which directs the Department of Justice to gather data on crimes motivated by the victim's race, religion, ethnicity, or sexual orientation. This law created a national mandate to identify such crimes, whereas previously only 12 states had monitored hate crimes. In 1994, data was released by law enforcement agencies covering about half of the United States. Over 8,000 hate-crime bias-motivated incidents were reported. While vandalism and intimidation were the most common, 16 percent of the incidents involved assault and even rape or murder (*Asianweek,* 1994).

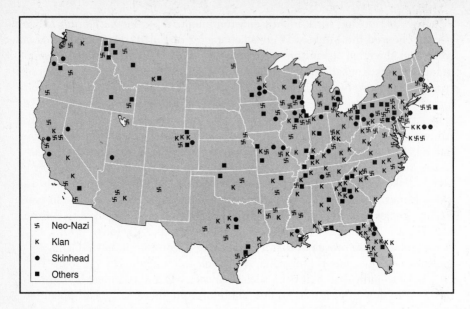

Figure 2.1 Racist Fringe Groups
No part of the nation is truly free of a variety of known fringe groups that espouse racial hatred and religious intolerance.

Source: Klanwatch in S. Shabad, "Beyond the Fringe," *Newsweek* 125 (May 1, 1995), p. 38.

What causes people to dislike entire groups of people? It is possible for such attitudes to be changed? This chapter tries to answer these questions about prejudice; Chapter 3 focuses on discrimination.

PREJUDICE AND DISCRIMINATION

Prejudice and discrimination are related concepts but are not the same. *Prejudice* is a negative attitude toward an entire category of people. The two important components in this definition are *attitude* and *entire category*. Prejudice involves attitudes, thoughts, and beliefs, not actions. Frequently, prejudice is expressed through the use of *ethnophaulisms*, or ethnic slurs, which include derisive nicknames such as *honkie, gook,* or *wetback.* Ethnophaulisms also include speaking about or to members of a particular group in a condescending way—"José does well in school for a Chicano"—or referring to a middle-aged woman as "one of the girls."

A prejudiced belief leads to categorical rejection. Prejudice is not disliking someone you meet because you find his or her behavior objectionable. It is disliking an entire racial or ethnic group, even if you have had little or no contact. A college student who requests a room change after three weeks of enduring his roommate's sleeping all day, playing loud music all night, and piling garbage on his desk is not prejudiced. He would be displaying prejudice, however, if he requested a change on arriving at school and learning from his roommate's luggage tags that his new roommate is of a different nationality group.

Prejudice is a belief or attitude; discrimination is action. *Discrimination* involves behavior that excludes all members of a group from certain rights, opportunities, or privileges. Like prejudice, it must be categorical. If an individual refuses to hire as a typist an Italian American who is illiterate, it is not discrimination. If an individual refuses to hire any Italian Americans because she thinks they are incompetent and does not make the effort to see if an applicant is qualified, it is discrimination.

Prejudice does not necessarily coincide with discriminatory behavior. Sociologist Robert Merton (1949, 1976, pp. 189–216), in exploring the relationship between negative attitudes and negative behavior, identified four major categories (see Figure 2.2 on p. 44). The folk label added to each of Merton's categories may more readily identify the type of individual being described. These are

1. The unprejudiced nondiscriminator: all-weather liberal
2. The unprejudiced discriminator: reluctant liberal
3. The prejudiced nondiscriminator: timid bigot
4. The prejudiced discriminator: all-weather bigot

Liberals, as the term is employed in Types 1 and 2, are committed to equality among people. The all-weather liberal believes in equality and practices it. Merton was quick to observe that all-weather liberals may be far removed from any real competition with African Americans or women. Furthermore, such people may be content with their own behavior and may do little to change. The reluctant liberal is not even this committed to equality among races. Social pressure may cause such a person to discriminate. Fear of losing employees may cause a manager to avoid promoting women to supervisory capacities. Equal-opportunity legislation may be the best way to influence the reluctant liberals.

Types 3 and 4 do not believe in equal treatment for racial and ethnic groups, but they vary in their willingness to act. The timid bigot, Type 3, will not discriminate if discrimination costs money or reduces profits or if he or she is pressured not to by peers or the government. The all-weather bigot unhesitatingly acts on the prejudiced beliefs he or she holds.

Merton's typology points out that attitudes should not be confused with behavior. People do not always act as they believe. More than half a century ago, Richard LaPiere (1934, 1969) measured the relationship between racial attitudes and social conduct. From 1930 to 1932, LaPiere traveled throughout the United States with a Chinese couple. Despite a climate of alleged intolerance of Asians, LaPiere observed that the couple was treated courteously at hotels, motels, and restaurants. He was puzzled by the good reception they received, for all the conventional attitude surveys showed extreme prejudice by Whites toward the Chinese.

It was possible that LaPiere had been fortunate during his travels and consistently stopped at places operated by the tolerant minority. To test this possibility,

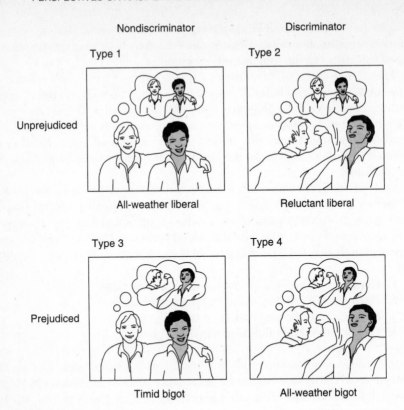

Figure 2.2 Prejudice and Discrimination
As sociologist Robert Merton's formulation shows, prejudice and discrimination are related to each other but are not the same.

he sent questionnaires asking the very establishments at which they had been served if the owner would "accept members of the Chinese race as guests in your establishment." More than 90 percent responded no, even though LaPiere's Chinese couple had been treated politely at all the establishments. How can this inconsistency be explained? People who returned questionnaires reflecting prejudice were unwilling to act based on those asserted beliefs: they were timid bigots.

The LaPiere study is not without its flaws. First, he had no way of knowing whether the respondent to the questionnaire was the same person who had served him and the Chinese couple. Second, he accompanied the couple, but the questionnaire suggested that the arrival was unescorted (and in the minds of some, uncontrolled) and perhaps consisted of many Chinese individuals. Third, personnel may have changed between the time of the visit and the mailing of the questionnaire (Deutscher et al., 1993).

Even with these shortcomings, the LaPiere technique has been replicated with similar results. This technique raises the question of whether attitudes are important if they are not completely reflected in behavior. But if attitudes are not important in small matters, they are important in other ways: lawmakers legislate and courts may reach decisions based on what the public thinks.

This is not just a hypothetical possibility. Legislators in the United States are often persuaded to vote in a certain way by what they perceive as changed attitudes toward open housing, school busing, nuclear wastes, and capital punishment. The same is true in other countries. In Great Britain, the first national survey of racial attitudes was conducted in 1969. Because it showed only 10 percent of White Britons highly prejudiced, members of Parliament cited it during the campaign for legislation outlawing discrimination.

Though prejudice is related to behavior, it is not the same. But that does not mean it is harmless. The schoolyard chant "Sticks and stones may break my bones, but names will never hurt me" is not true. Names do hurt people. To be subjected to ridicule is in itself detrimental.

Sociologists Jack and William C. Levin (1982) enumerated some of prejudice's functions. For the majority group, it serves to maintain privileged occupations and more power for its members. Although this effect seems self-evident, Levin and Levin go on to point out that prejudice may be viewed as having some functions even for subordinate groups. These functions include maintaining ingroup solidarity and reducing competition in some areas of employment, admittedly those with lower status or smaller rewards.

The following sections examine the theories of why prejudice exists and discuss the content and extent of prejudice today.

THEORIES OF PREJUDICE

The previous section pointed out that prejudice is learned. Friends, relatives, newspapers, books, movies, and television all teach it. Awareness that there are differences among people that society judges to be important begins at an early age. Several theories have been advanced to explain the rejection of certain groups in a society.

Exploitation Theory

Racial prejudice is frequently used to justify keeping a group in a subordinate position, such as a lower social class. Conflict theorists in particular stress the role of racial and ethnic hostility as a way for the dominant group to keep its position of status and power intact. Indeed, this approach maintains that even the less affluent White working class uses prejudice to minimize competition from upwardly mobile minorities.

This *exploitation theory* is clearly part of the Marxist tradition in sociological thought. Just as Karl Marx emphasized exploitation of the lower class as an integral part of capitalism, the exploitation or conflict approach explains how racism can stigmatize a group as inferior so that the exploitation of that group can be justified.

The exploitation theory of prejudice is persuasive. Japanese Americans were the object of little prejudice until they began to enter jobs that brought them into competition with Whites. The movement to keep Chinese out of the country became strongest during the latter half of the nineteenth century, when Chinese

Native Americans have been exploited. Here, actress Jane Fonda, Ted Turner (her husband and the Braves' owner), and former U.S. President Jimmy Carter join in the Tomahawk chop at a 1991 post-season baseball game.

immigrants and Whites fought over dwindling numbers of jobs. Both the enslavement of African Americans and the removal westward of Native Americans were to a significant degree economically motivated.

Related to the exploitation theory is the *caste approach* to race relations in the United States. The term *caste* describes a system of social inequality in which status is inherited and people have little, if any, opportunity to change their social positions. As we have seen through exploitation theory, economic subordination benefits the dominant group's financial interests. The caste approach, however, does not rely on Marxist theory for theoretical support. The caste explanation for racial subordination sees race and social class as closely related, because Blacks and other non-Whites are destined by the social structure to occupy a castelike position. Membership in the subordinate group is inherited and permanent.

The caste approach is basically descriptive and not very analytical; for example, sociologists using it make less effort to explain why caste relations originated than does the general exploitation approach of Oliver C. Cox. The caste approach, although acknowledging the importance of social class, argues that race is more important, whereas Cox's 1942 general exploitation theory sees racial discrimination as merely an example of class differences. The caste explanation seems somewhat limited. In a caste system, as strictly defined, the lower castes accept the system and their low status. But the increased numbers of Blacks in high-paying occupations and the continuous struggle for equal rights indicate that African Americans do not acquiesce (G. Berreman, 1960, 1973).

Although some cases support the exploitation theory, it is too limited to explain prejudice in all its forms. First, not all minority groups are exploited economically to the same extent. Second, many groups that have been the victims of prejudice have not been persecuted for economic reasons, for example, the Quakers and the Mormons. Nevertheless, as Gordon Allport (1979) concludes, the exploitation theory correctly points a finger at *one* of the factors in prejudice, that is, the rationalized self-interest of the upper classes.

Scapegoating Theory

Scapegoating theory says that prejudiced people believe they are society's victims. Exploitation theory maintains that intolerant individuals abuse others, whereas scapegoaters feel they are being abused themselves. The term *scapegoat* comes from a biblical injunction telling the Hebrews to send a goat into the wilderness to symbolically carry away the people's sins. Similarly, the theory of scapegoating suggests that an individual, rather than accepting guilt for some failure, transfers the responsibility for failure to some vulnerable group. In the major tragic twentieth-century example, Adolf Hitler used the Jews as the scapegoat for all of the social and economic ills of Germany in the 1930s. This premise led to the passage of laws restricting Jewish life in pre–World War II Germany and eventually escalated into the mass extermination of Europe's Jews.

Bettelheim and Janowitz (1964) studied prejudice in the United States and found that the downwardly mobile are usually more prejudiced. People who lose a job and are forced to accept a lower-status occupation experience increased tension and anxiety. Who is responsible, they ask, for their misfortune? At this time, a scapegoat, in the form of a racial, ethnic, or religious group, may enter the picture.

Like exploitation theory, scapegoating theory adds to our understanding of why prejudice exists but does not explain all its facets. For example, scapegoating theory offers little explanation of why a specific group is selected or why frustration may not be taken out on the real object when it is possible. Also, both the exploitation and the scapegoating theories suggest that every individual sharing the same general experiences in society would be equally prejudiced, but that is not the case. Prejudice varies among individuals who would seem to benefit equally from the exploitation of a subordinate group or who have experienced equal frustration. In an effort to explain these personality differences, social scientists developed the concept of the *authoritarian personality*.

Authoritarian Personality Theory

A number of social scientists do not see prejudice as an isolated trait that anyone can have. Several efforts have been made to detail the prejudiced personality, but the most comprehensive effort culminated in a volume entitled *The Authoritarian Personality* (Adorno et al., 1950). Using a variety of tests and relying on more than 2,000 respondents, ranging from middle-class Whites to inmates of San Quentin State Prison, the authors claimed they had isolated the characteristics of the authoritarian personality.

In these authors' view, the basic characteristics of the authoritarian personality were adherence to conventional values, uncritical acceptance of authority, and concern with power and toughness. With obvious relevance to the development of intolerance, the authoritarian personality was also characterized by aggressiveness toward people who did not conform to conventional norms or obey authority. According to the authors, this personality type developed from an early childhood of harsh discipline. A child with an authoritarian upbringing obeyed and then later treated others as he or she had been raised.

This study has been widely criticized, but the very existence of criticism indicates the influence of the study. Critics have attacked the study's equation of authoritarianism with right-wing politics (liberals can also be rigid); its failure to see that prejudice is more closely related to other individual traits, such as social class, than to authoritarianism as it was defined; and the research methods employed. Graham Kinloch (1974, p. 167), discussing personality in general and not just this study, added a fourth criticism: the authors concentrated on factors behind extreme racial prejudice, rather than on more common expressions of hostility.

Normative Approach

Although personality factors are important contributors to prejudice, normative or situational factors must also be given serious consideration. Analysis reveals how societal influences shape a climate for tolerance or intolerance. Societies develop social norms that dictate not only what foods are desirable (or forbidden) but also what racial and ethnic groups are to be favored (or despised). Social forces operate in a society to encourage or discourage tolerance. The force may be widespread, for example, the pressure on southerners to oppose racial equality while there was slavery, or it may be limited, for example, one male who finds himself becoming more sexist as he competes with three females for a position in a prestigious law firm.

Social psychologist Thomas Pettigrew (1958, 1959) collected data that substantiated the importance of such social norms in developing a social climate conducive to the expression of prejudice. Pettigrew found that Whites in the South were more anti-Black than Whites in the North, and that Whites in the United States were not as prejudiced as Whites in the Republic of South Africa.

Personality alone cannot account for such differences. Pettigrew's research revealed no significant variation between the two societies in terms of the presence of authoritarian individuals. He therefore concluded that structural factors explained differences in the levels of prejudice between these two regions. In the Republic of South Africa and the American South, Whites were socialized to have highly prejudiced attitudes toward Blacks. Not all Whites in these areas accepted prevailing racist ideas, however. Personality factors offer the best explanation for these differences in the degrees of prejudice among individuals living in the same region (J. Louw-Potgieter, 1988).

The four approaches to prejudice summarized in Table 2.1 should not be viewed as mutually exclusive. Social circumstances provide cues for a person's attitudes; personality determines the extent to which people follow social cues and the

Table 2.1   THEORIES OF PREJUDICE

There is no one explanation of why prejudice exists, but several approaches taken together offer insight.

Theory	Proponent	Explanation	Example
Exploitation	Oliver C. Cox Marxist theory	People utilize others unfairly to economic advantage.	A minority member is hired at lower wage level.
Scapegoating	Bruno Bettelheim Morris Janowitz	People blame others for their own failure.	An unsuccessful applicant assumes that a minority member or a woman got "his" job.
Authoritarian personality	Adorno and associates	Child rearing leads one to develop intolerance as an adult.	The rigid personality type dislikes people who are "different."
Normative	Thomas Pettigrew	Peer and social influences encourage tolerance or intolerance	A person from an intolerant household is more likely to be openly prejudiced.

likelihood that they will encourage others to do the same. Societal norms may promote or deter tolerance; personality traits suggest the degree to which a person will conform to norms of intolerance.

THE CONTENT OF PREJUDICE: STEREOTYPES

In Chapter 1, we saw that stereotypes play a powerful role in how people come to view dominant and subordinate groups. These exaggerated images have been subjected to numerous scientific studies.

The systematic study of stereotypes began with David Katz and Kenneth Braly's (1933) use of the *checklist approach*. College students were presented with a list of 84 adjectives (*sly, cruel, neat,* and so on) and were asked to list which traits they considered most characteristic of ten groups: Germans, Italians, Irish, English, Blacks, Jews, Americans, Chinese, Japanese, and Turks. The students' selection of traits for each group consistently agreed with one another, especially for Blacks and Jews. This technique has been confirmed by several other researchers. Table 2.2 presents the traits most frequently assigned to Blacks and Jews by students over a 60-year period.

Stereotyping of women and men is well documented, and we consider it in greater detail in Chapter 16. However, little research has been done on the stereotyping of women of color. Rose Weitz (1992) surveyed White undergraduates and found a definite willingness to characterize African-American women as "loud" and "argumentative," Mexican-American women as "lazy" and "quick-tempered," and Jewish women as "spoiled" and "shrewd." "American women" in general were seen as "intelligent," "materialistic," and "sophisticated"—quite a contrast to the labeling of women of color.

Table 2.2   STEREOTYPE TRAITS, 1932–1993

The compared responses of college students over a 60-year period show a softening of the stereotypes applied to Blacks and Jewish Americans.

Group and Trait	1932(%)	1950(%)	1969(%)	1982(%)	1993(%)
Blacks					
Superstitious	84	42	10	9	1
Lazy	75	32	18	18	5
Happy-go-lucky	39	17	5	1	2
Ignorant	38	24	8	9	5
Jews					
Shrewd	79	47	37	15	—
Mercenary	49	28	8	2	—
Grasping	34	17	1	1	—
Sly	20	14	8	9	—

Note: Data for Jewish Americans "not available" for 1993.

Source: L. Gordon (1986, p. 201); reprinted by permission of the author from *Sociology and Social Research* 70 (August 1988); J. Dovidio (1994).

Labels take on such strong significance that people often ignore facts contradicting their performed beliefs. People who believe Italian Americans to be members of the Mafia disregard law-abiding Italian Americans. Muslims are regularly portrayed in a violent, offensive manner which contributes to their being misunderstood and distrusted. We will consider later in the chapter how this stereotype has become especially widespread since the mid-1970s. Gradually the mass media—movies, television, newspapers, and periodicals—are presenting a more accurate, evenhanded portrayal of racial, ethnic, and religious groups; however, there is much room for improvement.

Research on stereotyping provides information on the content of prejudice but tells us little about the amount of prejudice. People may know what the stereotypes of a group are without believing them, or they may believe the stereotypes but also know that it is increasingly improper to use them, even on a questionnaire. Another limitation of this research is that some traits may be positive, or at least neutral, depending on individual interpretation (materialistic or pleasure-loving, for instance). Studies indicate that members of younger generations show more care in thinking about racial and ethnic groups, but this tendency in itself does not mean they are less prejudiced. The fading of one stereotype may mean only that it has been replaced by another. The image of many groups as docile and lazy was shattered by the social protest of the 1960s. Now, rather than being seen as weak, such groups are viewed as too aggressive.

Are stereotypes held only by dominant groups about subordinate groups? The answer is clearly no. White Americans even believe generalizations about themselves, although admittedly these are rather positive. Subordinate groups also hold exaggerated images of themselves. Studies before World War II showed a tendency for Blacks to assign to themselves many of the same negative traits that Whites assigned them. Now such stereotypes of themselves are largely rejected by African

Americans, Jews, Asians, and other minority groups, although subordinate groups will to some degree stereotype each other. The nature of the subordinate group's self-image is explored later in this chapter. The subordinate group also develops stereotyped images of the dominant group. Anthony Dworkin (1965) surveyed Chicanos and found that the majority agreed that Anglos were prejudiced, snobbish, hypocritical, tense, anxious, and neurotic and had little family loyalty.

If stereotypes are exaggerated generalizations, why are they so widely held and why are some traits more often assigned than others? First, evidence for traits may arise out of real conditions. For example, more Puerto Ricans live in poverty than Whites, and so the prejudiced mind associates Puerto Ricans with laziness. According to the New Testament, some Jews were responsible for the crucifixion of Jesus, and so, to the prejudiced mind, all Jews are Christ-killers. Some activists in the women's movement are lesbians, and so all feminists are lesbians. From a kernel of fact, faulty generalization creates a stereotype.

Black American artist Horace Pippin (1888–1946) produced this painting entitled *Mr. Prejudice.*

A second aspect of stereotypes is their role in the self-fulfilling prophecy discussed in Chapter 1. The dominant group creates barriers, making it difficult for a subordinate group to act differently from the stereotype. It also applies pressure toward conformity to the stereotype. Conformity to the stereotype, although forced, becomes evidence of the validity of the stereotype. Some evidence suggests that, even today, people accept to some degree negative stereotypes of themselves. The labeling process becomes complete as images are applied and in some cases accepted by those being stereotyped.

THE EXTENT OF PREJUDICE

Interest in developing theories of prejudice or studying its concept has been exceeded only by interest in measuring it. From the outset, efforts to measure prejudice have suffered from disagreement over exactly what constitutes intolerance, what differentiates prejudice from nonprejudice, and whether there is such a phenomenon as no prejudice. Add to these dilemmas the methodological problems of attitude measurement, and the empirical study of prejudice becomes an undertaking fraught with difficulty.

The extent of prejudice can be measured only in relative, rather than absolute, differences. We cannot accurately say, for example, that prejudice toward Puerto Ricans is four times greater than that toward Portuguese Americans. We can conclude that prejudice is greater toward one group than toward the other; we just cannot quantify how much greater. To assess differences in prejudice, the social distance scale is especially appropriate.

The Social Distance Scale

Robert Park and Ernest Burgess first defined social distance as the tendency to approach or withdraw from a racial group (1921, p. 440). A few years later, Emory Bogardus (1968) conceptualized a scale that could empirically measure social distance. So widely used is his social distance scale that it is frequently referred to as the *Bogardus scale*.

The scale asks people how willing they would be to interact with various racial and ethnic groups in specified social situations. The situations describe different degrees of social contact or social distance. The seven items used, with their corresponding distance scores, follow. People are asked if they would be willing to admit each group:

- To close kinship by marriage (1.00)
- To my club as personal chums (2.00)
- To my street as neighbors (3.00)
- To employment in my occupation (4.00)
- To citizenship in my country (5.00)
- As only visitors to my country (6.00)
- Would exclude from my country (7.00)

A score of 1.00 for any group would indicate no social distance and therefore no prejudice. The social distance scale has been administered to many different groups, even in other countries. Despite some minor flaws and certain refinements in the scale, the results of these studies are useful and can be compared.

The data in Table 2.3 summarize the results of studies using the social distance scale in the United States over a 65-year period. In the top third of the hierarchy are White Americans and northern Europeans. In the middle are eastern and southern Europeans, and generally near the bottom are racial minorities. This prestige hierarchy resembles the relative proportions of the various groups in the population. The arrows indicate some of the dramatic changes in the rankings. For example, the Japanese dropped from twenty-third to thirtieth during World War II and rose to twenty-fifth by 1966, only to fall again to twenty-ninth in 1991 as they became economic competitors. Two groups made marked upward progress between 1966 and 1991: Russians and Black Americans. The stability of rankings over more than half a century, however, is remarkable.

The similarity in the hierarchy during 65 years was not limited to White respondents. Several times, the scale was administered to Jewish, Chicano, Asian, Puerto Rican, Black African, and Black American groups. These groups generally shared the same hierarchy, although they placed their own group at the top. The extent of prejudice as illustrated in the ranking of racial and ethnic groups seems to be widely shared. Studies have also been performed in other societies and show that they have a racial and ethnic hierarchy as well.

A tentative conclusion we can draw from these studies is that the extent of prejudice is decreasing. At the bottom of Table 2.3 is the arithmetic mean of the racial reactions, on a scale of 1.0 to 7.0. Although the change was slight from survey to survey, it is consistently downward for all the groups. Many specific nationalities and races, however, experienced little change. The spread in social distance (the difference between the top- and bottom-ranked groups) also decreased or held steady from 1926 to 1991, a finding indicating that fewer distinctions were being made, although some were still being made. This result was also confirmed empirically in research on stereotypes (Crull and Bruton, 1985; Owen et al., 1981).

Attitude Change

Nationwide surveys over the years have consistently shown growing support by Whites for integration, even during the southern resistance and northern turmoil of the 1960s. Table 2.4 on p. 55 lists six questions that appeared on several opinion polls from 1942 to 1994. With few exceptions, the responses show an increase in the number of Whites responding positively to hypothetical situations of increased contact with African Americans. For example, 30 percent of the Whites sampled in 1942 felt that Blacks should not attend separate schools (Statement 3), but by 1970, 74 percent supported integrated schools, and fully 93 percent responded in that manner in 1991. Of course, this is what Whites *said* they wanted. As Andrew Greeley and Paul Sheatsley (1971) observed, "Attitudes are not necessarily predictive of behavior. A man may be a staunch integrationist and still feel his neighbor-

Table 2.3 CHANGES IN SOCIAL DISTANCE

The social distance scale developed by Emory Bogardus has been a useful measure of people's feelings of hostility toward different racial and ethnic groups.

I 1926 — Group	Score	II 1946 — Group	Score	III 1966 — Group	Score	IV 1977 — Group	Score	V 1991 — Group	Score
1. English	1.06	1. Americans (U.S. White)	1.04→	1. Americans (U.S. White)→	1.07→	1. Americans (U.S. White)→	1.25→	1. Americans (U.S. White)	1.00
2. Americans (U.S. White)→	1.10	2. Canadians	1.11	2. English	1.14	2. English	1.39	2. English	1.08
3. Canadians	1.13	3. English	1.13	3. Canadians	1.15	3. Canadians	1.42	3. French	1.16
4. Scots	1.13	4. Irish	1.24	4. French	1.36	4. French	1.58	4. Canadians	1.21
5. Irish	1.30	5. Scots	1.26	5. Swedish	1.42	5. Italians	1.65	5. Italians	1.27
6. French	1.32	6. French	1.31	6. Irish	1.46	6. Irish	1.68	6. Irish	1.30
7. Germans	1.46	7. Norwegians	1.35	7. Norwegians	1.50	7. Germans	1.69	7. Germans	1.36
8. Swedish	1.54	8. Hollanders	1.37	8. Italians	1.51	8. Swedish	1.83	8. Swedish	1.38
9. Hollanders	1.56	9. Swedish	1.40	9. Scots	1.53	9. Scots	1.83	9. Scots	1.50
10. Norwegians	1.59	10. Germans	1.59	10. Germans	1.54	10. Hollanders	1.84	10. Hollanders	1.56
11. Spanish	1.72	11. Finns	1.63	11. Hollanders	1.54	11. Norwegians	1.87	11. Norwegians	1.66
12. Finns	1.83	12. Czechs	1.76	12. Finns	1.67	12. Native Americans→	1.93	12. Native Americans	1.70
13. Russians→	1.88→	13. Russians→	1.83	13. Greeks	1.82	13. Greeks	1.98	13. Greeks	1.73
14. Italians	1.94	14. Poles	1.84	14. Spanish	1.93	14. Finns	2.00	14. Finns	1.73
15. Poles	2.01	15. Spanish	1.94	15. Jews→	1.97	15. Jews→	2.01	15. Poles	1.74
16. Armenians	2.06	16. Italians	2.28	16. Poles	1.98	16. Poles	2.02	16. Russians	1.76
17. Czechs	2.08	17. Armenians	2.29	17. Czechs	2.02	17. Spanish	2.03	17. Spanish	1.77
18. Greeks	2.38	18. Greeks	2.29	18. Native Americans→	2.12	18. Negroes→	2.11	18. Jews	1.84
19. Jews→	2.39→	19. Jews→	2.32	19. Japanese Americans→	2.14	19. Mexican Americans→	2.17	19. Mexicans (U.S.)	1.84
20. Native Americans→	2.47	20. Native Americans→	2.45	20. Armenians	2.18	20. Japanese Americans→	2.18	20. Czechs	1.90
21. Chinese	2.69	21. Chinese	2.50	21. Filipinos	2.31	21. Armenians	2.20	21. Americans (U.S. Black)	1.94
22. Mexican Americans	—	22. Filipinos	2.52	22. Chinese	2.34	22. Czechs	2.23	22. Chinese	1.96
23. Filipinos	2.80	23. Mexican Americans	2.76	23. Mexican Americans	2.37	23. Chinese	2.29	23. Filipinos	2.04
24. Mexicans	—	24. Mexicans	2.89	24. Russians→	2.38	24. Filipinos	2.31	24. Japanese (U.S.)	2.06
25. Turks	3.00	25. Japanese Americans→	2.90	25. Japanese→	2.41	25. Japanese→	2.38	25. Armenians	2.17
26. Japanese Americans→	3.28	26. Koreans	3.05	26. Turks	2.48	26. Mexicans	2.40	26. Turks	2.23
27. Koreans	3.30	27. Turks	3.30	27. Koreans	2.51	27. Turks	2.55	27. Koreans	2.24
28. Indians (from India)	3.36	28. Indians (from India)	3.43	28. Mexicans	2.56	28. Indians (of India)	2.55	28. Mexicans	2.27
29. Negroes→	3.60→	29. Negroes→	3.60→	29. Negroes→	2.56	29. Russians→	2.57	29. Japanese	2.37
30. Japanese→	3.91	30. Japanese→	3.61	30. Indians (from India)	2.62	30. Koreans	2.63	30. Indians (India)	2.39
Arithmetic mean	2.14	Arithmetic mean	2.12	Arithmetic mean	1.92	Arithmetic mean	1.93	Arithmetic mean	1.76
Spread in distance	2.85	Spread in distance	2.57	Spread in distance	1.56	Spread in distance	1.38	Spread in distance	1.39

Sources: Adapted from Emory S. Bogardus, "Comparing Racial Distance in Ethiopia, South Africa, and the United States," *Sociology and Social Research* 52 (January 1968), p. 152; Carolyn A. Owen, Howard C. Eisner, and Thomas R. McFaul, "A Half-Century of Social Distance Research: National Replication of the Bogardus Studies," *Sociology and Social Research* 66 (October 1981), p. 89; and Tae-H. Song, "Social Contact and Ethnic Distance Between Koreans and the U.S. Whites in the United States," unpub. paper, Macomb, Western Illinois University, 1991. Reprinted by permission.

Table 2.4 ATTITUDES OF WHITES TOWARD BLACKS, 1942–1994 (PERCENTAGE AFFIRMATIVE)

Attitudes of White Americans toward African Americans improved; however, most of this change took place in the 1950s and 1960s. There was relatively little change from 1963 to 1994.

	Year												
	1942	1956	1963	1965	1967	1970	1972	1976	1977	1978	1982	1985	1994
1. Negroes/Blacks have the same intelligence as White people given the same education and training.	42	77	78					72		75			
2. Negroes/Blacks should not push themselves where they are not wanted.			75			84	76	71	73		59	61	44
3. White students and Negroes/Blacks should go to the same schools, not separate ones.	30	49	63	67		74	86	85	86		91	93	
4. Do you favor the busing of Negro/Black and White schoolchildren from one district to another?							14	13	13	17	16	19	29
5. If a Negro/Black came to live next door, you would move.	67		45	35	35		19			13		7	
6. If Negroes/Blacks came to live in great numbers in your neighborhood, you would move.			78		69	71					51		

Note: Percentages indicate the proportion of the nationwide sample that agreed with the statement. The remaining respondents did not necessarily disagree: some did not answer and some expressed no opinion. The wording of the questions may have changed slightly from one year to the next. Questions not asked in a particular year are indicated by a blank.

Sources: Campbell and Schuman (1968); G. Gallup (1972); Greeley and Sheatsley (1971); Hyman and Sheatsley (1964); National Opinion Research Center (1995); Newsweek (1979); M. Schwartz (1967); J. Skolnick (1969); Smith and Sheatsley (1984).

hood is 'threatened'" (p. 9). Attitudes are still important, apart from behavior. A change of attitude may create a context in which legislative or behavioral change can occur. Such attitude changes leading to behavior changes did, in fact, occur in some areas during the 1960s. Changes in intergroup behavior mandated by law in housing, schools, public places of accommodation, and on the job appear to be responsible for making some new kinds of interracial contact a social reality. Attitudes translate into votes, peer pressure, and political clout, each of which can facilitate or hinder efforts to undo racial inequality.

The trend toward tolerance was not limited to any subgroup of Whites. The 1960s witnessed an increase in support for integration encompassing all regions (including the South), age groups (especially those under 25), income levels, levels of education, and occupational groups. The rise of support was a nationwide phenomenon.

During the civil disorders from 1965 to 1968, many people talked about a *White backlash*. The militancy of the Black Power movement had allegedly caused a hardening and reversal of White attitudes. The data in Table 2.4 and other surveys, however, present little evidence of a reversal of attitudes on the part of previously tolerant Whites. If that is so, how did the term *White backlash* become so widely used? The tumult of the 1960s made race more important to Whites in all regions, not just the South. Race also became important in many political issues, meaning that anti-Black feelings not only could be voiced as bigoted outbursts but could also be used as a political force to oppose open housing, affirmative action, and school busing. Over the years, Whites have shown greater resistance to new advances by African Americans while gradually accepting past advances. This change seems to be verified in Table 2.4: Whites increasingly supported accomplishments of the civil rights movement while consistently agreeing that Blacks should not push themselves where they were not wanted; Whites also displayed, begrudgingly, a very slow acceptance of busing. This resistance to further change came to be called the *White backlash*.

Surveying White attitudes toward African Americans makes two conclusions inescapable. First, attitudes are subject to change, and in periods of dramatic social upheaval, dramatic shifts can occur in one generation. Second, there is no consensus among Whites.

A third conclusion is that less progress has been made in the latter part of the twentieth century than was in the 1950s and 1960s. Economically less successful groups like African Americans and Hispanics tend to be credited with negative traits. In effect, we have another instance of "blaming the victim." A concern is that this view comes at a time when the willingness of government to address domestic ills is limited by increasing opposition to new taxes. While there is some evidence that fewer Whites are consistently prejudiced on all issues from interracial marriage to school integration, it is also apparent that Whites continue to endorse some anti-Black statements, and that negative images are widespread. In the 1990s, White attitudes hardened still further as issues such as affirmative action, immigration, and crime provoked strong emotions among Whites as well as members of subordinate groups (Schaefer, 1996).

MOOD OF THE SUBORDINATE GROUP

Opinion pollsters have been interested in White attitudes on racial issues longer than in the views of subordinate groups. This neglect of minority attitudes reflects, in part, the bias of the White researchers. It also stems from the contention that the dominant group is more important to study because it is in a better position to act on its beliefs. The results of nationwide surveys conducted in the United States in 1994 offer insight into the sharply different attitudes of African Americans, Hispanics, and Whites (see Figure 2.3).

Racial attitudes were also reassessed in the aftermath of the 1992 Los Angeles riots, the worst civil disturbance in the twentieth century. With 52 dead, this outbreak gave racism front-page attention. The riots were precipitated by a jury's failing to find four Los Angeles police officers guilty of beating a Black man, Rodney King. Since the beating had been videotaped and reshown numerous times on television, most people felt the police were guilty. In fact, a survey taken after the rioting began found 100 percent of African Americans and 86 percent of Whites believing that the jury's verdict was wrong. Yet, on other issues, there was more disagreement. Two-thirds of Whites compared to four-fifths percent of Blacks saw the Rodney King beating as evidence of widespread racism. Blacks definitely saw race relations worsening in the wake of the riots. Fully 43 percent felt they were poor, compared to 17 percent of the Whites questioned (M. Baumann, 1992).

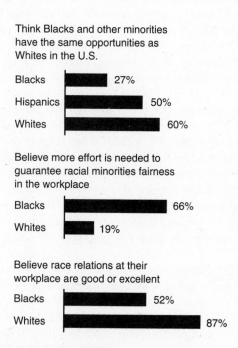

Figure 2.3 **Views of the United States, 1994**
Results of 1994 national surveys show very different views of the United States.

Source: J. Balzar (1994, p. A13); S. Fulwood (1994a, p. 8).

Annual surveys giving respondents an opportunity to identify what they feel to be the nation's major problems consistently show "civil rights" to be among the top six worries of African Americans. It barely makes the top 20 among White respondents, however (M. Gates, 1986). One might wonder whether this continued subordination has led Blacks to have anti-Black feelings as well, as some people contend.

We have focused so far on what usually comes to mind when we think about prejudice: one group's hating another group. But there is another form of prejudice: a group may come to hate itself. Members of groups held in low esteem by society may, as a result, have low self-esteem themselves. Many social scientists believe that members of subordinate groups hate themselves or, at least, have low self-esteem. Similarly, they argue that Whites have high self-esteem. High self-esteem means that an individual has fundamental respect for himself or herself, appreciates his or her own merits, and is aware of personal faults and will strive to overcome them. The research literature of the 1940s through the 1960s emphasized the low self-esteem of minorities. Usually, the subject was African Americans, but the argument has also been generalized to include any subordinate racial or ethnic group (J. Porter, 1985; Rosenberg and Simmons, 1971, p. 9).

This view is no longer accepted. Leonard Bloom (1971, pp. 68–69) cautions against assuming that minority status influences personality traits in either a good or a bad way. First, Bloom says, doing so may create a stereotype. We cannot accurately describe a Black personality any more than we can a White personality. Second, characteristics of minority group members are not completely the result of subordinate racial status; they are also influenced by low incomes, poor neighborhoods, and so forth. Third, many studies of personality imply that certain values are normal or preferable, but the values chosen are those of dominant groups.

If, as Bloom suggests, assessments of a subordinate group's personality are so prone to misjudgments, why is the belief in low self-esteem so widely held? Much of the research rests on studies with pre-school-age Black children asked to express preferences among dolls with different facial color. Indeed, one such study, by psychologists Kenneth and Mamie Clark (1947), was cited in the arguments before the U.S. Supreme Court in the landmark 1954 case *Brown v. Board of Education*. The Clarks's study showed that Black children preferred White dolls, a finding suggesting that the children had developed a negative self-image. While subsequent doll studies (Powell-Hopson and Hopson, 1988) have sometimes shown Black children's preference for white-faced dolls, other social scientists contend this shows a realization of what most commercially sold dolls look like rather than documenting low self-esteem.

The fact that African-American children, as well as other subordinate groups' children, can realistically see that Whites have more power and resources and therefore rate them higher does not mean that they personally feel inferior. Indeed, studies, even with children, show that when the self-images of middle-class or affluent African Americans are measured, their feelings of self-esteem are more positive than those of comparable Whites (W. Cross, 1991; Hughes and Demo, 1989; Martinez and Dukes, 1991; C. Raymond, 1991; Rosenberg and Simmons, 1971).

INTERGROUP HOSTILITY

Prejudice is as diverse as the nation's population. It exists not only between domi-nant and subordinate people but also among specific subordinate groups. Unfor-tunately, until recently, there was little research on this subject except for a few social-distance scales administered to racial and ethnic minorities.

A national survey conducted for the National Conference of Christians and Jews (1994) in 1993 revealed that, like Whites, many African Americans, Hispanic Americans, and Asian Americans held prejudiced and stereotypical views of other racial and ethnic minority groups. According to the survey:

- Majorities of Black, Hispanic, and Asian-American respondents agreed that Whites are "bigoted, bossy, and unwilling to share power." Majorities of these non-White groups also believed that they had less opportunity than Whites to obtain a good education, a skilled job, or decent housing.
- Forty-six percent of Hispanic Americans and forty-two percent of African Americans agreed with the statement that Asian Americans are "unscrupu-lous, crafty, and devious in business."
- Sixty-eight percent of Asian Americans and forty-nine percent of African Americans believed that Hispanic Americans "tend to have bigger families than they are able to support."
- Thirty-one percent of Asian Americans and twenty-six percent of Hispanic Americans agreed with the statement that African Americans "want to live on welfare."

Officials of the National Conference of Christians and Jews expressed concern about the extent to which subordinate group members agreed with negative stereotypes of other subordinate groups. At the same time, the survey also revealed positive views of major racial and ethnic minorities:

- More than eighty percent of respondents admired Asian Americans for "placing a high value on intellectual and professional achievement" and "having strong family ties."
- A majority of all groups surveyed agreed that Hispanic Americans "take deep pride in their culture and work hard to achieve a better life."
- Large majorities from all groups stated that African Americans "have made a valuable contribution to American society and will work hard when given a chance."

This was also a ground-breaking survey in that it explored attitudes toward Mus-lims, a group with increased visibility and increased labeling in the United States.

ARAB AMERICANS AND AMERICAN MUSLIMS: A CASE STUDY OF EMERGING PREJUDICE

The Arab-American and Muslim communities are among the largest growing sub-ordinate groups in the United States. Although they share some common demo-graphics, they are not the same, as many people believe.

An angry White youth bares the lip tattoo "100% White Skinhead."

Arab Americans are an ethnic group with origins in North Africa and the Middle Eastern countries of Syria, Iraq, Saudi Arabia, and the Palestine territory. However, to speak of Arabs (or Arab Americans) does not take into account the wide cultural differences and divisions within this group.

Muslims are followers of Islam, the world's largest faith after Christianity. While there are theological similarities to the Christian faith, such as belief in a common descent from Adam and Eve and reverence for the Virgin Mary, Islam is strongly influenced by the teachings of the Koran (or Al-Qur'an) of the seventh-century prophet, Muhammad. Islam is divided into a variety of faiths and sects. This division sometimes results in antagonistisms among its members, just as there are religious rivalries among Christians. However, many Muslims, such as Iranians and Pakistanis, are non-Arabs, and many Arabs, especially in the United States, are Christians. Yet many Westerners think that the ethnic group and the religious faith are one.

The stereotyping of Arabs by Westerners is vivid and almost cartoonlike—representing them as camel drivers, wealthy, and treacherous. Even Disney's 1993 animated film *Aladdin* referred to Arabs as "barbaric" and depicted, contrary to Islamic law, a guard threatening to cut off a young girl's hand for stealing food. The 1993 survey cited earlier by the National Conference of Christians and Jews found that over 40 percent of Americans view Muslims as supporting terrorism and that the majority see them as suppressing women. These images have crystallized not coincidentally as the number of Arabs in the United States has increased. While Arab immigration began in the late 1800s, it picked up dramatically in the 1960s. Initially, Arab immigrants were more likely to be Christian, and the first wave of Muslims assimilated many aspects of the American culture. However, there are now an estimated 870,000 Arab Americans and 4 million Muslims, many of whom cling to the traditions of their nation of origin (S. El-Badry, 1994; R. Niebuhr, 1990).

News events have fueled the anti-Arab, anti-Muslim feeling just as the "Communist menace" faded. Among the major events were the 1972 terrorist raid at the Munich Olympics, the 1973 oil crisis, the 1979 American hostage crisis in Tehran, the 1990 Gulf War, and the 1993 bombing of the World Trade Center in New York City. Media coverage of such events without much insight into Arab cultures and Islamic practices, served to polarize feelings. Contributing to this portrayal were stereotypical images in motion pictures such as *Cannonball Run* in 1979 and *True Lies* in 1994. Like so many other groups in the United States, Arab Americans and American Muslims have arrived only to encounter simplistic views of their beliefs and behavior (M. Siddiqi, 1993).

REDUCING PREJUDICE

Focusing on how to eliminate prejudice involves an explicit value judgment: Prejudice is wrong and causes problems for those who are prejudiced and for their victims. The obvious way to eliminate prejudice is to eliminate its causes: the desire to exploit, the fear of being threatened, and unacceptable personal failure. These might be eliminated by personal therapy, but therapy, even if it worked for everyone, is no solution. Such a program would not be feasible because of prohibitive cost and because it would have to be compulsory, which would violate civil rights. Furthermore, many of those in need of such therapy would not acknowledge their problem—the first step in effective therapy.

The answer would appear to rest with programs directed at society as a whole. Prejudice is indirectly attacked when discrimination is attacked. Despite prevailing beliefs to the contrary, we can legislate against prejudice; statutes and decisions do affect attitudes. In the past, people firmly believed that laws could not defy norms, especially racist ones. Recent history, especially after the civil rights movement began in 1954, has challenged that common wisdom. Laws and court rulings that have equalized the treatment of Blacks and Whites have led people to reevaluate their beliefs about what is right and wrong. The increasing tolerance by Whites during the civil rights period from 1954 to 1965 (see Table 2.3) seems to support this conclusion.

Much research has been done to determine how to change negative attitudes toward groups of people. The most encouraging findings point to the mass media, education, and intergroup contact.

Mass Media and Education

The research on the mass media and education consists of two types: research performed in artificially (experimentally) created situations and studies examining the influence on attitudes of motion pictures, television, and advertisements.

Leaflets, radio commercials, comic books, billboards, and classroom posters bombard people with the message of racial harmony. Television audiences watch a public service message that for 30 seconds shows smiling White and African-American infants reaching out toward each other. Law enforcement and military personnel attend in-service training sessions that preach the value of a pluralistic society. Does this publicity do any good? Do these programs make any difference?

Most but not all studies show that well-constructed programs do have some positive effect in reducing prejudice, at least temporarily. The reduction is rarely as much as one might wish, however. The difficulty is that a single program is insufficient to change lifelong habits, especially if little is done to reinforce the program once it ends. Persuasion to respect other groups does not operate in a clear field because, in their ordinary environments, individuals are still subjected to proprejudice arguments. Children and adults are encouraged to laugh at Polish jokes, or a Black adolescent may be discouraged by peers from befriending a White youth. All this serves to undermine the effectiveness of prejudice reduction programs (G. Allport, 1979).

Study results indicate the influence of educational programs specifically designed to reduce prejudice. For example, a special program in a small country town in Australia helped to reduce negative stereotypes of Aborigines, that nation's native people (Donovan and Levers, 1993). However, studies consistently document that increased formal education, regardless of content, is associated with racial tolerance. Research data show that more highly educated people are more likely to indicate respect and liking for groups different from themselves. Why should more years of schooling have this effect? It could be that more education gives a more universal outlook and makes a person less likely to endorse myths that sustain racial prejudice. Formal education teaches the importance of qualifying statements and the need at least to question rigid categorizations, if not reject them altogether. Christopher Bagley (1970) suggests that "education gives training in objective and dispassionate thought, dispositions which are obviously inimical to prejudice" (p. 72). An alternative explanation is that education does not actually reduce intolerance but simply makes individuals more careful about revealing it.

Formal education may simply instruct individuals in the proper responses, which in some settings could even be prejudiced views. Despite the lack of a clear-cut explanation, either theory suggests that the continued trend toward a better-educated population will contribute to a reduction in overt prejudice (R. Schaefer, 1986).

Education is not limited to formal schooling; increasingly, many forms of instruction are offered in the workplace. Remedies for intolerance can be taught there as well. With the entry of women and minority men into nontraditional work settings, training and support programs take on increased importance. Generally, when minorities enter an organization, they are thinly represented. Education programs have begun so that management does not treat these pioneers as "golden" (can do no wrong) or as hopeless cases doomed to failure (Pettigrew and Martin, 1987).

The mass media, like schooling, may reduce prejudice without the need of specially designed programs. Television, radio, motion pictures, newspapers, and magazines present only a slice of real life, but what effect do they have on prejudice if the content is racist or antiracist, sexist or antisexist? As with measuring the influence of antiprejudice programs, coming to strong conclusions on the mass media's effect is hazardous, but the evidence points to a measurable effect. The 1915 movie *The Birth of a Nation* depicts African Americans unfavorably and glorifies the Ku Klux Klan. A study of Illinois schoolchildren has shown that watching the movie made them more unfavorably inclined toward African Americans, a negative effect that persisted even five months later when the children were retested. Conversely, the 1947 movie *Gentleman's Agreement*, which took a strong stand against anti-Semitism, appears to have softened the anti-Semitic feelings of its audience (Commission on Civil Rights, 1977, 1980b).

Recent research has examined the influence of television because it commands the widest viewing audience among children and adolescents. A 1988 study found that almost a third of high school students felt that television entertainment was "an accurate representation" of African-American "real life" (Lichter and Lichter, 1988). Many programs, like "Amos 'n' Andy" or films with "dumb Injuns," which depict subordinate groups in stereotyped, demeaning roles, are no longer shown. Blacks and members of other subordinate groups are now more likely than before to appear in programs and commercials. As a result of the networks' greater sensitivity to the presentation of minority groups, people now see more balanced portrayals. Television programs showing positive African-American family life, as in "Family Matters," "Living Single," and "The Cosby Show," have been quite a change from "Diff'rent Strokes" and "Webster," which promoted the notion that African-American orphans are best off in White homes. Even the news, with its emphasis on crime and corruption, contributes to negative stereotypes, as noted by Patricia Raybon in "Listen to Their Voices."

But how far have the mass media really come? As Figure 2.4 shows, there have been modest increases in the presentation of African Americans over the last 30 years, but no positive change for Hispanics. The overwhelming majority of Black actors on prime-time television are employed in comedic roles or as criminals; no Black dramatic series has lasted a season, and very few are even given a chance. Asians and Hispanics have a similar image problem in contemporary television. The problem has been further complicated by the home-video revolution, which has led videocassette marketers to exhume many of the most stereotypical films.

Listen to Their Voices
A Case of "Severe Bias"

PATRICIA RAYBON

Former editor of The Denver Post's *Sunday* Contemporary *magazine, Patricia Raybon express-es concern about the one-sided presentation that African Americans receive in the media.*

Patricia Raybon

This is who I am not. I am not a crack addict. I am not a welfare mother. I am not illiterate. I am not a prostitute. I have never been in jail. My children are not in gangs. My husband doesn't beat me. My home is not a tenement. None of these things defines who I am, nor do they describe the other black people I've known and worked with and loved and befriended over these 40 years of my life.

Nor does it describe most of black America, period.

Yet in the eyes of the American news media, this is what black America is: poor, criminal, addicted and dysfunctional. Indeed, media coverage of black America is so one-sided, so imbalanced that the most victimized and hurting segment of the black community—a small segment, at best—is presented not as the exception but as the norm. It is an insidious practice, all the uglier for its blatancy.

In recent months, oftentimes in this very magazine, I have observed a steady offering of media reports on crack babies, gang warfare, violent youth, poverty and homelessness— and in most cases, the people featured in the photos and stories were black. At the same time, articles that discuss other aspects of American life—from home buying to medicine to technology to nutrition—rarely, if ever, show blacks playing a positive role, or for that matter, any role at all.

Day after day, week after week, this message—that black America is dysfunctional and unwhole—gets transmitted across the American landscape. Sadly, as a result, America never learns the truth about what is actually a wonderful, vibrant, creative community of people.

Most black Americans are *not* poor. Most black teenagers are *not* crack addicts. Most black mothers are *not* on welfare. Indeed, in sheer numbers, more *white* Americans are poor and on welfare than are black. Yet one never would deduce that by watching television or reading American newspapers and magazines. . . .

I am reminded, for example, of the controversial Spike Lee film, *Do the Right Thing,* and the criticism by some movie reviewers that the film's ghetto neighborhood isn't populated by addicts and drug pushers—and thus is not a true depiction.

In fact, millions of black Americans live in neighborhoods where the most common sights are children playing and couples walking their dogs. In my own inner-city neighborhood in Denver—an area that the local press consistently describes as "gang territory"—I have yet to see a recognizable "gang" member or any "gang" activity (drug dealing or drive-

Listen to Their Voices *Continued*

by shootings), nor have I been the victim of "gang violence."

Yet to students of American culture—in the case of Spike Lee's film, the movie reviewers—a black, inner-city neighborhood can only be one thing to be real: drug-infested and dysfunctioning. Is this my ego talking? In part, yes. For the millions of black people like myself—ordinary, hard-working, law-abiding, tax-paying Americans—the media's blindness to the fact that we even exist, let alone to our contributions to American society, is a bitter cup to drink. And as self-reliant as most black Americans are—because we've had to be self-reliant—even the strongest among us still crave affirmation.

I want that. I want it for my children. I want it for all the beautiful, healthy, funny, smart black Americans I have known and loved over the years.

And I want it for the rest of America, too.

I want America to know us—all of us—for who we really are. To see us in all of our complexity, our subtleness, our artfulness, our enterprise, our specialness, our loveliness, our American-ness. That is the real portrait of black America—that we're strong people, surviving people, capable people. That may be the best-kept secret in America. If so, it's time to let the truth be known.

From "A Case for 'Severe Bias'" by Patricia Raybon. *Newsweek* 114 (October 2, 1989), p. 11. Reprinted by permission of Patricia Raybon.

Even professional wrestling stars of the 1980s, such as the Iron Sheik, the Ugandan Giant, Mr. Fuji, and Chief Jay Strongbow, firmly reinforce stereotypes (H. Gates, 1989; Maguire and Wozniak, 1987).

The image of minorities in motion pictures is equally poor. The 1980s witnessed major movies distorting the image of minority groups. For example, *The Fiendish Plot of Dr. Fu Manchu*, starring Peter Sellers, appeared in 1980, and in the next year Paul Newman was featured in *Fort Apache, the Bronx*, which stereotypes the portrayal of both Black Americans and Puerto Ricans. The 1987 Oscar-winning film *Platoon* failed to show Black soldiers' leadership in the Vietnam war. By looking at the past, we can detect progress, but certainly the mass media image of women and racial groups does not uniformly cause people to discard the old definitions, the old stereotypes.

Because prejudice is acquired from our social environment, it follows that the mass media and educational programs, as major elements of that environment, influence the level of prejudice. The movement to eliminate the stereotyping of minorities and the sexes in textbooks and on television recognizes this influence. Most of the effort has been to avoid contributing to racial hostility; less effort has been made to attack prejudice actively, primarily because no one knows how to do that effectively. In looking for a way of directly attacking prejudice, many people advocate intergroup contact.

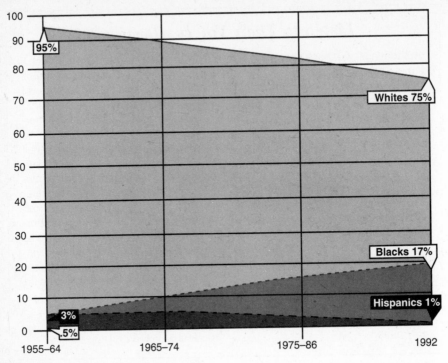

Figure 2.4 Television's Ethnic Portrayals
An analysis of prime-time entertainment (excluding reality-based syndicated series) shows an actual decline in the representation of Hispanics and an increase in the representation of African Americans.

Source: R. Du Brow (1994, p. A5).

Equal-Status Contact

An impressive number of research studies have been made of the *contact hypothesis.* This hypothesis, confirmed by numerous studies, states that interracial contact between people of equal status in harmonious circumstances will cause them to become less prejudiced and to abandon previously held stereotypes. Most studies indicate that such contact also improves the attitude of subordinate-group members. The importance of equal status in the interaction cannot be stressed enough. If a Puerto Rican is abused by his employer, little interracial harmony is promoted. Similarly, the situation in which contact occurs must be pleasant, making a positive evaluation likely for both individuals. Contact between two nurses, one Black and the other White, who are competing for one vacancy as a supervisor may lead to greater racial hostility (R. Schaefer, 1976, pp. 107–126).

The key factor in reducing hostility in addition to equal-status contact is the presence of a common goal. If people are in competition, as already noted, contact may heighten tension. However, bringing people together to share a common task has been shown to reduce ill feeling even when these people belong to different racial, ethnic, or religious groups (Sherif and Sherif, 1969, pp. 228–268; R. Slavin, 1985).

In a 1992 study of housing integration, researchers examined the harassment, threats, and fears that Blacks face in White schools in which low-income Black students are in the minority. Did these African-American youth experience acceptance, friendships, and positive interactions with their White classmates? The researchers (Rosenbaum and Meaden, 1992) interviewed youth who had moved to the suburbs and those who had relocated within the city of Chicago under the auspices of a federally funded program. In this program, low-income Black families received housing subsidies which allowed them to move from inner-city housing projects into apartment buildings occupied largely by middle-income Whites and located in middle-income, mostly White suburbs. The study found that these low-income Black youth did experience some harassment and some difficulty in gaining acceptance in the suburban schools, but the findings also suggest that they experienced great success in social integration and felt they fit into their new environments.

As African Americans and other subordinate groups slowly gain access to better-paying and more responsible jobs, the contact hypothesis takes on greater significance. Usually, the availability of equal-status interaction is taken for granted. Yet how often does intergroup contact in everyday life conform to the equal-status idea of the contact hypothesis? Probably not as often as we are assured by researchers who hope to see a lessening of tension (W. Ford, 1986).

CONCLUSION

This chapter has examined theories of prejudice and measurements of its extent. Prejudice should not be confused with discrimination. The two concepts are not the same: prejudice refers to negative attitudes, and discrimination to negative behavior toward a group.

Several theories try to explain why prejudice exists. Some emphasize economic concerns (the exploitation and scapegoating theories), whereas other approaches stress personality or normative factors. No one explanation is sufficient. Surveys conducted in the United States over 40 years point to a reduction of prejudice, but they also show that many Whites and Blacks are still intolerant of each other. Equal-status contact and the shared-coping approach may reduce hostility among groups. The mass media seem to be of limited value in reducing discrimination and may even intensify ill feeling by promoting stereotypical images.

Chapter 3 outlines the effects of discrimination. Discrimination's costs are high to both dominant and subordinate groups. With that in mind, we will examine some techniques for reducing discrimination.

KEY TERMS

authoritarian personality A psychological construct of a personality type likely to be prejudiced and to use others as scapegoats.

Bogardus scale Technique to measure social distance towards different racial and ethnic groups.

caste approach An approach that views race and social class as synonymous, with disadvantaged minorities occupying the lowest social class and having little, if any, opportunity to improve their social position.

checklist approach Technique of presenting respondents with traits to be applied to ethnic groups.

contact hypothesis An interactionist perspective stating that interracial contact between people of equal status in noncompetitive circumstances will reduce prejudice.

discrimination The denial of opportunities and equal rights to individuals and groups because of prejudice or for other arbitrary reasons.

ethnocentrism The tendency to assume that one's culture and way of life are superior to all others.

ethnophaulism Ethnic or racial slurs, including derisive nicknames.

exploitation theory A Marxist theory that views racial subordination in the United States as a manifestation of the class system inherent in capitalism.

normative approach The view that prejudice is influenced by societal norms and situations that serve to encourage or discourage the tolerance of minorities.

prejudice A negative attitude toward an entire category of people, such as a racial or ethnic minority.

scapegoat A person or group blamed irrationally for another person's or group's problems or difficulties.

White backlash White resistance to further improvement in the status of Black people.

FOR FURTHER INFORMATION

Irving Lewis Allen. *Unkind Words: Ethnic Labeling from Redskin to Wasp.* New York: Bergin & Garvey, 1990.

> A linguistic study of contemporary ethnic labeling in popular speech and usage in the United States.

Gordon W. Allport. *The Nature of Prejudice*, 25th anniversary ed. Reading, MA: Addison-Wesley, 1979.

> The various theories of prejudice are presented, and all the relevant studies available at the time this class work was published are summarized.

Irwin Deutscher, Fred P. Pestello, and H. Frances G. Pestello. *Sentiments and Acts.* New York: Aldine de Gruyter, 1993.

> Analyzes available research on the relationship between attitudes held and actual behavior.

Ed Guerrero. *Framing Blackness: The African American Image in Film.* Philadelphia: Temple University Press, 1993.

> Considers stereotyping in motion pictures from D. W. Griffiths' *The Birth of a Nation* through to Spike Lee's *Malcolm X.*

Milton Kleg. *Hate, Prejudice and Racism.* Albany, NY: State University of New York Press, 1993.

> Considers the problems and tensions precipitated by prejudiced attitudes ranging from the casual ethnic or racial joke to a lynch mob.

Gina Marchetti. *Romance and the "Yellow Peril": Race, Sex, and Discursive Strategies in Hollywood Fiction.* Chicago: University of Chicago Press, 1993.

> Focuses on how certain stereotypes have been reaffirmed through motion pictures that present Asians and interracial sexuality.

Paul M. Sniderman, Philip E. Tetlock, and Edward C. Carmines, eds. *Prejudice, Politics, and the American Dilemma.* Stanford, CA: Stanford University Press, 1993.

Drawing upon the latest survey data, the contributors consider the relationships among attitudes, behavior, and the political agenda in the United States.

Raymond William Stedman. *Shadows of the Indian: Stereotyping in American Culture.* Norman, OK: University of Oklahoma Press, 1982.

Covers the wide variety of stereotypes of Native Americans, including the "noble savage," the Indian maiden, and many more.

Donald M. Taylor and Fathali M. Moghaddam. *Theories of Intergroup Relations: International Social Psychological Perspectives,* 2d ed. Westport, CN: Preger, 1994.

A review of research on intergroup behavior drawing upon a cross-cultural perspective.

CRITICAL THINKING QUESTIONS

1. How are prejudice and discrimination both related and unrelated to each other?
2. Identify stereotypes associated with a group of people exclusive of their race, ethnic group, or gender.
3. What social issues do you think are most likely to engender hostility along racial and ethnic lines?
4. Besides Arab Americans and American Muslims, identify other groups recently subjected to prejudice, perhaps in your own community.
5. How do the media both reduce and inflame prejudice?

Chapter
3

Discrimination

Chapter Outline

Highlights

Just as social scientists have advanced theories to explain why people are prejudiced, they have also presented explanations of why discrimination occurs. Social scientists look more and more at the manner in which institutions, not individuals, discriminate. *Institutional discrimination* describes the pattern in social institutions that produces or perpetuates inequalities, even if individuals in the society do not intend to be racist or sexist. The data document that gaps do exist among racial and ethnic groups. Historically, attempts have been made to reduce discrimination, usually as a result of strong lobbying efforts by minorities themselves. More recently, *affirmative action* guidelines have been employed in an effort to equalize opportunity, but *glass ceilings* and *glass walls* remain.

Robert D. Thompson and five other African Americans stopped for breakfast in May 1993 at a Denny's—a nationwide chain sporting the slogan "Always Open"—in Maryland. The waitress did not serve them or even take their order. Meanwhile, 15 Whites who had come in at the same time were served. This case of the "invisible" restaurant patrons came to national attention because all the people—White *and* Black—were Secret Service agents en route to Andrews Air Force Base to provide protection for President Clinton. All were dressed alike right down to carrying guns. Poor service or outright discrimination? Lawsuits encompassing this complaint and 4,300 others involving treatment of African-American customers in various establishments were settled in 1994 for a total of $54 million.

A more obvious example of discrimination was the refusal of Holiday Spas, a health club chain, to allow African Americans to join. This refusal became very explicit when the Washington Lawyer's Committee documented in 1992 that the chain hired Whites and African Americans to pose as potential members to test their own membership application process. The health club chain wanted to be sure their discriminatory policies against Blacks were still in force. On being exposed, the chain agreed to pay $9.5 million in damages and to do away with the discriminatory practice.

Ill treatment of members of subordinate groups can intrude into even the most basic of services, such as housing. In 1994, federal marshals, FBI agents, and police protected four African-American adults and seven children in a housing project in Vidor, Texas. For nine years, Vidor and 36 East Texas counties had avoided complying with a federal court order to open public housing to Blacks. As one White resident said, "I don't care about them moving in. But I'm tired of all the [news] stories they write about it. They got us made out to be the most racist, hate-filled town" (M. Potok, 1994; also see D. Jones, 1995; J. Mathews, 1992).

Discrimination has a long history, right up to the present, of taking its toll on people. Despite legislative and court efforts to eliminate discrimination, members of dominant and subordinate groups pay a price for continued intolerance.

UNDERSTANDING DISCRIMINATION

Discrimination is the denial of opportunities and equal rights to individuals and groups because of prejudice or for other arbitrary reasons. Some people in the United States find it difficult to see discrimination as a widespread phenomenon. "After all," it is often said, "these minorities drive cars, hold jobs, own their homes, and even go to college." This does not mean that discrimination is rare. An understanding of discrimination in modern industrial societies such as the United States must begin by distinguishing between relative and absolute deprivation.

Relative Versus Absolute Deprivation

Conflict theorists have correctly said that it is not absolute, unchanging standards that determine deprivation and oppression. It is crucial that, although minority groups may be viewed as having adequate or even good incomes, housing, health care, and educational opportunities, it is their position *relative* to some other group that offers evidence of discrimination.

The term *relative deprivation* is defined as the conscious feeling of a negative discrepancy between legitimate expectations and present actualities. After settling in the United States, immigrants often enjoy better material comforts and more political freedom than were possible in their old country. If they compare themselves to most other people in the United States, however, they will feel deprived because, while their standard has improved, the immigrants still perceive relative deprivation.

Absolute deprivation, on the other hand, implies a fixed standard based on a minimum level of subsistence below which families should not be expected to exist. Discrimination does not necessarily mean absolute deprivation. A Japanese American who gets promoted to a management position may still be a victim of discrimination, if he or she had been passed over for years because of corporate reluctance to place an Asian American in such a visible position.

Dissatisfaction is also likely to arise from feelings of relative deprivation. Those members of a society who feel most frustrated and disgruntled by the social and economic conditions of their lives are not necessarily "worst off" in an objective sense. Social scientists have long recognized that what is most significant is how people *perceive* their situation. Karl Marx pointed out that, although the misery of the workers was important in reflecting their oppressed state, so, too, was their position relative to the ruling class. In 1847, Marx wrote that

> although the enjoyment of the workers has risen, the social satisfaction that they have has fallen in comparison with the increased enjoyment of the capitalist. (Marx and Engels, 1955, p. 94)

This statement explains why the groups or individuals who are most vocal and best organized against discrimination are not necessarily in the worst economic and

This Denny's restaurant in Annapolis, Maryland, generated a huge protest against the nationwide chain after it gave second-class treatment to African-American Secret Service agents in 1993.

social situation. They are likely, however, to be those who most strongly perceive that, relative to others, they are not receiving "their fair share."

Total Discrimination

Social scientists, and increasingly policymakers, have begun to use the concept of total discrimination. *Total discrimination,* as shown in Figure 3.1, refers to current discrimination operating in the labor market *and* past discrimination. Past discrimination includes the relatively poorer education and job experience of racial and ethnic minorities compared to that of White Americans. It is not enough, therefore, when considering discrimination, to focus only on what is being done to people now. Sometimes a person may be dealt with fairly but may still be at a disadvantage because he or she suffered from poorer health care, inferior counseling in the school system, less access to books and other educational materials, a poor job record resulting from absences to take care of brothers and sisters, and so forth.

We find another variation of this past-in-present discrimination when apparently nondiscriminatory present practices have negative effects because of prior

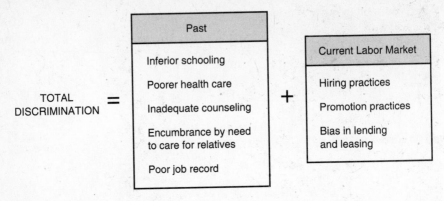

Figure 3.1 **Total Discrimination**

intentionally biased practices. Although unions that purposely discriminated against minority members in the past may no longer do so, some people are still prevented from achieving higher levels of seniority because of those past practices. A study of personnel records in the military shows that the cumulative record is vital in promotion and selection for desirable assignments. Blatantly discriminatory judgments and recommendations in the past, however, remain a part of a person's record.

INSTITUTIONAL DISCRIMINATION

Individuals practice discrimination in one-to-one encounters, while institutions practice discrimination through their daily operations. Indeed, a consensus is growing today that this institutional discrimination is more significant than that committed by prejudiced individuals.

Social scientists are particularly concerned with the ways in which patterns of employment, education, criminal justice, housing, health care, and government operations maintain the social significance of race and ethnicity. *Institutional discrimination* refers to the denial of opportunities and equal rights to individuals and groups that results from the normal operations of a society.

Civil rights activist Stokely Carmichael and political scientist Charles Hamilton are credited with introducing the concept of *institutional racism. Individual discrimination* refers to overt acts of individual Whites against individual Blacks; Carmichael and Hamilton reserved the term *institutional racism* for covert acts collectively committed against an entire group. James M. Jones (1972) provided this definition:

> Those established laws, customs, practices which systematically reflect and produce racial inequities in American society. If racist consequences accrue to institutional laws, customs, or practices, the institution is racist *whether or not the individuals maintaining those practices have racist intentions.* (p. 131)

This sign made by Black students shows that they have found institutional racism present in all aspects of life, including higher education.

Under this definition, discrimination can take place without an individual's intending to deprive others of privileges, and even without the individual's being aware that others are being deprived (Ture and Hamilton, 1992).

How can discrimination be widespread and unconscious at the same time? The following represent a few documented examples of institutional discrimination:

1. Standards for assessing credit risks work against potential African Americans in business who lack conventional credit references. Blacks in business also usually operate where insurance costs are much greater.
2. IQ testing favors middle-class children, especially the White middle class, because of the type of questions included.
3. The entire criminal justice system, from the patrol officer to the judge and jury, is dominated by Whites who find it difficult to understand ghetto life (Knowles and Prewitt, 1969).

In some cases, even apparently "neutral" institutional standards can turn out to have discriminatory effects. In 1992, African-American students at a midwestern state university protested a policy under which fraternities and sororities that wished to use campus facilities for a dance were required to post a $150 security deposit to cover possible damages. The Black students complained that this policy had a discriminatory impact on minority student organizations. Campus police countered that the university's policy applied to *all* student groups interested in using these facilities. However, since overwhelmingly White fraternities and sororities at the school had their own houses, which they used for dances, the policy indeed affected only African-American and other subordinate groups' organizations.

Institutional discrimination continuously imposes more hindrances on and awards fewer benefits to certain racial and ethnic groups than it does to others. This is the underlying and painful context of American intergroup relations.

DUAL LABOR MARKET

The secondary labor market affecting many members of racial and ethnic minorities has come to be called the *irregular economy*. The irregular economy is the transfer of money, goods, or services that is not reported to the government. This label describes much of the work in inner-city neighborhoods and poverty-stricken rural areas, in sharp contrast to the rest of the marketplace. Workers are employed in the irregular economy seasonally or infrequently. The work they do may resemble the work of traditional occupations, such as mechanic, cook, or electrician, but these workers lack the formal credentials to enter such employment. Indeed, workers in the irregular economy may work sporadically or may moonlight in the regular economy. The irregular economy also includes unregulated child-care services, garage sales, and the unreported income of craftspeople and street vendors.

The irregular economy, sometimes referred to as the *informal* or *underground economy,* exists worldwide. For example, in 1867 Karl Marx wrote of a stagnant layer of workers who were "part of the active labor army, with extremely irregular employment" (K. Marx, 1967, p. 643). Conflict sociologists in particular note that a significant level of commerce occurs outside traditional economies. Individually, the transactions are small, but they can be significant when taken together. They make up perhaps as much as 10–20 percent of all economic activity in the United States (J. Denton, 1985).

According to the *dual labor market* model, minorities have been relegated to the irregular economy. While the irregular economy may be profitable, it provides few safeguards against fraud or malpractice and gives little attention to the so-called fringe benefits of health insurance and pension that are much more likely to be present in the conventional marketplace. To be consigned to the irregular economy is therefore yet another example of social inequality.

Sociologist Edna Bonacich (1972, 1976) outlined the dual or split labor market that divides the economy into two realms of employment, the secondary one being populated primarily by minorities working at menial jobs. Labor, even when not manual, is still rewarded less when performed by minorities. In keeping with the conflict model, this dual market model emphasizes that minorities fare unfavorably in the competition between dominant and subordinate groups.

The workers in the irregular economy are ill prepared to enter the regular economy permanently or to take its better-paying jobs. Frequent changes in employment or lack of a specific supervisor leaves them without the kind of job résumé that employers in the regular economy expect before they hire. Some of the sources of employment in the irregular economy are illegal, such as fencing, narcotics pushing, pimping, and prostitution. More likely, the work is legal but not transferable to a more traditional job, such as that of an "information broker," who receives cash in exchange for such information as where to find good buys or how to receive maximum benefits in public assistance programs (S. Pedder, 1991).

THE UNDERCLASS

Many members of the irregular economy, along with some employed in traditional jobs, compose what has come to be called the underclass of American society.

The *underclass* consists of the long-term poor who lack training and skills. Conflict theorists, among others, have expressed alarm at the proportion of the nation's society living at this social stratum. Sociologist William Wilson (1987a, 1987b, 1988, p. 15; 1991) drew attention to the growth of this varied grouping of families and individuals who are outside the mainstream of the occupational structure. While estimates vary depending on the definition, in 1990 the underclass included more than 3 million adults of working age, not counting children or the elderly. In the central city, about 49 percent of the underclass in 1990 comprised African Americans; 29 percent, Hispanics; 17 percent, Whites; and 5 percent, other (O'Hare and Curry-White, 1992).

The discussion of the underclass has refocused attention on society's inability to address the problems facing the truly disadvantaged—many of whom are Black or Hispanic. Some scholars have expressed the concern that the portrait of the underclass seems to "blame the victim," making the poor responsible. Wilson and others have stressed that it is not bad behavior but structural factors, such as the loss of manufacturing jobs, that has hit ghetto residents so hard. As the labor market has become tighter, the subordinate groups within the underclass are at a significant disadvantage. Associated with this structural problem is isolation from social services. The disadvantaged lack contact or sustained interaction with the individuals or institutions that represent the regular economy. It is the economy, not the poor, that needs reforming (J. DeParle, 1991; W. Kornblum, 1991; S. Wright, 1993).

As part of a national survey of race relations commissioned by the NAACP Legal Defense and Educational Fund (1989), researchers conducted face-to-face interviews in mid-1988 with 347 chronically poor Blacks in eight American cities. Among the findings were the following:

- Women constituted 78 percent of the Black underclass.
- The median income of chronically poor Black households over the previous five years had been $4,900.
- At least 61 percent of those surveyed had not held a job in the last two years.
- Some 44 percent of those surveyed had either never held a job or had never received any training for work.

At the same time, members of the African-American underclass were found to share many of the most basic goals and aspirations of American society. For example, 55 percent of the respondents stated that they hoped their children would go to college.

Especially alarming is the high unemployment rate among teenagers in our metropolitan areas, not just the central cities. Even White teens experience 25 percent unemployment in poverty areas, as shown in Figure 3.2, but among Hispanic teens it reaches 30 percent, and among Blacks it is nearly 50 percent. Obviously, the irregular economy has a greater impact on the employment of young adults.

Poverty is not new. Yet the concept of an underclass describes a very chilling development: workers, whether employed or not in the irregular economy, are beyond the reach of any safety net provided by existing social programs. In addition, membership in the underclass is not an intermittent condition but a long-

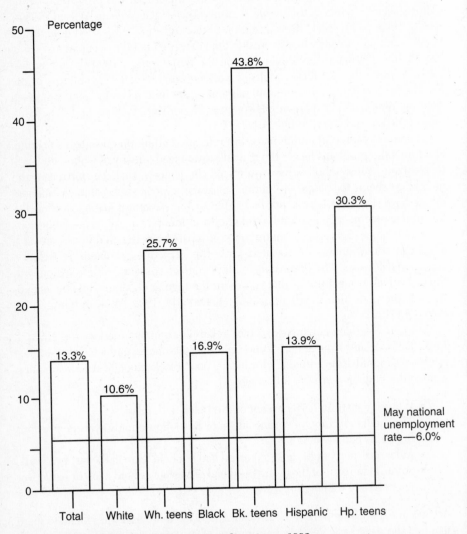

Figure 3.2 Unemployment Rates in Metropolitan Areas, 1993

Source: U.S. Bureau of the Census and Department of Labor data. R. Reich (1994, p. 4).

term attribute. The underclass is understandably alienated and engages sporadi-cally in illegal behavior. Alienation and illegal acts gain the underclass little support from the larger society to address the problem realistically.

Often, the term *underclass* is invoked to establish the superiority of the dom-inant group. Even if not stated explicitly, there is the notion that society and insti-tutions have not failed the underclass but that somehow they are beyond hope. All too frequently, the underclass is treated as a homogeneous group, the object of scorn, fear, and embarrassment.

In "Listen to Their Voices," sociologist and former president of the American Sociological Association William Julius Wilson makes a presentation to the U.S. House of Representatives' Ways and Means Committee on "The Plight of Black Male Job-Seekers." Based on the findings of his research, this presentation high-lights the shrinkage of manufacturing employment in urban America and its differ-ent affects on African Americans and Mexican immigrants. While many Hispanics are a part of the underclass, they are still generally perceived in a more positive light by potential White employers than their African-American counterparts.

DISCRIMINATION IN AMERICAN SOCIETY

Discrimination is widespread in the United States. It sometimes results from preju-dices held by individuals. More significantly, it is found in institutional discrimination and the presence of a dual labor market. It is even present in a subtle fashion among the affluent because, as we have just seen, more members of subordinate families must work in order to reach the type of moderately high incomes enjoyed by Whites.

Not so subtly, the face of discrimination shows itself even when people are prepared to be customers. A 1990 study had Black and White men and women fol-low a script to buy new cars in the Chicago area. After 164 visits, the results showed that a White woman could be expected to pay $142 more for a car than a White man, a Black man $421 more, and a Black woman $875 more. African Americans and women were perceived as less knowledgeable, and therefore, there could be more markup in prices. A similar study in housing, nationwide in 25 metropolitan areas, showed that African Americans and Hispanics faced discrimination in a majority of their responses to advertisements. Discrimination took the forms of failure to be shown real estate presented to Whites and less favorable terms, such as higher rents or higher fees for parking and utilities (I. Ayres, 1991; Turner, Struyck, and Yinger, 1991).

Discrimination also emerges when we look at data for groups other than Blacks and Hispanics. National studies have documented that White ethnics, such as Irish Catholics and Jewish Americans, are less likely to be in certain positions of power than White Protestants, despite their equal educational levels (Alba and Moore, 1982). The victims of discrimination are not limited to people of color.

Measuring Discrimination

How much discrimination is there? As in measuring prejudice, problems arise in quantifying discrimination. Measuring prejudice is hampered by the difficulties

Listen to Their Voices
The Plight of Black Male Job-Seekers

WILLIAM JULIUS WILSON

William Julius Wilson

In recent years, inner-city black males as a group have increasingly been maligned in films, television, and in the news media. The negative and worsening image of these men exacerbates racial hostility because it lends itself to overgeneralization about the entire black community. This image combined with the loss of traditional manufacturing and other blue-collar jobs in Chicago is partly responsible for increasing unemployment among inner-city black males and has contributed to their concentration in low-wage, high-turnover laborer and service jobs. Moreover, inner-city blacks tend to be parts of neighborhoods, networks, and households that are less conducive to employment. Hispanics have easier access to manufacturing jobs because many employers not only prefer them over blacks, but they also like to hire by referrals from current employees, which Hispanics can easily furnish, since they are well connected in immigrant networks.

Inner-city black men frequently express bitterness and resentment about their poor employment prospects and low wage work settings. Their attitudes and their erratic work histories in high-turnover jobs create the widely shared perception that black men are undesirable workers. That perception becomes the basis for employer discrimination that sharply increases in a weak economy.

Over the long term, discrimination has also grown because employers have been turning increasingly to an expanding immigrant and female labor force. . . .

The deterioration of the socioeconomic status of black men can be associated with increases in negative perceptions. Interviews of a representative sample of Chicago-area employers show that many consider inner-city blacks—especially young black males—to be uneducated, unstable, uncooperative, and dishonest. For example, a suburban drug store manager said:

> It's unfortunate, but in my business I think, overall, [black men] tend to be known to be dishonest. I think that's too bad but that's the image they have. (Interviewer: So you think it's an image problem?) Yeah, an image problem of being dishonest men and lazy. They're known to be lazy. (Interviewer: I see. How do you think that image was developed?) Go look in the jails.

Adding to the image problem is the hostility young black men hold toward their low paying jobs compared to immigrant Mexican men. Many young men demonstrated less willingness to be flexible in taking assignments or tasks not considered part of their job, and less willingness to work as hard for the same low wages.

Listen to Their Voices   *Continued*

These attitudes contrast with those of many Mexicans and other Third-World immigrants who are perceived to exhibit better "work ethics" than native workers because they are willing to tolerate harsh conditions, lower pay, and few opportunities to advance. Many immigrants are harder workers because they have migrated from areas of intense poverty, and even boring and grueling jobs look, by contrast, good to them. They also fear being deported if they fail to find employment.

Black men interviewed in the study strongly felt that they are victims of discrimination and complained that they get assigned the heaviest work or dirtiest jobs, were overworked, and paid less than nonblacks. Immigrant Mexicans also reported feeling exploited but tended to feel that this was to be expected because of the nature of the job. Richard Taub, a researcher on the project, concluded that the inner-city black men had a greater sense of "honor" and often viewed the work, pay, and treatment from bosses as insulting and degrading. This heightened sensitivity to exploitation, Taub believes, increases

anger and leads to a tendency, in some work settings, to just walk off the job. . . .

The more black males complain about low-paying jobs, poor working conditions, and restricted opportunities for upward mobility, the less desirable they seem to employers. They therefore experience greater discrimination when they seek employment and clash more often with supervisors when they find work. For all these reasons, it is important to link attitudinal and other cultural traits with structural realities of the economy and job market.

The employment struggles of black men in Chicago are clearly caused by several intermingled and mutually reinforcing factors. The shifting economy, race, and differing cultural orientations and attitudes all fuel the worsening employment opportunities for blacks. Effective public policy designed to address the employment problems of blacks must take these interrelated influences into account.

From "The Plight of Black Male Job-Seekers" by William J. Wilson. *Focus*, September 1992, pp. 7–8.

in assessing attitudes and by the need to take many factors into account. It is further restrained by the initial challenge of identifying different treatment. A second difficulty of measuring discrimination is assigning a number or cost to the discrimination.

Some tentative conclusions about discrimination can be made, however. Figure 3.3 uses government income data to show vividly the disparity in income between African Americans and Whites, men and women. The first comparison is of all workers. White men with a median income of $31,737 earn almost 38 percent more than Black men and almost twice as much as Hispanic women, who earn only $17,743 in wages. Clearly, White males earn most, followed by Black males, White females. Hispanic men, Black females, and Hispanic females. The sharpest drop is between White and Black males. Even worse, relatively speaking, is the plight of women. Black women earn less than half of what White males in American society earn. This disparity between Black women and White men has remained unchanged over the more than fifty years during which such data have been tabulated. It illustrates yet another instance of the double jeopardy experienced by minority women. Also, in Figure 3.3 are data for only full-time, year-round workers, and therefore, the figure excludes housewives and the unemployed. Even in this comparison, the deprivation of Blacks, Hispanics, and women is confirmed again.

Are these differences completely the result of discrimination in employment? No, individuals within the four groups are not equally prepared to compete for high-paying jobs. Past discrimination is a significant factor in a person's present ·social position. As discussed previously and illustrated in Figure 3.1, past discrimination continues to take its toll on modern victims. Taxpayers, predominantly White, were unwilling to subsidize the public education of African Americans and Hispanics at the same levels as White pupils. Even as these actions have changed, today's schools show this uneven spending pattern from the past. Education is clearly an appropriate variable to control. In Table 3.1, median income is compared, holding education constant, which means we can compare Blacks and Whites and men and women with approximately the same amount of formal schooling. The disparity remains. The gap between races does narrow as education increases. Women, however, lag behind men to an even greater extent (they earn 61 percent of what men earn). The contrast is dramatic: women with graduate work ($26,417) earn less than men who fail to finish college ($26,873).

Now that education has been held constant, is the remaining gap caused by discrimination? No, not necessarily. Table 3.1 measured only the amount of school-

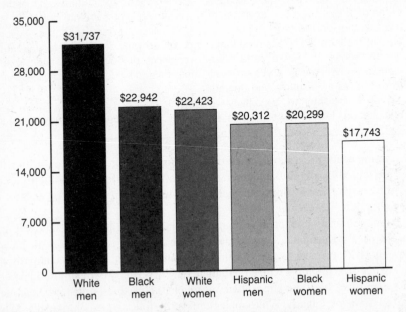

Figure 3.3 Median Income by Race, Ethnicity, and Gender, 1992
Even a brief analysis reveals striking differences in earning power between White men in the United States and other groups. Furthermore, the "double jeopardy" is apparent for Black and Hispanic women. (Median income is from all sources and is limited to year-round, full-time workers over 15 years old.)

Source: Bureau of the Census (1994, p. 472).

Table 3.1   MEDIAN INCOME BY RACE AND SEX, HOLDING EDUCATION CONSTANT

Even at the very highest levels of schooling, the income gap remains between Whites and Blacks. Education also has little effect, apparently, on the income gap between male and female workers.

	Race, 1993		Ratio	Sex, 1992		Ratio
	White	Black	Black to White	Male Workers	Female Workers	Women to Men
Total	$22,761	$17,121	.75	$26,472	$16,227	.61
High School						
1–3 years	12,667	10,586	.84	15,928	9,784	.61
4 years	19,104	14,930	.78	22,765	13,266	.58
College						
No degree	22,360	19,454	.87	26,873	16,111	.60
Bachelor's Degree or more	35,601	30,568	.86	40,590	26,417	.65

Note: Figures are median income from all sources except capital gain. Included are public assistance payments, dividends, pension, unemployment compensation, and so on. Incomes are for workers over twenty-five years of age. Data for Whites are for White non-Hispanics.

Source: C. Bennett, 1995, pp. 62, 66; Bureau of the Census, 1993c, pp. 94–95.

ing, not its quality. Racial minorities are more likely to attend inadequately financed schools. Some efforts have been made to eliminate disparities among school districts in the amount of wealth available to tax for school support, but with little success. In a 1973 case, *San Antonio Independent School District v. Rodriquez,* the U.S. Supreme Court ruled that attendance at an underfinanced school in a poor district does not constitute a violation of equal protection. The inequality of educational opportunity may seem less important in explaining sex discrimination. Even though women are usually not segregated from men, educational institutions encourage talented women to enter fields that pay less (home economics or elementary education).

Eliminating Discrimination

Two main agents of social change work to reduce discrimination: voluntary associations organized to solve racial and ethnic problems and the federal government. The two are closely related: most efforts initiated by the government were urged by associations or organizations representing minority groups, following vigorous protests against racism by African Americans.

All racial and ethnic groups of any size are represented by private organizations that are to some degree trying to end discrimination. Some groups originated in the first half of the twentieth century, but most have either been founded since World War II or have become significant forces in bringing about change only since then. These include church organizations, fraternal social groups, minor political parties, and legal defense funds, as well as more militant organizations operating under the scrutiny of law enforcement agencies. The purposes, membership, successes, and failures of these voluntary associations dedicated to eliminating discrimination are discussed throughout the balance of this book.

Government action toward eliminating discrimination is also part of only relatively recent history. Antidiscrimination actions have been generated by each branch of the government: the executive, the judicial, and the legislative.

The first antidiscrimination action at the executive level was President Franklin D. Roosevelt's 1943 creation of the Fair Employment Practices Commission (FEPC), which handled thousands of complaints of discrimination, mostly from African Americans, despite strong opposition by powerful economic and political leaders and many southern Whites. The FEPC had little actual power. It had no authority to compel employers to stop discriminating but could only ask for voluntary compliance. Its jurisdiction was limited to federal government employees, federal contractors, and labor unions. State and local governments and any business without a federal contract were not covered. Furthermore, the FEPC never enjoyed vigorous support from the White House, was denied adequate funds, and was part of larger agencies that were hostile to the commission's existence. This weak antidiscrimination agency was finally dropped in 1946 and was succeeded by an even weaker one in 1948.

The judiciary, charged with interpreting laws and the U.S. Constitution, has a much longer history of involvement in the rights of racial, ethnic, and religious minorities. Its early decisions, however, protected the rights of the dominant group, as in the 1857 U.S. Supreme Court *Dred Scott* decision, which ruled that slaves remained slaves even when living or traveling in states where slavery was illegal. Not until the 1940s did the Supreme Court revise earlier decisions and begin to grant African Americans the same rights as those held by Whites. The 1954 *Brown v. Board of Education* decision heralded a new series of rulings arguing, in effect, that to distinguish among races in order to segregate was inherently discriminatory. Unfortunately, the immediate effect of many such rulings was minimal because the executive branch and the Congress did not wish to violate the principle of *states' rights*, which holds that each state is sovereign in most of its affairs and has the right to order them without interference from the federal government.

Gradually, United States society became more committed to the rights of individuals. There was also an inherent fallacy in the states' rights argument. It perceived power as a finite quantity, where increased national power automatically meant reduced state and local authority. In reality, government activity expanded at all levels; those who lost power were individuals or businesses that wished to maximize their personal gain at the expense of others' rights. The proponents of states' rights sought to minimize federal government activity by keeping power in the state capitals, where the prospects of inaction were greatest because these proponents had greater influence to protect their own interests. The legislation of the 1960s committed the federal government to actively protecting civil rights, rather than merely leaving action up to state and local officials.

The most important legislative effort to eradicate discrimination was the Civil Rights Act of 1964. This act led to the establishment of the Equal Employment

Opportunity Commission (EEOC), giving it the power to investigate complaints against employers and to recommend action to the Department of Justice. If the Justice Department sued and discrimination was found, the court could order appropriate compensation. The act covered employment practices of all businesses with more than 25 employees, as well as nearly all employment agencies and labor unions. A 1972 amendment broadened the coverage to employers with as few as 15 employees.

The act also prohibited the application of different voting registration standards to White and Black voting applicants. It prohibited as well discrimination in public accommodations, that is, hotels, motels, restaurants, gasoline stations, and amusement parks. Publicly owned facilities, such as parks, stadiums, and swimming pools, were also prohibited from discriminating. Another important provision forbade discrimination in all federally supported programs and institutions, such as hospitals, colleges, and road construction.

The Civil Rights Act of 1964 covers discrimination based on race, color, creed, national origin, and sex. Although the inclusion of sex in employment criteria had been forbidden in the federal civil service since 1949, most laws and most groups pushing for change showed little concern about sex discrimination. There was little precedent for attention to sex discrimination even at the state level. Only Hawaii and Wisconsin had enacted laws against sex discrimination before 1964. As first proposed, the act did not include sex. One day before the final vote, opponents of the measure offered the amendment in an effort to defeat the entire act. The act did pass with sex bias included—an event that can only be regarded as a

DRESS FOR SUCCESS

Kirk Anderson, Ladysmith, WI.

milestone for women seeking equal employment rights with men (Commission on Civil Rights, 1975, pp. 19–20; E. Roth, 1993).

It is easy to overstate the significance of the Civil Rights Act of 1964; it was not perfect. Since 1964, several acts and amendments to the act itself have been added to compensate for the many areas of discrimination it left untouched, such as criminal justice and housing. Even in those areas singled out for enforcement in the Civil Rights Act of 1964, discrimination still occurs. Federal agencies charged with its enforcement complain that they are underfunded or are denied wholehearted support by the White House. Also, regardless of how much the EEOC may want to act in a case, the individual who has been discriminated against has to pursue the complaint over a long time, marked by long periods of inaction.

While civil rights laws have often established rights for other minorities, the Supreme Court made them explicit in two 1987 decisions involving groups other than African Americans. In the first of the two cases, an Iraqi-American professor asserted that he had been denied tenure because of his Arab origins; in the second, a Jewish congregation brought suit for damages in response to the defacing of its synagogue with derogatory symbols. The Supreme Court ruled unanimously that, in effect, any member of an ethnic minority may sue under federal prohibitions against discrimination. These decisions paved the way for virtually all racial and ethnic groups to invoke the Civil Rights Act of 1964 (S. Taylor, 1987).

A particularly insulting form of discrimination seemed to be finally on its way out in the late 1980s. Many social clubs had limitations forbidding membership to minorities, Jews, and women. For years, exclusive clubs argued that they were merely selecting friends, but in fact, a principal function of these clubs has been providing a forum where business is transacted. Denial of membership meant more than the inability to attend a luncheon; it also seemed to exclude one from part of the marketplace. The Supreme Court ruled unanimously in the 1988 case *New York State Clubs Association v. City of New York* that states and cities may ban sex discrimination by large private clubs where business lunches and similar activities take place. While the ruling does not apply to all clubs and leaves the issue of racial and ethnic barriers unresolved, it did serve to chip away at the arbitrary exclusiveness of private groups (S. Taylor, 1988).

The continuation of social club discrimination reemerged in the 1992 presidential campaign. In April 1992, independent presidential candidate Ross Perot appeared on "Larry King Live" and was asked by a caller if he belonged to any social clubs that excluded Jews or Blacks. Perot replied, "Yes, I do. All my Jewish friends in Dallas, they've had a great deal of fun with me over this. If it bothers people, I'll quit immediately." Perot's membership in restrictive Brook Hollow Country Club and the Dallas Country Club offended Blacks and Jews on his staff. Within a few days of the telecast, he resigned his memberships in these clubs. Yet such memberships and restrictive organizations remain perfectly legal (G. Cerio, 1992).

The inability of the Civil Rights Act, similar legislation, and court decisions to end discrimination is not due entirely to poor financial and political support. The number of federal employees' employers assigned to these tasks declined in the

1990s. By 1995, EEOC was looking at 188,000 unresolved complaints. Even if the EEOC had been given top priority, discrimination would remain. The civil rights legislation attacked the most obvious forms of discrimination. Many discriminatory practices, such as those described as institutional discrimination, are seldom obvious (Associated Press, 1995).

AFFIRMATIVE ACTION

Affirmative action is the positive effort to recruit subordinate-group members or women for jobs, promotions, and educational opportunities. The phrase *affirmative action* first appeared in an executive order issued by President Kennedy in 1963. The order called for contractors to "take affirmative action to ensure that applicants are employed, and that employees are treated during employment, without regard to their race, creed, color, or national origin." Four years later, the order was amended to prohibit discrimination on the basis of sex, but affirmative action was still vaguely defined. Today affirmative action has become a catch-all term for racial preference programs and goals.

Affirmative Action Explained

Affirmative action has become the most important tool for reducing institutional discrimination. Whereas previous efforts had been aimed at eliminating individual acts of discrimination, federal measures under the heading of affirmative action have been aimed at procedures that deny equal opportunities even if they are not intended to be overtly discriminatory. This policy has been implemented to deal with both the current discrimination and the past discrimination outlined earlier in this chapter.

The Commission on Civil Rights (1981, pp. 9–10) gave some examples of areas where affirmative action had been aimed at institutional discrimination:

- Height and weight requirements that are unnecessarily geared to the physical proportions of White males without regard to the actual requirements needed to perform the job and, therefore, exclude females and some minorities.
- Seniority rules, when applied to jobs historically held only by White males, that make more recently hired minorities and females more subject to layoff—the "last hired, first fired" employee—and less eligible for advancement.
- Nepotism-based membership policies of some unions that exclude those who are not relatives of members who, because of past employment practices, are usually White.
- Restrictive employment-leave policies, coupled with prohibitions on part-time work or denials of fringe benefits to part-time workers, which make it difficult for the heads of single-parent families, most of whom are women, to get and keep jobs and also meet the needs of their families.

- Rules requiring that only English be spoken at the workplace, even when not a business necessity, which result in discriminatory employment practices toward individuals whose primary language is not English.
- Standardized academic tests or criteria, geared to the cultural and educational norms of middle-class or White males, when these are not relevant predictors of successful job performance.
- Preferences shown by law and medical schools in the admission of children of wealthy and influential alumni, nearly all of whom are White.
- Credit policies of banks and lending institutions that prevent granting of mortgages and loans in minority neighborhoods or prevent granting of credit to married women and others who have previously been denied the opportunity to build good credit histories in their own name.

Employers have also been cautioned against asking leading questions in interviews, such as "Did you know you would be the first Black to supervise all Whites in that factory?" or "Does your husband mind your working on weekends?" Furthermore, the lack of minority-group (Blacks, Asians, Native Americans, and Hispanics) or female employees may in itself represent evidence for a case of unlawful exclusion (Commission on Civil Rights, 1975, p. 12).

Legal Debates

How far can an employer go in encouraging women and minorities to apply for a job before it becomes unlawful discrimination against White males? Since the late 1970s, a number of bitterly debated cases on this difficult aspect of affirmative action have reached the U.S. Supreme Court. These are summarized in Table 3.2.

In the 1978 *Bakke* case (*Regents of the University of California v. Bakke*), by a narrow 5–4 vote, the Court ordered the medical school of the University of California at Davis to admit Allan Bakke, a White engineer who had originally been denied admission. The justices ruled that the school had violated Bakke's constitutional rights by establishing a fixed quota system for minority students. The Court added, however, that it was constitutional for universities to adopt flexible admissions programs that use race as one factor in making decisions. In the following year, in the *Weber* case (*United Steelworkers of America v. Weber*), the Supreme Court ruled, by a vote of 5–2, that the labor union did not have to admit White laboratory technician Brian Weber to a training program in Louisiana. The justices held that it was constitutional for the union to run a program for training skilled technicians that, to promote affirmative action, admitted one African American for every White.

Even if the public in the United States acknowledges the disparity in earnings between White males and others, many people doubt that everything done in the name of affirmative action is desirable. In 1991, national surveys showed that 24 percent of respondents agreed that "affirmative action programs designed to help minorities get better jobs and education go too far these days." By 1995, 39 percent of respondents agreed with that statement. But further analysis of the survey data reveals sharp racial division. In 1995, 46 percent of Whites and only 8

Table 3.2   KEY AFFIRMATIVE ACTION DECISIONS

In a series of split and often very close decisions, the Supreme Court has been supportive of affirmative action as implemented, although it has had reservations in specific situations.

Year	Favorable/ Unfavorable to Policy	Case	Vote	Ruling
1978	–	Regents of the University of California v. Bakke	5–4	Prohibited specific number of places for minorities in college admissions
1979	+	United Steelworkers of America v. Weber	5–2	OK for union to favor minorities in special training programs
1984	–	Firefighters Local Union No. 1784 (Memphis, TN) v. Stotts	6–1	Seniority means recently hired minorities may be laid off first in staff reductions
1986	+	International Association of Firefighters v. City of Cleveland	6–3	May promote minorities over more senior Whites
1986	+	New York City v. Sheet Metal	5–4	Approved specific quota of minority workers for union
1987	+	United States v. Paradise	5–4	Endorsed quotas for promotions of state troopers
1987	+	Johnson v. Transportation Agency, Santa Clara, CA	6–3	Approved preference in hiring for minorities and women over better-qualified men and Whites
1989	–	Richmond v. Croson Company	6-3	Ruled a 30 percent set-aside program for minority contractors unconstitutional
1989	–	Martin v. Wilks	5–4	Ruled Whites may bring reverse discrimination claims against court-approved affirmative action plans
1990	+	Metro Broadcasting v. FCC	5–4	Supported federal programs aimed at increasing minority ownership of broadcast licenses
1995	–	Adarand Construction v. Peña	5–4	Benefits based on race are constitutional only if narrowly defined to accomplish a compelling interest

percent of African Americans indicated that affirmative action has gone too far (D. Lauter, 1995).

Beginning in the 1980s, the Supreme Court, increasingly influenced by conservative justices, has issued many critical rulings concerning affirmative action programs. In a key case in 1989, the Court invalidated, by a 6-3 vote, a Richmond, Virginia, law that had guaranteed 30 percent of public works funds to construction companies owned by minorities. In ruling that the Richmond statute violated the constitutional right of White contractors to equal protection under the law, the Court held that affirmative action programs are constitutional only when they serve the "compelling state interest" of redressing "identified discrimination" by the government or private parties. More recently in mid-1995, a divided Supreme Court, by a 5-4 vote in *Adarand v. Peña* held that federal programs that award benefits on the basis of race are constitutional only if they are "narrowly tailored" to accomplish a "compelling governmental interest." The Court's ruling was expected to encourage further legal challenges to federal affirmative action programs (L. Greenhouse, 1989).

Has affirmative action actually helped to alleviate employment inequality on the basis of race and gender? Sociologist Dula Espinosa (1992) studied the impact of affirmative action on a California municipal workforce whose hiring practices were traced from 1975 through 1985. As a federal contractor, the city was required to comply with federal guidelines regarding employment practices, including making "good faith efforts" to increase employment opportunities for women and minorities. Espinosa found that employment inequality by gender, race, and ethnicity had indeed decreased during the ten-year period studied.

Espinosa adds, however, that most of the reduction in the city's level of employment inequality occurred just after the affirmative action policy was first introduced. In Espinosa's view, once immediate progress can be seen, an organization may become less inclined to continue to implement an affirmative action policy. Moreover, while high levels of inequality may be relatively easy to address initially, sustaining positive results may take longer because of institutional discrimination. Care must also be taken not to interpret falsely as upward mobility positions that become inflated in status once they are filled by women or minorities. Espinosa concludes that affirmative action was successful to some degree in reducing employment inequality in the city studied but clearly had its limitations as well.

A study of income data and occupational mobility among Black and White male workers in the period 1974–1981 examined possible class polarization among Blacks. The researchers found that, while Black college graduates had made substantial gains as a result of affirmative action, less-advantaged Blacks had apparently not benefited from it. The researchers (Son, Model, and Fisher, 1989) concluded that the "racial parity achieved by young college-educated Blacks in the 1970s will be maintained only if the government's commitment to affirmative action does not slacken" (p. 325).

By the early 1990s, affirmative action had emerged as an increasingly important issue in state and national political campaigns. Generally, discussion focused on the use of quotas (or the "Q word," as it came to be known) in hiring practices. Supporters of affirmative action argue that hiring goals establish "floors" for minority inclusion but do not exclude truly qualified candidates from any group. Opponents insist that these "targets" are, in fact, quotas that lead to reverse discrimination. However, according to the Department of Labor, affirmative action

Hispanic-American professionals, like others, encounter glass ceilings and glass walls.

has caused very few claims of reverse discrimination by White people. Fewer than 100 of the more than 3,000 discrimination opinions in federal courts from 1990 to 1994 even raised the issue of reverse discrimination, and reverse discrimination was actually established in only six cases (*New York Times*, 1995b).

Despite such data, by mid-1995 affirmative action was "heating up" as a political issue and seemed likely to be a focus of the 1996 presidential campaign. The state of California, in particular, was a battleground over this controversial issue. In 1995, opponents of affirmative action launched the California Civil Rights Initiative, which would place on the ballot in 1996 a referendum to amend the state constitution and prohibit any programs that give preference to women and minorities for college admission, employment, promotion, or government contracts. In mid-1995, California's governor, Pete Wilson, issued an executive order dismantling some of the state's affirmative action programs. Wilson argued that these programs fostered hostility, pitting "group against group, race against race," but the Mexican American Legal Defense and Education Fund countered that "with one swoop of the pen, Governor Pete Wilson will become infamous for taking California back to an era where women and minorities 'knew their place'" (*New York Times*, 1995c, p. A15).

THE GLASS CEILING

We have been talking primarily about racial and ethnic groups as if they have uniformly failed to keep pace with Whites. While that is accurate, there are tens of thousands people of color who have matched and even exceeded Whites. For example, in 1991, there were over 133,000 Black households and over 134,000 Hispanic households that earned over $100,000. What can we say about affluent members of subordinate groups in the United States?

Prejudice does not necessarily end with wealth. Black newspaper columnist De Wayne Wickham (1993) wrote of the subtle racism he had experienced. He had witnessed a White clerk in a supermarket ask a White customer if she knew the price of an item the computer would not scan; when the problem occurred while the clerk was ringing up Wickham's groceries, she called for a price check. Affluent subordinate-group members routinely report being blocked as they move toward the first-class section aboard airplanes or seek service in upscale stores. Harvard-educated NBC vice president Jarobim Gilbert recalled when he and his secretary were trying to get separate cabs at the same location. She, who is White, got one on her first attempt; Gilbert, who is Black, eventually had to call his wife. "It's pretty hard to feel like you're mainstream," he said with a sigh, "when you're wearing $2,000 worth of clothes and you can't catch a cab at night" (R. Lacayo, 1989). Another journalist, Ellis Cose (1993), has termed these insults the soul-destroying slights that lead to the "rage of a privileged class."

Discrimination persists for even the educated and qualified of the best family backgrounds. As subordinate-group members are able to compete successfully, they sometimes encounter attitudinal or organizational bias that prevents them from reaching their full potential. They have confronted what has come to be called the *glass ceiling*. This refers to the barrier that blocks the promotion of a qualified worker in a multiracial work environment. The reasons are as many as the occurrences. It may be that one Black or one woman vice president is regarded as "enough," so the second potential candidate faces an end to the movement up through management. Decision makers may be concerned that their clientele will not trust them if they have "too many" people of color or concerned that a talented woman could become overwhelmed with her duties as a mother and wife.

Concern about the women and minorities climbing a broken ladder led to the formation in 1991 of the Glass Ceiling Commission with the U.S. Secretary of Labor chairing the 21-member group. Initially, it regarded some of the glass ceiling barriers as:

- Lack of management commitment to establishing systems, policies, and practices for achieving workplace diversity and upward mobility
- Pay inequities for work of equal or comparable value
- Sex-, race-, and ethnic-based stereotyping and harassment
- Unfair recruitment practices
- Lack of family-friendly workplace policies
- "Parent-track" policies
- Limited opportunities for advancement to decision-making positions (Department of Labor, 1993, 1995)

The commission report documented that the underrepresentation of women in managerial positions in a large part due to the presence of glass ceilings.

Glass ceilings are not the only barrier. Catalyst, a nonprofit research organization, conducted interviews in 1992 with senior managers and middle managers from larger corporations. The study found that, even before glass ceilings are encountered, women and racial and ethnic minorities face *glass walls* that keep them moving laterally. Specifically, the study found that women tend to be placed in staff or support positions in areas such as public relations and human resources and are often directed away from jobs in core areas such as marketing, production, and sales. Women are assigned, and therefore trapped, in jobs reflecting their stereotypical helping nature and encounter glass walls cutting off jobs that may lead to broader experience and advancement (J. Lopez, 1992).

How do members of subordinate groups respond to glass walls and ceilings? Some endure them, but others take their potential and begin their own businesses. Susan Crowe Chamberlain, past president of Women in Management, summarized it succinctly by saying that, for many women and minority men, the real way to get to the top is to get out. Instead of fighting the ceiling, they form their own companies (R. Richman, 1992, sect. 6, p. 11).

Focusing on the employed and even the relatively affluent should not lead us to ignore the underclass people employed in the irregular economy, or Native Americans without economic opportunities on isolated reservations. Surveying the past ten years, Urban League President John Jacob said in 1994 that Blacks can do only so much themselves; self-development cannot succeed without an "opportunity environment." He called on President Clinton to endorse a "Marshall Plan for America" that would focus on job creation and job training (*USA Today*, 1994). Yet even the affluent subordinate-group person is reminded of her or his second-class status through subtle racism or a glass ceiling.

CONCLUSION

Discrimination takes its toll, whether a person who is discriminated against is a part of the irregular economy or not. Even members of minority groups who are not today being overtly discriminated against continue to fall victim to past discrimination.

From the conflict perspective, it should not be surprising to find the widespread presence of a dual labor market and even an underclass. Derrick Bell

(1994), an African American law professor, has made the sobering assertion that "racism is permanent." He contends that the attitudes of dominant Whites prevail and society is only willing to advance programs on behalf of subordinate groups when they coincide with the needs as perceived by Whites. Bell observes that the criticism of the affirmative action program in the 1990s exceeded any concern over corporate downsizing which led to a loss of 1.6 million manufacturing jobs from 1989 to 1993 alone.

Women are a particularly vulnerable group, for whether the comparisons are within or across racial and ethnic groupings, they face significant social disparities. This inequality will be a recurring theme throughout this book, but we can cite the observations of two distinguished sociologists. Alice Rossi (1988) notes that, as a child during the Great Depression, she learned that homemaking tasks force a woman to think of employment as "a contingency" rather than "continuous." She goes on to recollect how opportunities, including federal research funds, went to aid the careers of men rather than women. More recently, Theda Skocpol (1988) has experienced difficulties she attributes to her gender. She notes that in 1984 she "was offered the Harvard tenured professorship that I am convinced would have been mine in 1981 if I had been 'Theodore' rather than 'Theda'" (p. 155). Whether it is among the underclass or in college classes, women are at a disadvantage.

The surveys presented in Chapter 2 show gradual acceptance of the earliest efforts to eliminate discrimination, but that support failing especially as it relates to affirmative action. Governmental programs are increasingly aimed at institutional discrimination, a form that some people feel is not really discrimination at all. As one might expect, attempts to attack institutional discrimination have met with staunch resistance. Partly as a result of this outcry from some of the public, especially White Americans, the federal government gradually deemphasized its efforts in affirmative action during the 1980s and 1990s.

As we turn to examine the various groups that make up the American people, through generations of immigration and religious diversity, look for the types of programs meant to reduce prejudice and discrimination that were discussed here. Most of the material in this chapter has been about racial groups, especially Black and White Americans. It would be easy to see intergroup hostility as a racial phenomenon, but that would be incorrect. Throughout the history of the United States, relations among White groups have been characterized by resentment and violence. The next two chapters examine the nature and relations of White ethnic groups.

KEY TERMS

absolute deprivation The minimum level of subsistence below which families or individuals should not be expected to exist.

affirmative action Positive efforts to recruit subordinate-group members or women for jobs, promotions, and educational opportunities.

discrimination The denial of opportunities and equal rights to individuals and groups because of prejudice or for other arbitrary reasons.

dual labor market Division of the economy into two areas of employment, the secondary one of which is populated primarily by minorities working at menial jobs.

glass ceiling The barrier that blocks the promotion of a qualified worker because of gender or minority membership.

glass wall A barrier to moving laterally in a business to positions that are more likely to lead to upward mobility.

institutional discrimination A denial of opportunities and equal rights to individuals or groups resulting from the normal operations of a society.

irregular economy Transfers of money, goods, or services that are not reported to the government. Common in inner-city neighborhoods and poverty-stricken rural areas.

relative deprivation The conscious experience of a negative discrepancy between legitimate expectations and present actualities.

states' rights The principle, reinvoked in the late 1940s, that holds that each state is sovereign and has the right to order its own affairs without interference by the federal government.

total discrimination The combination of current discrimination with past discrimination created by poor schools and menial jobs.

underclass Lower-class members who are not a part of the regular economy and whose situation is not changed by conventional assistance programs.

FOR FURTHER INFORMATION

Paula Burnstein, ed. *Equal Employment Opportunity: Labor Market Discrimination and Public Policy.* Hawthorne, NY: Aldine de Gruyter, 1994.

   Includes the work of scholars in economics, history, law, politics and sociology presenting important issues about equal-employment-opportunity laws.

Stephen Carter. *Reflections of an Affirmative Action Baby.* New York: Basic Books, 1991.

   A Black law professor at Yale offers an anecdotal account of his life that is critical of life as an African American in higher education under affirmative action and liberalism.

Robert Cherry. *Discrimination.* Lexington, MA: Lexington Book, 1989.

   An economist reviews the economic impact of discrimination on Blacks, Women, and Jews.

Philomena Essed. *Understanding Everyday Racism.* Newbury Park, CA: Sage, 1991.

   Interviews of 2,000 Black women in the United States and the Netherlands documenting personal and institutional racism.

Jacqueline Jones. *The Dispossessed: American's Underclasses from the Civil War to the Present.* New York: Basic Books, 1992.

   A study of the fate of the southern poor, both Black and White, from the close of the Civil War through the migration northward.

Louis L. Knowles and Kenneth Prewitt. *Institutional Racism in America.* Englewood Cliffs, NJ: Prentice-Hall, 1969.

   This book documents institutional racism in economic life, education, the courts, and the political process and describes how it is expressed in prejudice and discrimination.

Douglas S. Massey and Nancy A. Denton. *American Apartheid: Segregation and the Making of the Underclass.* Cambridge, MA: Harvard University Press, 1993.

   A thorough investigation of the economic impact that residential segregation has in the United States on African Americans and Hispanics.

Donald Tomaskovic-Derry. *Gender and Racial Inequality at Work: The Sources and Consequences of Job Segregation.* Ithaca, NY: Industrial and Labor Relations Press.

> Considers the social consequences of segregation by job titles in the workplace.

William J. Wilson. *The Truly Disadvantaged: The Inner City, the Underclass, and Public Policy.* Chicago: University of Chicago Press, 1987.

> A sociologist analyzes the continuing deterioration of the conditions facing the African-American urban poor.

Statistical Sources

Hundreds of federal government publications provide statistical data comparing racial and ethnic groups to each other and women to men. The Current Population Report Series P-20 and P-60 and the annual *Statistical Abstract of the United States* are among the best sources.

CRITICAL THINKING QUESTIONS

1. Why might people still feel disadvantaged even though their incomes are rising and their housing circumstances have improved?
2. Why does institutional discrimination sometimes seem less objectionable than individual discrimination?
3. In what way does an industrial society operate on several economic levels?
4. What are some objections people may raise to affirmative action?
5. How do glass ceilings and walls function in places you have observed?

PART Two

ETHNIC AND RELIGIOUS SOURCES OF CONFLICT

Chapter
4

Immigration and the United States

Chapter Outline

Early Immigration
   The Anti-Catholic Crusade
   The Anti-Chinese Movement
Restrictionist Sentiment Increases
   The National Origins System
   The 1965 Immigration and
      Naturalization Act
Contemporary Concerns
   The Brain Drain
   Population Growth

Illegal Immigration
   Scope of the Problem
   Reform and Amnesty
   Costs and Controversy
Refugees
Conclusion
Key Terms
For Further Information
Critical Thinking Questions

Highlights

The diversity of the American people is unmistakable evidence of the variety of places from which immigrants have come. The different immigrating people did not necessarily welcome one another. Instead they brought their European rivalries to the New World. The Chinese were the first to be singled out for restriction with the passage of the 1882 Exclusion Act. The Chinese became, in effect, the scapegoat for America's sagging economy in the last half of the nineteenth century. Growing fears that more un-American types were immigrating motivated the creation of the *national origins system* and the quota acts of the 1920s. These acts gave preference to certain nationalities, until the passage of the Immigration and Naturalization Act in 1965 ended that practice. Concern about illegal immigration has continued through the mid-1990s, leading to the 1994 passage of the controversial Proposition 187 in California. Controversy also continues to surround the policy of the United States toward refugees, particularly Haitians.

In the summer of 1986, a Taiwanese student arrived at Chicago's O'Hare Airport for her first time in the United States. She entered the customs and immigration area knowing there were two sections: one for Americans and the other for foreigners. She recalled, "At that moment, I felt that I had chosen the right line because in the line were a lot of Asian people and I thought that we are all foreigners who came to the United States. Later, I found that I was wrong because I saw everyone in this line carried American passports. So, from this event I suddenly realized that I could not judge a person's nationality by his appearance, especially in the United States" (S. Feng, 1988, p. 1).

The diversity of ethnic and racial backgrounds of Americans today is the living legacy of immigration. Except for descendants of Native Americans or of Africans brought here enslaved, today's population is entirely the product of individuals who chose to leave familiar places to come to a new country.

The social forces that cause people to emigrate are complex. The most important have been economic: financial failure in the old country and expectations of higher incomes and higher standards of living in the new homeland. Other factors included dislike of new regimes, racial or religious bigotry, and a desire to reunite families. All these factors push individuals from their homelands and pull them to other nations such as the United States. Immigration into the United States in particular has at times been facilitated by cheap ocean transportation and by other countries' removal of restrictions on emigration.

The reception given to immigrants in this country, however, has not always been friendly. Open bloodshed, restrictive laws, and the eventual return of close to one-third of the immigrants and their children to their home countries attest to the uneasy feeling toward strangers who wish to settle here. Nevertheless, vast numbers of immigrants have still come. Figure 4.1 indicates the high but fluctuating number of immigrants that have arrived during every decade from the 1820s through the 1980s. Opinion polls in the United States from 1946 through 1993 never show more than 13 percent of the public wanting more immigrants, and usually half want fewer. Yet, at any given time, around forty percent of those responding are either first- or second-generation residents or immigrants themselves (D. Moore, 1993; R. Simon, 1993; Warren and Kraly, 1985).

EARLY IMMIGRATION

European explorers of North America were soon accompanied by settlers, the first immigrants to the Western Hemisphere. The Spanish founded St. Augustine in Florida in 1565, and the English, Jamestown in Virginia in 1607. White Protestants from England emerged from the colonial period as the dominant force numerically, politically, and socially. The English accounted for 60 percent of the 3 million White Americans in 1790. Although exact statistics are lacking for the early years of the United States, the English were soon outnumbered by other nationalities, as the numbers of Scotch-Irish and Germans, in particular, swelled. The English colonists, however, maintained their dominant position, as Chapter 5 will examine.

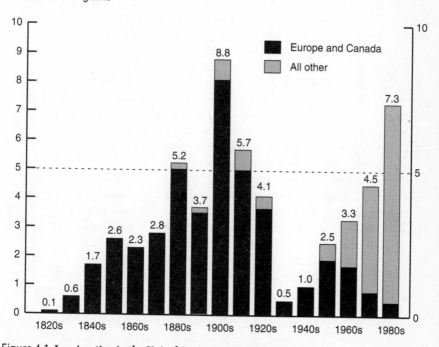

Figure 4.1 Immigration in the United States, 1820s through 1980s
Except during a period of tightening immigration policy in the 1930s and 1940s, the United States has received a consistent, sizable flow of immigrants, dominated since 1950 by non-Europeans.

Source: The Urban Institute in Fix and Passel (1991), based on Immigration and Naturalization Service statistics. Data for 1980s adjusted by author based on F. Barringer (1992).

Throughout American history, immigration policy has been a controversial political topic. The policies of the English king George III were criticized in the U.S. Declaration of Independence for obstructing immigration to the colonies. Toward the end of the nineteenth century, the American republic itself was criticized for enacting just such policies. But in the beginning, the country encouraged immigration. At first, legislation fixed the residence requirement for naturalization at five years, although briefly, under the Alien Act, it was 14 years, and "dangerous" people could be expelled. Despite this brief harshness, through most of the 1800s immigration was unregulated, and naturalization was easily available.

The Anti-Catholic Crusade

The absence of federal legislation from 1790 to 1881 does not mean that all new arrivals were welcomed. *Xenophobia* (the fear or hatred of strangers or foreigners) led naturally to *nativism* (beliefs and policies favoring native-born citizens over immigrants). Roman Catholics in general and the Irish in particular were among the first Europeans to be ill-treated. Anti-Catholic feeling originated in Europe and was brought by the early Protestant immigrants. The Catholics of colonial America, although few, were subject to limits on their civil and religious rights.

From independence until around 1820, little evidence appeared of the anti-Catholic sentiment of colonial days, but the cry against "popery" grew as Irish immigration increased. Prominent Americans encouraged hatred of these new arrivals. Samuel F. B. Morse, inventor of the telegraph and an accomplished painter, wrote a strongly worded anti-Catholic work in 1834 entitled *A Foreign Conspiracy Against the Liberties of the United States*. Morse felt the Irish were "shamefully illiterate and without opinions of their own" (1835, p. 61). In the mind of the prejudiced American, the Irish were particularly unwelcome because they were Roman Catholics. Many Americans readily believed Morse's warning that the pope planned to move the Vatican to the Mississippi River Valley (J. Duff, 1971, p. 34). Even poet and philosopher Ralph Waldo Emerson wrote of "the wild Irish . . . who sympathized, of course, with despotism" (J. Kennedy, 1964, p. 70).

This antagonism was not limited to harsh words. From 1834 to 1854, mob violence against Catholics across the country led to death, the burning of a Boston convent, the destruction of a Catholic church and the homes of Catholics, and the use of marines and state militia to bring peace to American cities as far west as St. Louis.

A frequent pattern saw minorities striking out against each other, rather than at the dominant class. Irish Americans opposed the Emancipation Proclamation and the freeing of the slaves because they feared Blacks would compete for the unskilled work open to them. This fear was confirmed when free Blacks were used to break a longshoremen's strike in New York. Hence, much of the Irish violence during the 1863 riot was directed against Blacks, not against the Whites who were most responsible for the conditions in which the immigrants found themselves (J. Duff, 1971; S. Warner, 1968).

In retrospect, the reception given to the Irish is not difficult to understand. Many came following the 1845–1848 potato crop failure and famine in Ireland. They fled not so much to a better life as from almost certain death. The Irish

Catholics brought with them a celibate clergy, who struck the New England aristocracy as strange and reawakened old religious hatreds. The Irish were worse than Blacks, according to the dominant Whites, because unlike the slaves and even the freed Blacks, who "knew their place," the Irish did not suffer their maltreatment in silence. Employers balanced minorities by judiciously mixing immigrant groups to prevent unified action by the laborers. For the most part, nativist efforts only led the foreign-born to emphasize their ties to Europe.

By the 1850s, nativism became an open political movement pledged to vote only for native Americans, to fight Roman Catholicism, and to demand a 21-year naturalization period. Party members were instructed to divulge nothing about their program and to say that they knew nothing about it. As a result, they came to be called the Know-Nothings. Although the Know-Nothings soon vanished, the antialien mentality survived and occasionally became formally organized into such societies as the Ku Klux Klan in the 1860s and the anti-Catholic American Protective Association in the 1890s. Revivals of anti-Catholicism continued well into the twentieth century. The most dramatic outbreak of nativism in the nineteenth century, however, was aimed at the Chinese. If there had been any doubt that the idea that the United States could harmoniously accommodate all was a fiction by the mid-1800s, debate on the Chinese Exclusion Act would settle the question once and for all (D. Gerber, 1993).

The Anti-Chinese Movement

Before 1851, official records show that only 46 Chinese had immigrated to the United States. In the next 30 years, more than 200,000 came to this country, lured by the discovery of gold and the opening of job opportunities in the West. Overcrowding, drought, and warfare in China also encouraged them to take a chance in the United States. Another important factor was improved transoceanic transportation; it was actually cheaper to travel from Hong Kong to San Francisco than from Chicago to San Francisco. The frontier communities of the West, particularly in California, looked on the Chinese as a valuable resource to fill manual jobs. As early as 1854, so many Chinese desired to come that ships had difficulty handling the volume.

During the 1860s, railroad work provided the greatest demand for Chinese labor, until the Union Pacific and Central Pacific railroads were joined at Promontory, Utah, in 1869. The Union Pacific relied primarily on Irish laborers, but 90 percent of the Central Pacific labor force was Chinese, because Whites generally refused the backbreaking work over the western terrain. Despite the contribution of the Chinese, White workers physically prevented their even being present when the golden spike was driven to mark the joining of the two railroads (Commission on Civil Rights, 1986; F. Hsu, 1971).

A variety of factors, rather than a single cause, motivated the anti-Chinese movement. The movement itself was twofold, including both legislative restrictions on the rights of Chinese immigrants and mob violence, vigilante groups, and spur-of-the-moment tribunals intended to intimidate the new arrivals. Although the legislators often chastised the mobs and vigilantes for their actions, both groups were inspired by the same fears.

Chinese men were recruited to immigrate into the United States beginning in the 1850s to do dangerous work on the railroads and in mines.

Reflecting their xenophobia, White settlers found the Chinese immigrants and their customs and religion difficult to understand. Indeed, relatively few people actually tried to understand these immigrants from Asia. Easterners and legislators, although they had had no firsthand contact with Chinese Americans, were soon on the anti-Chinese bandwagon, as they read sensationalized accounts of the way of life of the new arrivals.

Even before the Chinese immigrated, stereotypes of them and their country appeared. American traders returning from China, European diplomats, and Protestant missionaries consistently emphasized the exotic and sinister aspects of life in China. The sinophobes, people with a fear of anything associated with China, appealed to the racist theory developed during the slavery controversy. Similarly, Americans were beginning to be more conscious of biological inheritance and disease, and so it was not hard to conjure up fears of alien genes and germs. The only real challenge the anti-Chinese movement had was to convince people that the consequences of unrestricted Chinese immigration outweighed any possible economic gain from their presence. Perhaps briefly, racial prejudice was subordinated to industrial dependence on Chinese labor for the work that Whites shunned, but such positive feelings were short-lived. The fear of the "yellow peril" overwhelmed any desire to know more about Asian people and their customs (S. Miller, 1969; B. Schrieke, 1936).

Another nativist fear of Chinese immigrants was based on the threat they posed as laborers. Californians found support throughout the nation as organized labor feared that the Chinese would be used as strikebreakers. By 1870, Chinese workers had been used for that purpose as far east as Massachusetts. When Chinese workers did unionize, they were not recognized by major labor organizations. Samuel Gompers, founder of the American Federation of Labor (AFL), consistently opposed any effort to assist Chinese workers and refused to consider having a union of Chinese restaurant employees admitted into the AFL (H. Hill, 1967). Gompers worked effectively to see future Chinese immigration ended and produced a pamphlet entitled *Chinese Exclusion: Meat vs. Rice, American Manhood Against Asiatic Coolieism—Which Shall Survive?* (Gompers and Gustadt, 1908). Although employers were glad to pay the Chinese low wages, laborers came to loathe the Chinese rather than resenting their compatriots' willingness to exploit the Chinese. Only a generation earlier, the same concerns had been felt about the Irish, but with the Chinese, the hostility was to reach new heights because of another factor.

From the sociological perspective of conflict theory, we can explain how the Chinese immigrants were welcomed only when their labor was necessary to fuel the growth in the United States. When that labor was no longer necessary, the welcome mat for the immigrants was withdrawn. But as conflict theorists would further point out, restrictions were not evenly applied; a specific nationality group— the Chinese—was focused on to reduce overall the number of foreign workers in the nation. Because decision making at that time rested in the hands of the descendants of *European* immigrants, the steps to be taken were most likely to be directed against those least powerful; immigrants from China who, unlike Europeans seeking entry, had few allies among legislators and other policymakers.

In 1882, Congress enacted the Chinese Exclusion Act, which outlawed Chinese immigration for ten years. It also explicitly denied naturalization rights to those Chinese in the United States; that is, they were not allowed to become citizens. There was little debate in Congress, and discussion concentrated on *how* suspension of Chinese immigration could best be handled. No allowance was made for spouses and children to be reunited with their husbands and fathers in the United States. Only Chinese government officials, teachers, tourists, and merchants were exempted.

The balance of the nineteenth century saw the remaining loopholes allowing Chinese immigration closed. In 1884, Chinese laborers were not allowed to enter the United States from any foreign place, a ban that lasted ten years. Two years later, the Statue of Liberty was dedicated, with the poem by Emma Lazarus inscribed on its base. To the Chinese, the poem welcoming the tired, the poor, the huddled masses must have seemed a hollow mockery.

In 1892, Congress extended the Exclusion Act for another ten years and added that Chinese laborers had to obtain certificates of residence within a year or face deportation. After the turn of the century, the Exclusion Act was extended again. Two decades later, the Chinese were not alone; the list of people restricted by immigration policy expanded manyfold.

RESTRICTIONIST SENTIMENT INCREASES

As Congress closed the door to Chinese immigration, the debate on restricting immigration turned in new directions. Prodded by growing anti-Japanese feelings, the United States entered into the so-called Gentlemen's Agreement, completed in 1908. Japan agreed to halt further immigration to the United States, and the United States agreed to end discrimination against those Japanese who had already arrived. The immigration ended, but anti-Japanese feelings continued. Americans were growing uneasy that the "new immigrants" would overwhelm the culture established by the "old immigrants." The earlier immigrants, if not Anglo-Saxon or similar groups like the Scandinavians, the Swiss, and the French Huguenots, were more experienced in democratic political practices and had a greater affinity with the dominant Anglo-Saxon culture. But by the end of the nineteenth century, more and more immigrants were neither English-speaking nor Protestant and came from dramatically different cultures.

For four years, the United States Immigration Commission, known popularly as the Dillingham Commission, exhaustively studied the effects of immigration. The findings, presented in 1911, were determined by the commission's assumption that there were types of immigrants. The two types were the old immigrants, mostly Anglo-Saxons, who were characterized as hard-working pioneers, and the new immigrants from southern Europe, who were branded as opportunists (L. Fermi, 1971, p. 20; O. Handlin, 1957, pp. 78–110). Not surprisingly, pressure for a more restrictive immigration policy became insurmountable. A literacy test was one of the results of hostility against the new immigrants.

In 1917, Congress finally overrode President Wilson's veto and enacted an immigration bill that included the controversial literacy test. Critics of the bill, including Wilson, argued that illiteracy does not signify inherent incompetency but reflects lack of opportunity for instruction (*New York Times*, 1917a). Such arguments were not heeded, however. The act seems innocent at first glance—it merely required immigrants to read 30 words in any language—but it was the first attempt to restrict immigration from places other than western Europe. The act also prohibited immigration from the South Sea islands and other parts of Asia not already excluded. Curiously, this law that closed the door on non-Anglo-Saxons permitted waiver of the test if the immigrants came as a result of their government's discrimination against a race (*New York Times*, 1917b).

The National Origins System

Beginning in 1921, a series of measures was enacted that marked a new era in American immigration policy. Anti-immigration sentiment, combined with the isolationism that followed World War I, caused Congress to severely restrict entry privileges not just to the Chinese and Japanese but to Europeans as well. The national origins system was begun in 1921 and remained the basis of immigration policy until 1965. This system used the country of birth to determine whether an individual could enter as a legal alien, and the number of previous immigrants and their descendants was used to set the quota of how many from a country could enter annually.

To understand the effect that the 1929 act had on immigration, it is necessary to clarify the quota system. The quotas were deliberately weighted in favor of immigration from northern Europe. Because of the ethnic composition of the country in 1920, the quotas placed severe restrictions on immigration from the rest

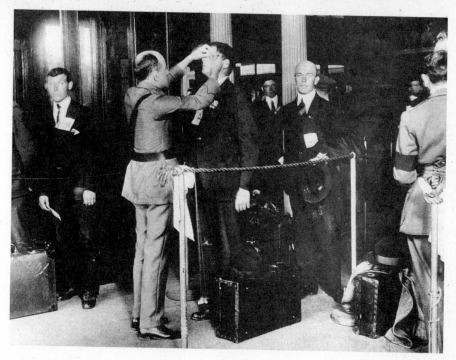

A doctor at Ellis Island examines a European immigrant in the early 1900s for signs of a disease that would bar entry.

of Europe and other parts of the world. Immigration from the Western Hemisphere (that is, Canada, Mexico, Central and South America, and the Caribbean) continued unrestricted. The quota for each nation was set at 3 percent of the number of people descended from each nationality recorded in the 1920 census. Once the statistical manipulations were completed, almost 70 percent of the quota for the Eastern Hemisphere went to just three countries: Great Britain, Ireland, and Germany.

The absurdities of the system soon became obvious, but the system continued. Britain was no longer a source of immigration, and so most of its quota of 65,000 went unfilled. The openings, however, could not be transferred, even though countries such as Italy, with a quota of only 6,000, had 200,000 people who wished to enter (F. Belair, 1970). However one rationalizes the purpose behind the act, the result was obvious: any English person, regardless of skill and regardless of any relation to anyone already here, could enter the country more easily than, say, a Greek doctor whose children were American citizens. The quota for Greece was 305, with the backlog of people wishing to come reaching 100,000.

By the end of the 1920s, annual immigration had dropped to one-fourth of its pre–World War I level. The worldwide economic depression of the 1930s decreased immigration still further. A brief upsurge in immigration just before World War II reflected the flight of Europeans from the oppression of expanding

Nazi Germany. The war virtually ended transatlantic immigration. The era of the great European migration to the United States had been legislated out of existence.

The 1965 Immigration and Naturalization Act

The national origins system was abandoned with the passage of the 1965 Immigration and Naturalization Act, signed into law by President Lyndon B. Johnson at the foot of the Statue of Liberty. The primary goals of the act were reuniting families and protecting the American labor market. After the act, immigration increased by one-third, but the act's influence was primarily on the composition rather than the size of immigration. The sources of immigration now included Italy, Greece, Portugal, Mexico, the Philippines, the West Indies, and South America. The effect is apparent when we compare the changing sources of immigration over the last hundred years, as in Figure 4.2. The most recent period shows that Asian and Latin American immigrants combined to account for 80 percent of the people who were permitted entry. This figure compares to the period of the national origins system, reflected approximately in the figure for the years 1931–1960, when 60 percent of the legal arrivals came from northern and western Europe and North America.

The liberalization of eligibility rules also brought a backlog of applications from relatives of American citizens who had earlier failed to qualify under the more restrictive national-origins scheme. Backlogs of applicants throughout the world still existed, but the equal treatment for all underlying the 1965 legislation gave them greater hope of eventually entering the United States (F. Belair, 1970; Dinnerstein and Reimers, 1975, pp. 88–89; D. Reimers, 1983).

CONTEMPORARY CONCERNS

While our current immigration policies compare favorably to other nations' restrictions, there are four continuing criticisms of our immigration policy: the brain drain, population growth, illegal immigration, and refugees. The first two, which have not been subject to specific legislation, will be examined first. We will then take an extended look at the concerns about illegal immigration and refugees.

The Brain Drain

How often have you identified your science or mathematics teacher or even your physician as someone who was not born in the United States? This nation has clearly benefited from attracting human resources from throughout the world, but this phenomenon has had its price in the sending nation.

The term *brain drain* refers to the immigration to the United States of skilled workers, professionals, and technicians who are desperately needed by their home countries. During the mid-twentieth century many scientists and other professionals from industrial nations, principally Germany and Great Britain, came to the United States. More recently, however, the brain drain has pulled emigrants from developing nations, including India, Pakistan, and newly independent African states.

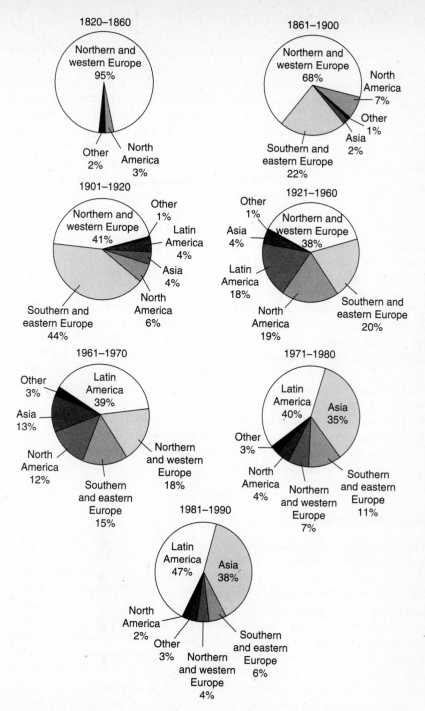

Figure 4.2 Legal Immigrants Admitted to the United States by Region of Last Residence, 1820–1990

Source: From Leon F. Bouvier and Robert W. Gardner, *Immigration to the U.S.: The Unfinished Story* (Washington, DC: Population Reference Bureau, 1986). Reprinted by permission. Data for 1981–1990 are author's estimates based on Immigration and Naturalization Service data cited in F. Barringer (1992).

The brain drain controversy was evident long before the passage of the 1965 Immigration Act. The 1965 act seemed, though, to encourage such immigration by placing the professions in one of the categories of preference. In the 1980s alone, 1.5 million college-educated immigrants joined the workforce in the United States. Increasingly, the nation's high-tech industries, from electronics to biotechnology, are depending on immigrants for engineers, scientists, and entrepreneurs to remain competitive in the global marketplace. Furthermore, these immigrants have links to their old countries and are boosting United States exports to the fast-growing economic regions of Asia and Latin America (Mandel and Farrell, 1992).

Conflict theorists see the current brain drain as yet another symptom of the unequal distribution of world resources. In their view, it is ironic that the United States gives foreign aid to improve the technical resources of African and Asian countries, simultaneously maintaining an immigration policy that encourages professionals in such nations to migrate to our shores. These are the very countries that have unacceptable public health conditions and need native scientists, educators, technicians, and other professionals.

Some of the effects of the brain drain have been lessened since 1982, when the entry of foreign-born and foreign-educated physicians was greatly restricted. Yet the United States continues to beckon to professionals and to retain highly motivated students, who remain in the United States after completing their education. A National Science Foundation study of Asian doctoral recipients found that 60 percent of the engineers and 85 percent of the scientists planned to stay in the United States (*Journal of Blacks in Higher Education,* 1994c).

One proposed solution to continuing international concern over the brain drain is to limit the number of professionals from a nation who may enter the United States in a year. Such legislation has not received widespread support with Congress, and the brain drain from developing countries continues.

Population Growth

The United States is almost alone among industrial nations in continuing to accept large numbers of permanent immigrants and refuges. Although such immigration has increased since the passage of the 1965 Immigration and Naturalization Act, the nation's birthrate has decreased. Consequently, the contribution of immigration to population growth has become more significant. Legal immigration accounted for one-fourth of the nation's growth in the 1990s. The impact is not evenly felt throughout the United States. If California had attracted no immigrants, in 1990, it would have gained two seats in the U.S. House of Representatives instead of seven. Illinois and New York would both have lost population in the 1980s rather than experiencing modest gains due to immigration (R. Warren, 1994).

Contrary to popular belief, immigrant women actually have a lower birthrate than native-born women, yet their contribution to population growth remains sizable. It is projected that immigrants who come to the United States in the period 1990–2080 and their descendants will add 72 million more people, or 25 percent, to the population. Assuming that native-born Americans maintain a low birthrate and the immi-

The Immigration and Naturalization Service (INS) is responsible for enforcing immigration laws in the United States.

Mike Konopacki, Huck-Konopacki Labor Cartoons.

grant contribution to the population of the United States is just 50 percent higher than at present, the contribution could run as high as 37 percent (Bouvier and Gardner, 1986; National Commission on Population Growth and the American Future, 1972).

ILLEGAL IMMIGRATION

The most bitterly debated aspect of U.S. immigration policy has been the control of illegal or undocumented immigrants. These immigrants and their families come to the United States in search of higher-paying jobs than are available in their home countries. The immigrants are pulled here by the lure of prosperity and better lives for their children, while they are pushed out of their native lands by unemployment and poverty. Despite fears to the contrary, immigrants—whether legal or illegal—have had only a slight impact on the employment prospects of longtime U.S. citizens. In general, immigrants are employed in jobs that employers find difficult to fill and that many residents do not want (G. Borjas, 1990).

Most recently, Florida joined California in 1994 in suing the U.S. government to secure strict enforcement of immigration laws and reimbursement for services rendered to illegal immigrants. Governor Lawton Chiles of Florida says his state spends $739 million annually, primarily for emergency medical services and education. California voters considered a 1994 referendum banning illegal immigrants from schools, public assistance programs, and all but emergency medical care. While the constitutionality of the proposal was in doubt, voters heavily favored the referendum which we will discuss in more detail later.

Scope of the Problem

There are over 3 million illegal immigrants in the United States, and that number is increasing annually. While Mexican nationals make up about 55–60 percent of this total, undocumented immigrants are here from throughout the world (T. Epenshade, 1990).

The cost of the federal government's attempt to police the nation's borders and locate illegal immigrants is sizable. There are significant costs for aliens and for other citizens as well. Civil rights advocates have expressed concern that the procedures used to apprehend and deport people are discriminatory and deprive many aliens of their legal rights. American citizens of Hispanic origin, some of whom were born in the United States, may be greeted with prejudice and distrust, as if their Spanish surnames automatically imply that they are "illegals." Furthermore, such American citizens may be unable to find work because employers wrongly believe that their documents are forged (Domestic Council Committee on Illegal Aliens, 1976; M. Farber, 1975).

Reform and Amnesty

In the context of this illegal immigration, Congress approved the Immigration Reform and Control Act of 1986, after debating it for nearly a decade. The act marked a historic change in immigration policy. For the first time, hiring illegal aliens became illegal, so that employers are subject to fines and even prison sentences. Just as significant was the extension of legal status to illegal aliens who had entered the United States before January 1, 1982 and had lived here continuously since then. After two years as lawful temporary residents of the United States, 3.1 million previously illegal aliens were allowed to become permanent residents eligible for American citizenship after another five years.

Support for the act was not unanimous. Some members of Congress, including Hispanic representatives, felt that employers might discriminate against Hispanics, fearing they were in the country illegally. Others opposed granting amnesty to people who had entered the country illegally, even if they had been here for several years. Some wondered about the millions of relatives of the now-legal aliens who might secure passage into the United States as permanent residents. It has been a bureaucratic challenge to determine which illegal immigrants have been in the United States long enough to qualify for legal status. Many people may be deported after unsuccessfully trying to document their residency in the United States.

It appears that the 1986 Immigration Reform and Control Act has had mixed results in terms of illegal immigration. According to data compiled by the U.S. Border Patrol, arrests along the border declined substantially in the first three years after the law took effect. However, in the fiscal year ending in September 1992, more than 1.2 million illegal immigrants were arrested crossing the border. As of 1994, it was estimated that 3.2 million illegal immigrants continued to live in the United States (Martin and Midgley, 1994).

Although the Immigration Reform and Control Act prohibited employers from discriminating against legal aliens because they were not American citizens, a 1990 report by the General Accounting Office revealed that the law had produced a "widespread pattern of discrimination" against people who looked or sounded like foreigners. The report estimates that some 890,000 employers had initiated one or more discriminatory practices in response to the 1986 immigration law. Although these firms employed nearly 7 million workers, fewer than 1,000 complaints of discrimination had been filed with government agencies—in good part because most employees were unaware of the protections included in the Immigration Reform and Control Act (C. Brown, 1990, p. 3).

Critics of the new immigration law emphasize that, while it has been extremely beneficial for many immigrants who qualified for amnesty, it has had a devastating impact on those who could not qualify. Many aliens in this situation are being overworked or underpaid by unscrupulous employers, who are well aware that these workers have few options. Consequently, millions of illegal immigrants continue to live in fear and hiding, subject to even more severe harassment and discrimination than before. From a conflict perspective, these immigrants—primarily poor and Hispanic—are being firmly entrenched at the bottom of the nation's social and economic hierarchies.

In February 1994, labor unions lend support in a parade for immigrant rights in Los Angeles. Nine months later, Californians overwhelmingly passed a measure that would block services such as education and health care to illegal immigrants.

Costs and Controversy

There is considerable public and scholarly debate about the economic effects of immigration and, particularly, illegal immigration. Research ranging from case studies focusing on how Korean immigrants have become dominant among New York City greengrocers to mobility studies charting the progress of all immigrants and their children has reached conflicting and varied conclusions.

For example, the overall impact of immigrants on the labor market is generally small; however, it can be significant in some occupations, such as farm work. In time, typically 18–20 years, immigrants' wages become comparable to or higher than those of the general population. There is even greater controversy over the receipt of welfare and health benefits by illegal immigrants. Generally, immigrants pay more in taxes than they receive in benefits, even if they reside in major cities like Los Angeles, with a large population of immigrants. However, since most of the taxes go to the federal government and do not totally relieve the local burden, some state and city municipalities are taking the matter into their own hands (Martin and Midgley, 1994).

A controversy occurred in November 1994 when voters in California approved Proposition 187, which supporters believe will deter illegal immigration. While 59 percent of the voters approved the measure, there were significant ethnic differences, with 65 percent of Whites, 47 percent of African and Asian Americans, and 33 percent of Hispanics favoring this proposition. Among the main provisions of the so-called Save Our State (or SOS) initiative are the following:

- *Public schools.* School districts are to verify the legal status of any new students to ensure that they are citizens of the United States. By 1996, schools must also verify the legal status of the parents or guardians of schoolchildren.
- *Higher education.* Illegal immigrants are prohibited from attending community colleges, the California state university system, and the University of California system.
- *Health.* Apart from emergency care, illegal immigrants are no longer eligible for any public health services. This includes no publicly funded immunizations and prenatal and postnatal care for women.
- *Law enforcement.* State offices providing health, welfare, and public education services are required to report any suspected illegal immigrants to law enforcement authorities.
- *False documents.* Providing false citizenship or resident-alien documents is a state felony, a crime punishable by five years in prison or a fine of $25,000.

Within hours after the polls closed on Election Day, opponents of Proposition 187 filed an array of lawsuits posing constitutional challenges to its implementation. A temporary restraining order was issued, blocking implementation of the measure's educational provisions. Legal experts predict that it may be years before the challenges to Proposition 187 are ultimately decided. Yet supporters hoped the proposition's success would lead to similar movements in other states. By 1995, congressmen began suggesting legislation that would include similar limitations of services to illegal immigrants (R. Cioe, 1994; Feldman and McDonnell, 1994).

REFUGEES

Refugees are persons living outside their country of citizenship for fear of political or religious persecution. An entire unsettled nation exists of refugees. There are approximately 17 million refugees worldwide. That makes the "nation" of refugees larger than Belgium or Sweden or Cuba.

The United States has touted itself as a haven for political refugees. The words of poet Emma Lazarus—"Give us your tired, your poor, your huddled masses yearning to breathe free"—are inscribed on the Statue of Liberty, long the symbol of hope for those who wanted to come to the United States. However, as we shall see, the welcome to political refugees has not always been evenhanded. It has even spurred controversies among immigrant communities themselves as indicated in "Listen to Their Voices": Bill Ong Hing's "Support the Chinese Boat People."

The United States, insulated by distance from wars and famines in Europe and Asia, has been able to be selective about which and how many refugees are welcomed. Since the arrival of refugees uprooted by World War II, the United States has allowed three groups of refugees to enter in numbers greater than regulations would ordinarily permit: Hungarians, Cubans, and Southeast Asians. Compared to the other two groups, the nearly 40,000 Hungarians who arrived following the abortive revolt against the Soviet Union of November 1956 were few indeed. At the time, however, theirs was the fastest mass immigration to this country since before 1922. With little delay, the United States amended the laws so that the Hungarian refugees could enter. Because of their small numbers and their dispersion throughout this country, the Hungarians are little in evidence four decades later. The much larger and longer period of movement of Cuban and Southeast Asian refugees into the United States has had a profound social impact.

Despite periodic public opposition, the United States government is officially committed to accepting refugees from other nations. According to the United Nations treaty on refugees, which our government ratified in 1968, countries are obliged to refrain from forcibly returning people to territories where their lives or liberty might be endangered. It is not always clear, though, whether an individual is fleeing for his or her personal safety or to escape poverty. Although persons in the latter category may be of humanitarian interest, they do not meet the official definition of refugees and are subject to deportation.

It is the practice of deporting people fleeing poverty that has been the subject of criticism. There is a long tradition in the United States of facilitating the arrival of people leaving Communist nations. Mexicans who are refugees from poverty, Liberians fleeing civil war, and black Haitians running from despotic rule are not similarly welcomed. The plight of Haitians has become of particular concern.

Haitians fled their country, often on small boats, from the time of the military coup in 1991 that overthrew the elected government of President Jean-Bertrand

Listen to Their Voices
Support the Chinese Boat People

BILL ONG HING

A Stanford University law professor since 1985, Hing serves as pro bono director of the Immigrant Resource Center in San Francisco. In 1994, a series of boats arrived with Chinese seeking asylum in the United States. Hing speaks about the alarm this arrival caused in the United States, even among some Chinese Americans.

These varied opinions epitomize the diversity of the Chinese American community, which ironically resulted in large part from the substantial numbers of Chinese immigrants that have arrived since 1965. I respect the opinions of those who are opposed to the new Chinese boat people, but I hope they will take the time to consider my reasons for believing that their position is wrong.

Bill Ong Hing

Chinese Americans who jump on the band wagon of anti-Chinese-boat-people rhetoric ought to take a close look at who's on the wagon. Many of the leaders of the anti-Chinese-boat-people crusade are the same folks who pushed for changes to refugee laws in 1980 when so many Southeast Asian refugees began arriving in the late 1970s, who tried to eliminate the sibling immigration category (the old fifth preference) in the 1980s, and who complained about Chinese signs on businesses in places like Monterey Park, Calif.

Don't kid yourself, the anti-Chinese-boat-people crusade is filled with individuals who don't like Asians. They are racists. They did not complain when thousands and thousands of Polish nationals fled to the United States in the 1980s, nor have they complained about the thousands and thousands of Irish nationals who have overstayed tourist visas.

I am not advocating that Chinese Americans stand by idly while the new Chinese boat people arrive. Go ahead and urge the prosecution of those who have exploited the new Chinese boat people. But while you're at it, urge the cleaning up of health, safety, and labor conditions in businesses which have contributed to the exploitation of many Chinese American workers. Push our leaders to better understand what's happening in China instead of using these incidents as an excuse to chime in with racist anti-immigrant groups.

Let them know that you will not take part in scapegoating refugees, because you understand that the poor economy and lack of community services is [*sic*] the result of an irresponsible national economic policy, urge that backlog be reduced with extra visas so that relatives can be reunited more quickly. But most of all, show some compassion in your words and actions to the new Chinese boat people who are our fellow human beings.

Source: Reproduced from *Asianweek*, June 3, 1994. Published by Pan Asia Venture Capital Corporation, 809 Sacramento St., San Francisco, CA 94108.

Aristide until he was restored to power in October 1994. The U.S. Coast Guard intercepted many Haitians at sea, saving some of these "boat people" from death due to their rickety and overcrowded wooden ships.

The Haitians feared detentions, torture, and execution if they remained in Haiti. However, the Bush administration viewed most of the Haitian exiles as economic migrants rather than political refugees and opposed granting them asylum and permission to enter the United States. During the 1992 presidential campaign, candidate Bill Clinton denounced the policy of interdiction as "cruel" and illegal, yet after assuming the presidency in 1993, he kept this policy in place. In 1993, the U.S. Supreme Court, by an 8–1 vote, upheld the government's right to intercept Haitian refugees at sea and return them to their homeland without asylum hearings. Steven Forester, an attorney at the Haitian Refugee Center in Miami, wondered how the justices could uphold a policy of forcibly returning Haitian refugees to "their military persecutors, . . . who the State Department condemns for their horrendous human rights practices" (L. Greenhouse, 1993b; L. Rohter, 1993c, p. 18).

In 1993, 119,000 people overseas sought to enter the United States as refugees, with the former Soviet Union and Vietnam accounting for the largest numbers. In addition, another 113,000 people were already here seeking asylum as refugees, with greatest numbers having arrived from Guatemala, El Salvador, China, and Haiti. In the meantime, there was a backlog of more than 400,000 residents who were waiting for hearings regarding their petitions. Refugees are a worldwide challenge to all nations, and the United States is no exception (R. Suro, 1994).

CONCLUSION

For its first hundred years, the United States allowed all immigrants to enter and become permanent residents. The federal policy of welcome did not mean, however, that immigrants would not encounter discrimination and prejudice. With the passage of the Chinese Exclusion Act, discrimination against immigrants became law. The Chinese were soon joined by the Japanese as peoples forbidden by law to enter and prohibited from becoming naturalized citizens. The development of the national origins system in the 1920s created a hierarchy of nationalities, with people from northern Europe encouraged to enter while other Europeans and Asians encountered long delays. The melting pot, which had always been a fiction, was legislated out of existence even as a possibility.

In the 1960s and again in 1990, the policy was liberalized so that the importance of nationality was minimized, and a person's work skills and relationship to an American were emphasized. This liberalization came at a time when most Europeans no longer desired to immigrate into the United States. The legacy of the arrival of nearly 50 million immigrants since 1820 is apparent today.

Throughout the history of the United States, as we have seen, there has been intense debate over the nation's immigration and refugee policies. In a sense, this debate reflects the deep value conflicts in the culture of the United States and parallels the "American dilemma" identified by Swedish social economist Gunnar

Myrdal (1944). One strand of our culture—well epitomized by the words "Give us your tired, your poor, your huddled masses"—has emphasized egalitarian principles and a desire to help people in their time of need. At the same time, however, hostility to potential immigrants and refugees—whether Chinese in the 1880s, European Jews in the 1930s and 1940s, or Mexicans, Haitians, and Arabs today—reflects not only racial, ethnic, and religious prejudice, but also a desire to maintain the dominant culture of the in-group by keeping out those viewed as outsiders. The conflict between these cultural values is central to the "American dilemma" of the 1990s.

This chapter has shown that the majority of Americans are not descended from the English, and that Protestants are outnumbered by other worshipers. This diversity of religious and ethnic groups will be examined next.

KEY TERMS

brain drain Immigration to the United States of skilled workers, professionals, and technicians who are desperately needed by their home countries.
nativism Beliefs and policies favoring native-born citizens over immigrants.
refugees Persons living outside their country of citizenship for fear of political or religious persecution.
xenophobia The fear or hatred of strangers or foreigners.

FOR FURTHER INFORMATION

Ray Allen Billington. *The Protestant Crusade, 1800–1860.* 1963; reprinted. Gloucester, MA: Peter Smith, 1963.

> Historian Billington traces American nativism from the anti-Catholicism of the 1820s to the rise and fall of the Know-Nothings in the 1850s.

Barry R. Chiswick, ed. *Immigration, Language, and Ethnicity: Canada and the United States.* Washington, DC: AEI Press, 1992.

> The contributions are organized around the topics of immigration history and policy, demographic characteristics and earnings, language, and women and minorities.

Ted Conover. *Coyotes.* New York: Vintage, 1986.

> A poignant look at illegal immigration, including the smugglers of Latin American aliens (known as *coyotes*).

Ann Crittenden. *Sanctuary: A Story of American Conscience.* New York: Weidenfeld & Nicholson, 1988.

> A detailed account of the sanctuary movement in the 1980s to provide asylum to refugees who were not granted legal status by the government.

Stanley Feldstein and Lawrence Costello, eds. *The Ordeal of Assimilation.* Garden City, NY: Anchor Books, 1974.

> This collection of speeches, magazine articles, and newspaper accounts presents a documentary history of European immigration from 1840 to the present. The concluding section stresses renewed ethnic consciousness.

Bill Ong Hing. *Making and Remaking Asian America Through Immigration Policy, 1850–1900.* Stanford, CA.: Stanford University Press, 1993.

An overview of the Asian immigration experience in light of the changing concept of Asian-American identity.

Philip Martin and Elizabeth Midgley. "Immigration to the United States: Journey to an Uncertain Destination." *Population Bulletin 40* (September 1994).

In a very concise format (47 pages), this issue reviews the economic and social aspects of immigration.

Susan Forces Martin. *Refugee Women.* London: Zed Books, 1991.

Discusses the key issues facing refugee women worldwide and the significant gaps in delivering humanitarian assistance to them.

Elmer Clarence Sandmeyer. *The Anti-Chinese Movement in California.* 1939; reprinted, Urbana, IL: University of Illinois Press, 1973.

This book, originally published in 1939, was the first modern account of the development of anti-Chinese racism in the West. In his introduction to the present edition, Roger Daniels places Sandmeyer's effort in the context of later research.

Periodicals

Both the *International Migration Review* (formerly the *International Migration Digest*), begun in 1966, and *Migration Today,* begun in 1972, are published by the Center for Migration Studies. The *Journal of Refugee Resettlement* (1981), the *Journal of Refugee Studies* (1988), and *Refugee Reports* (1979) were inaugurated in response to a renewed interest in refugees.

CRITICAL THINKING QUESTIONS

1. Why are nationality and religion used to oppose immigration?
2. What were the social and economic issues when public opinion mounted against Chinese immigration into the United States?
3. Can you find evidence of the brain drain in terms of the professionals with whom you come in contact?
4. Ultimately, what do you think is the major concern people have about contemporary immigration to the United States—the numbers of immigrants or their nationality?
5. What are the principles that appear to guide the refugee policy?

Chapter
5

Ethnicity and Religion

Chapter Outline

Highlights

The United States encompasses a multitude of ethnic and religious groups. Do they coexist in harmony or in conflict? How significant are they as sources of identity for their members? British Americans and Protestants may be the largest ethnic and religious groups, but both are outnumbered by all other groups combined. There was a resurgence of interest in their ethnicity among Whites in the 1960s and well into the 1970s, partly the result of the renewed pride in their ethnicity of Blacks, Hispanics, and Native Americans. White ethnics are the victims of humor (or "respectable bigotry") that many still consider socially acceptable, and they find themselves with little power in big business. Religious minorities have also experienced bigotry in the past; and conflicts between groups occasionally are taken to the U.S. Supreme Court.

The complexity of relations between dominant and subordinate groups in the United States is partly the result of its heterogeneous population. No one ethnic origin or religious faith encompasses all the inhabitants of the United States. Even though its period of largest sustained immigration is two generations past, an American today is surrounded by remnants of cultures and practitioners of religions whose origins are foreign to this country. Religion and ethnicity continue to be significant in defining an individual's identity.

ETHNIC DIVERSITY

The ethnic diversity of the United States in the 1990s is a social fact of life apparent to almost everyone. Passersby in New York City were undoubtedly surprised once when two street festivals met head-to-head. The procession of San Gennaro, the patron saint of Naples, marched through Little Italy to run directly into a Chinese festival originating in Chinatown. Teachers in many public schools frequently face students who speak only one language, and it is not English. In Chicago, there are many possibilities. Besides Spanish, students may know only Greek, Italian, Polish, German, Creole, Japanese, Cantonese, or the language of a Native American. In the Detroit metropolitan area, 21 languages are taught, including Arabic, Portuguese, Ukrainian, Latvian, Lithuanian, and Serbian. Recognition of different ethnic groups has led to the creation of White ethnic studies programs at colleges throughout the United States.

Germans are the largest ancestral group; the 1990 census showed almost one-fourth of Americans saying they had at least some German ancestry. While most German Americans are assimilated, it is possible to see the ethnic tradition in some areas and in particular in Milwaukee, which has 48 percent German ancestry. There three Saturday schools teach German, and one can affiliate with 34 German-American clubs and visit a German library that operates within the public library system (K. Johnson, 1992; M. Usdansky, 1992a).

Immigrants and their descendants often prosper by serving their ethnic community. In a Chicago deli, a clerk serves up a plate of olives.

RELIGIOUS PLURALISM

The more than 130 organized religions in the United States range from the over 50 million members of the Roman Catholic Church to sects with fewer than 1,000 adherents. In addition, there are growing numbers of non-Christian followers. Besides the long Jewish tradition in the United States, Muslims number close to 5 million. A smaller, but also growing, number of people adhere to such Eastern faiths as Hinduism, Buddhism, Confucianism, and Taoism. The diversity of American religious life is apparent from Figure 5.1, which shows the Christian faiths that numerically dominate areas of the country. For most nations of the world, a map of religions would hardly be useful because one faith accounts for almost all religious followers in the country. The diversity of beliefs, rituals, and experiences that characterizes religious life in the United States reflects both the nation's immigrant heritage and the First Amendment prohibition against establishing a state religion.

Sociologists use the word *denomination* for a large, organized religion not officially linked with the state or government. By far the largest denomination in the United States is Roman Catholicism; yet at least 21 other religious faiths have 1 million or more members (see Table 5.1). Protestants collectively accounted for about 56 percent of the nation's adult population in 1991, compared with 25 percent for Roman Catholics and about 3 percent for Jews (K. Bedell, 1995).

The diversity of faiths in the United States sharply contrasts with that in European countries, where a handful of faiths dominate. Religious statistics should be used with caution, however. Because census takers have not asked about religious affiliation since 1957, information about religious membership is supplied by the

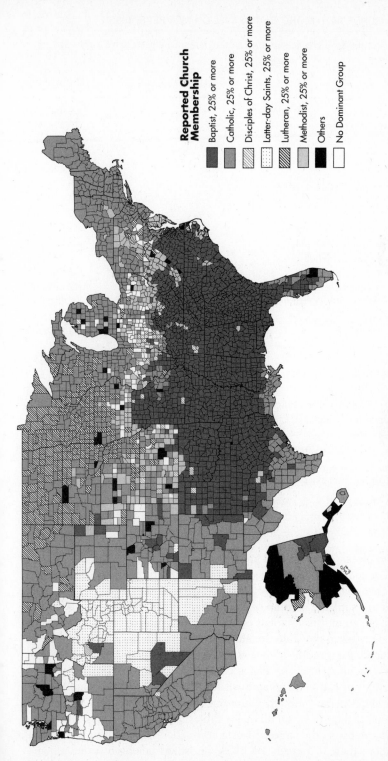

Reported Church Membership

- Baptist, 25% or more
- Catholic, 25% or more
- Disciples of Christ, 25% or more
- Later-day Saints, 25% or more
- Lutheran, 25% or more
- Methodist, 25% or more
- Others
- No Dominant Group

Figure 5.1 Predominant Christian Faiths by Counties of the United States, 1990
The diversity of Christian religious life in the United States is apparent in the figure. Many Christian faiths account for 25 percent or more of the church members in a county. Among non-Christian faiths, only Judaism may figure so significantly—in New York County (Manhattan) of New York City and in Dade County, Florida (which includes Miami Beach).

Source: Bradley, M.; Green, N. Jr.; Jones, D.; Lynn, M.; and McNeil, L., 1992.

Table 5.1   CHURCHES WITH MORE THAN A MILLION MEMBERS, 1995

Several hundred religions are practiced in the United States. Of these, 22 have at least 1 million members.

Religious Body	Membership
Roman Catholic Church	59,858,042
Southern Baptist Convention	15,398,642
United Methodist Church	8,646,595
National Baptist Convention, USA	8,200,000
Church of God in Christ	5,499,875
Evangelical Lutheran Church in America	5,213,785
Church of Jesus Christ of Latter-day Saints	4,520,000
Presbyterian Church (USA)	3,796,766
National Baptist Convention of America	3,500,000
African Methodist Episcopal Church	3,500,000
Lutheran Church–Missouri Synod	2,598,935
Episcopal Church	2,504,682
National Missionary Baptist Convention of America	2,500,000
Progressive National Baptist Convention, Inc.	2,500,000
Assemblies of God	2,271,718
Greek Orthodox Church	1,950,000
Churches of Christ	1,651,103
United Church of Christ	1,530,178
American Baptist Churches in the USA	1,516,505
Baptist Bible Fellowship	1,500,000
African Methodist Episcopal Zion Church	1,200,000
Christian Churches and Churches of Christ	1,070,616

Note: Data are the most recent reported in 1995, but some data back as early as 1977.

Source: From *Yearbook of American and Canadian Churches 1995,* edited by Kenneth B. Bedell. Copyright © 1995 by the National Council of Churches of Christ in the USA. Used by permission of the publisher, Abingdon Press.

churches themselves. Churches vary in whom they count as members: some count only baptized or confirmed members; others count only those in good standing.

One notable characteristic of religious practice in the United States is the almost completely separate worship of Blacks and Whites. During the 1976 presidential campaign, an unusual amount of attention was directed to the segregation practiced by churches in the United States. The church attended by Jimmy Carter in Plains, Georgia, captured headlines as it closed its doors to a Black civil rights activist seeking membership. The Plains church later opened its membership to African Americans at Carter's urging. Such formal racial restrictions are unusual, but today the church hour on Sunday mornings still fits the description "the most segregated hour of the week." Of all major Protestant denominations, the United Methodist Church boasts the largest Black constituency, but that is only 3 percent. Overall, no more than 10 percent of Black Christians belong to predominantly

White denominations. At the local or church level, it is estimated that only 1 percent of Black Christians belong to White churches (K. Briggs, 1976; R. Stark, 1987).

About seven in ten Americans (71 percent) are counted as church members, but great confusion exists over the degree of their religiosity or the strength of their religious commitment. A persuasive case can be made that religious institutions continue to grow stronger through an influx of new members despite mounting secularism in society. Some observers think that, after reaching a low in 1960s, religion is becoming important to people again. The upheavals in American religious life are reflected on the covers of *Time* magazine, which have cried out variously "Is God Dead?" (April 8, 1966), "Is God Coming Back to Life?" (December 26, 1969), and "The Jesus Revolution" (June 21, 1971). At present, there is little statistical support for the view that the influence of religion on society is diminishing.

Religion is important to Americans. According to a 1991 report, only 8 percent of the adults in the United States described themselves as "nonreligious." When residents of 11 nations were asked to indicate the importance of God in their lives, Americans registered the third highest score, slightly behind Mexicans and South Africans and far ahead of Hungarians, Japanese, Danes, and Swedes (B. Kosmin, 1991; Princeton Religion Research Center, 1986).

In reviewing data on church attendance and feelings about organized religion, however, we surmise that religion is not uniformly on the upswing. There is a great deal of switching of denominations and, as in the past, considerable interest in new ways of expressing spirituality. Some new groups encounter hostility from organized, established faiths that question the tactics used to attract members and financial support. It would be incorrect to conclude either that religion is slowly being abandoned or that Americans are turning to religion with the zeal of new converts. The future may bring not only periods of religious revivalism but also times of decline in religious fervor.

Throughout our discussion we have considered how the media distort if not stereotype racial and ethnic groups. While a 1994 national survey showed that 59 percent considered religion very important to them, one would not know that by watching television. Religion is relatively absent: only 5 percent of television characters practice religion in any way. Historically, spirituality has routinely appeared on such shows as "M*A*S*H" (Father Francis Mulcahy), "The Waltons," "Little House on the Prairie," and "Highway to Heaven," but in the 1990s, only "Dr. Quinn: Medicine Woman," "Northern Exposure," "Picket Fences," and "Touched by an Angel" have occasionally had a religion-oriented story line. Reverend Billy Graham views the lack of prime-time religion as a "cultural breakdown" and, recognizing how important religion is to people, has called on viewers to let the television "industry know how much it means to us when programs depict our Judeo-Christian values" (D. Gable, 1993a; Saad and McAneny, 1994).

THE REDISCOVERY OF ETHNICITY

After World War II, little thought was given by scholars to how White ethnicity might survive assimilation, but by the 1980s, the mass media and scholars had rediscovered the White ethnics.

Robert Park (1950, p. 205), a prominent early sociologist, wrote in 1913 that "A Pole, Lithuanian, or Norwegian cannot be distinguished, in the second generation, from an American, born of native parents." At one time, sociologists saw the end of ethnicity as nearly a foregone conclusion. W. Lloyd Warner and Leo Srole (1945) wrote in their often-cited Yankee City series that the future of ethnic groups seems to be limited in the United States and that they will be quickly absorbed. Oscar Handlin's *Uprooted* (1951) told of the destruction of immigrant values and their replacement by American culture. Although Handlin was among the pioneers in investigating ethnicity, assimilation was the dominant theme in his work (D. Cinel, 1969; R. Vecoli, 1970).

Many writers have shown almost a fervent hope that ethnicity would vanish. The persistence of ethnicity was for some time treated by sociologists as dysfunctional, for it meant a continuation of old values that interfered with the allegedly superior new values. Ethnicity was expected to disappear not only because of assimilation, but also because higher social class and status demanded that it vanish. Somehow, it was assumed that one could not be ethnic and middle class, much less affluent (H. Abramson, 1973; Yancey, Erickson, and Juliani, 1976; J. Yinger, 1976).

The Third-Generation Principle

Historian Marcus Hansen's (1937, 1952, 1987) *principle of third-generation interest* was an exception to the assimilationist approach to White ethnic groups. Simply stated, Hansen maintained that in the third generation—the grandchildren of the original immigrants—ethnic interest and awareness would actually increase; said Hansen, "What the son wishes to forget the grandson wishes to remember." Hansen's principle has been tested several times since it was first put forth. Although less research has been done on assimilation among third-generation women compared to men (R. Vecoli, 1987), in interviewing Irish and Italian Catholics, John Goering (1971) found that ethnicity was more important to members of the third generation than it was to the immigrants themselves.

Nathan Glazer and Daniel Moynihan admitted in the second edition of *Beyond the Melting Pot* (1970, p. viii) that perhaps they had been too hasty in concluding the first edition (1963) by saying, "Religion and race define the next stage in the evolution of the American peoples" (p. 315). Social-scientific dismissal of the ethnic awareness of blue-collar workers had begun the academic minimizing of the importance of ethnicity. Ethnicity was viewed as merely another aspect of White ethnics' alleged racist nature, an allegation that will be examined later in this chapter. Curiously, the very same intellectuals and journalists who bent over backward to understand the growing solidarity of Blacks, Hispanics, and Native Americans refused to give White ethnics the academic attention they deserved (D. Wrong, 1972).

The new assertiveness of Blacks and other non-Whites of their rights in the 1960s unquestionably presented White ethnics with the opportunity to reexamine their own position. "If solidarity and unapologetic self-consciousness might hasten Blacks' upward mobility, why not us?" asked the White ethnics, who were often only a half step above the Blacks in social status. The African-American movement pushed other groups to reflect on their past. The increased consciousness of Blacks and their positive attitude toward African culture and the contributions worldwide of African Americans are embraced in what we termed earlier (Chapter 1) the *Afrocentric perspective*. The mood, therefore, was set in the 1960s for the country to be receptive to ethnicity. By legitimizing the Black cultural difference from White culture, along with that of Native Americans and Hispanics, the country's opinion leaders legitimized other types of cultural diversity.

The Nature of Ethnicity

A vast amount of evidence pointed to the revival of ethnicity in the United States beginning in the mid-1960s (J. Roche, 1984). We have seen that social scientists then began to reconsider the inevitable disappearance of ethnic identity. Statistical evidence pointed to a growth in non-English-language homes that could not be explained by immigration alone. Non-English-language publications, churches, radio stations, and television programs grew throughout the 1960s. Even the conventional media seemed more sensitive to ethnic interests. By the 1980s, however, if not the late 1970s, the ethnic revival seemed to have subsided considerably, perhaps not to the levels of the 1950s, but the emergent ethnicity had peaked (J. Fishman, 1985).

The ethnicity of the 1990s embraced by English-speaking Whites is typically more symbolic. It does not include active involvement in ethnic activities or participation in ethnic-related organizations. In fact, sizable proportions of White ethnics have gained large-scale entry into almost all clubs, cliques, and fraternal groups. Such acceptance is a key indicator of assimilation (M. Gordon, 1964). Ethnicity has become increasingly peripheral to the lives of the members of the ethnic group. Although they may not relinquish their ethnic identity, other identities become more important.

The persistence of ethnic consciousness does not depend on foreign birth, a distinctive language, and a unique way of life. When the American dream of full acceptance does not materialize for many White ethnics, they reexamine their own roots. Appreciation of one's individual heritage is not automatic. Just because a person is of Italian descent and lives in an Italian-American neighborhood does not mean that he or she is acquainted with the writings of Dante, the thirteenth-century Italian poet. Frequently, the tradition that American ethnics preserve has little in common with life in the old country. Instead, it reflects experience in the United States as a unique group that developed a cultural tradition distinct from that of the mainstream (N. Glazer, 1971; Glazer and Moynihan, 1970).

Ethnicity gives continuity with the past, an affective or emotional tie. The significance of this sense of belonging cannot be emphasized enough. Whether reinforced by distinctive behavior or by what Milton Gordon (1964) called a sense of "peoplehood," ethnicity is an effective, functional source of cohesion. Proximity to fellow ethnics is not necessary for a person to maintain social cohesion and in-group identity. Even the ethnic neighborhoods that do exist are not ethnically homogeneous; most contain outsiders within their boundaries (G. Suttles, 1972, pp. 27, 251). Fraternal organizations or sports-related groups can preserve associations among ethnics who are separated geographically. Members of ethnic groups may even maintain their feelings of in-group solidarity after leaving ethnic communities in the central cities for the suburban fringe.

According to sociologist Herbert Gans (1979), ethnicity today increasingly involves the *symbols* of ethnicity, such as food, acknowledging ceremonial holidays, and supporting specific political issues or the issues confronting the "old country." This *symbolic ethnicity* may be more visible, but this type of ethnic heritage does not interfere with what people do, read, or say, or even whom they befriend or marry. Richard Alba (1990) surveyed Whites in the Albany, New York, area in the mid-1980s and found that, while there had been a decline in distinctions among ethnic groups, ethnic identity was still acknowledged. Heritage may not have disappeared, and indeed, the past, however defined, may even be important in today's frantic world.

Ethnicity cannot be ignored even among White Americans who seem fully assimilated. In "Listen to Their Voices," Michael Novak counters nine arguments frequently raised to devalue the promotion of ethnicity.

THE PRICE PAID BY WHITE ETHNICS

Many White ethnics shed their past and wish only to be Americans, with no ancestral ties to another country. Boris Shlapak, who played forward on a professional soccer team, changed his name to Ian Stone because "American kids need to identify with soccer players as Americans" (C. Terry, 1975). Stone, who by his own admission "never felt ethnic," was not concerned about being a figure to whom Slavic Americans would look as a hero. But some ethnics do not wish to abandon their heritage. To retain their past as a part of their present, however, they must pay a price because of prejudice and discrimination.

Prejudice Toward White Ethnic Groups

Our examination of immigration to the United States in Chapter 4 pointed out the mixed feelings that have greeted European immigrants. They are apparently still not well received. In 1944, well after most immigration from Poland had ended, the Polish-American Congress, an umbrella organization of 40 Polish fraternities, was founded to defend the image of Polish Americans. Young Polish Americans are made to feel ashamed of their ethnic origin when teachers find their names unpronounceable, and when they hear Polish jokes bandied about in a way that anti-Black or anti-Semitic humor is not. One survey found that half of second-generation Polish Americans encounter prejudice. Curiously, it was socially proper to condemn the White working class as racist, but quite improper to question the negative attitude of middle-class people toward White ethnics. Michael Lerner (1969) called this hostility toward White ethnics *respectable bigotry*. Polish jokes are acceptable, whereas anti-Black humor is considered in poor taste.

An important component of Lerner's respectable bigotry is not race prejudice but class prejudice. In 1973, researchers surveyed Whites living in areas of Florida that had undergone school desegregation. After identifying whether or not a respondent had protested against school desegregation, the researchers sought to determine if the opposition had been caused by racial prejudice. The affluent and well educated, the researchers found, were more disturbed by the possibility of interacting more with working-class people. Although not conclu-

Listen to Their Voices
How American Are You?

MICHAEL NOVAK

A scholar of ethnic relations, Michael Novak (1973b) draws upon his Slovak descent to understand the experience of White ethnics in the United States.

1. *Ethnic consciousness is regressive.* In every generation, ethnic consciousness is different. The second generation after immigration is not like the first, the third is not like the second. The native language begins to disappear; family and residential patterns alter; prosperity and education create new possibilities. The new ethnicity does not try to hold back the clock. . . .

Michael Novak

2. *Ethnic consciousness is only for the old; it is not shared by the young.* It is true that hardly anyone in America encourages ethnic consciousness. The church, the schools, the government, the media encourage "Americanization." So it is true that the young are less "conscious" of their ethnicity. This does not mean that they do not have it. It does not mean that they do not feel joy and release upon discovering it. . . .

3. *Ethnic consciousness is illiberal and divisive, and breeds hostility.* The truth is the reverse. What is illiberal is homogenization enforced in the name of liberalism. What is divisive is an enforced and premature unity, especially a unity in which some groups are granted cultural superiority as models for the others. What breeds hostility is the quiet repression of diversity, the refusal to allow others to be culturally different, the enforcement of a single style of Americanism. . . .

4. *Ethnic consciousness will disappear.* The world will end, too. The question is how to make the most fruitful, humanistic progress in the meantime. The preservation of ethnicity is a barrier against alienation and anomie, a resource of compassion and creativity and intergroup learning. . . .

5. *Intermarriage hopelessly confuses ethnicity.* Intermarriage gives children multiple ethnic models. The transmission of a cultural heritage is not a process clearly understood. But for any child a "significant other" on one side of the family or another may unlock secrets of the psyche as no other does. The rhythm and intensity of emotional patterns in families are various, but significant links to particular cultural traditions almost always occur. . . .

6. *Intelligent, sensitive ethnics, proud of their heritage, do not*

Listen to Their Voices   *Continued*

go around thumping their chests in ethnic chauvinism. Who would want chest-thumping or chauvinism? But be careful of the definition of "good" ethnics, "well-behaved" ethnics. Many successful businessmen, artists, and scholars of white ethnic background carry two sets of scars. On the one hand, they had to break from their families, neighborhoods, perhaps ghettoes, and they became painfully aware of the lack of education and experience among those less fortunate than they. On the other hand, they had to learn the new styles, new images, new values of the larger culture of "enlightenment". . . .

7. *The new ethnicity will divide group against group.* The most remarkable fact about the new ethnic consciousness is that it is cross-cultural. We do not speak only of "Polish" consciousness or "Italian" consciousness, but of "white ethnic" consciousness. The new ethnicity is not particularistic. It stresses the general contours of *all* ethnicity and notes analogies between the cultural history of the many groups. . . .

8. *Emphasis on white ethnics detracts from the first priority to be given Blacks.* On the contrary, blindness to white ethnics is an almost guaranteed way of boxing Blacks into a hopeless corner. A group lowest on the ladder cannot advance *solely* at the expense of the next group. . . .

9. *Ethnicity is all right for minorities, but not for the mainstream.* In America, every group is a minority. Even among white Anglo-Saxon Protestants there are many traditions. What is often called "mainline Protestantism," centered in the Northeast—Episcopal, Congregational, Presbyterian—is only one tradition within a far larger and more complex Protestant reality. . . .

Source: "How American Are You If Your Grandparents Came From Serbia in 1888?" from *The Rediscovery of Ethnicity,* edited by Sallie TeSelle. ©1973, by James S. Ozer Publishers, Inc.

sive, the study suggests that, even if the more affluent Whites are more tolerant of racial minorities, they may be less accepting of class differences (Giles, Gatlin, and Cataldo, 1976).

White ethnics in the early 1970s felt that the mass media unfairly ridiculed them and their culture while celebrating Black Power and African culture. Italian Americans, for instance, are concerned that their image is overwhelmed by stereotypes of organized crime, spaghetti, overweight mothers, and sexy women. Even television's Italian police seem to conform to the old stereotypes. In response to such stereotyping, the Columbian Coalition, founded in 1971, employs lawyers to handle cases of Italian Americans claiming they are victims of bigotry. Italian Americans are also not pleased by their conspicuous absence from the Roman Catholic Church hierarchy in the United States and in high political office. The Italians are well aware that another ethnic group, the Irish, dominates the American Catholic hierarchy, with 57 percent of the bishops in the country, although it has only 17 percent of the Catholic population. Not all Italian Americans are convinced that such self-help organizations as the Columbian Coalition, the Italian American Civil Rights League, or the Americans of Italian Descent are the answer. Despite disagreement over methods, most would agree that attitudes need changing. Italian Americans are just an example, however. Across the country and among all ethnic groups, appreciation of ethnic heritage is increasing (R. Gambino, 1974a, 1974b; Glazer and Moynihan, 1970; M. Novak, 1973a; N. Pileggi, 1971; R. Severo, 1970).

Income and Housing

Harsh words toward ethnics translate into lower incomes. A hierarchy of ethnic groups coinciding with a hierarchy of social classes has long been documented: disparities do exist among ethnic groups in socioeconomic status. A study of 1962 census data showed that national origin was not as important an explanation of the variance in education and occupation among contemporary ethnic men as it had been for their parents. For some ethnic groups, however, such as the Irish, Polish, and Italians, occupational success falls short of what would be expected for men of similar background and education. Other statistical analyses have not been clear about which disparities are caused by ethnic discrimination. Lower incomes do not necessarily mean that a group is the victim of discrimination. But in general, studies point to lower income and less likelihood of upward social mobility for White ethnic groups (Blau and Duncan, 1967; Duncan and Duncan, 1968; Duncan, Featherman, and Duncan, 1972; Levine and Herman, 1972; Warner and Srole, 1945).

The disparity between ethnics and other Whites is most apparent at the top rungs of the ladder of success in business. In 1972, and again in 1983, Russell Barta examined the ethnic background of the officers of the largest Chicago-area corporations. African Americans and Hispanics were grossly underrepresented as directors and officers. The two groups accounted for 29 percent of the area population but only 2 percent of the directorships and 5.6 percent of the officerships. White ethnics seemed to face exclusion as well. Poles made up 6.9 percent of the area population but only 0.5 percent of the directorships and 1.6 percent of the officerships. Italians fared somewhat better with 2.2 percent of the directorships and 2.2 percent of the corporation officerships, but they made up nearly 7 percent of the area population. Of the 92 corporations' boards, 87 had no Poles and 73 had no Italians. There had been some improvement in the presence of Blacks in the period studied, but no significant differences for Hispanics and White ethnics (R. Barta, 1974, 1984).

Some forms of discrimination are overt, as in housing. As recently as 1963, realtors in Michigan employed a point handicap system that made it difficult for Poles and Italians to purchase homes in better neighborhoods by penalizing people for being White ethnics (W. Bufalino, 1971). The result of such practices has been an ethnic segregation not unlike racial segregation. Ethnic groups form a Little Italy, a Greektown, or a Scandinavian "Andersonville" mostly because they want to stay together, but the difficulty of finding housing elsewhere has contributed as well. Many statistical studies have documented the ethnic segregation in American cities and the surrounding suburbs. Besides being segregated, ethnic neighborhoods are ripe for urban renewal programs and disruptive highway construction. White ethnics, like African Americans and Hispanics, have lacked the political power to prevent their neighborhoods from being physically destroyed.

An additional price was paid by White ethnics in the 1970s. They became labeled as typical bigots. The stereotype of the prejudiced "hard hat" has rarely been questioned. The danger of such a stereotype is that it becomes indistinguishable from fact. David Matza (1964) referred to these mental pictures, which "tend to remain beyond the reach of such intellectual correctives as argument, criticism and scrutiny. . . . Left unattended, they return to haunt us by by shaping or bending theories that purport to explain major social phenomena" (p. 1). This picture of ethnics and the degree of truth behind it will be examined next.

The Prejudice of Ethnics

In the 1960s, as the civil rights movement moved northward, White ethnics replaced the southern redneck as the typical bigot portrayed in the mass media. The chanting of protesters resulted in ugly incidents that made White ethnics and bigots synonymous. In 1951, Harvey Clark, an African-American war veteran, moved into a $60-a-month apartment in Cicero, Illinois. Cicero adjoins Chicago's Black ghetto, but no Blacks lived in the heavily Polish, Italian, and Czech town. Clark fled after being greeted by a mob aided by the local police. The Cicero police chief warned Clark, "Get out of Cicero and don't come back to town or you'll get a bullet through you." A grand jury handed down indictments against Clark's NAACP attorney, the apartment house owner, her lawyer, and her rental agent. The indictments, subsequently dropped, charged them all with conspiracy to injure property by causing "depreciation in the market selling price" (J. Epstein, 1972; W. Gremley, 1952; R. Margolis, 1972). Does this sort of incident typify White ethnic attitudes and justify the hard-hat image?

The first issue to resolve is whether White ethnic groups are more prejudiced than other Whites. Sociologist Andrew Greeley (1974a, 1977; Nie, Currie, and Greeley, 1974) examined attitudes toward race, social welfare, and American involvement in Vietnam. The evidence pointed to minimal differences between ethnics and nonethnics. Some of the differences actually showed greater tolerance and liberalism among White ethnics. White ethnics were more in favor of welfare programs and more opposed to this country's participation in the Vietnam war.

Even when more sophisticated statistical analysis is introduced, the overall finding remains unchanged. When income and region are accounted for, some differences between ethnics and nonethnics are reduced because White southerners are overwhelmingly nonethnics. Still, there is no evidence to support the hard-hat image. Greeley (1974a) concludes, "Our argument is not that ethnics are the last bastion of liberalism in American today, but rather that it is a misrepresentation of the facts to picture them as a vanguard of conservatism" (p. 202). Working-class ethnic neighborhoods, however, have undeniably been the scene of ugly racial confrontations. If ethnics are no more bigoted than nonethnics, how have such inci-

Tom Toles, The *Buffalo News*

dents occurred, and how has the hard-hat reputation developed? For that answer, the unique relationship between White ethnic groups and African Americans must be understood.

In retrospect, it should be no surprise that one group antagonistic to African Americans has been the White ethnics. For many citizens, including White ethnics, the America they had known seemed to change. When politicians told Americans, "We must fight poverty and discrimination," this translated to White ethnics as, "Share your job, share your neighborhood, pay your taxes" (M. Novak, 1973a; Sanders and Morawska, 1975; G. Tyler, 1972). Whites reflected on their movement several generations before from membership in a poor immigrant group to becoming a part of the prosperous working class. Government assistance to the poor was virtually nonexistent then, public education was more restricted, and subsidized training programs were absent (Glazer and Moynihan, 1970). Why was it different now? Many White ethnics found it difficult to understand why African Americans seemed to be singled out as a cause for concern.

White ethnics went so far as to turn their backs on federal aid offered them because they did not wish to have their neighborhoods marked as "poverty pockets," nor did they wish to be associated with Black-oriented programs. In Newark, New Jersey, Italians successfully prevented an antipoverty office from being established and thereby cut off the jobs that its programs would have created (F. Barbaro, 1974). This ethnic opposition to publicly sponsored programs was not new.

James Wilson and Edward Banfield (1964) studied elections in seven major cities between 1956 and 1963 for referenda to build new hospitals, parks, and schools. The results indicated that the least support came from White ethnics, who would have paid the least and benefited the most.

The prevailing conception of urban America is that the city is Black and the suburbs are White. Although the latter is almost true, the former is definitely not. Along with poor African Americans and Hispanics in the big city are many White ethnics who are "economically unmonied and geographically immobile" (G. Tyler, 1972). White ethnics thought they were being made to pay for past injustices even though they were not making the decisions or evaluating their consequences. White ethnics found it difficult to be happy with minority-group gains. The upward movement of Blacks would not have disturbed White ethnics if the ethnics had kept pace, but given the absence of economic-based programs for White ethnics, they have not even kept pace with the modest gains by African Americans (J. Conforti, 1974).

The real grievances of White ethnics were overlooked, and reformist bureaucrats of the 1960s neglected nationality groups, thinking they would fade into the White middle class. When residents of an ethnic neighborhood were threatened or when they perceived a potential threat (as in Cicero), they rose to defend themselves.

White ethnics have not only separated themselves from African Americans, but have chosen to distinguish themselves from WASPs (White Anglo-Saxon Protestants) as well, as the next section indicates. White ethnics have learned that they are not considered part of the dominant group and that, in order to achieve a larger slice of government benefits they must function as a self-interest group, just as racially subordinate groups have.

CASE EXAMPLE: THE ITALIAN AMERICANS

While each European country's immigration to the United States has created its own social history, the case of Italians, while not typical of each nationality, offers insight into the White ethnic experience. Italians immigrated even during the colonial period, and they played prominent roles during the American Revolution and the early days of the republic. Mass immigration, however, began in the 1880s, peaking in the first 20 years of the twentieth century, when Italians accounted for one-fourth of the European immigration. The immigration was concentrated not only in time, but also geographically. The majority of the immigrants were landless peasants from rural southern Italy, the Mezzogiorno.

Many Italians, especially in the early years of mass immigration in the nineteenth century, received their jobs through an ethnic labor contractor, the *padrone*. Similar arrangements have been used by Asian, Hispanic, and Greek immigrants, where the labor contractors, most often immigrants, have mastered sufficient English to mediate for their compatriots. Exploitation was common within the padrone system through kickbacks, provision of inadequate housing, and withholding of wages. By the time of World War I, 90 percent of Italian girls and 99 percent of Italian boys in New York City were leaving school at the age of

14 to work, but by that time, Italian Americans were sufficiently fluent in English to seek out work on their own, and the padrone system had disappeared.

Along with manual labor, the Roman Catholic church was a very important part of the Italian Americans' life at this time. Yet they found little comfort in a Catholic church dominated by an earlier immigrant group: the Irish. The traditions were different; weekly attendance for Italian Americans was overshadowed by the religious aspects of the *feste* (or festivals) held throughout the year in the honor of saints (the Irish viewed the *feste* as practically a form of paganism). These initial adjustment problems were overcome with the establishment of ethnic parishes—a pattern repeated by other non-Irish immigrant groups. Thus, parishes would be staffed by Italian priests, sometimes imported for that purpose. While the hierarchy of the church would adjust more slowly, Italian Americans were increasingly able to feel at home in their local parish church. Today, nearly 90 percent of Italian Americans are raised as Catholics (R. Alba, 1985; A. Rolle, 1972).

A controversial aspect of the Italian-American experience involves organized crime, as typified by Al Capone (1899–1947). Arriving in U.S. society in the bottom layers, Italians lived in decaying, crime-ridden neighborhoods that became known as Little Italies. For a minority of these immigrants, crime did serve as a significant means of upward social mobility. In effect, entering and leading criminal activity were one aspect of assimilation—admittedly not a positive one. Complaints linking ethnicity and crime actually began in colonial times with talk about the criminally-inclined Irish and Germans, and it continues with contemporary stereotyping about such groups as Colombian drug dealers and Vietnamese street gangs. Yet the image of Italians as criminals has persisted from Prohibition Era gangsters to the view of mob families today. As noted earlier, it is not at all surprising that groups such as the Columbian Coalition have been organized to counter such negative images.

The fact that Italians can be consistently characterized as criminal, even in the mass media, is another example of what we have termed *respectable bigotry* toward White ethnics. The persistence of linking Italians, or any other minority group, with crime is probably attributable to attempts to explain a problem by citing a single, naive cause: the presence of perceived undesirables (R. Alba, 1985; D. Bell, 1953; R. Daniels, 1990; R. Gambino, 1974a; P. Lupsha, 1981; J. O'Kane, 1992).

The immigration of Italians was halted by the national origins system, described in the previous chapter. As Italian Americans settled permanently, the mutual aid societies that had grown up in the 1920s to provide basic social services began to dissolve. More slowly, education came to be valued by Italian Americans as a means of upward mobility. But even becoming more educated did not defend them from prejudice. In 1930, for example, President Herbert Hoover rebuked Fiorello La Guardia, an Italian-American member of Congress from New York City, by stating that "the Italians are predominantly our murderers and bootleggers" and recommending that La Guardia "go back to where you belong" because, "like a lot of other foreign spawn, you do not appreciate this country which supports you and tolerates you" (E. Baltzell, 1964, p. 30). As a result of the U.S. troops' battling Italy during World War II, hatred and sporadic violence emerged against Italian Americans and their property. They were even confined by the federal government in specific areas of California by virtue of their ethnicity alone (S. Fox, 1990).

In politics, Italian Americans have been quite more successful, at least at the local level, where family and community ties could be translated into votes. But political success did not come easily, because many Italian immigrants anticipated returning to their homeland and did not always take neighborhood politics seriously. National politics were even more difficult for Italian Americans to break into: it was not until 1962 that an Italian American was named to a cabinet-level position. Geraldine Ferraro's being named the Democratic vice-presidential candidate in 1984 was every bit as much an achievement for Italian Americans as it was for women (Cornacchia and Nelson, 1992).

People of Italian ancestry accounted in 1990 for about 6 percent of the population, but less than 1 percent had actually been born in Italy. Yet Italian Americans still remain the seventh largest immigrant group. Just how ethnically conscious is the Italian-American community? While the number is declining, 1.3 million Americans speak Italian at home; only Spanish, French, and German are spoken more. But for another 10 million Italian Americans, the language tie to their culture is absent, and depending on their degree of assimilation, only traces of symbolic ethnicity may remain.

ETHNICITY, RELIGION, AND SOCIAL CLASS

Generally, several social factors influence a person's identity and life chances. Pioneer sociologist Max Weber described *life chances* as people's opportunities to provide themselves with material goods, positive living conditions, and favorable life experiences. Either religion or ethnicity or both may affect life chances.

Religion and ethnicity do not necessarily operate together. Sometimes, they have been studied as if they were synonymous. Groups have been described as Irish Catholic, Swedish Lutheran, or Russian Jewish, as if religion and ethnicity had been merged into some type of national church. Religious and ethnic divisions may reinforce each other, but they may also operate independently.

In the 1960s, sociologists felt that religion was more important than ethnicity in explaining behavior (Glazer and Moynihan, 1963; W. Herberg, 1983). They based this conclusion not on data, but on the apparently higher visibility of religion in society. Using survey data collected between 1963 and 1972, Andrew Greeley came to different conclusions (1974a; 1974b). He attempted to clarify the relative importance of religion and ethnicity by measuring four areas:

1. Personality characteristics, such as authoritarianism, anxiety, and conformity
2. Political participation, such as voting and civil activity
3. Civil liberties and civil rights, such as support for legislation
4. Family structure, such as the role of women, marital happiness, and sexual adjustment

The sample consisted of German and Irish Americans, both Protestant and Catholic. If religion was more significant than ethnicity, Protestants, whether of German or Irish ancestry, and Catholics, regardless of ethnicity, would be similar in outlook. Conversely, if ethnicity was the key, then the similarities would be among the Germans of either faith or among the Irish as a distinct group.

On 17 of the 24 items that made up the four areas measured, the differences were greater between German Catholics and Irish Catholics than between German Catholics and Protestants or between Irish Catholics and Protestants. Ethnicity was a stronger predictor of attitudes and beliefs than religion. In one area, political party allegiance, religion was more important, but this was the exception rather than the rule. (The significance of religion will be examined later in this chapter.)

In sum, Greeley found ethnicity to be generally more important than religion in predicting behavior. In reality, it is very difficult to separate the influences of religion and ethnicity on any one individual, but Greeley's research cautions against discounting the influence of ethnicity.

In addition, as already noted several times, social class is yet another significant factor. Sociologist Milton Gordon (1978) developed the term *ethclass* (ethnicity and class) to denote the importance of both factors. All *three* factors—religion, ethnicity, and class—combine to form one's identity, determine one's social behavior, and limit one's life chances. For example, in certain ethnic communities, friendships are limited, to a degree, to people who share the same ethnic background *and* social class. In other words, neither race and ethnicity nor religion nor class alone places one socially in a society such as the United States. One must consider several elements together as reflected in ethclass.

Muslims of a variety of nationalities gather in New York City to pray at the end of the holy period of Ramadan.

RELIGION AND AMERICAN SOCIETY

Divisive conflicts along religious lines are relatively muted in the United States compared with those in, say, Northern Ireland or the Middle East. Although not entirely absent, conflicts in religion in the United States seem to be overshadowed by civil religion. *Civil religion* refers to the religious dimension in American life that merges the state with sacred beliefs.

Sociologist Robert Bellah (1967, 1968, 1970, 1989; see also M. Marty, 1976; J. Mathisen, 1989) borrowed the phrase *civil religion* from the eighteenth-century French philosopher Jean-Jacques Rousseau to describe a significant phenomenon in the contemporary United States. Civil religion exists alongside established religious faiths and embodies a belief system incorporating all religions but not associated specifically with any one. It is the type of faith that presidents refer to in inaugural speeches and to which American Legion posts and Girl Scout troops swear allegiance. In 1954, Congress added the phrase "under God" to the Pledge of Allegiance as a legislative recognition of religion's significance. Bellah sees no sign that the importance of civil religion has diminished, but he does acknowledge that it is more conservative than during the 1970s (M. Marty, 1985).

In the following section we will explore the diversity among the major Christian groups in the United States, such as Roman Catholics and Protestants. However, as has already been noted, significant numbers of people in the United States are practicing religions long established in other parts of the world, such as Islam, Hindu, and Buddhism, to name the three major ones, in addition to Judaism, which is discussed in Chapter 15. The greater visibility of religious diversity in the United States is primarily the result of immigrants' bringing their religious faith with them and not assimilating to the dominant Christian rituals.

The New Denominationalism

The public awareness of White ethnicity has coincided with a less publicized recognition of the religious diversity among Christians in the United States—both among Roman Catholics and among Protestants. Will Herberg (1983) stressed the overall similarity among Americans within the tripartite division of Protestant, Catholic, and Jew. A rival model, focusing on the continued significance of underlying differences among the various groups, more adequately represents the reality of American social life. (For a different perspective, see E. Laumann, 1969, and H. Niebuhr, 1929.)

Diversity Among Roman Catholics   Social scientists have persistently tended to ignore the diversity within the Roman Catholic church in the United States. Recent research has not sustained the conclusion that Roman Catholics are melting into a single group, following the traditions of the American Irish Catholic model, and that foreign-language churches are long gone. A recent finding of special interest is that religious behavior has been different in each ethnic group. The Irish and the French Canadians left a society that was highly competitive culturally and socially. Their religious involvement in the United States is more relaxed than it was in Ireland and Quebec. The influence of American society, however, has increased German and Polish involvement in the Catholic church, but Italians have remained relatively inactive. Variations by ethnic background continue to emerge in studies of contemporary religious involvement in the Roman Catholic church. Perhaps the most prominent subgroup in the Catholic church is the Hispanics, who, according to a conservative estimate, will constitute the majority of Catholics by 2050.

Since the mid-1970s, the Roman Catholic church in America has received significant new members from the Philippines, Southeast Asia, and particularly Latin America. While these new members have been a stabilizing force offsetting the losses of White ethnics, they have also challenged a church that for generations was dominated by Irish, Italian, and Polish parishes.

The Roman Catholic church, despite its ethnic diversity, has clearly been a powerful force in reducing the ethnic ties of its members. It has also been a significant assimilating force. There is an irony in this role of Catholicism, in that so many nineteenth-century Americans heaped abuse on Catholics in this country for allegedly being un-American and having a dual allegiance. The history of the Catholic church in the United States may be portrayed as a struggle within the membership between the Americanizers and the anti-Americanizers with the former ultimately winning (A. Greeley, 1977). As a result, unlike the various Protestant churches that accommodated immigrants of a single nationality, the Roman Catholic church had to Americanize a variety of linguistic and ethnic groups. The Catholic church may have been the most potent assimilating force next to the public school system (Fishman, Hayden, and Warshaver, 1966). Comparing the assimilationist goal of the Catholic church and the present diversity in it leads us to the conclusion that ethnic diversity has continued in the Roman Catholic church in spite of, and not because of, this religious institution.

Diversity Among Protestants   Protestantism, like Catholicism, is often portrayed as a monolithic entity. Little attention is given to the doctrinal and attitudinal differences that sharply divide the various denominations, in both laity and clergy. Several studies document the diversity. Unfortunately, many opinion polls and surveys are content to learn if a respondent is a Catholic or a Protestant or a Jew. Stark and Glock (1968), in their massive undertaking, found sharp differences in religious attitudes within Protestant churches. For example, 99 percent of Southern Baptists had no doubt that Jesus was the divine Son of God, as contrasted to only 40 percent of Congregationalists. Based on the data, Glock and Stark (1965) identified four "generic theological camps" among Protestants:

1. Liberals: Congregationalists, Methodists, and Episcopalians
2. Moderates: Disciples of Christ and Presbyterians
3. Conservatives: American Lutherans and American Baptists
4. Fundamentalists: Missouri Synod Lutherans, Southern Baptists, and various small sects

Roman Catholics generally agreed with conservatives, except on essentially Catholic issues such as papal infallibility (the authority of the pope in all decisions regarding faith and morals). Whether or not there are four distinct camps is not important. The point is that the familiar practice of contrasting Roman Catholics and Protestants is clearly not productive. Some differences between Catholics and Protestants are inconsequential compared with the differences among Protestant sects.

Protestant faiths may be distinguished by secular criteria as well as doctrinal issues. Research has consistently shown that denominations can be arranged in a hierarchy based on social class. As Figure 5.2 reveals, certain faiths, such as Episcopalianism, Judaism, and Presbyterianism, have a higher proportion of affluent members. Members of other faiths, including Baptists and Evangelicals, are comparatively poor. Of course, all Protestant groups draw members from each social stratum. Nonetheless, the social significance of these class differences is that religion becomes a mechanism for signaling social mobility. A person who is "moving up" in wealth and power may seek out a faith associated with a higher social ranking. Similar contrasts are shown in formal schooling in Figure 5.3.

Protestant faiths have been diversifying, and their members have been seeking out more churches that follow strict codes of behavior or fundamental interpretations of biblical teachings. This trend is reflected in the decline of the five "mainline" churches: Baptist, Episcopalian, Lutheran, Methodist, and Presbyterian. In 1993, these faiths accounted for 42 percent of church membership, compared to 51 percent just 20 years earlier. It is unlikely that, with a broader accep-

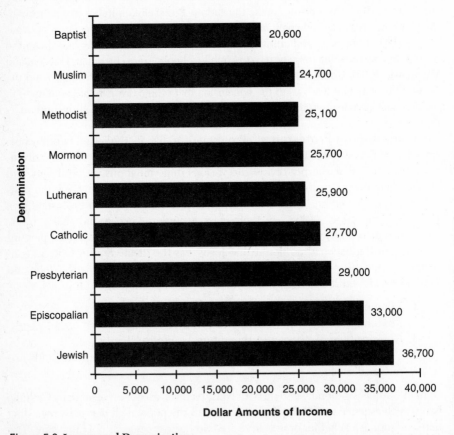

Figure 5.2 Income and Denominations
Denominations attract different income groups. All groups have both affluent and poor members, yet some have a higher proportion of members with high incomes, and others are comparatively poor.

Source: Kosmin and Lachman (1993, p. 260).

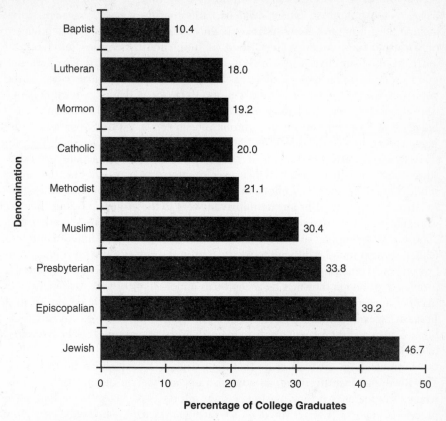

Figure 5.3 Education and Denominations
There are sharp differences in the proportion of college graduates by denomination.
Source: Kosmin and Lachman (1993, p. 258).

tance of new faiths and continuing immigration, the mainline churches will return to their dominance (Princeton Religion Research Center, 1994).

Women and Religion

Religious beliefs have often placed women in an exalted, but protected, position. As religions are practiced, this position has often meant being "protected" from becoming leaders. Perhaps the only major exception in the United States is the Christian Science church, in which the majority of practitioners and readers are women. Women may be evangelists, prophets, and even saints, but they find it difficult to become clergy*men* within their own congregations.

Even today, the largest denomination in the United States, Roman Catholicism, does not permit women to be priests. A 1993 Gallup survey found that 63 percent of Roman Catholics in this country favor the ordination of women, compared to only 29 percent in 1974, but internationally, the church has continued to maintain its long-standing teaching that priests should be male.

The largest Protestant denomination, the Southern Baptist Convention, has voted against ordaining women (even though some of its autonomous churches have women ministers). Other religious faiths that do not allow women clergy include the Lutheran Church–Missouri Synod, the Greek Orthodox Archdiocese of North and South America, the Orthodox Church in America, the Church of God in Christ, the Church of Jesus Christ of Latter-day Saints, and Orthodox Judaism.

Despite these restrictions, there has been a notable rise in female clergy in the last twenty years. The Bureau of the Census (1994) shows that six percent of clergy were women in 1983 but had increased to 11 percent in 1993. Increasingly, some branches of Protestantism and Judaism have been convinced that women have the right to become spiritual leaders. Yet a lingering question remains: Once ordained, are these female ministers and rabbis necessarily *accepted* by congregations? Will they advance in their calling as easily as their male counterparts, or will they face blatant or subtle discrimination in their efforts to secure desirable posts within their faiths?

It is too early to offer any definitive answers to these questions, but thus far, women clearly continue to face lingering sexism after ordination. According to a 1986 random sampling of 800 lay and ordained leaders of the United Church of Christ, women found it difficult to secure jobs in the larger, more prestigious congregations. Women ministers in other Protestant faiths have encountered similar problems. Although they may be accepted as junior clergy or as copastors, women may fail to receive senior clergy appointments. In both Reform and Conservative Judaism, women rabbis are rarely hired by the largest and best-known congregations. Consequently, women clergy in many denominations appear to be restricted to the low end of the pay scale and the hierarchy.

Women clergy are well aware that their struggle for equality is far from over. The Reverend Joan Forsberg, an administrator at the Yale Divinity School, tells women graduates that they must view their efforts as part of a larger, long-term process of change. "Even if you don't see change overnight," she notes, "you must remind yourself that you *are* making a difference for future generations" (A. Brooks, 1987, p. 15; Bureau of the Census, 1993a, p. 405; S. Cohen, 1991; R. Ostling, 1992; Princeton Religion Research Center, 1993).

Religion and the U.S. Supreme Court

Religious pluralism owes its existence in the United States to the First Amendment declaration that "Congress shall make no law respecting an establishment of religion, or prohibiting the free exercise thereof." The U.S. Supreme Court has consistently interpreted this wording to mean not that government should ignore religion but that it should follow a policy of neutrality to maximize religious freedom. For example, the government may not help religion by financing a new church building, but it also cannot obstruct religion by denying a church adequate police and fire protection. We will examine five issues that continue to require clarification: school prayer, parochial education, secessionist minorities, creationism, and the public display of religious symbols.

Among the most controversial and continuing disputes has been whether prayer has a role in the schools. Many people were disturbed by the 1962 Supreme Court decision in *Engel v. Vitale* that disallowed an allegedly nondenominational prayer drafted for use in the New York public schools. The prayer was "Almighty

God, we acknowledge our dependence upon Thee, and we beg Thy blessings upon us, our parents, our teachers, and our country." Subsequent decisions outlawed state laws requiring Bible reading in public schools, laws requiring recitation of the Lord's Prayer, and laws permitting a daily one-minute period of silent meditation or prayer.

What about prayers at public gatherings? In 1992, the Supreme Court ruled 5–4 in *Lee v. Weisman* that prayer at a junior high school graduation in Providence, Rhode Island, violated the U.S. Constitution's mandate of separation of church and state. The rabbi had given thanks to God in his invocation. The district court suggested that the invocation would have been acceptable without that reference. The Supreme Court did not agree with the school board that a prayer at a graduation was not coercive. The Court did say in its opinion that it was acceptable for a student speaker voluntarily to say a prayer at such a program.

The role of religion in public schools remains controversial. Jennifer Griffin, 18, won the right from the U.S. Supreme Court to read a prayer at her 1994 graduation.

Despite such judicial pronouncements, children in many public schools in the United States are led in regular prayer recitation or Bible reading. Many communities believe that schools should transmit the dominant culture of the United States by encouraging prayer. In a 1985 survey (the most recent available), 15 percent of school administrators (including 42 percent of school administrators in the South) reported that prayers were said in at least one of their schools. Moreover, according to a 1993 survey, 69 percent of adults in the United States favored a constitutional amendment that would permit organized prayer in public schools (J. Bacon, 1987; T. Mauro, 1993).

Parochial schools have long been guaranteed the right to function. In 1925, the Supreme Court (*Pierce v. Society of Sisters*) declared that parents may not be compelled to send their children to public schools, although they must send them to a properly accredited school. The degree to which the government can assist religious schools has not been resolved, however. Federal grants for lunches in all schools and the tax exemption for all religious institutions not engaged in business for profit have been upheld. The Court has refused to review state legislation that denies free bus transportation to parochial schoolchildren (R. Morgan, 1974). The lack of consensus on the Court was reflected in the May 19, 1975, decision in *Meed v. Pittinger* on assistance to parochial schools. Three justices voted against any assistance being given, three voted in favor of all types, and three voted that giving books and maps was acceptable but that giving projectors and lab paraphernalia was not because they could be "diverted to religious" purposes. The issues generated by the country's commitment to the separation of church and state will continue to face the Supreme Court and other judicial bodies.

Among religious groups are several that have been in legal and social conflict with the rest of society. Some can be called *secessionist minorities,* in that they reject assimilation as well as coexistence in some form of cultural pluralism. The Amish are one such group that comes in conflict with outside society because of their beliefs and way of life. The Amish shun most modern conveniences, such as electricity, television, radio, and automobiles. Their primary clash with the larger society has been on education because the Amish operate their own schools, which stop at the eighth grade. On May 16, 1972, the Supreme Court, in *Yoder v. Wisconsin,* upheld a lower court's decision that a Wisconsin compulsory-education law violated the Amish right to religious freedom (Kephart and Zellner, 1994).

Are there limits to the free exercise of religious rituals by secessionist minorities? Today, tens of thousands of members of Native American religions believe that the ingestion of the powerful drug peyote is a sacrament and that those who partake of peyote will enter into direct contact with God. In 1990, the Supreme Court ruled that prosecuting people who use illegal drugs as part of a religious ritual is *not* a violation of the First Amendment guarantee of religious freedom. The case arose because Native Americans were dismissed from their jobs for the religious use of peyote and were then refused unemployment benefits by the State of Oregon's employment division. In 1991, however, Oregon enacted a new law permitting the sacramental use of peyote by Native Americans (*New York Times,* 1991).

In another ruling on religious rituals in 1993, the Supreme Court unanimously overturned a local ordinance in Florida that banned ritual animal sacrifice. The high court held that this law violated the free-exercise rights of adherents of the Santeria religion, in which the sacrifice of animals (including goats, chickens, and other birds) plays a central role (L. Greenhouse, 1993a).

The fourth area of contention has been whether the biblical account of creation should be or must be present in school curricula and whether to give this account equal weight with scientific theories. In the famous "monkey trial" of 1925, Tennessee schoolteacher John Scopes was found guilty of teaching the scientific theory of evolution in public schools. Since then, however, Darwin's evolutionary theories have been presented in public schools with little reference to the biblical account in Genesis. Persons who support the literal interpretation of the Bible, commonly known as *creationists*, have formed various organizations to crusade for creationist treatment in American public schools and universities. In 1982, a critical defeat of the creationists came in *McLean v. Arkansas Board of Education* when the judge of a federal district court overturned an Arkansas law that called for a balanced treatment of evolution and the Genesis account. Judge William Ray Overton declared that "creation science . . . has no scientific merit or educational value." He added that the balanced-treatment law was "simply and purely an effort to introduce the Biblical version of creation into the public school curricula" and therefore violated the First Amendment guarantee of separation of church and state (R. Stuart, 1982).

The fifth area of contention has been a battle over public displays. Can manger scenes be erected on public property? Do people have a right to be protected from large displays such as a cross or a star atop a water tower overlooking an entire town? In a series of decisions in the 1980s, the Supreme Court ruled that religious displays on public government property may be successfully challenged, but not if they are made more secular. Displays that combine a crèche, the Christmas

The 1925 "monkey trial" of Tennessee schoolteacher John Scopes was an early test of the legality of teaching evolution. Scopes is pictured here (second from left) as he stands before the judge's bench.

manger scene depicting the birth of Jesus, or the Hanukkah menorah with reindeer or even Christmas trees have been ruled to be secular. These decisions have been dubbed "the plastic reindeer rules" and should be viewed as tentative, since the Court cases have been decided by close votes, and changes in the Supreme Court composition may alter the outcome of future cases (M. Hirsley, 1991).

Limits of Religious Freedom: Mormonism

Religious freedom is not absolute and must be balanced against other constitutional rights. The Church of Jesus Christ of Latter-day Saints (Mormons) has encountered severe persecution during its history, dramatizing the limits to which American secular society will tolerate a new religious order. Ironically, the obstacles in the way of the Mormons, as they are commonly called by nonmembers of the church, strengthened the young church as it grew throughout the nineteenth century. Leadership struggles and disputes over doctrine were forced into the background as the Mormons fought for life as a sect. In this instance, intergroup conflict maintained group identity and strengthened group cohesion (L. Coser, 1956; MacMurray and Cunningham, 1973).

The Mormon faith was founded in 1830 by Joseph Smith, who, by his own account, had earlier translated the *Book of Mormon* from a set of gold plates left by the angel Moroni. The followers of Smith encountered several decades of hostility as they moved from New York to Ohio, to Missouri, to Illinois, and finally to the Great Salt Lake basin in Utah. When they first arrived in a new community, the Mormons were usually well received because accounts of their persecution elsewhere had created sympathy. But non-Mormons soon grew suspicious of a religious group that had a lay priesthood, opposed slavery, and saw their church as the center of a planned community. The most violent disputes within as well as outside the church community took place in Illinois. They arose in response to the extraordinary political power that the Mormons were able to attain in the state and Smith's encouragement of plural marriage. The violence eventually led to Smith's arrest and assassination in 1844 and Brigham Young's assumption of the church's leadership. The majority of Mormons followed Young to Utah.

In Utah, the Mormons continued to have conflicts with non-Mormons. Anti-Mormon sentiment grew throughout the country to the extent that President Buchanan sent troops in 1857 to replace Young with a non-Mormon as territorial governor. The effort failed and Young remained, but during this short-lived "Mormon War," 120 non-Mormons were allegedly led into an Indian trap by overzealous Mormons in the Mountain Meadows Massacre. The anti-Mormon bandwagon grew, and concern grew, as well, over the issue of polygamy (more accurately, polygony, for Mormons permitted only men to take more than one spouse and did not practice polyandry, which permits women to have multiple husbands). Estimates of the proportion of polygynous households among Mormons ranged from 10 to 50 percent. In 1862, Congress enacted the Morill "anti-bigamy law," banishing the practice in the territories. In Utah, no grand jury would issue indictments for this offense, but the Supreme Court ruled finally in *Reynolds v. United States* in 1878 that the Morill Act must be upheld and did not represent an infringement of religious freedom. In 1890, the church officially abandoned polygamy in a manifesto that marked the end of Mormon separatism and the beginning of an uneasy compromise with non-Mormons. Six years later, Utah was admitted to the Union (T. O'Dea, 1957).

Unlike most Protestant faiths, the Latter-day Saints insist that theirs is the only true church of Christ and that they alone are the church for today's world. Mormons send missionaries out to seek converts even among those already associated with another Christian faith. This vigorous proselytizing is deeply resented by many non-Mormons. The Mormon church seems to maintain its solidarity as much because of the conflict it encounters as in spite of it. Thomas O'Dea (1957) remarks of this solidarity that the Latter-day Saints have come "closer to evolving an ethnic identity on this continent than any other comparable group" (p. 116).

Even today, Mormons have to defend their practices, but the charges they defend themselves against are of racism and sexism. The church followed Smith's declaration that Black skins are cursed "as pertaining to the priesthood" until 1978. The priesthood is still denied to women, who are expected to make their contribution through family-centered activities and auxiliary organizations. Although the church did not take an official position on the Equal Rights Amendment (ERA), the conservative attitude toward women's rights was fundamental to the defeat of the ERA in Utah (Miller and Linker, 1974). The practice of plural marriage by perhaps as many as 30,000 individuals who have been officially excommunicated from the church continues to embarrass church stalwarts (Kephart and Zellner, 1994).

Mormons still follow the strict life set forth over a century ago by Joseph Smith. The faithful are expected to forgo tobacco, liquor, cola drinks, coffee, and tea, and to follow a relatively puritanical code of sexual behavior. The more than 160-year history of the Church of Jesus Christ of Latter-day Saints encompasses a series of conflicts, some violent clashes, and other conflicts of social values. These conflicts have contributed to the transformation of a sect into a viable religious faith with nearly 9 million members worldwide and over 4 million adherents in the United States alone.

CONCLUSION

Any study of American life, but especially one focusing on dominant and subordinate groups, cannot ignore religion and ethnicity. The two are closely related, as certain religious faiths predominate in certain nationalities. People have been and continue to be ridiculed or to be deprived of opportunities solely because of their ethnic or religious affiliation. Women, in particular, may be at a disadvantage in organized religion. Reassertion of ethnicity has raised issues but has left them unresolved. How ethnic can a person be before society punishes him or her for the willingness to be different? How will the courts and society resolve the issues of religious freedom and freedom from religion? Today, ethnicity remains a viable source of identity for many citizens. Religious institutions may be under attack, but an examination of religious ties is fundamental to completing an accurate picture of a person's social identity.

Is the "new ethnicity" serious? That this question continues to be raised by liberal Whites may in itself be another example of Lerner's "respectable bigotry." Ethnicity is a part of today's social reality. The emotions, disputes, and debate over religion and ethnicity in the United States are powerful indeed.

KEY TERMS

civil religion The religious dimension in American life that merges the state with sacred beliefs.

creationists People who support a literal interpretation of the biblical book of Genesis on the origins of the universe and argue that evolution should not be presented as established scientific thought.

denomination A large, organized religion not officially linked with the state or government.

ethclass The merged ethnicity and class in a person's status.

life chances People's opportunities to provide themselves with material goods, positive living conditions, and favorable life experiences.

principle of third-generation interest Marcus Hansen's contention that ethnic interest and awareness increase in the third generation, among the grandchildren of immigrants.

respectable bigotry Michael Lerner's term for the social acceptance of prejudice against White ethnics, when intolerance against non-White minorities is regarded as unacceptable.

secessionist minority Groups, such as the Amish, that reject assimilation as well as coexistence.

symbolic ethnicity Herbert Gans's term that describes an emphasis on ethnic food and ethnically associated political issues rather than deeper ties to one's heritage.

FOR FURTHER INFORMATION

Richard D. Alba. *Ethnic Identity: The Transformation of White America.* New Haven: Yale University Press, 1990.

> An overview of the changing role of ethnicity among European Americans, with particular attention given to Italian Americans.

H. Paul Chalfant, Robert E. Beckley, and C. Eddie Palmer. *Religion in Contemporary Society,* 3d ed. Itasca. ILL.: Peacock, 1984.

> The authors draw upon sociological research in order to study the organization, leadership, and current trends of religious life in the United States.

Robert Coles and Jon Erickson. *The Middle Americans: Proud and Uncertain.* Boston: Little, Brown, 1971.

> Erickson's photographs, along with Coles's commentary, describe that segment of the population frequently called, perhaps inaccurately, "the silent majority," or the White lower-middle class.

Joshua Fishman, ed. *The Rise and Fall of the Ethnic Revival.* Berlin: Mouton, 1985.

> Drawing upon language patterns, Fishman critiques claims about the extent of the ethnic revival in the United States.

Andrew Greeley. *Ethnicity in the United States: A Preliminary Reconnaissance.* New York: Wiley, 1974.

Greeley summarizes the findings available on the attitudes, politics, religion, and socioeconomic status of White ethnic groups and stresses the need for further study. In *The American Catholic,* Greeley (1977) brings together similar data on Catholics.

Will Herberg. *Protestant—Catholic—Jew: An Essay in American Religious Sociology,* rev. ed. Chicago: University of Chicago Press, 1983.

Herberg presents his thesis that immigrant ties to the old country have been replaced by religious self-identification along the tripartite scheme of Protestant, Catholic, and Jew. Martin Marty provides a new introduction to this revision of the 1960 edition.

William M. Kephart and William M. Zellner. *Extraordinary Groups: The Sociology of Unconventional Life-Styles,* 5th ed. New York: St. Martin's Press, 1994.

Kephart and Zellner bring together for the first time in a sociological treatment the Romani (commonly known as the Gypsies), the Amish, the Oneida community, Hasidic Jews, the Jehovah's Witnesses, and the Mormons.

Barry A. Kosmin and Seymour P. Lachman. *One Nation Under God: Religion in Contemporary American Society.* New York: Harmony Books, 1993.

An overview of religion in the United States drawing upon the National Survey of Religious Identification.

Helena Znanieka Lopata. *Polish Americans.* Rutgers, NJ: Transaction Books, 1993.

Examines the Polish ethnic community in the United States created by immigration beginning in 1880.

Lionel Maldonado and Joan Moore, eds. *Urban Ethnicity in the United States.* Beverly Hills, CA: Sage, 1985.

This collection of ten articles reviews the historical and present situation of ethnics in the United States.

Randall M. Miller, ed. *The Kaleidoscopic Lens: How Hollywood Views Ethnic Groups.* Englewood, NJ: J. Ozer, 1980.

This illustrated book looks at how Blacks, Native Americans, Hispanics, Irish, Jews, Germans, Slovaks, and Asians have been treated stereotypically in the movies.

Charles H. Mindel, Robert W. Habenstein, and Roosevelt Wright, Jr., eds. *Ethnic Families in America: Patterns and Variations,* 3rd ed. New York: Elsevier, 1988.

The nature of family life is fundamental to comprehending minority groups. The editors of this book have brought together 15 original articles on family life in different racial and ethnic groups, including Italian Americans, Greek Americans, Mormons, Vietnamese Americans, and Irish-American Catholics.

Journals

Among the journals that focus on issues of race and ethnicity is *Ethnic and Racial Studies* (1978). The sociological study of religion is reflected in the *Journal for the Scientific Study of Religion, Review of Religious Research* (1958), *Sociological Analysis* (1940), and *Social Compass* (1954). The monthly newsletter *Emerging Trends,* published by the Princeton Religion Research Center beginning in 1979, provides the latest data on religious life.

CRITICAL THINKING QUESTIONS

1. In what respect are the ethnic and religious diversity of the United States related to each other?
2. Is assimilation automatic within any given ethnic group?
3. How can "blaming the victims" be applied to White ethnic groups?
4. Why has the U.S. Supreme Court ruled in favor of the Amish and Santeria and not the Native American use of peyote?
5. What evidence have you personally seen that religious activities are influenced by court rulings?

MAJOR RACIAL AND ETHNIC MINORITY GROUPS IN THE UNITED STATES

Chapter
6

The First Native Americans

Chapter Outline

Highlights

The first inhabitants of North America were the first to be subordinated by the Europeans. Those Native Americans who survived contact with the White people were removed from their ancestral homes, often far away. The U.S. government weakened tribal institutions through a succession of acts beginning with the *Allotment Act* of 1884. Even efforts to strengthen tribal autonomy, such as the 1934 *Reorganization Act,* did so by encouraging adoption of White society's way of life. The modern period of Native American–White relations is little different, as shown by such measures as the *Employment Assistance Program* and the *Termination Act,* both of which encourage Indians to assimilate. The *Red Power* and *pan-Indian* movements speak for a diverse Native-American people with many needs: settlement of treaty violations, increased employment opportunities, control over natural resources, improved educational programs, effective health care, religious freedom, and greater self-rule, to name a few.

Native Americans have been misunderstood and ill treated by their conquerors for several centuries. Assuming he had reached "the Indies," Christopher Columbus called them "people of India." It would be a mistake to think that the European immigrants who followed Columbus understood them any more than the Native Americans themselves comprehended their invaders. But because the Europeans had superior weaponry, it was the mistakes and misunderstandings of the English, French, Spanish, and Portuguese that became law.

Although our focus in this chapter is on the Native American experience in the United States, this same pattern of misunderstanding has been repeated with indigenous people in nations throughout the world. Except for those native people who have been entirely wiped out, indigenous people on every continent are familiar with the patterns of subjugation and the pressure to assimilate. The social patterns we see in the United States are those of subjugation, colonization, and assimilation, and of understandable resistance by the native peoples.

EARLY EUROPEAN CONTACTS

The first explorers of the Western Hemisphere came long before Columbus and Leif Ericson. Archaeologists estimate that between 25,000 and 40,000 years ago, Asians crossed over into North America on a land bridge that joined the two continents near present-day Alaska. The ancestors of today's Native Americans were hunters in search of wild game, including mammoths and long-horned bison. For thousands of years, the people spread through the Western Hemisphere, adapting to the many physical environments. Hundreds of cultures evolved, including the complex societies of the Mayas, Incas, and Aztecs.

It is beyond the scope of this book to describe the many tribal cultures of North America, let alone the ways of life of Native Americans in Central and South America and the islands of the Caribbean. We must appreciate that the term *Indian culture* is a convenient way of glossing over the diversity of cultures, languages, religions, kinship systems, and political organizations that existed—and in many instances, remain—among the peoples collectively referred to as *Native Americans* or *Americans Indians.* For example, in 1500, an estimated 700 individual languages were spoken in the area north of Mexico. At least 200 are still spoken by some tribal members today. For simplicity's sake we will refer to these many cultures as Native American, but we must be ever mindful of the differences this term conceals. Similarly, we will refer to non–Native Americans as *White people,* although in this context, this term encompasses a host of people, including African Americans and Hispanics in some instances (J. Schwartz, 1994; W. Swagerty, 1983).

Columbus commented in his diary, "It appears to me that the people [of the New World] are ingenious and would be good servants. . . . These people are very unskilled in arms. . . . With fifty men they could all be subjected to do all that one wishes" (*Akwesasne Notes,* 1972a, p. 22). The words of the first European explorer were prophetic. The period between initial European contact and the formation of the United States was characterized by cultural and physical conflict between Native Americans and Whites.

The number of Native Americans north of the Rio Grande, estimated at about 10 million in 1500, gradually decreased as their food sources disappeared or they fell victim to diseases like measles, smallpox, and influenza. By 1800, the Native American population was about 600,000, and by 1900, it had been reduced to 250,000. This loss of human life can only be judged as catastrophic. The United States does not bear total responsibility. The pattern had been well established by the early Spaniards in the Southwest, and by the French and English colonists, who sought to gain control of the eastern seaboard.

Occasionally, we read of warfare among tribes, which presumably reduces the guilt of European-initiated warfare. However, there is a significant difference. The Europeans launched large campaigns against the tribes, producing mass mortality. In the Americas, the tribes restricted warfare to specific campaigns designed for very specific purposes, such as recapturing some resource or avenging some loss.

Not all the initial contacts led to loss of life. Some missionaries traveled well in advance of settlements in an effort to Christianize the Native Americans before they came in contact with other, less "Christian," Europeans. Fur trappers, vastly outnumbered by Native Americans, were forced to learn their customs, but these trappers established routes of commerce that more and more Whites were to follow (C. Snipp, 1989; W. Swagerty, 1983, p. 21; R. Thornton, 1991).

As of the 1990 census, there were about 2 million Native Americans (including the Inuit and Aleut), 22 percent of them living on reservations. The Cherokee, followed by the Navajo, Chippewa, and Sioux, are the largest tribes today. The present Native American population reflects a significant growth in the last 10–20 years, primarily because of their increased willingness to claim their heritage (Bureau of the Census, 1993a; D. Harris, 1992).

History did not begin in North America with the arrival of the Europeans. In 1992, the American Indian Movement (AIM) staged a protest against a Texas pageant that displayed replicas of Columbus's ships.

TREATIES AND WARFARE

The United States formulated a policy toward Native Americans that followed the precedents established during the colonial period. The government policy was not to antagonize the Native Americans unnecessarily, but if the needs of tribes interfered with the needs, or even the whims, of Whites, Whites were to be victorious. The tribes were viewed as separate nations to be dealt with by treaties arrived at through negotiations with the central government. Fair-minded as that policy might seem, it was clear from the very beginning that the tribal groups that refused to agree to treaties suggested by the White people's government would be dealt with harshly. Federal relations with the Native Americans were the responsibility of the Secretary of War. Consequently, when the Bureau of Indian Affairs was created in 1824 to coordinate federal relations with the tribes, it was placed in the War Department. The government's primary emphasis was on maintaining peace and friendly relations along the frontier. As settlers moved the frontier westward, though, they encroached more and more on land that Native Americans had inhabited for centuries.

The Indian Removal Act, passed in 1830, called for relocating all eastern tribes across the Mississippi River. The act was very popular with Whites because it opened more land to settlement. Almost all Whites felt that the Native Americans had no right to block progress, defining progress as movement by White society. Among the largest groups relocated were the five tribes of the Creek, Choctaw, Chickasaw, Cherokee, and Seminole, who were resettled in Oklahoma. The movement, lasting more than a decade, has been called the Trail of Tears because the tribes left their ancestral lands under the harshest conditions. Poor planning, corrupt officials, little attention to those ill from a variety of epidemics, and inadequate supplies characterized the forced migration (Deloria and Lytle, 1983).

The Removal Act not only totally disrupted Native American culture itself but didn't move the tribes far enough or fast enough to stay out of the path of the ever-advancing White settlers. Following the Civil War, settlers moved westward at an unprecedented pace. The federal government negotiated with the many tribes but primarily legislated for them with minimal consultation. The goal was almost always to allow the settlers to live and work regardless of Native American claims.

The Case of the Sioux

The nineteenth century was devastating for every Native American tribe in the areas claimed by the United States. No tribe was the same after its association with federal policy. The treatment of the Sioux, or Dakotas, was especially cruel and remains fresh in the minds of tribal members even today.

In an effort to safeguard White settlers, the United States signed the Fort Laramie Treaty of 1868 with the Sioux, then under the leadership of Red Cloud. The government agreed to keep Whites from hunting or settling on the newly established Great Sioux Reservation, which included all of the land that is now South Dakota west of the Missouri River. In exchange the Sioux relinquished most of the remaining land they occupied at that time. The first few years saw relative peace, except for some raids by warrior bands under the leadership of the medicine man Sitting Bull. Red Cloud even made a much-publicized trip to Washington and New York in 1870.

The flood of White people eventually infiltrated the Sioux territory in an influx spurred on by Colonel George Custer's exaggerated 1874 reports of gold in the Black Hills. Hostilities followed, and bands of Native Americans were ordered to move during the winter, when travel was impossible. When the Sioux failed to move, Custer moved in to "pacify" them and the neighboring Cheyenne. Relying on Crow scouts, Custer underestimated the strength of the Sioux warriors under the leadership of Crazy Horse. The ensuing Battle of the Little Big Horn in 1876 was the last great Sioux victory. After the battle, the large encampment of warriors scattered throughout the plains into small bands, which were defeated one by one by a Congress and an Army more determined than ever to subdue the Sioux.

In 1876, the Sioux reluctantly sold the Black Hills and agreed to the reduction of the Great Sioux Reservation to five much smaller ones. The Sioux, unable to hunt game as they traditionally had, found life unbearable on the reservation. They sought escape through the supernatural—the Ghost Dance religion. The Ghost Dance was a religion that included dances and songs proclaiming the return of the buffalo and the resurrection of dead ancestors in a land free of the White people. The dance soon became a symbolic movement that social scientists call a *millenarian movement*—a movement founded on the belief that a cataclysmic upheaval will occur in the immediate future, followed by collective salvation. The movement had originated among the Paiutes of Nevada and, ironically, had spread northward to the Plains Indians via the cornerstone of the government's assimilationist policy:

the schools. The English that Native Americans learned in the mission or government schools gave them the means to overcome the barrier of tribal languages. By 1890, about 65 percent of the tribes in the West, according to sociologist Russell Thornton (1981), were involved in this movement.

From a functionalist perspective, this millenarian movement can be viewed as a means of coping with the domination of White intruders. Although the Ghost Dance was essentially harmless to Whites, Whites feared that the new tribal solidarity encouraged by the movement would lead to renewed warfare. As a result, more troops were summoned to areas where the Ghost Dance had become popular.

In late December 1890, anticipating that a massive Ghost Dance would be staged, a cavalry division arrived at an encampment of Teton Sioux at Wounded Knee Creek on the Pine Ridge, South Dakota, reservation. When the soldiers began disarming the warriors, a random shot was fired at the soldiers, touching off a close-range battle. The cavalry then turned its artillery on men, women, and children. Approximately 300 Sioux and 25 government soldiers were killed in the ensuing fighting, which is now referred to as the Battle of Wounded Knee. One Sioux witness later recalled, "We tried to run, but they shot us like we were a buffalo. I know there are some good white people, but the soldiers must be mean to shoot children and women" (D. Brown, 1971, p. 417).

For the federal government, the "Indian problem" remained; it had not vanished. Despite the effects of disease and warfare nearly 250,000 Indians still lived, according to the 1890 census. The reservation system constructed in the last

A U.S. Army photograph shows the burial of the Sioux dead at Wounded Knee, South Dakota in 1890.

decades of the nineteenth century to provide settlements for Native American peoples has formed the basis of the relationship of Native Americans to the government from then until the present.

LEGISLATING FOR THE NATIVE AMERICANS

Along with the military defeat of the tribes, the federal government tried to limit the functions of tribal leaders. If tribal institutions were weakened, it was felt the Native Americans would more rapidly assimilate. The government's intention to merge the various tribes into White society was unmistakably demonstrated in the 1887 Dawes, or General Allotment, Act. This failure to assist Native American people was followed by a somewhat more admirable effort—the Indian Reorganization Act of 1934. The Allotment Act and the Reorganization Act established the government's paternalistic approach, which was based on legislating *for* the Native Americans.

The Allotment Act

The Allotment Act bypassed tribal leaders and proposed to make individual landowners of tribal members. Each family was given up to 160 acres, under the government's assumption that, with land, they would become more like the White homesteaders who were then flooding the not-yet-settled areas of the West.

The effect of the Allotment Act on the Native Americans was disastrous. In order to guarantee that they would remain homesteaders, the act prohibited their selling the land for 25 years. Yet no effort was made to acquaint them with the skills necessary to make the land productive. Because many tribes were not accustomed to cultivating land and, if anything, considered such labor undignified, assistance to the new homesteaders would have been needed for them to adapt to homesteading, but none was forthcoming.

Much of the land initially deeded under the Allotment Act eventually came into the possession of White landowners. The land could not be sold legally, but it could be leased and was subsequently transferred through fraudulent procedures. Whites would even go so far as to arrange to become legal guardians of Native American youths who had received allotments. The Bureau of Indian Affairs (BIA) vainly tried to close such loopholes, but unscrupulous Whites and their Native American allies would inevitably discover new loopholes. For those Native Americans who managed to retain the land, the BIA required that, on the death of the owner, the land be equally divided among all descendants, regardless of tribal inheritance customs. In documented cases this division resulted in as many as 30 individuals trying to live off an 80-acre plot of worthless land. By 1934, Native Americans had lost approximately 90 million of the 138 million acres in their possession before the Allotment Act. The land left was generally considered worthless for farming and marginal even for ranching (Deloria and Lytle, 1983; W. Hagan, 1961; D. Holford, 1975; S. Tyler, 1973; M. Wax, 1971; S. Witt, 1970).

The Reorganization Act

The assumptions behind the Allotment Act and the missionary activities of the nineteenth century were that (1) it was best for Native Americans to assimilate into the White society, and (2) each individual was best considered apart from his or her tribal identity. Very gradually, in the twentieth century, government officials have accepted the importance of tribal identity. The Indian Reorganization Act of 1934, the Wheeler-Howard Act, recognized the need to use, rather than ignore, tribal identity. But assimilation, rather than movement toward a pluralistic society, was still the goal of the act.

Many provisions of the Reorganization Act, including revocation of the Allotment Act, benefited Native Americans. Still, given the legacy of broken treaties, many tribes distrusted the new policy at first. Under the Reorganization Act, tribes could adopt a written constitution and elect a tribal council with a chairperson. This system imposed foreign values and structures. The elected tribal chairperson actually represented an entire reservation, which might include several tribes, some of which were hostile to one another. Furthermore, the chairperson had to be elected by majority rule, a concept alien to many tribes. Many full-blooded Native Americans resented the provision that mixed-bloods were to have full voting rights. The Indian Reorganization Act did facilitate tribal dealings with government agencies, but the dictating of certain procedures common to White society alien to the tribes was another sign of assimilation to Native Americans.

As had been true of earlier government reforms, the Reorganization Act sought to assimilate Native Americans into the dominant society on the dominant group's terms. In this case, the tribes were absorbed within the political and economic structure of the larger society. Except for the chairpeople who were to oversee reservations that had several tribes, the Reorganization Act served to solidify tribal identity. Unlike the Allotment Act, it recognized the right of Native Americans to approve of some actions taken on their behalf. The act still maintained substantial non–Native American control over the reservations. As institutions, the tribal governments owed their existence not to their people, but to the BIA. These tribal governments rested at the bottom of a large administrative hierarchy (S. Cornell, 1984; V. Deloria, 1971; D. McNickle, 1973; W. Washburn, 1984; Wax and Buchanan, 1975).

RESERVATION LIFE AND FEDERAL POLICIES

Today, over 437,000 Native Americans live on 314 reservations and trust lands throughout the United States. While the majority live outside these tribal areas, the reservations play a prominent role in the identity of the Native American peoples (see Figure 6.1).

More than any other segment of the population, with the exception of the military, the reservation Native American finds his or her life determined by the federal government. From the condition of the roads to the level of fire protection to the quality of the schools, reservation life is effectively controlled by the federal government and such agencies as the Bureau of Indian Affairs and the Public

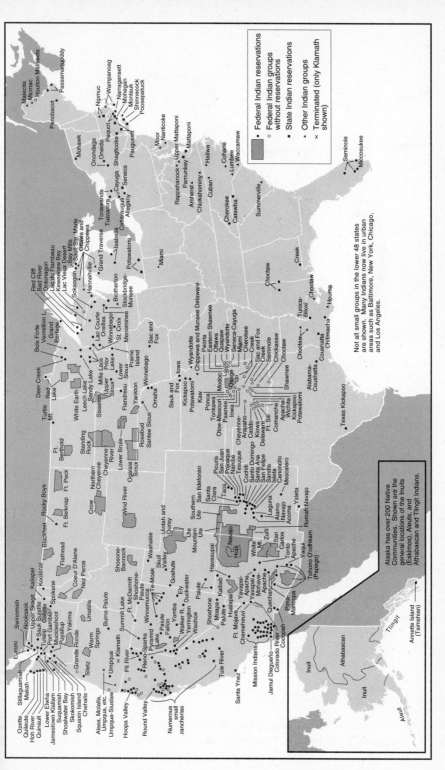

Figure 6.1 **Native American Lands and Communities**

Source: Bureau of Indian Affairs (1986, pp. 12–13).

Education programs developed for Native Americans have, until very recently, emphasized assimilation. This is a 1900 clothes-mending class at the Carlisle Indian School in Pennsylvania.

Health Service. Tribes and their leaders are now consulted more than in the past, but the ultimate decisions rest in Washington, D.C., to a degree that is not true for the rest of civilian population.

An April 1954 editorial in the *Washington Post* expressed sympathy with efforts of the federal government to "get out of the Indian business." Many of the policies instituted by the Bureau of Indian Affairs during the twentieth century have been designed with this purpose in mind. Most Native Americans and their organizations do not quarrel with this goal. They may only wish that the government and the White people had never gotten into "Indian business" in the first place. Disagreement between the BIA and the tribes and among Native Americans themselves has focused on how to reduce federal control and subsidies, not on whether they should be reduced. The government has taken three steps in this direction since World War II. Two of these measures have been the formation of the Indian Claims Commission and the passage of the Termination Act, examined next. The section following shows how the third step, the Employment Assistance Program, has created a new meeting place for Native Americans in cities, far from either their native homelands or the reservations (S. Tyler, 1973).

Native American Legal Claims

Native Americans have had a unique relationship with the federal government. As might be expected, little provision was ever made for them as individuals or tribes to bring grievances against the government. From 1863 to 1946, Native Americans could bring no claim against the government without a special act of Congress, a policy that effectively prevented most charges of treaty violations. Only 142 claims were heard during those 83 years. In 1946, Congress created the Indian Claims Commission, with authority to hear all tribal cases against the government. The three-member commission was given a five-year deadline. During the first five years, however, nearly three times as many claims were filed as had been filed during the 83 years of the old system. Therefore, the commission's term was extended and extended again, and its size was expanded. It continues to meet today, five decades after its establishment, and it now has five members.

The commission, although not a court, operates somewhat like one, with lawyers presenting evidence for both sides. Witnesses testify as to the legitimacy of land claims. If the commission concurs with the Native Americans, it then determines the value of the land at the time it was illegally seized. Native Americans do not usually receive payment based on present value, nor do they usually receive interest on the money due. Value at time of loss, perhaps a few pennies an acre, is considered "just compensation." Payments are then decreased by setoffs. *Setoffs* are deductions from the money due that are equal to the cost of federal services provided to the tribe. It is not unusual to have a case decided in favor of the tribe, only to have its settlement exceeded by the setoffs (V. Deloria, 1971; R. Ellis, 1972; G. Wilkinson, 1966).

One bitter dispute that continues unresolved illustrates the complexity of land claims. In 1882, the United States declared an end to a century-long conflict over which tribe—the Hopi or the Navajo—had the right to some lands in northeastern Arizona. The original inhabitants, the Hopi, were granted sole use of a group of mesas. These lands were surrounded by joint-use land to be used by both tribes, which itself was totally surrounded by the relatively populous Navajo reservation.

Although today the dispute seems to be between the tribes, the original conflict was created when the Navajos fled the U.S. Cavalry in New Mexico and entered neighboring Arizona. Even after joint use was declared, in the 1930s the government began issuing grazing permits to Navajos in these areas. In 1993, a new agreement (as shown in Fig. 6.2) was proposed that would allow some Navajos to remain with their homes and livestock on Hopi land. In exchange, the Hopis would receive land and money from the government to resolve lawsuits. The compromise was attacked by both tribes and White landowners. As the dispute continues, the lives of the Native Americans on these lands remain socially devastated because their future is in limbo (E. Benedek, 1993; O. Tamir, 1991).

In other legal cases, Native Americans are gaining success. The U.S. Supreme Court has begun to consider more tribe-related cases and to find in favor of the tribes. Other courts have reasserted such basic principles as that the tribes are separate governments; that the states have no jurisdiction over the reservations; that the federal government has a responsibility to the tribes; and that Native Americans have substantial rights to the resources on their land. Native American legal groups have organized to protect these and other legal rights, while various anti–Native American groups have organized to oppose what they regard as special privileges to tribes. The anti–Native American groups, openly linked to conservative extremist groups, argue that recognition of the tribes is a violation of the U.S. Constitution. Native Americans express concern about these groups, which have

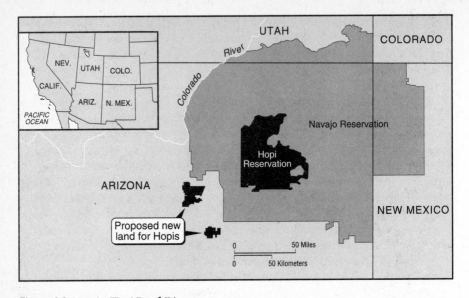

Figure 6.2 Navajo–Hopi Land Dispute
What sometimes appear to be disputes between tribes today actually stem from actions taken by the government. This is the case with the debate over awarding land to the Hopi to compensate for land they were recently forced to give up to the Navajo.

formed alliances on specific legal cases with such established groups as the National Wildlife Federation and the National Rifle Association (*Akwesasne Notes*, 1988; W. Schmidt, 1988).

Reservations contain a wealth of resources. In the past, Native Americans have lacked the technical knowledge to negotiate beneficial agreements successfully with private corporations, and when they did have this ability, the federal government often stepped in and made the final agreements more beneficial to the non–Native Americans than to the residents of the reservations. The native peoples have always been rooted in their land. It was their land that became the first source of tension and conflict with the Europeans. As the twenty-first century approaches, it is not surprising that land and the natural resources it holds continue to be major concerns. In 1976, the Council of Energy Resource Tribes (CERT) was formed by the leaders of 25 of the West's largest tribes. This new council reasoned that it could ensure more revenue from the tribes' vast mineral resources by being organized. Recently CERT, now representing over 45 tribes, has provided services to tribes monitoring nuclear waste management on their lands. Reservations are now expressing concern that their depleted lands are becoming dumping grounds for the Whites' toxic trash. The issues are similar to those faced nationwide: environmental concerns versus job opportunities and financial resources. For the tribes, which take their natural surroundings seriously but face economic depression, the choice is not always easy.

Native Americans increasingly express a desire to recover their land, rather than accept financial settlements. Following numerous legal decisions favoring the

Natural resources are yet another battleground for tribes and powerful outside interests. Navajos have successfully managed some of the coal mines on their reservation.

Sioux Indians, including a ruling of the U.S. Supreme Court, Congress finally agreed to pay $106 million for the land illegally seized in the aftermath of the Battle of the Little Big Horn, described earlier in this chapter. The Sioux rejected the money and lobbied for measures such as the 1987 Black Hills Sioux Nation Act in Congress to return the land to the tribe. No positive action has yet been taken on these measures. In the meantime, however, the original settlement, the subsequent unaccepted payments, and the interest brought the 1991 total of funds being held for the Sioux to over $330 million. Despite the desperate need for housing, food, health care, and education, the Sioux still wish to regain the land lost in the 1868 Fort Laramie Treaty and had not accepted payment as of 1995.

The Termination Act

The most controversial government policy toward reservation Native Americans during the twentieth century was initiated by the Termination Act of 1953. As might be said of many such policies, termination originated in ideas that were meant to be sympathetic to Native Americans. The BIA Commissioner, John Collier, had expressed concern in the 1930s over extensive governmental control of tribal affairs. In 1947, congressional hearings were held to determine which tribes had the economic resources to be relieved of federal control and assistance. The policy proposed at that time was an admirable attempt to give Native Americans greater autonomy and at the same time to reduce federal expenditures, a goal popular among taxpayers.

The special services the tribes received, like medical care and scholarships to college, should not be viewed as making them wards of the government. These services resulted from neither authoritarianism nor favoritism but merely fulfilled treaty obligations. The termination of the Native Americans' relationship to the government could then be viewed as a threat to reduce services rather than a release from arbitrary authority. Native Americans might be gaining greater self-governance, but the price was high.

Unfortunately, the Termination Act as finally passed in 1953 emphasized reducing costs and ignored individual needs. Recommendations for a period of tax immunity were dropped. Federal services such as medical care, schools, and road equipment were supposed to be withdrawn gradually. Instead, when termination was implemented, federal services were stopped immediately, with minimal coordination between local government agencies and the tribes themselves to determine whether the services could be continued by other means. The BIA Commissioner who oversaw termination was Dillon Myer, who had supervised the Japanese-American internment camps during World War II (see Chapter 14), and as it had been for the Japanese Americans, the effect of the government orders on the Native Americans was disastrous (V. Deloria, 1969; D. Fixico, 1988; S. Tyler, 1973; Wax and Buchanan, 1975).

The Case of the Menominee Tribe

The tragic treatment of the Menominee tribe of Wisconsin under termination is not typical. No other tribe that was terminated had been as well organized beforehand, and no other tribe was able to convince the federal government it was mistaken. The termination of the Menominees was preceded by a favorable Claims Commission settlement of $8 million from the government as compensation for the mismanagement of a forest on tribal land. The money, however, would not be paid unless Congress appropriated it, which was conditional on the Menominees' voting for termination. A vote for termination meant an almost immediate cash payment of $1,500 to each tribal member. Even with such a positive incentive, the Menominees at first overwhelmingly voted against termination. Finally, after six years of campaigning by members of Congress and the BIA, the Menominees voted for termination in 1959.

From the government's point of view, the 3,270 Menominees were prepared to be independent of federal services. They were one of only three tribes able to pay the costs of their own administration, which they could do because of a tribally owned sawmill. Twenty-five percent were unemployed, however, and the majority of tribal members met the standards of eligibility for surplus food. Even mill workers earned only $56 a week to support a typical family of eight. After termination they would also have to bear the burden of taxation, medical expenses, and utility payments.

On May 1, 1961, termination became final, and Menominee County, formerly a federal reservation, became the newest, smallest, least populated, least educated, and most poorly housed county in Wisconsin. The Menominees reluctantly started selling lakeshore property within a year of termination to provide the services previously financed by the federal government. Even with such drastic actions, the Menominees went without a full-time doctor for 11 years and had no school. Schoolchildren and patients had to be bused into neighboring communities, which did not appreciate the added burden on their limited medical and educational facilities.

In response to the growing problems, the Menominees created a grassroots organization called Determination of Rights and Unity for Menominee Shareholders (DRUMS). DRUMS struggled to stop the sale of land and the damming of rivers. Beginning in 1972, under the leadership of Ada Deer, DRUMS tried to persuade Congress that it should reverse the termination of the Menominees. To outsiders, it seemed puzzling to find the Menominees seeking the aid of the often-criticized BIA. Ada Deer herself said that the choice had not been easy, but that "determination" was the only choice, "because there is no alternative, no other way to hold on to our land" (P. Raymer, 1974, p. 248). Finally, in 1973, the Restoration Act was enacted, making Menominee County once again the Menominee Indian Reservation. The termination policy had been a failure. Two years later, when termination as a policy option was officially ended, the BIA estimated that the cost had been much greater to the federal government because of the additional economic assistance required once the Restoration Act had been passed (Spindler and Spindler, 1984).

Termination came to a halt with the passage in 1975 of the Indian Self-Determination and Education Assistance Act, which expanded tribal control over reservation programs, without necessarily suggesting that federal assistance would be decreased. The law also provided for parental groups to have increased authority over school programs—a special problem, as we will see later in this chapter (Bureau of Indian Affairs, 1981; E. Spicer, 1980).

NATIVE AMERICANS IN URBAN SETTINGS

The depressing economic conditions of reservation life might lead one to expect government initiatives to attract business and industry to locate on or near reservations. The government could provide tax incentives that would eventually pay for themselves. Such proposals, however, have not been advanced. Rather than take jobs to the Native Americans, the federal government decided to lead the more highly motivated away from the reservation. This policy has further devastated the reservations' economic potential.

In 1952, the BIA began programs to relocate young Native Americans. One of these programs, after 1962, was called the Employment Assistance Program (EAP). Assistance centers were created in Chicago, Cleveland, Dallas, Denver, Los Angeles, Oakland, San Jose, Oklahoma City, Tulsa, and Seattle. In some cities, the Native American population increased as much as fivefold in the 1950s, primarily because of the EAP. By 1968, more than 100,000 individuals had participated in the program, and 200,000, or one-fourth of the Native American population, had moved to urban areas. They have tended not to spread out throughout urban areas but to remain somewhat segregated. Though not as segregated as African

Americans or Hispanics, Native Americans often experience moderate segregation, similar to that of European ethnic groups (J. Bohland, 1982).

The EAP's primary provision was for relocation, individually or in families, at government expense, to urban areas where job opportunities were greater than those on the reservations. The BIA stressed that the EAP was voluntary, but as Howard Bahr (1972) correctly states, this voluntary aspect was "a fiction to the extent that the white man has structured the alternatives in such a way that economic pressures force the Indian to relocate" (p. 408). The program was not a success for the many Native Americans who found the urban experience unsuitable or unbearable. By 1965, one-fourth to one-third of the people in the EAP had returned to their home reservation. So great was the rate of return that, in 1959, the BIA actually stopped releasing data on the percentage of returnees, fearing that these would give too much ammunition to critics of the EAP.

Adjustment to a new way of life was the major challenge facing relocated Native Americans. Two studies (J. Price, 1968; R. Weppner, 1971) document the difficulties met by members of an agricultural tribe, the Navajo, in adjusting to urban life in Denver and Los Angeles. If the BIA had provided adequate vocational training and proper instruction in English, many more would undoubtedly have coped better with the new social environment. In the late 1960s, Merwyn Garbarino interviewed relocated Native Americans in Chicago. The 29-year-old man who told Garbarino (1971) the following could not be judged one of the EAP's successes:

> I don't like living in Chicago. I'm here on the relocation training program, and I'm glad to learn a trade, but I sure don't like the city. The BIA doesn't give us enough money to live in Chicago. It's awfully expensive here. But it's not just that. People are different here—even the Indians. They don't talk to you. Bus drivers are bastards, and I got lost on the "el" and no one could help me. City people are in such a hurry. As soon as I finish school, I'm going away—maybe back to the reservation, but to a small town anyhow. I'd rather be in a small town and not have such a good job as stay in the city. (p. 182)*

Other Native Americans were able to adjust to urban life in Chicago, as this interview with a 49-year-old man documents:

> I heard about relocation on the reservation. It's a good idea. Sometimes it doesn't work too well. When I first came, I had some training, and then things got bad and I lost my job. The BIA helped me get another one, but it didn't pay too good, and we had a hard time making out. We had to get some welfare at times. That sort of embarrassed me at first, but then in those days lots of people were out of work. At first it was just my wife and me. That wasn't so bad. She did some day jobs, you know, just line up each morning and see if there's a job for the day. That helped get some money. . . . I heard of a better job from a friend and I changed. No, I didn't think about going back to the reservation. Jobs were even worse there. There are things in the city that I like—the museums, movies, things like that. There are things to do, and the jobs did get better. We have

---

*From Merwyn Garbarino, "Life in the City," in Jack O. Waddell and O. Michael Watson, eds., *The American Indian in Urban Society.* Copyright © 1971 by Merwyn Garbarino. Reprinted by permission of the author.

quite a family now. Three girls and two boys, and I can take care of them all. Some people say that it is easier if you are alone, but I am glad that I have my family. I take the children to the zoo, and things. My wife never has to work any more. I think I'd like some other cities too. I like Chicago, but I have visited some smaller cities like Green Bay, and I think I might like to live there. But I can say I like a city. (pp. 179–180)°°

The Employment Assistance Program was not a total failure, but neither did it present an easy solution to the difficulties faced on the reservation.

The movement of Native Americans into urban areas has had many unintended consequences. It has further reduced the labor force on the reservation. Because those who leave tend to be better educated, it is the Native American version of the brain drain described in Chapter 4. Urbanization unquestionably contributed to the pan-Indian movement described in the next section of this chapter. The city became the new meeting place of Native Americans who learned of their common predicament both in the city and on the federally administered reservations. Government agencies also had to develop a policy of continued assistance to nonreservation Native Americans; despite such efforts, the problems of Native Americans in cities persist.

New programs are emerging to meet the needs of city-dwelling Native Americans. Founded in 1975, the Native American Education Service College in Chicago is an independent, accredited college trying to partially meet the need of that city's 16,000 Native Americans, who represent 100 tribes. It offers college degrees with specialized courses in Native American language and history. The college emphasizes small classes and individualized instruction. Yet this institution is not only unusual in higher education but is also unusual in offering urban Native Americans a pluralistic solution to being an American Indian in White America (C. Lauerman, 1993).

PAN-INDIANISM

The growth of pan-Indian activism is an example of both panethnicity and social protest. *Pan-Indianism* refers to intertribal social movements in which several tribes, joined by culture but not by kinship, unite to confront an enemy. Proponents of this movement see the tribes as captive nations or internal colonies. They generally see the enemy as the federal government. Until recently, pan-Indian efforts have usually failed to overcome the cultural differences and distrust among tribal groups. There have, however, been successful efforts to unite, even in the past. The Iroquois make up a six-tribe confederation dating back to the seventeenth century. The Ghost Dance briefly united the Plains tribes during the 1880s, some of which had earlier combined to withstand cavalry attacks. But these were the exceptions. It took nearly a century and a half of BIA policies to accomplish a significant level of unification.

The National Congress of American Indians (NCAI), founded in 1944 in Denver, Colorado, was the first national organization representing Native Americans. The NCAI registered itself as a lobby in Washington, D.C., hoping to make the

---

°°*Ibid.*

Native American perspective heard. Concern about "White peoples' meddling" is reflected in the NCAI requirement that White members pay twice as much in dues. The NCAI has had its successes. Early in its history, it played an important role in creating the Indian Claims Commission, and it later pressured the BIA to abandon the practice of termination. It is still the most important civil rights organization for Native Americans and uses tactics similar to those of the NAACP, although the problems facing African Americans and Native Americans are legally and constitutionally different.

A more recent arrival is the more radical American Indian Movement (AIM), the most visible pan-Indian group. The AIM was founded in 1968 by Clyde Bellecourt (of the White Earth Chippewa) and Dennis Banks (of the Pine Ridge Oglala Sioux), both of whom then lived in Minneapolis. Initially, AIM created a "patrol" to monitor police actions in order to document charges of police brutality. Eventually, it promoted programs for alcohol rehabilitation and school reform. By 1972, AIM was nationally known not for its neighborhood-based reforms but for its aggressive confrontations with the BIA and law enforcement agencies.

Fish-Ins and Alcatraz

Fish-ins began in 1964 to protest interference by Washington State officials with Native Americans who were fishing, as they argued, in accordance with the 1854 Treaty of Medicine Creek and were not subject to fine or imprisonment, even if they did violate White society's law. This protest was initially blocked by disunity and apathy, but several hundred Native Americans were convinced that civil disobedience was their only recourse to bring attention to their grievances with the government. Legal battles followed, and the U.S. Supreme Court confirmed the treaty rights in 1968. Other tribes continued to fight in the courts, but the fish-ins brought increased public awareness of the deprivations of Native Americans. One of the longest battles continues to the present: the Chippewas have rights to 50 percent of the fish, timber, and wildlife across the upper third of Wisconsin. In 1991, Wisconsin agreed with this long-standing treaty right, but Whites continue to demonstrate against what they feel is the unfair advantage extended to the Native Americans (L. Jolidon, 1991; S. Steiner, 1968).

The fish-ins were only the beginning. After the favorable Supreme Court decision in 1968, other events followed in quick succession. In 1969, members of the San Francisco Indian Center seized Alcatraz Island in San Francisco Bay. The 13-acre island was once a maximum-security federal prison that had been abandoned, and the federal government was undecided about how to use it. The Native Americans claimed "the excess property" in exchange for $24 in glass beads and cloth, following the precedent set in the sale of Manhattan more than three centuries earlier. The protesters left the island more than a year later, and their desire to transform it into an Native American cultural center was ignored. Despite the outcome, the event gained international publicity for their cause. Red Power was born, and those Native Americans who sympathized with the BIA were branded either "Uncle Tomahawks" or "apples" (red on the outside, white on the inside).

The federal government did not totally ignore calls for a new policy that involved Native Americans in its formulation. Nevertheless, no major breakthroughs came in the 1960s. One significant step, however, was passage of the Alaska Native Settlement Act of 1971. Alaskan Native American people—the Inuits and Aleuts—have maintained their claim to the land since Alaska was purchased from Russia in 1867. The federal government had allowed the natives to settle on about one-third of the land they claimed but had not even granted them title to that land. The discovery of huge oil reserves in 1969 made the issue more explosive, as the state of Alaska auctioned off mineral rights, ignoring Inuit occupation of the land. The Alaskan Federation of Natives (AFN), the major native Alaskan group, which had been organized in 1967, quickly moved to stop "the biggest land grab in the history of the U.S." as the AFN termed it. The AFN-sponsored bill was revised, and a compromise—the Native Claims Settlement Act—was passed in late 1971. The final act, which fell short of the requests by the AFN, granted control and ownership of 44 million acres to Alaska's 53,000 Inuits, Aleuts, and other peoples and gave them a cash settlement of nearly $1 billion. Given the enormous pressures from oil companies and conservationists, however, the Native Claims Settlement Act can be regarded as one of the more reasonable agreements reached between Native Americans and the government. Further reforms in 1988 helped to safeguard the original act, but as a major trade-off the Alaskan Native Americans surrendered future claims to all aboriginal lands (P. Iverson, 1993; S. Langdon, 1982; S. Nickerson, 1971).

Protest Efforts

The federal government, by closing the door to those presenting grievances and by the lack of positive movement, ensured that it would be only a matter of time before Native Americans took new steps to be heard.

It is little wonder, then, that the 1970s were marked by increasingly militant protests by Native Americans. One moderate group organized a summer-long caravan to reach the nation's capital just when the presidential election was being held in 1972. The Nixon administration, increasingly distrustful of protesting Native Americans, refused to meet with them. The militant AIM then emerged as the leader of those frustrated by government unresponsiveness.

The most dramatic confrontation between Native Americans and the government came early the next year in the Battle of Wounded Knee II. In January 1973, AIM leader Russell Means led an unsuccessful drive to impeach Richard Wilson as tribal chairman of the Oglala Sioux tribe on the Pine Ridge Reservation. In the next month, Means, accompanied by some 300 supporters, started a 70-day occupation of Wounded Knee, South Dakota, site of the infamous cavalry assault in 1890 and now part of the Pine Ridge Reservation. The occupation received tremendous press coverage.

Did this coverage affect the outcome? Negotiations between AIM and the federal government on the occupation itself brought no tangible results. Federal prosecutions were initiated against most participants. Although AIM leaders Russell Means and Dennis Banks were eventually cleared of all charges, they faced prosecution on a number of felony charges. Both men were eventually imprisoned. AIM has had less visibility as an organization since then. Russell Means wryly remarked in 1984, "We're not chic now. We're just Indians and we have to help ourselves" (N. Hentoff, 1984, p. 23; also see P. Matthiessen, 1983; J. Nagel, 1988; Roos et al., 1977; A. Trimble, 1976).

In the 1990s, AIM became less controversial than when it had confronted the establishment with protests and mass demonstrations. Recently, AIM members and others have brought attention to the use of Native Americans as the mascots of sports teams, such as the Washington Redskins, as well as to such spectator practices as the "Tomahawk chop" associated with the Atlanta Braves. Yet AIM meetings have also witnessed charges and countercharges hurled among the leaders of rival factions (S. Davis, 1994a; Wittstock and Salinas, 1994).

The most visible recent AIM activity has been its efforts to gain clemency for one of its leaders, Leonard Peltier. Imprisoned since 1976, Peltier was given two life sentences for murdering two FBI agents the year before on the embattled Sioux reservation of Pine Ridge, South Dakota. Fellow AIM leaders such as Dennis Banks organized a 1994 Walk for Justice to bring attention to Washington, D.C., to the view that Peltier is innocent. This view had been supported in two 1992 movie releases: the documentary *Incident at Oglala,* produced by Robert Redford, and the more entertaining, fictionalized *Thunderheart.* To date, clemency appeals to the president to lift the federal sentence have gone unheeded, but this issue remains the rallying point for today's remnants of AIM (V. Bielski, 1994; *Spirit of Crazy Horse,* 1994).

In 1994, a symbolic show of support for Native Americans took place in the nation's capital; only time will whether significant reforms will result. President Bill Clinton issued invitations to all 547 federally-recognized tribal leaders—the largest meeting ever with a U.S. president. On the lengthy agenda were issues such as:

- Tribal sovereignty
- Law enforcement and juvenile delinquency
- Casinos and the gaming industry
- Religious freedom
- Natural resources protection

Ada Deer, now director of BIA and earlier leader of the Menominee anti-Termination effort, declared that the historic meetings should erase the "vanishing Indian" image of an old warrior riding a horse alone down the last trail: "We have an opportunity, a moment in history now, to address many of these long-standing issues and problems. This is not just a show" (L. Kanamine, 1994, p. A2).

Clinton issued federal directives to accommodate Native Americans' need for eagle feathers for spiritual purposes and to consult with tribes over the use of their natural resources. Yet leaders have already expressed dismay over a proposed 13 percent cut in the 1995 budget for the Indian Health Service. The remaining years of the twentieth century will either support or refute Deer's hopeful statement (S. Davis, 1994b; D. Jehl, 1994).

Menominee tribe member Ada Deer, leader of the DRUMS effort to overturn termination policy in the 1970s, is sworn in to head the BIA in 1993. It is very unusual for Native Americans to have a leadership position in government.

Pan-Indianism: An Overview

Pan-Indianism, an example of panethnicity, has created a greater solidarity among Native Americans as they seek the solution to common grievances with government agencies. Whether through moderate groups like the NCAI or the more activist AIM, these developments have awakened Whites to the real grievances of Native Americans and have garnered the begrudging acceptance of even the most conservative tribal members who are more willing to cooperate with governmental action.

The results of pan-Indianism, however, have not all been productive, even when viewed from a perspective sympathetic to Native American self-determination. The national organizations are dominated by Plains tribes, not only politically but culturally as well. Powwow styles of dancing, singing, and costuming derived from the Plains tradition are spreading nationwide as common cultural traits.

The growing visibility of powwows is symbolic of Native Americans in the 1990s. The phrase *pau wau* referred to the medicine man or spiritual leader of the Algonquian tribes, but Europeans who watched medicine men dance thought the word referred to entire events. Over the last hundred years, *powwows* have evolved into gatherings in which Native Americans of many tribes come to dance, sing, play music, and visit. More recently, they have become organized events featuring competitions and prizes at over 1,000 locations. The general public sees them as entertainment, but for Native Americans, they are a celebration of their culture (M. Parfit, 1994).

NATIVE AMERICANS TODAY

The United States has taken most of the land from Native Americans, has restricted their movement, has unilaterally severed agreements, has created a special legal status for them, and, after World War II, has attempted to move them again. After all this ill treatment, how well are they doing today?

There is no easy answer for native peoples, who face a variety of challenges. Tribal women in the United States face the "double jeopardy" of gender and racial subordination. In "Listen to Their Voices," Yvonne Swan gives testimony to her experiences.

Any discussion of Native American socioeconomic status today must begin with an emphasis on the diversity of the people. Besides the variety of tribal heritages already noted, the contemporary Native American population is split between those on and off reservations and those living in small towns and in central cities. Life in these contrasting social environments is quite different, but there are enough similarities to warrant some broad generalizations on the status of Native Americans in the United States today.

The sections that follow summarize the status of contemporary Native Americans in employment and income, education, health care, and religious and spiritual expression.

Employment and Income

The Native Americans are an impoverished people. To even the most casual observer of a reservation, the poverty is a living reality and not merely numbers and percentages. Some visitors seem unconcerned, arguing that, because Native Americans are used to hardship and lived a simple life before the Europeans arrived, there is no need to worry now. In an absolute sense of dollars earned or quality of housing, Native Americans are no worse off now. But in a relative sense

Listen to Their Voices
The Light Within

Yvonne Swan

Swan, a member of Sinixt, Arrow Lakes Nation, is a mother and an advocate of prisoners' rights. In 1975, a known child molester broke into her home; she killed him in an effort to protect herself. She was charged with murder, and the case resulted in a U.S. Supreme Court case expanding women's right to self-defense.

I have been reflecting on the past eighteen years that I have been involved with AIM. I needed a lot of strength along the way because I faced a lot of obstacles as a woman and as a Native person. The one thing that helped me through all this turmoil was the spiritual strength, the teachings and the recognition that I received from the elders.

Yvonne Swan, Sinixt, Arrow Lakes Nation

each woman has to do is go within, find who she is, and cherish and hang on to that, because that is life itself.

Once you have that strength, that feeling of belonging and that pride, you can face anything. There is never any end to the learning. It becomes a driving force within to keep searching, and then the doors are always being opened. It is a beautiful experience. Daily prayer, no matter how brief, is the strength that keeps us going. Ask the ancestors, especially the grandmothers. They are waiting and wanting to help you.

When I was faced with a prison sentence, for example, I was terrified. There was nowhere to turn. I was facing a white court system and the prospect of going to prison and leaving my family and children. But I drew on the traditions, the culture, and the spiritual teachings. I went within. What

Source: Reprinted from Ronnie Farley, ed., *Women of the Native Struggle.* New York: Onion Books, 1993, p. 62.

that compares their position to that of Whites, they are dismally behind on all standards of income and occupational status. The 1990 census revealed that Native American families are about three times more likely to live below the poverty level and are much less likely to have a wage earner employed full-time. Nationwide, about a third of Native Americans live in poverty and have family incomes typically 35–40 percent lower than that of the total population (Bureau of the Census, 1993a). Furthermore, domination by Europeans, sociologist Murray Wax (1971) writes, has disrupted the Native Americans' "system of economic and social interdependence," a situation not measurable in statistics (p. 194).

Given the lower incomes and higher poverty rates, it is little surprise that the occupational distribution of Native Americans is similarly bleak. Those who are employed are less likely to be managers, professionals, technicians, salespeople, or administrators. Compared to the total population, employed Native Americans are more likely to be in farming, forestry, fishing, and repair occupations (Bureau of the Census, 1993a).

Tourism is an important source of employment for many reservation residents, who either directly serve the needs of visitors or provide souvenirs and craft items. Generally, such enterprises do not achieve the kind of success that significantly improves the tribal economy. Even if it did, sociologist Murray Wax (1971) argues, "It requires a special type of person to tolerate exposing himself and his family life to the gaze of tourists who are often boorish and sometimes offensively condescending in their attitudes" (p. 69).

Anthropologist Joan Laxson (1991) interviewed tourists visiting museums and reservations and found that, regardless of the presentation, the visitors interpreted their brief experiences to be consistent with their previously held stereotypes of and prejudices toward Native Americans.

Craft work rarely realizes the profits most Native Americans desire and need. Most Whites are interested in trinkets, not the more expensive and profitable items. The trading-post business has also taken its toll on Native American cultures. Many craft workers have been manipulated by Whites and other Native Americans to produce what the tourists want. Creativity and authenticity have frequently been replaced by mechanical duplication of "genuine Indian" curios. There is a growing concern and controversy surrounding alleged Native American art such as paintings and pottery fetching high prices that may not be produced by real Native Americans. The price of economic survival is very high (National Public Radio, 1992; M. Smith, 1982; C. Snipp, 1980; S. Steiner, 1976; J. Sweet, 1990).

A more recent source of significant income and some employment has been the introduction of gambling on reservations. Under the 1988 Indian Gaming Reg-

The growth of casinos is a mixed blessing to tribes such as Sisseton-Wapheton Sioux of South Dakota.

ulatory Act, states must negotiate gambling agreements with reservations and cannot prohibit any gambling already allowed under state law. By 1994, tribes in 23 states were operating a variety of gambling operations, including off-track betting, casino tables such as blackjack and roulette, lotteries, sports betting, video games of chance, telephone betting, slot machines, and high-stakes bingo. The gamblers are almost all non–Native Americans who sometimes travel long distances for the opportunity to wager money. The economic impact on some reservations has been enormous, and nationwide the profits from gambling were about $600 million in 1994 for the 200 tribes involved. Some successful casinos have led to staggering annual payments to small tribes: $400,000 in 1993 for a group of 100 in Mdevakantons in Minnesota is one such example. However, the more typical picture is of moderately successful gambling operations associated with tribes whose social and economic needs are overwhelming. The majority of native people living off-reservation receive little benefit.

Criticism is not hard to find, even among Native Americans who oppose gambling not only on moral grounds but because it is marketed in a form incompatible with Native American culture. Besides the majority of the gamblers not being Native Americans, virtually all of the reservation casinos are being managed by White-owned businesses. Some tribal members feel that the casinos trivialize and cheapen their heritage. In addition, established White gaming interests in Nevada and Atlantic City, New Jersey, are beginning to lobby Congress to restrict the tribes even though Native Americans generate only 5 percent of the nation's gambling revenue. On the Mohawk reservation along the Canada–New York State border, the battle over gambling combined with other issues has become extremely violent. Despite this tragic experience, gambling is on the rise (P. Annin, 1994; R. Denny, 1992; K. Johnson, 1994).

Another major source of employment is the government, principally the BIA, but also other federal agencies, the military, and state and local government. In 1970, one of every four employed Native Americans worked for the government. More than half the BIA's employees have tribal ancestry. In fact, since 1854, the BIA has had a policy of giving employment preference to Native Americans over Whites. This policy has been questioned, but the U.S. Supreme Court (*Morton v. Mancari*) upheld the policy in 1974. Although this is a significant source of employment opportunity, many criticisms have been leveled at Native American government workers, especially federal employees.

There is little question that government employees form a subculture in Native American communities. They tend to be Christians, educated in BIA schools, and sometimes the third generation born into government service. Discrimination against Native Americans in private industry makes government work attractive, and once a person is employed and has seniority, he or she is virtually guaranteed security. Of course, this security may lead some individuals (whether Native Americans or Whites) to smugness and less-than-efficient work. Finally, the large number of "feds," or BIA workers, further divides a community already in desperate need of unity (Bureau of Indian Affairs, 1970; C. Rachlin, 1970).

Tribal members who move to small towns near the reservations frequently encounter strong reactions against their being employed. Ralph Luebben (1964) found that, in areas bordering the massive Navajo reservation in Arizona, New Mexico, and Utah, members of the tribe were nearly always hired at the lowest level, regardless of the need for labor or the qualifications of the individual. The Navajos expected prejudice and discrimination, and their expectations in the employment sector were usually borne out.

We have examined the sources of employment, such as tourism, government service, legalized gambling, and businesses in towns adjoining reservations, but the dominant feature of reservation life is unemployment. A government report issued by the Full Employment Action Council opened with the statement that such words as *severe, massive,* and *horrendous* are appropriate to describe unemployment among Native Americans. Official unemployment figures for reservations range from 23 percent to 90 percent. It is little wonder that the 1990 Census showed that the poorest county in the nation was wholly on tribal lands: Shannon County, South Dakota, of the Pine Ridge Reservation had a 63 percent poverty rate. Unemployment rates for urban-based Indians are also very high; Los Angeles reports more than 40 percent, and Minneapolis 49 percent (Cornell and Kalt, 1990; L. Kanamine, 1992; T. Knudson, 1987; C. Sullivan, 1986).

The economic outlook for Native Americans need not be bleak. A single program is not the solution; the diversity of both them and their problems demands a multifaceted approach. The solutions need not be unduly expensive; indeed, because the Native American population is exceedingly small compared to the total population, programs with major influence may be financed without significant federal expenditures. Murray Wax (1971) observed that reformers often view the depressed position of Native Americans economically and quickly seize on education as the key to success. As the next section shows, improving the educational programs for Native Americans would be a good place to start.

Education

Government involvement in the education of Native Americans dates as far back as a 1794 treaty with the Oneida Indians. In the 1840s, the federal government and missionary groups combined to start the first school for American Indians. By 1860, the government was operating schools that were free of missionary involvement. Today, laws prohibit federal funds for Native American education from going to sectarian schools. Also, since the passage of the Johnson-O'Malley Act in 1934, the federal government has reimbursed public school districts that include Native American children.

Federal control of the education of Native American children has had mixed results from the beginning. Several tribes started their own school systems at the beginning of the nineteenth century, completely financing the schools themselves. The Cherokee tribe developed an extensive school system that taught both English and Cherokee, the latter using an alphabet developed by the famed leader Sequoyah. Literacy for the Cherokees was estimated by the mid-1800s at 90 percent, and they even published a bilingual newspaper. The Creeks, Chickasaws, and Seminoles also maintained school systems. But by the end of the nineteenth century, all these schools had been closed by federal order. Not until the 1930s did the federal government become committed to ensuring an education for Native American children. Despite the push for educational participation, by 1948 only a quarter of the children on the Navajo reservation, the nation's largest, were attending school (D. Adams, 1988; Bureau of Indian Affairs, 1970, 1974; Fuchs and Havighurst, 1972).

Educational Attainment A serious problem in Native American education has been the unusually high level of underenrollment. Many children never attend school, or they leave while in elementary school and never return. Enrollment rates are as low as 30 percent for Alaska Eskimos (or Inuits). Another discouraging sign is the high dropout rate, which is at least 50 percent higher than that of Blacks or Hispanics and nearly three times that of Whites. The term *dropout* is misleading because many tribal American schoolchildren have found their educational experience so hostile that they had no choice but to leave (D. Kelly, 1991).

Rosalie Wax (1967) conducted a detailed study of the education among the Sioux on the Pine Ridge Reservation of South Dakota. She concluded that terms like *kickout* or *pushout* are more appropriate. The children are not so much hostile to school as they are set apart from it; they are socialized by their parents to be independent and not to embarrass their peers, but teachers reward docile acceptance and expect schoolchildren to correct one another in public. Socialization is not all that separates home from school. Teachers are often happy to find parents not "interfering" with their job. Parents do not visit the school, and teachers avoid the homes, a pattern that only furthers the isolation of school from home. This lack of interaction is partly due to the predominance of non-Native American teachers, although the situation is improving.

Quality of Schooling The quality of Native American education is more difficult to measure than the quantity. How does one measure excellence? And excellence for what? White society? Tribal life? Both? Chapter 1 discussed the disagreement over measuring intellectual achievement (how much a person has learned) and the greater hazards in measuring intellectual aptitude (how much a person is able to learn). It is not necessary to repeat the arguments. Studies of reservation children, using tests of intelligence that do not require a knowledge of English, consistently show scores at or above the levels of intellectual middle-class urban children. Yet, in the upper grades, a *crossover effect* appears when the tests used assume lifelong familiarity with English. Native American students drop behind their White peers and so would be classified by the dominant society as underachievers (Bureau of Indian Affairs, 1988, pp. 69–72; Coleman et al., 1966, p. 450; Fuchs and Havighurst, 1972, pp. 118–135).

Preoccupation with such test results perhaps avoids the more important question: Educational excellence for what? It would be a mistake to assume that the tribal peoples have reached a consensus. They do wish, however, to see a curriculum that, at the very least, considers the unique aspects of their heritage. Charles Silberman (1971, p. 173) reported visiting a sixth-grade English class in a school on a Chippewa reservation where the students were all busily at work writing a composition for Thanksgiving: "Why We Are Happy the Pilgrims Came." A 1991

Department of Education report entitled "Indian Nations at Risk" still found the curriculum presented from a European perspective. It is little wonder when a 1990 national survey found that, at 48 percent of all schools Native American children attend, there is not a single Native American teacher.

Some positive changes in education are occurring. About 23 percent of the students in BIA-funded schools receive bilingual education, but as yet, no coordinator exists in the BIA for this important activity. There is growing recognition of the need to move away from past policies that suppressed or ignored the native language and to acknowledge that educational results may be maximized when the native language is included (Bureau of Indian Affairs, 1988; R. Wells, 1991).

Higher Education   The picture for Native Americans in higher education is decidedly mixed with some progress and some promise. Enrollment in college steadily increased from the mid-1970s through the mid-1990s, but degree completion, especially the completion of professional degrees, may actually be declining. The economic and educational background of Native American students, especially reservation residents, makes considering entering a predominantly White college a very difficult decision. Native American students may soon feel isolated and discouraged, particularly if the college does not help them understand the alien world of European-style higher education. Even at campuses with large Native American student bodies, there are few Native American faculty or advisers to serve as role models. About 53 percent of the students leave at the end of their first year (Carnegie Foundation for the Advancement of Teaching, 1990; R. Wells, 1989).

The most encouraging development in higher education in recent years has been the creation of tribally controlled colleges—usually two-year community colleges. The Navajo Community College, the first such institution, was established in 1968, and by 1993 there were 27 nationwide. Besides serving in some rural areas as the only educational institution for many miles, tribal colleges also provide services such as counseling and child care. Tribal colleges enable the students to maintain their cultural identity while training them to succeed outside the reservation. About 90 percent of Native American students who leave the reservation for traditional college drop out, but 35 percent entering tribal colleges go on to complete their bachelor's degree, and another 53 percent find jobs after leaving tribal college.

Funding for tribal colleges is a major problem. When Congress passed the Tribally Controlled Community College Assistance Act in 1978, it proposed $5,280 per year in federal funds for every full-time student. Over the years, the assistance has been under $3,000, jeopardizing the ability to maintain adequate educational programming (B. Campbell, 1992; J. Kleinhuizen, 1991b; L. McMillen, 1991).

As the levels advance, Native Americans virtually disappear from the educational scene. In 1992, of the 25,759 doctorates awarded to U.S. citizens, 148 went to Native Americans, compared to the over 13,000 that went to citizens of foreign countries (Carter and Wilson, 1993).

Summary   "Dine bizaad beeyashti!" Unfortunately this declaration, "I speak Navajo!" is not commonly heard from educators. Gradually, schools have begun to encourage the preservation of native cultures. Until the 1960s, BIA and mission schools forbade speaking in the native languages, so it will take time to produce an educated teacher corps knowledgeable in and conversant with native cultures (L. Linthicum, 1993).

As we have seen, there are many failures in our effort to educate, not just assimilate, the first Americans. These primary problems are as follows:

1. Underenrollment at all levels, from the primary grades through college
2. The need to adjust to a school with values sometimes dramatically different from those of the home
3. The need to make the curriculum more relevant
4. The underfinancing of tribal community colleges
5. The unique hardships encountered by reservation-born American Indians who later live in and attend schools in large cities
6. The language barrier faced by the many children who have little or no knowledge of English.

Other problems include lack of educational innovation (the BIA had no kindergartens until 1967) and a failure to provide special education to children who need it.

Health care received by Native Americans is another area in need of reform.

Native Americans have often been vulnerable to economic challenges.

Jerry Fearing, *St. Paul Pioneer Press.*

Health Care

For Native Americans, "health care" is a misnomer, another broken promise in the array of unmet promises that the government has made. Native Americans are more likely to die before age 45 than any other racial and ethnic group. What is equally frustrating, in 1994 they died of treatable diseases like tuberculosis, at rates 500 percent higher than the national rate (L. Kanamine, 1994). This dramatic difference arises out of their poverty, and also out of the lack of health services. There are only 96 doctors per 100,000 Native Americans, compared to 208 per 100,000 of the general population. Similarly there are 251 nurses per 100,000 Native Americans, contrasted to 672 per 100,000 for the nation as a whole (R. Coddington, 1991; L. Kanamine, 1992, 1994).

In 1955, the responsibility for health care for Native Americans was transferred from the BIA to the Public Health Service (PHS), and although their health has improved markedly since the mid-1960s, serious problems remain. As is true of industrial development and education, advances in health care are hampered by the poverty and geographic isolation of the reservation. Also, as in the educational and economic sectors, health policies, in effect, initiate a cultural war in which Native Americans must reject their traditions to secure better medical treatment.

With the pressure to assimilate Native Americans in all aspects of their lives, there has been little willingness to recognize their traditions of healing and treating illnesses. In the 1990s, there emerged a pluralistic effort to recognize alternative forms of medicine, including those practiced by Native Americans. In addition, reservation health-care workers have begun to accommodate traditional belief systems as they administer the White culture's medicine (N. Angier, 1993; E. Fox, 1992).

It is not merely that Native Americans have more diseases and shorter life spans than the rest of the population. Indians have acute problems in such areas as mental health, nutrition, the needs of the elderly, and alcoholism, which have been documented for generations but have only recently been addressed through innovative programs. Further improvement can be expected, but it will be some time before the gains make health care for Native Americans comparable to that for the general population (P. Edmonds, 1992).

Subordinate groups in the United States, including Native Americans, have made tremendous gains and will continue to do so in the years to come. But the rest of the population is not standing still. As Native American income rises, so, too, does White income. As Native American children stay in school longer, so, too, do White children. American Indian health care improves, but so, too, does White health care. Advances have been made, but the gap remains between the descendants of the first Americans and those of later arrivals. Low incomes, inadequate education, and poor health care spurred Native American–White relations to take a dramatic turn in the 1960s and 1970s, when Native Americans demanded a better life in America (American Indian Policy Review Commission, 1976a; 1976b; 1976c).

Religious and Spiritual Expression

Like other aspects of Native American culture, the expression of religion is diverse, reflecting the variety of tribal traditions and the assimilationist pressure of the Europeans. Indeed, Christopher Columbus's diary recorded on his very first day in the New World, October 12, 1492, "They ought to be good servants and of good intelligence. . . . I believe that they would easily be made Christians because it seems to me that they had no religion" (W. Echo-Hawk, 1992, p. 1).

Following generations of formal and informal pressure to adopt Christian faiths and their rituals, in 1978 Congress enacted the American Indian Religious Freedom Act, which declares that it is the government's policy to "protect and preserve the inherent right of American Indians to believe, express, and practice their traditional religions." However, the act contains no penalties or enforcement mechanisms. For this reason, Hopi leader Vernon Masayesva (1994) refers to it as "the law with no teeth" (p. 93). Therefore, Native Americans are lobbying to strengthen this 1978 legislation. They are seeking protection for religious worship services for military personnel and incarcerated Native Americans, as well as better access to religious relics such as eagle feathers and better safeguards against the exploitation of sacred lands (M. Burgess, 1992; V. Deloria, 1992; Friends Committee on National Legislation, 1993).

In recent years, significant publicity has been given to an old expression of religion: the peyote cult, which dates back to 1870. The sacramental use of peyote was first observed in the 1640s. First a Southwest-based religion, it has spread since World War II among northern tribes. In 1918, the religious use of peyote, a plant that creates mild psychedelic effects, was organized as the Native American Church (NAC). The use of the substances is a relatively small part of a long and moving ritual. The exact nature of NAC rituals varies widely. Clearly, it maintains the tradition of ritual curing and the seeking of individual visions. However, practitioners also embrace elements of Christianity representing a type of religious pluralism of "Indian" and "European" identities. Peyote is a hallucinogen, however, and the government has been concerned about NAC use of it. Several states passed laws in the 1920s and 1930s prohibiting the use of peyote. The federal government and the states began to exempt the religious use of peyote from criminal penalties—a policy that defenders view as an application of the First Amendment guarantee of the free exercise of religion. However, the State of Oregon did not accept peyotism; its refusal to do so became the center of a controversy that made its way to the U.S. Supreme Court in *Oregon v. Alfred Smith*, a Sioux. Eventually, in 1990, the Supreme Court held, by a 6–3 vote, that prosecuting people who use illegal drugs as a part of religious rituals is not a violation of the First Amendment guarantee of religious freedom. Dissenting justices and civil libertarians worried that this ruling would inevitably be used against the rituals of "minor" (but not "major") religions. Indeed, Justice Sandra Day O'Connor called the majority opinion "incompatible with our nation's fundamental commitment to individual religious liberty" (L. Greenhouse, 1990, p. A10). The following year, Oregon passed a law protecting the Native American use of peyote, but the specter of prosecution remains in much of the nation. Now 28 states offer some type of protection from prosecution (H. Dellios, 1993; Lawson and Morris, 1991).

Another area of spiritual concern is the stockpiling of Native American relics, including burial remains. Contemporary Native Americans are increasingly seeking the return of their ancestors' remains and artifacts, alarming museums and archaeologists. Legislation is proposed which would require an inventory of such collections and provide for the return of materials if a claim can be substantiated. Many scholars believe the ancient bones and burial artifacts to be valuable clues to humanity's past. Yet, in part, this belief reflects a difference in cultural traditions. Western scientists have been dissecting cadavers for hundreds of years, but many tribes believe that disturbing the graves of ancestors will bring spiritual sickness to the living. Today's Native Americans are asking for their traditions to be recognized as an expression of pluralist rather than assimilationist coexistence. These traditions are also closely tied to religion. The need to reform the 1978 American Indian Religious Freedom Act was underscored when the Supreme Court held in *Lyng v. Northwest Indian Cemetery Protection Association* (1988) that the U.S. Forest Service could construct a road through a mountain area sacred to three tribes. The Court declared that the government could act only if its purpose was secular and did not specifically aim to harm a religion. Sacred sites of Native Americans are clearly under attack as well as their religious practices (G. Cowley, 1989; W. Echo-Hawk, 1992; R. Schmidt, 1994).

CONCLUSION

Do Native Americans have to choose between assimilating to the dominant White culture and maintaining their identity? It is not easy to maintain one's tribal identity outside the reservations. One has to consciously seek out one's cultural heritage amid the pressure to assimilate. Even on a reservation, it is not easy to integrate being Native American with elements of contemporary society. The dominant society needs innovative approaches to facilitate pluralism. For example, anthropologist George Esber, Jr. (1987) was hired to work with some Apaches in Arizona and a group of architects to design a new community for the Apaches. The architects were expected to accommodate the distinctive traditions and customs of this Native American tribe; as a result, Esber was hired to obtain relevant information concerning the Apaches' housing needs and preferences. To do so, he reviewed written records of the Apaches and conducted fieldwork, overcoming the Apaches' understandable concerns about an outsider coming into their community, asking personal questions, and observing their day-to-day interactions.

Esber was ultimately successful in discussing important issues with the Apaches and communicating to the architects those features of Apache life that should guide the community design. Consequently, when the Apaches moved into their new homes in 1981, they entered a community that had been designed with their participation and with their specific traditions in mind. For example, it was essential that each new house have a large, open living space. The culture of the Apaches requires that all participants in a social situation remain in full view, so that each person can observe the behavior of all others and act appropriately according to Apache norms and values.

The Apaches are also accustomed to major social gatherings at people's homes, at which an offering of food precedes other social interactions. Consequently, based on Esber's findings, the architects designed large kitchens (with extra-large sinks, cupboards, and worktables) that were conveniently near the dining areas and living rooms. In these ways and others, the planners of this new community took into account and respected the unique cultural traditions of the Apaches. We need more pluralistic approaches such as this one.

Amid the diversity of the United States, the first Americans are not alone in experiencing subordination. Both African Americans and Native Americans are more likely than Whites to have lower incomes, to suffer from poor health, and to experience prejudice and discrimination. Both groups have protested against these injustices for centuries. Beginning in the 1960s, these protests gained a new sense of urgency. But there, the similarities between the nearly 29 million African Americans and the 2 million Native Americans in the United States end.

The reservation is not a ghetto. It is economically depressed, but it is the home of the Native American people even, if not always physically, then ideologically. Furthermore, the reservation's isolation means that the frustrations of reservation life and the violent outbursts against them do not alarm large numbers of Whites as do disturbances in Black ghettos. Native Americans today, except in motion pictures, are out of sight and out of mind. The federal government, since the BIA was created in 1824, has had much greater control over Native Americans than over any other civilian group in the nation. For Native Americans, the federal government and White people are virtually synonymous. The typical White, however, tends to be more sympathetic, if not paternalistic, toward Native Americans than toward African Americans.

As Chapter 7 will show, African Americans have achieved a measure of recognition in Washington, D.C. that Native Americans have not. They are only 5 percent as numerous as the Black population, so that their collective voice is weaker. Only a handful of Native Americans have ever served in Congress, and many of the Whites representing states with large numbers of Native Americans emerged as their biggest foes, much less their advocates.

Another enemy of the Native American people is their disunity: full-bloods are pitted against mixed-bloods, reservation residents against city dwellers, tribe against tribe, conservative against militant. This disunity reflects the diversity of cultural backgrounds and historical experiences represented by the people collectively referred to as Native Americans. This disunity is also counterproductive when it comes to confronting a central government. Pan-Indianism has made tremendous strides since the weak alliances formed by a few tribes hundreds of years ago, but the current mood serves as much to split as to unify Native Americans nationally. Symptomatic were government hearings in 1989 that, rather than focusing on the BIA bureaucracy, quickly shifted attention to alleged corruption among tribal leaders. One does not need to be a sociologist to see this as another case of "blaming the victim."

The greatest challenge to and asset of the descendants of the first Americans is their land. Although only a small slice of what they once occupied, the land they still possess is a rich natural resource. It is barren and largely unproductive agriculturally, but it is unspoiled, relatively free of pollution, and often rich in natural resources. No wonder many large businesses, land developers, and casino managers covet their land. For Native Americans, the land they still occupy, as well as much of that occupied by other Americans, represents their roots, their homeland.

On Thanksgiving Day 1988, one scholar noted that, according to tradition, at the first Thanksgiving in 1621 the Pilgrims and the Wampanoag ate together. The descendants of these celebrants increasingly sit at distant tables with thoughts of equality equally distant. Today's Native Americans are the "most undernourished, most short-lived, least educated, least healthy." For them, "That long ago Thanksgiving was not a milestone, not a promise. It was the last full meal" (M. Dorris, 1988).

KEY TERMS

crossover effect An effect that appears as previously high-scoring Native American children become "below average" in intelligence when tests are given in English rather than their native languages.

fish-ins Tribes' protests over government interference with their traditional rights to fish as they would like.

kickouts or **pushouts** Native American school dropouts, who leave behind an unhealthy academic environment.

millenarian movements Movements, such as the Ghost Dance, that prophesy a cataclysm in the immediate future, followed by collective salvation.

pan-Indianism Intertribal social movements in which several tribes, joined by culture but not by kinship, unite, usually to confront an enemy such as the federal government.

powwows Native American gatherings of dancing, singing, music playing, and visiting, accompanied by competitions.

setoffs Deductions from money due in U.S. government settlements with Native Americans, equal to the cost of federal services provided to the tribe.

FOR FURTHER INFORMATION

Ronet Bachman. *Death and Violence on the Reservation: Homicide, Family Violence, and Suicide in American Indian Populations.* New York: Auburn House, 1992.

Death and violence on contemporary reservations as aggravated by economic deprivation and social disorganization.

Dee Brown. *Bury My Heart at Wounded Knee.* New York: Holt, Rinehart & Winston, 1971.

Focuses on what the author calls the "incredible era of violence, greed, audacity, sentimentality, [and] undirected exuberance" toward Native Americans from 1860 to 1890.

Stephan Cornell and Joseph P. Kalt, eds. *What Can Tribes Do? Strategies and Institutions in American Indian Economic Development.* Los Angeles: American Indian Studies Center, 1992.

This anthology addresses the economic problems and solutions facing Native Americans.

Vine Deloria, Jr. *Custer Died for Your Sins: An Indian Manifesto.* New York: Avon, 1969.

Although much has happened since Deloria wrote this book, it remains an excellent, readable explanation for non–Native Americans about why Native Americans are tired of being oppressed. In often witty writing, Deloria touches on termination policy, missionaries, Native American leadership, and the BIA.

Al Gedicks. *The New Resource Wars.* Boston: South End Press, 1993.

An analysis of the challenges facing the tribal control of natural resources in light of the role played by multinational corporations.

M. Annette Jaimes, ed. *The State of Native America.* Boston: South End Press, 1992.

Drawing mostly on Native American writers, Jaimes, a Juaneño-Yaqui, explores the various circumstances confronted by Native Americans in the contemporary United States.

Alvin M. Josephy, ed. *America in 1492.* New York: Random House, 1991.

A collection of anthropological writings about the world of Native Americans before the arrival of Columbus.

Edward Lazarus. *Black Hills White Justice.* New York: HarperCollins, 1991.

A detailed account of the ongoing legal fight of the Sioux Nation from 1755 to the present.

Nicholas C. Peroff. *Menominee Drums.* Norman: University of Oklahoma Press, 1982.

Political scientist Peroff traces the history of the Wisconsin tribe from termination to the successful restoration of reservation rights in 1974.

Stephen L. Pevar. *The Rights of Indians and Tribes,* 2d ed. Carbondale: Southern Illinois University Press, 1992.

Completed under the auspices of the American Civil Liberties Union, this book summarizes Native American rights without resorting to too much legal jargon.

Linda Shorten. *Without Reserve: Stories from Urban Natives.* Edmonton, Alberta: NeWest Press, 1991.

A collection of autobiographical profiles of individual native people who live in urban Canada.

C. Matther Snipp. *American Indians: The First of This Land.* New York: Sage, 1989.

A detailed demographic study of American Indians, including analyses of housing, household composition, education, occupation, and migration.

Christopher Vecsey, ed. *Handbook of American Indian Religious Freedom.* New York: Crossroad, 1991.

Examines how religious practices are undermined.

Periodicals

Many tribes publish regular newspapers, and there are also national papers: *Akwesasne Notes,* founded in 1969, and *News from Indiana Country,* founded in 1986. Journals include the *American Indian Culture and Research Journal* (1977), a quarterly published by University of California at Los Angeles (UCLA); *American Indian Religions: An Interdisciplinary Journal* (1994), a quarterly of the UCLA American Indian Studies Center; *Indian Historian* (1967), a quarterly published by the American Indian Historical Society; the *Journal of American Indian Education* (1961), published three times a year by Arizona State University; and *Tribal College* (1989), a quarterly. In terms of indigenous peoples worldwide, Amnesty International publishes numerous reports, and *CovertAction Information Bulletin* (1983) appears quarterly.

CRITICAL THINKING QUESTIONS

1. What contact have you had either directly (face-to-face) or indirectly (through the media) with Native Americans?
2. How has land rights been a continuing theme in White–Native American contact?
3. Why have Native American issues been easier to ignore than those advanced by African Americans or Hispanics?
4. How much, if at all, should Native Americans shed of their cultural heritage to become a part of contemporary society?
5. Do casinos and other gaming outlets represent a positive force for Native American tribes today?

Chapter
7

The Making of
African Americans
in a White America

Chapter Outline

Highlights

The African presence in America began almost simultaneously with permanent White settlement. Unlike Europeans, however, the African people were brought involuntarily and in bondage. The end of slavery heralded new political rights during Reconstruction, but this was a short-lived era of dignity. The twentieth century witnessed the movement of Blacks northward and the beginning of a Black protest movement that was assisted by some sympathetic Whites.

Despite advocacy of nonviolence by leaders such as the Reverend Martin Luther King, Jr., the civil rights movement was met with violent resistance throughout the South. In the middle 1960s, the nation's attention was diverted to urban violence in the North and the West. Blacks responded to the absence of significant change despite years of protest by advocating Black Power, which, in turn, was met with White resistance. Religion was and continues to be a major force in the African-American community.

The United States, with more than 30 million Blacks (or African Americans), has the sixth largest Black population in the world; only Brazil, Ethiopia, Nigeria, South Africa, and Zaire have larger Black populations. Despite their large numbers, Blacks in this country have had virtually no role in major national and political decisions and have been allowed only a peripheral role in many crucial decisions influencing their own destiny.

The history of African Americans, to a significant degree, is the history of the United States. Black people accompanied the first explorers, and a Black man was among the first to die in the American Revolution. The enslavement of Africans was responsible for the South's wealth in the nineteenth century and led to the country's most violent domestic strife. Their continued subordination has led to sporadic outbreaks of violence in the rural South and throughout urban America. This chapter concentrates on the history of African Americans into the 1990s, and their contemporary situation is the subject of Chapter 8.

The Black experience in what came to be the United States began as something less than citizenship yet slightly better than slavery. In 1619, twenty Africans arrived in Jamestown as indentured servants. Their children were born free people. These Blacks in the British colonies were not the first in the New World, however, for some Blacks had accompanied Spanish explorers, perhaps even Columbus. But all this is a historical footnote. By the 1660s, the British colonies had passed laws making Africans slaves for life, forbidding interracial marriages, and making children of slaves bear the status of their mother. Slavery had begun in North America; more than three centuries later we still live with its legacy.

SLAVERY

Slavery seems far removed from the debates over issues that divide Whites and Blacks today. Both contemporary institutional and individual racism, however, which are central to today's conflicts, have their origins in the institution of slavery. Slavery was not merely a single aspect of American society for three centuries; it has been an essential part of our country's life. For nearly half of this country's history, slavery not only was tolerated but was legally protected by the U.S. Constitution and the U.S. Supreme Court. Because it was so fundamental to our culture, it continues to exert influence on Black–White relations in the 1990s.

Slave Codes

Slavery in the United States rested on four central conditions: first, that slavery was for life and was inherited; second, that slaves were considered merely property; third, that slaves were denied rights; and fourth, that coercion was used to maintain the system (D. Noel, 1972). As slavery developed in colonial America and the United States (see Table 7.1), *slave codes* were created to clarify the position of slaves. Although the rules varied from state to state and from time to time and were not always enforced, the more common features demonstrate how completely subjugated the Africans were.

1. A slave could not marry or even meet with a free Black.
2. Marriage between slaves was not legally recognized.
3. A slave could not buy or sell anything unless by special arrangement.
4. A slave could not possess weapons or liquor.
5. A slave could not quarrel with or use abusive language with Whites.
6. A slave could not possess property (including money), except as allowed by his or her owner.
7. A slave could make no will, nor could he or she inherit anything.
8. A slave could not make a contract or hire himself or herself out.
9. Slaves could not leave a plantation without a pass noting their destination and time of return.
10. No one, including Whites, was to teach slaves (and in some areas even free Blacks) to read or write, or to give them books, including the Bible.
11. Slaves could not gamble.
12. Slaves had to obey established curfews.
13. A slave could not testify in court except against another slave (S. Elkins, 1959; Franklin and Moss, 1994; K. Stampp, 1956).

Violations of these rules were dealt with in a variety of ways. Mutilation and branding were not unknown. Imprisonment was rare; most violators were whipped. An owner was virtually immune from prosecution for any physical abuse of slaves. Because slaves could not testify in court, a White's actions toward enslaved African Americans was practically above the law.

Slavery, as enforced through the slave codes, controlled and determined all facets of the lives of the enslaved Africans. The organization of family life and religious wor-

Table 7.1   BLACK POPULATION, 1790–2000

Blacks accounted for a decreasing proportion of the total population until the 1940s, primarily because White immigration to the United States far outdistanced population growth by Blacks.

Census	Black Population (in thousands)	Black Percentage of Total Population
1790	757	19.3
1810	1,378	19.0
1830	2,329	18.1
1850	3,639	15.7
1870	4,880	12.7
1890	7,489	11.9
1910	9,828	10.7
1930	11,891	9.7
1950	15,042	10.0
1970	22,581	11.1
1990	29,986	12.1
1995	32,117	12.6
2000 (projection)	35,469	12.8
2050 (projection)	61,586	15.7

Source: Bureau of the Census (1960, p. 9; 1995, p. 18).

ship were no exceptions. Naturally, the Africans had brought to America their own cultural traditions. In Africa, people had been accustomed to a closely regulated family life and a rigidly enforced moral code. The slave trade rendered it impossible for them to retain family ties in the New World. The demand for male Africans created an extreme imbalance in the sexes in the slave population. It was not until 1840, two centuries after African slave labor had begun, that the number of Black women equaled the number of Black men in America. Religious life in Africa was rich with rituals and beliefs, but like family structures, the religious practices of the slaves were to undergo a major transformation in the New World (W. Du Bois, 1970; K. Stampp, 1956).

The slave family had no standing in law. Marriages among slaves were not legally recognized, and masters rarely respected them in selling adults or children. Slave breeding—deliberate efforts to maximize the number of offspring—was practiced with little attention to the emotional needs of the slaves themselves. The owner, not the parents, decided at what age children should begin working in the fields. The slave family could not offer its children shelter or security, rewards or punishments. The man's only recognized family role was that of siring offspring, being the sex partner of a woman. In fact, slave men were often identified as if they were the woman's possession, for example, as "Nancy's Tom." Southern law consistently ruled that "the father of a slave is unknown to our law." This is not to imply that the male slave did not occupy an important economic role. Men held virtually all the managerial positions open to slaves.

Unlike the family, which slavery victimized, a strong religious tradition survived slavery. In fact, an owner wishing to do "God's work on earth" would encourage the slave church, finding it functional in dominating the slaves. Of course, African religions were forbidden, and the White people's Christianity flourished, but Blacks still used West African concepts in the totally new way of life caused by slavery. The preacher maintained an intense, dependent relationship with the congregation, similar to the role played by the elder in West Africa. The Christianity to which the slaves were introduced stressed obeying their owner. Complete surrender to Whites meant salvation and eternal happiness in the hereafter. To question God's will, to fight slavery, caused everlasting damnation. Obviously, this twisted version of Christianity was intended to make slaves acquiesce to their owners' wishes in return for reward after death. However, to some degree, religion did keep alive in slaves the desire for freedom, and to some extent, it formed the basis of their struggle for freedom: nightly prayer meetings and singing gave a sense of unity and common destiny necessary for that struggle. On a more personal level, religion made the slaves' daily lives more bearable (E. Frazier, 1964; G. Rawick, 1972; K. Stampp, 1956).

African Americans and Africa

The importance of Africa to Black Americans can be seen in the aspects of African culture that became integral parts of Blacks' lives in the United States. This importance was recognized long before the emergence of the Afrocentric perspective in the 1990s. Black scholars W. E. B. Du Bois (1939) and Carter Woodson (1968), along with respected White anthropologist Melville Herskovits (1930, 1941), have all argued persuasively for the continued influence of the African heritage.

Scholars debate to what degree African culture was able to persist despite efforts by slave owners to rid their human property of any vestiges of African traditions. It would appear that the survival of African culture can be most easily documented in folklore, religion, and music. It is difficult to clarify the degree of survival because Africans came from many different cultures, and while they all encountered oppression, the form of the forced assimilation differed in the Americas. Furthermore, the Afrocentric perspective argues that there are some aspects of African culture such as certain art forms, that have so permeated Western culture that we mistake its origin as being European.

Africa has had and will always have an importance to Blacks that many Blacks and most Whites do not appreciate, and this importance is unlikely to be influenced by the continued debate over which aspects of Black life today can be traced back to African culture. The significance of Africa to Black Americans is one of the most easily identifiable themes in the Black experience. During certain periods (the 1920s and the late 1960s), the Black cultural tradition was the rallying point of many Blacks, especially those living in the cities. Studies continue to document the survival of African culture in North America. Research on the Sea Islands along the coast of

Kwanzaa is a nonreligious cultural celebration of African-American values developed in the United States in 1966. This annual event, which starts on December 26, is gaining in popularity and, to the concern of its proponents, is becoming more commercialized.

South Carolina and Georgia shows movement and dance among Blacks similar to that in African folklore. The Sea Island inhabitants have been isolated from the mainland and therefore are less assimilated into the rest of society (R. Toner, 1987; M. Twining, 1985). The social significance of African culture in America rests not in its integrity or availability to scientific study, as in the Sea Islands studies, but in the extent to which it becomes real and significant to African Americans (R. Blauner, 1972).

The Attack on Slavery

Although the slave was vulnerable to his or her owner's wishes, slavery as an institution was vulnerable to outside opinion. For a generation after the American Revolution, restrictions on slaves increased as southerners accepted slavery as permanent. Slave revolts and antislavery propaganda only accelerated the intensity of oppression. This change led to the ironic situation that, as slavery was attacked from within and without, it became harsher and its defenders became more outspoken in asserting what they saw as its benefits (G. Fitzhugh, 1857).

The antislavery, or *abolitionist,* movement involved both Whites and free Blacks. Many Whites who opposed slavery, such as Abraham Lincoln, did not believe in racial equality. In their minds, slavery was a moral evil, but racial equality was unimaginable. This apparent inconsistency did not lessen the emotional fervor of the efforts to end slavery. Antislavery societies had been founded even before the American Revolution, but the Constitution dealt the antislavery movement a blow. In order to appease the South, the writers of the Constitution recognized and legitimized slavery's existence. The Constitution even allowed slavery to increase southern political power. A slave was counted as three-fifths of a person in determining population representation in the House of Representatives.

Another aspect of Black enslavement was resistance to servitude by the slaves themselves. Slaves did revolt, and between 40,000 and 100,000 actually escaped from the South and slavery. Yet fugitive slave acts provided for the return even of slaves who had reached free states. Enslaved Blacks who did not attempt escape, which, in failure, often led to death, resisted slavery through such means as passive resistance. Slaves feigned clumsiness or illness; pretended not to understand, see, or hear; ridiculed Whites with a mocking, subtle humor that their owners did not comprehend; and destroyed farm implements and committed similar acts of sabotage (Bauer and Bauer, 1942; L. Bennett, 1966; J. Oakes, 1993).

SLAVERY'S AFTERMATH

On January 1, 1863, President Lincoln issued the Emancipation Proclamation. The document created hope in slaves in the South, but many Union soldiers resigned rather than participated in a struggle to free slaves. The proclamation freed slaves only in the Confederacy, over which the president had no control. The 800,000 slaves in the border states were unaffected. The proclamation was a war measure effective in gaining the support of European nations for the Union cause. Shortly after the surrender of the Confederacy in 1865, abolition became a fact when the Thirteenth Amendment abolished slavery throughout the nation.

From 1867 to 1877, during the period called Reconstruction, Black–White relations in the South were unlike what they had ever been. The Reconstruction Act of 1867 put each southern state under a military governor until a new state constitution could be written with Blacks fully participating in the process. Whites and Blacks married each other, went to public schools and state universities together, and rode side by side on trains and streetcars. The most conspicuous evidence of the new position of Blacks was their presence in elected office. In 1870, the Fifteenth Amendment was ratified, prohibiting the denial of the right to vote on grounds of race, color, or previous condition of servitude. Black men put their vote to good use; Blacks were elected as six lieutenant governors, 16 major state officials, 20 members of the House of Representatives, and two U.S. senators. Despite accusations that they were corrupt, Black officials and

Black-dominated legislatures created new and progressive state constitutions. Black political organizations, such as the Union League and the Loyal League, rivaled the church as the focus of community organization (L. Bennett, 1965, 1966; W. Du Bois, 1969b).

With the fall of Reconstruction governments, segregation became entrenched in the South. Evidence of Jim Crow's reign was apparent by the close of the nineteenth century. The term *Jim Crow* appears to have its origin in a dance tune, but by the 1890s it was synonymous with segregation and referred to the statutes that kept African Americans in an inferior position. Laws, C. Vann Woodward (1974) argues, were not always "an adequate index of the extent and prevalence of segregation and discriminatory practices in the South" (p. 102). Segregation often preceded laws and often went beyond their provisions. The institutionalization of segregation gave White supremacy its ultimate authority. In 1896, the U.S. Supreme Court ruled in *Plessy v. Ferguson* that state laws requiring "separate but equal" accommodations for Blacks were a "reasonable" use of state government power (L. Bennett, 1966; C. Woodward, 1974).

It was in the political sphere that Jim Crow exacted its price soonest. In 1898, the Court's decision in *Williams v. Mississippi* declared constitutional the use of poll taxes, literacy tests, and residential requirements to discourage Blacks from voting. In Louisiana that year, 130,000 Blacks were registered to vote. Eight years later only 1,342 were. Even all these measures did not deprive all African Americans of the vote, and so White supremacists erected a final obstacle. By the turn of the century, the South had a one-party system, making the primary the significant contest and the general election a mere rubber stamp. Beginning with South Carolina in 1896 and spreading to 12 other states within 20 years, statewide Democratic Party primaries were adopted. The party explicitly excluded Blacks from voting, an exclusion that was constitutional because the party was defined as a private organization free to define its membership. The *White primary* brought a virtual end to the political gains of Reconstruction (D. Lacy, 1972; P. Lewinson, 1965; C. Woodward, 1974).

THE CHALLENGE OF BLACK LEADERSHIP

The institutionalization of White supremacy precipitated different responses from African Americans, just as slavery had. In the late 1800s and early 1900s, a number of articulate Blacks attempted to lead the first generation of freeborn Black Americans. Most prominent were Booker T. Washington and W. E. B. Du Bois. The personalities as well as the ideas of these two men contrasted with one another. Washington was born a slave in 1856 on a Virginia plantation. He worked in coal mines after emancipation and attended elementary school. Through hard work and driving ambition, Washington became the head of an educational institute for Blacks in Tuskegee, Alabama. Within 15 years, his leadership brought Tuskegee Institute national recognition and made him a national figure. Du Bois, on the other hand, was born in 1868 of a free family in Massachusetts. He attended Fisk University and the University of Berlin and became the first Black to receive a doctorate from Harvard. Washington died in 1915, while Du Bois died in self-imposed exile in Africa in 1963.

The Politics of Accommodation

Booker T. Washington's approach to White supremacy is referred to as the *politics of accommodation*. He was willing to forego social equality until White people saw Blacks as deserving of it. Perhaps his most famous speech was the one made in Atlanta on September 18, 1895, to an audience that was mostly White, and mostly wealthy. Introduced by the governor of Georgia as "a representative of Negro enterprise and Negro civilization," Washington (1900) made a five-minute speech in which he pledged the continued dedication of Blacks to Whites:

> As we have proved our loyalty to you in the past, in nursing your children, watching by the sick-bed of your mothers and fathers, and often following them with tear-dimmed eyes to their graves, so in the future, in our humble way, we shall stand by you with a devotion that no foreigner can approach, ready to lay down our lives, if need be, in defense of yours. (p. 221)

The speech catapulted Washington into the public forum, and he became the anointed spokesperson for Blacks for the next 20 years. President Grover Cleveland congratulated Washington for the "new hope" he gave Blacks. Washington's essential theme was compromise. Unlike Frederick Douglass, who had demanded for Blacks the same rights as for Whites, Washington asked that Blacks receive more education because it would be a wise investment for Whites. Racial hatred he referred to as "the great and intricate problem which God has laid at the doors of the South." The Blacks' goal should be economic respectability. Washington's accommodative attitude ensured his popularity with Whites. His recognition by Whites contributed to his large following of Blacks, who were not used to seeing their leaders achieve fame among Whites (H. Hawkins, 1962; R. Logan, 1954; A. Pinkney, 1994).

It is easy in retrospect to be critical of Washington and to write him off as simply a product of his times. Booker T. Washington entered the public arena when the more militant proposals of Douglass had been buried. Black politicians were losing political contests and influence. To become influential as a Black, Washington reasoned, required White acceptance. His image as an accommodator allowed him to fight discrimination covertly. He assisted presidents Roosevelt and Taft in appointing Blacks to patronage positions. Washington's goal was for African Americans eventually to have the same rights and

A 1935 lynching in Ft. Lauderdale of an African American who had been charged with "threatening and frightening" a White woman. Over 3,200 Blacks were executed by lynching between 1889 and 1938.

opportunities as Whites. Just as people disagree with leaders today, some Blacks disagreed over the means that Washington chose to reach that goal. No African American was more outspoken in his criticism of the politics of accommodation than W. E. B. Du Bois (L. Harlan, 1972; H. Hawkins, 1962; Meier and Rudwick, 1966).

The Niagara Movement

The rivalry of Washington and Du Bois has been overdramatized. Actually, they enjoyed fairly cordial relations for some time. In 1900, Washington recommended Du Bois, at his request, to be superintendent of Black schools in Washington, D.C. By the time the Niagara Movement arose in 1905, however, relations between the two had cooled. Du Bois spoke critically of Washington's influence, arguing that his power was being used to stifle African Americans such as himself who spoke out against the politics of accommodation. He also charged that Washington had caused the transfer of funds from academic programs to vocational education. Du Bois's greatest objection to Washington's statements was that they encouraged Whites to place the burden of the Blacks' problems on the Blacks themselves (W. Du Bois, 1961; see also H. Hawkins, 1962).

As an alternative to Washington's program, Du Bois (1903) advocated the theory of the *talented tenth,* which reflected his atypical educational background. Unlike Washington, Du Bois was not at home with both intellectuals and sharecroppers. Although the very words *talented tenth* have an aristocratic ring to them, Du Bois argued that the privileged Blacks must serve the other nine-tenths. This argument was also Du Bois's way of criticizing Washington's emphasis on vocational education. He thought education for African Americans should emphasize academics, which would be more likely to improve their position. Drawing on the talented tenth, Du Bois invited 29 Blacks to participate in a strategy session near Niagara Falls in 1905. Out of a series of meetings came several demands that unmistakably placed the responsibility for the problems facing African Americans on the shoulders of Whites.

The Niagara Movement, as it came to be called, was closely monitored by Booker T. Washington. Du Bois encountered difficulty gaining financial support and recruiting prominent people, and Du Bois (1968) himself was to write, "My leadership was solely of ideas. I never was, nor ever will be, personally popular" (p. 303). The movement's legacy was the education of a new generation of African Americans in the politics of protest. After 1910, the Niagara Movement ceased to hold annual conventions. In 1909, however, the National Association for the Advancement of Colored People (NAACP), with White and Black members, was founded by the Niagara Movement leaders. It was through the work of the NAACP that the Niagara Movement accomplished most of the goals set forth in 1905. The NAACP also marked the merging of White liberalism and Black militancy, a coalition unknown since the end of the abolition movement and Reconstruction (L. Bennett, 1966; E. Rudwick, 1957).

THE EXODUS NORTHWARD

The most significant event for African Americans during the first half of the twentieth century was not in the realm of legal or social rights, but the demographic change in the distribution of Black people. In 1900, 90 percent of African Americans lived in the South. As shown in Figure 7.1, Blacks have moved out of the South and into the West and North, especially the urban areas

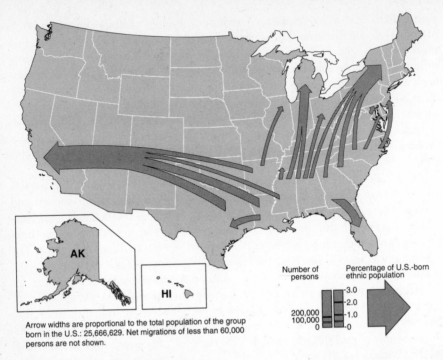

Arrow widths are proportional to the total population of the group born in the U.S.: 25,666,629. Net migrations of less than 60,000 persons are not shown.

Figure 7.1 Migration of Black Americans
This map shows the origin of Black Americans based on their residence in 1980. It shows net internal migration out of the southeastern part of the United States.

Source: Reprinted with permission of Macmillan Publishing Company from *We the People: An Atlas of Ethnic Diversity,* p. 148, by James Paul Allen and Eugene James Turner. Copyright © 1988 by Macmillan Publishing Company, a division of Macmillan, Inc.

in those regions, during the post–Civil War period and continuing through the 1950s and 1960s. However, most African Americans still live in the South in the 1990s.

Life in the North was generally better than it had been in the South, where agricultural conditions had considerably worsened. Although the migrants entered the job market at the bottom and lived in the worst housing the North offered, they were still better off than in the rural South. The principal reason for Black migration out of the South was similar to the motivation for the many millions of Europeans who came to the United States: the search for better economic opportunities.

The pattern of violence, with Blacks usually the victims, started in the South during Reconstruction, continued into the twentieth century, and moved northward. In 1917, a riot in East St. Louis, Illinois, claimed the lives of 39 Blacks and nine Whites. The several days of violence resulted from White fear of social and economic gains made by Blacks. The summer of 1919 saw so much violence that it is commonly referred to as the *"red summer."* Twenty-six riots broke out through-out the country as White soldiers returned from World War I fearing the new com-petition that Blacks represented. This period of violence against African Ameri-cans also saw a resurgence of the Ku Klux Klan, which at its height had nearly nine million members (E. Bonacich, 1976; A. Grimshaw, 1969; R. Schaefer, 1969, p. 20, 1971, pp. 146–151, 1980).

The competition between African Americans and Whites for jobs was short-lived. The unionization of industrial plants by the all-White American Federation of Labor (AFL) generally meant the expulsion of all Blacks, regardless of their skills or seniority. The National Urban League, founded in 1911 by Blacks and Whites allied with Booker T. Washington, wrestled unsuccessfully with the mass unemployment of Blacks. The NAACP did not involve itself at this time with job discrimination. Basically, the needs and frustrations of African Americans in the growing ghettos of the North were unmet by the government and the existing organizations (L. Bennett, 1966; Franklin and Moss, 1994; D. Lacy, 1972; Meier and Rudwick, 1966).

REEMERGENCE OF BLACK PROTEST

American involvement in World War II signaled prosperity for both Whites and Blacks. Nearly a million African Americans served in the military in rigid-ly segregated units. Generally, more Blacks could participate in the armed ser-vices in World War II than in previous military engagements, but efforts by Blacks to contribute to the war effort at home were hampered by discrimina-tory practices in defense plants. A. Philip Randolph, president of the Brother-hood of Sleeping Car Porters, threatened to lead 100,000 Blacks in a march on Washington in 1941 to ensure their employment. Randolph's proposed tactic was nonviolent direct action, which he modeled on Mahatma Gandhi's prac-tices in India. Randolph made it clear that he intended the march to be all-Black, because he saw it as neither necessary nor desirable for Whites to lead Blacks to their own liberation. President Franklin Roosevelt responded to the pressure and agreed to issue an executive order prohibiting discrimination if Randolph would call off the march. Although the order and the Fair Employ-ment Practices Commission (FEPC) it set up did not fulfill the original promis-es, a precedent had been established for federal intervention in job discrimi-nation (H. Garfinkel, 1959).

Racial turmoil during World War II was not limited to threatened marches. Racial disturbances occurred in cities throughout the country, the worst riot being in Detroit in June 1943. In that case, President Roosevelt sent in 6,000 soldiers to quell the violence, which left 25 Blacks and nine Whites dead. The racial disor-ders were paralleled by a growth in civil disobedience as a means to achieve equality for Blacks. The Congress of Racial Equality (CORE) was founded in 1942 to fight discrimination with nonviolent direct action. This interracial group used sit-ins to open restaurants to Black patrons in Chicago, Baltimore, and Los Angeles. In 1947, CORE sent "freedom riders" to test a court ruling that prohibited segregation in interstate bus travel. In contrast to the red summer of 1919, the end of World War II was not followed by widespread racial violence, in part because the continued expansion of the postwar economy reduced competition between Whites and Blacks for employment (A. Grimshaw, 1969; Meier and Rudwick, 1966).

The 1933 Scottsboro trials involved nine Black youths charged with raping two White women. There were no less than seven retrials, and the result was several important U.S. Supreme Court decisions, including those stating that one cannot be denied an attorney and that Blacks cannot be automatically excluded from juries.

The war years and the period following saw several U.S. Supreme Court decisions that suggested that the High Court was moving away from tolerating racial inequities. The White primary elections endorsed in Jim Crow's formative period were finally challenged in the 1944 *Smith v. Allwright* decision. The effectiveness of the victory was limited, for many states simply passed new devices to frustrate the Black electorate.

A particularly repugnant legal device for relegating African Americans to second-class status was restrictive covenants. A *restrictive covenant* was a private contract entered into by neighborhood property owners stipulating that property could not be sold or rented to certain minority groups, thus ensuring that they could not live in the area. In 1948, the Supreme Court finally declared in *Shelley v. Kramer* that restrictive covenants were not constitutional, although it did not actually attack their discriminatory nature. The victory was in many ways less substantial than symbolic of the new willingness by the Supreme Court to uphold the rights of Black citizens.

The Democratic Party administrations of the late 1940s and early 1950s made a number of promises to Black Americans. The party adopted a strong civil rights platform, but its provisions were not enacted. Once again, union president Randolph threatened Washington, D.C., with a massive march. This time, he insisted that, as long as Blacks were subjected to a peacetime draft, the military must be desegregated. President Truman responded by issuing Executive Order No. 9981 on July 26, 1948, desegregating the armed forces. The U.S. Army abolished its quota system in 1950, and training camps for the Korean War were integrated. Desegregation was not complete, however, especially in the reserves and the National Guard, and even today charges of racial favoritism confront the armed forces. Whatever its shortcomings, the desegregation order offered African American an alternative to segregated civilian life (C. Moskos, 1966).

THE CIVIL RIGHTS MOVEMENT

It is difficult to say exactly when a social movement begins or ends. Usually, a movement's ideas or tactics precede the actual mobilization of people and continue long after the movement's driving force has been replaced by new ideals and techniques. This description applies to the civil rights movement and its successor, the continuing struggle for African American freedom. The civil rights movement gained momentum with a Supreme Court decision in 1954 and ended as a major force in Black America with the civil disorders of 1965 through 1968. Even prior to 1954, there were some confrontations of White supremacy: the CORE sit-ins of 1942 and efforts to desegregate buses in Baton Rouge, Louisiana, in 1953. However beginning in 1954, toppling the traditional barriers to full rights for Blacks was the rule, not the exception.

Struggle to Desegregate the Schools

For the majority of Black children, public school education meant attending segregated schools. Southern school districts assigned children to school by race, rather than by neighborhood, a practice that constituted *de jure* segregation. It was this form of legal humiliation that was attacked in the landmark decree of *Linda Brown et al. v. Board of Education of Topeka.*

Seven-year-old Linda Brown was not permitted to enroll in the grade school four blocks from her home in Topeka, Kansas. Rather, school board policy dictated that she attend the Black school almost two miles from her home. This denial led the NAACP Legal Defense and Educational Fund to bring suit on behalf of Linda Brown and 12 other Black children. The NAACP argued that the Fourteenth Amendment was intended to rule out segregation in public schools. Chief Justice Earl Warren of the Supreme Court wrote the unanimous opinion that "in the field of public education the doctrine of 'separate but equal' has no place. Separate educational facilities are inherently unequal."

The freedom that African Americans saw in their grasp at the time of the *Brown* decision essentially amounted to a reaffirmation of American values. What Blacks sought was assimilation into White American society. The motivation for the *Brown* suit came not merely because Black schools were inferior, although they were. Blacks were assigned to poorly ventilated and dilapidated buildings, overcrowded classrooms, and unqualified teachers. Less money was spent on Black schools than on White schools throughout the South, in both rural and metropolitan areas. The issue was not such tangible factors, however, but the intangible factor of not being allowed to go to school with Whites. All-Black schools could not be equal to all-White schools. Even in this victory, Blacks were reaffirming White society and the importance of an integrated educational experience.

Although *Brown* marked the beginning of the civil rights movement, the reaction to it showed just how deeply prejudice was held in the South. Resistance to court-ordered desegregation took many forms: some people called for impeachment of all the Supreme Court justices, others petitioned Congress to declare the Fourteenth Amendment unconstitutional, cities closed schools rather than comply, and the governor of Arkansas even used the State's National Guard to block Black students from entering a previously all-White high school in Little Rock.

The issue of school desegregation was extended to higher education, and Mississippi state troopers and the State's National Guard confronted each other over the 1962 admission of James Meredith, the first African American admitted to the University of Mississippi. Scores were injured and two were killed in this clash between segregationists and the law. A similar defiant stand was taken a year later by Governor George Wallace, who "stood in the schoolhouse door" to block two Blacks from enrolling in the University of Alabama. President Kennedy federalized the Alabama National Guard in order to guarantee admission of the students. *Brown* did not resolve the school controversy, and many questions still remain unanswered. More recently, the issue of school segregation resulting from neighborhood segregation has been debated. In the next chapter, another form of segregation, called *de facto* segregation, is examined more closely.

Civil Disobedience

The success of a year-long boycott of city buses in Montgomery, Alabama, dealt Jim Crow another setback. On December 1, 1955, Rosa Parks defied the law and

Linda Brown, of *Brown v. Board of Education,* standing in front of the school near her home that she could not attend because the schools of Topeka, Kansas, were segregated.

refused to give her seat on a crowded bus to a White man. Her defiance led to the organization of the Montgomery Improvement Association, headed by 26-year-old Martin Luther King, Jr., a Baptist minister with a Ph.D. from Boston University. The bus boycott was the first of many instances in which nonviolent direct action was employed as a means of obtaining for Blacks the rights that Whites already enjoyed. Initially, the boycott protested discourtesies to Blacks and asked that Black drivers be hired for bus routes in predominantly Black areas. Eventually, the demands included the outright end of segregated seating. The *Brown* decision woke up all of America to racial injustice, but the Montgomery boycott marked a significant shift away from the historical reliance on NAACP court battles (L. Killian, 1975).

The belief that individuals have the right to disobey the law under certain circumstances was not new; it had been used by Blacks before. Under King's leadership, however, *civil disobedience* became a widely used tactic and even gained a measure of acceptability among some prominent Whites. King, in his celebrated "Letter from Birmingham Jail" (1963), clearly distinguished between the laws to be obeyed and those to be disobeyed: "A just law is a man-made law of God. An unjust law is a code that is out of harmony with the moral law" (p. 82). In disobeying unjust laws, King (1958) developed this strategy.

1. *Active* nonviolent resistance to evil
2. Not seeking to defeat or humiliate opponents, but to win their friendship and understanding
3. Attacking the forces of evil rather than the people who happen to be doing the evil
4. Willingness to accept suffering without retaliating
5. Refusing to hate the opponent
6. Acting with the conviction that the universe is on the side of justice. (pp. 101–107)

King, like other Blacks before him and since, made it clear that passive acceptance of injustice was intolerable. He hoped that, by emphasizing nonviolence, southern Blacks would display their hostility to racism but that violent reaction by Whites would be undercut.

The pattern had now been established and a method devised to confront racism. But civil disobedience did not work quickly. The struggle to desegregate buses in the South, for example, took seven years. Civil disobedience was also not spontaneous. The success of the civil rights movement rested on a dense network of local efforts. People were spontaneously attracted to the efforts, but organized tactics and targets were crucial to dismantling racist institutions that had existed for generations (A. Morris, 1993).

The Battle of Birmingham

Beginning in April 1963, the Southern Christian Leadership Conference (SCLC), founded by King, began a series of marches in Birmingham to demand fair employment opportunities, desegregation of public facilities, and the release of 3,000 people arrested for participating in the marches. King, himself arrested, tells in "Listen to Their Voices" why civil disobedience and the confrontation that followed were necessary. In May, the Birmingham police used dogs and water from high-pressure hoses on the marchers, who included many schoolchildren.

The violence touched off sympathetic demonstrations of support throughout the country. In the next month, Medgar Evers, leader of the Mississippi NAACP,

Listen to Their Voices
Letter from Birmingham Jail

You may well ask: "Why direct action? Why sit-ins, marches and so forth? Isn't negotiation a better path?" You are quite right in calling for negotiation. Indeed, this is the very purpose of direct action. Nonviolent direct action seeks to create such a crisis and foster such a tension that a community which

Martin Luther King

has constantly refused to negotiate is forced to confront the issue. It seeks so to dramatize the issue that it can no longer be ignored. My citing the creation of tension as part of the work of the nonviolent-resister may sound rather shocking. But I must confess that I am not afraid of the word "tension." I have earnestly opposed violent tension, but there is a type of constructive, nonviolent tension which is necessary for growth. Just as Socrates felt that it was necessary to create a tension in the mind so that individuals could rise from the bondage of myths and half-truths to the unfettered realm of creative analysis and objective appraisal, so must we see the need for nonviolent gadflies to create the kind of tension in society that will help men rise from the dark depths of prejudice and racism to the majestic heights of understanding and brotherhood.

The purpose of our direct-action program is to create a situation so crisis-packed that it will inevitably open the door to negotiation. I therefore concur with you in your call for negotiation. Too long has our beloved Southland been bogged down in a tragic effort to live in monologue rather than dialogue. . . .

You express a great deal of anxiety over our willingness to break laws. This is certainly a legitimate concern. Since we so diligently urge people to obey the Supreme Court's decision of 1954 outlawing segregation in the public schools, at first glance it may seem rather paradoxical for us consciously to break laws. One may well ask: "How can you advocate breaking some laws and obeying others?" The answer lies in the fact that there are two types of laws: just and unjust. I would be the first to advocate obeying just laws. One has not only a legal but a moral responsibility to obey just laws. Conversely, one has a moral responsibility to disobey unjust laws. I would agree with St. Augustine that "an unjust law is no law at all."

Source: Excerpt from "Letter from Birmingham Jail," in *Why We Can't Wait,* by Martin Luther King, Jr. Copyright © 1963 and 1964 by Martin Luther King, Jr. Copyright © renewed 1991 by Coretta Scott King. Reprinted by permission of HarperCollins Publishers, Inc..

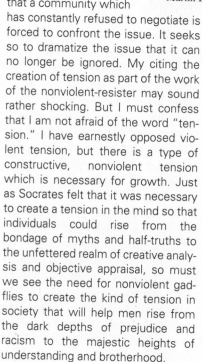

was shot in the back outside his house, an incident that touched off nationwide sit-ins, school strikes, and marches. His murderer was finally convicted in 1994. Following that violent summer of 1963, President Kennedy could delay no longer and submitted to Congress legislation to secure voting rights and to broaden government protection of Blacks' civil rights. But this initiative was followed by inaction, as Congress delayed.

Following the example of A. Philip Randolph in 1943, Blacks organized the March on Washington for Jobs and Freedom on August 28, 1963. With more than 200,000 people participating, the march was the high point of the civil rights movement. The mass of people, middle-class Whites and Blacks, looking to the federal government for support, symbolized the struggle. However, a public opinion poll conducted shortly before the march documented the continuing resentment of the majority of Whites: 63 percent were opposed to the rally (G. Gallup, 1972, p. 1836).

King (1971) delivered his famous "I Have a Dream" speech before the large crowd; he looked forward to a time when all Americans "will be able to join hands and sing in the words of the old Negro spiritual, 'Free at last! free at last! thank God almighty, we are free at last!'" (p. 351). Just 18 days later, a bomb exploded in a Black church in Birmingham, killing four little girls and injuring 20 others.

Despair only increased as the November 1963 elections saw segregationists successful in their bid for office. Most distressful was the assassination of President Kennedy on November 22. As president, Kennedy had significantly appealed to Blacks despite his previously mediocre legislative record in the U.S. Senate. His death left doubt as to the direction and pace of future actions on civil rights by the executive branch under President Lyndon Baines Johnson. Now, no time could be lost. Two months later, the Twenty-fourth Amendment was ratified, outlawing the poll tax that had long prevented Blacks from voting. The enactment of the Civil Rights Act on July 2, 1964 was hailed as a major victory and provided for at least a while what historian John Hope Franklin called "the illusion of equality" (Franklin and Moss, 1994).

In the months that followed, the pace of the movement to end racial injustice slowed. The violence continued, however, from the Bedford-Stuyvesant section in Brooklyn to Selma, Alabama. Southern state courts still found White murderers of Blacks innocent, and they had to be tried and convicted in federal civil, rather than criminal, court cases, on the charge that by killing a person one violates that person's civil rights. Government records, which did not become public until 1973, revealed a systematic campaign by the FBI to infiltrate civil rights groups in an effort to discredit them, claiming that such activist groups were subversive (N. Blackstock, 1976). It was in such an atmosphere that the Voting Rights Act was passed in August 1965, but this significant, positive event was somewhat overshadowed by violence in the Watts section of Los Angeles in the same week.

EXPLAINING URBAN VIOLENCE

Riots involving Whites and Blacks did not begin in the 1960s. As we saw earlier in this chapter, urban violence occurred after World War I and even during World War II, and violence against Blacks is nearly 350 years old. But the urban riots of the 1960s influenced Blacks and Whites in the United States and throughout the world so extensively that they deserve special attention. We must remember, however, that most violence between Whites and Blacks has not been large-scale collective action but has involved only a few people.

The summers of 1963 and 1964 were a prelude to riots that were to grip the country's attention. Although most people knew of the civil rights efforts in the South and legislative victories in Washington, everyone realized that the racial problem was national after several Northern cities experienced violent disorders. The riot in Los Angeles in August 1965 first shocked those who thought that racial harmony had been achieved. Thirty-four were killed in the Black ghetto of Watts in the worst riot since Detroit in 1943. Americans were used to tension between Whites and Blacks, but in the South, not the North, and certainly not in California (R. Blauner, 1972; R. Conot, 1967; C. Degler, 1969; A. Oberschall, 1968).

The next two years saw major riots in Cleveland, Newark, and Detroit. Violence was not limited to a few urban ghettos, however. One estimate for 1967 alone identifies 257 disorders in 173 cities claiming 87 lives, injuring 2,500, and leading to 19,200 arrests. In April of 1968, after the assassination of Martin Luther King, more cities exploded than had in all of 1967. Even before the summer of 1968 began, there were 369 civil disorders. Communities of all sizes were hit. More than one-fourth of race-related disturbances occurred in cities with populations of less than 25,000. Most of the civil disorders were relatively minor and probably would have received no publicity if the major riots had not created increased awareness (Baskin et al., 1971, 1972).

As the violence continued and embraced many ghettos, a popular explanation was that riot participants were mostly unemployed youths who had criminal records, often involving narcotics, and who were vastly outnumbered by the African Americans who repudiated the looting and arson. This explanation was called the *riff-raff* or *rotten-apple theory* because it discredited the rioters and left the barrel of apples, White society, untouched. On the contrary, research shows that the Black community expressed sympathetic understanding toward the rioters and that the rioters were not merely the poor and uneducated but included middle-class, working-class, and educated residents (Sears and McConahay, 1969, 1973; T. Tomlinson, 1969).

Several alternatives to the riff-raff theory explain why Black violent protest increased in the United States at a time when the nation was seemingly committed to civil rights for all. Two explanations stand out. One ascribes the problem to Black frustration with rising expectations in the face of continued deprivation relative to Whites. The other explanation points to increased national consciousness.

Rising Expectations and Relative Deprivation

The standards of living of African Americans improved remarkably after World War II, and it continued to do so during the civil rights movement. White income and occupation levels, however, did not remain unchanged either. Chapter 3 showed that feelings of relative deprivation are often the basis for seeing discrimination. *Relative deprivation* is the conscious feeling of a negative discrepancy between legitimate expectations and present actualities.

It is of little comfort to African Americans that their earning power matches that of Whites eight to ten years earlier. As shown in Figure 7.2, in 1959 the Black median family income was little more than half of White income. Five years later, Black income had jumped 21 percent, but White income had increased 16 percent, leaving the gap between the two intact. Most Blacks made no tangible gains in housing, education, jobs, or economic security. African Americans were doing better in absolute numbers, but not relative to Whites. As we consider the effect of this situation on African Americans, we must determine whom they select as an appropriate reference or comparison group. Frustration comes not from a group's absolute level of attainment, but from its position relative to the appropriate comparison group. David Matza (1971) wrote that "profound degradation in an absolute sense may be tolerable or even pass unnoticed if others close at hand fare no better or if one never had any reason to expect better" (p. 607n). The Blacks' situation was thus intolerable in both ways, because the continued greater affluence of Whites was apparent to Blacks at the same time that Blacks were consistently being promised.

Blacks felt that they had legitimate aspirations, and the civil rights movement reaffirmed that discrimination had blocked upward mobility. The civil rights movement gave higher aspirations to Black America, yet for the majority life remained basi-

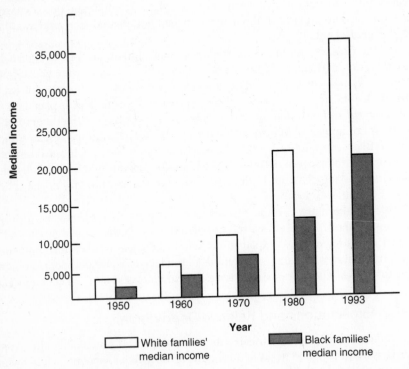

Figure 7.2 Black-White Income Gap
For the more than 40 years of available data, Black income has been only a fraction of White income.

Source: Bureau of the Census (1994, p. 48).

cally unchanged. Not only were their lives unchanged, but the feeling was widespread that the existing social structure held no prospect for improvement (Sears and McConahay, 1970, p. 133; also see Thomas and Thomas, 1984).

Developing a National Consciousness

The first riots in the 1960s were examined in an effort to find causes in the community: Had the chief of police misjudged the situation? Had it been crucial that the governor was vacationing out of the country? Would the riot have occurred if the unemployment rate had been slightly lower? As the rioting became a national phenomenon, such localized explanations were replaced by statistical efforts to find similarities among riot cities that contrasted them to nonriot cities.

The nature of the community was not important in explaining the outbreak of racial conflict, both because the federal government played a pivotal role, and because of the influence of the mass media in transforming local issues into national ones: The federal government was responsible for promoting or failing to promote racial equality. Blacks in Jacksonville and Boston were in many respects more affected by decisions in the nation's capital than in their own city halls. In addition, coverage of civil rights in the mass media, especially national television newscasts, created national interest and a national racial identity that transcended community boundaries. The mass media were criticized for emphasizing the emotional side of the riots, but the Kerner Commission, established to investigate the riots and their causes, found reporting to be calm and factual. Prior to the riots, however, the mass media coverage of the civil rights movement, documenting recognition by Whites or Black leaders, had served to develop a national consciousness. Blacks had become aware not of deprivation unique to their own neighborhood but of the deprivation common to all ghettos. Given this increased awareness of their low status despite years of promises, almost any Black community could explode (National Advisory Commission on Civil Disorders, 1968).

BLACK POWER

The riots in the northern ghettos captured the attention of Whites, and Black Power was what they heard. Appropriately enough, Black Power was born not of Black but of White violence. On June 6, 1966, James Meredith was carrying out a one-person march from Memphis to Jackson, Mississippi, to encourage fellow African Americans to overcome their own fears and vote, following the passage into law of the Voting Rights Act. During that march, an unidentified assailant shot and wounded Meredith. Blacks from throughout the country immediately continued the march, led by King of the SCLC, Floyd McKissick of CORE, and Stokely Carmichael of the Student Nonviolent Coordinating Committee (SNCC). Responding to King's pressure and his threat to withdraw financial support, McKissick and Carmichael agreed to open up the march to Whites. This was the last integrated effort by all the major civil rights organizations. During the march, Carmichael proclaimed to a cheering Black crowd, "What we need is Black Power." King and others later urged "Freedom Now" as the slogan for the march. A compromise dictated that no slogan would be used, but the mood of Black America dictated something else (M. King, 1967; L. Lomax, 1971).

In retrospect, it may be puzzling that the phrase *Black Power* frightened Whites and offended so many Blacks. It was not really new. The National Advisory Commission on Civil Disorders (1968, pp. 234–235) correctly identified it as old wine in new bottles: Black consciousness was not new even if the phrase was. Furthermore, it was the type of umbrella term that could mean everything or nothing. A survey of Detroit Blacks in the following year showed many respondents confused or vague about the concept (Aberbach and Walker, 1973). But to many Whites, the meaning was clear enough. Set against the backdrop of riots in the North, Black Power signaled to many that the civil rights movement was over. And indeed, they were right.

By advocating Black Power, Carmichael was distancing himself from the assimilationism of King. Carmichael rejected the goal of assimilation into White middle-class society. Instead, he said, Blacks must create new institutions. To succeed in this endeavor, Carmichael argued that Blacks must follow the same path as the Italians, Irish, and other White ethnic groups. "Before a group can enter the open society, it must first close ranks. . . . Group solidarity is necessary before a group can operate effectively from a bargaining position of strength in a pluralistic society" (Ture and Hamilton, 1992, p. 44). Prominent Black leaders opposed the concept; many feared that Whites would retaliate even more violently. King (1967) saw Black Power as a "cry of disappointment" but acknowledged that it had a "positive meaning."

Eventually Black Power gained wide acceptance among Blacks and even many Whites. Although it came to be defined differently by nearly every new proponent, support of Black Power generally implied endorsing Black control of the political, economic, and social institutions in Black communities. One reason for its popularity among African Americans was that it gave them a viable option for surviving in a segregated society (J. Ladner, 1967; A. Pinkney, 1994). The civil rights movement strove to end segregation, but the White response showed how committed White society was to maintaining it. Black Power presented restructuring society as the priority item on the Black agenda.

One aspect of Black Power clearly operated outside the conventional system. The Black Panther Party was organized in October 1966 in Oakland, California, by Huey Newton, aged 24, and Bobby Seale, aged 30, to protect Blacks from police abuse. The Panthers were controversial from the beginning. From 1969 to 1972, internal weaknesses, a long series of trials involving most of the leaders, intraparty strife, and several shoot-outs with police combined to bring the organization to a standstill. The Panthers, although they were frequently portrayed as the most separatist of the Black militant movements, were willing to form alliances with non-Black organizations, including Students for a Democratic Society (SDS), the Peace and Freedom Party, the Young Lords, the Young Patriots, and the Communist

Party of the United States. Despite, or perhaps because of, such coalitions, the Panthers were not a prominent force in shaping contemporary Black America. Newton himself admitted in 1973 that the party had alienated Blacks and had become "too radical" to be a part of the Black community (J. Abron, 1986; K. Cleaver, 1982; C. Woodward, 1974, p. 105).

The militant Black Panthers encountered severe difficulties during the 1970s and fell victim to both internal political problems and external surveillance. Finally, their formerly outspoken leaders moved in new directions. Eldridge Cleaver became a born-again Christian and confined himself to lecturing on the virtues of his evangelical faith. Cofounder Bobby Seale ran unsuccessfully for mayor of Oakland, California, in the kind of traditional campaign he had formerly denounced as unproductive. Following that unsuccessful bid, Seale became an organizer of moderate community groups. Former Panther defense minister Bobby Rush became deputy chairman of the Illinois State Democratic Party and was successfully elected to the U.S. Congress in 1992. The role of spokesperson for a minority group in the United States is exhausting, and people who have assumed that role for a time often turn to more conventional, less personally demanding roles, especially if public support for their programs wanes.

THE RELIGIOUS FORCE

It is not possible to overstate the role religion has played, good and bad, in the social history of African Americans. Historically, Black leaders have emerged from the pulpits to seek out rights on behalf of all Blacks. Churches have served as the basis for community organization in neighborhoods abandoned by businesses and even government. Religion has been a source of antagonism as well. For example, at least 93 southern Black churches were bombed or burned because they were leading the way in voter registration and in the promotion of community integration (Kosmin and Lachman, 1993).

As we saw earlier in this chapter, because the Africans who were brought involuntarily to the Western Hemisphere were non-Christian, they were seen as heathens and barbarians. To "civilize" the slaves in the period before the Civil War, southern slaveowners encouraged and often required their slaves to attend church and embrace Christianity. The Christian churches to which Blacks were introduced in the United States encouraged them to accept the inferior status enforced by Whites, and the religious teaching that the slaves received equated whiteness with salvation, presenting whiteness as an acceptable, if not preferred, object of reverence.

Despite being imposed in the past by Whites, the Christian faiths are embraced by most African Americans today. As shown in Figure 7.3, African Americans are overwhelmingly Protestant, half being Baptist. The Methodists and Roman Catholics account for another 9 percent each. Therefore, almost seven out

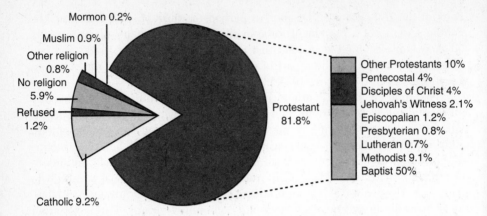

Figure 7.3 **Religious Profile of African Americans**
Based on a 1990 national sample, most African Americans are Baptist, Roman Catholic, or Methodist.
Source: Kosmin and Lachman (1993, p. 131).

of ten African Americans are members of these three faiths, compared to less than half of Whites.

However, a variety of non-Christian groups have exerted a much greater influence on African Americans than the reported numbers of their followers would suggest. The Nation of Islam, for example, which became known as the Black Muslims, has attracted a large number of followers and received the most attention. The Muslim religion was first introduced to Black Americans in 1930, with the arrival of Wali D. Fard, later called Mr. W. Fard Muhammad, in Detroit.

Under the leadership of Elijah Muhammad, Fard's most trusted follower and his successor, the Nation of Islam became a well-known, controversial organization. While Black Muslims were preaching racial hatred and suffering internal violence, they built a financial empire. Elements of White society have respected the Nation of Islam for its impressive use of capitalism to the organization's advantage and for the strict moral code its members follow. The membership of the group, now officially called the American Muslim Mission, dropped from 250,000 in the mid-1970s to 100,000 a decade later. W. Deen Muhammad, successor and son of Elijah Muhammad, has opened the faith to people of all races, although he acknowledges that it is basically an African-American organization. In 1985, Muhammad dissolved the sect, leaving the 200 mosques and worship centers to operate independently.

Malcolm X, originally a member of the Nation of Islam, became the most powerful and brilliant voice of Black self-determination in the 1960s. He was an authentic folk hero to his sympathizers. Besides his own followers, he commanded an international audience and is still referred to in a manner befitting a prophet. Indeed, Spike Lee's 1993 movie based on the *Autobiography of Malcolm X* reintroduced him to another generation. Malcolm X was highly critical of the civil rights movement in general and of Martin Luther King, Jr., in particular.

Malcolm X is not remembered for his stiff attacks on other Black leaders, for his break with the Nation of Islam, or even for his apparent shift to support the formation of coalitions with progressive Whites. Rather, he is remembered for teaching Blacks lessons which came to haunt the champions of nonviolent direct action—among them, that Blacks must resist violence "by any means necessary." During his last year, Malcolm X (by then known as Malik El-Shabazz) created the nonreligious Organization of Afro-American Unity, which was meant to internationalize the civil rights movement. Malcolm X's life was ended by three assassins in 1964. "His philosophy can be summarized as pride in Blackness, the necessity of knowing Black history, Black autonomy, Black unity, and self-determination for the Black community" (A. Pinkney, 1975, p. 213, 1993; see also L. Lomax, 1971; C. Woodward, 1974).

Minister Louis Farrakhan has been the most visible spokesperson among the various Muslim groups in the African-American community. Farrakhan broke with W. Deen Muhammad in 1977 and named his group Nation of Islam, adopting, along with the name, the more orthodox ideals of Elijah Muhammad, such as Black moral superiority. Farrakhan's endorsement of the candidacy of Rev. Jesse Jackson for both the 1984 and 1988 Democratic Party nomination for the presidency propelled Farrakhan into the limelight, although his public statements about Jews and Israel gave an anti-Semitic taint to Farrakhan's teachings. The split between Farrakhan and Muhammad is not new to the Black followers of Islam, as Malcolm X's life indicates (W. Henry, 1994; C. Lincoln, 1994).

While Farrakhan's statements against Whites—Jews in particular, and pro-Israel foreign policy—have attracted the media's attention, many of his speeches

Louis Farrakhan of the Nation of Islam is an outspoken leader who attracts support from many Blacks and much hostility from Whites.

and writings reflect the basic early tenets of the Nation of Islam. Abortion, drugs, and homosexuality are condemned. Self-help, bootstrap capitalism, and strict punishment are endorsed. He is not pessimistic about the future of race relations in the United States. As leader of the 1995 Million Man March, he encouraged those present and African Americans nationwide to register to vote and work for positive change (D. Terry, 1994; B. Turque, 1993).

CONCLUSION

The dramatic events affecting African Americans today have their roots in the fact that their ancestors were forcibly brought to the United States as slaves. In the South, whether as slaves or as victims of Jim Crow, Blacks were not a real threat to any but the poorest Whites, although even affluent Whites feared the potential threat that Blacks posed. During the time of slavery, revolts were met with increased suppression, but after emancipation, leaders calling for accommodation were applauded.

As Blacks moved to the urban North, a new social order was being defined. Whites found it more difficult to ignore Blacks as residents of the ghetto than as sharecroppers in the rural South. The Black urban voter had potential power, no longer excluded by the "White primary" as in the South. The federal government and city halls slowly began to acknowledge the presence of Blacks. From the Black community came voices that spoke of pride and self-help: Douglass, Washington, Du Bois, King, and Malcolm X.

Black and White Americans dealt with the continued disparity between the two groups by endorsing several ideologies. Assimilation was the driving force behind the civil rights movement, which sought to integrate Whites and Blacks into one society. People who rejected any contact with the other group endorsed separatism. The government and various Black organizations began to recognize cultural pluralism as a goal, at least paying lip service to the desire of many African Americans to exercise some autonomy over their own lives. Although Blacks differed on their willingness to form coalitions with Whites, they would have concurred with Du Bois's (1903) comment that a Black person "simply wishes to make it possible to be both a Negro and an American, without being cursed and spit upon by his fellows, without having the door of opportunity closed roughly in his face" (pp. 3–4). The object of Black protest seems simple enough, but on many, including presidents, the point was lost.

How much progress has been made? When covering several hundred years, beginning with slavery and ending with rights constitutionally recognized, it is easy to be impressed. Yet let us consider Topeka, Kansas, the site of the 1954 *Brown v. Board of Education* case. Linda Brown, one of the original plaintiffs, has recently seen another segregation case. In 1992, the courts held that Oliver Brown, her grandchild, was being victimized because the Topeka schools were still segregated, now for reasons of residential segregation. The remedy to separate schools in this Kansas city is still unresolved (K. Hays, 1994).

Chapter 8 assesses the status of African Americans today. Recall the events chronicled in this chapter as you consider the advances that have been made. These events are a reminder that any progress has followed years—indeed, generations—of struggle by African Americans, enlisting the support of Whites sympathetic to the removal of second-class status for African Americans in the United States.

KEY TERMS

abolitionists Whites and free Blacks who favored the end of slavery.

civil disobedience A tactic promoted by Martin Luther King, Jr., based on the belief that individuals have the right to disobey unjust laws under certain circumstances.

Jim Crow Southern laws passed during the latter part of the nineteenth century that kept Blacks in their subordinate position.

relative deprivation The conscious experience of a negative discrepancy between legitimate expectations and present actualities.

restrictive covenants Private contracts or agreements that discourage or prevent minority-group members from purchasing housing in a neighborhood.

riff-raff theory Also called the *rotten-apple theory;* the belief that the riots of the 1960s were caused by discontented youths, rather than by social and economic problems facing all African Americans.

slave codes Law that delineated the position held by enslaved Blacks in the United States.

White primary Legal provisions forbidding Black voting in election primaries, which in one-party areas of the South effectively denied Blacks their right to select elected officials.

FOR FURTHER INFORMATION

Molefi Kete Asante. *The Afrocentric Idea.* Philadelphia: Temple University Press, 1987.

Historians, philosophers, and others are taken to task for promoting a Eurocentric view of life so rigid that it ignores the experience and the contributions of African Americans.

Arthur R. Ashe, Jr., with Kip Branch, Ocania Chalk, and Francis Harris. *A Hard Road to Glory: A History of the African-American Athlete,* 3 vols. New York: Amistad Books, 1989.

A comprehensive examination of African Americans in sports that is both a history and a cry of protest.

Clayborne Carson et al., eds. *The Eyes on the Prize Civil Rights Reader.* New York: Penguin Books, 1991.

The documents, speeches, and firsthand accounts of the African-American struggle, from 1954 through Nelson Mandela's address in Atlanta in 1990.

W. E. B. Du Bois. *The Philadelphia Negro: A Social Study.* New York: Schocken Books, 1967.

This, the first important sociological study of a Black community, was originally published in 1899 and is worth reading today. Du Bois discusses family life, interracial relations, education, occupations, and other aspects of the North's largest Black community just three decades after the end of slavery.

John Hope Franklin and Alfred A. Moss, Jr. *From Slavery to Freedom: A History of Negro Americans*, 7th ed. New York: McGraw Hill, 1994.

> The most authoritative historical account of the African-American experience in the United States.

Alex Haley. *Roots: The Saga of an American Family*. Garden City, NY: Doubleday, 1976.

> Drawing on the knowledge of his relatives and the oral history retold by a *griot* in the Gambian village of Kinte-Kundah, plus archival research, Haley managed to trace his ancestry back to Kunta Kinte, who was abducted in 1767 and eventually sold to a Virginia planter.

James H. Jones. *Bad Blood: The Tuskegee Syphilis Experiment*. New York: Free Press, 1981.

> Historian James Jones details the horrors of a Public Health Service survey in which 412 Black Alabama men with syphilis were used as experimental subjects from 1932 to 1972. The study's purpose was to assess the long-term effects of syphilis *without* medical treatment. It was not until newspaper publicity in 1972 that the victims, their infected wives, and their offspring born with the disease were given any treatment.

C. Eric Lincoln and Lawrence H. Mamiya. *The Black Church in the African American Experience*. Durham, NC: Duke University Press, 1990.

> An overview of the role of organized religion from the days of slavery through the challenges experienced today in the United States.

Malcolm X. *The Autobiography of Malcolm X*. New York: Grove Press, 1964.

> Just before his assassination, Malcolm X related his experiences leading to his leadership in the Nation of Islam and his subsequent disenchantment with that organization.

Raphael J. Sonenshein. *Politics in Black and White: Race and Power in Los Angeles*. Princeton: Princeton University Press, 1993.

> A political scientist draws upon interviews and voting analyses to look at interracial cooperation and conflict in Los Angeles.

Kenneth M. Stampp. *The Peculiar Institution: Slavery in the Ante-Bellum South*. New York: Random House, 1956.

> An objective, scholarly account of what slavery was like and what effects it had on Blacks, Whites, and the South.

Brent Staples. *Parallel Time: Growing Up Black and White*. New York: Pantheon Books, 1994.

> A Black journalist reflects on his life as a successful journalist and that of his young brother, who was murdered by one of his cocaine clients.

Wallace Terry. *Bloods: An Oral History of the Vietnam War by Black Veterans*. New York: Random House, 1984.

> Journalist Terry, who covered the war for *Time*, provides vivid testimony by 20 veterans.

Periodicals

Numerous mass-circulation magazines deal primarily with African Americans, including *Black Collegiate, Black Enterprise, Black World* (formerly *Negro Digest*), *Ebony, Essence,* and *Jet.* Journals include *Black Politics* (first issued in 1969), *Black Scholar* (1969), *Journal of Negro Education* (1931), *Journal of Negro History* (1916), *Negro History Bulletin* (1946), and *Race Relations Reporter* (1970; formerly *Southern School News*, 1954).

CRITICAL THINKING QUESTIONS

1. In what ways were slaves defined as property?
2. How did slavery provide a foundation for both White and Black America today?
3. If civil disobedience is nonviolent, why is so much violence associated with it?
4. How does the research on the 1960s urban riots help us to better understand more recent disturbances like those in Los Angeles in 1992?
5. Why has religion proved to be a force of both unity and disunity among African Americans?

Chapter
8

African Americans Today

Chapter Outline

Highlights

African Americans have made significant progress in many areas, but inequality relative to White Americans remains in all sectors. African Americans have advanced in formal schooling to a remarkable degree, although public schools remain mostly segregated. Higher education also reflects the legacy of a nation that has operated two schooling systems: one for Blacks and another for Whites. Gains in earning power have barely kept pace with inflation, and the gap between Whites and Blacks has remained relatively unchanged. African-American families are susceptible to the problems associated with a low-income group that also faces discrimination and prejudice. Housing remains segregated, despite growing numbers of Blacks in suburban areas. African Americans are more likely to be victims of crimes as well as to be arrested for violent crimes. The subordination of Blacks is also apparent in the delivery of health care. African Americans have made substantial gains in elective office, but still are underrepresented.

By the 1990s, a superficial sense of complacency about the position of African Americans in the United States was evident. Uninformed, casual observers saw the increasing presence of African Americans inside city halls and Congress rather than marching outside, and some concluded that everything was going well in Black America.

Yet, this complacency was interrupted by the events in Southern California in 1991 and 1992. Rodney King, a Black construction worker, sustained nearly a dozen head fractures when he was beaten by Los Angeles Police Department officers following a high-speed chase. The beating of 56 blows in 81 seconds happened to be captured on a videotape that shocked the nation as it was replayed numerous times on television. Four White officers were tried, a year later, on a variety of charges but were found not guilty by a jury of ten Whites, one Hispanic, and one Asian.

The verdict touched off rioting in Los Angeles and smaller disturbances in several cities, but the California riots became the worst in the twentieth century: 52 dead, 2,400 injured, and 8,800 arrested. The 1992 Los Angeles riot area of South-Central borders the 1965 Watts riot area. Except for a few government buildings and 500 units of low-income housing, Watts remains a ghetto. South-Central was virtually leveled by fires and looting that, like the original Rodney King beating, shocked the United States. Yet the expressions of concern over lawless civilians, police brutality, and insufficient government policies for the ghetto seemed all too familiar (A. Stone, 1992).

By 1995, the complacency had returned. The plans to address inner-city problems were low on the nation's list of priorities. Instead, the dismantling of affirmative action emerged as the major race issue.

As you read this chapter, try to keep the profile of African-Americans in the United States today in perspective. This chapter will assess education, employment and income, family life, housing, criminal justice, health care, and politics among the nation's African Americans. Progress has occurred, and some of the advances are nothing short of remarkable. The deprivation of the African-American people relative to Whites remains, however, even if absolute deprivation has been softened. A significant gap remains between African Americans and the dominant group, and to this gap a price is assigned: the price of being African Americans in the United States.

EDUCATION

The African-American population in the United States has always placed special importance on acquiring education, beginning within the home of the slave family through the creation of separate, inferior schools for Black children because the regular schools were closed to them by custom or law. Today, long after the old civil rights coalition has disbanded, education remains a controversial issue. Formal schooling is the key to social mobility in the United States. Because racial and ethnic groups realize that it is, they wish to maximize their opportunities for upward mobility, and so they demand better schooling. White Americans also appreciate the value of formal schooling and do not wish to do anything that they perceive will jeopardize their own position.

Quality and Quantity of Education

Several measures document the inadequate education received by African Americans, for example, the quantity of formal education. They generally drop out of school sooner and are therefore less likely to receive high school diplomas, let alone college degrees. Table 8.1 shows the gap in the amount of schooling African Americans receive compared to Whites. It also illustrates progress in reducing this gap in recent years. Yet, despite this progress, the gap remains substantial, with twice the proportion of Whites holding a college degree when compared with Blacks in 1994.

A second aspect of inadequate schooling, many educators argue, is that many students do not drop out of school but are pushed out by the combined inadequacies of their education. Among the deficiencies noted have been

1. Insensitive teachers
2. Poor counseling
3. Unresponsive administrators
4. Overcrowded classes
5. Irrelevant curricula
6. Dilapidated school facilities

Middle- and upper-class children occasionally face these barriers to a high-quality education, but they are more likely than the poor to have a home environment favorable to learning. Because African-American students are less likely to have such a home environment, these barriers to learning are particularly damaging to

Maintaining positive role models for Black youth is a major concern in educational institutions. A principal speaks to students at the predominantly male Malcolm X Academy in Detroit.

them. Even African-American schoolchildren who stay in school are not guaranteed success in life. Many high schools do not prepare students who are interested in college for advanced schooling. The problem is that schools are failing students, not that students are failing in schools.

School Segregation

It has been over 40 years since the U.S. Supreme Court issued its unanimous ruling in *Brown v. Board of Education* (Topeka, Kansas) that "separate educational facilities are inherently unequal." What has been the legacy of that decision? Initially, the courts, with the support of the federal government, ordered southern school districts to end racial separation. But as attention turned to larger school districts, especially in the North, the challenge was to have integrated schools even though the neighborhoods were segregated. In addition, some cities' school districts were predominantly African American and Hispanic surrounded by suburban school districts that were predominantly White. In 1974, the Supreme Court ruled in *Millikin v. Bradley* that it was improper to order Detroit and the suburbs to have a joint metropolitan busing solution. The Court also ended an 11-year-old

Table 8.1   YEARS OF SCHOOL COMPLETED (PERCENTAGES OF PERSONS 25 YEARS
              OLD AND OVER)

Among adults, the gaps remain between Black and Whites in the proportion completing high
school and college.

	1960	1980	1994
Completing High School			
Black			
Male	18.2%	51.1%	71.7%
Female	21.7	51.3	73.8
White			
Male	41.6	71.0	82.1
Female	44.7	70.1	81.9
Completing College			
Black			
Male	2.8	7.7	12.8
Female	3.3	8.1	13.0
White			
Male	10.3	22.1	26.1
Female	6.0	14.0	20.0

Source: C. Bennett (1995, p. 10); Bureau of the Census (1988).

school desegregation program which was limited to one city, Kansas City, in its
1995 ruling *Missouri v. Jenkins.* These and other Supreme Court decisions have
effectively ended initiatives to overcome residential segregation in schools.
Indeed, even in Topeka, one-third of the schools are once again segregated today
(J. Kozol, 1994; D. Savage, 1995a; E. Wiley, 1994).

Even as the courts debated the merits of busing, there was a great deal of controversy about it within the Black and White communities. Initially, it was bitterly
opposed by White students and their parents, who objected both to their children's
being bused to previously Black schools and to African Americans being bused into
their local school. While research has shown the positive outcomes of desegregated classrooms, African-American parents have come to question sending their children into hostile environments, preferring to take control of their own schools,
even within large, troubled urban school districts. In the absence of racial equality
outside the educational system, significant integration in education has become
impossible. At least, African Americans contend, let us have the same degree of
influence over our children's education as White parents do. In some urban areas,
the response by African Americans has been to create all-Black or even all-Black
male schools, with the expectation that separate classes will foster positive self-
images and role models (P. King, 1989; J. Morgan, 1991; P. Walters, 1994).

On the other hand, a diverse student population does not guarantee an integrated, equal schooling environment. For example, tracking in schools, especially
middle and high schools, serves to intensify segregation at the classroom level.
Tracking is the practice of placing students in specific curriculum groups on the

basis of test scores and other criteria. It also has the effect of decreasing White-Black classroom interaction as African-American children are disproportionately classified in general classes, while White children are placed in college-bound classes. Some studies indicate that African-American students are more likely than White students to be placed in classes for the learning-disabled or emotionally disturbed (J. Berger, 1995; J. Hilkevitch, 1995; J. Oakes, 1995; Serwatka, Deering, and Grant, 1995).

While there are successes in public education, true integration is clearly not one of them. This same general conclusion holds for higher education.

Higher Education

The overall picture of African-American education is not promising. While strides were made in the period following the civil rights movement, a plateau was reached in the mid-1970s. African Americans are more likely to be part-time students and in need of financial aid, which began to be severely cut back in the 1980s. They are also finding the social climate on predominantly White campuses less than positive. As a result, the Historically Black Colleges and Universities (HBCU) are once again playing a significant role in educating African Americans. For a century, they were the only real source of college degrees for Blacks. Then, in the 1970s, predominantly White colleges began to recruit African Americans. Yet in 1992, the just 105 HBCUs still accounted for almost 20 percent of all Black college students (N. Sheppard, 1994).

As shown in Table 8.1, while African Americans are more likely today to be college graduates, the upward trend has declined. Several factors have been identified for this reversal in progress:

1. A reduction in financial aid and more reliance on loans than on grants-in-aid, coupled with rising costs, have tended to discourage students who would be the first members of their families to attend college.
2. Pushing for "higher standards" and "excellence" in educational achievement without providing compensatory resources have locked out many minority students.
3. Employment opportunities, though slight for African American without some college, have continued to lure young people who must contribute to their family's income.
4. Negative publicity about affirmative action may have discouraged some African Americans from even considering college.
5. Increasing attention to what appears to be a growing number of racial incidents on predominantly White college campuses.

Colleges and universities seem uneasy about these problems but publicly appear to be committed to addressing them.

There is little question that special challenges face the African-American student at a college with an overwhelmingly White student body, faculty, advisers, coaches, and administrators. The campus culture may, at best, be neutral and is often hostile to the presence of members of racial minorities. The high attrition rate of African-American students on predominantly White college campuses confirms the need for a positive environment (H. Edwards, 1970; R. Schaefer, 1996).

As noted above, there have been a growing number of widely publicized racial incidents on college campuses. They have included cross burnings, discrimination, racist literature, physical attacks, derogatory behavior, and racist remarks. In addition, there are more subtle aspects, such as campus bars that discourage minority-student patronage by not playing minority-oriented music and local law-enforcement officials who more closely monitor the activities of African-American students. As a consequence of the lack of continued success of African Americans in college, relatively fewer are available to fill faculty and administrative positions. This means that there are no more, and perhaps fewer, role models standing in the fronts of college classrooms for students from subordinate groups to see. In "Listen to Their Voices," Nikki Giovanni, writer and college professor, offers advice to African-American college students for some of the "stupid questions" they will inevitably be asked at predominantly White colleges and universities.

The disparity in schooling becomes even more pronounced at the highest levels, and the trends are negative. Only 2.8 percent of all doctorates awarded in 1993 were to African Americans; that proportion had been 3 percent or higher in the 1980s. Since the early 1980s, the proportion of African Americans receiving medical degrees has remained steady at 5–6 percent. Despite the prevailing view that financial assistance is widely available to subordinate-group students, data released in 1993 showed only 47 percent of Black doctoral students receiving any aid, compared to 56 percent of Whites. Blacks were also less likely than White graduate students to receive grants (*Journal of Blacks in Higher Education,* 1994a, 1994b; C. Leatherman, 1994; K. Manzo, 1994).

In Chapter 1, we said that one of the consequences of subordinate-group status is segregation. This is certainly true in education. *De facto* segregation is present in the public schools, and indeed, some state university systems, such as Mississippi's, are accused of promoting segregation. African Americans who attend predominantly White colleges often encounter a chilly climate that isolates them from their classmates and even their teachers. The apparent gains of the 1970s in educational advancement have not continued.

EMPLOYMENT AND INCOME

By almost every measure of employment and income, the lot of African Americans has improved in absolute terms in the last four decades. Progress has not always been even, and the rate of improvement varies considerably by region, education, age, and gender. More important than this overall improvement by Blacks are the similar gains made by Whites. As the discussion of relative deprivation in Chapter 3 showed, the gap between Black and White income remains. Figure 8.1 vividly shows the lack of significant change in the ratio between African-American and White family income. Median income, which is the middle level of earnings (half of the families make more and half less), offers a realistic view of the earning power

Listen to Their Voices
Racism 101

NIKKI GIOVANNI

Q: What's it like to grow up in a ghetto?

A: I don't know.

Q: (from the teacher). Can you give us the Black perspective on Toni Morrison, Huck Finn, slavery, Martin Luther King, Jr., and others?

Nikki Giovanni

A: I can give you *my* perspective. (Do not take the burden of 22 million people on your shoulders. Remind everyone that you are an individual, and don't speak for the race or any other individual within it.)

Q: Why do all the Black people sit together in the dining hall?

A: Why do all the white students sit together?

Q: Why should there be an African-American studies course?

A: Because white Americans have not adequately studied the contributions of Africans and African-Americans. Both Black and white students need to know our total common history. . . .

Q: How can whites understand Black history, culture, literature, and so forth?

A: The same way we understand white history, culture, literature, and so forth. That is why we're in school: to learn.

Q: Should whites take African-American studies courses?

A: Of course. We take white-studies courses, though the universities don't call them that.

Comment: When I see groups of Black people on campus, it's really intimidating.

Comeback: I understand what you mean. I'm frightened when I see white students congregating.

Comment: It's not fair. It's easier for you guys to get into college than for other people.

Comeback: If it's so easy, why aren't there more of us?

Comment: It's not our fault that America is the way it is.

Comeback: It's not our fault, either, but both of us have a responsibility to make changes.

Source: Nikki Giovanni, *Racism 101* (pp. 104–106). New York: William Morrow and Co., 1994. By permission of William Morrow and Co., Inc., 1350 Avenue of the Americas, New York, NY 10019.

of a particular group. One cannot help but be struck by the lack of progress in closing this gap over a 24-year period.

Three factors take a toll on African-American incomes. First, the African-American family is more likely to depend on two sources of income, with both hus-

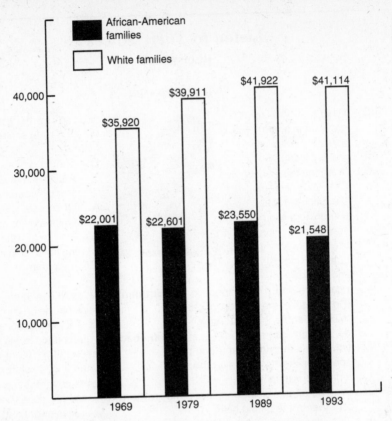

Figure 8.1 African-American and White Median Family Income, 1969–1993
African-American median family income has not closed the gap with White income since 1969 and, indeed, has fallen slightly behind.

Note: 1993 data for White, not Hispanic.

Source: C. Bennett (1995, p. 21).

band and wife working. Second, Blacks have consistently migrated to areas with higher living costs, say, from farms to cities, where increased income barely keeps pace with the increased costs. Third, Blacks are especially hard hit at times of increased unemployment. As shown in Figure 8.2, higher unemployment rates for Blacks have persisted since 1960 and can be documented even further back. Recessions have also taken their toll on African Americans. The Reverend Joseph Lowery, former aide to Martin Luther King, Jr., appropriately said that "when America catches a cold, the black community gets pneumonia" (K. Zinsmeister, 1988, p. 41).

The employment picture is especially grim for young African-American workers aged 16–24. Many live in the central cities and fall victim to the unrecorded, irregular economy outlined in Chapter 3. Many factors have been cited by social scientists to explain why official unemployment rates for young African Americans exceed 40 percent:

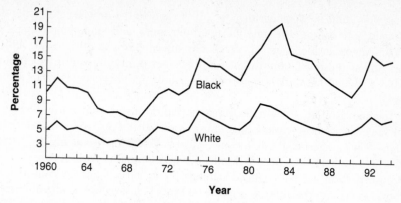

Figure 8.2 African-American and White Unemployment Rates, 1960–1992
Even in the healthy economy of the early 1960s, African-American unemployment did not fall below 9 percent until 1965.

Note: African-American data for 1960–1971 are for "Blacks and other races."

Source: Rates through 1981, from John Reid, "Black America in the 1980s." *Population Bulletin* 37 (December 1982). Reprinted by permission of the Population Reference Bureau. Data for 1980–1992 from Bureau of the Census; C. Bennett (1995, p. 20).

1. Many African Americans live in the depressed economy of the central cities.
2. Immigrants and illegal aliens are increased competition.
3. White middle-class women have entered the labor force.
4. Illegal activities at which youths find they can make more money have become more prevalent.

None of these factors is likely to change soon, so that depressionlike levels of unemployment are likely to persist (R. Farley, 1993; Massey and Gross, 1993).

The picture grows even more somber when we realize that we are considering only official unemployment. The federal government's Bureau of Labor Statistics regards as unemployed only those persons *actively* seeking employment. Thus, in order to be counted as unemployed, a person must not hold a full-time job, must be registered with a government employment agency, and must be engaged in writing job applications and seeking interviews.

Quite simply, the official unemployment rate leaves out millions of Americans who are effectively unemployed. It does not count persons so discouraged that they have temporarily given up looking for employment. The problem of unemployment is further compounded by underemployment. The term *underemployment* refers to working at a job for which one is overqualified, or involuntarily working part-time, or being intermittently employed.

The official unemployment rate for African-American teenagers in a central city is about 40–45 percent, well above the 25 percent jobless rate for the nation as a whole during the depression of the 1930s. Again, such official statistics do not include youths who have dropped out of the system: those who are not at school, not at work, and not looking for a job. If we add to the official figures the discouraged job seeker, the rate of unemployment and underemployment of African-American teenagers in central-city areas climbs to 90 percent. As discouraging as these data are, the picture becomes even grimmer as we consider studies showing that underemployment remains high for young African Americans.

Income data are equally discouraging. Unfortunately, the words *Black* and *poor* have always been closely related in these statistics. As we have seen, Black income falls far short of White income. African Americans are nearly three times as likely to be below the poverty level. This relationship of African Americans to the poverty level has not changed significantly in the last quarter century. Low incomes are counterbalanced to some extent by Medicare, Medicaid, public assistance, and food stamps. The income of the affluent is underestimated, however, because capital gains and other types of income received by the more well-to-do are excluded from census data. That an African-American family in 1993 had a 28 percent probability of being poor showed that the degree of social inequality is staggering.

African-American Businesses

Many people aspire to run their own businesses, but it is clearly attractive to subordinate groups, including African Americans. Going into business alone offers the opportunity to make it into the middle class. It is also a way to avoid some of the racism in business: the "glass ceilings" that block the promotion of a qualified worker and the tensions of a multiracial work environment.

Historically, the first Black-owned business developed behind the wall of segregation. African Americans provided other African Americans services that Whites would not provide, such as insurance, hairdressing, legal assistance, and medical help. While this is less true today, African-American entrepreneurs usually cater first to the market demand within their own community in such areas as music and mass media. However, if these new ventures become profitable, the entrepreneur usually faces stiff competition from outside the African-American community.

In the 1970s, there were strong cries to help African-American businesses. Community leaders launched "Buy Black" campaigns, and the government spoke of assisting Black capitalists. African-American businesses have increased, but they are relatively few in number. African Americans own only about 3 percent of the nearly 14 million firms in the United States. These firms tend to be very small, 83 percent having no paid employees. Only 189 out of the 400,000 African-American firms have 100 or more employees, but these few enterprises account for 14 percent of all receipts (Bureau of the Census, 1991a).

The situation is not improving. Among the factors creating new obstacles are the following:

1. Continuing backlash against affirmative action programs.
2. Difficulty in obtaining loans and other capital.

3. A changing definition of minority that allows women, veterans, and the disabled to qualify for special small-business-assistance programs.

4. A reduction in the number and scope of set-aside programs.

The last item requires further explanation. *Set-asides* are stipulations that government contracts must be awarded in a minimum proportion, usually 10–30 percent, to minority-owned businesses. However, in 1989, the U.S. Supreme Court determined that the city of Richmond, Virginia, had acted illegally in its set-aside programs (see Table 3.2). Since *City of Richmond v. Croson,* cities and government have abandoned such programs, jeopardizing already fragile African-American businesses. Then, in 1995, amid criticism of affirmative action, set-aside programs at the federal level also came under attack (D. Savage, 1995a).

In the aftermath of the 1992 South-Central Los Angeles riots, President George Bush advanced his policy of creating *enterprise zones* in urban areas. While not directly aimed at minority-owned businesses, the policy intends to encourage employment and investment in blighted neighborhoods through the use of tax breaks. Following this lead, President Bill Clinton proposed *empowerment zones* to be created in 1993, with a total of 50 by 1997. The idea of offering tax incentives to attract investment is not new and has been used by 30 states, with varying degrees of success. Locally, in Los Angeles, successful African-American business leaders began to develop their own strategies to create business opportunities in the ghetto. Ironically, Los Angeles was passed over when the first group of zones was named. Critics contend that this approach is just the latest half-hearted attempt in efforts at community development that stretch back to urban renewal in 1949 and the Model Cities program in 1966 (N. Lemann, 1994; Wolf and Benedetto, 1992).

Even if programs that stress increasing the number of African-American businesses succeeded, most ghetto Blacks would still be left poor. Writing more than a generation ago, W. E. B. Du Bois (1968) mentioned this potentially negative effect of Black capitalism. Encouraging a few African Americans to move up the capitalistic ladder, he said, "will have inserted into the ranks of the Negro race a new cause of division, a new attempt to subject the masses of the race to an exploiting capitalist class of their own people" (p. 208). Du Bois's alternative was a program that would substantially improve the economic conditions of all African Americans, not just a few.

Occupational Patterns

The limits of African-American capitalism are evident if one examines how Whites have succeeded. Most Whites achieve upward mobility by climbing the ladder of jobs in established businesses or by entering financially rewarding professions. It is through these methods of economic improvement, rather than by establishing their own businesses, that some African Americans have begun to make progress. Admittedly, the continued dependence on White firms that this method implies does little to assist the large numbers of Blacks relegated to work or unemploy-

Mike Konopacki, Huck/Konopacki Labor Cartoons.

ment in the ghetto, distant from the high-paying, stable jobs in the suburbs or in urban corporate enclaves (O'Hare et al., 1991; W. Wilson, 1987a).

While relatively few African Americans have crashed the "glass ceiling" and made it into the top echelons of American business or government, more have entered a wider variety of jobs. The taboo against putting them in jobs in which they would supervise Whites has weakened, and the percentage of African Americans in professional and managerial occupations rose from 4 percent in 1949 to 14 percent in 1993, a remarkable improvement. However, most of this advancement came prior to 1980. There has been little advancement since then.

As shown in Table 8.2, African Americans, who constitute 12–15 percent of the labor force, are underrepresented in high-status, high-paying occupations. Less than 5 percent of lawyers, judges, physicians, financial managers, public relations specialists, architects, pharmacists, and dentists are African American. On the other hand, they account for over 15 percent of cooks, health aides, hospital orderlies, maids, janitors, and stock handlers (Bureau of the Census, 1994, pp. 407, 409).

In summary, the economic differences between Whites and Blacks are striking. The same generalizations that were made prior to the civil rights movement are still accurate as the twenty-first century approaches. African Americans have a higher unemployment rate, a greater rate of business failures, and occupy lower-paying jobs. As might be expected, this disparity in income takes its toll on family life.

Table 8.2   PERCENTAGE OF AFRICAN-AMERICAN EMPLOYEES IN SELECTED
OCCUPATIONS, 1972 AND 1993

In professional and managerial positions, progress has been modest since 1972.

Occupation	1972	1993
Professional workers	6	7
Engineers	2	4
Lawyers and judges	2	3
Physicians	3	5
Registered nurses	6	8
College teachers	4	5
Other teachers	8	9
Social workers	16	21
Managers	3	6
Sales workers	3	7
Clerical workers (including administrative support)	8	11
Service workers	17	17
Cleaners and servants	64	22
Firefighters	4	8
Police and detectives	8	18

Source: Bureau of the Census (1982b, pp. 419–420; 1994, pp. 407–409).

FAMILY LIFE

In its role as a social institution providing for the socialization of children, the family is crucial to its members' life satisfaction. The family also reflects the influence, positive or negative, of income, housing, education, and other social factors. For African Americans, the family reflects both amazing stability and the legacy of racism and low income across many generations.

Challenges to Family Stability

It is the conventional view that the typical African-American family is female-headed. Yet it is only since about 1989 that the majority of African-American families have not been two-parent households. In 1994, about 8 million African-American families lived in the United States. In more than 3 million of them, both a husband and a wife were present. But in 4 million, a single parent was raising children under age 18 (see Figure 8.3). It is as inaccurate to assume that a single-parent family is necessarily "deprived" as it is to assume that a two-parent family is always secure and happy. So, while single-parent African-American families are not uncommon, they are not typical. In comparison, such single-parent arrangements were also present among about one in five White families in 1994.

Nevertheless, life in a single-parent family can be extremely stressful. Speaking about all single parents, and not just those who are members of subordinate groups, Ronald Haskins, director of the Child Development Institute at the Uni-

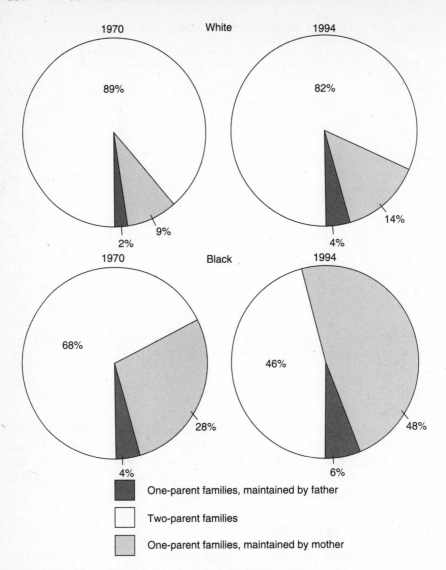

Figure 8.3 **One-Parent Families among Blacks and Whites, 1970 and 1994**
In 1994, 54 percent of African-American families and 18 percent of White families were headed by one adult.
Sources: C. Bennett (1995, p. 8); Bureau of Labor Statistics (1986).

versity of North Carolina, observes, "It's a big and risky undertaking when so many parents try to raise so many children alone" (J. Mann, 1983, p. 62). There is also the very real issue that the lack of a male presence, the absent parent typically being the father, means almost always the lack of a male income. This monetary impact of a single-parent household is not to be minimized (A. Hacker, 1995).

Looming behind the woman-headed families is the plight of the African-American man. Simply stated, the economic status of Black men is deteriorating. Historically, it has not always been a problem. Despite the absence of legal protection for the slave family, African Americans were able to establish significant kinship relationships. After emancipation, males preferred that their wives remain at home because a working woman was considered a mark of slavery. But it was hard for Black men to find work as anything other than strikebreakers, and so women were the more important source of wages. In 1900, about 41 percent of Black women were employed, compared to only 16 percent of White women. The twentieth-century movement from the rural South to the ghettos of the North increased the employment opportunities for Black men, but Black women found job opportunities as well, including relatively high-paid positions in nursing and teaching. Ever since labor statistics on African Americans were first collected in 1890, Black men have had more jobs than Black women, but when Blacks are compared to Whites, Black women fare better. As we saw in Chapter 3, the employment gap is narrower between Black and White women than it is between Black and White men. In the 1990s, renewed attention has been given to the unfavorable stereotype of African-American males, especially young men, that follows them wherever they go in society (B. Baker, 1992; R. Mincy, 1994).

For many African-American women living in poverty, marriage after having a child is an added burden. The absence of a husband does not mean that no one shares in child care: 85 percent of the out-of-wedlock children born to Black teenage mothers live with their grandparents and form three-generational households. Stronger religious beliefs contribute to teenage Blacks' being almost half as likely as Whites to terminate a pregnancy by abortion. A variety of social factors combine to explain the frustration felt by many African Americans who are beginning to rear a family (C. Billingsley, 1992; Staples and Johnson, 1993).

No one explanation accounts for the rise in single-parent households. The rapid expansion is attributed by sociologists primarily to shifts in the economy that have kept Black men, especially in urban areas, out of work. The phenomenon of expansion in female-headed families certainly is not limited to African Americans. Increasingly, White and Black women both bear children before they marry. More and more parents, both White and Black, divorce, so that the children live with only one parent.

Strengths of African-American Families

In the midst of ever-increasing single parenting, another picture of African-American family life becomes visible: success despite discrimination and economic hardship. Robert Hill (1972, 1987) of the National Urban League listed five strengths of African-American families that allow them to function effectively in a hostile (racist) society.

1. *Strong kinship bonds.* Blacks are more likely than Whites to care for children and the elderly in an extended family network.
2. *A strong work orientation.* Poor Blacks are more likely to be working, and poor Black families often include more than one wage earner.
3. *Adaptability of family roles.* In two-parent families, the egalitarian pattern of decision making is the most common. The self-reliance of Black women who are the primary wage earners best illustrates this adaptability.

4. *A high achievement orientation.* Working-class Blacks indicate a greater desire for their children to attend college than working-class Whites. Even a majority of low-income African Americans desire to attend college.

5. *A strong religious orientation.* Black churches since the time of slavery have been the source of many significant grassroots organizations.

Social workers and sociologists have confirmed these strengths noted by Robert Hill through actual social research (J. Hudgins, 1992). Within the African-American community, these are the sources of family strengths, just as economic deprivation fosters instability.

Increasingly, social scientists are learning to look at both aspects of African-American family life: the weaknesses and strengths. Expressions of alarm about instability date back to 1965, when the Department of Labor issued the report *The Negro Family: The Case for National Action.* The document, commonly known as the Moynihan Report after its principal author, Daniel Patrick Moynihan, outlined a "tangle of pathology" with the Black family at its core. More recently, two studies, the Stable Black Families Project and the National Survey of Black Americans, sought to learn how Black families encounter problems and resolve them successfully with internal resources. The coping mechanisms paralleled those outlined by Hill in his highly regarded work (F. Chideya, 1993; Department of Labor, 1965, p. 30; Gary et al., 1983; Hatchett, Cochran, and Jackson, 1991).

The most consistently documented strength of African-American families is the presence of an extended family household—the first strength listed above. The most common feature is having grandparents residing in the home. Extended living arrangements are twice as common among Black as among White households. These arrangements are recognized as having the important economic benefit of pooling limited economic resources. Because of the generally lower earnings of African-American heads-of-household, income from second, third, and even fourth wage earners is required to achieve a desired standard of living or, in all too many cases, simply to meet daily needs (Farley and Allen, 1987; Taylor et al., 1990).

The African-American Middle Class

Many characterizations of African-American family life have been attacked because they overemphasize the poorest segment of the African-American community. An opposite error is the exaggeration of the success that African Americans have achieved. Social scientists face the challenge of avoiding a selective, one-sided picture of Black society. The problem is similar to viewing a partially filled glass of water. Does one describe it as half empty and emphasize the need for assistance? Or does one describe the glass as half full to give attention to what has been accomplished? The most complete description would acknowledge both perspectives (A. Gouldner, 1970, p. 4.

A clearly defined African-American middle class has emerged. In 1993, one-third of African Americans earned more than the median income for Whites (Bennett, 1994). At least 30 percent of Blacks, then, are middle class. Many have debated the character of this middle class. E. Franklin Frazier (1957), a Black sociologist, wrote an often-critical study of the African-American middle class, in which he identified its overriding goal as achieving petty social values and becoming acceptable to White society.

Yet African Americans are still aware of their racial subordination even when they have achieved a superficial economic equality. The Black middle class may not be militant, but neither do its newest members forget their roots. They are more likely than Whites to be first-generation middle class, dependent on two or more sources of income, and precariously close to the lower class both financially and residentially. Yet with their relative success has come a desire to live in better surroundings. The migration of middle-class African Americans out of the ghetto in the 1970s and 1980s has left a vacuum. They may still care about the problems of the Black poor, but they are no longer present as role models (Durant and Louden, 1986; B. Landry, 1987; N. Lemann, 1986a, 1986b).

Members of the African-American middle class do not automatically accept all aspects of the White middle class. For years, for example, Whites have relied on books and magazines on infant and child care; such materials treated African-American children as if they did not exist. To counter this neglect, James Comer and Alvin Poussaint wrote *Raising Black Children* (1992), in which the authors advise parents on how to deal with questions like "What is Black?", a child's first encounter with prejudice, and a teenage girl's being watched by store security.

Directing attention to the Black middle class also requires that we consider the relative importance of the two components in *ethclass*, Milton Gordon's concept introduced in Chapter 5. The degree to which relatively affluent Blacks identify themselves in class terms or racial terms is an important ideological question. W. E. B. Du Bois (1952) argued that, when racism decreases, class issues become more important. As Du Bois saw it, exploitation would remain and many of the same people would continue to be subordinate. Black elites might become economically successful, either as entrepreneurs (Black capitalists) or professionals (Black white-collar workers), but they would continue to identify with and serve the dominant group's interest.

Social scientists have long recognized the importance of class. *Class* is a term that was used by sociologist Max Weber to refer to persons who share a similar level of wealth and income. The significance of class in people's lives is apparent to all. In the United States today, roughly half the lower-class population suffers from chronic health conditions that limit their activity, compared with only one in 11 among the affluent. The poor are more likely to become victims of crime, and they are only about half as likely as the affluent to send their children to colleges or vocational schools (Schaefer and Lamm, 1995).

The complexity of the relative influence of race and class was apparent in the controversy surrounding the publication of sociologist William J. Wilson's *The Declining Significance of Race* (1980). Pointing to the increasing influence of African Americans, Wilson concluded that "class has become more important than race in determining black life-chances in the modern world" (p. 150). The policy implications of his conclusion are that programs must be developed to confront class subordination rather than ethnic and racial discrimination. Wilson did not deny the legacy of discrimination reflected in the disproportionate number of

African Americans who are poor, less educated, and living in inadequate and over-crowded housing. He pointed, however, to "compelling evidence" that young Blacks were successfully competing with young Whites.

Critics of Wilson comment that focusing attention on this small educated elite ignores vast numbers of African Americans relegated to the lower class (A. Pinkney, 1984; C. Willie, 1978, 1979). Wilson himself was not guilty of such an oversimplification and indeed expressed concern over lower-class, inner-city African Americans' seemingly falling even further behind, like those who become a part of the irregular economy discussed in Chapter 3. He pointed out that the poor are socially isolated and have shrinking economic opportunities (1987a, 1987b). It is easy to conclude superficially, however, that because educated Blacks are entering the middle class, race has ceased to be of concern.

As many African Americans have learned, prejudice and discrimination do not end with affluence. Jerobim Gilbert, a graduate of Harvard University and a vice president of NBC, recalls an evening when he and his secretary attempted to hail separate taxicabs at the same location. The secretary, who is White, was successful in her first attempt; by contrast, Gilbert, who is African American, could not get a cab and eventually had to call and ask his wife to pick him up. "It's pretty hard to feel mainstream," he says with a sigh, "when you're wearing $2,000 worth of clothes and you can't catch a cab at night" (R. Lacayo, 1989).

A study of 209 affluent African Americans identified a number of strategies that they use to contend with prejudice and discrimination. Among these are avoidance, laughter, placing the hostility in its proper place, confrontation, and legal action. One important aspect of coping with racism involves preparing African-American children for racial slights and obstacles. These lessons are taught by example (as children see their parents contend with racism) and through explicit family discussions about these issues (also see J. Hochschild, 1993).

HOUSING

Housing plays a major role in determining the quality of a person's life. For African Americans, as for Whites, housing is the result of personal preferences and amount of income. African Americans differ from Whites, however, in that their housing has been restricted in a manner not used against Whites. Black housing has improved, as indicated by statistics on home ownership, new construction, density of living units, and quality as measured by plumbing facilities. Despite such gains, African Americans remain behind Whites. The quality of Black housing is inferior to that of Whites at all income levels, yet Blacks pay a larger share of their income for shelter.

Housing was the last major area to be covered by civil rights legislation. The delay was not due to its insignificance; quite the contrary, it was precisely because housing touches so many parts of the American economy and relates to private property rights that legislators were slow to act. After an executive order by President Kennedy, the government required nondiscrimination in federally assisted housing, but this ruling included only 7 percent of the housing market. In 1968, the Federal Fair Housing Law (Title VIII of the 1968 Civil Rights Act) and the U.S. Supreme Court decision in *Jones v. Mayer* combined to outlaw all racial discrimination in housing. Enforcement has remained weak, however, and many aspects of housing, real estate customs, and lending practices remain untouched.

Residential Segregation

Typically in the United States, as was noted earlier, White children attend predominantly White schools, Black schoolchildren attend predominantly Black institutions, and Hispanic schoolchildren attend predominantly Hispanic schools. This school segregation is not only the result of the failure to accept busing but also the effect of residential segregation. In their studies on segregation, Douglas Massey and Nancy Denton (1993) concluded that racial separation "continues to exist because white America has not had the political will or desire to dismantle it" (p. 8). In Chapter 1, we noted the pervasiveness of residential segregation. This racial isolation in neighborhoods has not improved since the beginnings of the civil rights movement in the 1950s.

What are the factors that create residential segregation in the United States? Among the primary factors are that:

1. Because of private prejudice and discrimination, people refuse to sell or rent to people of the "wrong" race, ethnicity, or religion.
2. The prejudicial policies of real estate companies steer people to the "correct" neighborhoods.
3. Government policies enforcing antibias legislation are ineffective.
4. Public housing policies today, as well as past construction patterns, reinforce housing for the poor in inner-city neighborhoods.
5. Policies of banks and other lenders create barriers to financing home purchasing based on race.

This last issue of racial-basis financing deserves further explanation. In 1988, new attention was given to the persistence of *redlining*, a practice in which financial lenders designated minority and racially changing neighborhoods as poor investments for home and commercial loans. Research documented that, in many cities, the including Atlanta, Baltimore, Chicago, Philadelphia, and Washington, D.C., the neighborhoods of subordinate groups received fewer and smaller loans than White neighborhoods, even when economic factors were taken into account. Particularly compelling data emerged from a 1991 study by the Federal Reserve Board, which showed that White borrowers with the lowest incomes were approved for mortgages more often than Black borrowers with median incomes over $66,000 per year. The disparity continued whether mortgages were sought from local banks, the Federal Housing Administration, or the Veteran's Administration. Redlining exists primarily because of the continuation of residential segregation.

Although the African-American concentration in the central cities has increased, a small but growing number of Blacks have moved into suburban areas.

By 1990, 32 percent of the nation's metropolitan African Americans lived in sub-urban areas. Yet the most significant growth in the percentage of suburban African Americans has come from movement into suburbs that are predominantly Black or are adjacent to predominantly Black areas. In many instances, therefore, it represents further ghettoization and spillover from city slums. It is not necessarily a signal of two cars and a backyard pool. In many instances, the suburbs with large Black populations are isolated from surrounding White communities and have less satisfactory housing and municipal services, but ironically pay higher taxes (D. Dent, 1992; J. Poe, 1992; D. Schemo, 1994).

A dual housing market is part of today's reality, although attacks continue against the remaining legal barriers to fair housing. Zoning laws, in theory, are enacted to ensure that specific standards of housing construction will be satisfied. These regulations can also separate industrial and commercial enterprises from residential areas. Some zoning laws in suburbs, though, have seemed to curb the development of low- and moderate-income housing that would attract African Americans who want to move out of the central cities.

For years, the construction of low-income public housing in the ghetto has furthered racial segregation. Yet the courts have not ruled consistently in this matter in recent years, so that, as with affirmative action and busing, public officials lack clear guidance. In the suburban Chicago community of Arlington Heights, the courts decided in 1977 that a community could refuse to rezone to allow low-income housing, a policy that effectively kept out African Americans. Yet in 1988, the courts fined Yonkers, a city adjoining New York City, for failing to build public housing for low- and middle-income households in a way that would foster integration.

Even if court decisions continue to dismantle exclusionary housing practices, the rapid growth of integrated neighborhoods is unlikely. In the future, African-American housing (1) will continue to improve, (2) will remain in all-Black neighborhoods, and (3) will remain inferior in quality to White housing. This gap is greater than can be explained by differences in social class.

CRIMINAL JUSTICE

A complex, sensitive topic affecting African Americans is their role in criminal justice. It encompasses the paucity of lawyers (2.7 percent of attorneys in 1993 were Black) as well as the large proportion of inmates facing death sentences (more than 42 percent are Black).

Data collected annually in the FBI's *Uniform Crime Report* show that Blacks account for 25 percent of arrests, even though they represent only about 12 percent of the nation's population. Conflict theorists point out that the higher arrest rate is not surprising for a group that is disproportionately poor and therefore much less able to afford private attorneys, who might be able to prevent formal arrests from taking place. Even more significantly, the *Uniform Crime Report* focuses on index crimes (mainly property crimes), which are the type of crimes most often committed by low-income persons.

Interestingly—and in contrast to popular misconceptions about crime—African Americans and the poor are especially likely to be the victims of serious crimes. This fact is documented in *victimization surveys,* which are systematic interviews of ordinary people carried out annually to reveal how much crime occurs. These Bureau of Justice statistics show that African American households are 50 percent more likely to be burglarized, and their automobiles are twice as likely to be stolen (Department of Justice, 1993).

The videotaped beating of Rodney King and the subsequent initial not-guilty verdict given four Los Angeles police officers touched off the 1992 South-Central Los Angeles riots. These events gave very different messages to the public. For Blacks, many minorities, and sympathetic Whites, the events called for renewed attention to police procedures and the handling of citizen complaints. For others, the televised looting and arson pointed to the need for a stronger law-enforcement presence in the inner city (R. Schaefer, 1996).

Central to the concern that minorities often express about the criminal justice system is *differential* justice; that is, Whites are dealt with more leniently than Blacks whether at time of arrest, indictment, conviction, sentencing, or parole.

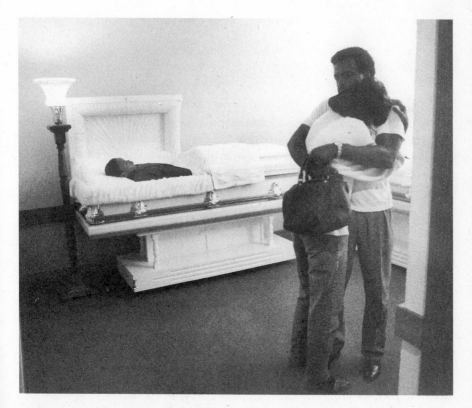

Crime is a major concern to African Americans. In Chicago, parents mourn the death of their 11-year-old son, the victim of a drive-by shooting.

Several studies demonstrate that police often deal with African-American youths more harshly than with White youngsters.

Conflict theorists argue that the criminal justice system, through these differential applications of social control, serves to keep certain groups in their deprived systems. A 1983 report documented that African Americans and Hispanics received stiffer prison sentences and served more time in jail than Whites convicted of similar felonies (J. Petersilia, 1983; also see Bridges and Crutchfield, 1988; Klein, Turner, and Petersilia, 1988). In this two-year study, prepared for the National Institute of Corrections of the U.S. Department of Justice, the data showed that minorities were less able to make bail than Whites and more likely to have court-appointed lawyers. The study surveyed three states—California, Michigan, and Texas—which accounted for 22 percent of the nation's prison inmates. Although no racial differences were found in the type of prison programs to which inmates were assigned, the study did find significant differences in the length of sentences:

- In California, Hispanics' sentences were about 6.5 months longer than Whites'; Blacks' were almost 1.5 months longer than Whites'.
- In Texas, Hispanics' sentences were more than 2 months longer than Whites'; Blacks' were 3.5 months longer than Whites'.
- In Michigan, Blacks' sentences averaged more than 7 months longer than Whites'.
- Differential justice was not limited to adult offenders. Black juveniles appeared to be at greater risk of being charged with more serious offenses than Whites involved in comparable levels of delinquent behavior (Huizinga and Elliott, 1987).

In the 1990s, the concerns within the African-American community over the toll that crime was taking became more visible. The concerns were twofold: first, that the growth of Black-on-Black crime was not being dealt with as seriously as when Whites were victimized. Researchers on crime have come to call this *victim discounting*, that is, society's viewing crimes as less socially significant if the victim is viewed as less worthy. African-American men aged 12–24 are especially likely to be victimized—at a rate double that of the victimization of Whites. Young African-American men are also more likely to be victimized by violent crimes (robberies and assaults). In 1992, one out of every six Black males aged 16–19 sustained a violent crime, compared to one out of 11 in 1973 (Bastian and Taylor, 1994; T. Gibbons, 1985).

Perhaps the most extreme form of victim discounting comes in homicide cases. Although half of all homicide victims in the United States from 1977 to 1992 were African American, 85 percent of prisoners executed were convicted of killing Whites. Viewed from a conflict perspective, such data suggest that, in applying the death penalty, the judicial system in the United States considers Black lives less valuable than White lives. Prosecutors are less likely to argue for a death sentence—and juries and judges less likely to impose it—when the murder victim is Black (E. Zorn, 1995).

The second community concern revolves around the impact that crime is having on the quality of life of African Americans. Housing, health, education, and employment opportunities are all being adversely affected by the presence of crime. In response, a 1994 summit of African-American notables, including Jesse Jackson, Bill Cosby, Spike Lee, and Al Sharpton, declared that crime is becoming a premier civil rights issue. C. Deloris Tucker of the National Political Congress of Black Women declared, "Our great fear is not from hurricanes or earthquakes, not from disease or war, but from violence against one another" (T. McNulty, 1994, p. 7). There is also a reluctant acceptance that the government cannot be counted on to address inner-city problems: between 1980 and 1990, federal grants to state and local governments to support the poor were cut by $26 billion, almost in half. There has been less action than talk about private enterprise becoming involved, and empowerment zones have not really been given a chance. The solution will not be simple. As one writer noted, "There is no magic bullet to reduce youth violence" (K. McFate, 1994, p. 4).

HEALTH CARE

The price of being an African American took on new importance with the release in 1990 of a shocking study in a prestigious medical journal that revealed that a man in Harlem, a predominantly Black neighborhood in New York City, was less likely to live to the age of 65 than was a man in Bangladesh, one of the poorest nations of the world. Whereas 55 percent would reach age 65 there, the same would be true of only 40 percent of men in Harlem. According to this study, based on data from the period 1979–1981, the factors contributing to Harlem's high mortality rate, in order, were cardiovascular disease, cirrhosis, homicide, tumors, and drug dependency. However, as the researchers noted, the problem of mortality among 25- to 44-year-olds in Harlem had become even more severe since 1980, with acquired immunodeficiency syndrome (AIDS) now established as the most common cause of death in this age group. The researchers added that Harlem's high mortality rate was not unique; they had identified 53 other health areas, predominantly inner-city neighborhoods with high Black or Hispanic populations, that had age-adjusted mortality rates approximately twice the national average for Whites (McCord and Freeman, 1990).

The morbidity and mortality rates for African Americans as a group, and not just Harlem men, are equally distressing. Compared with Whites, Blacks have higher death rates from diseases of the heart, pneumonia, diabetes, and cancer. In 1987, the death rate for strokes was twice as high among African Americans as it was among Whites. Such epidemiological findings reflect in part the higher proportion of Blacks found among the nation's lower classes. White Americans in the year 2000 can expect to live 77.6 years. By contrast, life expectancy for African-American men will be only 65.3 years (Bureau of the Census, 1994; *New York Times*, 1990). Drawing on the conflict perspective, sociologist Howard Waitzkin (1986) suggests that racial tensions contribute to the medical problems of African Americans. In his view, the stress resulting from racial prejudice and discrimination helps to explain the higher rates of hypertension found among African Americans (and Hispanics) than among Whites. Hypertension is twice as common in

Baltimore Mayor Kurt Schmoke is pictured with Rev. Jesse Jackson participating in a Washington march for more assistance to urban areas.

Blacks as in Whites; it is believed to be a critical factor in Blacks' high mortality rates from heart disease, kidney disease, and stroke. Although there is disagreement among medical experts, some argue that the stress resulting from racism and suppressed hostility exacerbates hypertension among African Americans (D. Goleman, 1990).

Studies presented by the American Medical Association in 1994 reported that African Americans and Whites receive different levels of health care. One study compared 33,641 African Americans and Whites treated at Veteran's Affairs Medical Centers from 1988 to 1990. Black heart attack patients were treated with surgery or angioplasty about half as often as White patients, yet Blacks had a slightly higher rate of survival. While discrimination may contribute to the lower incidence of surgery among African Americans, it is also possible that Black patients had less severe problems than Whites or were more likely to decline surgical procedures (Peterson et al., 1994; see also J. Ayaniun, 1994).

A second study of 9,932 Medicare patients found that African Americans and low-income people of all races received less care than affluent Whites, regardless of the type of hospital (rural hospital, urban nonteaching hospital, or urban teaching hospital). However, six months after hospitalization, survival rates were similar, regardless of race or class. Researchers note that African Americans and low-income patients are disproportionately treated in urban teaching hospitals, which generally offer higher-quality care (Kahn et al., 1994).

The previous section noted that African Americans are underrepresented in the criminal justice system among lawyers. A similar phenomenon emerges in

Table 8.3   BLACK ELECTED OFFICIALS, 1972–1994

Although the rate of increase has leveled off, the number of Black elected officials has continued to increase.

Year	Number	Percentage Change During Preceding 4 Years	Percentage Increase Since 1972
1972	2,264	—	—
1976	3,979	58	58
1980	4,912	23	117
1984	5,700	16	152
1988	7,225	27	219
1992	7,552	5	234
1994	7,984	—	252

Source: From data in *National Roster of Black Elected Officials, 1995,* by the Joint Center for Political Studies. Reprinted by permission. Also Bureau of Census (1994).

health care. Blacks represent only 5 percent of practicing physicians. They are also underrepresented in other areas of medicine. The fact that they are even underrepresented in clinical and research trials of new drugs suggests that insufficient data have been generated to accurately assess the safety of these chemicals for African Americans (Lloyd and Miller, 1989; N. Miller, 1987; C. Svensson, 1989).

Just how significant is the impact of poorer health on the lives of the nation's less educated people, less affluent classes, and subordinate groups? Drawing on a variety of research studies, population specialist Evelyn Kitagawa (1972) estimated the "excess mortality rate" to be 20 percent. In other words, 20 percent more people were dying than otherwise might have because of poor health linked to race and class. Using Kitagawa's model, we can calculate that, if every African American in the United States were White and had at least one year of college education, some 54,000 fewer Blacks would have died in 1994 and in each succeeding year (Bureau of the Census, 1994, p. 89).

POLITICS

African Americans have never received an equal share of the political pie. After Reconstruction, it was not until 1928 that a Black was again elected to Congress. Now, over 60 years and several civil rights acts later, there are still only 40 African-American congressional representatives. Recent years have brought some improvement. In fact, between 1970 and 1994, the number of Black elected officials has increased more than fivefold (see Table 8.3).

While African Americans have a long way to go to reach equality in the political arena, two events show the beginnings of their full-scale entry. First, in 1973, Councilman Tom Bradley, a Black sharecropper's son, defeated the incumbent to become mayor of Los Angeles at a time when the city was only 15 percent African

Figure 8.4 Race-Based Congressional District
This odd-shaped district stretching across Georgia links predominantly African-American neighborhoods. It triggered a 1995 Supreme Court ruling that such a race-based district is unconstitutional.

American. Bradley served in that capacity for almost 20 years. Second, in 1983, Bobby Rush was elected to Chicago's City Council and later, in 1992, to the U.S. House of Representatives. This elected official began his public career as the defense minister of the Black Panther Party. The political landscape is definitely changing (J. McCormick, 1992).

The Reverend Jesse Jackson is the most visible African-American political figure today, even though he has never been elected to office. Well known for his civil rights activity, Jackson campaigned for the 1984 Democratic Party nomination for president. His expressed goal was to create a "Rainbow Coalition" of disenfranchised Americans, including African Americans, Hispanics, Asian Americans, women, and gay people. Aided by a dramatic turnout of Black voters across the country, Jackson made a strong showing, winning 18 percent of the votes cast in Democratic presidential primaries. His success appeared to encourage more African Americans to run for national and statewide offices. Jackson ran for president again in 1988 and won 29 percent of the votes in Democratic primaries, second only to the 43 percent won by Massachusetts governor Michael Dukakis (*Congressional Quarterly,* 1984; E. Dionne, 1988).

African Americans continue to hold a disproportionately small share of elective and appointive offices in the United States. They usually serve in predominantly Black areas and rarely represent mixed constituencies. White political leaders, however, continue to represent many areas populated by racial minorities. As they have since passage of the Voting Rights Act of 1965, African Americans continue to grow as a political force, but they still fall far short of parity in elective and appointive offices (A. Pinkney, 1994).

The political gains by African Americans, as well as Hispanics, have been placed in jeopardy by legal actions that question race-based districts. Especially beginning with the 1992 presidential election, states drew boundaries for congressional districts so that African-American residential areas were grouped together to virtually guarantee the success of a minority candidate.

Civil rights pioneers meet in Greensboro, North Carolina, at the lunch counter where they were refused service in 1960, an event that triggered sit-ins to desegregate the South.

Some of these new minority districts were redrawn in such a way as to raise cries of gerrymandering. *Gerrymandering* dates from 1810 and refers to bizarrely outlining districts to create politically advantageous outcomes. Most controversial was the North Carolina 12th District, which meandered through ten counties for 160 miles along Highway I-85 to pick up concentrations of African-American voters in several cities (see Figure 8.4). In 1993, the U.S. Supreme Court, in *Shaw v. Reno,* ruled by a 5-4 vote that individuals could challenge such computer-generated districts. In 1995, the Supreme Court declared unconstitutional a strangely shaped Georgia district, calling into question race-based districts in other states. The conflict view in sociology would note that such attacks on race-based minority districts fail to acknowledge that these districts have routinely been drawn based on a commonality of interests, such as rural versus urban interests, or to maximize the likelihood of electing a representative from a certain political party. The use of race-based districts and the subsequent legal attacks demonstrate the vulnerability of racial and ethnic groups' role in the U.S. political system (K. Cooper, 1994; D. Kaplan, 1993).

CONCLUSION

Black and White Americans have dealt with the continued disparity between the two groups by endorsing several ideologies. Assimilation was the driving force behind the civil rights movement, which sought to integrate Whites and Blacks into one society. People who rejected any contact with the other group endorsed separatism. Both Whites and Blacks, as Chapter 2 showed, generally lent little support to separatism. The government and various Black organizations in the latter 1960s began to recognize cultural pluralism as a goal, at least paying lip service to the desire of many African Americans to exercise cultural and economic autonomy. Perhaps on no other issue is this condition more evident than in the schools.

As the future of African-American people in the United States unfolds, one element of the population generally unnoticed thus far may move into prominence. An evergrowing proportion of the Black population consists of people of foreign birth. In the 1980 census, 816,000 foreign-born Blacks were counted, or 3.1 percent of the Black population, the highest ever recorded. Yet by 1994 the number had nearly doubled to 1,596,000, which constituted 5.1 percent of the Black population. Fully 20 percent of of foreign-born Black population arrived in the preceding four years with the primary sources of the immigration being the island nations of the Caribbean. The numbers are expected to increase as is the proportion of the African American population which is foreign-born. Diversity exists in a significant degree with the Black community today (Farley and Allen, 1987; Hansen and Bachu, 1995; J. Reid, 1986).

Twice in this nation's history, African Americans have received significant attention from the federal government and, to some degree, from the larger White society. The first period extended from the Civil War to the end of Reconstruction. The second period was during the civil rights movement of the 1960s. In both periods, the government acknowledged that race was a major issue, and society made commitments to eliminate inequality (R. Farley, 1993). As we noted in the previous chapter, Reconstruction was followed by decades of neglect, and on several measures, the position of Blacks deteriorated in the United States. While the 1980s and 1990s have not been without their successes, race is clearly not a major issue on the nation's agenda. Even riots in Miami and Los Angeles only divert our attention, while attacks on school integration and affirmative action seem to persist.

The gains that have been made are substantial, but will the momentum continue? Improvement has occurred in a generation inspired and spurred on to bring about change. If the resolve to continue toward that goal lessens in the United States, the picture may become bleaker, and the rate of positive change may decline further.

KEY TERMS

class As defined by Max Weber, persons who share similar levels of wealth.

gerrymandering Redrawing districts bizarrely to create politically advantageous outcomes.

redlining The practice of financial lenders' refusing to grant home and commercial loans in minority and racially changing neighborhoods.

set-asides Programs stipulating a minimum proportion of government contracts that must be awarded to minority-owned businesses.

tracking The practice of placing students in specific curriculum groups on the basis of test scores and other criteria.

underemployment Work at a job for which the worker is overqualified, involuntary part-time instead of full-time employment, or intermittent employment.

victim discounting Society's viewing crimes as less socially significant if the victim is viewed as less worthy.

victimization surveys Annual attempts to measure crime rates by interviewing ordinary citizens who may or may not have been crime victims.

zoning laws Legal provisions stipulating land use and the architectural design of housing, often used to keep racial minorities and low-income persons out of suburban areas.

FOR FURTHER INFORMATION

Andrew Billingsley. *Climbing Jacob's Ladder: The Enduring Legacy of African-American Families.* New York: Simon & Schuster, 1992.

Sociologist Billingsley considers the strengths of African-American families and relates them to the studies of the underclass.

John H. Bunzel. *Race Relations on Campus: Stanford Students Speak.* Stanford, CA: Portable Stanford, 1992.

Bunzel, a former president of Stanford University and member of the U.S. Commission on Civil Rights, analyzes campus racial tensions and draws heavily on interviews with students.

Andrew Hacker. *Two Nations: Black and White, Separate, Hostile, Unequal.* New York: Scribner's, 1992.

Political scientist Hacker analyzes the relative status of African Americans in terms of family, income, employment, education, criminal justice, and government.

Douglas S. Massey and Nancy A. Denton. *American Apartheid: Segregation and the Making of the Underclass.* Cambridge: Harvard University Press, 1993.

In the view of the authors, the persistence of the ghetto is no accident and is a significant factor in perpetuating poverty among African Americans.

Alphonso Pinkney. *Black Americans,* 4th ed. Englewood Cliffs, NJ: Prentice-Hall, 1994.

Pinkney presents an excellent profile of African Americans and devotes a chapter to Black nationalism, although that subject is described in even greater detail in the author's 1976 work. He evaluates Milton Gordon's seven assimilation variables in the context of contemporary Black life.

William Pleasant, ed. *Independent Black Leadership in America.* New York: Castillo International, 1990.

A collection of statements by three controversial African American: minister Louis Farrakhan, Dr. Lenora Fulani, and Rev. Al Sharpton.

Brent Staples. *Parallel Time: Growing Up Black and White.* New York: Pantheon Press, 1994.

Staples, an editorial writer for the·*New York Times,* reflects on his life and that of his younger brother, who was murdered by a rival drug dealer.

Cornel West. *Race Matters.* Boston: Beacon Press, 1993.

The director of Afro-American Studies at Princeton University examines the basic racial problems confronting the United States.

William J. Wilson. *The Declining Significance of Race: Blacks and Changing American Institutions,* 2d ed. Chicago: University of Chicago Press, 1980.

Although acknowledging Black Americans' disadvantaged position compared to that of Whites, Wilson argues that, for the first time in the nation's history, class is more important than race in determining Black people's access to privilege and power.

CRITICAL THINKING QUESTIONS

1. To what degree have the civil rights movement initiatives in education been realized or do they remain unmet?

2. What challenges face the middle class within the African-American community?
3. What are the biggest assets and problems facing African-American families?
4. How are differential justice and victim discounting related?
5. How is race-based gerrymandering related to affirmative action?

Chapter 9

Hispanic Americans

Chapter Outline

Highlights

The group label *Hispanic American* links a diverse population of people who share a common language heritage but otherwise have many significant differences. The language barrier in an assimilationist-oriented society has been of major importance to Hispanics. For generations, schools made it difficult for Spanish-speaking children to succeed. The United States has only recently recognized its *bilingual, bicultural* heritage and allowed knowledge of a language other than English to be an asset, rather than a liability. The strength of resistance even to elements of pluralism has been exhibited by the *language purity* movement. Hispanics include several major groups, of which Chicanos, Puerto Ricans, and Cubans are the largest. Cuban Americans constitute a significant presence in southern Florida. Immigrants and refugees from Central and South America have also increasingly established communities throughout the United States.

More than one out of 11 of the U.S. population are of Spanish or Latin American origin. The Census Bureau estimates that by the year 2050, Hispanics will constitute about one-quarter of the U.S. population and that, collectively, Hispanics (or Latinos) will outnumber African Americans long before that date. Today, the majority of Hispanics in the United States are Chicanos, or Mexican Americans. Puerto Ricans and Cuban Americans account for the largest segment of the remaining 8 million Hispanics. The diversity of Hispanics is shown in Figure 9.1 and Table 9.1 (Bureau of the Census, 1993b).

The Hispanic influence is everywhere. Motion pictures such as *La Bamba, Born in East L.A., Stand and Deliver, Salsa,* and *The Mambo Kings* did not cater to Hispanic audiences alone. Cuban-born fashion designer Adolfo was a favorite of Nancy Reagan. Politicians address the needs and desires of Hispanic Americans. Music groups such as Los Lobos and the Miami Sound Machine attract listeners throughout the United States. Are these significant signs of acceptance or remnants of tolerant curiosity? In this and the next two chapters, we will examine the vibrant, growing group of Hispanic citizens in the United States (G. Firmat, 1994; R. Lacayo, 1988).

The various segments of the Hispanic population live in different regions: Chicanos are mostly in the Southwest, Puerto Ricans in the Northeast, and Cuban Americans in Florida (see Figure 9.2). The political strength of Hispanics is felt most in the Southwest. Over sixty percent of the nation's Hispanics are located in Arizona, California, Colorado, New Mexico, and Texas. This Hispanic population is dominated by Chicanos, of course, who account for almost ninety percent of the Southwest's Hispanics and are also a major factor in that region's growth. Chicanos accounted for half of population growth in Texas of over 2.7 million during the 1980s.

Some prevailing images of Hispanic settlements in the United States are no longer accurate. Hispanics do not live in rural areas. They are generally urban dwellers: 86 percent of Hispanics live in metropolitan areas, contrasted to 73 percent of the total population. Hispanics have moved away from their traditional areas of settlement. Many Chicanos have left the Southwest, and many Puerto

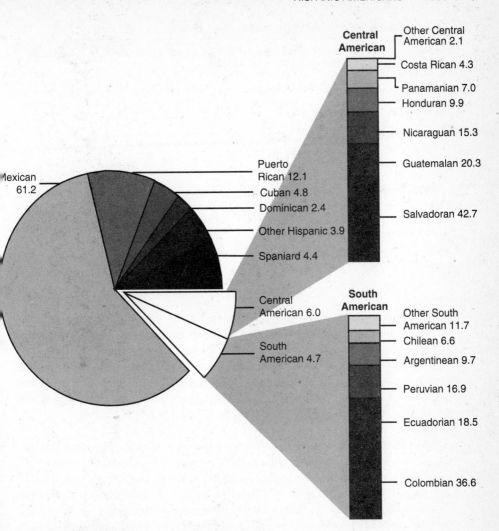

Figure 9.1 Hispanic Population in the United States by Origin, 1990
The percentage, per place of origin, of the Hispanic or Latino people in the United States, ranging from the largest group, Mexican or Chicano, to a variety of Latin-American nationalities.
Source: Bureau of the Census (1993f, p. 4).

Ricans have left New York City. In 1940, 88 percent of Puerto Ricans residing in the United States lived in New York City, but by the 1980 census, the proportion had dropped to less than half.

HISPANIC IDENTITY

Is there a common identity among Hispanics? Is a panethnic identity emerging? Non-Hispanics often label this diverse group of native-born Hispanic Ameri-

Table 9.1 HISPANIC POPULATION, 1993

Hispanics account for 1 out of 11 members of the U.S. population. Chicanos form the largest group.

Group	Percentage of Hispanics	Percentage of Population	Number (in thousands)
Chicano	64.2	5.8	14,628
Puerto Rican	10.6	.9	2,402
Cuban	4.7	.4	1,071
Central and South Americans	13.4	1.2	3,052
Other	7.0	.6	1,598
Total	100.0	8.9	22,752

Source: P. Montgomery (1994, pp. 10–11).

cans and immigrants as one group. This labeling by the out-group is similar to the dominant group's way of viewing "American Indians" or "Asian Americans" as one collective group. For example, sociologist Clara Rodriquez has noted that Puerto Ricans, who are American citizens, are viewed as an immigrant group and lumped with all Latinos or Hispanics. She observes that, to most Anglos, "all Hispanics look alike. It's the tendency to see all Hispanics as the same. It's unfortunate lack of attention to U.S. History" (R. Rodríguez, 1994, p. 32).

Are Hispanics themselves developing a common identity? To some degree, the actions of the dominant group do have an impact in culturally defining Hispanic identity. Hispanics are brought together through language, national cable TV stations such as Univision and Telemundo, and periodicals both in English and in Spanish aimed at them. These advances are significant because they counter the Anglo-dominated media. For example, in 1994, a survey reported that only 11 of the 800 prime-time television parts are Hispanic roles (N. Kanellos, 1994; H. Waters, 1994).

There are sharp divisions among Hispanics on the identity issue. Only a minority, one out of four as we noted in Chapter 1, prefer to refer to themselves by panethnic names such as *Hispanic* or *Latino* or Spanish American. Even among those born in the United States, fewer than one-third use such names, the majority preferring single-group names like *Mexicans, Mexican Americans, Chicanos, Puerto Ricans, Cubans,* and *Dominicans.* Indeed, in Miami, one can see bumper stickers proclaiming "No soy Hispano, soy Cubano"—"I am not Hispanic, I am Cuban" (D. Gonzalez, 1992). Such "name issues" or "language battles," as they have been termed, are not inconsequential, but they do distract attention from working together for common concerns. For example, bridging differences is important in politics, where the diverse Latino or Hispanic groups meet to support

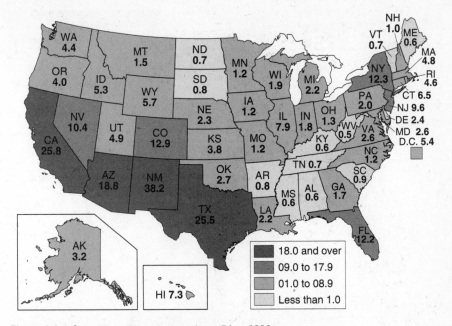

Figure 9.2 Where Most Hispanic Americans Live, 1990
In 1990, nearly 86 percent of the Hispanics in the United States lived in nine states. Chicanos, the largest Hispanic group, are concentrated in the Southwest, particularly in California and Texas. Most Puerto Ricans live in New York and New Jersey. Cubans are primarily in Florida. The largest numbers of the fourth, more scattered group, "other Hispanics," live in California and New York.

Source: Bureau of the Census (1993f).

candidates or certain legislative initiatives (de la Garza et al., 1992; E. Shorris, 1992; H. Waters, 1994).

THE LANGUAGE BARRIER

Hispanics, wherever they reside in the United States, share the heritage of the Spanish language. They do not all speak Spanish all the time. About one-third speak Spanish at work, and over 60 percent speak Spanish at home. Three-quarters listen to Spanish-language television and radio stations. Cubans, Mexican Americans (or Chicanos), Puerto Ricans, Dominicans, and other Hispanic groups can instantly identify their own forms of Spanish, but others, in particular Anglos, note more similarities than differences (P. Braus, 1993; N. Kanellos, 1994).

The myth of Anglo superiority has rested in part on language differences. (The term *Anglo* in the following text is used to mean all non-Hispanics, but primarily Whites.) First, the criteria for economic and social achievement usually include proficiency in English. By such standards, Spanish-speaking pupils are judged less

The increase in the Hispanic population has encouraged the growth of media targeting this population segment. Pictured here is Cuban-born Carlos Barber, who heads up Univision, the Spanish-language cable station.

able to compete. Many Anglos perceive French and German to be the only cultured foreign languages. Further, many Anglos believe that, occupationally, Spanish is not an asset. Only recently, as government agencies have belatedly begun to serve Hispanic people, and as businesses recognize the growing Hispanic consumer market, have Anglos recognized that knowing Spanish is not only useful but necessary to carry out certain tasks.

Quality of Hispanic Schooling

The devaluing of the Spanish language has, until recently, resulted in a conscious effort to discourage Hispanics from using it. This intent has been most evident in the schools. In the recent past in the Southwest, Chicanos (or Mexican Americans) were assigned to "Mexican schools," which were substantially under-funded in comparison to the regular public schools. Legal action against such schools dates back to 1945, but it was not until 1970 that the U.S. Supreme Court ruled in *Cisneros v. Corpus Christi Independent School District* that the *de jure* segregation of Chicanos was unconstitutional. Appeals delayed implementation of that decision, and not until September 1975 was the *de jure* plan forcibly overturned in Corpus Christi, Texas (Commission on Civil Rights, 1976a).

Even in integrated schools, Hispanic children were given separate, unequal treatment. "No Spanish" was a rule enforced throughout the Southwest, Florida, and New York City by school boards in the 1960s. Children speaking Spanish on school grounds, even on the playground, might be punished with detention after school, fines, physical reprimands, and even expulsion for repeated violations. From 1855 to as recently as 1968, teaching in any language other than English was illegal in California. Such laws existed despite a provision in the 1848 Treaty of Guadalupe Hidalgo between the United States and Mexico that guaranteed the right of Mexicans to maintain their culture. All official publications were to be bilingual, but "English only" became the social norm. Young schoolchildren were not allowed to go to the washroom unless they made their request in perfect English. Spanish-speaking children were then humiliated in front of their classmates as they wet their pants.

As late as 1971, 22 states specifically forbade bilingual instruction by law, and no state required it. Finally, in 1974, the Supreme Court unanimously ruled in *Lau v. Nichols* that it is a violation of civil rights to use English to teach pupils who cannot understand it. This ruling opened the way for the bilingual instruction of Spanish-speaking schoolchildren. Ironically, this precedent involved Chinese students in San Francisco (R. Macias, 1973; M. Sheils, 1977; E. Stoddard, 1973; D. Vidal, 1977).

The campaign to discourage the use of Spanish has naturally taken its toll on Hispanic schoolchildren's performance. The devastating fact that most Spanish-speaking Texans spend twice as long as Anglos in the first grade is attributed to the children's speaking only Spanish. Through the twisted logic of the dominant society, the children are held responsible and become the victims. As early as the 1930s, George Sanchez (1934) was warning his fellow educators about the fallacy of using tests in English to measure the potential of non-English-speaking children. Many of these pupils were classified as retarded or slow learners when, in fact, their only difficulty was lack of fluency in English. Such mistaken labeling impairs the learning of Hispanics and perpetuates in their own eyes, as well as those of Anglos, the notion that they are less qualified to compete (D. Aspy, 1970; Commission on Civil Rights, 1974; *New York Times,* 1979; S. Steiner, 1974).

The language barrier extends beyond school into employment. Hispanics are more likely to learn about jobs by word of mouth and less likely than Anglos or Blacks to read job listings in newspapers or to use employment agencies. Furthermore, the government has done little to help. Ironically, job training programs designed to help the poor compete are rarely offered in bilingual form (Commission on Civil Rights, 1976c).

The importance of Spanish to Hispanics cannot be overstated. Even to English-speaking Hispanics, the language represents a cultural heritage centuries old. This recognition is particularly important because rules against using Spanish have generally extended to the suppression of the Hispanic cultures. Even in those places without the "no Spanish" rule, positive treatment of the Hispanic experience was still rare. As recently as 1969, California was alone in the Southwest in offering any courses on Mexican-American heritage in schools that were at least 10 percent Chicano (Commission on Civil Rights, 1972).

Bilingualism

Should the United States place greater emphasis on respect for cultural diversity, or should it promote shared cultural standards? Is it essential that English be the sole language of instruction in American schools and universities? Such questions are part of the passionate debate on bilingualism currently under way in the United States.

Bilingualism is the use of two or more languages in places of work or educational facilities, according each language equal legitimacy. Thus, a program of bilingual education may instruct children in their native language (such as Spanish) while gradually introducing them to the language of the dominant society (English). If such a program is also bicultural, it will teach children about the culture of both linguistic groups. Bilingualism has most often appeared as an issue in the voting booth and in the classroom.

Voting Rights   In 1975, Congress moved toward recognizing the multilingual background of the U.S. population. Federal law now requires bilingual or even multilingual ballots where census data show a substantial number of non-English-speaking people. Even before Congress acted, the federal courts had been ordering cities like Chicago, Miami, and New York City to provide bilingual ballots where necessary.

Historically, language minorities have not participated in elections to the extent that Anglos have, and they have produced even fewer officeholders than the Black community has. Table 9.2 documents the relatively small proportion of Hispanics, compared to Blacks and to all U.S. citizens, who reported being registered to vote and reported voting in both the 1972 and the 1992 presidential elections.

The poor turnout was not because Hispanics were not interested in voting. Many were ineligible because they were noncitizens. In the November 1992 general election, 62 percent of Hispanics who did not vote were noncitizens, compared to only 12 percent of non-Hispanics. This handicap may help to explain why only 29 percent of Hispanics, compared to 61 percent of the people as a whole, reported voting in 1992. By contrast, Puerto Rican voters on the island of Puerto Rico turn out in proportions that exceed those of Anglos on the mainland, but they have a dismal record on the mainland, where they face English ballots (with some exceptions in New York City). Similarly, states with literacy tests have sub-

Table 9.2   VOTER PARTICIPATION REPORTED, 1972 AND 1992

Numerical minorities such as Blacks and Hispanics are at a disadvantage in national elections, but the problem is compounded when they register and vote in smaller proportions than Whites.

Group	1972		1992	
	Percentage Registered	Percentage Voted	Percentage Registered	Percentage Voted
Whites	73.4	64.5	63.6	70.1
Hispanics	44.4	37.5	28.9	35.0
Blacks	65.5	52.1	54.0	63.9
Total population	72.3	63.0	61.3	68.2

Source: J. Jennings (1993, pp. v–vi).

stantially lower voter registration in areas populated by Hispanics than states without such tests. The result of multilingual ballots should be more Hispanic officeholders, from school board members to legislators (J. Jennings, 1993; N. Kanellos, 1994).

Bilingual Education   *Bilingual education* allows students to learn academic material in their own language, while they are learning a second language. Ideally bilingual education programs also allow English-speaking pupils to be bilingual, but generally they are directed only to making non-English-speakers proficient in more than one language.

Belatedly, bilingualism has become recognized as an asset. In the past, school systems' suppression of Spanish made many Hispanics *aliterate,* that is, illiterate in both languages. Although the children were superficially able to speak both English and Spanish, they could not speak and write either language correctly. Finally, in 1965, the Elementary and Secondary Education Act (ESEA) provided for bilingual education. Implementation of the ESEA provisions and subsequent programs has been slow.

Programs teaching English as a Second Language (ESL) have been the cornerstone of bilingual education, but they are limited in approach. For example, ESL programs tend to emphasize bilingual, but not bicultural, education. As a result, the method can unintentionally contribute to ethnocentric attitudes, especially if it seems to imply that a minority group is not really worthy of attention. As conflict theorists are quick to note, the interests of the less powerful—in this case, millions of non-English-speaking children—are those that are least likely to be recognized and respected. One alternative to the ESL approach, viewed with much less favor by advocates of bilingualism, is *English immersion,* in which students are taught primarily in English, using their native languages only when they do not understand their lessons. In practice, such instruction usually becomes an English-only "crash program" (F. Hechinger, 1987).

Bilingual education remains a controversial issue, despite its positive impact on young people's development of facility in English.

Bilingual education has been beset by problems. Its early supporters were disillusioned by the small number of English-speaking children participating and by the absence of a bicultural component in most programs. The frustration has been most clearly visible in the lack of consensus among educators on how best to implement bilingual programs. Even when a consensus is reached in a school district, superintendents find it difficult to get qualified instructors. The problem is further complicated by the presence of children speaking languages other than the predominant second language, so that superintendents must mount bilingual programs in many languages. Indeed, federally supported programs now operate in an estimated 125 languages.

Do bilingual programs help children to learn English? It is difficult to reach firm conclusions on the effectiveness of the bilingual programs in general because they vary so widely in their approach to non-English-speaking children. Research studies evaluating bilingual programs for Navajo-speaking children in Arizona, Chinese-speaking children in New York City, French-speaking children in Louisiana and Minnesota, and Spanish-speaking children in several states have all demonstrated that a quality bilingual program can be effective in improving both general learning skills and performance in reading and speaking English. But some educational researchers seem to agree that studies on bilingual education have been methodologically unsound and thus remain inconclusive (Ramirez, Yuen, and Ramey, 1991; L. Soto, 1991).

Drawing on the conflict sociological perspective, we can understand some of the attacks on bilingual programs. The criticisms do not necessarily result from careful educational research. Rather, they stem from the effort to assimilate children and to deprive them of language pluralism. This view is expressed by those who wish to stamp out "foreignness" wherever it occurs, especially in our schools. Research findings have little influence on those who, holding such ethnocentric views, try to persuade policymakers to follow their thinking. Success in bilingual education may begin to address the problem of high school dropouts and the paucity of Hispanics in colleges and universities.

Language Purity Attacks on bilingualism both in voting and in education have taken several forms and have even broadened to question the appropriateness of U.S. residents using any language other than English. Federal policy has become more restrictive. Local schools have been given more authority to determine appropriate methods of instruction; they have also been forced to provide more of their own funding for bilingual education. Early in 1981, the federal government decided to scrap new proposals requiring school districts to offer bilingual education to non-English-speaking children. The government's action was bitterly protested by Representative Robert Garcia, a Puerto Rican congressman from New York City, who stated, "This is a signal to the rest of the country that does not want civil rights for Hispanics that school districts can say, 'The hell with it, why should we bother?' It will be back to business as usual, which in many states is back to bigotry" (Barrett and Cooper, 1981, p. 24).

The congressman's warnings were not heeded. Beginning in 1985, federal funds for bilingual education could also be used for alternative types of programs, which included the English immersion of Spanish-speaking children in English-language programs. Furthermore, a 1988 law stipulates that no student can be in a federally funded transitional bilingual program for more than three years unless special requirements are met.

Attacks on bilingualism have come on a number of fronts. In a 1983 nonbinding referendum, San Francisco voters approved by a 2-to-1 vote a proposition opposing the practice of printing city ballots in Spanish and Chinese as well as English. In 1984, Californians passed by almost a 3-to-1 margin a statewide proposition supporting repeal of a federal requirement that ballots be printed in foreign languages as well as in English. The proposition passed even though a survey in California found that, in 1984, about the same proportion of White ethnics used non-English ballots as did Hispanics. In response to this mood and in an overall effort to reduce federal spending, the Reagan administration issued new regulations, beginning with the 1984 general election, sharply reducing the number of counties required to provide bilingual ballots for Hispanic Americans and other voters in need of bilingual services.

The momentum continues to establish English as the "official" language of the nation. National surveys show up to 78 percent of the U.S. population favoring English as the official language of government. As of 1995, 22 states had passed laws or constitutional amendments to that effect, and many more were considering such measures. The courts are dealing with cases questioning the legality of these provisions, but there is clearly significant support for such declarations. These challenges come just as Hispanic voter registration has been showing signs of growth. The Census Bureau estimates that there were over 5 million Hispanic voters by 1992. This number represented an increase of 106 percent over 1972, compared to a 52 percent increase for African Americans and a 25 percent increase for Whites (L. Chavez, 1994; J. Jennings, 1993).

A major force behind a proposed constitutional amendment and other efforts to restrict bilingualism is U.S. English, a nationwide organization, which by 1990 claimed to have 350,000 members. Its adherents echo the view of Idaho senator Steve Symms that "many Americans now feel like strangers in their own neighborhoods, aliens in their own country." By contrast, Hispanic leaders see the U.S. English campaign as a veiled expression of racism. "I wonder whether the movement has as part of its agenda whitening the complexion of the country," asks Joe Trevino, head of the League of United Latin American Citizens (J. Ridgeway, 1986 p. 33; also see R. Bernstein, 1990).

The challenges to bilingualism continue. In 1995, legislators in Illinois seriously considered a proposal to allow school districts to drop bilingual programs involving 82,000 students. While the arguments were financial, many other education programs remained unaffected. Also in 1995, Congress began the consideration of yet another constitutional amendment. This version would both ban federal funding of bilingual education and establish English as the official language (M. Garza, 1995).

The discouraging lack of movement toward bilingualism in the United States makes this country unusual. Switzerland has four official languages and India more than 20, and most nations elevate more than one language to some kind of official status. It is depressing to see businesses but not the government or the general public recognizing more than one language as viable. Again, conflict sociologists would see this condition as an instance of the interests of the powerful being given primacy. McDonald's touts its "hamburguesas," and Anheuser-Busch insists that "Budweiser es para usted" ("is for you"). Perhaps, at some time in the future, teachers and poll watchers will more often offer the greeting, "Se habla inglés y español."

Bilingual education, however, is not an issue just for Spanish-speaking people. The plaintiff Kinney Lau, after all, in the initial landmark ruling *Lau v. Nichols,* was a Chinese student failing in his San Francisco school because he could not understand the language of instruction. More than 5 million children of immigrants are expected to have entered public schools by the end of the 1990s speaking more than 150 languages. While Spanish will be the major minority-language, seven states will have schools where 25 percent or more of the students do not speak English as their primary language (C. Leslie, 1991).

CUBAN AMERICANS

Third in numbers only to Chicanos and Puerto Ricans, Cuban Americans represent a significant ethnic Hispanic minority in the United States. Their presence in this country is a relatively long one, Cuban settlements in Florida dating back to as early as 1831. These tended to be small, close-knit communities organized around a single enterprise, such as a cigar-manufacturing firm.

Until recently, however, the number of Cuban Americans was very modest. The 1960 census showed that 79,000 people who had been born in Cuba lived in the United States. By 1993, over a million people of Cuban birth or descent lived

By 1990, 18 states had declared English the official language. Copyright 1988, USA Today. *Reprinted with permission.*

By 1995, 22 states had declared English the official language.

Copyright 1988, *USA Today.* Reprinted with permission.

in the United States. This tremendous increase followed Fidel Castro's assumption of power after the 1959 Cuban Revolution.

Immigration

Cuban immigration to the United States since the 1959 revolution has been a continuous stream, but there have been three significant influxes of large numbers of immigrants. First, the initial exodus of about 200,000 following Castro's assumption of power lasted for a period of about three years. Regular commercial air traffic continued despite the U.S. severing of diplomatic relations with Cuba. This first wave stopped with the missile crisis of October 1962, when all legal movement between the two nations was halted.

The second major migration has been the most controversial. In 1980, more than 124,000 refugees fled Cuba in the "freedom flotilla." In May of that year, a few boats from Cuba began to arrive in Key West, Florida, with people seeking asylum in the United States. President Carter, reflecting the nation's hostility toward Cuba's Communist government, told the new arrivals and anyone else who might be listening in Cuba that they were welcome "with open arms and an open heart." As the number of arrivals escalated, it became apparent that Castro had used the invitation as an opportunity to send prison inmates and addicts. The majority of the refugees, though, were neither marginal to the Cuban economy nor social deviants.

The Cuban refugees of this migration were soon given the derisive name *Marielitos*. The word, meant to suggest that these refugees were undesirable, refers to Mariel, the fishing port west of Havana where Cuban authorities herded people into boats. The term *Marielitos* became and remains a stigma in the media and in Florida, suggesting that this group of people is inferior, in surprising agreement with Castro's evaluation of them, and to the embarrassment of the Carter administration that first welcomed them. Because of their negative reception by longer-established Cuban immigrants, coupled with the group's relatively modest skills and little formal education, this Latin American group had the most difficulty in adjusting to their new life in the United States.

Government assistance to these immigrants was limited, but help from some groups of Cuban Americans in the Miami area was substantial. For many members of this "freedom flotilla," a smooth transition has been difficult. Unlike the earlier wave, they grew up in a country bombarded with anti-American images. Despite these problems, acceptance into the Hispanic community has been impressive, and many members of this second significant wave have found employment. Most have applied for permanent-resident status. However, for a small core group of 3,700, adjustment was impossible. The legal status of a few of these detainees was ambiguous because of alleged offenses committed either in Cuba or the United States or both. Major prison riots in Louisiana and Georgia by some of these detainees brought attention to their plight, which is still largely unresolved (Boswell and Curtis, 1984; Hufker and Cavender, 1990; J. LeMoyne, 1990; Portes and Stepick, 1985; H. Silva, 1985).

A smaller, but also controversial, third wave occurred in 1994 when Cuba faced particularly harsh economic conditions and social unrest created by the end of the significant Russian aid that Cuba had received for so many years. Castro encouraged migration, and the Clinton administration acquiesced at first by picking up the refugees at sea and transporting them to the U.S. mainland. Opposition grew to this welcome, particularly in Florida, where the governor expressed the need for vast amounts of assistance to help with the influx of Cubans. President Clinton then revised the policy, relocating the refugees temporarily to the U.S. Naval Base in Guantanomo, Cuba, as well as to other nations, such as Panama. An estimated 20,000 arrived at the base during this migration (T. Post, 1994).

The Present Picture

Compared to other recent immigrant groups and to Hispanics as a whole, Cuban Americans are doing relatively well. As shown in Table 9.3, young Cubans (those 25–34 years old) have college completion rates twice those of other Hispanics and comparable to those of Anglos. Unemployment rates are low, especially for Cuban-American women, who are unlikely to seek employment unless positions are available. The close-knit structure of Cuban-American families encourages women to follow the traditional roles of homemaker and mother.

The presence of Cubans has been felt in urban centers throughout the United States, but most notably in the Miami, Florida, area. Throughout their various immigration phases, Cubans have been encouraged to move out of southern Florida, but many have returned to Dade County (metropolitan Miami), with its warm climate and proximity to other Cubans and Cuba itself. As of 1990, 53 percent of all Cuban Americans lived in Miami; another 15 percent lived in New York City, and 5

The most recent influx of 20,000 Cuban immigrants came in 1994 as Cuba's social and economic problems mounted.

Table 9.3   SELECTED SOCIAL AND ECONOMIC CHARACTERISTICS OF CUBANS, 1993

Compared to other Hispanics, Cuban Americans are doing well, except for their low incomes.

	Total Non-Hispanic White	Total Hispanic	Cuban
Median age	34.4	26.7	43.6
Percentage completing college			
25–34 years	25.5	9.0	25.1
35 years and over	22.0	9.0	14.7
Percentage unemployed			
Male	8.1	12.4	7.6
Female	5.8	11.1	7.3
Percentage living below poverty level	13.1	29.3	18.1
Median income (year-round workers)			
Male	$31,765	$20,054	$23,437
Female	$21,930	$17,124	$19,687

Source: P. Montgomery (1994, pp. 10–15).

percent lived in Los Angeles. Metropolitan Miami itself now has a Hispanic majority compared to only a 4 percent Hispanic minority in 1950 (M. Winsberg, 1994).

Probably no ethnic group has had more influence on the fortunes of a city in a short period of time than have the Cubans on Miami. Some consider the Cubans' influence positive; the president of the University of Miami declared, "Castro is the best thing that ever happened to Miami." The Cuban and other Latin-American immigrants have transformed Miami from a languishing resort to a boomtown (T. Talbot, 1993). Their relations with other groups have not been perfect. For example, Miami's other Hispanics, such as the Venezuelans, Ecuadorians, and Colombians, resent being mistaken for Cubans and feel that their own distinctive nationality is being submerged. Perhaps the primary criticism heard in Miami's Anglo community is that the Cubans invest their profits in other Cuban-owned businesses and have little to do with Anglos and Blacks. Non-Cuban Americans feel that the economic resurgence of Miami is bypassing them. Disadvantaged African Americans resent Cuban Americans who seek public assistance because, as a group, they are better off than other subordinate groups. The Cubans respond that self-help among Cuban Americans is not clannishness but merely the kind of self-help that so many immigrant groups before them have undertaken (Pérez-Stable and Uriarte, 1993; L. Rohter, 1993b; T. Talbot, 1993).

The Cuban immigrants had much to adjust to, and they could not immediately pick up from where they had left off in Cuba. Although those who fled Cuba were sometimes forced to give up their life's savings, the early immigrants of the first wave were generally well educated, had professional or managerial backgrounds, and therefore met with greater economic success (Portes and Stepick, 1993).

The long-range prospects for Cubans in the United States depend on several factors. Of obvious importance are events in Cuba, for many Cuban refugees publicly proclaim their desire to return if the Communist government is overturned. A

Cuban American–African American relations are strained in Miami, primarily as the result of economic competition. In 1990, Cuban Americans protested the visit of South African leader Nelson Mandela following his favorable comments about Cuba's Fidel Castro.

powerful force in politics in Miami is the Cuban-American National Foundation, which takes a strong anti-Castro position. They have not looked favorably on proposals by the Clinton administration that the United States develop a more flexible policy toward Cuba. More moderate voices in the Cuban exile community have not been encouraged to speak out. Indeed, there has even been sporadic violence within the community over United States–Cuban relations (L. Rohter, 1992, 1993d).

As the years pass and as the refugees' prosperity increases, however, fewer and fewer are likely to return even if a political reversal occurs. A hard core of Cubans in the United States are still active anti-Castro militants. In addition, the growing economic and social problems of Cuba are causing elder Cubans in Miami to have second thoughts about wanting to return. Even over ten years ago, in 1983, while 68 percent of Miami's Cuban Americans surveyed favored an invasion, only 24 percent indicated that they would return if Castro were actually ousted. Assimilation may not be dampening their anti-Castro feelings, but it is deepening their roots in the United States (T. Morganthau, 1994; R. Morin, 1983; D. Rieff, 1993).

Social scientist José Llanes (1982), formerly of the University of Havana, has worked among and interviewed Cuban exiles in the United States. In "Listen to Their Voices," he explores the duality that Cuban Americans feel for Cuba and the United States.

More dramatic than efforts to change Cuba politically has been the transformation in Miami politics. Miami was once a liberal Democratic Party stronghold, but Cuban Americans' overwhelming Republican orientation has elected a number of conservatives to office. Miami elected a Cuban American, Xavier Suarez, as mayor in 1985 over

Listen to Their Voices
"Shores of Liberty"

JOSÉ LLANES

José Llanes

No matter how we feel about Fidel and the revolution, the word Cuba is never far from our lips. The fantasy of the nation, either as it was (*la Cuba de ayer*) in our rose-colored memories or how it will be in lavender-colored myths of the future, is alive in all of us. Yet many of us belong to two nations now. Officially we are citizens of the United States (68 percent to 46 percent depending on estimates chosen), and circumstantially we are an important part of recent U.S. history. In brief, we are as American as the previous immigrants and Cuban to the last!

Our search for political and social equality started with American citizenship. Before becoming U.S. citizens, we viewed ourselves as invited guests, willing to demand fair treatment but conscious of our alien status. The search for the "central value of the American system and its legitimating agent"—equality—is some-thing for "Americans" to do. Along the way we encounter Mexican-Americans, Puerto Ricans, Central Americans, Blacks, Chinese-Americans, and we embrace democracy—U.S.-style democracy as a means of attaining institutional equality. Our own view is somewhat more jaundiced, nurtured in the totalitarianism of our heritage. Ironically, our struggle for equality is helped along by the progress made already, before inequality was actually perceived. This struggle will occupy our attention in the decades ahead, as our *ethnos* becomes part of our self-identity.

What will become of us here in the United States? What will become of Cuba? If Cuban society changes, will we be part of that change? When, if ever, will we stop feeling Cuban?

Source: From José Llanes, *Cuban Americans: Masters of Survival,* Cambridge, Massachusetts: Abt Books, 1982, p. 206; Abt Books, 55 Wheeler Street, Cambridge, MA 02138.

another Cuban American. In 1989, Havana-born Ileana Ros-Lehtinen became the first Cuban American in Congress representing Miami. A Republican, she had come to the United States during the first wave of immigration following Castro's rise to power.

Cubans have selectively accepted Anglo culture. One especially vulnerable Cuban practice has been the tradition of chaperoning adolescents. But Cuban culture has been tenacious; Cubans do not feel that they need to forget Spanish, as other immigrant children have shunned their linguistic past. Still, a split between the original exiles and their children is evident. As a result, Miami has become the most bilingual of any city in the United States not on the Mexican border. At the annual Orange Bowl Parade on New Year's Eve, tourists are greeted with dual-language signs warning "No se siente en la acera" ("Don't sit on the curb").

The Cuban experience in the United States has not been completely positive. Some detractors worry about the Cubans' vehement anticommunism and about the apparent growth of an organized crime syndicate that engages in ganglike violence and lucrative trade in illegal drugs. Miami's Cubans have also recently expressed concern over what they feel is the indifference of Miami's Roman Catholic hierarchy. Cubans, like other Hispanics, are underrepresented in leadership positions throughout the church. Although there is one Anglo priest for every 855 English-speaking Catholics, there is only one Hispanic priest for every 5,000 Spanish-speaking parishioners. The Catholic leadership counters by affirming their long commitment to assisting the exiles. In addition, Cuban Americans in Miami as group, despite individual success stories, fall behind Anglos in income, proportion of professionals, and employment rate.

Bilingualism has become an emotional issue in southern Florida, where concern about language purity has been strong. In a 1980 election, the electorate, by a 3-to-2 vote, reversed a 1978 resolution designating Dade County a bilingual county. Through this referendum, voters prohibited public expenditure "for the purpose of utilizing any language other than English or promoting any culture other than that of the United States." This vote ended the practice of translating county legal documents into Spanish, although bilingual education programs continue.

This 1980 vote was a statement by the overwhelming majority of non-Cubans that they were uncomfortable with the "Latinization" of their area. But it was for the most part an ideological statement; it has had little practical effect. Just as Cubans are at a clear disadvantage if they cannot communicate effectively in English, Anglo businesspeople have increasingly realized the value, as reflected in profit statements, of being able to communicate in Spanish as well as English (R. Mohl, 1986).

CENTRAL AND SOUTH AMERICANS

More than 1 million immigrants have come from Central and South America, not including Mexico, since 1820. This diverse population has not been closely observed. Indeed, most government statistics treat them collectively as "other" and rarely differentiate them by nationality. Yet people from Chile and Costa Rica have little in common other than their hemisphere of origin and the Spanish language. Not all Central and South Americans have Spanish as their native tongue; for example, immigrants from Brazil speak Portuguese, immigrants from French Guiana speak French, and those from Surinam speak Dutch.

Many of the nations of Central and South America have a *color gradient* placing people into a myriad of racial groups. African slaves were brought to almost all of these countries, and these people of African descent, in varying degrees, have intermarried with each other or with indigenous Indians, as well as with the European colonizers. Rather than placing people in two or three distinct racial groupings, these societies describe skin color in a continuum from light to dark. Terms such as "mestezo Hondurans," "mulatto Colombians," or "African Panamanians" reflect this continuum. The discussion of Puerto Ricans in Chapter 11 and of race relations in Brazil in Chapter 17 will consider color gradients in greater detail.

Added to language diversity and the color gradient are social class distinctions, religious differences, urban versus rural backgrounds, and differences in dialect even among those speaking the same language. We can understand historians Ann Orlov and Reed Ueda's (1980) conclusion that "social relations among Central and South American ethnic groups in the United States defy generalization" (p. 212). Central and South Americans do not form, nor should they be expected to form, a cohesive group, nor do they "naturally" form coalitions with Cuban Americans or Chicanos or Puerto Ricans.

Immigration Patterns

Immigration from the various Central and South American nations has been sporadic—influenced by both our immigration laws and social forces operating in the home country. Perceived economic opportunities escalated the northward movement in the 1960s. By 1970, Panamanians and Hondurans represented the largest national groupings, most of them being identified in the census as "nonwhite."

Since the mid-1970s, increasing numbers of Central and South Americans have fled unrest. While Hispanics as a whole are a fast-growing minority, Central and South Americans increased in numbers even faster than Mexicans or any other group during the 1980s. In particular, from about 1978, war and economic chaos in El Salvador, Nicaragua, and Guatemala prompted many to seek refuge in the United States. Not at all a homogeneous group, they range from Guatemalan Indian peasants to wealthy Nicaraguan exiles. These latest arrivals have probably had some economic motivation for migration, but this concern is overshadowed by their fear of being killed or hurt if they remained in their home country (A. Camarillo, 1993).

The Present Picture

The contemporary settlement of Central and South Americans has been clouded by two issues. First, many of the arrivals are illegal immigrants. Among those uncovered as undocumented workers, citizens from El Salvador, Guatemala, and Colombia are outnumbered only by Mexican nationals. Second, significant numbers of highly trained and skilled people have left these countries, which most desperately need these professional workers. While the results are difficult to document, this *brain drain* worsens conditions in these professionals' countries of origin.

Economically, as a group, Central and South Americans experience high unemployment levels compared to other Hispanics; yet, they are better educated, as shown in Table 9.4. This disparity reflects the plight that frequently faces recent immigrants. Upon relocating in a new country, they initially experience downward mobility in terms of occupational status.

The settlement patterns of this diverse group have been consistent over time. Central and South Americans have congregated in urban areas, especially in very large metropolitan areas such as Los Angeles, San Francisco, Chicago, and Washington, D.C. (A. Camarillo, 1993).

The challenges to immigrants from Latin America are reflected in the experience of Colombians. The initial arrivals from this South American nation after World War I were educated middle-class people who quickly assimilated to life in the United States. Rural unrest in Colombia later triggered large-scale movement to the United States, where the Colombian immigrants had to adapt to a new culture *and* to urban life. The adaptation of this later group has been much more difficult. Some have found success through catering to their other Colombians. For example, enterprising immigrants have opened *bodegas* (grocery stores) to supply traditional, familiar foodstuffs. Similarly, Colombians have established restaurants, travel agencies, and realtors that serve other Colombians. Yet many find themselves obliged to take menial jobs and to require that several family members combine incomes to stay abreast of the high cost of urban life. Colombians of mixed African descent also face racial as well as ethnic and language barriers (Orlov and Ueda, 1980).

What is likely to be the future of Central and South Americans in the United States? While much will depend on future immigration, they could assimilate over the course of generations. One alternative is that they will become trapped with Chicanos as a segment of the dual labor market of the urban areas where they have taken residence. A more encouraging possibility is that they will retain an independent identity, like the Cubans, and establish an economic base. An examination of the urban economy of the San Francisco metropolitan area in the 1980s seemed to show that they were entering the same irregular economy and poverty populated by the Chicanos there. Little evidence of the establishment of a local economic base was found. Whether this initial assessment has continued and can be generalized to other cities will await subsequent analysis (S. Wallace, 1989).

In 1991, violence broke out in the Hispanic Mount Pleasant area of Washington, D.C., heavily populated by Central American immigrants. El Salvadorans figured prominently among those arrested during the several days of rioting that followed the police shooting of a Salvadoran man being arrested. In the aftermath, many concerns were raised similar to those after the riots in African-American neighborhoods in the 1960s: no jobs, police brutality, an unresponsive city government, exploitive employers, and uncaring teachers. One difference was that many

Table 9.4   SELECTED SOCIAL AND ECONOMIC CHARACTERISTICS OF CENTRAL AND SOUTH AMERICANS, 1993

People of Central or South American origin have less formal schooling and are more likely to be poor, compared to other Hispanic Americans and non-Hispanics.

	Total Non-Hispanic	Total Hispanic	Central and South Americans
Median age	34.4	26.7	28.6
Percentage completing college			
25–34 years	25.5	9.0	13.5
35 years and over	22.0	9.0	16.3
Percentage unemployed			
Male	8.1	12.4	12.4
Female	5.8	11.1	14.4
Percentage living below poverty level	13.1	29.3	26.7
Median income (year-round workers)			
Male	$31,765	$20,054	$14,358
Female	$21,930	$17,124	$10,249

Source: P. Montgomery (1994, pp. 10–15).

neighborhood residents had come to our nation's capital fleeing violent warfare in their home country (W. Raspberry, 1991; S. Sanchez, 1991).

CONCLUSION

The signals are mixed. A number of movies and television programs and much music have a Hispanic flavor. Candidates for political office seek Hispanic votes and sometimes even speak Spanish to do so. Yet the poverty rate of Hispanic families reported in 1993 was 29 percent, compared to 10 percent for non-Hispanic Whites (P. Montgomery, 1994, p. 13).

The successes are there. Texas Tech University president Lauro Cavazos was named by Ronald Reagan in 1988 to head the Department of Education—the first Hispanic cabinet appointee in this nation's history. George Bush subsequently asked him to continue in that position. Yet, in 1987, a study found that Hispanic schoolchildren—unlike Black students—were far more likely to attend segregated schools than they had been 20 years before. In 1991, 73 percent of the Hispanics attend predominantly minority schools, compared to 55 percent in 1968. Of the 36 schools listed as overcrowded in Chicago, 33 were in Hispanic neighborhoods (G. Orfield, 1987, 1993).

Ballots are printed in Spanish and other languages. Bilingual education at taxpayer expense is available throughout the United States. Yet more and more states are declaring English the "official" language, and even Congress from time to time considers a constitutional amendment to that effect. Many Hispanics feel that to be bilingual is not to be less a part of the United States. Espousing pluralism rather than assimilation is not "un-American." This contrast of images and substance is evident again in the chapters that follow on Chicanos and Puerto Ricans. "In World War II, more Hispanics won Medals of Honor than any other ethnic group," said Democratic Representative Matthew Martinez, a former U.S. Marine who represented part of Los Angeles. "How much blood do you have to spill before you prove you are a part of something?" (D. Whitman, 1987, p. 49).

KEY TERMS

bilingual education A program designed to allow students to learn academic concepts in their native language while they learn a second language.

bilingualism The use of two or more languages in places of work or education and the treatment of each language as legitimate.

brain drain Immigration to the United States of skilled workers, professionals, and technicians who are desperately needed by their home countries.

color gradient The placement of people along a continuum from light to dark skin color rather than in distinct racial groupings by skin color.

English immersion Teaching in English by teachers who know the students' native language but use it only when students do not understand the lessons.

Marielitos People who arrived from Cuba in the second wave of Cuban immigration, most specifically those forcibly deported via Mariel Harbor. The term is generally reserved for those refugees seen as especially undesirable.

FOR FURTHER INFORMATION

Gustavo Pérez Firmat. *Life on the Hyphen*. Austin: University of Texas Press, 1994.

A look at the culture of the Cuban-American community and its impact on the United States, with special attention to media and music.

Denis Lynn Daly Heyck. *Barrios and Borderlands: Cultures of Latinos and Latinas in the United States*. New York: Routledge, 1994.

Linguist Heyck brings interviews, poetry, and essays together with her own chronicle of the Hispanic experience in the United States.

Nicolás Kanellos. *The Hispanic Almanac: From Columbus to Corporate America*. Detroit: Visible Ink, 1994.

A compendium of history and cultural events, including sections on the media, the performing arts, Hispanic literature, and sports.

Edwin Melendez, Clara Rodriquez, and Janis Barry Figueroa, eds. *Hispanics in the Labor Force: Issues and Policies*. Washington, DC: Plenum, 1991.

Considers many aspects of Hispanics in the workplace, with special attention to women workers and the government as a potential force for positive change.

Joan Moore and Harry Pachon. *Hispanics in the United States*. Englewood Cliffs, NJ: Prentice-Hall, 1985.

Two sociologists present an analysis of people in the United States whose identity is based on national origins in Mexico, Puerto Rico, Cuba, and other Latin-American nations.

Frank Morales and Frank Bonilla, eds. *Latinos in a Changing U.S. Economy*. Newbury Park, NJ: Sage, 1993.

Besides national treatments, there is a more focused consideration of Chicanos in Los Angeles and San Antonio, Cubans in Miami, and Puerto Ricans in New York City.

Periodicals

Journals devoted exclusively to the Hispanic experience are *Aztlán* (founded in 1969) and the *Hispanic Journal of Behavioral Sciences* (1979). *Latina* and *Hispanic* are among the popular periodicals oriented to the Hispanic audience.

CRITICAL THINKING QUESTIONS

1. What different factors seem to unite and to divide the Hispanic community in the United States?
2. How do Hispanics view themselves as a group? How are they viewed by "outsiders"?
3. Why do language and bilingualism become almost ideological issues in the United States?
4. To what extent has the Cuban migration been positive, and to what degree do significant challenges remain?
5. How have Central and South Americans contributed to the diversity of the Hispanic peoples in the United States?

Chapter
10

Chicanos: The Nation's Largest Ethnic Group

Chapter Outline

Highlights

Chicanos make up over 60 percent of the largely Spanish-speaking Hispanic population. The history of Chicanos is closely tied to immigration, which has been encouraged (*Los Braceros* program) when Mexican labor is in demand, or discouraged (*repatriation* and *Operation Wetback*) when Mexican workers are unwanted. Chicanos find themselves on the periphery of formal education, facing a curriculum unsuited to their needs and colleges ill prepared to receive them. As is true of other subordinate groups, the strength of Chicanos rests in their organizations: political groups, the church, and the family. The continuing gap between Chicanos and Anglos has given birth to an awakened consciousness and has contributed to the popularity of such charismatic leaders as César Chávez and Reies Tijerina.

Chicanos, immigrants of Mexican origin, are the largest ethnic group in the United States. Numbering more than 14 million, they are part of a still larger group, Hispanics. Chicanos have a long history in the United States, stretching back before the nation was even formed to the early days of European exploration. Santa Fe, New Mexico, was founded more than a decade before the Pilgrims landed at Plymouth. The Chicano people trace their ancestry back to the merging of Spanish settlers with the Native Americans of Central America. This ancestry reaches back to the brilliant Mayan and Aztec civilizations, which attained their height about A.D. 700 and 1500, respectively. Roots in the land do not guarantee a group dominance over it. Over several centuries, the Spaniards conquered the land and merged with the Native Americans to form the Mexican people. In 1821, Mexico obtained its independence, but this independence was short-lived, for domination from the north began less than a generation later (Meier and Rivera, 1972).

Today, the Southwest, once a part of Mexico, is dominated by the descendants of Europeans, although heavily populated by Chicanos. The Chicano people are a varied group, differing in their retention of Spanish heritage, in their history, and in their culture. Even the term *Chicano* is not universally adopted, because many wish to be called "Mexican-American," "Hispanic," "Mexican," "Spanish-American," or "Latin-American." Regardless, most see themselves as a distinctive group and not merely as assimilated Americans (de la Garza et al., 1992; N. Kanellos, 1994).

Assimilation may be the key word in the history of many immigrant groups, but for Chicanos the key term is *La Raza. La Raza* literally means *the people,* but among contemporary Chicanos, the term connotes pride in a pluralistic Spanish, Native American, and Mexican heritage. Chicanos cherish their legacy and, as we shall see, strive to regain some of the economic and social glory that once was theirs. Compared to Anglos, and to even Hispanics as a group, Chicanos are more likely to be unemployed and poor, as shown in Table 10.1. We will explore the historical factors that have led to this subordinate status in the United States.

Table 10.1 SELECTED SOCIAL AND ECONOMIC CHARACTERISTICS OF CHICANOS, 1993

Compared both to Hispanics as a group and to non-Hispanics, several social indicators show the poor economic status of Chicanos.

	Total Non-Hispanic Whites	Total Hispanic	Chicanos
Median age	34.4	26.7	24.6
Percentage completing college			
25–34 years	25.5	9.0	5.8
35 years and over	22.0	9.0	6.0
Percentage unemployed			
Male	8.1	12.4	12.1
Female	5.8	11.1	11.1
Percentage living below poverty level	13.1	29.3	30.1
Median income (year-round workers)			
Male	$31,765	$20,054	$18,422
Female	$21,930	$17,124	$16,399

Source: P. Montgomery (1994, pp. 10–15).

LEGACY OF THE NINETEENTH CENTURY

Many Chicanos trace their ancestors as far back as the sixteenth century on land that is today the United States. The Spanish and Mexican heritage therefore lives on in people, not just in place names like San Francisco, the Pecos River, or the San Joaquin Valley. Approximately 1.3 million Chicanos today are descended from Mexicans residing in the Southwest as far back as 1848 (L. Hernandez, 1969).

These people first became Mexican Americans with the conclusion of the Mexican-American War. In the Treaty of Guadalupe Hidalgo, signed February 2, 1848, Mexico acknowledged the annexation of Texas to the United States and ceded California and most of Arizona and New Mexico to the United States for $15 million. In exchange, the United States granted citizenship to the 75,000 Mexican nationals who still remained on the annexed land after one year. With citizenship, the United States was to guarantee religious freedom, property rights, and cultural integrity, that is, the right to continue Mexican and Spanish cultural traditions and to use the Spanish language.

The descendants of these Mexican nationals are today called *Hispanos*. Though often placed in the same category as Chicanos, the Hispanos' ancestry in North America is similar to that of the earliest European settlers on the East Coast. For this reason, some of the estimated 850,000 Hispanos repudiate the label of *Chicano* or *Mexican American* (C. Cortés, 1980; Moore and Pachon, 1985; Moquin and Van Doren, 1971; F. Quintana, 1980).

The beginnings of the Chicano experience were as varied as the Chicano people themselves. Some Chicanos were affluent, with large landholdings. Others were poor peasants barely able to survive. Along such rivers as the Rio Grande, commercial towns grew up around the growing river traffic. In New Mexico and Arizona, many Chicano people welcomed the protection that the U.S. government offered against several Native American tribes. In California, life was quickly dominated by the gold miners, and Anglos controlled the newfound wealth. One generalization can be made about the many segments of the Chicano population in the nineteenth century. They were regarded as a conquered people. In fact, even before the war, Whites who traveled into the West brought feelings against people of mixed blood (in this instance, against Mexicans). Whenever Chicano and Anglo interests conflicted, Anglo interests won out (M. Servin, 1974).

Although a pattern of second-class treatment for Chicanos emerged well before the twentieth century, it was not pursued consistently. Gradually, the Anglo system of property ownership replaced the Native American and Hispanic systems. Chicanos inheriting land proved no match for Anglo lawyers. Court battles provided protection for poor Spanish-speaking landowners. Unscrupulous lawyers occasionally defended Chicanos successfully, only to demand half the land as their fee. Anglo cattle ranchers gradually pushed out Chicano ranchers. By 1892, the federal government was granting grazing privileges on public grasslands and forests to anyone but Chicanos.

In California, laws passed to drive the Chinese out of mine work except as menial laborers also banned Chicanos. Prior to 1860, Californios (that is, Chicanos in California) owned all parcels of land valued at more than $10,000. By the 1870s, they owned only a quarter of this land. Anglos saw an end of landowning among Californios and the transfer of their fortunes to Whites as a price the Californios ought to pay for injustices that some Mexican governors had committed against the Native Americans. This explanation was accepted widely, yet few thought that Anglos should suffer for abusing both the Native Americans and the Chicanos. Chicanos did not respond to such obvious violations of the 1848 treaty with passive acceptance. Chicanos frequently resorted to violence and formed vigilante groups to protect what they saw as their rights. These efforts, however, were met with even greater retaliatory force and mob hysteria, culminating in countless lynchings (C. McWilliams, 1968; R. Padilla, 1973; L. Pitt, 1966; E. Stoddard, 1973).

The Mexican-American War ended with the Mexicans losing much more than they gained. By the end of the nineteenth century, the Chicanos had lost more than they had won with American citizenship. Wayne Moquin and Charles Van Doren (1971) called this the period of Anglo-American conquest, when the Chicanos "became outsiders in their own homeland" (p. 251). In retrospect, the Anglos' land grab left the Chicanos as unable to escape it as the Native Americans had been. The expansion of the cattle and sheep industries, farming, and mining was financed by Anglos who profited from Chicano labor and experience. The ground was laid for the social structure of the Southwest in the twentieth century, an area of growing productivity in which minority groups have increased in size but have remained subordinate.

THE IMMIGRANT EXPERIENCE

Nowhere else in the world do two countries with such different standards of living and wage scales share a relatively open border. Immigration from Mexico is unique in several respects. First, it has been a continuous large-scale movement for most of this century. The United States did not restrict immigration from Mexico through legislation until 1965. Therefore, the flow of new immigrants has been continuous. Second, the proximity of Mexico encourages past immigrants to maintain strong cultural and language ties with the homeland through friends and relatives. Return visits to the old country are only one- or two-day bus rides for Chicanos, not once-in-a-lifetime voyages, as they have been for most European immigrants. The third point of uniqueness is the aura of illegality that has surrounded the Mexican migrant. Throughout the twentieth century, the suspicion in which Anglos have held Chicanos has contributed to mutual distrust between the two groups.

The years preceding World War I brought large numbers of Mexicans into the expanding agricultural industry of the Southwest. The Mexican revolution of 1909–1922 thrust even more refugees into the United States, and World War I curtailed the flow of people from Europe, leaving the labor market open to the Chicanos. After the war, continued political turmoil in Mexico and more prosperity in the Southwest brought still more Mexicans across the border.

Simultaneously, American corporations, led by agribusinesses, invested in Mexico in such a way as to maximize their profits but minimize the amount of money remaining in Mexico to provide needed employment. Conflict theorists view this investment as a part of the continuing process in which American businesses have used Mexican people when it has been in corporate leaders' best interests (first, as we shall see, as braceros, then either as cheap laborers in their own country or as undocumented workers here) and have dismissed them when they are no longer judged to be useful (first during a program called *repatriation* and sporadically now during crackdowns on "illegal" immigration). During the 1920s, nearly a half million Mexicans immigrated. The Southwest welcomed the laborers onto the bottom rungs of the social and economic ladders of Anglo-dominated society (C. Guerin-Gonzales, 1994).

Repatriation

The influx of Mexicans slowed markedly after 1929 as the Great Depression gripped the United States. Unemployed city workers flocked to agriculture, but the dust bowl decreased the need for farm labor. More Mexicans were not needed by Anglo businesses, and those already here were seen as a burden.

Government officials developed a quick way to reduce welfare rolls and eliminate people seeking jobs: ship Mexicans back to Mexico. This program of deporting Mexicans during the 1930s was referred to as *repatriation*. As officially stated, the program was constitutional, for only illegal aliens were to be repatriated. Actually, it was much more complex. Border records were incomplete because, before 1930, the United States had shown little interest in whether Mexicans had entered with all the proper credentials. Also, many Mexicans who could be classified as illegal aliens had resided in the United States for decades. Because they had children who were citizens by birth, they therefore could not legally be deported. The legal process of fighting a deportation order was overwhelming, however, especially to a poor Spanish-speaking family. The Anglo community virtually ignored this outrage against the civil rights of those deported, nor did it show interest in assisting repatriates to ease the transition (Meier and Rivera, 1972).

For those Chicanos and Mexicans who were allowed to remain, the 1930s were not good times. Many Chicano landholders lost their real estate because they were unable to pay taxes. They flocked to the growing concentrations of Chicanos living in segregated areas, called *barrios*, of the urban Southwest. Meanwhile, many in the cities lost their jobs and left for rural areas that were merely less densely populated poverty areas. The Roosevelt administration's efforts to alleviate the Depression were helpful to Chicanos, but many were disqualified from participation by local or state requirements (Meier and Rivera, 1972; Guerin-Gonzales, 1994).

Los Braceros Program

When the Depression ended, Mexican laborers again became attractive to industry. In 1942, the United States and Mexico agreed to a program allowing migration across the border by contracted laborers, or *braceros*. Within a year of the initiation of Los Braceros program, more than 80,000 Mexican nationals had been brought in; they made up one-eleventh of the farm workers on the Pacific Coast. The program continued with some interruptions until 1964. It was devised to recruit labor from Mexican poverty areas to U.S. farms. In a program that was supposed to be jointly supervised by Mexico and the United States, minimum standards were to be maintained for the transportation, housing, wages, and health care of the braceros. Ironically, these safeguards placed the braceros in a better economic situation than Chicanos, who often worked alongside the protected Mexican nationals. The Mexicans were still regarded as good only when useful, and the Chicano people were merely tolerated (E. Galarza, 1964; R. Scott, 1974; E. Stoddard, 1973). While Mexican laborers were sometimes welcomed, their families rarely were.

In "Listen to Their Voices," historian Camille Guerin-Gonzales (1994) describes the social reality of Mexican immigrants who were drawn to the United States to fill jobs unwanted by others. As she points out, the Mexican arrivals were in many respects fulfilling the "American dream" as well as their own ambition.

World War II brought new opportunities for employment for Chicanos, but not without the resentment of the non-Hispanic Whites whom they replaced. Incidents during the war emphasized the deep hatred that Anglos felt for the Chicano community. In California, and especially in Los Angeles and San Diego, public fears about wartime juvenile delinquency grew.

In the minds of Anglos, Chicano youth was synonymous with delinquency. Carey McWilliams (1968) wrote, "Los Angeles had revised the old saying that 'boys will be boys' to read 'boys, if Mexican, will be gangsters!'" (p. 239). Newspapers minimized Anglo violence and focused on Chicano gangs and boys who dressed in bizarre "drapes" and *zoot suits* (broad hats, long coats, and baggy trousers with tight-fitting cuffs). In June 1943, tension ran high following a sensational murder case. Servicemen roamed the streets of Los Angeles for a week, attacking those they though were *zoot-suiters*. An undeclared war developed

Listen to Their Voices
Mexican Workers and American Dreams

CAMILLE GUERIN-GONZALES

Camille Guerin-Gonzales

Mexican American and Mexican immigrant women and men who had stayed behind in the U.S. during the 1930s survived the depression with the knowledge that Mexicans were an unwanted people who could be expelled at any time. Repatriation and the publicity surrounding it not only reinforced existing ideas about Mexican immigrants and Mexican Americans as foreigners who were primarily young men working temporarily in the U.S., but actually gave credence to the idea that Mexicans indeed were not Americans—that repatriation was a consequence and a manifestation of their foreignness, and therefore proof of it. The construction of Mexican Americans and Mexican immigrants as alien made it possible for government agencies to continue to sponsor and support repatriation and to intimidate Mexicans in the U.S. without fear of sanctions.

Government involvement legitimized and established a precedent for the use of intimidation and expulsion to solve economic problems, a precedent that other agencies and groups could draw upon with relative impunity. Between 1939 and 1954, the federal government expelled three million Mexican immigrants and Mexican Americans from the country, using the military to carry out "Operation Wetback"—a name that both drew upon and naturalized the construction of Mexican Americans and Mexican immigrants as foreign, temporary, and illegitimate.

The conflict over who was entitled to economic opportunity in the United States and the strategies agricultural employers and Mexican farm workers used in this conflict revealed that the contestation was over not one, but two very different concepts of the American Dream. It was also an argument about how the imagined community of the American nation was to be peopled. Growers, aided by state power, struggled to perpetuate an essentialized, normative image of who was American, based on racial and gender ideologies of white male individualism. Mexican farm workers, on the other hand, fought to reinscribe a promise of America that was dynamic and inclusive.

Thus, the American Dream was not one dream, but two dreams, each transformed through contestation for cultural, ethnic, and racial leadership among different immigrant and native-born groups. Rather than a story of exclusion from access to economic security—a story that includes a call for social justice through inclusion— the history of Mexican immigrants and Mexican Americans, as well as other immigrant groups in the United States, is one of violent conflict over the cultural, social, and political meanings of the American Dream. The meanings Mexican workers brought to California's fields hold a different set of keys to the doors of social justice.

Source: Camille Guerin-Gonzales, *Mexican Workers and American Dreams: Immigration, Repatriation, and California Farm Labor 1900–1939,* New Brunswick, New Jersey: Rutgers University Press, 1994, pp. 137–138.

against all Chicanos, with law enforcement officials arresting the Chicano victims of the attack, not the Anglo attackers. Similar outbreaks followed in several California towns. At this time, the riots were blamed entirely on the Chicanos. The sailors and soldiers were said to be acting in self-defense. Later reports completely reversed this assessment (P. Adler, 1974; C. McWilliams, 1968; Meier and Rivera, 1972; C. Mills, 1943).

Operation Wetback

Another crackdown on illegal aliens was to be the third step in dealing with "the Mexican problem." Alternately called Operation Wetback and Special Force Operation, it was fully inaugurated by 1954. The term *wetbacks,* or *mojados,* the derisive slang for Mexicans who enter illegally, refers to those who secretly swim across the Rio Grande. Like other roundups, this effort did not stop the illegal flow of workers. For several years, some Mexicans were brought in under the bracero program, while other Mexicans were being deported. With the end of the bracero program in 1964 and stricter immigration quotas for Mexicans, illegal border crossings increased because legal crossings became more difficult (W. Gordon, 1975; E. Stoddard, 1973, 1976a, 1976b).

Although Operation Wetback was formally phased out by 1956, the deportations have continued to the present. As we discussed in Chapter 4, illegal immigration remains controversial. Illegal aliens take jobs from U.S. citizens, but generally, they get only the least desirable ones. César Chávez, the late organizer of migrant farm workers, repeatedly expressed concern that illegal aliens are used as strikebreakers (R. Severo, 1974).

More dramatic than the negative influence that continued immigration has had on employment conditions in the Southwest is the effect on the Mexican and Chicano people themselves. Routinely the rights of Mexicans, even the rights to which they are entitled as illegal aliens, are ignored. Of those illegal immigrants deported, less than 2 percent have been expelled through formal proceedings. The remaining 98 to 99 percent have left for Mexico under the threat of legal action, frequently taking their children who were born in the United States. These children, of course, are U.S. citizens. The Mexican American Legal Defense and Education Fund (MALDEF) has repeatedly expressed concern over the government's handling of illegal aliens. The organization argues that Mexican nationals do not waive their rights by crossing the border (V. Briggs, 1975; J. Bustamante, 1972; V. Martinez, 1976; Meier and Rivera, 1972; S. Rosen, 1974).

Despite passage of the Immigration Reform and Control Act of 1986, the apprehension of illegal aliens is not likely to end. Chicanos will continue to be more closely scrutinized by law enforcement officials because their Mexican descent makes them more suspect as potential illegal aliens. But officials have been restrained from acting overzealously. Indiscriminate raids on Hispanic neighborhoods in 1974 led to a lawsuit to block "sweeps" aimed at migrant workers and other Hispanics. In October 1975, in response to a court decision, the Immigration and Naturalization Service announced that it would discontinue mass raids and that, before entering a home or business, its agents would require probable cause.

The Mexican border created in 1848 is not an impenetrable barrier. Many employers in the Southwest wish the laborers of Mexico to be readily available and try to keep wages for manual labor low. The Mexicans themselves are eager to earn higher wages. They view employment in the United States as a means to move upward socially and economically. Foreign wage labor has become a regular feature in the economy of many Mexican households. By the mid-twentieth century, a certain momentum was established through bonds of friendship and kinship which meant that migrants were not so much pioneers as merely reuniting with familiar people.

In the United States, Chicanos have mixed feelings toward the illegal Mexican immigrants. Many are their kin, and Chicanos realize that entry into the United States brings Mexicans better economic opportunities. Massive deportations, however, only perpetuate the Anglo stereotype of Mexican and Chicano alike as surplus labor. Chicanos, largely the product of past immigration, find that the continued controversy over illegal immigration places them in the ambivalent role of citizen and relative. Chicano organizations opposing illegal immigration must confront people to whom they are closely linked by culture and kinship, and they must cooperate with government agencies they deeply distrust (D. Massey, 1986; Massey et al., 1987; A. Portes, 1974).

As the Chicano population has increased, organizations of Chicanos have grown. These groups, as we will see in the next section, have used different tactics to meet many goals, as the number of Chicanos grew from 382,000 in 1910 to more than 14 million in 1993.

ORGANIZATIONS WITHIN THE CHICANO COMMUNITY

The earliest Chicano community organizations were similar to those created by other immigrant groups. These organizations provided mutual aid as the Mexican immigrants pooled their meager resources. An exception to these was the Order of the Sons of America (*La Orden de los Hijos de América*), organized in San Antonio, Texas, in 1921. The order restricted its membership to Chicanos who were citizens of the United States. This limitation permitted the group to work for the election of public officials who would better represent the needs of Chicanos. In 1929, because of a disagreement over the speed with which the group was moving, some members split away to form the League of United Latin American Citizens (LULAC). From the beginning, LULAC was committed to total assimilation and asked its members to be the "most perfect type of a true and loyal citizen of the United States of America." Today, local LULAC councils are found in 43 states and Puerto Rico. The organization has gradually changed from being conservative and middle class to showing concern for the residents of the barrios and the rural areas (C. Cortés, 1980; M. Galvan, 1982; M. Tirado, 1970).

Immediately after World War II, two organizations were founded in the Chicano community. Both the Community Service Organization (CSO) and the GI Forum responded to the needs of younger, generally less affluent Chicanos. The

CSO was founded in 1947 in Los Angeles to address the social problems and the need for educational reform in that city's barrio. It quickly became apparent that the group's aims could be accomplished only by more responsive public officials. In 1949, the CSO finally succeeded in electing the first Chicano to the city council since 1881. Eventually, the CSO became less involved in promoting political leaders and developed mutual benefit programs such as resource centers and credit unions. From the CSO have come such Chicano leaders as Congressman Edward Roybal and activist César Chávez (M. Tirado, 1970).

Chicanismo

The social protests that characterized much of the political activity in the United States of the mid-1960s touched the Chicano community as well. In Southern California in 1966, young Chicanos in college were attracted to the ideology of *Chicanismo* (or *Chicanozaje*) and joined what is popularly called the Chicano movement. Like Black Power, Chicanismo has taken on a variety of meanings, but all definitions stress a positive self-image and place little reliance on conventional forms of political activity. Followers of Chicanismo, unlike the more assimilation-oriented older generations, have been less likely to accept the standard claim that the United States is equally just to all.

The origin of the word *Chicano* is not clear, but until the 1960s it was a derogatory term that Anglos used for Mexican Americans. Now the word *Chicano* has taken on a new, positive meaning (A. Cuellar, 1970; Gutiérrez and Hirsch, 1970; M. Vigil, 1990).

Besides a positive self-image, Chicanismo and the movement of La Raza include renewed awareness of the plight of Chicanos at the hands of Anglos. Chicanos are a colonial minority, as Joan Moore (1970) wrote, because their relationship with Anglos was originally involuntary, Mexican culture has been either transformed or destroyed by Anglos, and the Chicano people themselves have been victims of racism (see also Barrera et al., 1972; Moore and Pachon, 1985). The colonial model points out the ways in which societal institutions have failed Chicanos and perpetuated their problems. Militant Chicanos refer to assimilationists, who they say would sell out to the White people, as *vendidos,* or traitors. The ultimate insult is the term *Malinche,* the name of the Native American woman who became the mistress of the Spanish conqueror, Cortés. Many in the Chicano movement believe that, if one does not work actively in the struggle, one is working against it.

The best known of the urban Chicano leaders has been Rodolfo ("Corky") Gonzáles of Denver. Gonzáles is the author of an epic poem entitled *Yo Soy Joaquin,* (1972), which is a statement of the Chicanos' unconquerable quest for freedom (R. Gonzáles, 1972). In 1966, leaving behind brief careers as a professional boxer, and in the War on Poverty Gonzáles organized the Crusade for Justice. The Crusade for Justice is a civil rights organization that strives to reform the police and the courts, improve housing and education for Chicanos, and diversify employment opportunities.

Police–Chicano relations have continued to be a source of tension. Many Chicanos still fear the Texas Rangers and the border patrol, nor is it a coincidence that the two landmark U.S. Supreme Court decisions limiting police interrogation (*Escobedo v. Illinois* and *Miranda v. Arizona*) involved Chicano suspects (R. Acuña, 1981; *Time*, 1969).

Tijerina and Land Rights   Perhaps as well as any recent Chicano, Reies López Tijerina captures the spirit of Chicanismo. In fact, Tijerina in New Mexico, César Chávez (the late head of the United Farm Workers) in California, Gonzáles (leader of the Crusade for Justice) in Colorado, and José Gutiérrez (head of *La Raza Unida Partido*) in Texas share the responsibility for popularizing Chican-ismo. Born in a cotton field worked by migrant farmers, Tijerina became a pente-costal preacher and in the late 1950s took an interest in old Spanish land grants. From research in Mexico, Spain, and the Southwest, he concluded that the Chi-canos—and more specifically, the Hispanos—had lost significant tracts of land through quasi-legal chicanery and other questionable practices.

In 1963, he formed the *Alianza Federal de Mercedes* (Federal Alliance of Land Grants), whose purpose is to recover the lost land. To publicize his purpose when few Anglos would pay attention, he seized part of the Kit Carson National Forest in New Mexico. Arrested for trespassing, Tijerina spent the next few years either in jail or awaiting trial. Tijerina's quest for restoration of land rights has sometimes been violent. During one trial in 1967, Tijerina sympathizers became involved in a gun battle at the Tierra Amarilla courthouse, which ended with two law enforcement officials shot. The land dispute was partially resolved in 1975, when more than a thousand acres of the national forest were transferred to 75 His-panic families. For his participation in the protest, Tijerina was sentenced to two years in prison but was paroled in 1971, on the condition that he hold no official position in the *Alianza*. By 1987, Tijerina was leading an isolated existence outside a small town in New Mexico (P. Blawis, 1971; T. Callanan, 1987; P. Nabokov, 1970).

Tijerina and the *Alianza* were not as active in the 1980s as they were in the late 1960s, but they were not forgotten. Even as individuals like Corky Gonzales and Reies Tijerina passed from center stage, their presence was still felt. The problems they fought have continued to exist, and Chicanos still press for solutions. The Chi-canos who were in college from 1965 to about 1972 are those most aware of Chi-canismo; they have been unlikely to forget its significance to them as individuals and as Chicanos. They continue to carry on the fight for their rights. As they do, an action foremost in their memory has been the struggle by César Chávez on behalf of migrant farm workers in Southern California.

Chávez and the Farm Laborers   The best-known Chicano labor leader was César Chávez, who crusaded to organize migrant farm workers. These laborers had never won collective bargaining rights, partly because their mobility made it difficult for them to organize into a unified group. Efforts to organize agricultural laborers date back to the turn of the century, but Chávez was the first to enjoy any success.

In 1962, Chávez, 35 years old, resigned from leadership in the Community Service Organization to form the National Farm Workers Association (NFWA), later to become the United Farm Workers union (UFW). Organizing migrant farm

César Chávez, in his role as president of the United Farm Workers, leads the picketing of a supermarket urging shoppers not to buy nonunion grapes or lettuce.

workers was not easy, for they had no savings to pay for organizing or to live on while striking. Growers could rely on a virtually limitless supply of Mexican laborers to replace the Chicanos and Filipinos who struck for higher wages and better working conditions.

Chávez's first success was the grape boycott launched in 1965, which carried the struggle into the kitchens of families throughout the country. It took five years for the grape growers to sign three-year contracts with Chávez's union, which had affiliated with the AFL-CIO. This victory signaled a new era in labor relations and made Chávez a national folk hero (J. Levy, 1975; R. McVeigh, 1993).

Despite their success, Chávez and the United Farm Workers were plagued with problems:

1. There was continual opposition by agribusiness.
2. The increased mechanization of agriculture reduced the need for migrant farm workers.
3. Chicanos in urban areas did not offer mass support.

4. The UFW became increasingly dependent for money and guidance on the AFL-CIO, with which it is affiliated.
5. Chávez was criticized for his refusal to take a broader leadership role in the Chicano movement.
6. The union leaders, while dedicated, lacked administrative experience.

A particular problem in the early years was competition from the Teamsters Union. Chávez charged that the teamsters offered growers "sweetheart contracts," which brought raises to the farm workers but were not as good for them as the agreements backed by the UFW. The long, bitter, and sometimes violent struggle between the unions ended in March 1977, when a five-year agreement was signed, giving the field hands to the UFW and the canners, packers, and farm-truck drivers to the Teamsters Union.

Problems resurfaced in the 1980s as California's governor and lawmakers, many of whom had been elected with the strong support of agribusiness, became less supportive of Chávez. This was about the time when the UFW was also trying to heighten the public consciousness of the pesticides in the fields worked by laborers. Research into the long-term effects of pesticides had only begun. Although Chávez's 1988 fast to bring attention to this issue was widely publicized, his efforts did not gain the support he had hoped for. Despite objections from some UFW members, Chávez turned his attention to consumer boycotts rather than organizing the workers.

Chávez had difficulty in fulfilling his objectives. Union membership had dwindled from a high of 70,000 to 20,000 in 1989, and to a low of 10,000 by 1994. Nevertheless, what he and the UFW accomplished was considerable. First, they succeeded in making federal and state governments more aware of the exploitation of migrant laborers. Second, the migrant workers, or at least those organized in California, developed a sense of their own power and worth that will make it extremely difficult for growers to abuse them in the future as they have in the past. Third, working conditions improved. California agricultural workers were paid an average of less than $2 an hour in the mid-1960s. By 1987, they were being paid an average of about $5.85 an hour, but by 1994, as the entire California economy suffered, wages had dropped to $4.75 an hour.

Migrant workers still face a very harsh life. Under pressure to reduce government spending in general, the federal government in the 1980s reduced its enforcement of migrant worker laws. Only two Labor Department officers inspect North Carolina's 1,000 migrant worker camps. Tuberculosis, alcoholism, and malnutrition remain common among migrant farm workers. Chávez died in 1993, and a year later, hundreds of supporters of the UFW arrived in Sacramento, California, to commemorate his death and to acknowledge the full agenda that remains (F. Bardacke, 1993; J. DeParle, 1991; P. Matthiessen, 1993; *The Nation*, 1993; National Public Radio, 1994; J. Nordheimer, 1988).

Political Organizations

More directly involved in effective political representation than the organizations just described is the Mexican American Political Association (MAPA), founded in

FARM WORKERS' SANITATION FACILITIES...

Recent efforts on behalf of farm workers have protested their working conditions and pesticide use that may threaten their lives.

Gary Huck/UE, Huck/Konopacki Labor Cartoons.

1958 in California. Although primarily middle class in membership, it has sought to promote political organization among lower-class Chicanos. MAPA conducts political education efforts and voter registration drives. It strives to be nonpartisan, but most of its support usually comes from Democrats; it in turn endorses Democratic Party political candidates. In the early 1960s, concern that other Hispanics were being excluded from MAPA led to the creation of PASSO (Political Association of Spanish-Speaking Organizations). PASSO's success in California has been less dramatic than in Texas. PASSO was the first Hispanic political coalition in Texas during the twentieth century that succeeded without the consent of the local Democratic Party. In 1963, PASSO successfully elected a completely Chicano slate to the Crystal City, Texas, city council. Two years later, Anglos and conservative Chicanos voted them out of office, however (A. Juarez, 1972; M. Tirado, 1970).

Political activity varies widely among Chicanos in the Southwest. Chicanos have had the greatest political representation in New Mexico, both when it was a territory and since being granted statehood in 1912. Unlike California, where the Hispanics were driven out, or Texas, which was the site of a full-scale war between Anglos and Hispanics, New Mexico had a continuous heritage of leadership by the Hispanos, or descendants of the colonized Mexicans. This role was barely interrupted by Anglo settlements. The state constitution provides that individuals who speak only Spanish may vote and hold office. Not too surprisingly, a third of New Mexico's state legislators are Hispano, and that state has been the location of the only mass movement among Hispanos, Tijerina's *Alianza*. Although New Mexico's

Chicanos play a pivotal political role within the Democratic Party, Hispanics in other states are less fortunate. Despite MAPA and PASSO, they have been less successful in California. In Texas, however, until recently, the outlook for Chicanos in politics has been bleakest. As we have seen, PASSO marked increasing politicization among Chicanos in Texas. But Chicanos received no help from regular party organizations and had to take an even more dramatic step, forming a new political party (R. Lindsey, 1978; J. Moore, 1970).

La Raza Unida Partido (United Peoples Party) is the latest stage of Chicano political organization. *La Raza Unida* (LRU) has been a third party supporting candidates who offer alternatives to the Democratic and Republican Parties. It was organized by José Angel Gutiérrez in Texas in 1970 and has had remarkable successes. The LRU candidate for governor captured 6 percent of the vote in 1972. Most notable has been the party's success in Crystal City, where Chicanos ran the community without forming any political coalition with Anglos. But Crystal City is not typical. It has fewer than 10,000 people and has had a very large Chicano majority for some time, which is unusual even for southern Texas. Nonetheless, the Chicanos made changes that have been welcomed by some Anglos as well. By the mid-1970s, the LRU had fallen into disarray. Disagreements within the party as well as delays by established state politicians in supplying federal money to Crystal City hastened its demise. Even more discouraging, some of the reforms introduced, such as Chicano studies in high school, have been undone (B. Marquez, 1987; D. Pedersen, 1987).

Organized in 1967, the Mexican-American Legal Defense and Education Fund (MALDEF) has emerged as a potent force to protect Chicanos' constitutional rights. While not endorsing candidates, it has made itself felt in the political arena, much as has the NAACP has for African Americans. On the education side, it has addressed segregation, biased testing, inequities in school financing, and failure to address bilingualism. MALDEF has been involved in litigation concerning employment practices, immigration reform, and voting rights. It has emerged as the primary civil rights group for Chicanos and other Hispanics (M. Vigil, 1990).

Representative of the types of battles that are fought on behalf of Chicanos is one that occurred in Los Angeles County. The powerful county board of supervisors was elected by districts whose boundaries divided the county's 3 million Hispanics. Consequently, the board was all-White. Various voting-rights suits led to districts' being redrawn for the county board and other elected offices, and to many successful campaigns by Hispanics (F. López, 1992).

The politically successful movements have increasingly appealed to conventional political parties, and the Democrats serve as standard bearer. A 1992 survey showed 67 percent of Chicanos leaning toward the Democrats. Acknowledging the growing numbers of Chicanos, however, the Republicans have also begun to cater to them with some success. Some observers decry the *fiesta politics*, in which, every four years, presidential candidates make blatant overtures to the Chicano community, although their special needs are forgotten between elections (de la Garza et al., 1992).

The Church

The most important organization in the Chicano community is the church, specifically the Roman Catholic church. In 1994, about 70 percent of Hispanics were Roman Catholic. The strong identification of Chicanos and Mexican immigrants with Catholicism has reinforced the already formidable barriers between them and the predominantly Protestant Southwest. By virtue of its size, wealth, and widespread support, the Catholic church has the potential to be a significant force in bringing about social justice for Chicano people (A. Herrmann, 1994).

The church has only sporadically involved itself in the Chicano movement, and rarely have the upper levels of the church hierarchy supported Chicanismo. Many Chicanos have found this relative inactivity frustrating because two-thirds of the church's membership in the Southwest are Chicanos. They are highly spiritual in their religious beliefs but are somewhat less likely to go to church, seek penance, or receive communion. It remains to be seen if the church can accept a form of participation in the faith that cares less about organizational matters dictated by the European heritage and that cares more about celebrating the spirit in the Latin fashion (K. Briggs, 1983; de la Garza et al., 1992).

Leaders of the Hispanic community are outspoken in their views on the Roman Catholic church. César Chávez (1973), speaking as early as 1968, explained what Chicanos want the Roman Catholic church to do:

> We don't ask for more cathedrals. We don't ask for bigger churches or fine gifts. We ask for its presence with us, beside us, as Christ among us. We ask the Church to *sacrifice with the people* for social change, for justice, and for love of brother. We don't ask for words. We ask for deeds. We don't ask for paternalism. We ask for servanthood. (p. 218)

In spite of this criticism, the Catholic church is important to the future of Chicanos.

The Catholic church has basically taken an assimilationist role, whether with Mexican Catholics or with other minority Catholics. Because the Chicano movement rejects assimilation, the Catholic church appears to be at odds with Chicanismo. Even Chicano priests, because of their middle-class training, support programs with long-range goals, whereas barrio residents seek instant results. The Church has, in fact, spoken out against high school protests and against militants who embrace communism; it has defended itself against charges that its own parochial schools suppress Mexican culture. Nevertheless, efforts have been made to give the Chicanos a bigger voice within the church. In 1969, a nationwide association of Chicano priests named PADRES (*Padres Asociados para Derechos Religiosos, Educativos y Sociales,* Priests United for Religious, Educational, and Social Rights) was formed to urge the church to provide more assistance for social projects and adequate education in barrio parochial schools. At the local level, the Catholic church has supported aspects of the Chicano movement. Chávez asked for, and usually received, approval for his UFW from priests throughout Southern California.

Not only is the Roman Catholic church important to Hispanics, but Hispanics also play a significant role for the church. The population growth of Chicanos and other Hispanics has been responsible for the Roman Catholic church's continued growth in recent years while mainstream Protestant faiths have declined in size. Hispanics account for 38 percent of Roman Catholics in the United States. However, they continue to be underrepresented among bishops: only 7 percent are Hispanic (de la Garza et al., 1992; S. Parker, 1992).

While Hispanics are predominantly Roman Catholic, their membership in Protestant and other Christian faiths is growing in strength. Pentecostalism, a type of evangelical Christianity, is growing in Latin America and is clearly making a significant impact on Hispanics in the United States. Pentecostalism and similar faiths are attractive to many because they offer followers the opportunity to openly express their religious fervor. Furthermore, many of the churches are small and thus offer a sense of community, often with Spanish-speaking leadership. Gradually, the more established faiths are recognizing the desirability of offering Hispanic parishioners a greater sense of belonging (N. Kanellos, 1994).

EDUCATION

Although statistics on Chicanos and formal schooling seem positive at first glance, they become disturbing on closer examination. While the number of Hispanic college students has increased, their gains have not kept pace with the population increase. As is apparent in Table 10.1, Chicanos fall well behind other Hispanics, and even further behind Anglos. While bilingual education is still endorsed in the United States, the implementation of effective, quality programs has been difficult, as the previous chapter showed. In addition, attacks on funding bilingual education have continued into the 1990s. Two other areas of concern in education are the increasing segregation of Chicano students and their absence from higher education.

Social Isolation

While Black students have managed to hold to early gains in school desegregation, Hispanics, including Chicanos, have become increasingly isolated. In 1968, 54.8 percent of all Hispanics attended predominantly minority schools, that is, schools where at least half of the students were minorities. By 1993, this rate was 73.6 percent—a level of segregation higher than that for Black students. Significantly, the schools in certain states with large numbers of Hispanics, such as Illinois, New York, and Texas, are more segregated than in the national averages. In a parallel development, between 1970 and 1985, the percentage of Whites in the typical Chicano student's school in Los Angeles County dropped from 45 percent to 17 percent. The trend toward the growing isolation of Hispanics is found in virtually all parts of the nation and, since 1968, has prevailed in almost every period in which national data have been collected (G. Orfield, 1993).

Three factors explain this increasing social isolation of Chicanos from other students in school. First, Hispanics are increasingly concentrated in the largest cities, where minorities dominate. Second, the numbers of Hispanics have increased dramatically since the 1970s, when efforts to desegregate schools began to lose momentum. Third, schools once desegregated have become "resegregated" as the numbers of school-aged Chicanos in an area have increased, and as the determination to maintain balances in schools, as noted, has lessened (Moore and Iadicola, 1981).

Higher Education

Chicanos are missing from higher education—in all roles. Recent reports have documented the absence of Hispanics among college teachers and administrators. The situation is similar in this respect to that of Blacks; however, there are no Hispanic counterparts to historic Black colleges, such as Tuskegee Institute, to provide a source of leaders.

The problem of students seeing few teachers and administrators like themselves is perpetuated through what is often termed the *educational pipeline:* insufficient numbers of Hispanic university students have been prepared to serve as teachers and administrators. In 1993, only 46 percent of Chicanos aged 25 years or over completed high school, compared to 84 percent of non-Hispanic Whites. Even these data are deceptively encouraging with respect to Hispanics. Chicanos who do choose to continue their education beyond high school are more likely to select a proprietary, or technical, school or community college, in order to acquire work-related skills. The pipeline narrows still further as we reach the baccalaureate level (P. Montgomery, 1994).

Chicanos face challenges similar to those that Black students meet on predominantly White campuses. Given the social isolation of Hispanic high schools, Chicanos are likely to have to adjust for the first time to an educational environment almost totally populated by Anglos. They may experience racism for the first time, just as they are trying to accommodate to a heavier academic load. Chicanos at more selective universities report that classmates accuse them of having benefited from affirmative-action admissions policies and of not really belonging (E. Fiske, 1988a, 1988b).

The plight of Hispanics sometimes leads to innovative responses. The University of Texas at El Paso, for example, has allowed Mexicans to commute over the border since 1989 and, if they demonstrate financial need, to pay in-state tuition. In 1992, there were 927 Mexican students, of whom 84 percent qualified for the lower tuition rate. Since many of the commuters are not fluent in English, the university provides an array of support services for non-English-speaking students (K. Manigan, 1991).

The admissions policy of the University of Texas at El Paso reflects the growing recognition of the *borderlands.* The borderlands are the area adjoining the Mexican–United States border, which is a common cultural area. The growing immigration, legal and illegal; the exchange of media; workers crossing on a daily basis; and the passage in 1994 of the North American Free Trade Act (NAFTA)—all make the notions of a separate Mexican and U.S. culture increasingly obsolete along the border. Gradually, social institutions like universities are recognizing the social reality of the borderlands.

The next section considers family life among Chicanos and looks at how close family ties can contribute to and support educational achievement. Yet college recruiters report that some Chicanos are hesitant to leave home to attend a residential college. Data show that African Americans and Hispanics who drop out of college, more than other minorities, are likely to report that they did so to provide financial assistance for their families—another sign of the close-knit character of many Hispanic households. Stress over family-related issues is frequently cited by college counselors working with Chicano students. This is not at all surprising, given Table 10.1's report of the high proportion of Chicano families living below the poverty level. Stress is particularly noticeable for Chicanas, that is, Chicano women, who are often the first of their gender in their families to enter college (K. Bergheim, 1995).

FAMILY LIFE

In 1987, San Antonio mayor Henry Cisneros, the first Chicano ever to serve as chief executive of a major U.S. city, announced that he would drop out of the governor's race. He was regarded as a popular front-runner, but his reasons were not political. His new son was ailing from birth defects, and he chose his family role over staying in the political landscape. Many people saw Cisneros's choice of family first as typical of many other Chicanos who value the family. (He later became President Clinton's Secretary of Housing and Urban Development.)

The most important organization or institution among Chicanos, or for that matter any group, is the family. The structure of the Chicano family differs little from that of the families of other people in the United States, a statement remarkable in itself given the impoverishment of Chicanos. In 1983, most White families (82 percent) and most Hispanic families (69 percent) were headed by both a husband and a wife. Only 7.3 percent of Hispanics were divorced, compared to 16.7 percent of the population generally (Bureau of the Census, 1994, pp. 55, 62).

Much writing on the Chicano family, as well as on the family in Mexico, has repeated the error of describing it as homogeneous. It is often characterized as a simple peasant family surviving upward mobility. Even the concept of the peasant family has received little qualification. Good and bad traits, but usually the latter, have been assigned to Chicano families regardless of the truth. We shall briefly examine the characteristics of the "culture of poverty," machismo and marianismo, and familism to determine their usefulness in descriptions of the Chicano family (E. Stoddard, 1973).

The "Culture of Poverty"

Like the Black American families described in Chapter 8, Chicano families are labeled as having traits that, in fact, describe poor families rather than specifically Chicano families. Indeed a 1980 report of the Commission on Civil Rights (1980b, p. 8) states that the two most prevalent stereotypical themes appearing in works on Hispanics show them as (1) exclusively poor and (2) prone to commit violence.

Similarly, movies from *Tony the Greaser* in 1911 to *Fort Apache, The Bronx* in 1981, have done little to change this image (A. Woll, 1981).

Social scientists have also relied excessively on the traits of the poor to describe a minority group like Chicanos. Anthropologist Oscar Lewis (1959, 1965, 1966), in several publications based on research conducted among Mexicans and Puerto Ricans, identified the "culture of poverty." The *culture of poverty* embraces a deviant way of life according to its theorists, which involves no future planning, no enduring commitment to marriage, and absence of the work ethic. This culture supposedly follows the poor, even when they move out of the slums or the barrio. Hispanic groups protested the remarks of a Housing and Urban Development official who showed little concern about overcrowding because, he said, it was "a cultural preference" of families to double up (*New York Daily News*, 1984; F. Penalosa, 1968).

The culture-of-poverty view is another way of "blaming the victim" (W. Ryan, 1976): the affluent are not responsible for social inequality, nor are the policymakers; it is the poor who are to blame. This stance allows government and society to blame the failure of antipoverty and welfare programs on Chicanos and other poor people, rather than on the programs themselves. These are programs designed and largely staffed by middle-class, English-speaking Anglo professionals (L. Shannon, 1979). Conflict theorists join Ryan in saying that it is unfair to blame the poor for their lack of money, low education, poor health, and low-paying jobs.

Lewis's hypothesis about the culture of poverty, whether exaggerated or not, came to be used indiscriminately to explain continued poverty. Critics argue that Lewis sought out exotic, pathological behavior, ignoring the fact that, even among the poor, most people live fairly conventionally and strive to achieve goals similar to those of the middle class. A second criticism challenges the use of the term *culture of poverty* to describe an entire ethnic group. Because Lewis's data were on poor people, social scientists have increasingly stressed that his conclusions may be correct as far as the data permit, but the data cannot be generalized to all Hispanics because the sample was not a representative cross section drawn from different economic and educational levels (J. Burma, 1970; E. Casavantes, 1970; Moore and Pachon, 1985; C. Valentine, 1968).

Social science research has since been conducted that, unlike Lewis's, does sample Chicano families across a broad range of socioeconomic levels. This research shows that, when Anglo and Chicano families of the same social class are compared, they differ little in family organization and attitudes toward child rearing. In addition, comparisons of work ethics find no significant differences between Chicanos and Anglos. Poverty is present among Chicanos; there is no doubt about that. However, that does not mean there is a *culture* of poverty or a permanent underclass. Institutions such as the family and the church seem viable, although the schools are in disrepair and the picture on businesses is mixed. To question the label of *culture of poverty* does not deny the poor life chances facing many Chicanos (R. Aponte, 1991; T. Caine, 1972; Irelan et al., 1969; Isonio and Garza, 1987; E. Martinez, 1988; J. Moore, 1989; Moore and Pinderhughes, 1993; K. Winkler, 1990b).

Machismo and Marianismo

Chicanos, like other people, are expected to fulfill certain roles as men and women. Among Chicanos and other Hispanics, there are particular versions of masculinity and femininity. Hispanic men are expected to take great pride in their maleness, and women in being females.

For men, the sense of virility, of personal worth in one's own eyes and in those of one's peers, is called *machismo*. The idea of male dominance and superiority is probably the characteristic emphasized in most descriptions of both Chicano and Mexican families. Machismo is often misrepresented or exaggerated. First, it may be demonstrated differently by different men. For some, it may entail resorting to weapons or fighting, but for others, it may mean being irresistible to women. Generally, the machismo of a man is more imagined than real; that is, it consists of claiming achievements never accomplished.

Marianismo describes the qualities of femininity that are complementary to those of machismo in men. A good woman accepts the dominance of men and consistently places the needs of the family first. The few research studies that have focused on machismo and marianismo had limited sample sizes. Yet there is little evidence to date that male-dominated or patriarchal households are typical of Chicanos and other Hispanics. Research data collected in Los Angeles, New York City, and San Antonio suggest that common notions of machismo are disappearing or perhaps were never very prevalent after all. More recent research has found no important differences between Anglos and Chicanos in wives' labor-force participation and male versus female dominance in family decision making (Vega et al., 1986).

Several factors have contributed to the decline of machismo. The feminist movement in both the United States and Latin America has changed the way in which men and women react to one another. Feminists argue that male Chicanos have falsely glorified machismo, giving this aspect of Mexican culture more attention than it deserves. Urbanization, upward mobility, and assimilation are all combining to make machismo more of a historical footnote with each passing generation of Chicanos (Moore and Pachon, 1985; E. Stevens, 1973; K. Winkler, 1990a).

Familism

Chicanos are described as laudably more familistic than other people in the United States. By *familism* is meant pride and closeness in the family, which result in family obligation and loyalty coming before individual needs. The family, therefore, is the primary source of both social interaction and caregiving.

Familism has been viewed as both a positive and a negative influence on individual Chicanos. It may have the negative effect of discouraging youths with a bright future from taking advantage of opportunities that would remove them from the family. Familism is generally regarded as good, however, because an extended family provides emotional strength in times of family crisis. Close family ties maintain the mental and social well-being of the elderly. The family, therefore, is seen as a norm and as a nurturing unit that provides support throughout the individual's

Familism refers to pride and closeness within Hispanic families.

lifetime. The many significant aspects of familism include (1) the importance of *compadrazgo* (the godparent–godchild relationship); (2) the benefits of the financial dependency of kin; (3) the availability of relatives as a source of advice; and (4) the active involvement of the elderly within the family.

Familism and machismo are two traits associated with the traditional Mexican family. These traditional values, whether judged good or bad, are expected to decline in importance with urbanization, industrialization, and the acquisition of middle-class status. Characteristics that marked differences between Chicano and Anglo family life were sharper in the past. Even among past generations, the differences were of degree, not of kind; that is, Chicano families tended to exhibit some traits more than Anglos, not different traits altogether. A comparison between similar Anglo and Chicano families in San Diego found no significant differences in family life between the two groups. The variations that did appear as the result of statistical analysis tended, as stated above, to be of degree rather than of kind. Some of these differences are disappearing; the "culture of poverty" is a somewhat different matter because of sharp disagreement over whether it exists, let alone whether it is vanishing. The Chicano family, in summary, displays all the variety of American families in general. Unlike Anglos, however, Chicanos are subject to prejudice and discrimination (Vega et al., 1986; see also N. Kanellos, 1994).

HEALTH CARE

Earlier, in Chapter 5, we introduced the concept of *life chances*, which are people's opportunities to provide themselves with material goods, positive living conditions, and favorable life experiences. We have consistently seen Chicanos and other Hispanic groups as having more limited life chances. Perhaps in no other area does this apply so literally as in the health care system.

Hispanics as a group are locked out of the health care system more often than any other racial or ethnic group. A third have no health insurance (or other coverage such as Medicaid) compared to 14 percent of Whites and 20 percent of Blacks. Predictably, the uninsured are less likely to have a regular source of medical care. This means waiting for a crisis before seeking care. Fewer are immunized, and rates of preventable diseases like lead poisoning are higher. Noncoverage is increasing, a circumstance that may reflect a further breakdown in health care delivery or may be a result of continuing immigration (Bureau of the Census, 1994).

The health care dilemma facing Chicanos and other Hispanic groups is complicated by the lack of Hispanic health professionals. They account for 5 percent or less of dentists, nurses, pharmacists, and physicians, yet are approaching 10 percent of the population. Less than 5 percent of students in medical school are Hispanic, so the situation will not soon change. Obviously, one does not need to be administered health care by someone in one's own ethnic group, but the paucity of Hispanic professionals increases the likelihood that the group will be underserved (Bureau of the Census, 1994).

Given the circumstances of the high proportion of uninsured individuals and the low number of Hispanic health-care personnel, it is not surprising to learn of the poor status of Hispanics' health care as a group. They are at increased risk for certain medical conditions, including diabetes, hypertension, tuberculosis, AIDS, alcoholism, and specific cancers. The situation begins to deteriorate at the start of life. Only about 60 percent of Chicanos and Puerto Ricans initiate prenatal care in the first trimester, compared to 80 percent of Whites. Yet infant mortality rates are generally lower for Chicano children than for Whites. Experts suggest that familism may account for the surprising advantage in infants' health, in that they receive more help even if it is not "professional." However, this is less true of Hispanics born in the United States to parents who show signs of assimilating to some U.S. habits such as poor diet and smoking. Women's health has not received sufficient attention, and this is especially true of minority women. The American Medical Association acknowledges, for example, that not enough is known about why Hispanic women are especially vulnerable to cervical cancer and AIDS. There is a challenge to develop a health care system that can respond to these needs (Becerra et al., 1991; Council on Scientific Affairs, 1991; J. Kleinhuizen, 1991a; Novello et al., 1991).

Some Chicanos and many other Hispanics have cultural beliefs that inhibit the use of the medical system. They may interpret their illnesses according to folk practices or *curanderismo*—Hispanic folk medicine, a form of holistic health care and healing. This orientation influences how one approaches health care and even how one defines illness. The use of folk healers, or *curanderos*, is probably infrequent, but perhaps 20 percent rely on home remedies. While these are not necessarily without value, especially if a dual system of folk and establishment medicine is followed, reliance on natural beliefs may be counterproductive. Another aspect of folk beliefs is the identification of folk-defined illnesses such as *susto* (or fright sickness) and *atague* (or fighting attack). While these complaints, alien to Anglos, often have biological bases, they need to be dealt with carefully by sensitive medical professionals who can diagnose and treat illnesses accurately (Council on Scientific Affairs, 1991; G. Rivera, 1988).

Surgeon General Antonia Novello was one of the most visible Hispanic women, and also one of the few Hispanic Americans who have held a major government office.

PREJUDICE AND DISCRIMINATION

The term *taco circuit* has an unpleasant meaning for FBI agents. It refers to the dead-end jobs in dreary Southwest cities that have too often been the lot of the bureau's Hispanic agents. In 1988, a federal judge ruled that the FBI had systematically discriminated against its Hispanic agents by assigning them to the least rewarding or, in some cases, the most hazardous assignments. In all, 311 plaintiffs, more than three-fourths of all the bureau's Hispanic agents, successfully charged that they had been harassed by their superiors in the nation's most prestigious law-enforcement agency (M. Isikoff, 1988).

Discrimination is not limited to the "taco circuit" for Chicanos. They, like other racial and ethnic groups, continue to be victims of prejudice and discrimination. Movies and advertisements that perpetuate stereotypes continue to reinforce prejudice. The stereotypical Mexican village in movies or advertisements has residents who are either sleeping around a fountain or walking around in bored laziness. In the late 1960s, several Chicano groups protested against portrayals of Mexicans as either bandits or lazy peasants. The mass media and advertisers have responded mostly by avoiding such negative stereotyping. The result is that Chicanos are now altogether absent from advertisements and films, with the exception of taco advertisements (T. Martinez, 1973; Moore and Pachon, 1985).

The prevailing poverty of Chicanos affects the quality of their life. They are more likely to live in overcrowded, substandard housing than are Anglos, and in the Southwest, they fall far behind Blacks as well. The urban Chicano finds barrio life depressing because it lacks city services and opportunities for employment. Disease, death, and mental illness are more likely in the Chicano household. Not only are crime rates higher among Chicanos than among Whites, but they are more likely to be the victims of assault or theft. Whether assessed through statistics or in-depth descriptive studies, the conclusion remains that the standard of living of Chicanos falls far short of the minimal standards that U.S. society has set. The life of the urban poor in the barrio has been graphically described by several Chicano authors (O. Acosta, 1972; E. Galarza, 1971; R. Gonzales, 1972).

Language proficiency serves as a barrier to upward mobility for Chicanos more than for Anglos. Sometimes, however, language difference is merely an excuse for discrimination. Speaking English is used as a job requirement either unnecessarily or artificially, placing standards of proficiency higher than needed for the employment sought (Moore and Pachon, 1985).

Data indicate that, on most measures of socioeconomic status, Chicanos' lives are improving. Figure 10.1 shows that the median family income for Chicanos increased from $10,300 to $23,714 from 1976 to 1993. Yet the gains of minority groups have been matched by the increased economic prosperity of the dominant group. In 1970, Chicano family income was 70 percent of White family income. In 1993, it was 59 percent. The gap in income has not only not narrowed but actually widened with the influx of more immigrants (see Figure 10.1).

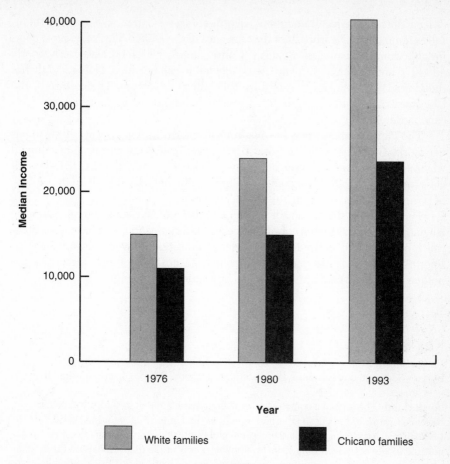

Figure 10.1 **Median Family Income of Whites and Chicanos**
Chicanos' family income has increased since 1976, but not as rapidly as White income.
Source: Bureau of the Census (1991f, p. 12); P. Montgomery (1994).

CONCLUSION

David Gomez (1971) described Chicanos as "strangers in their own land." The Chicano people were native to the Southwest long before the expansion westward of European immigrants and the redrawing of U.S. boundaries. Possession of the land did not guarantee dominance, however. In fact, title to the land was soon lost, and today, many individuals, following the lead of Reies Tijerina, have attempted to reclaim the land on behalf of the Chicano people.

Not all Chicanos are descended from the Mexicans who lived in the territory ceded to the United States following the Mexican-American War. Many are descendants of Mexican immigrants, like the braceros and mojados, or are themselves immigrants. Nearly half of the Chicanos in the United States feel most comfortable communicating in Spanish. Consequently, Chicanos have been poorly educated and have had difficulty being elected to public office. Only recently has the United States begun to recognize this bilingual heritage. The culture of the Chicanos is a rich one that is receiving renewed attention in the contemporary Chicano movement.

The Chicano movement has made itself known in several ways. Individuals like Corky Gonzales, Tijerina, César Chávez, and José Gutiérrez have questioned why Anglos dominate Chicanos as if they were a conquered minority. This second-class treatment is found in accounts of Chicano life that have described the culture of poverty as typical of the life of most Chicanos.

Puerto Ricans share many of the characteristics of Chicanos: they also face the language barrier, are victims of prejudice and discrimination, and have poor political representation. It would be an oversimplification, however, to assume that Puerto Ricans are indistinguishable from Chicanos. Chapter 11 describes the unique history and contemporary status of Puerto Ricans.

KEY TERMS

barrios Segregated urban slums populated by Chicanos, Puerto Ricans, or other Hispanic groups.

borderlands The area of a common culture along the United States–Mexican border.

bracero Contracted Mexican laborers brought to the United States during World War II.

Chicanismo An ideology emphasizing pride and positive identity among Chicanos.

culture of poverty According to its proponents, a way of life that involves no future planning, no enduring commitment to marriage, and no work ethic; this culture follows the poor even when they move out of the slums or the barrio.

curanderismo Hispanic folk medicine.

educational pipeline The process that begins when pupils pass through formal schooling and travel in an ever-narrowing funnel, attaining professional degrees at the end.

familism Pride and closeness in the family that result in placing family obligation and loyalty before individual needs.

fiesta politics Blatant overtures by presidential candidates to Chicanos for their support.

La Raza "The People"; a term referring to the rich heritage of Chicanos, and hence used to denote a sense of pride among Chicanos today.

life chances People's opportunities to provide themselves with material goods, positive living conditions, and favorable life experiences.

machismo A male's sense of virility, of personal worth, in his own eyes and in those of his peers.

marianismo A female's acceptance of males' dominance and the placing of family needs first.

mojados "Wetbacks"; derisive slang for Mexicans who enter illegally, supposedly by swimming the Rio Grande.

repatriation The program of deporting Mexicans during the 1930s.

zoot-suiters Chicano youth during the mid-1940s in Southern California; a derisive term based on their dress.

FOR FURTHER INFORMATION

Rodolfo Acuña. *Occupied America: A History of Chicanos*, 2d ed. New York: Harper & Row, 1981.

The author reexamines conventional accounts of the Chicano experience and argues that they are biased. He feels that the exploitation of Chicanos is comparable to that of a colonized people.

Irene I. Blea. *Toward a Chicano Social Science.* New York: Praeger, 1988.

An overview of the Chicano experience, with an emphasis on seeing it from an ethnic perspective.

Leo R. Chavez. *Shadowed Lives: Undocumented Immigrants in American Society.* Fort Worth, TX: Harcourt Brace Jovanovich, 1992.

An anthropological study of illegal Mexican immigrants, ranging from temporary farmworkers to skilled craftspeople.

Rodolfo O. de la Garza, Frank D. Bean, Charles M. Bonjean, Ricardo Romo, and Rodolfo Alvarez. *The Mexican American Experience: An Interdisciplinary Anthology.* Austin: University of Texas Press, 1985.

This collection of 45 articles has many selections previously published in the *Social Science Quarterly.*

Gilbert G. Gonzalez. *Chicano Education in the Era of Segregation.* Philadelphia: Balch Institute Press, 1990.

An overview of Chicano education in the U.S. Southwest.

Camille Guerin-Gonzales. *Mexican Workers and American Dreams.* New Brunswick, NJ: Rutgers University Press, 1994.

A history of how Mexican immigrants and Mexican Americans were used as workers in the first part of this century.

Z. Anthony Kruszewski, Richard L. Hough, and Jacob Ornstein-Galicia. *Politics and Society in the Southwest: Ethnicity and Chicano Pluralism.* Boulder, CO: Westview Press, 1982.

This anthology covers such topics as language, identity, social class, and politics as they affect Chicanos in the Southwest.

John Shockley. *Chicano Revolt in a Texas Town.* Notre Dame, IN: University of Notre Dame Press, 1974.

Shockley describes the rise of La Raza Unida in Crystal City, Texas, in 1969, one of the few successful contemporary grassroots political movements of Chicanos.

Peter Skerry. *Mexican-Americans: The Ambivalent Minority.* New York: Free Press, 1994.

A view of contemporary Chicano politics in Los Angeles and San Antonio.

Richard Steven Street. *New Voices from Rural Communities.* Portland, OR: NewSage Press and California Rural Legal Assistance, 1992.

This illustrated look at rural California workers profiles Chicano and Asian laborers.

CRITICAL THINKING QUESTIONS

1. In what respects has Mexico been viewed as a source of workers and a place to leave unwanted laborers?
2. How does Chicanismo relate to the issue of Hispanic identity?
3. What role does religion play in the Chicano community?
4. What problems serve as barriers to Chicanos' enjoying the kind of success that Anglos have had in higher education?
5. How does the notion of the "culture of poverty" relieve society of responsibility for the poor?

Chapter
11

Puerto Ricans: Divided Between Island and Mainland

Chapter Outline

Highlights

The Puerto Rican people are divided between those who live on the island commonwealth and those who live on the mainland itself. Although they are citizens of the United States, Puerto Ricans on the island do not have the same privileges as non-Puerto Ricans. Self-rule is the continuing major political issue, overshadowed only by the dire poverty of the island. Those who migrate to the mainland most often come in search of better jobs and housing. A significant proportion return to the island and take on the ambivalent position of *Neoricans*. Because Puerto Rico is so poor, living in the United States does provide an opportunity for advancement, but most Puerto Ricans on the mainland are confined to the lower class and the barrio.

Puerto Ricans share the major problems of their fellow citizens of the United States, especially those who belong to subordinate groups. Nearly 6 million Puerto Ricans face prejudice and discrimination. More than 2 million of them who live on the mainland are seen by many as outsiders, occupying an unenviable social and economic position (see Table 11.1). For the more than 3.6 million residents of the island commonwealth of Puerto Rico, citizenship carries different responsibilities and privileges from their fellow citizens on the mainland.

For no other minority group in the United States is citizenship so ambiguous. Even Native Americans, who are subject to some unique laws and are exempt from others because of past treaties, have a future firmly dominated by the United States. This description does not necessarily fit Puerto Ricans. They and their island home are the last major U.S. colonial territories, and, for that matter, one of the few colonial areas remaining in the world. Before assessing, as one author wrote, "the evidence for success or survival" of Puerto Ricans on the mainland, we will assess the relationship of the United States to Puerto Rico (Bureau of the Census, 1994).

THE ISLAND OF PUERTO RICO

Puerto Rico, located about a thousand miles from Miami, has never been the same since it was discovered by Columbus in 1493 (see Figure 11.1). The original inhabitants of the island were wiped out in a couple of generations by disease, tribal warfare, hard labor, unsuccessful rebellions against the Spanish, and fusion with their conquerors. Among the institutions imported to Puerto Rico by Spain was slavery. Although slavery in Puerto Rico was not as harsh as in the southern United States, the legacy of the transfer of Africans is present in the appearance of Puerto Ricans today, many of whom are seen by people on the mainland as Black.

During the four centuries of Spanish rule, life for most Puerto Ricans was difficult. A few rich landowners and multitudes of poor workers labored in a country still underdeveloped when the United States seized the island in 1898 during the Spanish-American War. Spain relinquished control of it in the Treaty of Paris. The

Table 11.1   SELECTED SOCIAL AND ECONOMIC CHARACTERISTICS OF PUERTO
RICANS, 1993

The urban-based Puerto Ricans, like other Hispanics, have less formal schooling, experience
more unemployment, and have high levels of poverty, compared to non-Hispanics.

	Total Non-Hispanic White	Total Hispanic	Puerto Ricans
Median age	34.4	26.7	26.9
Percentage completing college			
25–34 years	25.5	9.0	10.4
35 years and over	22.0	9.0	6.8
Percentage unemployed			
Male	8.1	12.4	17.2
Female	5.8	11.1	11.0
Percentage living below poverty level	13.1	29.3	36.5
Median income (year-round workers)			
Male	31,765	20,054	23,749
Female	21,930	17,124	20,178

Source: P. Montgomery (1994, pp. 10–15).

value of Puerto Rico for the United States, as it had been for Spain, was mainly its
strategic location, which was advantageous for maritime trade.

The beginnings of rule by the United States quickly destroyed any hope that
Puerto Ricans had for self-rule. All power was given to officials appointed by the
president, and any act of the island's legislature could be overruled by Congress.
Even the spelling was changed briefly to *Porto Rico* to suit North American pro-
nunciation. English, previously unknown on the island, became the only language
permitted in the school systems. The people were colonized—politically, then culturally, and finally economically (Aran et al., 1973; D. Christopulos, 1974).

Citizenship was extended to Puerto Ricans by the Jones Act of 1917, but Puerto Rico remained a colony. This political dependence altered in 1948 when Puerto
Rico elected its own governor and became a commonwealth, rather than a colony.
This status, officially *Estado Libre Asociado,* or Associated Free State, extends to
Puerto Rico and its people privileges and rights different from those of people on
the mainland. Although Puerto Ricans are U.S. citizens and elect their own governor, they may not vote in presidential elections and have no voting representation
in Congress. They are subject to military service, selective service registration, and
all federal laws. Courts on the island are patterned after those in the United States,
and appeals may be made to the U.S. Supreme Court. Puerto Ricans pay a local
income tax but no federal income tax. Most federal grants-in-aid, however, are significantly lower in Puerto Rico than those on the mainland.

The commonwealth period has been a most significant one for Puerto Rico.
Change has been dramatic, though whether it has all been progress is debatable.
On the positive side, Spanish has been reintroduced as the language of classroom
instruction, but the study of English is also required. The popularity in the 1980s
of groups such as the rock singers Menudo shows that even Puerto Rican young

Figure 11.1 **Puerto Rico**
Puerto Rico is a bit smaller than Connecticut and lies twice as far from Florida as it does from Venezuela.

people wish to maintain ties with their ethnicity. Such success is a challenge, because Puerto Rican music is almost never aired on non-Hispanic radio stations. The Puerto Rican people have had a vibrant and distinctive cultural tradition, as clearly seen in folk heroes, holidays, sports, and contemporary literature and drama. Dominance by the culture of the United States makes it difficult to maintain the culture on the mainland and even on the island itself.

The fragile nature of Puerto Rican culture is illustrated by its issue of language. From 1902, English was the official language of the island, but Spanish was the language of the people, serving to reaffirm the island's cultural identity independent of the United States. However, in 1992, Puerto Rico also established Spanish as the official language.

In reality, the language issue is related more to ideology than to substance. While English is once again required in primary and secondary schools, textbooks may be written in English while the classes are conducted in Spanish. Indeed, Spanish remains the language of the island; only 20 percent of the islanders speak

English, and another 10 percent are fully bilingual (D. Heyck, 1994; R. Rodriquez, 1993; Third World Journalists, 1994).

Issues of Statehood and Self-Rule

Puerto Ricans have periodically argued and fought for independence for most of the 500 years since Columbus landed. They continue to do so in the 1990s. The contemporary commonwealth arrangement is popular with many Puerto Ricans, but others prefer statehood, while some call for complete independence from the United States.

Since 1948, the *Partido Popular Democratico* (PPD), or Popular Democratic Party, has dominated the island's politics. The party has consistently favored commonwealth status. Why should commonwealth status be continued? The arguments embrace the serious and the trivial. The idea of statehood invokes among some island residents the fear of higher taxes and an erosion of their cultural heritage. Some even fear the end of separate Puerto Rican participation in the Olympics and the Miss Universe pageant. On the other hand, while independence may be attractive, commonwealth supporters argue that it includes too many unknown costs, and therefore they embrace the status quo.

Proponents of independence have a long, vocal history emphasizing the need of Puerto Rico to regain its cultural and political autonomy. Some of the supporters of independence have even been militant. In 1950, nationalists attempted to assassinate President Truman, killing a White House guard in the process. Four years later, another band of nationalists opened fire in the gallery of the U.S. House of Representatives, wounding five members of Congress. Beginning in 1974, a group calling itself the Armed Forces of National Liberation (FALN, for *Fuerzas Armadas de Liberación Nacional*) took responsibility for more than 100 explosions continuing through 1987. The FALN is not alone, for at least four other militant groups advocating independence were identified as having been at work in the 1980s. The island itself is occasionally beset by violent demonstrations, often reacting to U.S. military installations there—a symbol of U.S. control (M. Breasted, 1977; D. Kleinman, 1977; R. McFadden, 1983; M. Suarez, 1985).

Concerns about Puerto Rico's status are not entirely internal. As many of the colonies of Africa and Asia gained their independence, world attention shifted to the few remaining dependent states. Consequently, in 1978, the United Nations passed a resolution proclaiming that, despite whatever the United States said, Puerto Rico was a colony. Further, the resolution called on Puerto Rico to determine its own future.

The issue of Puerto Rico's political destiny is in part ideological. Independence is the easiest way for the island to retain and strengthen its sense of cultural as well as political identity. Some nationalists express the desire that autonomous Puerto Rico develop close political ties with communist Cuba. The crucial arguments for independence are probably economic. An independent Puerto Rico would no longer be required to use U.S. shipping lines, which are more expensive than those of foreign competitors. An independent Puerto Rico, however, might be faced by a tariff wall when trading with its largest current customer, the mainland United States. Also, Puerto Rican migration to the mainland could be restricted.

Puerto Rico's future status most recently faced a vote in 1993, the first such opportunity since a vote in 1967. In the latest referendum, 48 percent favored con-

A demonstration in San Juan urging voters to participate in a referendum on Puerto Rico's future relationship with the United States.

tinuing commonwealth status, and 46 percent backing statehood. Less than 5 percent favored independence. While the vote was nonbinding, the issue of statehood, much less independence, is not likely to be put to another vote for some time to come. It is also unlikely that there will be sufficient support in Congress to move toward statehood, given the greater support, even if modestly greater, for commonwealth status. Yet, with half expressing a preference for a change, it is clear that discontent with the current arrangement prevails and remains a "colonial dilemma" (Meléndez and Meléndez, 1993; also see W. Booth, 1994; J. Passalacqua, 1994; *Sentinel*, 1993).

Economic Development

Depending on what the Puerto Rican economy is compared to and what part of it is being studied, the influence of the mainland United States either has been very progressive or has stagnated the island's economy. The major economic initiative has been Operation Bootstrap, begun in 1947, which exempted U.S. industries locating in Puerto Rico from taxes on profits for at least ten years. Later this exemption was extended, so that today, 600 U.S. corporations based on the mainland are exempted from paying taxes on profits they earn on the island. By 1993, this amount was over $11 billion in profits subject only to modest taxation. In addition, the federal government's program of enterprise zones that grants tax incentives to promote private investment in inner cities has also been extended to Puerto Rico. Unquestionably, Puerto Rico has become attractive to mainland-based corporations. Skeptics point out that, as a result, the island's agriculture has been virtually ignored. Furthermore, the economic benefits are limited. Businesses have spent the profits they have gained on Puerto Rico back on the mainland (L. Rohter, 1993a).

Puerto Rico's economy is already in severe trouble. Its unemployment rate has always been at least double that of the mainland. By 1983, unemployment islandwide exceeded 22 percent—three times the average on the mainland. In addition, the per capita income was less than half that of Mississippi, the poorest state on the mainland. Efforts to raise the wages of Puerto Rican workers only make the island less attractive to "labor-intensive" businesses, that is, those employing larger numbers of unskilled people. "Capital-intensive" companies, like the petrochemical industries, have found Puerto Rico attractive, but they have not created jobs for the semiskilled. A growing problem is Puerto Rico emerging as a major gateway to the United States for illegal drugs from South America, which has led the island to experience waves of violence and the social ills associated with the drug trade (M. Navarro, 1995).

Another major factor of Puerto Rico's economy is tourism. Government subsidies have encouraged the construction of luxury hotels. After U.S. citizens' travel to Cuba was closed in 1962, tourists discovered Puerto Rico's beaches and warm climate. Critics complain that the major economic beneficiaries of tourism are not local, being primarily investors from the mainland, and that high prices prevent the less affluent from visiting, thus unnecessarily restricting tourism. The irony of the tourist boom was seen by historian Mary Vaughan (1974): "The vegetables on the table at the Puerto Rican Sheraton have been picked in New Jersey by Puerto Rican migrant workers whose fathers once worked the now uncultivated land of Puerto Rico" (p. 281). As has been true of other aspects of the island's economic development, the tourist boom has had little positive effect on most Puerto Ricans.

Puerto Rico continues to face new challenges. First, with congressional approval in 1994 of NAFTA (the North American Free Trade Agreement), Mexico, Canada, and the United States became integrated into a single economic market. The reduction of trade barriers with Mexico, coupled with that nation's lower wages, may combine to undercut Puerto Rico's commonwealth advantage. Second, many more island nations now offer the sun-bound tourist from the mainland alternatives to Puerto Rico. In addition, cruise ships present another attractive option for tourists. Given the economic problems of the island, it is not surprising that many Puerto Ricans migrate to the mainland (L. Rohter, 1993a).

For years, migration to the mainland has served as a safety valve for Puerto Rico's population, which has annually grown at a rate 50 percent faster than that of the United States. Typically, migrants from Puerto Rico represent a broad range of occupations. There are seasonal fluctuations, as Puerto Rican farmworkers leave the island in search of seasonal employment. Puerto Ricans, particularly agricultural workers, earn higher wages on the mainland. Yet a significant proportion return despite their relatively higher wages (E. Meléndez, 1994).

BRIDGE BETWEEN ISLAND AND MAINLAND

In Chapter 10, we pointed out that the proximity of Mexico accounts for the stronger cultural distinctiveness of Chicanos than one finds among Whites of European descent. This is even more true of Puerto Ricans, because as U.S. citizens they may go to and from the mainland without legal restriction. Citizenship does not mean that they can move without meeting difficulties, however. Despite

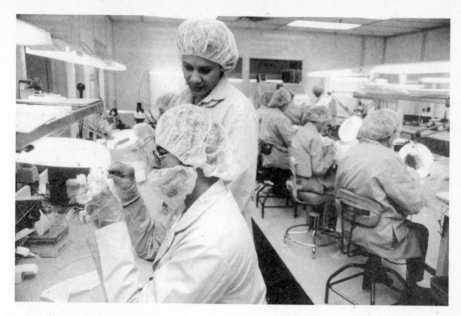

Economic development programs in Puerto Rico have not lived up to expectations. Here, pharmaceutical workers assemble pacemakers.

their citizenship, Puerto Ricans are occasionally challenged by immigration officials. Because other Latin Americans may attempt to enter the country posing as Puerto Ricans, Puerto Ricans find their papers more closely scrutinized than do other U.S. citizens.

Puerto Ricans came in relatively small numbers during the first half of the century, often encouraged by farm labor contracts similar to those extended to Mexican braceros. During World War II, the government recruited hundreds of Puerto Ricans to work on the railroads, in food manufacturing plants, and in copper mines on the mainland. But migration has been largely a post–World War II phenomenon. The 1940 census showed fewer than 70,000 Puerto Ricans on the mainland, or 10,000 fewer Puerto Ricans than lived in Massachusetts alone in 1970. Among the factors that have contributed to migration are (1) the economic pull away from the underdeveloped island, (2) the absence of legal restrictions against travel, and (3) the growth of relatively cheap air transportation. As the migration continued, the mainland offered the added attraction of a large Puerto Rican community in New York City, which makes adjustment easier for new arrivals.

New York City still has a formidable population of Puerto Ricans, compared to metropolitan San Juan's, but Puerto Ricans are now more dispersed throughout the mainland's cities, with sizable numbers in New Jersey, Illinois, Florida, California, Pennsylvania, and Connecticut.

The Puerto Ricans who have moved out of the large ethnic communities in cities like New York City, Chicago, and Philadelphia are a group more familiar with U.S. culture and the English language. This movement from the major set-

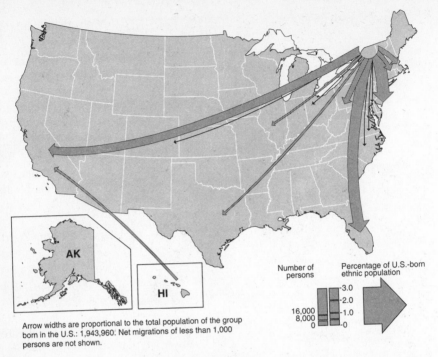

Number of persons

Percentage of U.S.-born ethnic population

-3.0
-2.0
-1.0
-0

16,000
8,000
0

Arrow widths are proportional to the total population of the group born in the U.S.: 1,943,960. Net migrations of less than 1,000 persons are not shown.

Figure 11.2 U.S.-Born Puerto Rican Origin Population

Source: Reprinted with permission of Macmillan Publishing Company from *We the People: An Atlas of Ethnic Diversity* by James Paul Allen and Eugene James Turner. Copyright © 1988 by Macmillan Publishing Company, a division of Macmillan, Inc.

tlements has been hastened as well by the loss of manufacturing jobs in these cities, a loss that hits Puerto Rican men especially hard. Figure 11.2 illustrates this dispersal of Puerto Ricans on the mainland out of New York City (L. Stains, 1994).

As the U.S. economy underwent recession in the 1970s and 1980s, unemployment among mainland Puerto Ricans, always high, increased dramatically. This increase shows in migration. In the 1950s, Puerto Ricans were half of the Hispanic arrivals. By the 1970s, they accounted for only 3 percent. Indeed, in some years during the 1980s, more Puerto Ricans went from mainland to island than the other way around.

Puerto Ricans returning to the island have become a significant force. Indeed, they have come to be given the name *Neoricans* (or *Nuyoricans*)—a term the islanders also use for Puerto Ricans in New York. Long-time islanders direct a modest amount of hostility toward these Neoricans. They usually return from the mainland with more formal schooling, more money, and a better command of English than native Puerto Ricans. Not too surprisingly, Neoricans compete very well with the islanders for jobs and land (C. Muschkin, 1993).

RACE IN PUERTO RICO AND ON THE MAINLAND

As the balance of this chapter will discuss, Puerto Rican migrants to the mainland must make adjustments in language, housing, and employment. These changes are required of most immigrants, but Puerto Ricans must also adapt to new racial identities. Racism does exist in Puerto Rico. People are arbitrarily denied opportunities merely because of their skin color. The racism, however, is not the same as on the mainland. Slavery was not as significant on the island as it was in the U.S. South, and Puerto Rico has a long history of accepting interracial marriages. Puerto Rico did not experience the mainland practices of segregation, antimiscegenation laws, and Jim Crow. More recently, however, Puerto Rico has started to resemble the mainland in taking on rigid racial attitudes (J. Fitzpatrick, 1987; J. Flores, 1985; C. Rodriquez, 1989).

The most significant difference between the meaning of race on Puerto Rico and on the mainland is that Puerto Rico, like so many other Caribbean societies, has a color gradient. The phrase *color gradient* describes distinctions based on skin color made on a continuum, rather than by sharp categorical separations. Rather than being either "black" or "white," people are judged in such societies as "lighter" or "darker" than others. Puerto Rico has such a color gradient. The presence of a color gradient rather than two or three racial categories does not necessarily mean that prejudice is less. Generally, however, societies with a color gradient permit more flexibility and are therefore less likely to impose specific sanctions against a group of people based on skin color alone.

Although Puerto Rico has not suffered interracial conflict or violence, its people are conscious of the different racial heritages. Rather than seeing people as either black or white in skin color, they perceive people as ranging from pale white to very black. Puerto Ricans are more sensitive to degrees of difference and make less effort to pigeonhole a person in one of two categories. Studies disagree on the amount of prejudice in Puerto Rico, but all concur that race is not as clear-cut an issue on the island as it is on the mainland.

Racial identification in Puerto Rico depends a great deal on the attitude of the individual making the judgment. If one thinks highly of a person, he or she may be seen as a member of a more acceptable racial group. A variety of terms are used in the color gradient to describe people racially: *blanco* (white), *triqueño* (almost white or black), *prieto, moreno,* or *de color* (dark-skinned), and *negro* (black) are a few of these. Factors such as social class and social position determine race, but on the mainland race is more likely to determine social class. This situation may puzzle people from the mainland, but racial etiquette on the mainland may be just as difficult to comprehend and accept for Puerto Ricans (J. Egerton, 1971; C. Rodriquez, 1989; Tumin and Feldman, 1961).

The Puerto Rican in the United States finds a new identity thrust on him or her by the dominant society. On the island, distinctions are by social class, but on the mainland, people are preoccupied with color. Many, taken for Blacks, are forced to emphasize that they are Puerto Rican. Still others are sometimes mistaken for Blacks at other times are identified as Puerto Rican, which also makes adjustment difficult. In fact, evidence indicates that those Puerto Ricans whose skin color is intermediate, between black and white, have the most difficulty adapting to or being accepted by American society. A study of Puerto Rican college students in New York found that most considered themselves "white" or "tan" and that less than 7 percent viewed themselves as "black." Yet, when asked how Anglos saw them, they dropped any reference to an intermediate category like "tan": 58 percent said "white" and 42 percent indicated "black." These differences can even be more difficult for younger children as they adjust to the color that is being assigned to them (Alaracón et al., 1994; A. Martinez, 1988).

Mainland-born Puerto Ricans feel the challenge of defining a racial identity less acutely than do the migrants. In "Listen to Their Voices," Aurora Levins Morales eloquently contemplates her Jewish Puerto Rican heritage. We will consider the many challenges Puerto Ricans face on the mainland in the sections that follow.

EL BARRIO

Whether outsiders referred to it as East Harlem or Spanish Harlem or El Barrio, a section of upper Manhattan was the most important Puerto Rican neighborhood on the mainland during the 1950s and much of the 1960s. It is less significant now because Puerto Ricans no longer migrate only to New York City, and even those who do are more likely to live outside El Barrio. By 1970, more Puerto Ricans lived in either the Bronx or Brooklyn than in this section of Manhattan. Like other minority groups, Puerto Ricans are generally concentrated in certain neighborhoods. They are segregated by both their social class and their darker skin. The latter factor clearly matters, because Puerto Ricans are more segregated from Whites than are Chicanos in such cities as Los Angeles. Puerto Ricans coming of age in the barrio are challenged simply to survive, let alone succeed (J. Fitzpatrick, 1987; Glazer and Moynihan, 1970, pp. 107–108; N. Kantrowitz, 1973; Massey and Bitterman, 1985).

The Puerto Rican neighborhoods need tremendous improvement in housing quality. The Bronx and Brooklyn, the two New York City boroughs where most Puerto Ricans live, accounted for more than 80 percent of the net loss of housing units in the entire nation between 1970 and 1980. Even more specifically, the South Bronx—the densest and largest Puerto Rican settlement in the United States—suffered such devastation that its very name came to mean urban blight. With the vanished housing went social networks, ethnic stores, and dance clubs. Such changes underscore that the Puerto Rican neighborhoods have little of the charm conveyed in *West Side Story*. All social institutions—political, educational, familial, and religious—suffer as a result (P. Guzman, 1995).

As revolving-door migration between island and mainland has become more common, Puerto Rican organizations have gone through a transition. The home-town clubs on the mainland, where ties to one of the island's 72 municipalities were central to social life, have withered and have no clear successor group. The militancy of the 1960s, reflected in the Young Lords Party, orga-

Listen to Their Voices
Child of the Americas

AURORA LEVINS MORALES

I am a child of the
    Americas,
a light-skinned mestiza
    of the Caribbean,
a child of many diaspo-
    ra, born into this
    continent at a
    crossroads.

I am a U.S. Puerto
    Rican Jew,
a product of the ghet-
    tos of New York I have never
    known.
An immigrant and the daughter and
    granddaughter of immigrants.
I speak English with passion: It's the
    tool of my consciousness,
a flashing knife blade of crystal, my
    tool, my craft.

I am Caribeña, island grown, Spanish
    is in my flesh,
ripples from my tongue, lodges in my
    hips:
the language of garlic and man-
    goes,

Aurora Levins Morales

the singing in my
    poetry, the flying
    gestures of my
    hands.
I am of Latinoamerica,
    rooted in the histo-
    ry of my continent:
I speak from that body.

I am not african. Africa
    is in me, but I can-
    not return.
I am not taína. Taíno is in me, but
    there is no way back.
I am not european. Europe lives in
    me, but I have no home there.

I am new. History made me. My first
    language was spanglish.
I was born at the crossroads
and I am whole.

Source: From Denis Lynn Daly Heyck, *Barrios and Borderlands: Cultures of Latinos and Latinas in the United States.* New York: Routledge, 1994, p. 447; reproduces poem © 1986 by Aurora Levins Morales and Rosario Morales, *Getting Home Alive.* Ithaca, N. Y.: Firebrand Books, 1986, p. 50.

nized along lines similar to the Black Panther Party, has also faded as a basis of social organization. As the second—and third—generations of Puerto Ricans on the mainland grow, political action groups working on behalf of and in Puerto Rican communities on the mainland may well grow stronger and more numerous. As the twentieth century draws to a close, however, this promise has yet to be fulfilled (Jennings and Rivera, 1984; Stevens-Arroyo and Díaz-Ramírez, 1982).

The problems of the South Bronx and other urban Puerto Rican settlements raise again the thoughts of "underclass" and "culture of poverty." The high proportion of low-income households is certainly present. The unemployment that creates the poverty has certainly been exacerbated if not triggered by the loss of hundreds of thousands of jobs from the central city. Studies of labor force participation document the declining opportunities of the early 1980s, especially in the "Rust-belt," where mainland Puerto Ricans reside, compared to the "Sunbelt" home of Chicanos and Cubans. Whether Puerto Ricans are moving out of the labor market permanently or can begin to return to gainful employment remains to be seen (N. Lemann, 1991; M. Tienda, 1989).

Education

Puerto Ricans confront several problems in education that are similar to those faced by Chicanos. Relative to Whites, both groups have lower educational attainment and are more likely to complete the same amount of schooling at an older age than Whites. In addition, Puerto Ricans have an even higher dropout rate than Chicanos. In 1993, 56 percent of Puerto Ricans aged 25 and older had completed high school, compared to 82 percent of non-Hispanics. Approximately 8 percent of Puerto Ricans have college degrees, in contrast to 23 percent of non-Hispanics (Bureau of the Census, 1994).

The challenge of being a Puerto Rican in a society dominated by Anglos is evident in the public schools. Part of the difficulty, as we have seen with other Hispanics, is the language barrier. Puerto Ricans on the island applying to colleges often take special standardized admissions tests in addition to such exams as the Scholastic Aptitude Test (SAT) and American College Test (ACT). Studies document that, regardless of high aptitude on the Spanish test, proficiency in English is almost as important a factor as aptitude for success on the conventional examinations in English. These findings are especially important since Puerto Ricans taking SATs are even more likely than Chicanos to indicate that English is not their best language (M. Pennock-Román, 1986).

These problems with standardized examinations are compounded by tracking. *Tracking* is the practice of placing students in specific classes or curriculum groups on the basis of test scores and other criteria. Tracking begins very early in the classroom, often in reading groups during first grade. These tracks may reinforce the disadvantages of Puerto Rican children from less affluent families and non-English-speaking households who have not been exposed to English reading materials in their homes during early childhood (C. Rodriquez, 1989; Schaefer and Lamm, 1995).

The usual problems of low-income youth are compounded for Puerto Ricans by the disruptive transfer of public school children between Puerto Rico and the mainland. The New York City Board of Education records that, from 1964 to 1973, 108,000 children transferred to New York City and another 106,000 transferred to the island. In New York City, Puerto Rican parents have shown interest in their children's education. Some of this interest erupted into an emotional battle during the 1968–1969 school strike over decentralization. The parents favored substantial local control, but the teachers' union, which supported more centralized control was stronger, and only a moderately decentralized program was eventually adopted. The benefits to Puerto Ricans that giving local school boards in New York City autonomy from the central board would have had is not completely clear. Modest gains in the number of Puerto Rican teachers and administrators have recently been made, but because of centralization, parental involvement in important school decisions remains marginal (Commission on Civil Rights, 1976c; J. Fitzpatrick, 1987).

Employment and Income

The board comparisons in Chapter 9 between Hispanics and the rest of the U.S. population document the poor economic situation of Puerto Ricans. Their position relative to that of Whites has grown worse over the years; it has not even remained the same, as it has with Blacks. In 1959, Puerto Rican family earnings were 71 percent of the national average. As Figure 11.3 indicates, Puerto Rican income had dropped to 50 percent that of Whites by 1993.

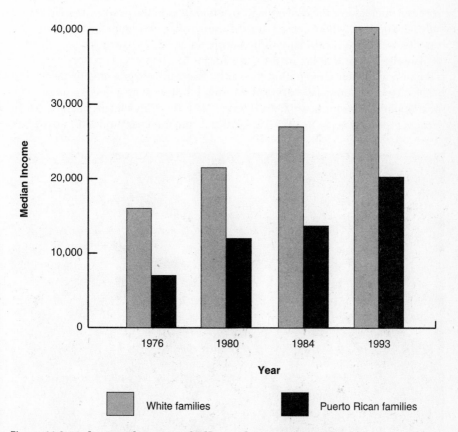

Figure 11.3 Median Family Income of Whites and Puerto Ricans, 1993
Puerto Rican family income on the mainland has increased since 1976 but has fallen behind gains made by Whites.

Note: 1990 data are for households.

Source: Bureau of the Census (1994, pp. 18–19).

Whatever economic measure is used, the conclusion is the same: Puerto Ricans fall desperately short of parity with Whites. A staggering 37 percent of Puerto Rican families lived below the poverty level in 1993. This figure compares to 30 percent of Chicanos and 13 percent of the nation's non-Hispanic families. Nationally in 1993, 12.8 percent of Puerto Ricans were unemployed, compared to the national figure of 6.8 percent. Economic recessions are especially hard on Puerto Ricans. Like other subordinate groups, Puerto Ricans are concentrated in the low-paying jobs subject to frequent layoffs and seasonal unemployment (Bureau of the Census, 1994, p. 396).

Several barriers keep Puerto Ricans from receiving a fair share of the better-paying jobs. The first is the language barrier, an obstacle described in detail in Chapter 9. Puerto Ricans who are not fluent in English falter in schools that lack effective bilingual programs. They are also placed in jobs that do not require language skills or training. These jobs are low-paying and do not lead to advancement up the occupational ladder. A second factor is the lack of work experience. Rural migrants do not have the skills sought by employers in the cities of the Northeast and the Midwest, where most Puerto Ricans reside. Without the necessary job experience, Puerto Ricans have difficulty obtaining better-paying jobs.

Another factor that has kept Puerto Ricans in a depressed economic position is the timing of their immigration. The cities they have congregated in, particularly New York, not only have stopped growing but have seen a decline in employment opportunities for newcomers. During New York City's financial crisis, which became especially acute in 1975 and 1976 and continue into the 1980s, nearly half

Labor unions (such as members pictured here of the International Lady Garment Workers Union) have helped to represent Puerto Ricans in the workforce, although some mainland union groups have protested the tax advantages that cause some mainland industries to relocate to Puerto Rico.

the Puerto Ricans holding civil service appointments lost their jobs in cutbacks. Even when the New York City economy began to rebound, the new jobs required skills that neither the local Puerto Ricans nor those migrating from the island were likely to have. In addition, jobs had moved out into the metropolitan area away from the Puerto Rican communities.

These hindrances to the Puerto Rican workforce in New York City have continued into the 1990s and have been repeated in other cities with significant Puerto Rican populations. Industrial Bridgeport, Connecticut, has a growing Puerto Rican community, but as its numbers increase, its economic situation has worsened, as factories and the jobs that went with them have left the city for suburbs and small towns (J. Fitzpatrick, 1989; Leebaw and Heyman, 1976; C. Rodriquez, 1989; Torres and Bonilla, 1993).

The Commission on Civil Rights (1976c) concluded that, even after factors like language and job experience are taken into account, "the evidence is compelling that racial, ethnic, and sex discrimination are barriers to job opportunities for Puerto Ricans" (p. 61). Arbitrary job requirements disqualify Puerto Ricans. Height standards used by law enforcement agencies are gradually being revised, but while in effect, they eliminate short-statured Puerto Ricans from consideration. Even when they do have work experience that should qualify them for a position, Puerto Ricans may be denied employment because they lack a high school diploma. A 1985 survey of Hispanics in Chicago found that 51 percent of Puerto Ricans felt that Anglos discriminated against them. This proportion perceiving mistreatment was even larger than that among foreign-born Hispanics (Ogletree and Ujlaki, 1985).

The courts and various government agencies have sought to eliminate the barriers to effective labor-force participation by Puerto Ricans. The inequities remain, however, and Puerto Ricans are underrepresented even in agencies that serve Puerto Ricans. As might be expected given their low incomes, a large number of Puerto Rican families receive public assistance or welfare. Many other immigrant groups have depended on social services, but the earlier arrivals from Europe were aided by settlement houses that manifested a deeper concern for the individual. Today's welfare bureaucracy primarily coordinates paper forms and people, seeming to see the two as interchangeable. Consequently, today more than ever, public aid workers must be responsive to their clients (Commission on Civil Rights, 1976c; Glazer and Moynihan, 1970; E. Mizio, 1972).

Family Life

Education in the public schools can support or detract from the maintenance of traditional values. Schooling introduces ethnic children, whether they are Puerto Ricans or come from immigrant groups, to the traditions of the host society. This exposure usually puts the school in conflict with ethnic traditions and also weakens parental authority during the crucial period of adolescence. In this way, the Puerto Rican family resembles the families of European immigrants in the past and Chicanos today. Like the former, the Puerto Rican migrant family has experienced the cultural shock of adjusting to a new society. Even though they are citizens of the United States, island-born migrants find life different on the mainland. Many Puerto Rican migrants hold some child-rearing and self-image values in common with Chicanos.

Traditional values fade in conjunction with the length of time since permanent residence in Puerto Rico. Also, the more schooling one has received on the mainland, the less familism is observed. The extended family takes on a less important role, so that of a significant source of social support is lost. But a decline in familism also means a fading of machismo and marianismo, which is generally viewed as a positive change (D. Cortés, 1995).

As familism declines and the extended family weakens, Puerto Ricans are forced to turn to impersonal bureaucratic agencies for the services that used to be provided by their kin. One manifestation of the decline already taking place in machismo is the fact that women on the mainland are more likely to work than they are on the island. It remains to be seen whether such positive attributes found among many Puerto Ricans as a zest for life, sociability, a sense of pride, and emotional warmth will be maintained as Puerto Ricans become residents on the mainland (J. Fitzpatrick, 1987; E. Francis, 1976; E. Preble, 1968).

As is so often the case with subordinate groups, poverty takes its toll on family life. In 1993, in 53 percent of Puerto Rican families no man was present, while in comparison, 84 percent of non-Hispanic families had both husband and wife present. Puerto Rican female-headed families, even after one considers government transfer payments like public assistance and Social Security, are the poorest segment in the mainland United States (Bureau of the Census, 1994).

Religious Life

The church has been an important element of immigrant family life. For Puerto Ricans, however, religion has not played a major unifying role. About four-fifths of Puerto Ricans are Roman Catholic, because of conversions during the Spanish colonial period. The balance of the population is Protestant, the legacy of missionaries who came shortly after the American acquisition of the island.

The number of Protestants is growing on the island as evangelicals and pentecostals step up recruiting. *Evangelical faiths* are Christian religions that emphasize a personal relationship between the individual and God. Evangelicals believe that each adherent must spread the faith and bear personal witness. Adherents to *pentecostal faiths* have beliefs similar to those of the evangelicals but, in addition believe in the infusion of the Holy Spirit into services and in religious experiences such as faith healing. Puerto Rican Catholics, even more than other Hispanics, do not have their own clergy and consequently lack the strong support that ethnic parishes provided for the Irish and the Poles. The Catholic church might have been a stabilizing factor, but the American presence in Puerto Rico has reduced its positive influence. Until 1961, the Catholic church on the island was under the leadership of American bishops. Even as recently as 1984, fewer than 15 percent of the island's priests had been born on Puerto Rico.

With this background, the traditional sense of religious identity that might have developed was weakened, as the typical Puerto Rican was forced to choose between loyalty to the Americanized Catholic church and her or his identity as a

Puerto Rican. Even on the mainland, Catholic parishes populated by Puerto Ricans have usually been under the direction of Anglos or Chicanos. Consequently, the Puerto Ricans who migrate have not found the church as useful in assisting them in their adjustment as other immigrants have. By contrast, the pentecostal congregation has provided a warmth and a more emotional form of worship that more closely mirrors the culture of the island (J. Fayer, 1985; Glazer and Moynihan, 1970; R. Stuart, 1984).

Political Organizations

As it does among other groups, political activity among Puerto Ricans takes two forms. The first is the work to elect individuals to office, and the second is to organize into political action groups, which are sometimes scrutinized by law enforcement agencies because of their activities.

As a group, Puerto Ricans do not play a decisive role in electoral politics and have less influence than Black U.S. citizens. On the whole, the Puerto Rican population is much smaller than the Black population, but even in New York City, where, coupled with other Hispanics, they make up 20 percent of the population, their effect has been slight. Steps such as providing election information in Spanish and registration drives may encourage greater Puerto Rican participation. Despite legal remedies, voter turnout is likely to continue to be modest.

Puerto Rican voters are often alienated from the political process because (1) they move frequently because of job layoffs; (2) they find life in cities impersonal when contrasted to Puerto Rico's small towns; (3) district boundaries are drawn in some instances to divide Hispanic communities, effectively diluting the power base; and (4) some may assume that their stay in the United States will be temporary. Puerto Ricans may also have little desire to participate actively in a political system that appears to be retreating from its earlier commitment to special social and economic programs for minorities. This relative political inactivity is not typical of the Puerto Rican people. For example, in the 1993 referendum on the island's future status, fully 80 percent of the electorate voted (V. Irwin, 1987; D. Nelson, 1980; J. Passalacqua, 1994).

There are some encouraging signs. Puerto Ricans are consistently being elected to the House of Representatives, from districts primarily in Chicago and New York City. In Congress, they participate in the increasingly large Congressional Hispanic Caucus first organized in 1987. In addition, Puerto Ricans have been appointed to important positions, such as Antonia C. Novello, who was appointed U.S. surgeon general in 1990. A 1992 national survey showed Puerto Ricans to be heavily Democratic in terms of party allegiance. About 64 percent viewed themselves as Democrats, compared to 44 percent of Anglos (N. Kanellos, 1994).

Not all organizations in the Puerto Rican community are concerned with electoral politics. Founded in 1961, *Aspira* (Spanish for "strive" or "aspire") encourages Puerto Rican youths to undertake higher education and to enter professional schools. A number of grassroots groups representing special interests, such as merchants, fraternal social organizations, and various occupational groups, have also formed to better represent the needs of the diverse Puerto Rican community (J. Fitzpatrick, 1987).

CONCLUSION

In 1998, Puerto Rico will "celebrate" its five hundredth anniversary as a colony—four centuries under Spain and another century under the United States. Its dual status as a colony and as a developing nation has been the defining issue for Puerto Ricans, even those who have migrated to the mainland (R. Perusse, 1990).

The Puerto Rican people share many problems with other subordinate groups: poor housing, inadequate health care, weak political representation, and low incomes. Like Chicanos, they have a language and cultural tradition at variance with that of Anglo society. The dominant society has removed some barriers to achievement by Spanish-speaking people in the United States but public concerns grow about bilingual and bicultural programs. Chicanos and Puerto Ricans are poorly represented among key decision makers in both corporate offices and governmental agencies. Both Chicanos and Puerto Ricans, however, are close to or are actually in their home country, a situation that facilitates maintaining a rich cultural tradition. Hispanics' ability to maintain their original identity and solidarity means they have not been as compelled as European immigrants to assimilate White American customs and values.

The situation of Puerto Ricans is unique. Those on the island must resolve the issues of its political relationship to the mainland and must set the proper pace and emphasis for economic development. Those migrating to the mainland must adapt to a social definition of race different from that on the island and must adjust to a system that leaves some Puerto Ricans in an ambiguous social position.

The problems of Puerto Rican barrios throughout the United States are not just cold statistics or symptoms subject to the latest government program. Their real, human meaning has frequently been brought out by civil disturbances, as in Chicago in 1966, New York City in 1967, and Newark in 1974, when Puerto Ricans participated in desperate riots. A survey conducted in Chicago shortly after that disorder rated police relations and unemployment as the major problems (F. Forni, 1971). Puerto Rican respondents seemed to turn more eagerly to individual solutions (getting more education and other forms of self-improvement) than to work through public agencies. In part, this attitude reflects the public agencies' ineffectiveness in dealing with the problems facing Puerto Ricans. Once again, Myrdal's observation, in *An American Dilemma* (1944), that the problems of a subordinate group are actually the problems of the dominant group seems apt.

The Puerto Rican mainland population is also distinct. Many first-generation immigrants have endured poverty in the past; in this respect the Puerto Rican migrant is not unique. The Commission on Civil Rights (1976c) however, 20 years ago, concluded its report on Puerto Ricans this way:

> The United States has never before had a large migration of citizens from offshore, distinct in culture and language and also facing the problem of color prejudice. After 30 years of significant migration, contrary to conventional wisdom that once Puerto Ricans learned the language the second generation would move into the mainstream

of American society, the future of this distinct community in the United States is still to be determined. (p. 145)

Puerto Ricans are still among the groups who find themselves economically on the outside despite Hispanics' long history of immigration to the United States. Another group with such a history has also met problems of racial prejudice and economic discrimination: Asian Americans.

KEY TERMS

color gradient The placement of people on a continuum from light to dark skin color rather than in distinct racial groupings by skin color.

evangelical faiths Christian faiths that place great emphasis on a personal relationship between the individual and God and believe that each adherent must spread the faith and bear personal witness by openly declaring the religion to nonbelievers.

Neoricans Puerto Ricans who return to the island to settle after living on the mainland of the United States (also *Nuyoricans*).

pentecostal faiths Religious groups similar in many respects to evangelical faiths which, in addition, believe in the infusion of the Holy Spirit into services and in religious experiences such as faith healing.

tracking The practice of placing students in specific curriculum groups on the basis of test scores and other criteria.

FOR FURTHER INFORMATION

Edna Acosta-Belén, ed. *The Puerto Rican Woman: Perspectives on Culture, History, and Society*, 2d ed. New York: Praeger, 1986.

This collection of 11 articles deals with Puerto Rican women both on the island and the mainland.

Alba N. Ambert and María D. Alvarez, eds. *Puerto Rican Children on the Mainland: Interdisciplinary Perspectives*. New York: Garland, 1992.

Examines mainland children in terms of language, education, health, and family.

Ronald Fernandez. *The Disenchanted Island: Puerto Rico and the United States in the Twentieth Century*. New York: Praeger, 1992.

A critical analysis of the relationship between the mainland United States and Puerto Rico.

Joseph P. Fitzpatrick. *Puerto Rican Americans: The Meaning of Migration to the Mainland*, 2d ed. Englewood Cliffs, NJ: Prentice-Hall, 1987.

A good sociological treatment of Puerto Ricans, this book emphasizes the degree to which they have been assimilated into Anglo society. Chapters are devoted to education, welfare, mental illness, drug abuse, religion, and the differing definitions of race on the island and the mainland.

Edwin Meléndez and Edgardo Meléndez, eds. *Colonial Dilemma: Critical Perspectives on Contemporary Puerto Rico*. Boston: South End Press, 1993.

Examines the impact of the mainland United States on Puerto Rico in terms of the economy and politics.

Felix M. Padilla. *The Gang as an American Experience*. New Brunswick, NJ: Princeton University Press, 1992.

A profile of a Puerto Rican drug-dealing gang based on interviews in Chicago.

Roland I. Perusse. *The United States and Puerto Rico: The Struggle for Equality.* Malabar, FL; Krieger, 1990.

An overview of the political association of Puerto Rico with the mainland United States. Includes an appendix of 100 pages of major acts and legislation from 1876 to 1982 relating to this relationship.

Edward Rivera. *Family Installments: Memories of Growing Up Hispanic.* New York: Morrow, 1982.

English professor Rivera was born in Puerto Rico and draws on his own experience of growing up in El Barrio.

Clara E. Rodriquez. *Puerto Ricans: Born in the U.S.A.* Boston: Unwin Hyman, 1989.

This authoritative book concentrates on Puerto Ricans in New York City, with a special emphasis on education and housing. It includes a look at the impact of the pop group Menudo.

Piri Thomas. *Down These Mean Streets.* New York: Signet, 1967.

In an autobiographical account of life in El Barrio, Thomas discusses the especially difficult existence of a dark-skinned Puerto Rican.

CRITICAL THINKING QUESTIONS

1. What do you see as the major issues facing Puerto Rico?
2. How does Puerto Rico function differently from Mexico as a source of migration to the United States?
3. How does the case of Puerto Rico support the notion of race as a social concept?
4. What are the special challenges that Puerto Ricans face in the schools?
5. Consider how the concepts of ethnicity, race, and nationality apply to Puerto Ricans.

Chapter *12*

Asian Americans: Growth and Diversity

Chapter Outline

Highlights

Asian Americans are a diverse group that is one of the fastest-growing segments of the U.S. population. Immigration is the primary source of growth among Koreans, Filipinos, and refugees from Southeast Asia. All Asian groups, along with Blacks and Whites (or *Haoles,* as they are known) coexist in Hawaii. Asian Americans are often viewed as a *model minority* that has successfully overcome discrimination. This inaccurate image disguises lingering maltreatment and anti-Asian-American violence. Further, it denies Asian Americans the opportunities afforded other racial minorities.

Two characteristics of the people in the United States of Asian descent are growth and diversity. Asian Americans in 1990 number 7.2 million, up from 1.5 million in 1970 (see Table 12.1). Although they are just 3 percent of the U.S. population, they form collectively the third largest racial or ethnic minority after Blacks and Hispanics.

Asia is a vast region with more than half the world's population. The successive waves of immigrants to the United States from that continent constitute a vast array of nationalities and cultures. Besides the eight groups listed in Table 12.1, the Census Bureau enumerates the Bangladeshi, Bhutanese, Bornean, Burmese, Celebesian, Cernan, Indochinese, Iwo-Jiman, Malayan, Maldivean, Nepali, Okinawan, Sikkimese, Singaporean, and Sri Lankan. Knowing this variety among Asian people, we can apply to Asian Americans several generalizations made earli-

Table 12.1 ASIAN-AMERICAN POPULATION

The Asian-American population doubled in the 1970s and doubled again during the 1980s.

Group	Population (in thousands)			Change (percentage)	
	1970	1980	1990	1970–1980	1980–1990
Chinese Americans	453	806	1,640	85	104
Filipino Americans	343	775	1,407	126	82
Japanese Americans	591	701	848	19	21
Asian Indians	—	362	815	—	125
Korean Americans	69	355	799	413	116
Vietnamese	—	262	615	—	135
Laotian	—	48	149	—	210
Cambodian	—	16	147	—	819
All other	80[a]	176	854	—	485
Total	1,539	3,501	7,274	127	108

[a]Includes Asian Indians, Vietnamese, Laotian, and Cambodian.

Source: Bureau of the Census data reported in J. Ng (1991).

er about Native Americans. Both groups are a collection of diverse peoples with distinct linguistic, social, and geographic backgrounds. The stereotyped portrait of Asians as expressionless people with their heads bowed is just as useless as the stereotype of the cigar-store Indian. It is easy to lump together all people of the same color, but doing so ignores the sharp differences among them. Any examination of Asian Americans quickly reveals their diversity.

As is true of all the minority groups discussed so far, to be accepted, Asians in the United States have been pressured to assimilate. The effects of this pressure vary. For recent refugees from Asia, assimilation is a new experience, whereas the grandchildren of Japanese immigrants may be culturally indistinguishable from Whites. As is evident in Table 12.2, many Asian Americans cluster on the West Coast and in Hawaii, but significant settlements of most Asian-American groups can be found in a number of the larger cities. Figure 12.1 shows how Asian Americans combine with other groups to form the diversity typical of an American metropolitan area such as Los Angeles.

This chapter examines Asian Americans in general and three of the larger groups—Koreans, Filipinos, and refugees from Southeast Asia—in greater depth. The chapter concludes with an examination of the coexistence of a uniquely mixed group of peoples—Hawaiians—among whom Asian Americans form the numerical majority. Chapters 13 and 14 concentrate on the Chinese and the Japanese, the two Asian groups with the longest historical tradition in the United States.

KOREAN AMERICANS

The population of Korean Americans is now nearly as large as that of Japanese Americans. Yet Korean Americans are often overlooked in favor of the larger groups from Asia.

Historical Background

Today's Korean-American community is the result of three waves of immigration. The initial wave, of a little more than 7,000 immigrants, came to the United States between 1903 and 1910, when laborers migrated to Hawaii. Under Japanese colonial rule (1910–1945), Korean migration was halted except for a few hundred "picture brides" allowed to join their prospective husbands.

The second wave followed the end of the Korean War, accounting for about 14,000 immigrants from 1951 through 1964. Most of these immigrants were war orphans and wives of American servicemen. Relatively little research has been done on these first two periods of immigration.

The third wave was initiated by the passage of the 1965 Immigration Act, which greatly facilitated movement from Korea. For the four years prior to the act, Koreans accounted for only seven out of every 1,000 immigrants. In the first four years after the act, Koreans were 38 out of every 1,000 immigrants to the

Table 12.2   LARGEST ASIAN-AMERICAN POPULATIONS, BY STATES, 1990

Asian Americans have settled mostly in a few states, particularly California and Hawaii. Five states account for anywhere from 55 percent (Korean Americans) to 74 percent (Japanese Americans) of these four groups.

Rank	Population	Percentage of Group
Chinese Americans		
1. California	704,850	43
2. New York	284,144	17
3. Hawaii	68,804	4
4. Texas	63,232	4
5. Massachusetts	53,792	3
6. Other states	470,650	29
Total	1,645,472	100
Filipino Americans		
1. California	731,685	52
2. Hawaii	168,682	12
3. Illinois	64,224	5
4. New York	62,259	4
5. New Jersey	53,146	4
6. Other states	326,774	23
Total	1,406,770	100
Japanese Americans		
1. California	312,989	37
2. Hawaii	247,486	29
3. New York	35,281	4
4. Washington	34,366	4
5. Illinois	21,831	3
6. Other states	195,609	23
Total	847,562	100
Korean Americans		
1. California	259,941	33
2. New York	95,648	12
3. Illinois	41,506	5
4. New Jersey	38,540	5
5. Texas	31,775	4
6. Other states	331,439	41
Total	798,849	100

Source: Bureau of the Census data reported in J. Ng (1991).

United States. This third wave, continuing to the present, has reflected the admission priorities set up in the 1965 immigration law. These immigrants have been well educated and have arrived in the United States with professional skills (P. Min, 1995).

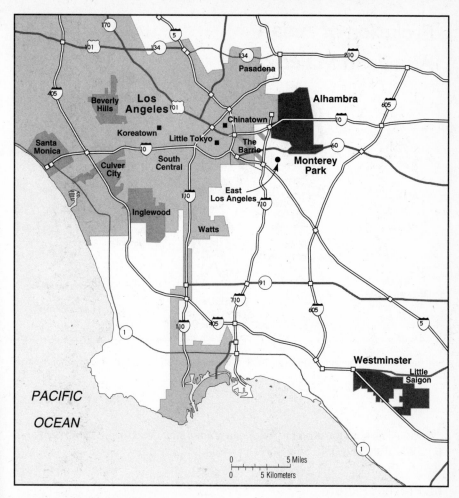

Figure 12.1 Ethnic Diversity in Los Angeles
The diversity of life in Los Angeles, the second largest city in the United States, reflects migration from
Mexico (the barrio), Korea (Koreatown), China and Hong Kong (Chinatown), Taiwan (Monterey Park
and Alhambra), Vietnam (Little Saigon in Westminister), and Japan (Little Tokyo). Also noted on the
map are the locations of the 1965 riots (Watts) and 1992 riots (South-Central Los Angeles).

Many of the most recent immigrants, though, must settle at least initially for
positions of lower responsibility than those they held in Korea and must suffer
through a period of "exigency" or disenchantment, as described in Chapter 2. The
problems that have been documented, such as stress, loneliness, alcoholism, family strife, and mental disorders, reflect the pain of adjustment. They have also been
termed the *ilchomose*, or "1.5 generation": The Korean-American immigrants who
accompanied their parents to the United States when young now occupy a middle,
marginal position between the cultures of Korea and the United States. They
are today middle-aged, remain bilingual and bicultural, and tend to form the

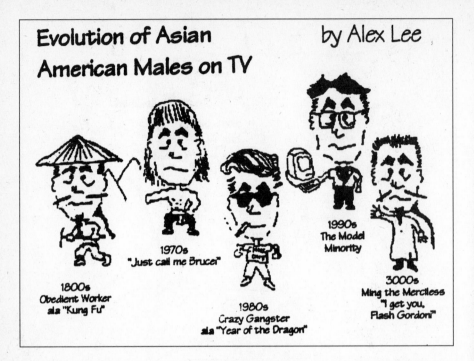

A cartoonist satirizes the stereotypical portrayal of Asian-American men on television in the United States.

Courtesy, Alex Lee.

professional class in the Korean-American community (W. Hurh, 1990; Hurh and Kim, 1984, 1987, 1988; L. Shin, 1971).

The Present Picture

Today's young Korean Americans face many of the cultural conflicts common to any first generation born in a new country. The parents may speak the native tongue, but the road to opportunity is paved with U.S. culture and the English language. It is very difficult to maintain a sense of Korean culture in the United States; the host society is not particularly helpful. Although the United States fought a war there and U.S. troops remain in South Korea, Korean culture is very foreign to contemporary Americans. The few studies of attitudes toward Korean Americans show Americans responding with vague, negative attitudes or simply lumping Korean Americans with other Asian groups (W. Hurh, 1977b; Hurh and Kim, 1982, 1984; Kitano and Matsushima, 1981; R. Rodriquez, 1982).

Studies by social scientists indicate that Korean Americans face many problems typical for immigrants, like difficulties with language. In Los Angeles, where the largest concentration of Koreans lives, more than 100 churches have only Korean-language services, and local television stations feature several hours of Korean programs. The Korean immigrants' high level of education should help them cope with the challenge. In 1980, 40 percent of Korean Americans 20–24 years old were enrolled in school, compared to 24 percent of Whites. While Korean Americans stress conventional schooling as a means to success, Korean schools have also been begun in major cities. Typically operated on Saturday afternoons, they offer classes on Korean history, customs, music, and language to help students maintain their cultural identity (Gardner, Robe, and Smith, 1985; W. Hurh, 1977a; H. Kim, 1980; Kim and Hurh, 1983; D. Lee, 1992).

Korean-American women commonly participate in the labor force, as do many Asian-American women. About 60 percent of native-born Korean-American women and half the women born abroad work in the labor force. These figures may not seem striking compared with the data for White women, but the cultural differences make the figures more significant. Korean women immigrate from a family system that establishes well-defined marital roles: the woman is expected to serve as homemaker and mother only. Although these roles are carried over to the United States, women are pressed, because of their husband's struggles to establish themselves, to support their families.

Many Korean-American men begin small service or retail businesses and gradually involve their wives in the business. Wages do not matter, as the household mobilizes to make a profitable enterprise out of a marginal business. Under economic pressure, Korean-American women must move away from traditional cultural roles. The move, however, is only partial; studies show that despite the high rate of participation in the labor force by Korean immigrant wives, first-generation immigrant couples continue in sharply divided gender roles in other aspects of daily living (Kim and Hurh, 1984, 1985a, 1985b; P. Min, 1995).

Korean-American businesses should not be regarded as major operations, most are relatively small. They do benefit from a special form of development capital (or cash) used to subsidize businesses, called a *kye* (pronounced "kay"). Korean Americans pool their money through the kye—an association that grants members money on a rotating basis to gain access to even more additional capital. Kyes depend on trust and are not protected by laws or insurance like bank loans. Kyes work as follows: Say for example, that 12 people agree to contribute $500 a month. Then, once a year, one of these individuals receives $6,000. Few records are kept, as the entire system is built on trust and friendship. Rotating credit associations are not unique to Korean Americans; for example, they have been used in the United States by West Indians and Ethiopians. Not all Korean business entrepreneurs use the kye, but it does represent a significant source of capital. A 1984 Chicago survey revealed that 34 percent of Korean merchants relied on a kye (M. Goozner, 1987; I. Kim, 1988; Light and Bonacich, 1988; L. Sun, 1995).

In the early 1990s, nationwide attention was given to the apparent friction between Korean Americans and another subordinate group, African Americans. In New York City, Los Angeles, and Chicago, the scene was replayed where a Korean-American merchant confronted an African-American allegedly threatening or robbing her or him. The African-American neighborhood responded with hostility to what they perceived as the disrespect and arrogance of the Korean-American entrepreneur. Such friction is not new; earlier generations of Jewish, Italian, and even Arab merchants encountered similar hostility from what to outsiders seems an unlikely source, another oppressed subordinate group. The contemporary conflict was even dramatized in Spike Lee's 1989 movie *Do the Right Thing*, in which African Americans and Korean Americans clashed. The situation stems from Korean Americans' being the latest immigrant group prepared to cater to the needs of the inner city abandoned by those who have moved up the economic ladder (Commission on Civil Rights, 1992; H. El Nasser, 1991a; L. Goodstein, 1990).

The tension that can arise between subordinate groups gained national attention during the 1992 South-Central Los Angeles riots. In that city's poor areas, the only shops in which to buy groceries or liquor or gasoline are owned by Korean immigrants. They have largely replaced the White businesspeople who left the ghetto area after the 1965 Watts riot. African Americans were well aware of the dominant role Korean Americans played in their local retail market. Some Blacks expressed resentment that had previously been fueled by the 1991 fatal shooting of a 15-year-old Black girl by a Korean grocer in a dispute over a payment for orange juice. The resentment grew when the grocer, convicted of manslaughter, had her prison sentence waived by a judge in favor of a five-year probation period.

The 1992 riots focused in part on retailers in South-Central Los Angeles, and therefore on Korean Americans. During the unrest 2,000 Korean businesses valued at $350 million were destroyed. In a postriot survey of those African Americans arrested, 80 percent felt that Korean Americans were disrespectful, compared to 56 percent who felt similarly about Whites. Desire to succeed had Korean

Kibok Yoo, whose liquor store was ruined in the Los Angeles riots, learned that her insurance did not cover the loss. About 2,000 other Korean-American businesses were also destroyed.

Americans' led them to the inner city, where they did not face competition from Whites. But it also meant that they had to deal on a daily basis with the frustration of another minority group (Commission on Civil Rights, 1992, pp. 32–39; S. McIntosh, 1992; S. Mydans, 1992, 1993).

Among Korean Americans the most visible organization holding the group together is the church. Half the immigrants have been affiliated with Christian churches prior to immigrating. One study of Koreans in Chicago and Los Angeles found that 70 percent were affiliated with Korean ethnic churches, mostly Presbyterian, with small numbers of Roman Catholics and Methodists. Korean ethnic churches are the fastest-growing segment of the Presbyterian and Methodist faiths. The church performs an important function, apart from the manifest religious one, giving Korean Americans a sense of attachment and a practical way to meet other Korean Americans. The churches are much more than simple sites for religious services; they assume multiple, secular roles for the Korean community. The fellowship that Korean Americans participate in is both spiritual and ethnic (Hurh and Kim, 1984, 1989, 1990).

FILIPINO AMERICANS

Relatively little has been written about the Filipinos (also spelled *Philipinos*) although they are the second largest Asian-American group in the United States, now at more than a million. Social science literature considers them Asians for geographical reasons, but physically and culturally, they are very different because of centuries of Spanish rule.

Immigration Patterns

The earliest Filipino immigrants came as American nationals, when, in 1899, the United States gained possession of the Philippine Islands at the conclusion of the Spanish-American War. In 1934, the islands gained commonwealth status. Yet, despite the close ties, immigration was sharply restricted to only 50 to 100 persons annually until the 1965 Immigration Act lifted these quota limitations. Before the restrictions were removed, pineapple growers in Hawaii successfully lobbied to import workers to the islands. Another exception was the U.S. Navy, which put Filipino citizens to work in kitchens aboard ship; as recently as 1970, 14,000 Filipinos were employed as mess stewards. Many of them later settled on the mainland of the United States. However, many of these ex-sailors felt they were not welcomed as veterans but as unwanted immigrants. A long-standing concern was their understanding that, given their military service, the U.S. citizenship of Filipino World War II veterans would be expedited. This problem was only partially resolved in a 1994 federal court ruling—almost a half century after the end of World War II (S. Cacas, 1995; P. Calica, 1995; Gardner et al., 1985; H. Melendy, 1980; R. Takaki, 1989).

Filipino immigration can be divided into four distinct periods:

1. The first generation, immigrating in the 1920s, was mostly male and employed in agricultural labor.

2. A second group, coming also in the early twentieth century, immigrated into Hawaii to serve as contract workers on Hawaii's sugar plantations.
3. The post–World War II arrivals included many war veterans and brides of U.S. servicemen.
4. The newest immigrants, who include many professionals (physicians, nurses, and others), arrived under the 1965 Immigration Act (H. Kitano, 1991; P. Min, 1995; A. Pido, 1986).

As in other Asian groups, the people are diverse. Besides these stages of immigration, the Filipinos can also be defined by different states of immigration—different languages, regions of origin, and religions—differences that sharply separate the people in their homeland as well. In the Philippines and among Filipino immigrants to the United States, eight distinct languages with 200 dialects are spoken (A. Pido, 1986, p. 17).

The Present Picture

As shown in Table 12.1, the Filipino population increased dramatically when restrictions on immigration were eased in 1965. More than two-thirds of the new arrivals qualified for entry as professional and technical workers, but like Koreans, they have often worked at jobs below those they left in the Philippines. Surprisingly, U.S. born Filipinos often have less formal schooling and lower job status (see Figure 12.2 on page 340). They come from poorer families unable to afford higher education and have been relegated to unskilled work, including migrant farm work. Their relatively poor economic background that means they have little start-up capital for businesses. Therefore, unlike other Asian-American groups, Filipinos have not developed small-business bases such as retail or service outlets capitalizing on their ethnic culture.

The volume of Philippine exports to the United States is low—one-fourth of Korean exports. The Filipino exports are mostly agricultural, and so their volume and the content of the products do not provide an opening for small businesses. Filipinos, therefore, have been absorbed into primarily low-wage, private-sector jobs. Prospects for immediate economic advancement for Filipino Americans as a group seem dim (Bureau of the Census, 1994; P. Min, 1987, 1995; Nee and Sanders, 1985).

Despite their numbers, no significant Filipino social organization has formed, for several reasons. First, Filipinos' strong loyalty to family and church, particularly Roman Catholicism, works against time-consuming efforts to create organizations. Second, the people's diversity makes forming ties here difficult. Third, though Filipinos have organized many groups, these tend to be clublike or fraternal. They do not seek to represent the general Filipino population and therefore remain invisible to Anglos. Fourth, although Filipinos have initially stayed close to events in their homeland, they show every sign of seeking involvement in broader non-Filipino organizations and avoiding group exclusiveness. The election of Filipino-American Benjamin Cayetano as governor of Hawaii in 1994 would be such an example of involvement in mainstream political organization (Lin and

Arguelles, 1995; H. Melendy, 1980; R. Morales, 1976; D. Nakanishi, 1986; V. Rabaya, 1971; E. Yu, 1980).

For similar reasons, Filipinos, unlike other Asian Americans, do not have visible commercial centers like Chinatowns. Only in the 1990s, because of the sheer size of the Filipino community in Los Angeles County, are such ethnic enclaves beginning to emerge, but they barely exceed the "Manilatowns" of the 1920s (Lin and Arguelles, 1995; P. Min, 1995).

SOUTHEAST ASIAN AMERICANS

The people of Southeast Asia—the Vietnamese, Cambodians (Kampucheans), and Laotians—were part of the former French Indochinese Union. *Indochinese* is only a term of convenience, for the peoples of these areas are ethnically and linguistically diverse. The ethnic Laotians constitute only half of the Laotian people, for example; a significant number of Mon-Khmer, Yao, and Hmong form minorities (Kitano and Daniels, 1988; M. Wright, 1980).

The Refugees

The problem of U.S. involvement in Indochina did not end when all U.S. personnel were withdrawn from South Vietnam in 1975. The final tragedy was the reluctant welcome given to the refugees from Vietnam, Cambodia (Kampuchea), and Laos by Americans and people of other nations. One week after the evacuation of Vietnam in April 1975, a Gallup poll reported that 54 percent of Americans were against giving sanctuary to the Asian refugees, with 36 percent in favor and 12 percent undecided. The primary objection to Vietnamese immigration was that it would further increase unemployment (Schaefer and Schaefer, 1975).

Many Americans offered to house refugees in their homes, but others declared that the United States had too many Asians already and was in danger of losing its "national character." This attitude toward the Indochinese, has been characteristic of the feeling that Harvard sociologist David Riesman named the *gook syndrome. Gook* is a derogatory term for an Asian, and the syndrome refers to the tendency to stereotype these people in the very worst of lights. Riesman believed that the American news media created an unflattering image of the South Vietnamese and their government, leading the American people to believe they were not worth saving (C. Luce, 1975, p. E19).

The initial 135,000 Vietnamese refugees who fled in 1975 were joined by more than a million running from the later fighting and religious persecution that plagued Indochina. The United States accepted about half of the refugees, some of them the so-called boat people, who took to the ocean in overcrowded vessels, hoping that some ship would pick them up and offer sanctuary. Hundreds of thousands were placed in other nations or remain in overcrowded refugee camps administered by the United Nations.

As immigration to the United States continued, so, too, did mixed feelings among Americans. Surveys in the 1980s showed that, although few Americans regarded the Vietnamese and others as undesirable, 30 to 50 percent still worried that the refugees would be an economic drain. Furthermore, some critics argued that the movement which began as a genuine refugee flow had clearly shifted to a migratory flow composed of some refugees, a growing number of people seeking family reunification, and an even larger economic migrant component (B. Gwertzman, 1985; Starr and Roberts, 1981).

The Present Picture

As has been so of other immigrants, the refugees from Vietnam, Laos, and Cambodia face a difficult adjustment. Few expect to return to their country for visits, and fewer still hope ever to return to their homeland permanently. Therefore, many look to the United States as their future home and the home of their children. They may still, however, have to accept jobs well below their occupational positions in Southeast Asia; geographic mobility has been accompanied by downward social mobility. For example, of those who had been employed as managers in Vietnam, only 5 percent have been employed in similar positions in the United States. The available data indicate that these refugees have increased their earnings at a relatively fast rate, often by working long hours. Partly because the Southeast Asian people comprise significantly different subgroups, assimilation as well as acceptance is not likely to occur at the same rate for all (Bach and Bach, 1980; G. Kelly, 1986).

Even though most refugee children spoke no English on their arrival here, they have done extremely well in school. One study of 350 refugee children

With increased participation in U.S. culture, Asian-American youth may become increasingly defiant of family and rules just like their White counterparts. Pictured are Vietnamese American youth in Falls Church, Virginia.

showed 27 percent scoring in the 90th percentile on national standardized tests of math achievement—almost three times better than the national average. More than a quarter earn top marks in their English courses.

The picture for young Southeast Asians in the United States is not completely pleasant. Crime is not unknown, of course, but some fear that it has two very ugly sides. Some of this crime may represent reprisals for the war: militant nationalists who dream of toppling the communist government of Vietnam may strike out at their fellows in the United States who do not take such a stance. Also, it has been charged that gangs have organized intending to link communities into an organization. The allegations continue, but no strong evidence has surfaced to support them. By contrast, violent episodes directed at Southeast Asians by Whites and others expressing resentment over their employment or even their mere presence have been clearly documented (Burke and O'Rear, 1990; M. Ingrassia, 1994; *New York Times*, 1992).

In contrast with its inaction concerning earlier immigrant groups, the federal government involved itself conspicuously in locating homes for the refugees from Vietnam, Cambodia, and Laos. Pressured by many communities afraid of being overwhelmed by immigrants, goverment agencies attempted to disperse the refugees throughout the nation. Such efforts failed, though, mostly because the refugees, like European immigrants before them, sought out their compatriots. As a result, Southeast Asian communities and neighborhoods have become visible, especially in California and Texas. In such areas of the nation where refugees from Asia have reestablished some cultural practices from their homeland, a more pluralistic solution to their adjustment seems a possible alternative to complete assimilation. Also for those living outside of metropolitan areas, the Southeast Asians may make frequent trips to urban areas such as Chicago where they can stock up on food, books, and even videotapes in their native language.

In 1995, the United States initiated normal diplomatic relations with Vietnam which may lead to more movement between the nations. However, there is little evidence that Vietnamese Americans or other Asian Americans wish to relocate to Asia. Indeed, there are still 40,000 Vietnamese boat people in refugee camps in Hong Kong and the Philippines who would still like to resettle in the United States (S. Salgado, 1995). Despite this desire to come to the United States, however, as the following case study illustrates, barriers to even modest acceptance remain.

Case Study: A Hmong Community

Wausau (population 37,000) is a community located in rural Wisconsin best known, perhaps, for the insurance company bearing its name. To sociologists, it is distinctive for its sizable Hmong population. Wausau finds itself with the greatest percentage of Hmong of any city in Wisconsin. These Southeast Asians account for 10 percent of the city's population and 22 percent of its kindergarten pupils. But because the Hmong are concentrated in the more affordable downtown area of Wausau, they constitute as much as 62 percent of the students in some schools. The Hmong immigrated to the United States from Laos and Vietnam following the April 1975 end of the U.S. involvement in Vietnam.

Progress in teaching the Hmong English in Wausau was stymied in the view of school officials because the newcomers continued to associate with each other and spoke only their native tongue. The Wausau school board decided in the fall of 1993 to distribute the Hmong and other poor students more evenly by restructuring its elementary schools in a scheme that requires two-way busing.

The desegregation has divided the city, and its residents voted in a 1993 special recall election to decide whether to fire the five school board members who had backed the plan. "People feel this decision was just stuffed down their throats," said Peter Beltz, the director of Families Approve Neighborhood Schools (FANS), which fielded candidates and gathered the signatures for the recall (R. Worthington, 1993).

Wausau school officials said that their plan, which is not federally mandated, is aimed less at integration and more at achieving an equitable socioeconomic balance and learning environment. The busing, they say, had been begun as a convenience for parents, whose children now travel an average of two miles farther than before.

Recalls of elected officials are rare in the United States, but in December of 1993 opponents of the busing plan organized a special election which led to the removal of fire board members. Therefore the Wausau Board now had a majority who opposed the busing plan that had integrated Asian-American youngsters into mostly white grade schools. "Busing and partner schools as envisioned is over," Don Langlois, one of the winners, declared after the votes were counted on a Tuesday night. "We plan to have a neighborhood school plan for the fall 1994 school year," Langlois said (*Chicago Tribune*, 1993).

But defeated board president Richard Allen said that he expected supporters of the busing plan to take the matter to court, claiming that removing the plan would cause segregation. Christopher Ahmuty, executive director of the American Civil Liberties Union of Wisconsin, said, after the recall, that his group was willing to file a lawsuit to stop the school board from overturning the changes: "Where a governmental body by law engages in an intentional act of resegregation, that would violate all kinds of constitutional standards" (*Chicago Tribune*, 1993, p. 3; also see E. Lee, 1994).

How events will unfold in Wausau are unclear. The community has undergone significant change since 1980, when the U.S. Census found Wausau one of the most ethnically homogeneous cities in the nation, less than 1 percent of the population being non-White. While Wausau's confrontation in the schools received national attention, smaller cities throughout the United States, such as Gwinnett, Georgia, and Collin, Texas, experienced 600 percent increases in their Asian-American population in the 1980s. Asian groups, including those unknown in the United States a generation earlier, such as the Hmong, are contributing to the diversity of the nation (R. Beck, 1994; S. Chan, 1994; M. Usdansky, 1992b).

HAWAII AND ITS PEOPLE

Social relationships among racial groups in Hawaii (or Hawai'i) are very different from conditions on the mainland; assumptions that might be valid elsewhere are not valid in Hawaii. That Hawaii has no Japantown or Little Tokyo of the sort in which one-third of Japanese Americans on the mainland reside is no indication that local Japanese Americans are not interested in Japanese culture. On the contrary, the entire state reinforces cultural diversity. It has six television stations

Wausau, Wisconsin, classrooms such as this have been the object of heated debates over whether Hmong schoolchildren should be integrated with Whites.

broadcasting in Japanese, along with many Japanese-run retail establishments (Research Committee, 1986). Nevertheless, prejudice, discrimination, and pressure to assimilate are present in Hawaii because life on the island is much closer to that in the rest of the country than to the ideal of a pluralistic society. Hawaii's population is unquestionably diverse, as shown in Table 12.3. To grasp contemporary social relationships, we must first understand the historical context that brought races together on the islands—the various Asian peoples plus the *Haoles* (pronounced "hah-oh-lehs"), the term frequently used to refer to Whites in Hawaii.

Historical Background

Geographically remote, Hawaii was initially populated by Polynesian people who had their first contact with Europeans in 1778, when English explorer Captain James Cook arrived. The Hawaiians were rather tolerant of the subsequent arrival of plantation operators and missionaries. Fortunately, the Hawaiian people were united under a monarchy and received respect from the European immigrants, a respect that developed into a spirit of goodwill. Slavery was never introduced, even during the colonial period, as it was in so many areas of the Western Hemisphere. Nevertheless, the effect of the White arrival on the Hawaiians themselves was disastrous. Civil warfare and disease had reduced the number of full-blooded natives to fewer than 30,000 by 1900, and the number is probably well under 10,000 now. Meanwhile, large sugarcane plantations imported laborers from China, Portugal, Japan, and, in the early 1900s, the Philippines, Korea, and Puerto Rico.

In 1893, a revolution encouraged by foreign commercial interests overthrew the monarchy. During the revolution, the United States landed troops, and five

Table 12.3   HAWAII: RACIAL COMPOSITION, 1950 AND 1990

Since 1950, the relative proportion of Hawaii's people who are of Japanese, Hawaiian, or Chinese ancestry has declined.

Racial Group	1950 Percentage	1950 Total	1990 Percentage	1990 Total
White	23.0	114,793	33.4	369,616
Japanese	36.9	184,598	22.3	247,486
Filipino	12.2	61,062	15.2	168,682
Hawaiian	17.2	86,090	11.7	129,663
Chinese	6.5	32,376	6.2	68,804
Black	.5	2,651	2.4	27,195
Korean	1.4	7,030	2.2	24,454
All other	2.2	11,169	6.6	72,329
Total	99.9	499,769	100.0	1,108,229

Sources: A. Lind (1969, p. 47); Bureau of the Census (1991a); J. Ng (1991). Hawaiian 1990 count is the author's estimate.

years later, Hawaii was annexed as a territory to the United States. The 1900 Organic Act guaranteed racial equality, but foreign rule dealt a devastating psychological blow to the proud Hawaiian people. American rule had mixed effects on relations among the races. Citizenship laws granted civil rights to all those born on the islands, not just the wealthy Haoles. But the anti-Asian laws still applied, excluding the Chinese and Japanese from political participation.

The twentieth century has witnessed Hawaii's transition from a plantation frontier to the fiftieth state and an integral part of the economy. During that transition, Hawaii became a strategic military outpost, although that role has had only a limited effect on race relations. Even the attack on Pearl Harbor had relatively little influence on Japanese Americans in Hawaii.

The Present Picture

Hawaii's racial mixture was not always admired. Congressional opposition to statehood was based chiefly on opposition to admitting to citizenship so many non-Whites. But Hawaii has now achieved some fame for its good race relations. In fact, tourists, who are predominantly White, have come from the mainland and have seen and generally accepted the racial harmony. Admittedly, Waikiki Beach, where most tourists congregate, is atypical of the islands, but even there, the tourist cannot ignore the difference in intergroup relations.

One clear indication of the multicultural nature of the islands is the degree of exogamy—marrying outside one's own group. The out-group marriage rate varies annually but seems to be stabilizing, with about 45 percent of all marriages in the state performed involving residents being exogamous. The rate varies by group from a low of 34–39 percent among Koreans and Haoles to 58 percent among Chinese and Blacks (Hawaii, 1994).

A closer look shows that equality among the people is not absolute, let alone among the races as groups. The pineapple and sugarcane plantation legacy persists. A 1972 estimate placed 97 percent of Hawaiian workers in the employ of 40 landholders. One estate alone owned nearly one-tenth of the state's territory. Native Hawaiians tend to be least well off, working land they do not own. The economy is dominated by Japanese Americans and Haoles. The *AJAs* (Americans of Japanese ancestry, as they are called in Hawaii) are especially important in education, where they account for nearly 58 percent of teachers, and in politics, where they dominate. The political activity of the AJAs certainly contrasts to that of mainland Japanese Americans. In 1976, Hawaii's governor, both representatives in the U.S. House of Representatives, one senator, and the majority of the state legislators were AJAs. Chinese Americans have been successful businesspeople in Hawaii, but top positions are almost all filled by Haoles. Recent immigrants from Asia and, more significantly, even long-term residents of Filipino and Hawaiian descent, show little evidence of sharing in Hawaii's overall picture of affluence (T. Kaser, 1977; H. Kitano, 1976, pp. 73–79; *Time,* 1975; W. Turner, 1972; Wright and Gardner, 1983).

Prejudice and discrimination are not alien to Hawaii. Attitudinal surveys show definite racial preferences and sensitivity to color differences. Housing surveys taken prior to the passage of civil rights legislation showed a commitment to nondiscrimination, but racial preferences were still present. Residential neighborhoods are sometimes dominated by certain groups, but there are no racial ghettos. As shown in Figure 12.2, the various racial groups are not uniformly distributed among the islands, but they are clustered rather than segregated. All civilian census tracts in Honolulu have residents of the five largest groups: Haoles, Japanese, Chinese, Hawaiian, and Filipino.

Discrimination by exclusive social clubs exists but is diminishing. Groups like the Rotary and Lions' clubs opened their doors to Asians in Hawaii before they did on the mainland. Undoubtedly, Hawaii has gradually absorbed the mainland's racial consciousness, but a contrast between the islands and the rest of the nation remains. Evidence of racial harmony is much more abundant. Hawaii has never known forced school segregation, Jim Crow laws, slavery, or laws prohibiting racial intermarriage (Ball and Yamamura, 1960; B. Hormann, 1972, 1982; A. Lind, 1969; R. Rapson, 1980; F. Samuels, 1969, 1970).

The multiracial character of the islands will not change quickly, but the identity of the native Hawaiians has already been overwhelmed. Today, there are fewer than 10,000 pure Hawaiians. While rich in cultural heritage, they tend to be very poor and often view the 1898 U.S. occupation as the beginning of their cultural and economic downfall. The organization *Ka Lahui Hawaii,* or Hawaiian Nation, is seeking to have Hawaiian native people receive federal recognition similar to that accorded mainland tribes; to date, that recognition has not occurred. This growing effort, often referred to as the prosovereignty movement, has also sought a restoration of the land or its value that has been lost to Anglos over the last century. Sometimes, the native Hawaiians successfully form alliances with environmental groups that wish to halt further commercial development on the islands. In fact, in 1978, the state of Hawaii created an Office of Hawaiian Affairs to serve as a receptacle

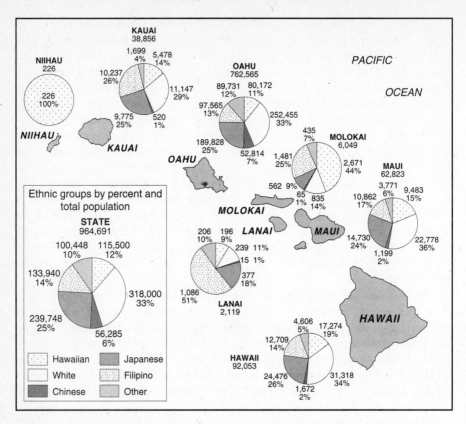

Figure 12.2 Racial Distribution in the Hawaiian Islands
There are few racial enclaves in Hawaii. The best known is Niihau, a privately owned island populated entirely by Hawaiians.

Source: Department of Geography, University of Hawaii, *Atlas of Hawaii,* 2d ed. Honolulu: University of Hawaii Press, 1983, p. 113.

for any reparations awarded, but virtually no progress has been made in that direction (H. El Nasser, 1993; J. Kamakahi, 1994; R. Reinhold, 1992; H. Trask, 1993).

In an absolute sense, Hawaii is not a racial paradise. Certain occupations and even social classes tend to be dominated by a single racial group. Hawaii is not immune to intolerance, and it is expected that the people will not totally resist prejudice as the island's isolation is reduced. By the same token, newcomers to the islands set aside some of their old stereotypes and prejudices (R. Adams, 1969). The future of race relations in Hawaii is uncertain, but relative to the mainland and much of the world, Hawaii's race relations more closely resemble harmony than bigotry.

THE "MODEL-MINORITY" IMAGE EXPLORED

President Ronald Reagan called Asian Americans "our exemplars of hope and inspiration." *Time* and *Newsweek* articles have featured headlines such as "A Formula for Success" and "The Drive to Excel." CBS's "60 Minutes" presented a glow-

Beginning to speak out for their ancestral land, Hawaiian Americans gather for a 1994 protest at the Iolani Palace, home of the Hawaiian monarchs of the last century.

ing report. "Why are Asian Americans doing so exceptionally well in school?" Mike Wallace asked and quickly added, "They must be doing something right. Let's bottle it" (Commission on Civil Rights, 1980c; B. McLeod, 1986; A. Ramirez, 1986; R. Takaki, 1989, p. 474).

Many other Americans also see Asian-American groups as constituting a *model* or *ideal minority* because, despite past sufferings from prejudice and discrimination, they are believed to have succeeded economically, socially, and educationally without resorting to political or violent confrontations with Whites. Some observers point to the existence of a model minority as a reaffirmation that anyone can get ahead in the United States. Proponents of the model-minority view declare that, because Asian Americans have achieved success, they have ceased to be a minority and are no longer disadvantaged. This is only a variation of "blaming the victim"; with Asian Americans, it is "praising the victim." An examination of areas of socioeconomic status will allow a more thorough exploration of this view (K. Gould, 1988; Hurh and Kim, 1989; E. Wong, 1985).

Education

Asian Americans as a group do have impressive school enrollment rates in relation to the total population. As shown in Table 12.4, 43 percent of Asian-American men have a bachelor's degree compared to 23 percent of the total population. Yet, for

Table 12.4   ASIAN AMERICANS' EDUCATIONAL ATTAINMENT, 1990: PERCENTAGE 25
YEARS OLD AND OLDER

Education is highly valued in Asian-American communities, but the educational attainment of different groups varies widely.

	High School Graduate or Higher		Bachelor's Degree or Higher	
	Male	Female	Male	Female
Total population	75.7	74.8	23.3	17.6
Total Asian	81.7	73.9	43.2	32.7
Chinese	77.2	70.2	46.7	35.0
Filipino	84.2	81.4	36.2	41.6
Japanese	89.9	85.6	42.6	28.2
Asian Indian	89.4	79.0	65.7	48.7
Korean	89.1	74.1	46.9	25.9
Vietnamese	68.5	53.3	22.3	12.2
Cambodian	46.2	25.3	8.6	3.2
Hmong	44.1	19.0	7.0	3.0
Laotian	49.4	29.8	7.0	3.5
Thai	88.6	66.2	47.7	24.9
Other Asian	85.9	78.7	47.5	34.2

Source: Bureau of the Census (1993e, p. 4).

Southeast Asian groups such as the Vietnamese, Cambodian, Hmong, and Laotians, the proportions are much less favorable (Bureau of the Census, 1993a).

Asian-American youths are also more likely to be at work as well as in school, as is evident from the very low inactivity rate for Asian Americans. The *inactivity rate* is the proportion of people neither in school nor in the labor force. In 1980, 8 percent of Whites aged 16–19 were inactive, compared to 3 percent of Korean Americans. The pattern was similar for other groups. Only recently arrived Vietnamese-born youths had inactivity rates higher than those of Whites (Gardner et al., 1985, p. 32; Hirschman and Wong, 1986).

This encouraging picture does carry some qualifications of the optimistic model-minority view. Asian Americans maintain that, at some universities, they must have better records than other applicants to gain admission, and even when they have such records, they are turned down. Some observers therefore claim that some institutions adopt unofficial quotas to reduce Asian Americans' disproportionately high representation among college students. At the very least, many colleges fail even to acknowledge that some Asian Americans deserve the same consideration given to talented members of other minorities.

By 1990, there were growing charges that well-known universities were using unofficial quotas (similar to those historically used against Jewish applicants) to restrict the percentage of Asian-American students. In 1989, several selective universities announced plans to revise their admissions policies substantially to correct what they termed "possible unintentional discrimination" against Asian-American students. However, in 1990, the Department of Education charged that the mathematics department of the University of California at Los Angeles (UCLA) had been guilty of racial discrimination in denying admission to five Asian-American applicants. In addition, incidents of racial harassment on college campuses have begun to receive public attention (Commission on Civil Rights, 1992; S. Jaschik, 1990).

A study of Californias state university system, released in 1991, casts further doubt on the model-minority stereotype of Asian Americans. According to the report, while Asian Americans are often viewed as successful overachievers, they suffer from unrecognized and overlooked needs, discomfort, and harassment on campus—as well as from a shortage of Asian faculty and staff members to whom they can turn for support. The report noted that an "alarming number" of Asian-American students appear to be experiencing intense stress and alienation, problems which have often been "exacerbated by racial harassment" (K. Ohnuma, 1991, p. 5; D. Takagi, 1992).

Even the positive stereotype of Asian-American students as "academic stars" can be dysfunctional. Asian Americans who do only modestly well in school may face criticism from their parents or teachers for their failure to conform to the "whiz kid" image. In fact, despite the model-minority label, the high school dropout rate for Asian Americans is increasing rapidly. California's special program for low-income, academically disadvantaged students has a 30 percent Asian-American clientele, and the proportion of Asian students in the programs is on the rise (F. Lee, 1991; J. Tachibana, 1990).

The Work Force

The fact that Asian Americans as a group work in the same occupations as Whites suggests that they have been successful, but the pattern shows some differences (see Figure 12.3). Asian immigrants, like other minorities and immigrants before them, are found disproportionately in the low-paying service occupations. Even among these immigrants, though, substantial proportions are also concentrated at the top in professional, managerial, and executive positions. Yet, as we'll see, they rarely get to be at the very top. Among engineers, for example, they form a large minority of about 6 percent overall and almost 20 percent of engineers with doctorates. However, they hit the "glass ceiling" (or, some others say, "climb a broken ladder") before they reach management (E. Lee, 1993).

A comparison in Figure 12.3 of the occupational profiles of Asian-American groups with those of Whites, African Americans, and Hispanics, shows that the middle or "other" category is smaller for most Asian-American groups, particularly the Chinese Americans. Wen Lang Li (1982) describes the *bipolar occupational structure* of Chinese Americans (which also applies to other Asian-American groups), referring to the clustering of workers in both high-paying professional occupations and low-paying service jobs with relatively few in between (M. Wong, 1995). Figure 12.3 shows the bipolarity for native-born Chinese Americans, 53 percent of whom are employed in these extreme categories. The large numbers of service workers reflect the type of employment Asian Americans were restricted to in the past. The strong representation at the other end of the occupational ladder partly results from upward mobility, but also from selective immigration. Many Asian Americans still find themselves in service occupations, just as their ancestors did.

The absence of Asian-American executives in firms also indicates that success is not complete. Asian Americans have become middlemen in the economy, doing well in small businesses and modest agricultural ventures. While self-employed and managing their own businesses, Asian Americans' operations have been of very modest size. Because of the long hours, the income from such a business may be below prevailing wage standards, so even when they are "business owners," they may well still constitute cheap labor. Chinese restaurants, Korean-American clean-

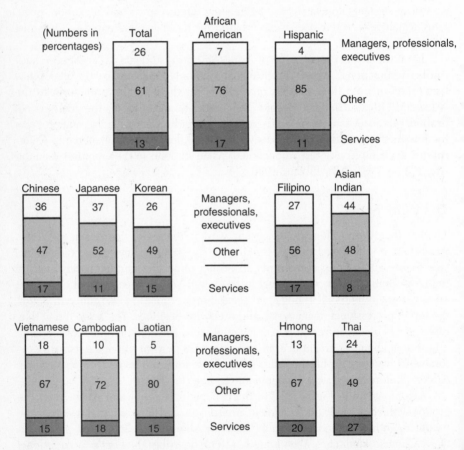

Figure 12.3 Occupational Status of Asian Americans Compared to Total Population, African Americans, and Hispanics
While some Asian-American groups are relatively well represented at the managerial levels, they also tend to be found disproportionately in low-paying service occupations.

Note: Data are from 1990 for Asian Americans and from 1993 for total, Black, and Hispanic.

Source: Bureau of the Census, 1993e, 1994.

ing businesses and fruit and vegetable stores, and motels, gasoline stations, and newspaper-vending businesses operated by Asian Indians fall into this category.

Asian Americans are therefore typical of what sociologists refer to as *middlemen minorities*—groups that occupy middle positions rather than positions at the bottom of the social scale, where racial and ethnic minorities are typically located. Asian Americans involved in small businesses tend to maintain closer ties with other Asian Americans than do individuals who join larger corporations. These ethnic owners generally hire other ethnics, who are paid low wages in exchange for paternalistic benefits such as on-the-job training or even assistance in creating their own middleman businesses. The present disproportionality of Asian Americans as middlemen, however, is the result of exclusion from other work, not of success (E. Bonacich, 1988; Bonacich and Modell, 1981; D. Lee, 1995; W. Zenner, 1991).

Income

Wide publicity was given to the 1992 census figure of $38,153: the median family income of Asian Americans as a group. This income exceeded the comparable figure for Whites by nearly $8,000. Once again, the model racial minority appeared successful. Yet these family income figures are misleading. Asian Americans are more likely to live in urban areas, where incomes are higher. They are also concentrated in parts of the nation where the prevailing wages are higher. For example, in the high-wage area of New York City, Asian Americans do have high incomes; yet a 1989 study found 30 percent living in poverty compared to 25 percent of non-Asians (M. Howe, 1989). Furthermore, several workers are more likely to contribute to that family income. As we have also seen, Asian Americans are better educated than Whites, a situation which adds to their earning power.

Asian-American family income approaches parity with that of Whites because of their greater achievement than Whites in formal schooling. However, the reason is that Asian Americans have more education as a group. If we look at specific educational levels, Whites earn more than their Asian counterparts of the same age. In 1990, Asian Americans' average earnings increased $2,300 each additional year, while Whites gained almost $3,000 (O'Hare and Felt, 1991; Zhou and Kamu, 1994).

Even more than income, Asian Americans differ from Whites in the way they mobilize their households. They are more likely to have two or more paid workers, compared to Whites. Their rates per worker show earning power comparable to that of Whites. While figures for recent arrivals show low incomes, these reflect only paid labor, and a significant number of Asian Americans operate family businesses (the proportion of Korean Americans is three times that of Whites), to which all family members contribute long hours to make these businesses a success. Moreover, the talk of "model minority" ignores the diversity among Asian Americans. There are rich and poor Japanese, rich and poor Filipinos, and rich and poor among all other Asian immigrants (D. Bell, 1985; Gardner et al., 1985).

According to a report issued in mid-1994 by the Asian Pacific American Public Policy Institute and the Asian American Studies Center at the University of California at Los Angeles, more than 30 percent of all Southeast Asian households received welfare benefits. Among Cambodians and Laotians in California, the proportion of households on welfare was as high as 77 percent.

The report underscores the complex situation and striking contrasts among Asian Americans. Asian Americans have the lowest divorce rate of any racial group in the United States (3 percent), the lowest unemployment rate (3.5 percent), the lowest rate of teen pregnancy (6 percent), and the highest median family income ($35,900). Nevertheless, for every Asian-American family with an annual income of $75,000 or more, there is roughly one earning less than $10,000 a year. In New York City's Chinatown neighborhood, about one-quarter of all families live below the poverty level. Even relatively successful Asian Americans continue to face obstacles because of their racial heritage. According to a study of three major public hospitals in Los Angeles, Asian Americans account for 34 percent of all physicians and nurses; yet they fill only 12 percent of management positions at these hospitals (A. Dunn, 1994).

In "Listen to Their Voices," Bong Hwan Kim, director of the Korean Youth and Community Center in Los Angeles, argues how inappropriate the model-minority image is in describing the diverse Asian-American population.

At first glance, one might be puzzled to see a positive generalization such as "model minority" criticized. Why should the stereotype of adjusting without problems be a disservice to Asian Americans? This incorrect view serves to exclude Asian Americans from social programs and conceals unemployment and other social ills. When representatives of Asian groups do seek assistance for those in need, they are resented by those who are convinced of the model-minority view. If a minority group is viewed as successful, it is unlikely that its members will be included in programs designed to alleviate the problems they encounter as minorities. We have seen how important small businesses are in Asian Americans' economic life. Yet laws to support the development of small businesses often fail to include Asian Americans as an eligible minority. The stereotype means that the special needs of recent immigrants may be ignored. Although few foreign-born Asian Americans have yet succeeded, the positive stereotype reaffirms the American system of mobility: they and other minorities ought to achieve more merely by working within the system. Viewed from the conflict perspective outlined in Chapter 1, this becomes yet another instance of "blaming the victims," for Blacks and Hispanics must be irresponsible if Asian Americans have succeeded (Commission on Civil Rights, 1980c; Hurh and Kim, 1986; M. Ichiyama, 1991; W. Ryan, 1976; M. Wong, 1991).

THE DOOR HALF OPEN

Despite the widespread belief these "model minority," Asian Americans are victims of both prejudice and violence. On June 19, 1982, in a Detroit lounge, two White males began arguing with a Chinese American, Vincent Chin. Believing him to be of Japanese descent, they blamed Chin for the dire straits of the American automobile industry. They chased Chin into the parking lot, where they repeatedly beat him with a baseball bat. He died four days later. Through plea-bargaining,

Listen to Their Voices
Toward Social Justice and Equality

BONG HWAN KIM

I am always amazed at how pervasive this stereo-type of Asian Americans as a model minority is. It doesn't benefit us for whites to believe we are smarter or "better" than other people of color. Instead of mutely accepting a designated place in the social hierarchy, we must work toward a completely different

Bong Hwan Kim

social structure based not on hierarchy but on social justice and equality, as espoused in the U.S. Constitution. Immigrant Korean parents often view themselves as sacrificial lambs, believing that even though they go to their graves deaf, dumb, and blind, they are doing it so that their children can achieve the so-called American dream. Their kids work incredibly hard, knowing that only they can vindicate their parents for their sacrifice. In the end, they may think that as Korean Americans with college degrees they are fulfilling their parents' expectations according to the myth of the American dream. But instead, they become the target of resentment from all sides: white resentment and fear of Asian yellow peril takeover and black and brown resentment because of the perception that Asian Americans are honorary white people unconcerned about social justice issues.

People don't realize that a large percentage of Asian immigrants are from the middle classes of their homelands. When they come to the United States, they suffer socioeconomic decline, but ironically this decline is perceived as achievement. The Southeast Asian refugees who didn't come from the middle class share a lot with Spanish-speaking working-class immigrants. Those Asians who don't conform to the model minority stereotype are invisible in mainstream society. There are going to be more and more Korean American high school dropouts and juvenile delinquents succumbing to urban deterioration. There's only so much that the much-touted "family values" can do to defend against these pressures. The family unit can't operate all alone, in a vacuum, indefinitely.

Source: Elaine H. Kim, "Between Black and White: An Interview with Bong Hwan Kim," pp. 90–91. In Karin Aguilar-San Juan, *The State of Asian America,* pp. 71–100. Boston: South End Press, 1994.

the two laid-off automobile workers were found guilty of manslaughter. Much to the shock of the Asian-American community, the accused killers of Vincent Chin were sentenced to three years' probation and fined $3,700 each. Subsequently they were tried in federal courts for interfering with Chin's civil rights. The one not directly involved in beating Chin was acquitted, and the other was sentenced to 25 years in prison (Commission on Civil Rights, 1986).

The Chin case is an extreme example of how Asian Americans have been made to feel unwelcome in U.S. society, but it is not the most recent. In 1989, a Chinese American was killed in Raleigh, North Carolina, by Whites mistaking him for a Vietnamese and wishing to avenge the war in Southeast Asia. Organized hate groups killed an Asian Indian in New Jersey in 1987 and a Vietnamese boy in Houston, Texas in 1990. Most dramatically, a man with intense racial hatred, and for no other reason, entered a Stockton, California, elementary school in 1989 and killed four Southeast Asian children with an assault rifle. In 1993, at least 30 Asian Americans died as a result of racially motivated homicides. Asian Americans are certainly being victimized throughout the United States (Commission on Civil Rights, 1992; *Daily Citizen,* 1994; *Harvard Law Review,* 1993; P. Min, 1995).

This anti-Asian American feeling is built on a long cultural tradition. The concept *yellow peril* comes from the view of Asian immigration, particularly from China, as unwelcome. *Yellow peril* came to refer to the generalized prejudice toward Asian people and their customs. The immigrants were characterized as heathen, morally inferior, drug-addicted, savage, or lustful. While the yellow peril has been associated with anti-Asian sentiment around the turn-of-the-century, it is very much alive today. This intolerance is very unsettling for many contemporary Asian Americans, given their conscientious efforts to extend their education, seek employment, and conform to the norms of society (W. Hurh, 1994).

Prejudice against Asian Americans is fueled by the way they are represented in the media, such as newspapers and television news reports. The Asian American Journalists Association (1991, 1993, 1994) initiated Project Zinger to identify how mainstream news media use ethnic slurs and stereotypes, demonstrate insensitivity, and otherwise exhibit bias in reporting. We can identify several ways in which this occurs—some subtle, some more overt.:

- *Inappropriate use of metaphors.* News reports use "Asian invasion" even when referring to a small number of Asian Americans. For example, a 1994 *Sports Illustrated* article about Asians trying out for major league baseball was billed "Orient Express" and "Asian invasion," yet the story gave a total of only two Asians as examples.
- *Mistaken identity.* Not only are Asians identified by the wrong nationality, but American citizens of Asian descent are presented as if they were foreigners.
- *Overgeneralizations.* Inappropriate assumptions are made and too widely applied. For example, an article discussing the growth of Chinatown was headlined "There Goes the Neighborhood," implying that any increase in the number of Chinese Americans was undesirable.
- *Ethnic slurs.* While the print media are generally free of racially derogatory terms, radio talk shows offer frequent examples of racism. Even U.S. Senator Alfonse D'Amato engaged in a pidgin-English mockery of Judge Lance Ito of the O. J. Simpson trial (B. Frankel, 1995b) during a morning radio broadcast.

- *Inflammatory reporting.* Unbalanced coverage of such events as World War II or Asian investment in the United States can needlessly contribute to ill feelings.
- *Japan bashing.* News accounts may unfairly blame Asian nations for economic problems in the United States. For example, as Japan-based automakers gained a foothold in the United States, much of the coverage failed to note that U.S. carmakers had not maintained their own competitive advantage.
- *Media invisibility.* News reports may ignore Asian Americans and rarely seek their views on issues that are viewed as Asian-oriented.
- *Model minority.* This positive portrayal can also have a negative effect as we noted earlier.

In its own way, each of these biases contributes to the unbalanced view we have developed of the large, diverse Asian-American population.

Why do these beliefs in the shortcomings of Asian Americans persist? A significant factor is that Asian Americans are underrepresented among the reporters and decision makers in the media. The San Francisco Bay Area is about 15 percent Asian; yet a 1991 study found that only 4 percent of news sources and 8 percent of reporters and photographers for television and newspapers were Asian (E. Smith, 1991).

ASIAN-AMERICAN IDENTITY

Despite the diversity among groups of Asian Americans, they have spent generations being treated as a monolithic group. Out of similar experiences have come panethnic identities in which people share a self-image, as among African Americans or Whites of European descent. As we noted in Chapter 1, *panethnicity* is the development of solidarity among ethnic subgroups.

Are Asian Americans finding a panethnic identity? It is true that, in the United States, extremely different Asian nationalities have been lumped together in past discrimination and present stereotyping. Asian Americans can be seen as having called on unifying principles that are clearly products of contact with Whites. After centuries of animosity between ethnic groups in Asia, any feelings of community among Asian Americans must develop anew here; they bring none with them. We find some structural signs of a unitary identity: the development of Asian studies programs in various colleges and the growth of organizations meant to represent all Asian Americans, such as the Asian Law Collective in Los Angeles. In addition, the rise of interethnic marriages among Asian Americans has further blurred boundaries between nationalities and cultures. Groups are also forming that reflect special alliances, such as feminists who have formed Asian Women United (E. Greene, 1987; S. Shah, 1994; R. Trottier, 1981).

Yet, even with a common agenda, there is a diversity of concerns and issues. Despite these signs of a panethnic identity, compelling evidence shows that Americans of Asian descent define their identity by their status as a racial minority, their ancestry, and their participation in American society as contributing members.

Asian Americans have not appeared in a television series except in minor, often subservient roles. Stand-up comedian Margaret Cho broke through that barrier with her weekly series *All-American Girl*, which was on television 1994–1995.

Asian Americans have immigrated at very different stages in U.S. history, so that their patterns of work, settlement, and family life have varied greatly. Even though all have been subjected to many of the same policies and laws, those ones that denied cultural differences have not been in effect for at least 40 years. Most Asian Americans can rejuvenate their ethnic culture because the traditions live on in the home countries: China, Japan, Korea, and the Philippines. Although the people of Southeast Asia, such as the Hmong and the Vietnamese in the United States, have trouble keeping close contact with their homelands, continuing immigration revives distinctive traditions that separate rather than unite Asian-American groups (Ong and Umemoto, 1994).

CONCLUSION

To some people, Asian Americans seem to be a cohesive, easy-to-understand group, but like other subordinate groups, Americans of Asian descent represent varied ways of life. They immigrated into the United States at different times, leaving behind a bewildering array of cultural experiences. Yet they have been expected to assimilate rather than preserve elements of this rich cultural heritage.

Asian Americans are a rapidly growing group, of well over 7 million. Despite striking differences among them, they are frequently viewed as if they came from one culture, all at once. They are characterized, too, as being a successful or model minority. Individual cases of success and some impressive group data do not imply, however, that the diverse group of peoples who make up the Asian-American community are uniformly successful. Indeed, despite significantly high levels of formal schooling, Asian Americans earn far less than Whites with comparable education and continue to be victims of discriminatory employment practices (Commission on Civil Rights, 1980c, p. 24).

The diversity within the Asian-American community belies the similarity suggested by the panethnic label of *Asian American*. The Chinese and Japanese Americans share a history of several generations in the United States. The Filipinos are veterans of a half century of direct U.S. colonization and a cooperative role with the military. In contrast, the Vietnamese, Koreans, and Japanese are associated in a negative way with three wars. Korean Americans come from a nation that still has a major U.S. military presence and a persisting "cold war" mentality. Korean Americans and Chinese Americans have taken on middleman roles, while Filipinos and Japanese Americans tend to avoid the ethnic enclave pattern.

Who are the Asian Americans? This chapter has begun to answer that question by focusing on three of the larger groups: the Korean Americans, the Filipino Americans, and the Southeast Asian Americans. The ties of the United States to all three groups came out of warfare, but today, these groups' descendants work to succeed in civilian society. Hawaii is a useful model because its relatively harmonious social relationships cross racial lines. Though not an interracial paradise, Hawaii does illustrate that, given proper historical and economic conditions, continuing conflict is not inevitable. Chinese and Japanese Americans, the subjects of Chapters 13 and 14, have experienced problems in American society despite striving to achieve economic and social equality with the dominant majority.

KEY TERMS

AJAs Americans of Japanese ancestry in Hawaii.
bipolar occupational structure Clustering at the higher and lower-paying ends of the occupational scale, with relatively few in the middle—a situation in which Chinese Americans, and other Asian Americans, find themselves.

gook syndrome David Riesman's phrase describing Americans' tendency to stereotype Asians and to regard them as all alike and undesirable.

Haoles Hawaiian term for Caucasians.

ilchomose The 1.5 generation of Korean Americans—those who immigrated into the United States as children.

inactivity rate Proportion of a population neither in school nor in the labor force.

kye A rotating credit system used by Korean Americans, to subsidize the start of businesses.

middlemen minorities Groups, such as Japanese Americans, that who typically occupy middle positions in the social and occupational stratification system.

model or ideal minority A group that, despite past prejudice and discrimination, succeeds economically, socially, and educationally without resorting to political or violent confrontations with Whites.

panethnicity The development of solidarity among ethnic subgroups, as reflected in the term *Asian American*.

yellow peril A term denoting a generalized prejudice toward Asian people and their customs.

FOR FURTHER INFORMATION

Karin Aguilar-San Juan, ed. *The State of Asian America: Activism and Resistance in the 1990s*. Boston: South End Press, 1994.

> An anthology of articles dealing with confrontations with the media and the political establishment. This book also deals with the panethnicity question.

Sucheng Chan, ed. *Hmong Means Free: Life in Laos and America*. Philadelphia: Temple University Press, 1994.

> Accounts written by the Hmong of the difficult transition from life in South Asia to the United States.

Won Moo Hurh and Kwang Chung Kim. *Korean Immigrants in America: A Structural Analysis of Ethnic Confinement and Adhesive Adaptation*. Rutherford, NJ: Farleigh Dickinson University Press, 1984.

> Besides presenting the results of the authors' empirical research in the Korean-American communities in Chicago and Los Angeles, this book offers theoretical and historical insights into this fast-growing group.

Yen Le Espiritu. *Asian American Panethnicity: Bridging Institutions and Identities*. Philadelphia: Temple University Press, 1992.

> A consideration of the degree to which a combined identity has developed among people in the United States of Chinese, Japanese, Filipino, Korean, and Vietnamese origin.

Paul Ong, ed. *The State of Asian Pacific America: Economic Diversity, Issues and Policies*. Los Angeles: Leadership Education for Asian Pacifics, 1994.

> An overview of the contemporary status of Asian Americans.

Linda S. Parker. *Native American Estate: The Struggle over Indian and Hawaiian Lands*. Honolulu: University of Hawaii Press, 1989.

> Parker, an attorney and a Cherokee, discusses the similarities and differences between land claims of native Hawaiians and the American Indians.

Antonio J. A. Pido. *The Filipinos in America*. New York: Center for Migration Studies, 1986.

> Sociologist Pido offers the most detailed available examination of this significant minority group.

Dana Y. Takagi. *The Retreat from Race: Asian-American Admissions and Racial Politics.* New Brunswick, NJ: Transaction Books, 1992.

> Sociologist Takagi analyzes the controversy surrounding Asian Americans' admissions to colleges and universities.

William Wei. *The Asian American Movement.* Philadelphia: Temple University Press, 1993.

> An overview of the rising consciousness of Asian Americans by an historian.

Periodicals

Amerasia Journal (founded in 1971) is an interdisciplinary journal focusing on Asian Americans. Periodicals presenting contemporary coverage of Asian Americans include *Asian American Review* (1972), *Bridge* (1971), *Jade* (1974) and *Viet Now* (1995). The *Aloha Aina* is a newspaper that represents the interests of native Hawaiians. *Asianweek,* published in San Francisco, stresses concerns and events in the Chinese-American, Japanese-American, and Korean-American communities.

CRITICAL THINKING QUESTIONS

1. In what respects has the mass media image of Asian Americans been both undifferentiated and negative?
2. How has the tendency of many Korean Americans to help each other been an asset but also viewed with suspicion by those outside their community?
3. What were the critical events or legislative acts that increased each Asian-American group's immigration into the United States?
4. To what degree do "race relations" offer both promise and a chilling dose of reality to the future of race and ethnicity on the mainland?
5. How is the "model-minority" image a disservice to both Asian Americans and other subordinate racial and ethnic groups?

Chapter
13

Chinese Americans: Continued Exclusion

Chapter Outline

Highlights

Present-day Chinese Americans are both descendants of pre-Exclusion Act immigrants and of post–World War II immigrants. Non-Chinese Americans associate Chinese Americans with Chinatown and its glitter of tourism. This glitter, however, is a facade hiding the poverty of the *fob*s (the newly arrived Chinese) and the discontent of the American-born *jook-sings*. As the Chinese-American population has stabilized, patterns have begun to develop in such social institutions as the family, religion, and politics.

China, the most populous country in the world, has been a source of immigrants for centuries. Many nations have a sizable Chinese population, whose history may be traced back more than five generations. The United States is such a nation. Even before the great migration from Europe began, more than 100,000 Chinese were in the United States. Today, Chinese Americans number 1.6 million.

LEGACY OF THE YELLOW PERIL

In the nineteenth century, Chinese immigration was welcome because it brought to these shores needed hard-working laborers. It was also unwelcome because it brought an alien culture that the European settlers were unwilling to tolerate. As detailed in Chapter 4, the anti-Chinese mood led to the passage of the Exclusion Act in 1882, which was not repealed until 1943. Even then, the group that lobbied for repeal, the Citizens Committee to Repeal Chinese Exclusion, encountered the old racist arguments against Chinese immigration.

Very gradually, the Chinese were permitted to enter the United States after 1943. Initially, only 105 a year were allowed, then several thousand wives of servicemen were admitted, and later, college students were allowed to remain after finishing their education. Also, in 1943 for the first time, foreign-born Chinese Americans were eligible to become citizens. American-born Chinese had become citizens at birth since an 1898 U.S. Supreme Court ruling. Not until after the 1965 Immigration Act did Chinese immigrants arrive again in large numbers, almost doubling the Chinese-American community (R. Lee, 1960; H. Melendy, 1972).

Immigration continues to exert a major influence on the growth of the Chinese-American population. It has approached 100,000 annually, with many immigrants entering illegally. Desperate for the opportunities they may find in the United States, illegal arrivals may pay up to $30,000 to be smuggled into the United States. Even if we limit the discussion to legal immigration, arrivals in the 1980s exceeded the total number for the previous 70 years (R. Benjamin, 1993; M. Wong, 1995).

Explicit in all but the most recent immigration legislation has been the fear that the Chinese, by their very numbers, threaten the U.S. mainland. This fear of the *yellow peril* has gradually given way to other images. In the movies, the sinister Dr. Fu Manchu (1929) was replaced by the benevolent Charlie Chan (various movies from 1931 to 1981 show Chinese Americans as law enforcers instead of lawbreakers). During the 1930s, China's heroic resistance to Japan won favor in the United States. Later, as a wartime ally, China again gained esteem in the eyes of many White Americans (B. Cosford, 1981; R. Oehling, 1980; I. Paik, 1971; C. Wu, 1972). The rise of a communist government in China and the wars in Korea and Vietnam undoubtedly took their toll on attitudes toward the Chinese. Opinion polls conducted before and after President Richard Nixon's trip to China, however, showed that the trip had fostered a far more favorable image of the Chinese.

These changes in White attitudes have affected Chinese Americans themselves. In one study, Chinese-American students acknowledged increased pride in being Chinese after this country established closer ties with China. Some of this enthusiasm was political and took the form of support for the teachings of Mao Tse-tung. Generally, the new spirit has meant greater interest in the rich cultural heritage of the Chinese people. One sign of this spirit is the growth and popularity of Asian-American studies on college campuses (F. Ching, 1973; L. Huang, 1975; Kagiwada and Fujimoto, 1973).

The character of the Chinese-American community is the result of past and present immigration. That the Chinese brought not only their culture but their institutions as well is most apparent in the Chinatowns scattered throughout the United States.

CHINATOWNS TODAY

Chinatowns represent a paradox. The casual observer or tourist sees them as thriving areas of business and amusement, bright in color and lights, exotic in sounds and sights. They have, however, large poor populations and face the problems associated with slums. Most Chinatowns are in older, deteriorating sections of cities. There are exceptions such as Monterey Park outside Los Angeles where Chinese Americans dominate the economy. However in the older enclaves, the problems of Chinatowns include the entire range of the social ills that infest low-income areas, but here, the difficulties are greater because the glitter sometimes conceals the problems from the outsider and even from social planners. A unique characteristic of Chinatowns, distinguishing them from other ethnic enclaves, is the variety of social organizations they encompass.

Organizational Life

The Chinese have a rich history of organizational membership, much of it carried over from China. Chief among such associations are the clans, or tsu; the benevolent associations, or hui kuan; and the secret societies, or tongs.

The clans, or *tsu*, that operate in Chinatown have their origins in the Chinese practice that families with common ancestors unite. Immigrant Chinese continued to affiliate themselves with those sharing a family name, even if a blood relation-

Chinese immigrants, while actively recruited in the mid-1800s to come to the United States, were viewed as a threat embodied in the fear of the "yellow peril."

ship was absent. Even today, some families dominate in certain cities, for example, Toms in New York, Moys and Chins in Chicago, and Lees in Philadelphia. Social scientists agree that the influence of clans is declining as young Chinese become increasingly acculturated. The clans in the past provided mutual assistance, a function increasingly taken on by government agencies. The strength of the clans, although less today, points to the extended family's important role for Chinese Americans. Social scientists have found parent-child relationships stronger and more harmonious than those among non-Chinese Americans. Just as the clans have become less significant, however, so has the family structure undergone change. The differences between Chinese and non-Chinese family life are narrowing with each new generation (W. Li, 1976; S. Lyman, 1986; B. Sung, 1967).

The benevolent associations, or *hui kuan,* assist their members in adjusting to a new life. But instead of being organized along kinship ties like the clans, hui kuan membership is based on the person's district of origin in China. Besides extending assistance, the hui kuan give loans to and settle disputes among their members. They have thereby exercised wide control over their members. The various hui kuan are traditionally, in turn, part of an unofficial supragovernment in each city called the Chinese Six Companies, or later the Chinese Consolidated Benevolent Association (CCBA). The president of the CCBA is sometimes called the mayor of a Chinatown. The CCBA often protects newly arrived immigrants from racism. The organization actively works to promote political involvement among Chinese Americans and to support the democracy movement within the People's Republic of China. Some members of the Chinese community have resented, and still resent, the CCBA's authoritarian ways and its attempt to speak as the sole voice of Chinatown.

The Chinese have also organized in *tongs,* or secret societies. The secret societies' membership has been determined not by family or locale, but by interest. Some have been political, attempting to resolve the dispute over which China (the People's Republic of China or the Republic of China) is the legitimate government, and others have protested the exploitation of Chinese workers. Other tongs provide illegal services, like drugs, gambling, and prostitution. Because they are secret, it is difficult to determine accurately the power of tongs today. Most observers concur that their influence has dwindled over the last 50 years and that their functions, even the illegal ones, have been taken over by elements not so closely tied to Chinatown.

Some conclusions can be reached about these various social organizations. First, all have followed patterns created in traditional China. Even the secret societies had antecedents, organizationally and historically, in China. Second, all three types have performed similar functions, providing mutual assistance and representing their members' interests to a sometimes hostile dominant group. Third, because all these groups have had similar purposes and have operated in the same locale, conflict among them has been inevitable. Such conflicts were very violent in the nineteenth century, but in the twentieth century, they have tended to be political. Fourth, the old associations have declined in significance, notably since the mid-1979s, as new arrivals have come from urban metropolises of Asia, with little respect for the old rural ways to which such organizations were important. Fifth, when communicating with dominant society, all these groups have downplayed the problems that afflict Chinatowns. Only recently has the magnitude of social problems become known (Kessner and Caroli, 1981; H. Lai, 1980; S. Lyman, 1974, 1986; L. Sherry, 1992; B. Sung, 1967; W. Wei, 1993; D. Ziegler, 1992).

Social Problems

It is a myth that Chinese Americans and Chinatowns have no problems. This false impression grows out of our tendency to stereotype groups as being all one way or the other, as well as the Chinese people's tendency to hide the problems they face.

In the late 1960s, White society became aware that all was not right in the Chinatowns. The awareness grew not from suddenly deteriorating living conditions in Chinese-American settlements, but from the inability of the various community organizations to continue maintaining the facade that hid Chinatown's social ills. Despite Chinese American's remarkable achievements as a group, the inhabitants suffered by most socioeconomic measures. Poor health, high suicide rates, run-down housing, rising crime rates, poor working conditions, inadequate care for the elderly, and the weak union representation of laborers were a few of the documented problems.

These problems have grown more critical as Chinese immigration has increased. For example, the population density of San Francisco's Chinatown in the late 1980s was ten times that of the city as a whole. The problems faced by elderly Chinese are also exacerbated by the immigration wave because the proportion of older Chinese immigrants is more than twice that of older people among immigrants in general (M. Wong, 1995).

Life in Chinatown has been and is still particularly dreary for Chinese-American women. Often above a restaurant, dozens of women labor over sewing machines ten hours a day. According to one recent estimate, 75 percent of Chinatown's women work under such conditions. While newly arrived Chinese men who settle in Chinatown seem to fare better economically than those who locate elsewhere, the same is not true of women. Their labor is poorly rewarded, and there is little advancement in the stratification system (Lum and Kwong, 1989; M. Spector, 1990; Zhou and Logan, 1989).

Chinatown in New York City remains a prime site of sweatshops in the 1990s. These small businesses, often in the garment industry, consist of workers sewing 12 hours a day, six and seven days a week, and earning about $200 weekly—well below minimum wage. The workers—most of whom are women—can be victimized because they are either illegal immigrants, who may owe labor to the smugglers who brought them into the United States, or legal residents unable to find better employment (A. Finder, 1995; P. Kwong, 1994).

Chinatown communities continue to grow in population and continue to diversify. For example, Toysanese, Cantonese, and Fuzhounese are just a few of the languages spoken. Several dialects are now found, thus dividing somewhat an enclave that was once more cohesive. The diversity has also led new Chinese firms to appeal to more varied preferences in cuisine, reading material, and so forth. Although to outsiders Chinatowns may appear "untouched by time," they are not (P. Kwong, 1994; B. Wong, 1982).

Language, regardless of dialect, insulates many Chinese Americans from the rest of society. A third of adults whose primary language is Chinese have difficulty with English. Even 11 percent of people under 18 who speak Chinese have yet to master the dominant tongue of the United States. Theirs is like the difficulty Spanish-speaking people have today, which makes Chinatown an attractive place to live and seek employment, despite the social problems (Bureau of the Census, 1982a).

The barrier that Chinese Americans have created around their settlements may have protected them in the past, but it now denies them needed social services. No Chinatown was designated to receive funds under the Model Cities Program, even though 150 cities developed such programs. Nevertheless, Chinatowns

The outward excitement of contemporary Chinatowns keeps from our view the presence of poverty, particularly among women and children.

have undergone urban renewal, although it has sometimes threatened their existence. In Honolulu, Chicago, New York City, and Philadelphia, the massive relocation of residents caused by renovation in the 1960s and 1970s required many to leave Chinatown altogether. However, Chinatowns are not disappearing (Commission on Civil Rights, 1980a; Light and Wong, 1975; S. Lyman, 1974; K. Quan, 1986; B. Rice, 1977; B. Sung, 1967; M. Yee, 1972b).

Beyond Chinatown

Not all Chinese live in Chinatowns; most have escaped them or have never experienced their social ills. Only one out of six Chinese Americans in Chicago and one out of four in New York actually lives in Chinatown. Of course, Chinatown remains important for many of those who live outside its borders, but not as important as in the past. For many Chinese, movement out of Chinatown is itself a sign of success. On moving out, however, they soon encounter discriminatory real estate practices and White parents' fears about their children playing with Chinese-American youths.

D. Y. Yuan (1963) traced four hypothetical stages of the development of a Chinatown. The first is *involuntary choice,* the result of discrimination and prejudice. The next two stages are *defensive insulation,* the need for mutual help, followed by *voluntary segregation.* Yuan identified a number of reasons why ethnic groups continue these enclaves voluntarily. The reasons include relatives' desire to live together, language difficulties, and the desire to preserve customs, including religious faiths (in this case Buddhism). The final stage is *gradual assimilation*, as Chinese move out of Chinatown and increase their contact with White Americans. The upwardly mobile, acculturated Chinese American has gone beyond the first stages of involuntary choice and defensive insulation. To remain in Chinatown would be voluntary segregation, and so most opt for gradual assimilation and movement out of Chinatown. For the newly arrived Chinese immigrant, however, Chinatowns perform almost the same functions they did for immigrants a century ago.

Another development has taken place which amends Yuan's formulation. In certain locales, Chinese Americans have assimilated but moved together into new, middle-class Chinese communities. While the suburban Los Angeles community Monterey Park has a distinct presence of Chinese Americans, new arrivals from Taiwan have caused it to be referred to as "Little Taipei" (see Figure 12.1).

As recently as 1960, Monterey Park's residents had been 85 percent white, 12 percent Spanish surname, and only 3 percent Asian and of other minorities. Ten years later, Japanese represented 9 percent and Chinese 4 percent of the city's 49,166 residents. Since then, the Chinese have become the largest ethnic group, totaling over 50 percent of the 61,000 residents in 1988. During the early 1980s, the city elected its first Chinese-American mayor, Lilly Chen. But not everyone has welcomed the new Chinese presence. In 1986 a sign at a gas station near the city limits, for example, displayed two slanted eyes with the inscription "Will the last American to leave Monterey Park please bring the flag?" (T. Fong, 1994; R. Takaki, 1989).

The movement of Chinese Americans out of Chinatowns parallels the movement of White ethnics out of similar enclaves. It signals the upward mobility of Chinese Americans coupled with their growing acceptance by the rest of the population. This mobility and acceptance are especially evident in occupations.

INDUSTRY AND OCCUPATIONS

Asian Americans are employed in all aspects of the economy, and the Chinese are no exception. Superficially, they appear to do very well. They have lower unemployment rates and are better represented in professional occupations than the population as a whole (refer to Figure 12.3).

The background of the contemporary Chinese-American labor force lies in Chinatown. For generations, Chinese Americans were virtually barred from working elsewhere. The Chinese Exclusion Act was only one example of discriminatory legislation. Many laws were passed that made it difficult or more expensive for Chinese Americans to enter certain occupations. Whites did not object to Chinese in domestic service occupations or in the laundry trade, for White males were uninterested in such menial, low-paying work. When given the chance to enter better jobs, as they were in wartime, Chinese Americans jumped at the opportunities. Without those opportunities, however, many Chinese Americans sought the relative safety of Chinatown. The tourist industry and the restaurants dependent on it grew out of the need for employment of the growing numbers of idle workers in Chinatown (R. Lee, 1960; I. Light, 1973, 1974).

The new immigration has added to Chinatown's economic dependence on tourism. First, new immigrants have difficulty finding employment outside Chinatown. Potential employers who are not Asian American are reluctant to hire Chinese Americans because they believe that many Asians are illegal aliens. Instead, they hire a White job applicant to avoid the issue. Also, potential employers are unwilling to work with the new arrivals and their language problems.

Second, because many new immigrants speak little English, they flock to Chinatowns, where they are frequently employed as restaurant workers. Women may end up in the sweatshops described earlier.

A continuing force in Chinatowns is the role of tourism. The tourist industry is a double-edged sword. It does provide needed jobs, even if some are at substandard wages. But it also forces Chinatown to keep its problems quiet and not seek outside assistance. Slums do not attract tourists. This dilemma is being resolved by events beyond Chinese Americans' control. The tourist industry has not kept pace with the population growth of Chinatowns caused by immigration. Increasingly, outside assistance has to be sought, regardless of its consequences for the lights and glitter of Chinatown. This parallel between Chinese Americans and Native Americans finds both groups depending on the tourist industry even at the cost of hiding problems (Light et al., 1994).

The Chinese-American architect I. M. Pei has risen to the top of his profession in the United States. Here, he appears in front of one of his sites, the East Building of the National Gallery of Art in Washington, D.C.

FAMILY AND RELIGIOUS LIFE

Family life and religious worship are major forces shaping all immigrant groups' experience in the United States. Generally, assimilation takes its toll on distinctiveness in cultural behavior. Family life and religious practices are no exceptions. For Chinese Americans, the latest immigration wave has helped preserve some of the old ways. But traditional cultural patterns have undergone change even in the People's Republic of China, and so the situation is most fluid.

The contemporary Chinese-American family is often indistinguishable from its White counterpart, except that it is victimized by prejudice and discrimination. Immigration policy has imposed two points of difference. In the past, Chinese-American families had to overcome immigration laws forbidding entry by other family members left outside the United States. The reuniting of families that European immigrants took for granted was not possible. Because nineteenth-century Chinese immigrant men came for economic reasons, a significant imbalance of men over women resulted. Statistical data are lacking, but it appears that, even though the sex ratio for Chinese Americans as a whole is now balanced, the imbalance remains in Chinatowns.

Where acculturation has taken hold less strongly, the legacy of China remains. Parental authority, especially the father's, is more absolute, and the extended family is more important than is typical in middle-class families. Divorce is rare, and attitudes about sexual behavior tend to be strict because the Chinese generally frown on public expressions of emotion. We noted earlier that, in Chinatown, Chinese immigrant women survive a harsh existence. A related problem that is beginning to surface is domestic violence. While the available data do not indicate that Asian-American men are different from other groups, their wives, as a rule, are less willing to talk about their plight and to seek help. The nation's first shelter for Asian women was established in Los Angeles in 1981, but increasingly, the problem is being recognized in more cities (Commission on Civil Rights, 1992; D. Rubien, 1989).

Change in family life is one of the most difficult cultural changes to accept. The questioning of parental authority by children that most Americans grudgingly accept is a painful experience for tradition-oriented Chinese. The youthful rebellion among Chinese Americans of the 1960s, discussed in the next section, was not simply seen by many elders as a challenge to their authority as business leaders. The political protest also amounted to a challenge to their authority as parents (L. Huang, 1976).

As is true of the family and other social organizations, religious life has its antecedents in China, which has no single Chinese faith. In China, religious beliefs tend to be much more accommodating than Christian beliefs are: one can be a Confucian, Buddhist, and Taoist at the same time. Consequently, when they came to the United States, Chinese immigrants found it easy to accept Christianity, even though doing so ultimately meant rejecting their old faiths. In the United States, a Christian cannot also be a Taoist. As a result, with each generation, Chinese Christians depart from traditional ways. About 20 percent of Chinese Americans are Christian, and almost two-thirds of those are Protestant.

The extended family is an important part of the Chinese-American community.

Although traditional Chinese temples are maintained in most Chinese-American communities, many exist only as museums, and few are places of worship with growing memberships. Religion is still a source of community attachment, but it is in the Protestant Chinese church, not in the temple (F. Hsu, 1971; H. Lai, 1980; R. Lee, 1960; S. Lyman, 1974, 1986).

POLITICS

In the past, Chinese Americans have mostly been interested in the events of their homeland: the People's Republic of China, the Republic of China (Taiwan), and Hong Kong. Party politics for many brings to mind the Communist Party and a deep distrust of government. It has proved difficult for some to make the transition to U.S. political systems. However, as the number of U.S.-born Chinese Americans has grown, the relative lack of interest in U.S. politics has begun to change. The process has been gradual.

Since relatively few Chinese Americans have been politically active, their role in partisan politics is difficult to assess. Those who have long been in the United States appear more likely to follow Republican Party candidates, remembering that party's strong stance against the People's Republic of China stand in the 1960s. More recent immigrants tend to be attracted to the Democratic Party's support of social welfare measures aimed at the poor and unemployed. In San Francisco, where there are proportionately more Chinese Americans (15 percent of the population) than in any other major city, they are 60 percent Democrat and 40 percent Republican. Evidence suggests, however, that when a Chinese American is on the ticket, ethnic unity takes over, and Chinese Americans will cross party lines to support their fellow citizen. Indeed, Chinese-American candidates receive significant financial help from other Chinese Americans living outside the area they seek to represent. Delaware Lieutenant Governor S. B. Woo, who ran unsuccessfully for governor in 1988, raised 70 percent of his campaign funds from Chinese Americans outside his state.

Newly emerging politicians from the Chinese-American community face tough scrutiny. Will they speak out on ethnic issues? If so, they may confront power interests within the minority community. For example, housing advocates want politicians to fight against zoning-law changes and high-rise developments that real estate interests support. Similarly, union activists want candidates who take policy positions against Chinese restaurant and factory owners to combat violations of labor laws and improve sweatshoplike conditions.

At least six factors have been identified that explain why Chinese Americans— and to a large extent, Asian Americans in general—have not been more active in politics:

1. To become a candidate means to take risks, bring on criticism, be assertive, and be willing to extol one's virtues. These are traits alien to Chinese culture.
2. Older people remember when the discrimination was blatant and tell others to "be quiet" and not attract attention.
3. As noted earlier, many recent immigrants have no experience with democracy and arrive with a general distrust of government.
4. Like many new immigrant groups, Chinese Americans have concentrated on getting ahead economically and educating their children rather than thinking in terms of the larger community.
5. The careers pursued by the brightest tend to be in business and science, rather than in law or public administration, and therefore provide poor preparation for politics.
6. Chinatowns notwithstanding, Chinese and other Asian American groups are dispersed and cannot control the election even of local candidates.

Yet Asian Americans are regarded as a future political force in the United States. Frustrated by conventional politics, whether headed by Chinese Americans or not, some Chinese Americans seek to change the status quo through more militant means (J. Gross, 1989).

MILITANCY AND RESISTANCE

Younger Chinese Americans, unlike their elders, are not content to be grateful for what they have been given in exchange for their labor; they but expect the full rights and privileges of citizenship. More than their parents, they refuse to tolerate continued discrimination in employment.

In the 1960s, Chinese-American students and their peers started to speak out against injustice. The activity was first noticeable on college campuses in the western states but soon involved noncollege youths in Chinatowns. Some Chinese Americans created reform movements, like Leway, Inc., founded in 1967 in San Francisco. *Leway*, which stood for "legitimate way," tried to improve opportunities for youths through self-help and community contributions. Local police and the Chinese Chamber of Commerce gave this innovative approach little chance to succeed. Disgruntled, radical Leway members left Leway in 1969 to form the Red Guards. They took their lead from the Red Guards in China, who were purging that country of outside influences. The Red Guards of San Francisco's Chinatown similarly wished to purify the community by eliminating what they regarded as the the excessive control that Chinese elders and White outsiders exercised over Chinatown. The traditional Chinese elders were called Chinatown's "Uncle Tongs." The Red Guard movement lasted only until 1971 and did not attract the active support of large numbers of youth (R. Chin, 1971; M. Yee, 1972b).

Another problem has been the rise in gang activity since the mid-1970s. Battles between opposing gangs have taken their toll, including the lives of some innocent bystanders. Some trace the gangs to the tongs and thus consider them an aspect, admittedly destructive, of groups trying to maintain cultural traditions. However, a more realistic interpretation is that Chinese-American youth from the lower classes are not part of the "model minority." Upward mobility is not in their future. Alienated, angry, and with prospects of low-wage work in restaurants and laundries, they turn to gangs like Ghost Shadows and Flying Dragons and force Chinese-American shopkeepers to give them extortion money. Asked why he became involved in crime, one gang member replied, "To keep from being a waiter all my life" (R. Takaki, 1989, p. 451; also see F. Butterfield, 1985; *Seward World*, 1988).

Chinese-American youths cannot be typed any more than the adolescent population of any other minority group. Two segments of the new generation stand out, however: those sometimes referred to as the *jook-sings* and those called the *fobs*. Jook-sing is the hollow part of a bamboo pole, the name implying that an individual is Chinese on the outside but hollow in cultural knowledge. The *jook-sings* are American-born youths who are acculturated and yet rejected because of bigotry in the wider society. They may either see their ethnicity as a handicap and reject it or have pride in their Chinese heritage in a society that tends to look down on it. The fobs, for *"fresh off the boat,"* are the newly arrived immigrant youths. They adapt differently, of course, depending on whether they come from westernized Hong Kong or rural China. The less acculturated immigrants face the double barrier of racial prejudice and adjustment to an alien culture (M. Chan, 1986; P. Chen, 1970; Kuo and Lin, 1977; W. Miller, 1977; Nee and DeBary, 1973; B. Rice, 1977; C. Watanabe, 1973).

Some Chinese Americans wish to maintain their cultural identity, whereas others are eager to be as American as possible. But as a group, Chinese Americans are not as silent a minority as they once were. While Chinese Americans were not particularly a target in the 1992 Los Angeles riots, the violence against Korean Americans served to unify the entire Asian-American community.

Drawing on the lessons learned in the aftermath of the Rodney King riots, Chinese-American playwright David Henry Hwang expresses a need, in "Listen to Their Voices," to rethink interethnic, interracial cooperation in the United States.

REMNANTS OF PREJUDICE AND DISCRIMINATION

The Fu Manchu image may be gone, but the replacement is not much better. In the popular television series *Kung Fu,* the only Chinese American able to win fights was half-White, a Eurasian. In *Dr. No,* the title character, an Asian, threatened everyone's hero, James Bond. In the Oscar-nominated movie *Chinatown,* the Chinese played servants, and the leading character spoke derisively of Chinese sexual behavior (F. Chin, 1974). The 1980s continued with disturbing portrayals of Chinese Americans in movies such as *Sixteen Candles* and *Big Trouble in Little China,* which seemed to overshadow Japanese-American Noriyuki "Pat" Morita's sensitive roles in the *Karate Kid* movies (B. Fong-Torres, 1986; D. Hwang, 1985).

Chinese Americans are ignored or misrepresented in history books. Even past mistakes are repeated. When the transcontinental railroad was completed in Utah in 1869, Chinese workers were barred from attending the ceremony. Their contribution is now well known, one of the stories of true heroism in the West. However, in 1969, when Secretary of Transportation John Volpe made a speech marking the hundredth anniversary of the event, he neglected to mention the Chinese contribution. He exclaimed, "Who else but Americans could drill tunnels in mountains 30 feet deep in snow? Who else but Americans could chisel through miles of solid granite? Who else but Americans could have laid 10 miles of track in 12 hours?" (A. Yee, 1973, p. 100). The Chinese contribution was once again forgotten (F. Hsu, 1971, p. 104; L. Huang, 1976).

Although they avoid obvious anti-Black slurs, Whites somehow continue to see anti-Chinese slurs as less harmful. Pekin High School in Illinois called its athletic teams the "Chinks" and featured a student dressed up as a "Chinaman" who

Listen to Their Voices
Facing the Mirror

DAVID HENRY HWANG

As a native of Los Angeles, I felt the profound limitations of the isolationist/nationalist model during the 1992 uprising that followed the first Rodney King verdict. In the wake of simmering tensions between African American and Korean American communities in New York as

David Henry Hwang

well as Los Angeles, repressed hostilities exploded into outright violence. One cannot help but feel that "multiculturalism," as defined during the late 1970s and 1980s, had not been sufficiently inclusive; it operated under the assumption of a Euromajority nation. Under such circumstances, to "explain ourselves" seemed a pathetic attempt to win favor from whites, the very people who had taught us self-loathing.

In the 1990s, however, we see the rise of a new demographic reality: a nation with no majority race. Certainly whites continue to control a wildly disproportionate amount of power in the United States; that injustice has not changed. But the fact that people of color will soon numerically dominate this nation means that in "explaining ourselves," we are now building bridges to Latino, African, and Native Americans as well as those of European origin. The need to forge such bonds speaks to the explosion of another belief from an earlier decade: the myth of "Third World" solidarity. White America has traditionally set minorities to war against each other over scraps from its pie. As Anglos

react to their shrinking powerbase, such battles will become fiercer and more commonplace. Thus, "multiculturalism," it seems to me, must evolve into a sort of "interculturalism" which attempts to outline commonalities as well as differences. For example, the question, "What do Asian American and African American cultures have in common?" has not yet been properly posed. In the past we may have replied, "We're all non-white." Such a reactionary response is of limited value as we approach the new millennium.

In fact, the 1990s seem to me to question the very definition of Asian America itself. With increasing bi- and multiracialism among our children, with the expanding diversity of Asian Americans among us, the boundaries of our community have become blurred. When a Caucasian woman who was adopted and raised by working-class *nisei* parents argues with a college student whose parents are wealthy Japanese diplomats, who is the "real" Asian American? Does it matter? Addressing such questions forces us to confront an issue many of us have sidestepped: class. To say that an upper-class Chinese-American corporate lawyer has more in common with a newly arrived Laotian cabdriver than, say, a wealthy African American Ivy Leaguer is a necessary lie. It is necessary because Asians are perceived monolithically in America

---

Listen to Their Voices   *Continued*

and must therefore band together. It is a lie, however, because it ignores the line that class cuts through our community and that many Asian Americans, myself included, have often swept under the carpet.

In fact, what most irks white America in the 1990s is that it is increasingly losing control of the political agenda. In the sixties and seventies, white liberalism could be dispensed from above, the majority magnanimously handing over a larger piece of the pie to powerless minorities. In the nineties, people of color are making our own rules, redefining a national identity that certainly includes European Americans, but as only one element in a diverse picture. As we move toward empowerment, however, we find ourselves facing an entirely new set of realities and responsibilities. . . . In the 1990s, Asian American activism and resistance looks into the mirror, and discovers something frightening and wonderful: Our faces are changing.

Source: from David Henry Hwang "Forward: Facing the Mirror," pp. x–xi. In Karin Aguilar-San Juan, *The State of Asian America*, pp. ix–xii. Boston: South End Press, 1994.

---

paraded at halftime at football games and struck a gong when the team scored. Despite pressure in 1974 from the Organization of Chinese Americans and the Illinois Department of Human Relations and brief consideration of more neutral nicknames, the school retained the "Chinks" nickname until 1980, when they finally became the Dragons (D. Holmberg, 1974; G. Sloan, 1980).

Chinese Americans believe that prejudice and discrimination have decreased in the United States, but subtle reminders remain. Third-generation Chinese Americans feel insulted when they are told, "You speak English so well." Adopting new tactics, Chinese Americans have organized to fight racist and exclusionary practices. Organized in 1974, the Asian Americans for Fair Employment work for better job opportunities for Asian Americans, especially in the building trades. Discriminatory treatment causes Chinese Americans to take renewed interest in their cultural heritage (K. Lem, 1976).

Maintaining links with a tradition different from that of the dominant group is difficult. In 1971, a court-ordered busing plan caused Chinatown residents to be transported to other neighborhoods in San Francisco. Many parents expressed concern when programs tailored to their children's needs and cultural background were dropped. A subsequent U.S. Supreme Court decision in 1974 (*Lau v. Nichols*) ruled that San Francisco must provide special classes for non-English-speaking youth. But this decision did not affect the virtual elimination of special Chinese cultural classes. In response, some Chinese Americans created "freedom schools," which often took a decidedly anti-White approach. Educating Chinese-American youth is another example of the difficulty of maintaining pluralism in an assimilationist society (T. Wolfe, 1969; M. Yee, 1972a, 1972b).

Marriage statistics also illustrate the problem. At one time 29 states prohibited or severely regulated marriages between Asians and non-Asians. Today, intermarriage, though not typical, is certainly more common, and more than one-fourth of Chinese Americans under 24 marry someone not Chinese. Endogamy, marrying within the same group, has decreased, and out-group marriage is no longer the rare exception. Among all three major groups of Asian Americans—the Chinese, Japanese, and Filipinos—youths are more likely to marry a member of another racial group than was true of the older generation, partly because a greater proportion of the older generation was foreign-born and already married before arrival (Department of Health, Education, and Welfare, 1974; L. Huang, 1975; C. Lee, 1965).

The increased intermarriage indicates growing White acceptance of Chinese Americans. It also suggests that Chinese cultural ties are weakening and that the traditionally strong authority of Chinese parents is shrinking. The dating attitudes and sex roles of each successive generation have become more Americanized. As happened with the ways of life of European immigrants, the traditional norms are being cast aside for those of the host society. In one sense, these changes make Chinese Americans more acceptable and less alien to Whites. However, increased interaction with other Americans also increases the likelihood that Chinese Americans will face hostility (S. Fong, 1965, 1973).

Acceptance is not complete. Chinese Americans are still excluded in an informal, extralegal fashion from several labor unions on the grounds that they are too short. One critic has pointed out the inappropriateness of this justification, since the Chinese constructed the Great Wall in China and worked on the transcontinental railway in the West (S. Lyman, 1974, p. 139). Even American-educated professionals of Chinese ancestry are not welcomed by many non-Chinese. Some Chinese Americans have responded by arguing against accepting Anglo ways and by being more Chinese. Most continue to accept the American way of life but speak out more militantly against the examples of racism that remain.

CONCLUSION

It would be simple to say that Asian Americans are one group, easy to understand. But like other minority groups, Americans of Asian descent represent a variety of ways of life. They differ in their country of origin and their length of residency in the United States. As will be further apparent in Chapter 14, Asian Americans share little except the part of the world from which their ancestors came and the subordinate role they have been forced into in this society.

The Chinese-American experience illustrates the efforts to which a group will go to overcome second-class citizenship. Barred from most high-paying occupations, Chinese Americans have sought to maximize the opportunities left. Because of housing restrictions and bigotry, Chinatowns have become havens of escape from anti-Chinese hostility. Social organizations like the clans and the benevolent associations have provided valuable help to both the newly arrived immigrant and the lifelong resident of Chinese ancestry.

The future of the Chinese-American community is uncertain. Reduced prejudice and an end to overt discrimination will mean a better life for individuals. As a group, Chinese Americans have undergone great changes. Chinatowns are now slowly shedding their glitter so that finally, perhaps too late, they will receive governmental assistance. The continued influx of Chinese immigrants brings a mixture of English-speaking professionals who head for suburbia and non-English-speaking laborers looking about for any kind of employment, however menial. The problems are complex and the prospects unclear. Although it seems that, for at least the present, this country is more willing than ever before to accept Chinese Americans as people and not as aliens, full acceptance has not taken place and is not necessarily inevitable.

KEY TERMS

defensive insulation The framework of social structures for mutual help found in enclaves like Chinatowns.

fobs Recent immigrants from China, *fresh off the boat.*

hui kuan Chinese American benevolent associations organized on the basis of the district of the immigrant's origin in China.

jook-sings Chinese Americans who fail to carry on the cultural traditions of China or to maintain a sense of identification with other Chinese Americans.

tongs Chinese-American secret associations.

tsu Clans established along family lines and forming a basis for social organization by Chinese Americans.

yellow peril A term denoting a generalized prejudice toward Asian people and their customs.

FOR FURTHER INFORMATION

Jeffery Paul Chan, Frank Chin, Lawson Fusan Inada, and Shawn Wong, eds. *The Big Aiiieeeee: An Anthology of Chinese American and Japanese American Literature.* New York: Merdu, 1991.

  Short stories, poetry, and autobiographical accounts give an effective look at the diversity of the Chinese-American and Japanese-American experiences in the United States.

Frank Ching. *900 Years in the Life of a Chinese Family.* New York: Morrow, 1988.

  A journalist of the *Wall Street Journal* traces his ancestry through many generations, offering a biographical tour of Chinese history.

Roger Daniels. *Asian American: Chinese and Japanese in the United States Since 1850.* Seattle: University of Washington Press, 1988.

  A historical analysis of two of our largest Asian-American minorities.

Timothy P. Fong. *The First Suburban Chinatown*. Philadelphia: Temple University Press, 1994.

>A case study of how Monterey Park, outside of Los Angeles, evolved into a predominantly Chinese-American community.

Francis L. K. Hsu. *The Challenge of the American Dream: The Chinese in the United States*. Belmont CA: Wadsworth, 1971.

>This book is especially strong in its treatment of the Chinese backgrounds of the life of Chinese Americans.

Stanford M. Lyman. *Chinatown and Little Tokyo*. Millwood, NY: Associated Faculty Press, 1986.

>A useful comparison of Chinese and Japanese immigrants to the United States with an emphasis on social organizations and kinship patterns.

Ruthanne Lum McCunn. *Chinese American Portraits*. San Francisco: Chronicle Books, 1988.

>In this excellently illustrated book are profiles of Chinese Americans that reflect their diversity, ranging from railroad baron to cowboy to immigrant.

Bernard P. Wong. *Chinatown: Economic Adaptation and Ethnic Identity of the Chinese*. New York: Holt, Rinehart & Winston, 1982.

>Anthropologist Wong provides a detailed, systematic view of New York City's Chinatown, emphasizing its occupational and family structure.

Cheng-Tsu Wu. *Chink!* New York: Meridian, 1972.

>This documentary history of anti-Chinese prejudice has a fine concluding chapter outlining the extent of the hostility.

Walter P. Zenner. *Minorities in the Middle: A Cross-Cultural Analysis*. Albany: State University of New York Press, 1991.

>An anthropologist analyzes "middleman minorities" throughout the world, including Chinese Americans in the United States.

CRITICAL THINKING QUESTIONS

1. What has been the legacy of the "yellow peril"?
2. In what respects does diversity characterize Chinatowns?
3. How do contemporary Chinatowns differ from those in the past?
4. Has family life or political life changed more for Chinese Americans?
5. What stereotypical images of Chinese Americans can you identify in the contemporary media?

Chapter
14

Japanese Americans: Overcoming Exclusion

Chapter Outline

Highlights

Japanese Americans encountered discrimination and ill treatment during the early twentieth century. Like the Chinese, they found their employment opportunities severely limited. The involuntary wartime internment of 113,000 Japanese Americans was the result of sentencing without charge or trial. Merely to be of Japanese ancestry was reason enough to be suspected of treason. For the *internees,* the economic effect of the internment camps was devastating, and the psychological consequences were incalculable. A little more than a generation later, Japanese Americans did very well, with high educational and occupational attainment. Assimilation is incomplete because Japanese Americans are still readily identified as Japanese Americans, not just Americans.

The Japanese-American experience in the United States is a study of contrasts. Not once, but twice, has the government launched a conscious effort to exclude the Japanese from U.S. society, first by not letting them enter the country and later by placing those already here in concentration camps. Both episodes occurred well after slavery was abolished and the Native American–cavalry wars were over. The actions against Japanese Americans cannot be written off as caused by the ignorance of people of long ago.

The Japanese-American story does not end with another account of oppression and hardship. Today, Japanese Americans have achieved success by almost any standard. We must qualify, however, the progress that *Newsweek* (1971) once billed as their "Success Story: Outwhiting the Whites." First, it is easy to forget that the achievements of several generations of Japanese Americans were accomplished by overcoming barriers that U.S. society had created, not because Japanese Americans had been welcomed. However, many, if not most, have become acculturated. Nevertheless, successful Japanese Americans are still not wholeheartedly accepted into the dominant group's inner circle of social clubs and fraternal organizations. Second, Japanese Americans today may represent a stronger indictment of society than economically oppressed African Americans, Native Americans, and Hispanics. There are few excuses apart from racism that Whites can use to explain why they continue to look on Japanese Americans as different, as "them."

EARLY IMMIGRATION

The nineteenth century was a period of vast social change for Japan: the end of feudalism and the beginning of rapid urbanization and industrialization. Only a few pioneering Japanese came to the United States prior to 1885, for Japan prohibited emigration. After 1885, the numbers remained small relative to the great immigration from Europe at the time (see Table 14.1).

Since 1934, Nisei Week activities in Los Angeles and some other cities have tried to reaffirm the ancestral heritage of Japanese Americans.

Table 14.1 CHINESE-AMERICAN AND JAPANESE-AMERICAN POPULATION, 1860–1990

Although Chinese and Japanese patterns of immigration into the United States have been quite different, the two groups had reached relatively similar proportions of the U.S. population until Chinese immigration escalated in the 1980s.

Year	Chinese Americans	Japanese Americans
1860	34,933	—
1880	105,465	148
1900	89,863	24,326
1930	74,954	138,834
1950	117,629	141,768
1960	198,958	260,059
1960[a]	237,292	464,332
1970[a]	435,062	591,290
1980[a]	806,027	700,747
1990[a]	1,640,000	848,000

[a]Includes Alaska and Hawaii
Source: J. Ng (1991).

Japanese Americans sharply distinguish among themselves according to the number of generations an individual's family has been in the United States. Generally, each succeeding generation is more acculturated, and each is successively less likely to know any Japanese. The *Issei* (pronounced "EE-say") are the first generation, the immigrants born in Japan. Their children, the *Nisei* ("NEE-say") are American-born. The third generation, the *Sansei* ("SAHN-say"), must go back to their grandparents to reach their roots in Japan. The *Yonsei* ("YAWN-say") are the fourth generation. Because Japanese immigration is relatively recent, these four terms describe virtually the entire contemporary Japanese-American population. Some Nisei were sent by their parents to Japan for schooling and to have marriages arranged. Such people, referred to as the *Kibei* ("KEE-boy") are expected to be less acculturated than other Nisei. These terms are sometimes used rather loosely, and occasionally, *Nisei* is used to describe all Japanese Americans. But we will use them as they were intended, to differentiate the four generational groups.

THE ANTI-JAPANESE MOVEMENT

The Japanese who immigrated into the United States in the 1890s took jobs as laborers at low wages with poor working conditions. Their industriousness in such circumstances made them popular with employers but unpopular with unions and other employees. The Japanese had the mixed blessing of arriving just as bigotry toward the Chinese had been legislated in the harsh Chinese Exclusion Act of 1882. For a time after the act, the Issei were welcomed by powerful business interests on the West Coast. They replaced the dwindling number of Chinese laborers in some industries, especially agriculture. In time, however, anti-Japanese feeling grew out of the anti-Chinese movement. The same Whites made the same charges about the yellow peril. Eventually, a stereotype developed of Japanese Americans as lazy, dishonest, and untrustworthy.

The attack on Japanese Americans concentrated on limiting their ability even to earn a living. In 1913, California enacted the Alien Land Act, amended to become still stricter in 1920. The act prohibited anyone who was ineligible for citizenship from owning land and limited leases to three years. Initially, federal law had allowed only Whites to be citizens, but the law was amended to include Blacks in 1870 and some Native Americans in 1887. What about Asians? They had not been mentioned in the amendments. The U.S. Supreme Court repeatedly saw this not as an oversight, but as a constitutional prohibition against citizenship for Asians. As Chapter 13 noted, this omission was finally remedied for the Chinese in 1943. Those born in Japan were excluded from citizenship until 1952.

The anti-Japanese laws permanently influenced the form that Japanese-American business enterprise was to take. In California, the land laws drove the Issei into cities. In the cities, however, government and union restrictions prevented large numbers from entering the available jobs, leaving self-employment. Japanese, more than other groups, ran hotels, grocery stores, and other medium-sized businesses. Although this specialty limited their opportunities to advance, it did give the urban Japanese Americans a marginal position in the expanding economy of the cities (E. Bonacich, 1972; I. Light, 1973; S. Lyman, 1986).

Three aspects of the anti-Japanese movement distinguish it from the anti-Chinese movement. The first, and most obvious, is the difference in time. The anti-Chinese efforts preceded and provided the groundwork for the anti-Japanese movement. Second, Japanese Americans spoke out more vehemently against the racist legislation than their Chinese-American counterparts. The Issei and Nisei constantly organized demonstrations, led boycotts to counter boycotts of Japanese products, published books, and enlisted the support of sympathetic Whites. Third, Japan took a more active interest in what was happening to its citizens in the United States than did China. The discriminatory legislation that the United States and especially California consistently passed later strengthened the hand of militarists in Japan who wished to attack the United States (F. Chuman, 1976; R. Daniels, 1967; Y. Ichioka, 1988; Y. Kimura, 1988; L. Mosley, 1966; K. Yoneda, 1971).

THE WARTIME EVACUATION

The decades following the end of immigration in 1924 were not easy for Japanese Americans. The Issei and their Nisei children adapted to a new way of life while preserving aspects of their ancestral home. Whether they lived in the "Little Tokyos" of the West Coast or on farms, the obligation they felt to help fellow Japanese Americans was strong. In 1929, the Nisei founded the Japanese American Citizens League (JACL), which is still influential among Japanese Americans today. The JACL grew in strength as the Nisei grew in numbers. Generally such groups represented a conscious effort to become acceptable to Whites. Few were under the delusion that this change could be completely accomplished. If they were, the wartime evacuation proved how wrong they had been (A. Zich, 1986).

Japan's attack on Pearl Harbor on December 7, 1941, began World War II for the United States and a painful tragedy for the Issei and Nisei. Almost immediately, public pressure mounted to "do something" about the Japanese Americans living on the West Coast. Many feared that if Japan attacked the mainland, Japanese Americans would fight on behalf of Japan, making a successful invasion a real possibility. Pearl Harbor was followed by successful invasions of one Pacific island after another. A Japanese submarine actually attacked a California oil-tank complex early in 1943.

Rumors mixed with racist bigotry rather than facts explain the events that followed. Japanese Americans on Hawaii were alleged to have cooperated in the attack on Pearl Harbor by using signaling devices to assist the pilots from Japan. Front-page attention was given to pronouncements by the secretary of the navy that Japanese Americans had the greatest responsibility for Pearl Harbor. Newspapers covered in detail FBI arrests of Japanese Americans allegedly engaging in sabotage by assisting the attackers. They were accused of poisoning drinking water, cutting sugarcane fields to form arrows directing enemy pilots to targets, and blocking traffic along highways to the harbor. None of these charges was substantiated, despite thorough investigations. It made no difference. In the 1940s, as it had been a generation earlier, the treachery of the Japanese Americans was a foregone conclusion regardless of evidence to the contrary (Y. Kimura, 1988; A. Lind, 1946; ten Brock, Barnhart, and Matson, 1954).

Executive Order 9066

On February 13, 1942, President Franklin Roosevelt signed Executive Order 9066. It defined strategic military areas in the United States and authorized the removal from those areas of any people considered threats to national security. Subsequent congressional action, with bills often passed overwhelmingly by a voice vote, designated General John DeWitt to make the western portions of California, Washington, Oregon, and part of Arizona "militarily secure."

The events that followed were tragically simple. All people on the West Coast of at least one-eight Japanese ancestry were taken to assembly centers for transfer to concentration camps. These camps are identified in Figure 14.1. This order covered 90 percent of the 126,000 Japanese Americans on the mainland. Of those evacuated, two-thirds were citizens and three-fourths were under age 25. Ultimately 120,000 Japanese Americans were in the camps. Of mainland Japanese Americans, 113,000 were evacuated, but to those were added 1,118 "evacuated" from Hawaii, 219 voluntary residents (Caucasian spouses, typically), and, most poignantly of all, the 5,981 who were born in the camps (M. Weglyn, 1976).

The evacuation order did not arise from any court action. No trials took place. No indictments were issued. Merely having a Japanese great-grandparent was enough to mark an individual for involuntary confinement. The evacuation was carried out with little difficulty. For Japanese Americans to have fled or militantly defied the order would only have confirmed the suspicions of their fellow Ameri-

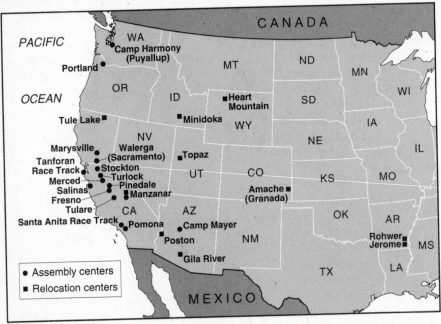

Figure 14.1 Evacuation Camps
Japanese Americans were first ordered to report to "assembly centers" from which, after a few weeks or months, they were resettled in "relocation centers."

Source: Adapted from Michi Weglyn, *Years of Infamy: The Untold Story of America's Concentration Camps.* Copyright 1976 by Michi Nishura Weglyn. By permission of William Morrow and Company, Inc.

cans. The JACL even decided not to arrange a court test of the evacuation order. It felt that cooperating with the military might lead to sympathetic consideration later when tensions subsided.

Japanese Americans were as shocked as other citizens by the attack on Pearl Harbor. In "Listen to Their Voices," Congressman Norman Mineta recalls what it was like at the time and during the war.

Even before reaching the camps, the *evacuees,* as Japanese Americans being forced to resettle came officially to be called, paid a price for their ancestry. They were instructed to carry only personal items. No provision was made for shipping their household goods. The federal government took a few steps to safeguard the belongings they left behind, but the evacuees assumed all risks and agreed to turn over their property for an indeterminate length of time. These Japanese Americans were economically destroyed. Merchants, farmers, and business owners had to sell all their property at any price they could get. The short time and the large number of people liquidating possessions left the Japanese Americans in a difficult position. For example, one woman sold a 37-room hotel for $300. Precise figures of the loss in dollars are difficult to obtain, but after the war, the Federal Reserve Bank estimated it to be $400 million. To place this amount in perspective, one estimate stated that, in 1993 dollars, the economic damages sustained, excluding personal income, would be in excess of $9 billion (Commission on Wartime Relocation and Internment of Civilians, 1982a, 1982b; B. Hosokawa, 1969; Thomas and Nishimoto, 1946).

The Camps

Ten camps were established in seven states. Were they actually *concentration* camps? Obviously, they were not concentration camps constructed for the murderous purposes of those in Nazi Germany, but such a positive comparison is no compliment to the United States. To refer to them by their official designation, *relocation centers,* ignores these facts: the Japanese Americans did not voluntarily come there, had been charged with no crime, and could not leave without official approval.

Milton S. Eisenhower, brother of Dwight Eisenhower (military chief of staff, later to become president), headed the War Relocation Authority (WRA). He saw to it that the Japanese Americans would be able to work at wage labor. The maximum wage was set at $19 a month, which meant that camp work could not possibly recoup the losses incurred by evacuation. The evacuees had to depend on the government for food and shelter, a situation they had not experienced in prewar civilian life. More devastating than the economic damage of camp life was the psychological damage. Guilty of no crime, the Japanese Americans moved through a monotonous daily routine with no chance of changing the situation. Forced community life, with such shared activities as eating in mess halls, weakened the strong family ties that Japanese Americans, especially the Issei, took so seriously (Kitsuse and Broom, 1956).

Amid the economic and psychological devastation, the concentration camps began to take on some resemblance to U.S. cities of a similar size. High schools were established, complete with cheerleaders and yearbooks. Ironically, Fourth of

Listen to Their Voices
Pearl Harbor and Japanese Americans

NORMAN MINETA

In 1974, Norman Mineta became the first mainland Japanese American elected to the House of Representatives. But years earlier, he had been one of many interned in the relocation centers. On the occasion of the fiftieth anniversary of the attack on Pearl Harbor, he provided his recollections.

Norman Mineta

We all knew that when the Japanese attacked Pearl Harbor they attacked every American, including Americans of Japanese ancestry. But the historical discrimination in the United States against Japanese Americans was too well-known to pretend that our lives would be unaffected after the attack. Federal exclusion laws had long prevented Asian immigrants from becoming citizens and California state laws had long prevented residents who were ineligible to become citizens from owning land. But, we wondered, would the attack on Pearl Harbor become an excuse for a new round of home-grown injustice directed against Japanese Americans?

There was no question that our community was loyal to the United States. I remember a young friend of mine—an American of Japanese ancestry—who climbed the roof of his house in Mountain View, pointed his BB-gun up at the sky and stood ready to defend his family against Japanese planes. But would that depth of patriotism, which ran through the entire community, protect us against injustice?

We didn't have to wait long for an answer.

That Sunday afternoon, I vividly recall my neighborhood friend Joyce Hirano running through the break in the hedge between our houses screaming, "They're taking my father away!" The "they" were the FBI. For the next two months, the Hiranos had no idea where he'd been taken.

Later toward the evening, after the initial shock in the neighborhood had died down, I remember seeing my father walk into his office, which was in a separate part of our house. He closed the office door, but not completely. I looked in at him through the doorway as he sat down at his desk. He looked through some papers, leaned back in his chair and started to cry. That shook me. The full weight of what had happened must have just hit him then, and that moment was when I began to understand that, even though I was only a 10-year-old, my life had significantly changed.

Later that month, my father and mother sat us down as a family: my brother, two sisters and I. My father said that he did not know what would happen to him and my mother, since they were not citizens. But he did believe that because his children were American-born and therefore American citizens that we would be safe.

He was wrong.

In February after President Roosevelt signed Executive Order 9066

Listen to Their Voices   *Continued*

and set the stage for the internment of Japanese Americans, I remember being struck for the first time by the stigma of disloyalty written into the notices that the Army had posted throughout the West Coast. The signs addressed us as "aliens and non-aliens." Imagine. Even though I was born a citizen in the United States, the only status my government would grant me was the rank of "non-alien."

When your own government disowns you—a 10-year-old child whose only alleged crime was his ancestry—the only hope you have are the rights endowed by our Constitution. But as Japanese Americans learned then, even our Constitution can be ignored by those who control access to the corridors of political power and influence. The result was the internment. . . .

We fought for another 45 years to redress the injustices of the internment. In 1988 we finally achieved that

victory. We achieved that victory because we educated the Congress, the President and our fellow Americans that the internment wasn't merely a Japanese American issue or an Asian American issue. It was, and is, an American issue.

But even with that victory, the anniversary of Pearl Harbor will never lose its sting for Americans of Japanese ancestry. For us, it was a multiple tragedy. That day, attackers from the land of our ancestry killed and maimed thousands of our fellow Americans. And on that same day, our rights and freedoms as Americans of Japanese ancestry began to fall victim to wartime hysteria, racism and weak political leadership.

Fifty years later, our prayer is that tragedies like these will never occur again.

Source: "Pearl Harbor and Japanese Americans" by Rep. Norman Mineta, *Asianweek* 13 (December 6, 1991), p. 14. Reprinted by permission of *Asianweek.*

July parades were held, with camp-organized Boy Scout and Girl Scout troops marching past proud parents. But the barbed wire remained, and the Japanese Americans were asked to prove their loyalty.

The loyalty test came in 1943 on a form all had to fill out, the "Application for Leave Clearance." The Japanese Americans were undecided how to respond to two questions:

No. 27. Are you willing to serve in the armed forces of the United States on combat duty, wherever ordered?

No. 28. Will you swear to abide by the laws of the United States and to take no action which would in any way interfere with the war effort of the United States? (R. Daniels, 1972, p. 113)

The questions were not clear-cut, leaving many confused about how to respond. For example, if an Issei said yes to the second question, would she or he be without any citizenship? The Issei would be ending allegiance to Japan but was unable, at the time, to gain U.S. citizenship. Similarly, would a Nisei who responded yes be suggesting that she or he had been a supporter of Japan? For whatever reasons,

Hisako Hibi was a wife and the mother of two children when she painted this picture in Topaz Relocation Center, Utah, in 1943. Entitled *Mothers Bathing Children in Laundry Room,* it reflects everyday life in the camps.

6,700 Issei and Nisei were transferred to the high-security camp at Tule Lake for the duration of the war (R. Bigelow, 1992).

Japanese Americans consistently showed loyalty to the government that had created the camps. In general, security in the camps was not a problem. Heart Mountain, Wyoming, with 10,000 evacuees, had only 3 officers and 124 enlisted men in the guard detail. The army, which had overseen the removal of the Japanese Americans, recognized the value of the Japanese Americans as translators in the war ahead. About 6,000 Nisei were recruited to work as interpreters and translators, and by 1943, a special combat unit of 23,000 Nisei volunteers had been created to fight in Europe. The predominantly Nisei unit was unmatched and concluded the war as the most decorated of all American units.

Milton Eisenhower, as WRA head, had hoped initially to relocate some of the evacuees in western states nearer their homes, but when he met with western governors and attorneys general, he saw that such a plan was unacceptable. Wyoming Governor Nels Smith warned that, if Eisenhower's plan were attempted, "There would be Japs hanging from every pine tree" (A. Zich, 1986, p. 528). Eventually, the WRA allowed some evacuees to leave the camps to attend college, and it later allowed more to leave to work in wartime industry, but they always went to areas far from the West Coast (R. Daniels, 1972; Girdner and Loftis, 1969; B. Hosokawa, 1969).

Japanese-American behavior in the concentration camps can be seen only as reaffirming their loyalty. True, some refused to sign an oath, but that was hardly a treasonous act. More typical were the tens of thousands of evacuees who contributed to the American war effort.

The Road Out

A few Japanese Americans resisted the evacuation and internment. They took their case to the courts. They received little support even from those segments of the White community usually sympathetic to minority causes. A 1942 survey of members of the American Civil Liberties Union in northern California showed overwhelming support for Executive Order 9066 (W. Petersen, 1971).

Several cases arising out of the evacuation and the detention in concentration camps reached the U.S. Supreme Court during the war. Amazingly, the Court upheld lower court decisions on Japanese Americans without even raising the issue of the whole plan's constitutionality. Essentially, the Court upheld the idea of the collective guilt of an entire race. Finally, after hearing *Mitsuye Endo v. United States,* the Supreme Court ruled on December 18, 1944, that the defendant (and

The postwar welcome to evacuees returning home from the camps was generally not pleasant. A Nisei family is shown in 1945 in front of their home in Seattle, Washington, which they found had been vandalized while they were in an Idaho relocation center.

presumably all evacuees) must be granted their freedom. Two weeks later, Japanese Americans were allowed to return to their homes for the first time in three years (ten Brock et al., 1954).

The immediate postwar climate was not pro–Japanese American. Whites terrorized returning evacuees, in attacks similar to those against Blacks a generation earlier. Labor unions called for work stoppages when Japanese Americans reported for work. Portland refused to grant any business license to any Issei. Fortunately, the most blatant expression of anti-Japanese feeling disappeared rather quickly. Japan stopped being a threat as the atomic bomb blasts destroyed Nagasaki and Hiroshima. For the many evacuees who lost relatives and friends in the bombings, however, it must have been a high price to pay for marginal acceptance (M. Maykovich, 1972a, 1972b; W. Petersen, 1971).

The Evacuation: What Does It Mean?

The wartime evacuation cost the U.S. taxpayer a quarter of a billion dollars in construction, transportation, and military expenses. Japanese Americans, as already noted, effectively lost several billion dollars. These are only the tangible costs to the nation. The relocation was not justifiable on any security grounds. No verified act of espionage or sabotage by a Japanese American was recorded. How could it happen?

Racism cannot be ignored as an explanation. Japanese Americans were placed in camps, though German Americans and Italian Americans were ignored by comparison. Many of those whose decisions brought about the evacuation were of German and Italian ancestry. The fact was that the Japanese were expendable. Placing them in camps posed no hardship for the rest of society, and in fact, some profited by their misfortune. The secretary of California's Grower-Shipper Vegetable Association responded, "We do," to the charge that they wanted to get rid of the Japanese Americans for selfish reasons (F. Taylor, 1942, p. 66). That Japanese Americans were evacuated because they were seen as expendable is evident from the decision not to evacuate Hawaii's Japanese. In Hawaii, the Japanese were an integral part of the society; removing them would have destroyed the islands economically (B. Hosokawa, 1969; Y. Kimura, 1988; S. Miyamoto, 1973).

Some argue that Japanese nonresistance made internment possible. Certainly, this seems a weak effort to transfer guilt—to "blame the victim." Curiously, the Sansei and Yonsei are the quickest to show concern about the alleged timidity of their parents and grandparents when faced with evacuation orders. Probably many, if not most, evacuees did not really believe what was happening. "It just cannot be that bad," they thought. At worst, the evacuees can be accused of being naive. But even if their reactions were realistic, what alternatives were open? None (G. Haak, 1970; H. Kitano, 1976; Y. Takezawa, 1991).

The year 1952 marked a watershed in the civil rights of Japanese Americans. As we have seen, in that year the Issei could finally become citizens. Japanese immigration was again legal, and relatives of Japanese Americans were given preference. The California Supreme Court finally declared the 40-year-old Alien Land

Act unconstitutional. The civil rights enjoyed by Whites had finally been extended to Japanese Americans (R. Daniels, 1972).

After lobbying efforts by the JACL, President Carter created the Commission on Wartime Relocation and Internment of Civilians. In 1981, the commission held hearings on whether additional reparations should be paid to evacuees or their heirs. The final commission recommendation in 1983 was for a formal apology from the government and $20,000 tax-free to each of the approximately 66,000 surviving internees. Congress began hearings in 1986 on the bill authorizing these steps, and President Ronald Reagan signed the Civil Liberties Act of 1988, which authorized the payments. The payments, however, were slow in being authorized because other federal expenditures had higher priorities. Yet the aging internees were dying at a rate of 200 a month. In 1990, the first checks were finally issued, accompanied by President Bush's letter of apology. Many Japanese Americans were disappointed by and critical of the begrudging nature of the compensation and the length of time it had taken to receive compensation (Commission on Wartime Relocation and Internment of Civilians, 1982a, 1982b; T. Squitieri, 1989; Y. Takezawa, 1991).

POSTWAR SUCCESS

Aside from the legacy of the camps, the Japanese-American community of the 1950s was very different from that of the 1930s. Japanese Americans were more widely scattered. In 1940, 89 percent lived on the West Coast. By 1950, only 58 percent of the population had returned on the West Coast. Another difference was that a smaller proportion than before were Issei. The Nisei and even later generations accounted for 63 percent of the Japanese population.

More dramatic than these demographic changes was the upward mobility that Japanese Americans collectively and individually accomplished. Occupationally and academically, two indicators of success, Japanese Americans are doing very well. The educational attainment of Japanese Americans as a group, as well as their family earnings, are higher than those of Whites, but caution should be used in interpreting such group data. Obviously, large numbers of Asian Americans, as well as Whites, have little formal schooling and are employed in poor jobs. Furthermore, Japanese Americans are concentrated in areas of the United States such as Hawaii, California, Washington, New York, and Illinois, where wages, as well as the cost of living, are far above the national average. Also, the proportion of Japanese-American families with multiple wage earners is higher than that of White families. Nevertheless, the overall picture for Japanese Americans is remarkable, especially for a racial minority that had been discriminated against so virulently (M. Inoue, 1989; H. Kitano, 1980; S. Nishi, 1995; E. Woodrum, 1981).

Even after many years, not all Japanese Americans were successful. Some remained on the West Coast and served as sharecroppers in a role similar to the freed slaves after the Civil War. Sharecropping involved working the land of others who provided shelter, seeds, and equipment and sharing any profits at the time of harvest. The Japanese Americans used the practice to gradually get back into farming after being stripped of their land during World War II (M. Parrish, 1995).

After the war, leadership changed among Japanese Americans. The Issei had dominated through loosely coordinated relationships and Buddhist religious organizations. Gradually, during the war, the Nisei, through the JACL, gained prominence. The shift was not simply a progression of generations. The policy of dispersing the evacuees throughout the country made community-based groups more difficult to maintain. During the evacuation, community-based organizing had been threatened because the JACL had cooperated with the WRA, in a position not supported by all Nisei. Although the JACL is the primary organization of its type today, it still does not enjoy uncontested leadership. Politically, individual Japanese Americans have achieved success. Several have been elected to Congress, and in Hawaii, a Japanese American became governor. As a group, Japanese Americans show virtually no evidence of the political organization of many other racial or ethnic groups (J. Burma, 1953; B. Hosokawa, 1982b; H. Kitano, 1976; D. Nakanishi, 1987; C. Powers, 1976).

The contemporary Japanese-American family seems to continue the success story. The divorce rate has been low, although it is probably rising. Similar conclusions apply to crime, delinquency, and mental illness. Data on all types of social disorganization show Japanese Americans with a lower incidence of such behavior than all other minorities; it is also lower than that of Whites. Japanese Americans find it possible simultaneously to be good Japanese and to be good Americans. Japanese culture demands high in-group unity, politeness, respect for authority, and duty to community, all traits highly acceptable to middle-class Americans. Basically, psychological research has concluded that Japanese Americans share the high achievement orientation held by many middle-class White Americans. One might expect, however, that, as Japanese Americans continue to acculturate, the breakdown in Japanese-oriented behavior will be accompanied by a rise in social deviance (S. Nishi, 1995).

ASSIMILATION AMID CONFLICT

In reflecting on the Japanese Americans, it is easy to emphasize their assimilation in education and business. In addition, census data show that each successive generation of Japanese Americans is less segregated from Whites. Yet these facts must be viewed against a backdrop of the conflict created by government policy during World War II and the subsequent intolerance expressed against people of Japanese ancestry. Despite advances, the assimilation of Japanese Americans has been clearly blocked (S. Nishi, 1995).

Young Japanese Americans are very ambivalent today about their cultural heritage. The pull "to be American" is intense, but so are the reminders that, in the eyes of others, Japanese Americans are "they," not "we." Sansei youth indicate they would like to learn Japanese. It is questionable whether many will. The very success of Japanese Americans seems to argue that they will not maintain a unique cultural tradition. In fact, their success has been in part the result of their assimilating, forsaking the cultural heritage of Japan. Their emphasis on college educa-

The emergence of anti-Japan feelings in the 1990s was, for this illustrator, reminiscent of the internment camps of the 1940s.

The emergence of anti-Japanese feelings in the 1990s was, for this illustrator, reminiscent of the internment camps of the 1990s.

Reprinted with special permission of King Features Syndicate.

tion and advanced training makes it likely that Japanese Americans will scatter throughout the country. Dispersal will make cultural ties difficult to maintain. Little Tokyos do exist, but even in some major cities, such a basic symbol of ethnic solidarity is absent (T. Garrison, 1974; H. Kitano, 1971; Levine and Montero, 1973).

The results of the UCLA Japanese American Research Project, begun in 1963, emphasize the degree of acculturation that had already taken place in the Nisei, especially among the well educated. Half of the high-school-educated were Buddhists and spoke Japanese fluently. On the other hand, only about 10 percent of the college graduates had similar cultural ties to Japan. In summary, it appears that the Nisei have acquired knowledge, habits, and attitudes that more closely resemble those of the United States than those of Japan. Although the Issei may have successfully merged the Japanese and American cultures, the Nisei have adapted themselves to American culture. Further research into the third generation, the Sansei, indicates that assimilation has continued. There is little evidence of Marcus Hansen's principle of third-generation interest in the homeland's culture, as described in Chapter 5. Yet many of the Sanseis' lives have been shaped by the internment experience as they choose careers intended to finish the unfulfilled dreams of their previously interned relatives (D. Montero, 1981; D. Nagata, 1991; S. Nishi, 1995)

The Japanese-American community struggles to maintain its cultural identity. Despite being viewed as "racially different," young Japanese Americans are readily adopting mainstream culture. Nisei Week celebrations have been held in August since 1934 as a festive effort to showcase the tea ceremony, bonsai ornamental plant techniques, and Kamans (family crests). But other customs, such as eating

While Japanese-American students, such as these pictured at the University of Southern California, have enjoyed a measure of success, they have also found it difficult to maintain any unique cultural identity.

traditional foods like sushi (uncooked fish) and namasu (radish and carrots marinated in vinegar), are fading in popularity (M. Becker, 1995).

In addition to geographical mobility, the degree of out-marriage by Japanese Americans indicates further assimilation. Census data show a higher rate of exogamy among younger Japanese Americans than in their parents' generation. Obviously, if such trends continue, it will be increasingly difficult to make a sense of cultural continuity last beyond the present generation. Furthermore, increasing numbers of interracial children are being born to such unions: There are now 39 percent more Japanese–White mixed births than births to parents who are both of Japanese ancestry (S. Kalish, 1992, 1995; S. Nishi, 1995).

It would be incorrect to interpret assimilation as an absence of protest. Because militancy characterized the attitudes of a sizable segment of the college youth of the 1960s and early 1970s, and because the Sansei are more heterogeneous than their Nisei and Issei relatives, it was to be expected that some Japanese Americans, especially the Sansei, would be militant. For example, the Japanese and other Asian Americans have emerged as activists for environmental concerns ranging from contaminated fish to toxic working conditions, and the targets of Japanese Americans' anger have included the apparent rise in hate crimes in the United States against Asian Americans in the 1990s. They also lobbied for passage of the Civil Rights Restoration Act extending reparations to the evacuees. They have expressed further activism through Hiroshima Day ceremonies, marking the anniversary of the detonation in World War II of the first atomic bomb over a major Japanese city. Also, each February, a group of Japanese-American youths makes a pilgrimage to the site of the Tule Lake evacuation camp in a "lest we forget" observance. Such protests are modest, but they are a militant departure from the almost passive role played by the Nisei (G. Shaffer, 1994; Y. Takezawa, 1991; W. Wei, 1993).

It is clear that, even for the Sansei or Yonsei, assimilation is incomplete. Conflict with the dominant White majority continues. Although the ties to Japanese culture may be weakened, or even completely broken, Japanese Americans are still readily identified as *Japanese* Americans, not as Americans. Indeed, the 1990s saw a reemergence of anti-Japanese feeling in the United States. The growing trade competition between Japan and the United States brought strong feelings that Japan was somehow not "playing fair" as the only explanation of why we are suffering a trade imbalance. Each time a Japanese company has bought a U.S. company, the media have given the event tremendous attention; yet similar action by Australian, British, or German investors has been relatively unnoticed. Particularly chilling was the 1982 murder in Detroit of Vincent Chin, a Chinese American, whom two White unemployed automobile workers mistook for Japanese in their outrage over Japan's success in exporting cars to the United States. The fiftieth anniversary of the attack on Pearl Harbor rekindled feelings that people from Japan cannot be trusted. Sporadic vandalism of symbols of Japanese-American presence occurred at the time. And in 1995, on the fiftieth anniversary of the dropping of bombs on Nagasaki and Hiroshima, there were once again strong anti-Japanese reactions in the United States. In this light, it is not surprising to learn that 44 percent of Sansei surveyed, who had had both parents interned during World War II, agreed that Japanese Americans would be held captive again if the United States and Japan were to go to war (E. Cose, 1989; H. El Nasser, 1991b; L. Foderaro, 1990; P. Min, 1995; S. Muto, 1991; D. Nagata, 1990).

Even cartoons showed anti-Japanese sentiment in the 1990s amid growing concerns about Japan's economic power. "Kudzu," by 1988 Pulitzer Prize–winning cartoonist Doug Marlette, satirizes the takeover of a small town by a Japanese corporation (Sayonara Inc.). The series was criticized for the use of stereotypes and Japan-bashing. Marlette, who was asked to respond, defended his work and said that his critics don't have a sense of humor and are trying to impose their beliefs on him. "My experience is that here are two kinds of racial groups—one has a sense of humor, the other doesn't," he is quoted as saying.

KUDZU by Doug Marlette. By permission of Doug Marlette and Creators Syndicate.

The insults, while minor but still symbolic, continue. For example, the Japanese American Citizens League has been unsuccessful in getting Texas communities to change the name of their roads "Jap Lane" and "Jap Road"—holdovers from a Japanese immigrant agricultural colony founded in 1908 (G. Muranaka, 1993).

Is pluralism developing? Japanese Americans give little evidence of wanting to maintain a distinctive way of life. The Japanese values that have endured are attitudes, beliefs, and goals shared by and rewarded by the White U.S. middle class. The Japanese American is caught in the middle. He or she is culturally a part of a society that is dominated by a group that excludes him or her because of racial distinctions.

Sociologist Minako Maykovich (1972a) distinguished among the three generations by the "three y's" and the "three b's." Specifically, they are (1) Issei—yellow peril and bamboo; (2) Nisei—yellow pansy and banana; and (3) Sansei—yellow power and bee (pp. 78–79). The first Japanese Americans, the Issei, were attacked by the yellow peril stereotype but did not accept this image. Like bamboo, the Issei easily bent in whatever direction the wind blew, only to eventually spring back straight and proud. Their children became quiet and wishy-washy, hence the name *yellow pansy.* They were bananas, yellow on the outside but white inside. Their children, the Sansei, were less accommodating. It was in this generation that yellow power emerged. The bee, active and with a sting that hurts, is a more suitable image. Maykovich acknowledged the oversimplification. Not all Sansei would identify with the bee, for example. Although the labels may be misleading, they do underscore once again that the Japanese-American experience has not been one long success story. Nor has the story been uniform throughout the country. The conclusions on the assimilation of Japanese Americans apply most accurately to the mainland. Hawaii's acceptance of Japanese Americans, as well as other Asians and Whites, has been different (see Chapter 12).

COMPARING CHINESE-AMERICAN AND JAPANESE-AMERICAN EXPERIENCES

Most White adults are confident of their ability to distinguish Asians from Europeans. Unfortunately, though, White Americans frequently cannot tell Asians apart and are not disturbed about their confusion. There are, however, definite differences in the experience of the Chinese and the Japanese, several of which should now be obvious. The Chinese arrived in large numbers before the Japanese, although movements to discriminate predictably followed the same pattern. Japanese-American immigrants, mostly male, began sending back to Japan for brides soon after their arrival. As a result, the preponderance of males did not last as long as it did among urban Chinese Americans.

There are also obvious differences in the degree of assimilation. The Chinese Americans have maintained their ethnic enclaves more than the Japanese Americans. Chinatowns live on, but Little Tokyos are few because of the differences in the cultures of China and Japan. China was almost untouched by European influence, but even in the early 1900s, Japan had been influenced by the West. Relatively speaking, then, the Japanese arrived somewhat more assimilated than their Chinese counterparts. The continued migration of Chinese in recent years has also meant that Chinese Americans as a group have been less assimilated than Japanese Americans (W. Beach, 1934; S. Lyman, 1974, 1986).

Both groups have achieved some success, but only to a degree. For Chinese Americans, a notable exception to success is the prevalence of Chinatowns, which, behind the tourist front, are just other poverty areas in American cities. Neither Chinese Americans nor Japanese Americans have figured prominently in the executive offices of the nation's large corporations and financial institutions. Compared to other racial and ethnic groups, they have had relatively little impact in their political activity and militancy.

CONCLUSION

Japanese Americans embody a success story better than the rags-to-riches saga of some enterprising inventor. Here is a group that, in little more than a generation, went from total rejection by society to success, at least by middle-class standards.

The success, however, is that of the Japanese Americans, not of U.S. society. First, they have been considered a success only because they conform to the dominant society's expectations. The acceptance of Japanese Americans as a group does not indicate that the United States is moving toward pluralism. Second, the ability of the Nisei to recover from the camps cannot be taken as a precedent for other racial minorities. The Japanese Americans left the camps a skilled group, ambitious to overcome their adversity, and placing a cultural emphasis on formal education. They entered a booming economy in which Whites and others could not afford to discriminate even if they wished to. African Americans after slavery and Hispanic immigrants have entered the economy without skills at a time when the demand for manual labor has been limited. Many of them have been forced to remain in a marginal economy, whether that of the ghetto, the barrio, or subsistence agriculture. For Japanese Americans, the post–World War II period marked the fortunate coincidence of their having assets and ambition when they could be used to full advantage. Third, some Whites, though not many, use the success of the Japanese Americans to prop up their own prejudice. Japanese-American success is twisted by bigoted individuals to show that racism cannot possibly play a part in another group's subordination. If the Japanese can do it, why cannot African Americans, the illogical reasoning goes. Or more directly, and even less frequently, Japanese Americans' success serves as an excuse for another's failure ("They advanced at my expense") or as a sign that they are clannish or too ambitious. Regardless of what a group does, to a prejudiced eye the group can do no right.

As for other racial and ethnic minorities, assimilation seems to be the path most likely to lead to tolerance but not necessarily to acceptance. But assimilation has a price that is well captured in the Chinese phrase *Zhancao zhugen:* "To eliminate the weeds, one must pull out their roots." To work for acceptance means to uproot all traces of one's cultural heritage and former identity (L. Wang, 1991).

KEY TERMS

evacuees Japanese Americans interned in camps for the duration of World War II.
Issei First-generation immigrants from Japan to the United States.
Kibei Americans of the Nisei generation sent back to Japan for schooling and to have marriages arranged.
Nisei Children born of immigrants from Japan.
Sansei The children of the Nisei, that is, the grandchildren of the original immigrants from Japan.
Yonsei The fourth generation of Japanese Americans in the United States, the children of the Sansei.

FOR FURTHER INFORMATION

Maisie Conrat and Richard Conrat. *Executive Order 9066.* Los Angeles: Los Angeles Asian American Studies Center, 1992.

> The Conrats constructed a very moving photographic essay of the relocation and internment of the Japanese Americans.

Roger Daniels. *Asian America: Chinese and Japanese in the United States Since 1850.* Seattle: University of Washington Press, 1988.

> A balanced, authoritative look at two racial minorities that have experienced success and continued bigotry.

William Minoru Hohri. *Repairing America: An Account of the Movement for Japanese-American Redress.* Pullum: Washington State University Press, 1988.

> A summary of the testimony that led to the presidential apology and the payment of $20,000 to each surviving evacuee.

Bill Hosokawa. *JACL in Quest of Justice.* New York: Morrow, 1982.

> A well-illustrated, detailed account of the Japanese American Citizens League (JACL) from its founding through its efforts to gain reparations in the 1980s.

Japanese American Evacuation and Resettlement Study.

> This six-year study (1942–1948), based at the University of California, produced the most detailed report on the camps and was published in three volumes by the University of California Press: *The Spoilage,* by Dorothy S. Thomas and Richard S. Nishimoto (1946); *The Salvage,* by Thomas (1952); and *Prejudice, War, and the Constitution,* by Jacobus ten Brock, Edward N. Barnhart, and Floyd W. Matson (1954).

Japanese American National Museum. *The View from Within: Japanese American Art from the Internment Camps, 1942–1945.* Los Angeles: Japanese American National Museum, 1992.

> Besides a brief chronology, this book includes photography and color reproductions of paintings depicting internment life.

Harry H. L. Kitano. *Japanese Americans: The Evolution of a Subculture,* 2d ed. Englewood Cliffs, NJ: Prentice-Hall, 1976.

Kitano gives a thorough review of Japanese Americans with unusually detailed coverage of such aspects of contemporary life as family, cultural beliefs, mental illness, and crime. A chapter is devoted to the Japanese in Hawaii. The author graduated from high school while in the Topaz internment camp.

Yoshiko Uchida. *Desert Exile*. Seattle: University of Washington Press, 1982.

A chronicle of life in an internment camp written by someone who experienced the hardships of the camps and the recovery that followed.

Government Documents

The federal government carefully recorded the relocation from beginning to end. Documents can be consulted that were issued by these now-defunct agencies: War Agency Liquidation Unit, War Relocation Authority (both of the Department of the Interior), the Western Defense Command (U.S. Army), and the Select Committee Investigating National Defense Migration (House of Representatives, 1942). Still another source is the Commission on Wartime Relocation and Internment of Civilians, which met in the 1980s.

CRITICAL THINKING QUESTIONS

1. In what respects were the early anti-Japanese-American movements more a product of feelings against Asians in general than of a specific antagonism toward people of Japanese ancestry?
2. What made the placement of Japanese Americans in internment camps unique?
3. What do you think is the most significant legacy of the internment camp experience?
4. How would you distinguish between the Issei, the Nisei, and the Sansei?
5. How has Japanese-American assimilation been blocked in the United States?

Chapter 15

Jewish Americans: Quest to Maintain Identity

Chapter Outline

Highlights

The Jewish people are an ethnic group. Their identity rests not on the presence of physical traits or religious devoutness, but on a sense of belonging that is tied to Jewish ancestry. The history of *anti-Semitism* is as ancient as the Jewish people themselves. Yet there is evidence that in both thought and action, this intolerance persists today. Jews in the United States may have experienced less discrimination than did earlier generations in Europe, but some opportunities are still denied them. Contemporary Jews figure prominently in the professions and as a group exhibit a strong commitment to education. Many Jews share a concern about either the lack of religious devotion of some or the division within American Judaism over the degree of orthodoxy. Jews in the United States practice their faith as Orthodox, Conservative, or Reform. Paradoxically, the acceptance of Jews by Gentiles has made the previously strong identity of Jews weaker with each succeeding generation.

The United States has the largest Jewish population in the world. This nation's 5.6 million Jews account for 43 percent of the world's Jewish population. Jewish Americans not only are a significant group in the United States but also play a prominent role in the worldwide Jewish community. The nation with the second largest Jewish population, Israel, is the only one in which Jews are in the majority, accounting for 82 percent of that nation's population, compared to less than 3 percent in the United States. Figure 15.1 depicts the worldwide distribution of Jews (Schmelz and Della Pergola, 1994).

The Jewish people form a contrast to the other subordinate groups we have studied. It has been at least 1,500 years since Jews were the dominant group in any nation. Israel, created in 1948, is the exception, but even there, Jews are in competition for power. American Jews superficially resemble Asian Americans in their relative freedom from poverty compared to Chicanos or Puerto Ricans. Unlike that of any of these groups, however, the Jewish cultural heritage is not nationalistic in origin. Perhaps the most striking difference is that the history of anti-Jewish prejudice and discrimination (usually referred to as *anti-Semitism*) is nearly as old as relations between Jews and Gentiles (non-Jews).

Statistical data on Jewish Americans are unreliable. Because the Bureau of the Census no longer asks people their religions, the kinds of statistical information available on other minority groups, who are identified in the census, are lacking. The last count the Bureau of the Census made in 1957, placed the Jewish population over age 14 at nearly 4 million. Estimates for 1992 placed the Jewish population at about 5.6 million. The Jewish birthrate remains well below that of the national population, and so growth of the Jewish population during the 1980s did not keep pace with that of the nation as a whole. Indeed, the proportion of the U.S. population that is Jewish has been estimated to be the lowest since the first decade of the century.

The most distinctive aspect of the Jewish population is its concentration in urban areas and in the Northeast. The most recent estimates (for 1993) place 48 percent of the Jewish population in the Northeast (see Table 15.1). The special 1957 census of religion showed 96 percent of Jews living in urban areas, compared to 64 percent for the whole population. Although these data are old, they probably still reflect accurately the distribution of Jews today.

Jews are especially concentrated in New York City. One-fourth of the nation's Jewish population in 1993 lived in New York City and neighboring cities in New York state and New Jersey. There are more Jews in this area than in Israel's largest city, Tel Aviv. While a much larger portion of the Jewish population lived in New York City in the past, New York remains the focus of the Jewish community (Kosmin and Scheckner, 1994).

THE JEWISH PEOPLE: RACE OR RELIGION OR ETHNIC GROUP?

Jews are a subordinate group. They fulfill all the criteria set forth in Chapter 1.

1. Jews have characteristics that distinguish them from the dominant group.
2. Jews do not choose to be Jewish, in the same way that Whites do not choose to be White or Chicanos to be Chicano.
3. Jews have a strong sense of group solidarity.
4. Jewish men and women tend to marry one another rather than marrying Gentiles.
5. Jewish Americans experience unequal treatment from non-Jews in the form of prejudice, discrimination, and segregation.

The first criterion for classification as a subordinate group on this list requires special attention. What are the distinguishing traits? Are they physical features, thus making Jews a racial group? Are these characteristics matters of faith, suggesting that Jews are best regarded as a religious minority? Or are they cultural and social, making Jews an ethnic group? Answering these questions requires an approach to the ancient and perennial question: What is a Jew?

The question of what a Jew is is not only a scholarly question, for in Israel, it figures in matters of policy. Following the 1988 general election, Israeli prime minister Yitshak Shamir was under great pressure from tradition-minded Jews in both his own country and the United States to redefine Israel's Law of Return. This law defines who is a Jew and extends Israeli citizenship to all Jews. Currently, the law recognizes all converts to the faith, but pressure has grown recently to limit citizenship to those whose conversions were performed by Orthodox rabbis. While the change would have had little practical impact, symbolically it showed the tension and lack of consensus even among Jews over who is a Jew (R. Watson, 1988).

The definition of race used here is fairly explicit. The Jewish people are not physically differentiated from non-Jews. True, many people believe they can tell a Jew from a non-Jew, but actual distinguishing physical traits are absent. Jews today come from all areas of the world and carry a variety of physical features. Most Jew-

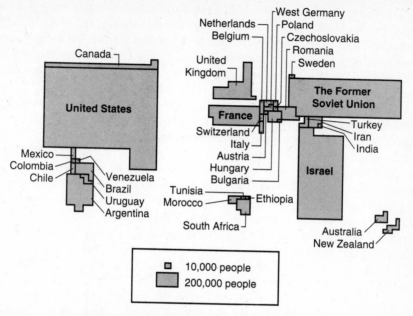

Figure 15.1 The Worldwide Distribution of Jews
While the United States, Israel, and the former Soviet Union have the largest numbers of Jews, significant Jewish populations can also be found in France, Great Britain, Canada, and Argentina.

Source: Atlas of the World Today by Neil Grant and Nick Middleton, 1987. Copyright © by Itex Publishers. Reprinted by permission of Harper & Row Publishers, Inc.

Table 15.1   JEWISH POPULATION DISTRIBUTION IN THE UNITED STATES
(PERCENTAGES)

Region	1900		1993	
	Jewish	Total	Jewish	Total
Northeast	56.6	27.7	48.2	20.0
Midwest	23.7	34.6	11.6	23.8
South	14.2	32.2	20.8	34.6
West	5.5	5.4	19.4	21.6

Note: Percentages may not add up to 100 because of rounding.

Source: S. Goldstein (1981, p. 63); Kosmin and Scheckner (1994). Data reproduced with the permission of the American Jewish Committee and the Council of Jewish Federation.

ish Americans are descended from Northern and Eastern Europeans and have the appearance of Nordic and Alpine people. Many others carry Mediterranean traits that make them indistinguishable from Spanish or Italian Catholics. Many Jews reside in North Africa, and although they are not significantly represented in the United States, many people would consider them Black. The wide range of variation among Jews makes it inaccurate to speak of a "Jewish race" in a physical sense (J. Gittler, 1981; A. Montagu, 1972).

To define Jews by religion would seem the obvious answer, because there are Judaic religious beliefs, holidays, and rituals. But these beliefs and practices do not distinguish Jews from non-Jews. To be a Jewish American does not mean that one is affiliated with one of the three religious groups: the Orthodox, the Reform, and the Conservative. A large segment of Jewish Americans, more than a third, do not participate as adults in religious services or even belong, however tenuously, to a temple or synagogue. They have not converted to Christianity, nor do they cease to think of themselves as Jews. This is not to say that Jewish religious beliefs and the history of religious practices are not significant legacies for all Jews today, however secularized their everyday behavior.

The trend for some time, especially in the United States, has been toward a condition that Herbert J. Gans (1956) called *Judaization,* the lessening importance of Judaism as a religion and the substitution of cultural traditions as the tie that binds Jews. Depending on one's definition, Judaization has caused some Jews to become so assimilated in the United States that more traditional Jews would cease to consider them acceptable spouses. Predictions of the proportion of "problematic" Jews by the year 2000 range from 4 to 20 percent (American Jewish Committee, 1987).

Jewish identity is ethnic. Jews share cultural traits, not physical features or uniform religious beliefs. The level of this cultural identity differs for the individual Jew. Just as some Apaches may be more acculturated than others, the degree of assimilation varies among Jewish people. Judaization, as defined by Gans, may base identity on such things as traditional Jewish foods, Jewish jokes, and the Star of David. For others, this cultural identity may be the sense of a common history of centuries of persecution. For still others, it may be a relatively unimportant identification. They say, "I am a Jew," just as they say, "I am a resident of California."

The question of what constitutes Jewish identity is not easily resolved, except that it is not based on physical features or religiosity. The most appropriate explanation of Jewish identity may be the simplest. A Jew in contemporary America is an individual who thinks of himself or herself as a Jew (H. Himmelfarb, 1982).

MIGRATION OF JEWS TO THE UNITED STATES

As every schoolchild knows, 1492 was the year in which Christopher Columbus reached the Western Hemisphere, exploring on behalf of Spain. That year also marked the expulsion of all Jews from Spain. The exodus that the expulsion caused was not the first migration of Jews, nor was it the last. One of the most significant movements among Jews is the one that created history's largest concentration of Jews: the migration to the United States. The first Jews arrived in 1654 and were of Sephardic origin, meaning that they were from Spain and Portugal. These immigrants came looking for refuge after they were expelled from European countries.

When the United States gained its independence from Great Britain, there were only 2,500 Jews in the population. By 1870 the Jewish population had climbed to about 200,000, supplemented mostly by Jews of German origin. They did not immediately merge into the older Jewish-American settlements any more than the German Catholics fused immediately with native Catholics. Years passed before the two groups' common identity as Jews overcame nationality differences (L. Dinnerstein, 1994; F. Jaher, 1994).

The greatest migration of Jews to the United States occurred around the turn of the nineteenth century and was simultaneous with the great European migration described in Chapter 4. This similarity in timing does not mean that the movement of Gentiles and of Jews was identical in all respects. One significant difference was that Jews were much more likely to stay in the United States; few returned to Europe. Although between 1908 and 1937, one-third of immigrants returned to Europe, only 5 percent of Jewish immigrants did. The legal status of Jews in Europe at the turn of the century had improved since medieval times, but their rights were still revoked from time to time (C. Sherman, 1974).

Despite the legacy of anti-Semitism in Europe, past and present, most of the Jews who migrated to the United States up to the early twentieth century came voluntarily. Sociologist Marshall Sklare (1971) wrote, "The immigration of the European Jew was basically elective rather than enforced" through expulsions (p. 16). These immigrants tended to be less pious and less observant of Judaic religious customs than those who remained in Europe. As late as 1917, there were only five small day schools, as Jewish parochial schools were called, in the entire nation. Although the earliest Jewish immigration did not come directly in response to fear, the United States had special meaning for the Jewish arrival. The United States had no history of anti-Semitism like that of Europe. Many Jews must have felt a new sense of freedom, and many clearly demonstrated their commitment to their new nation by becoming citizens at a rate unparalleled in other ethnic groups (W. Herberg, 1983).

The immigration acts of the 1920s sharply reduced the influx of Jews, as it did that of other European groups. Beginning in about 1933, the Jews arriving in the United States were not merely immigrants; they were also refugees. The tyranny of the Third Reich began to take its toll well before World War II. German and Austrian Jews fled Europe as the impending doom became more evident. Many of the refugees from Nazism in Poland, Hungary, and Ukraine tended to be more religiously orthodox and adapted slowly to the ways of the earlier Jewish immigrants, if they adapted at all. The concentration camps, the speeches of Hitler, the atrocities, the war trials, and the capture of Nazi leaders undoubtedly made all American Jews—natives and refugees, the secular and the orthodox—acutely aware of their Jewishness and the price one may be required to pay for ethnicity alone.

Because the Immigration and Naturalization Service does not identify an immigrant's religion, precise data are lacking for the number of people of Jewish background migrating recently to the United States. Estimates of 500,000 have been given, however, for the number of Jews who made the United States their home during the 1960s and 1970s. The majority came from Israel, but 75,000 came from the Soviet Union and another 20,000 from Iran, escaping persecution in those two nations. As the treatment of Jews in the Soviet Union improved in the late 1980s, the U.S. immigration officials began to scrutinize requests for entry to see if refugee status still needed to be granted. While some Soviet Jews had diffi-culty demonstrating that they had a "well-founded fear of persecution," the Unit-ed States admitted over 13,600 in 1988 (through Rome alone). The situation grew more complicated with the collapse of the Soviet Union in 1991. Throughout the period, the immigrants' arrival brought about a growth in the Jewish community in the United States.

The large number of Jews immigrating to the United States from Israel has obvious significance for that small nation, and those who leave for North America or Europe are often regarded as "traitors" by those left behind in the besieged land of Israel. Some of the emigrants, and especially those from the Soviet Union, are referred to pejoratively as *noshrim*, or dropouts, having discarded their faith and abandoned membership in Jewish organizations. The Iranian Jews, who have tend-ed to cluster in Los Angeles, are more traditional but are linked to a culture alien to that of most American Jews (S. Gold, 1988; Kass and Lipset, 1980, 1982; D. Shipler, 1981; Simon and Simon, 1982).

ANTI-SEMITISM PAST AND PRESENT

The historical tradition of the Jewish people has included the struggle to overcome centuries of hatred. Several religious observances, like Passover, Hanukkah, and Purim, commemorate the past sacrifices or conflicts Jews have experienced. Anti-Jewish hostility, or anti-Semitism, has followed the struggle of the Jewish people from the beginning of the Christian faith to the present.

Origins

Many anti-Semites justify their beliefs by pointing to the role of some Jews in the crucifixion of Jesus Christ, who was a Jew. For nearly 2,000 years various Christians have argued that all Jews share in the responsibility of the Jewish elders who con-demned Jesus Christ to death. Much anti-Semitism over the ages bears little direct relationship to the crucifixion, however, and has more to do with the persisting stereotype that sees Jews as behaving treacherously to members of the larger soci-ety in which they live. As Chapter 2 showed, people may continue to be familiar with a stereotype, whether or not they accept it as true. Table 2.1 shows the change in the stereotype of Jews from 1932 to 1982. Although negative aspects were cited less frequently, many still saw Jews in a less-than-positive light. Studies such as the one shown in Table 2.1 and that of Bruno Bettelheim and Morris Janowitz (1964) confirm that many Gentiles believe that Jews use underhanded methods in busi-ness and finance, and that Jewish people tend to be clannish (B. Glassman, 1975; R. Wuthnow, 1982).

What truth is there in such stereotypes? Even prominent political leaders have publicly expressed stereotyped opinions about Jews. In 1974, the chairman of the Joint Chiefs of Staff of the U.S. armed forces declared that Jews "own, you know, the banks in this country" (*Time*, 1974b, p. 16). Yet the facts show that Jewish Americans are dramatically underrepresented in management positions in the nation's leading banks. Even in New York City—where Jews account for half the college graduates—Jewish Americans represent only 4 percent of that city's senior banking officials (Slavin and Pradt, 1979, 1982). Similarly, sociologists Richard Alba and Gwen Moore (1982), using national data for the period 1972–1980, concluded that Jews account for 8.9 percent of college-educated men but only 6.9 percent of the business elite.

If the stereotype of being money-minded is false, how did it originate? Social psychologist Gordon Allport (1979), among others, advanced the *fringe-of-values theory*. Throughout history, Jews have occupied positions economically different from those of Gentiles, often because laws forbade them to farm or practice trades. For centuries, the Christian church prohibited the taking of interest in the repayment of loans, calling it the sin of usury. Most Jews were not moneylenders, and most of those who were did not charge interest. In fact, many usurers were Christians, but because they worked in secret, it was only the reputation of the Jews that was damaged. In the minds of Europeans, the sinful practice of moneylending was equated with the Jew. To make matters worse, the nobles of some European countries used Jews to collect taxes, which only increased the ill feeling. To the Gentile, such business practices by the Jews constituted behavior on the *fringes* of proper conduct, hence this theory about the perpetuation of anti-Semitism is called *fringe of values* (American Jewish Committee, 1965, 1966a, 1966b; De Fleur, D'Antonio, and De Fleur, 1976; *Time*, 1974a).

A similar explanation is given for such other stereotypes as the assertion that Jews are clannish, that they stay among themselves and do not associate with others. In the ancient world, Jews in the Near East area were frequently under attack by neighboring peoples. This experience naturally led them to unify and rely on themselves rather than others. In more recent times, the stereotype that Jews are clannish has gained support because Jews have been more likely to interact with Jews than with Gentiles. But this behavior is reciprocal, for Gentiles have tended to stay among their own kind, too. It is another example of *in-group virtues* becoming *out-group vices*. Sociologist Robert Merton (1968) described how proper behavior by one's own group becomes unacceptable when practiced by outsiders. For Christians to take their faith seriously is commendable; for Jews to withstand secularization is a sign of backwardness. For Gentiles to prefer Gentiles as friends is understandable; for Jews to choose other Jews as friends suggests clannishness. The assertion that Jews are clannish is an exaggeration and ignores the fact that the dominant group shares the same tendency. It also fails to consider to what extent anti-Semitism has logically encouraged—and indeed, forced—Jews to seek out other Jews as friends and fellow workers (G. Allport, 1979).

This has been only the beginning of an exploration of the alleged Jewish traits, their origin, and the limited value that such stereotypes have in accurately describing several million Jewish people. Stereotypes are only one aspect of anti-Semitism: another has been discrimination against Jews. In A.D. 313, Christianity became the official religion of Rome. Within another two centuries, Jews were forbidden to marry Christians or to try to convert them. Because Christians shared with Jews both the Old Testament and the origin of Jesus, they felt ambivalent toward the Jewish people. Gentiles attempted to purge themselves of their doubts about the Jews by projecting exaggerated hostility onto the Jews. The expulsion of the Jews from Spain in 1492 is only one example. Spain was merely one in a list of countries, which included England and France, that the Jews were expelled from. During the middle of the fourteenth century, the bubonic plague wiped out a third of Europe's population. Because of their social conditions and some of their religious prohibitions, Jews were less likely to die from the plague. Anti-Semites pointed to this fact as evidence that the Jews were in league with the devil and had poisoned the wells of non-Jews. Consequently, from 1348 to 1349, 350 Jewish communities were exterminated, not by the plague, but by Gentiles.

The injustices to the Jewish people continued for centuries. It would, however, be a mistake to say that all Gentiles were anti-Semitic. History, plays, and literature do record daily, presumably friendly, interaction between Jew and Gentile. At particular times and places, anti-Semitism was an official government policy. In other situations, it was the product of a few bigoted individuals and sporadically became mass movements. Anti-Semitism was a part of Jewish life, something Jews were forced to contend with. By 1870, most legal restrictions aimed at Jews had been abolished in western Europe. Since then, however, Jews have again been used as scapegoats by opportunists who blame them for a nation's problems.

The most tragic example of such an opportunist was Adolf Hitler, whose "final solution" to Germany's problems led to the Holocaust, the extermination of six million Jewish civilians beginning in 1933 and becoming systematic during World War II. Two-thirds of Europe's total Jewish population was killed; in Poland, Germany, and Austria, 90 percent were murdered. Despite the enormity of the tragedy, a small but vocal proportion of the world community, perhaps 3 percent, are *Holocaust revisionists*, claiming that the Holocaust did not happen. There are also debates between those who contend that this part of modern history must be remembered and others, in the United States and Europe, who feel that it is time to go on. However, the poignant statements by Holocaust survivors, as well as the release of such films as *Schindler's List* (1993) keep the tragedy of the destruction of European Jews in our minds (L. Collette, 1994; L. Dawidowicz, 1967, 1975).

With the collapse of eastern European Communist governments and the Soviet Union in 1991, there has emerged a concern that the absence of authoritarian states will allow old hatreds to resurface. The fear is that, with freedom of speech, bigotry is beginning to be expressed openly. Anti-Semitic literature has been distributed, and expressions of alarm over Jews migrating from the former Soviet Union to western Europe are not uncommon. Yet, even a half century after Nazi Germany mounted its war on the Jews of eastern Europe, the Jewish population is relatively small. Hungary has the most, with about 60,000, but many of the 1.5 million Jews in the countries formerly controlled by Moscow are expected to leave. The future of the Jewish community in Europe even without the threat of Communist repression, like many other aspects of life, is uncertain (T. Mathews, 1990).

American Anti-Semitism: Past

Compared to the brutalities of Europe from the time of the early Christian church to the rule of Hitler, the United States cannot be described as a nation with a history of severe anti-Semitism. The United States has also had its outbreaks of anti-

The 1993 Oscar-winning film *Schindler's List* reminded many of the horrors of the Holocaust. Here German industrialist Oskar Schindler (Liam Neeson) searches for his plant manager among a trainload of Polish Jews about to be deported to Auschwitz-Birkenau.

Semitism, however, though none have reached the scope of western Europe's. An examination of the status of Jewish Americans today will indicate the extent of discrimination against Jews that remains. Contemporary anti-Semitism, however, must be seen in relation to past injustices.

In 1654, the year Jews arrived in colonial America, Peter Stuyvesant, governor of New Amsterdam (the Dutch city later named New York), attempted to expel them from the city. Stuyvesant's efforts failed, but they were the beginning of an unending effort to separate Jews from the rest of the population. Because the pre-1880 immigration of Jews was relatively small, anti-Semitism was little noticed except, of course, by Jews. Most nineteenth-century movements against minorities were targeted at Catholics and Blacks and ignored Jews. In fact, Jews occasionally joined in such movements. By the 1870s, however, signs of a pattern of social discrimination against Jews had appeared. Colleges limited the number of Jewish students or excluded Jews altogether. The first Jewish fraternity was founded in 1898 to compensate for the barring of Jews from campus social organizations. As Jews began to compete for white-collar jobs early in the twentieth century, job discrimination became the rule, rather than the exception (J. Higham, 1966; M. Selzer, 1972).

The 1920s and the 1930s were the period of the most virulent and most overt anti-Semitism. During these decades, the myth of an internationally organized Jewry took shape. According to a forged document entitled the *Protocols of the Elders of Zion,* Jews throughout the world planned to conquer all governments, and the major vehicle for this rise to power was communism, said by anti-Semites to be a Jewish movement. Absurd though this argument was, some respected Americans accepted the thesis of an international Jewish conspiracy and believed in the authenticity of the *Protocols.* Henry Ford, founder of the automobile company that bears his name, was responsible for the publication of the *Protocols. The Dearborn Independent,* a weekly newspaper owned by Ford, published anti-Semitic material for seven years. Finally in 1927, faced with several million dollars' worth of civil suits for slandering well-known Jewish Americans, he published a halfhearted apology. In his later years, Ford expressed regret for his espousal of anti-Semitic causes, but the damage had been done; he had lent an air of respectability to the most exaggerated charges against Jewish people.

It is not clear why Henry Ford was, even for a short period of his life, so willing to accept anti-Semitism. But Ford was not alone. Groups like the Ku Klux Klan and the German-American Bund, as well as radio personalities like the Catholic priest Charles E. Coughlin, preached about the Jewish conspiracy as if it were fact. By the 1930s, those who held such sentiments usually expressed a fondness for Hitler and showed little concern about Germany's actions against Jews. Even the famed aviator Charles Lindbergh made speeches to gatherings claiming that Jews were forcing the United States into a war so that Jewish people could profit by wartime production. When the barbarous treatment of the Jews by Nazi Germany was exposed, most Americans were horrified by such events, and individuals like Lindbergh were as puzzled as anyone about how some Americans could have been so swept up by the pre–World War II wave of anti-Semitism (G. Meyers, 1943; M. Selzer, 1972).

The next section examines anti-Semitic feelings in contemporary America. But first, consider several crucial differences between anti-Semitism in Europe and in the United States. First, and most important, the U.S. government has never promoted anti-Semitism. Unlike its European counterparts, the U.S. government has never embarked on an anti-Semitic program of expulsion or extermination. Second, because anti-Semitism was never institutionalized in the United States as it has sometimes been in Europe, American Jews have not needed to develop a defensive ideology to ensure the survival of their people. A Jewish American can make a largely personal decision about how much to assimilate or how secular to become. For Jewish Europeans, on the other hand, the major question of life has more often been how to survive, not whether to assimilate (B. Halpern, 1974).

Contemporary Anti-Semitism

Next to social research on anti-Black attitudes and behavior of Whites, anti-Semitism has been the major focus of studies of prejudice by sociologists and psychologists. Most of the conclusions described in Chapter 2 apply equally to the data collected on anti-Semitism. Relatively little concern was expressed by Jews in the United States about anti-Semitism immediately after World War II. From the latter 1960s into the 1990s, however, anti-Semitism has appears to be a threat again in many parts of the world. For example, the infamous *Protocols,* used earlier to promote the notion of an international conspiracy of Jews, resurfaced in the Soviet Union in the 1970s and in Japan in the 1980s (D. A. Harris, 1987; G. Johnson, 1987; T. Smith, 1994).

That anti-Semitism has not disappeared in the United States is shown by this swatiska painted on a high school running track in 1993, the day before graduation ceremonies.

Anti-Semitic incidents in the United States, ranging from desecration to murder, occur annually. In recent years, a rash of anti-Semitism and of "JAP-baiting" has been impossible to ignore on several college campuses. *JAP* is an acronym for "Jewish-American Princess," a stereotyped presentation of young Jewish women as materialistic and obnoxious. "JAP-baiting" has gone beyond joke-telling and has manifested itself as chanting and group harassment at public events such as athletic games (S. Chayat, 1987; L. Dinnerstein, 1988; L. Shapiro, 1988; G. Spencer, 1987).

The Anti-Defamation League (ADL) of B'nai B'rith, founded in 1913, makes an annual survey of anti-Semitic incidents. Although the number has fluctuated, the 1994 tabulation reached the highest level in the 15 years during which the ADL has been recording such incidents. Figure 15.2 shows the rise of harassments, threats, and assaults, which, adding episodes of vandalism, bring the total to 2,066 incidents, including a gunman opening fire on a van filled with Hasidic students in New York City, killing one and wounding three others. A portion of the incidents were inspired by neo-Nazi skinheads—groups of young people who champion racist and anti-Semitic ideologies (Anti-Defamation League of B'nai B'rith, 1993, 1995).

Particularly disturbing has been the upward trend in anti-Semitic incidents on college campuses. In 1994, 143 incidents were reported on 79 campuses—a rise of 17 percent over the year before. Anti-Jewish graffiti, anti-Semitic speakers, and swastikas affixed to predominantly-Jewish fraternities were among those incidents documented (Anti-Defamation League of B'nai B'rith, 1995).

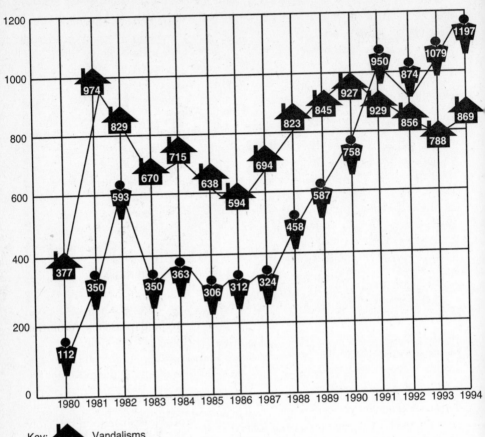

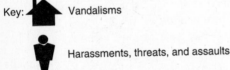

Figure 15.2 **Anti-Semitic Incidents, 1980–1994**
During the 1980s and 1990s, the number of anti-Semitic incidents has fluctuated but in 1994 was at the highest level since the tabulations began in 1980.

Source: Anti-Defamation League of B'nai B'rith (1995, p. 10).

Acts of anti-Semitic violence in the United States, along with the continuing Middle East conflict and the expression of anti-Semitic themes by some African Americans, have prompted renewed national attention to anti-Semitism.

American Jews and Israel When the Middle East became a major hot spot in international affairs in the 1960s, a revival of 1930s anti-Semitism was rekindled. Many Jewish Americans expressed concern that, because Jews are freer in the United States than they have been in perhaps any other country in their history, they would ignore the struggle of other Jews. Israel's precarious status has proven to be a strong source of identity for Jewish Americans. Major wars in the Middle East in 1967, 1973, and 1991 reminded the world of Israel's vulnerability. Palestinian uprisings in the Occupied Territories and international recognition of the Palestine Liberation Organization (PLO) in 1988 eroded the strong pro-Israeli front among the Western powers. A few Jewish Americans have shown their commitment to the Israeli cause by actually emigrating to Israel. Although not all American Jews agree with Israel's actions, many Jews express support for Israel's struggles by contributing money and by trying to influence American opinion and policy to be more favorable to Israel.

The Anti-Defamation League has carefully watched for any trends in disfavor toward Israel. The 1973 oil embargo by the Arab states and the subsequent rise in American gasoline prices led to what some leaders of the ADL identified as an "oil backlash" of people in the United States holding Jews responsible for empty gas tanks. The ADL saw the oil embargo as signaling an end to "the golden age of Jewish life in America," when anti-Jewish feelings were minimal. Arab nations pressured American corporations not to invest in Israel and even not to place Jews in high management positions. The U.S. Army acknowledged in 1975 that it had not sent Jewish soldiers to Saudi Arabia because of that government's pressure. Such stipulations ended during the massive buildup for the 1991 Persian Gulf War (Lichtenstein and Denenberg, 1975; T. Smith, 1994).

In the year after the oil embargo (1974), the United Nations General Assembly ignored American and Israeli objections and passed a resolution declaring that "Zionism is a form of racism and racial discrimination." *Zionism,* which initially referred to the old Jewish religious yearning to return to the biblical homeland, has been expressed in the twentieth century in the movement to create a Jewish state in Palestine. Ever since the diaspora, the exile of Jews from Palestine several centuries before Christianity began, many Jews have seen the destiny of their people only as the establishment of a Jewish state in the Holy Land. The Zionism resolution, finally repealed UN in 1991, had no lasting influence and did not change any nation's foreign policy. It did, however, increase Jewish fears of reawakened anti-Semitism thinly disguised as attacks on Zionist beliefs. Even the development of agreements between Israel and its Arab neighbors and the international recognition of Palestinian autonomy in Israel did not end the concern of Jewish Americans that continuing anti-Israeli feeling reflected anti-Semitism (R. Carroll, 1975; T. Smith, 1994; I. Spiegel, 1973a, 1973b).

American Jews and African Americans   The contemporary anti-Semitism of African Americans is of special concern to Jewish Americans. There is no reason why anti-Semites should be exclusively White, but Jews have been especially troubled by Blacks' expressing ethnic prejudices. Jewish Americans have been active in civil rights causes and have contributed generously to legal defense funds. Jewish neighborhoods and employers have also been quicker to accept African Americans than their Gentile counterparts. There is, therefore, a positive Black-Jewish alliance with a long history. For these reasons, some Jews find it especially difficult to understand why another group experiencing prejudice and discrimination should express anti-Semitic sentiments.

Surveys do not necessarily show significant differences between Blacks and Whites in anti-Semitism, but studies do show a rise among African Americans.

Added to this attitudinal component have been highly publicized events that have brought attention to alleged Black anti-Semitism as well as anti-Black feelings among Jewish Americans (T. Smith, 1990).

Beginning in the 1960s, some African-American activists and the Black Panther Party supported the Arabs in the Middle East Conflict and called on Israel to surrender. Black–Jewish relations were again inflamed during the 1984 campaign by the Reverend Jesse Jackson for the Democratic-Party nomination for the presidency. His off-the-record reference to Jews as "Hymies" and the publicly broadcast anti-Semitic remarks by one of his supporters, the Nation of Islam minister Louis Farrakhan, gave rise to new tensions between Blacks and Jews. During the 1988 campaign, Jackson distanced himself from anti-Semitic rhetoric, stating, "The sons and the daughters of the Holocaust and the sons and the daughters of slavery must find common ground again" (W. Schmidt, 1988, p. 14).

In the 1990s, unrelated events again seemed to draw attention to the relationship between Jews and African Americans. On several college campuses, invited African-American speakers made anti-Israeli statements, inflaming the Jewish students in attendance. In a 1991 New York City incident, a Hasidic Jew ran a red light, killing an African-American child, and the ambulance that regularly serves the Hasidic community did not pick up the child. In the emotional climate that resulted, an Australian Jewish researcher was stabbed to death, and several days of rioting in the Brooklyn, New York, neighborhood of Crown Heights followed (L. Duke, 1993; H. Gates, 1992; R. Morin, 1994; Morris and Rubin, 1993; T. Smith, 1991; K. Stern, 1991).

The 1991 auto tragedy in the Crown Heights area of Brooklyn, New York, heightened tensions between Jews and African Americans. An impromptu memorial appeared for 7-year-old Gavin Cato, killed in the car accident.

In response to these and other events, many Jewish and African-American leaders perceived a crisis in intergroup relations and calls for unity became very public. As just one example, in 1994, Rev. Jesse Jackson sought to distance himself from the statements of Khalid Abdul Muhammad, an aide of Farrakhan, calling him "racist, anti-Semitic, divisive, untrue and chilling" (A. Finder, 1994, p. 21).

African-American resentment, in many situations attracting notoriety, has rarely been anti-Jewish as such but has been opposed to White institutions. As author James Baldwin (1967) said, Blacks "are anti-Semitic because they're anti-White" (p. 114). That racial prejudice is deep in the United States is shown by the fact that two groups suffering discrimination, groups that might unite in opposition to the dominant society, fight each other instead.

An old Yiddish saying, "Schwer zu sein a Yid," means "It is tough to be a Jew." Anti-Semitism past and present is related. The old hostilities seem never to die. The atrocities of Nazi Germany have not been forgotten, nor should they be. Racial and ethnic hostility, whatever group is the victim, unifies the group against its attackers, and Jewish Americans are no exception. The Jewish people of the United States have come together, regardless of nationality, to form a minority group with a high degree of group identity.

POSITION OF JEWISH AMERICANS

Jewish Americans have an important role in contemporary America. They are active participants in the fight for civil rights and work on behalf of Israel. These efforts are important, but for most of the five to six million Jews in the United States they do not involve full-time participation. For a better perspective on Jewish people in the United States, a summary follows of their present situation with respect to (1) employment and income, (2) education, (3) organizational activity, and (4) political activity.

Employment and Income

Discrimination conditions all facets of a subordinate group's life. Jews have experienced, and to a limited extent still experience, differential treatment in the American job market. As recently as 1956, in a survey of employers in San Francisco, one out of four acknowledged that it either barred Jews altogether or limited their employment to a predetermined level. Civil rights acts and U.S. Supreme Court decisions have made it illegal to discriminate in employment. Through perseverance and emphasis on education, Jewish Americans as a group have overcome barriers to full employment and now enjoy high incomes. Survey data indicate that Jews are the wealthiest group of White Americans (A. Greeley, 1976; also see S. Steinberg, 1977).

This high income level does not mean that Jews find it as easy to enter all occupations as Gentiles do. Jewish Americans are conspicuously absent from banks, savings-and-loan institutions, utilities, insurance companies, and major industrial occupations. The legal profession is attractive to Jews, but few enter the prestigious private law firms. Many Jewish professionals find it easiest to work for Jewish law firms or to affiliate with Jewish hospitals (American Jewish Committee, 1965, 1966a, 1966b; De Fleur et al., 1976; J. Porter, 1981; M. Sklare, 1971; Slavin and Pradt, 1982; Zweigenhaft and Domhoff, 1982).

Social science studies using a variety of techniques have shown declining evidence of discrimination against Jews in the business world. Sociologist Samuel Klausner interviewed business school graduates, comparing Jews with Protestants and Roman Catholics who graduated from the same university in the same year. Klausner (1988) concludes that: "(1) Jewish MBAs are winning positions in the same industries as their Catholic and Protestant classmates; (2) they are rising *more* rapidly in corporate hierarchies than their Catholic and Protestant colleagues; (3) they are achieving *higher* salaries than their Catholic and Protestant colleagues" (p. 33). Klausner adds that researchers tested seven indicators of discrimination and, in each case, *failed* to find evidence of discrimination against Jewish executives. Interestingly, however, this same study detected substantial discrimination against African Americans and women.

The economic success of the Jewish people as a group does obscure the poverty of many individual Jewish families. We reached a similar conclusion in Chapter 12 from income data on Asian Americans and their image as a "model minority." Sociologists largely agree that Jews in 1930 were as likely to be poverty-stricken and to be living in slums as any minority group today. Most have escaped poverty, but there remains what Ann Wolfe (1972) calls "the invisible Jewish poor," invisible to the rest of society. Like Chinese Americans, the Jewish poor were not well served by the Economic Opportunity Act and other federal experiments to eradicate poverty in the 1960s and 1970s. Although the proportion of the poor among the Jews is not as substantial as among Blacks or Hispanics, it does remind us that affluence and the lifestyle of all Jewish families are not the same (M. Gold, 1965; A. Lavender, 1977; Levine and Hochbaum, 1974).

Education

Jews are unique among ethnic groups in their emphasis on education. This desire for formal schooling stems, it is argued, from the Judaic religion, which places the rabbi, or teacher, at the center of religious life. In the United States today, all Jewish congregations emphasize religious instruction more than Protestants typically do. The more religiously orthodox require instruction on Sundays as well as on weekday afternoons following attendance at public schools. Eighty-four percent of young men (15–19 years) and 72 percent of young women receive some Jewish education (A. Goren, 1980, p. 596). Jews have created summer camps in which Hebrew is the only language spoken. Theological seminaries provide rabbinic training. The Jewish-sponsored component of higher education, however, is not limited to strict religious instruction. Beginning in 1947, Jews founded graduate schools of medicine, education, social work, and mathematics, along with Brandeis University, which offers both undergraduate and graduate degrees. These institutions are nonsectarian (that is, admission is not limited to Jews) and are conceived of as a Jewish-sponsored contribution to higher education (S. Greenberg, 1970; C. Waxman, 1983).

The religiously based tradition of lifelong study has left as a legacy a value system that stresses education. The poverty of Jewish immigrants kept them from devoting years to secular schooling, but they were determined that their children should do better. Despite their high levels of educational attainment, some members of the Jewish community express concern about Jewish education. They express disappointment with its highly secularized nature—not just that religious teaching has been limited, but that the Jewish sociocultural experience has been avoided altogether. It may even contribute to Judaization, the lessening of Judaism. A group of sociologists (Glock et al., 1975; I. Spiegel, 1975), after uncovering anti-Semitism among a sample of grade school and high school children, recommended that public schools not ignore the history of Judaism or sidestep anti-Semitism. There is no evidence that American public schools have changed curriculum materials to consider the Jewish experience as they have the role of Black Americans. With this secularization of Jewish children, the survival of Jewish identity may be threatened. Secularization may, however, be compensated for by the high level of organizational activity among Jews of all ages.

Organizational Activity

The American Jewish community has encompassed a variety of organizations from the beginning. These groups serve many purposes: some are religious, and others are charitable, political, or educational. No organization, secular or religious, represents all American Jews, but there are more than 300 nationwide organizations. Among the most significant are the United Jewish Appeal (UJA), the American Jewish Committee, the American Jewish Congress, and the B'nai B'rith. The UJA was founded in 1939 and serves as a fund-raising organization for humanitarian causes. Recently, Israel has received the largest share of the funds collected. The American Jewish Committee (founded in 1906) and Congress (1918) work toward the similar purpose of improving Jewish–Gentile relations. B'nai B'rith (Sons of the Covenant) was founded in 1843 and claims 500,000 members in 40 nations. It promotes cultural and social programs and, through its Anti-Defamation League, fights anti-Semitism.

Besides those on the national level, there are many community-based organizations. Some local organizations, such as social and business clubs, were founded because the existing groups barred Jews from membership. The U.S. Supreme Court has consistently ruled that private social organizations like country clubs and business clubs may discriminate against Jews or any ethnic or racial group. Jewish community centers are also prominent local organizations. To Gentiles, the synagogue is the most visible symbol of the Jewish presence at the community level. The Jewish community center, however, serves as an important focus of local activity. In many Jewish neighborhoods throughout the United States, it is the focus of secular activity. Hospitals, nurseries, homes for the elderly, and child care agencies are only a few of the community-level activities sponsored by Jewish Americans (S. Rabinove, 1970; M. Sklare, 1971).

Political Activity

American Jews play a prominent role in politics as both voters and elected officials. Jews as a group are not typical in that they are more likely than the general population to label themselves liberal. Although upper-middle-class voters tend to vote Republican, Jewish voters have been steadfastly Democratic. In the 14 presidential elections beginning in 1940, Jews have voted at least 82 percent Democratic seven times and have always given the Democrats more of their votes than the Republicans. Jewish suburban voters, unlike those in the central cities, tend to be more supportive of Republican candidates but are still more Democratic than their Gentile neighbors. Jews have long been successful in being elected to office, but it was not until 1988 that an Orthodox Jew was elected to the U.S. Senate, from Connecticut. Joseph Lieberman refrained from campaigning on the Sabbath each week; his religious views were not an issue.

While the Democratic candidate, Bill Clinton, was successful in his bid to unseat President George Bush in 1992, with only 43 percent of the vote, an estimated 80 percent of Jewish Americans supported Clinton. After the same election, 44 of the members of the House and 10 members of the Senate were Jewish— about 10 percent of the total membership of Congress. However, the Jewish community does not blindly support Jewish candidates. For example, New York senator D'Amato was heavily backed financially by Jewish lobbyists over his contender, a Jewish candidate, because of D'Amato's strong pro-Israeli position (J. Chanes, 1994).

As in all subordinate groups, the political activity of Jewish Americans has not been limited to conventional electoral politics. Radical Jewish politics has been dominated by college students. At the height of their involvement in the late 1960s, Jewish youths were active with Gentiles in the New Left movement as well as working alone for causes unique to Jews, like the support of Israel. Into the 1980s and 1990s, some Jews backed the more extreme responses to the friction between Israel and its Arab neighbors. A few even settled in Israel and, while small in number, were often vocal backers of resistance to any accommodation to the Arab nations or the Palestinian refugees (J. Porter, 1970).

RELIGIOUS LIFE

Jewish identity and participation in the Jewish religion are not the same. Many Americans consider themselves Jewish and are considered Jewish by others even though they have never participated in Jewish religious life. The available data suggest that about half of American Jews are affiliated with a synagogue, but only one-quarter attend services monthly. Even in Israel, only 30 percent of Jews are religiously observant. Nevertheless, the presence of a religious tradition is an important tie among Jews, even secular Jews (S. Cohen, 1991).

As at this temple in Everett, Washington, many, but not all, Jewish Americans participate in their religious activities.

The unitary Jewish tradition developed in the United States into three sects beginning in the middle of the nineteenth century. The differences among Orthodox, Conservative, and Reformed Judaism are based on the acceptance of traditional rituals. The differences developed out of a desire by some Jews to be less distinguishable from other Americans. Another significant factor in explaining the development of different groups is the absence of a religious elite and bureaucratic hierarchy. This facilitated the breakdown in traditional practices. All three sects embrace a philosophy based on the Torah, the first five books of the Old Testament. Orthodox Jewish life is very demanding, especially in a basically Christian society like the United States. Almost all conduct is defined by rituals that require an Orthodox Jew to reaffirm his or her religious conviction constantly. Most Americans are familiar with *kashrut,* the laws pertaining to permissible and forbidden foods. When strictly adhered to, kashrut governs not only what foods may be eaten (kosher), but how the food is prepared and how it is served and eaten (I. Shenker, 1979). Besides day-to-day practices, Orthodox Jews have weekly and annual observances. Marshall Sklare (1971) summarized the contrast between the Jewish faith and that of the dominant society: "The thrust of Jewish religious culture is sacramental [while] the thrust of American religious culture is moralistic" (p. 111).

Orthodox Jews differ in the degree of their adherence to traditional practices. Among the ultraorthodox are the Hasidic Jews, or Hasidim, who reside chiefly in several neighborhoods in Brooklyn. These neighborhoods and their residents are like another world. To the Hasidim, following the multitude of mitzvahs, or commandments of behavior, is important in the 1980s as it was in the time of Moses.

They wear no garments that mix linen and wool. Men wear a yarmulka, or skullcap, constantly, even while sleeping. Attending a secular college is frowned on. Instead the, men undertake a lifetime of study of the Torah and the accompanying rabbinic literature of the Talmud. Women's education consists of instruction on how to run the home in keeping with Orthodox tradition.

Orthodox children attend special schools so as to meet minimal New York State educational requirements. The devotion to religious study is reflected in this comment by a Hasidic Jew: "Look at Freud, Marx, Einstein—all Jews who made their mark on the non-Jewish world. To me, however, they would have been much better off studying in a *yeshivah* [a Jewish school]. What a waste of three fine Talmudic minds" (H. Arden, 1975, p. 294). Although devoted to their religion, the Hasidim participate in local elections, politics, and employment in outside occupations. All such activities are influenced by their orthodoxy and a self-reliance rarely duplicated elsewhere in the United States (M. Danzger, 1989; C. Liebman, 1973; E. Schoenfeld, 1976; R. Schultz, 1974; *Time*, 1972).

Reformed Jews, though deeply committed to the religious faith, have altered many of the rituals. Women and men usually sit together in Reformed congregations, and some congregations have introduced organ music and choirs. A few have even experimented with observing the Sabbath on Sunday. Circumcision is not mandatory for males. Civil divorce decrees are sufficient and recognized, so that a divorce granted by a three-man rabbinic court is not required before remarriage. Reformed Jews recognize the children of Jewish men and non-Jewish women as Jews with no need to convert. All these practices would be unacceptable to the Orthodox Jew.

Conservative Judaism is a compromise between the rigidity of the Orthodox and the extreme modification of the Reformed. Because of the middle position, the national organization of Conservatives, the United Synagogue of America, strives to create its own identity and seeks to view its traditions as an appropriate, authentic approach to the faith. In Table 15.2 are displayed some results of a national survey on Jewish identification. The three sects include here *both* members *and* nonmembers of local congregations. Reformed Jews are the least likely of the three religious groups to participate in religious events, to be involved in the Jewish community, or to participate in predominantly Jewish organizations. Yet, in Reformed temples there has been an effort in the 1990s to observe religious occasions such as Rosh Hashana (*Religion Week*, 1995).

The one exception in Reformed Jews' relatively low levels of participation is on issues concerning world Jewry, such as Israel or the treatment of Jews in such nations as the former Soviet Union and Iran. For the Orthodox Jew these issues are less important than those strictly related to the observance of the faith. Although no nationwide organized movement advocates this, in recent years Reformed Jews seem to have reclaimed traditions they once rejected. Yet one survey reported that Reformed temples record that anywhere from 7 to 22 percent of the membership is made up of non-Jews (National Jewish Family Center, 1982).

Unlike those of most faiths in the United States, Jews historically have not embarked on recruitment or evangelistic programs to attract new members. Beginning in the late 1970s, Jews, especially Reformed Jews, debated the possibil-

Table 15.2   JEWISH IDENTIFICATION BY GROUP (PERCENTAGES)

Orthodox Jews are the strictest in ritual. The denominations do not differ in their concern about worldwide Jewry. The data are based on a national survey in 1989 of Jewish adults. Higher scores mean greater endorsement of the index factor listed.

Indices	Orthodox	Conservative	Reformed	"Just Jewish"
Ethnic pride	86	79	73	65
Closeness to Jews	90	83	71	54
Observance of Jewish holidays	73	42	28	18
Observance of Christian holidays	6	6	17	28
Pro-Israel	78	71	56	50

Note: Steven M. Cohen, *Content or Continuity? Alternative Bases for Commitment.* New York: American Jewish Committee.

Source: S. Cohen (1991, pp. 58, 63, 74).

ity of outreach programs. Least objectionable to Jewish congregations were efforts begun in 1978 aimed at non-Jewish partners and children in mixed marriages. In 1981, the program was broadened to invite conversions by Americans who had no religious connection, but these modest recruitment drives are still far from resembling those that have been carried out by Protestant denominations for decades (K. Briggs, 1978; *New York Times,* 1982).

The Judaic faith embraces a number of factions or denominations that are similar in their roots but marked by sharp distinctions. No precise data reveal the relative numbers of the three groups. Part of the problem is the difficulty of placing individuals in the proper group. It is common, for example, for a Jew to be a member of an Orthodox congregation but consider himself or herself Conservative. The following levels of affiliation are based on the 1990 National Jewish Population Study (Kosmin et al., 1991) and show ranges depending upon whether one considers only those born Jewish or also those who converted:

- Orthodox: 6–7 percent
- Conservative: 31–38 percent
- Reformed: 42–49 pecent
- Other: 13–14 percent

As with denominations among Protestants, Jewish denominations carry social class, nationality, and other social differences. The Reformed Jews are the wealthiest and best formally educated of the group, the Orthodox are the poorest and least educated in years of formal secular schooling, and the Conservatives occupy a position between the two, as shown in Table 15.3. A fourth branch of American Judaism, Reconstructionism, an offshoot of the Conservative movement, has only recently developed an autonomous institutional structure. Many of the ritual and other differences among the three branches shown in the table may be rooted in

Table 15.3   SOCIAL CHARACTERISTICS OF GROUP (PERCENTAGES)

For every social characteristic there are significant differences among the three groups, as shown in these data from the 1970–1971 National Jewish Population Survey.

Characteristics	Orthodox	Conservative	Reformed
Age: 60 or over	33	30	21
Foreign-born	45	23	8
Parents U.S.-born	5	14	24
College graduates	24	30	37
Income: $20,000+	15	19	31

Source: B. Lazerwitz (1993). Used by permission of the author. Copyright © 1983 by Bernard Lazerwitz and Michael Harrison.

social class. Religious identification is also associated with generation: immigrants tend to be Orthodox and their grandchildren are more likely to be Reformed (S. Cohen, 1988; Goldstein and Goldscheider, 1968; C. Liebman, 1973).

JEWISH IDENTITY

Ethnic and racial identification can be positive or negative. Awareness of ethnic identity can contribute to an individual's self-esteem and give him or her a sense of group solidarity with similar people. When an identity experienced only as a basis for discrimination or insults, the individual may want to shed his or her identity in favor of one more acceptable to society. Unfavorable differential treatment can also encourage closer ties among members of the community being discriminated against, as it has for Jews. Louis Wirth, in his study of Jewish-American slum life, *The Ghetto* (1928), wrote:

> What has held the Jewish community together . . . is . . . the fact that the Jewish community is treated as a community by the world at large. The treatment which the Jews receive at the hands of the press and the general public imposes collective responsibility from without. (p. 270)

Most would judge the diminishing of out-group hostility and the ability of Jews to leave the ghetto as a positive development (G. Friedman, 1967).

The improvement in Jewish–Gentile relations also creates a problem in Jewish social identity not present before. It has become possible for Jews to shed their "Jewishness," or *Yiddishkait*. Many retain their Yiddishkait even in suburbia, but it is more difficult there than in the ghetto. In the end, however, Jews cannot lose their identity entirely. Jews are still denied total assimilation in the United States no matter how much the individual ceases to think of himself or herself as Jewish. Social clubs will still refuse membership and prospective in-laws will still deny their child's hand in marriage. Events in the world also remind the most assimilated Jew of the heritage left behind. A few such reminders in the past generation include Nazi Germany, the founding of Israel in 1948, the Six-Day War of 1967,

Soviet interference with Jewish life and migration, the terrorist attack at the 1972 Munich Olympics, the Yom Kippur War of 1973, the 1973 oil embargo, the UN's 1974 anti-Zionism vote, and the Scud missile attacks during the 1991 Gulf War.

A unique identity issue presents itself to Jewish women, whose religious tradition has placed them in a subordinate position. For example, it was not until 1968 that a Jewish seminary in the United States finally accepted women and men on an equal basis. Jewish feminism has its roots in the recent women's movement, several of whose leaders were Jewish. There have been some changes in *halakha* (Jewish law covering obligations and duties), but it is still difficult for a woman to get a divorce recognized by the Orthodox Jewish tradition. Sima Rabinowicz of upstate New York has been hailed as the "Jewish Rosa Parks" for her recent bus battle. Rabinowicz refused to give up her seat, in the women's section of a Hasidic-owned, publicly subsidized bus, to Orthodox men who wanted to pray in private, segregated from women as required by halakha. The courts defended her right to ride as she wished, just as an earlier court had ruled with Rosa Parks in the Birmingham bus boycott. Jewish women contend that they should not be forced to make a choice between their identities as a woman and as a Jew (D. Cohen, 1994; B. Frankel, 1995a; B. Greenberg, 1992; S. Tenenbaum, 1993).

We will now examine three factors that influence the ethnic identity of Jews in the United States: family, religion, and cultural heritage.

Role of the Family

The Jewish family has been the subject of more novels than the families of probably any other ethnic group. A common theme is the child's struggle to free himself or herself from the mother's domination. Unfortunately, no wealth of social science studies matches the fictional literature. In general, the family performs the functions of childhood socialization and the adult management of sexual desires, but for religious Jews it also fulfills a religious commandment. In the past this compulsion was so strong that the shadchan (the marriage broker or matchmaker) fulfilled an important function in the Jewish community by ensuring marriage for all eligible people. The emergence of romantic love in modern society made the shadchan less acceptable to young Jews, but recent statistics show Jews more likely to marry than any other group.

Jews have traditionally remained in extended families, intensifying the transmission of Jewish identity. Numerous observers have argued that the Jewish family today no longer maintains its role in identity transmission and that the family is consequently contributing to assimilation. The American Jewish Committee released a report in 1976 identifying ten problems that are endangering "the family as the main transmission agent of Jewish values, identity, and continuity" (B. Conver, 1976, p. A2). The following issues are still relevant to Jews nearly two decades later:

1. More Jews marry later than members of other groups.
2. Most organizations of single Jews no longer operate solely for the purpose of matching. These groups are now supportive of singles and the single way of life.

3. The divorce rate is rising; there is no presumption of the permanence of marriage and no stigma attached to its failure.
4. The birthrate is falling, and childlessness has become socially acceptable.
5. Financial success has taken precedence over child raising in importance and, for many has become the major goal of the family.
6. The intensity of family interaction has decreased, although it continues to be higher than in most other religious and ethnic groups.
7. There is less socializing across generational lines, partly as a result of geographic mobility.
8. The sense of responsibility of family members to other family members has declined.
9. The role of Jewishness is no longer central to the lives of Jews.
10. Intermarriage has lessened the involvement of the Jewish partner in Jewish life and the emphasis on Jewish aspects of family life.

Data and sample surveys have verified these trends. To use a term introduced in Chapter 10 in connection with the Chicano family, Jewish Americans still have a higher than typical degree of *familism*. Jews are more likely than other ethnic or religious groups to be members of a household that interacts regularly with kinfolks. Nonetheless, the trend is away from familism, a trend that could further erode Jewish identity.

These problems or concerns are not unique to Jews. Similar problems face other religious or ethnic groups. As a part of the "family values" debate of the 1990s, these same issues of divorce and family disintegration have become a wide concern (B. Farber et al., 1976; M. Sklare, 1971; I. Spiegel, 1974; J. Wertheimer, 1994).

Without question, of the ten problems cited by the American Jewish Committee, intermarriage has received the greatest attention from Jewish leaders. Since Christianity's influence has grown, a persistent fear among Jews has been that their children or grandchildren would grow up to be *amhaaretz*, ignorant of the Torah. Even worse, a descendant might become *apikoros*, an unbeliever who engages in intellectual speculation about the relevance of Judaism. Intermarriage, of course, makes a decrease in the size of the Jewish community in the United States more likely. As the tolerance of mixed marriages rises in the United States, so, too, does Jewish leaders' concern over it, especially since the decrease in cultural differences between Jews and Gentiles makes such marriages a greater possibility. In marriages around 1970, over 70 percent of Jews married Jews or people who converted to Judaism. In marriages since 1985, that proportion has dropped to 48 percent. This change means that American Jews today are just as likely to marry a Gentile as a Jew. Three-quarters of the children of these Jewish–Gentile marriages are not raised as Jews (Kosmin et al., 1991; P. Steinfels, 1992).

Intermarriage, however, need not mean a decline in the number of the faithful. Non-Jewish spouses can convert to Judaism and raise their children in the faith. For example, 60 percent of intermarried Jews still participate in Passover rituals. However, some more traditional Jews question the integrity of these occasional ventures into the faith and see them as further evidence of Judaization. Yet many Jewish leaders respond that intermarriage is inevitable and that the Jewish community must build on whatever links the intermarried couple may still have

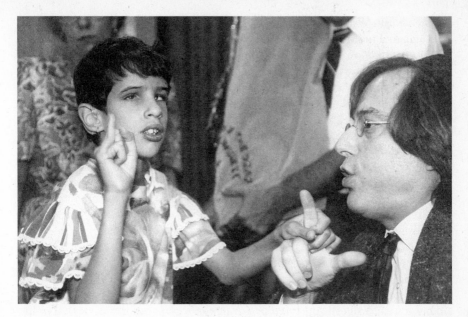

As in other faiths, Jewish leaders seek to reach out to their diverse following. At her bas mitzvah, a girl recites passages from the Torah by signing them to a rabbi who provides outreach to Jews who are deaf.

with their ethnic culture. The increase in intermarriage leads to further anxiety about the survival of religious and cultural traditions. Indeed, there are nearly 600 programs in the United States to help Gentile spouses of Jews feel welcome so that the faith will not lose them both. Yet, other Jews feel that such efforts may be sending a dangerous signal that intermarriage is inevitable (P. Steinfels, 1992; J. Wertheimer, 1994; K. Woodward, 1991).

Role of Religion

Devotion to Judaism appears to be the clear way to preserve ethnic identity. Yet Jews are divided about how to practice their faith. Many of the Orthodox see Reformed Jews as little better than nonbelievers. Even among the Orthodox, some sects like the Lubavitchers try to awaken less observant Orthodox Jews to their spiritual obligation. Added to these developments is the continuing rise in Jewish out-marriages noted above. Many Jewish religious rituals are centered in the home rather than in the synagogue, from lighting Sabbath candles to observing dietary laws. Jews are far more likely, therefore, to feel that children cannot be brought up in the faith without that family support.

The religious question facing Jews is not so much one of ideology as of observing the commandments of traditional Jewish law. The religious variations among the nearly six million Jewish Americans are a product of attempts to accommodate traditional rituals and precepts to life in the dominant society. It is in adhering to such rituals that Jews are most likely to be at odds with the Christian theme advanced in public schools, even if it appears only in holiday parties. In Chapter 1, we introduced the term *marginality* to describe the status of living in two distinct cultures simultaneously. Walter Gerson's (1969) study of Jews at Christmastime was cited as an example of individuals' accommodating themselves to two cultures. For all but the most Orthodox, this acceptance means disobeying commandments or even accepting non-Jewish traditions by singing Christmas carols or exchanging greeting cards.

In "Listen to Their Voices," a college student, Jaclyn Foreman, relates her experience of being Jewish on a predominantly Gentile college campus. For her, the experience of marginality ironically made her more aware of her Yiddishkait, or "Jewishness." Her response is not unlike the third-generation principle advanced by Marcus Hansen (1952) and discussed in Chapter 5. He maintained that ethnic interest and awareness, which decreased among the children of immigrants, would increase in the third generation: "What the son wishes to forget the grandson wishes to remember." Paul Cowan, for example, a writer whose father changed his name from Cohen, embraced Judaism in middle age. Cowan's wife, a Protestant, converted to Judaism as well (C. Silberman, 1985).

Is there a widespread pattern among Jewish Americans of reviving the "old ways"? Some Jews, especially those secure in their position, have taken up renewed orthodoxy. It is difficult to say whether the rise of traditionalism among Jews is a significant force or a fringe movement as it was viewed in the 1960s. Jewish leaders in North America and Europe are much more likely in the 1990s to express concern about the increase in the number of secularized Jews than to find reasons to applaud an increase in Yiddishkait (R. Gledhill, 1992).

Role of Cultural Heritage

For many Jews, religious observance is a very small aspect of their Jewishness. They express their identity instead in a variety of political, cultural, and social activities. For them, acts of worship, fasting, eating permitted foods, and the study of the Torah and the Talmud are irrelevant to being Jewish. Religious Jews, of course, find such a position impossible to accept (C. Liebman, 1973).

Many Gentiles mistakenly suppose that a measure of Jewishness is the ability to speak Yiddish. Few people have spoken as many languages as the Jews through their long history. Yiddish is only one, and it developed in Jewish communities in eastern Europe between the tenth and twelfth centuries. Fluency in Yiddish in the United States has been associated with the immigrant generation and the Orthodox. Sidney Goldstein and Calvin Goldscheider (1968) reported that evidence overwhelmingly supports the conclusion that linguistic assimilation among Jews is almost complete by the third generation (see also I. Shenker, 1974). The 1960s and 1970s, however, brought a slight increase in the use of Hebrew. This change was probably due to increased pride in Israel and a greater interaction between that nation and the United States.

Overall, the differences between Jews and Gentiles have declined in the United States. To a large extent, this reduction is a product of generational changes typical of all ethnic groups. The first-generation Mexican American in Los Angeles contrasts sharply with the middle-class White living in suburban Boston. The con-

Listen to Their Voices
Being Jewish Among Gentiles

JACLYN FOREMAN

I am a college student at a somewhat small Midwestern University. There are people here of all backgrounds, races, ethnicities, and religions. One religion, or ethnicity, that is not as abundant is Judaism. I know, because I am Jewish. I now know what it feels like to be a minority.

Jaclyn Foreman

Where I come from, a medium-sized suburb of Chicago, I am not different. It is not unknown to people how Jewish people live. I grew up in a predominantly Jewish neighborhood, and I did not feel like an outcast. People were not ignorant of the Jewish religion. I was part of the majority.

When I started attending an out-of-school town, I noticed that there were not many Jewish people. Most of the people that I have met are very curious about my lifestyle and do not judge me because of my religion. Many questions are asked, and I answer them to the best of my knowledge. Then there are those that make very rude comments about me: "No kike jokes, there's one present," or "You must be cheap." And the not-so-rude ones, but just stupid, like the ever-popular, "Where's your beanie?" I realize that if people are not around Jewish people, they may not know how we live. From what I've heard, most people think that all Jewish people are Hassidic like they see on television. I explain to them that all Jewish people are not the same.

Before coming here to school, I was not very into my religion. I did not attend temple, and I was not very faithful to my family's religious beliefs. After hearing what I have heard and seeing what I have seen, I have come to realize how important it is to be faithful to my religion. I wear a Star of David, which I get many comments on, some of them very cruel, and I am proud to be Jewish. If someone finds it necessary to condemn me because of my beliefs, then I would rather not associate with them.

Most people do not believe that I am Jewish because, according to them, I am not a JAP (Jewish-American Princess). I am not the "typical" Jewish girl. "What is the typical Jewish girl?" I wonder. People are not typical; they just have different kinds of lifestyles. Of all the Jewish people I know, very few are what Jewish people are said to be.

Of course, times have changed a bit since the 1940s and 1950s, when my grandfather was fired from a job as soon as his religion was found out, or when my father was harassed and picked on because he was Jewish. Unfortunately, there are still many people who feel as if we should not exist. It is very hard for me to understand those views, and I probably never will. I am a person, just like everyone else.

Listen to Their Voices   *Continued*

The hardest time for me is the holidays. On Chanukah, I was not able to find a card, except for a few in a popular national chain store; much less was I able to find decorations. My family sent me the traditional Chanukah gelt, a dradel, and some decorations from home, so I could join in the festivities of the holidays. Being surrounded by only Christmas fun was not bad, but it made me feel like an outcast. It was then that I really felt different. When Passover arrived, I had brought kosher Passover foods from home, because these foods are not easily found where I live. I had a little Passover service with my friends, so I could sort of show them what its like. It was fun, but not the same. It would have helped if there had been a place to go so I could have a service with others who were in the same boat as I was. There was no place like that to be found. No place to worship. No place to be myself and pray on the holiday.

I took a class about minorities, and found out what a small population there is of Jewish people in this world. In order for us to survive, we need to put the past behind and live as we were meant to.

I am a minority, even though it is not apparent on the outside. I do not need to look like one, because I feel like one.

There is no cure for anti-Semitism, just as there is no cure for any type of racism. I have a responsibility to myself and to my family to carry on with my religion. Ignorance will not ever take that away from me, no matter how hard people try. People should not be judged by their religious beliefs, but by their human beliefs. I am not inferior nor superior; I am an equal. If everyone felt this way and banded together, maybe prejudice will fade away, just as the smoke did after the Holocaust.

vergence in culture and identity is much greater between the fourth-generation Chicano and his or her White counterpart. A similar convergence is occurring among Jews. This change does not mean the eventual demise of the Jewish identity. Moreover, Jewish identity is not a single identity, as we can see from the heterogeneity in religious observance, dedication to Jewish and Israeli causes, and participation in Jewish organizations.

Being Jewish comes from the family, the faith, and the culture, but it does not require any one criterion. Jewishness transcends nation, religion, or culture. A sense of *peoplehood* is present that neither anti-Semitic bigotry nor even an ideal state of fellowship would destroy. American life may have drastically modified Jewish life in the direction of dominant society values, but it has not eliminated it. Milton Gordon (1964) refers to peoplehood as a group with a shared feeling (pp. 23–24). For Jews this sense of identity originates from a variety of sources, past and present, both within and without (S. Heilman, 1982; H. Himmelfarb, 1982; C. Liebman, 1973).

CONCLUSION

Jewish Americans are the product of three waves of immigration originating from three different Jewish communities: the Sephardic, the western European, and the eastern European. They brought different languages and, to some extent, different levels of religious orthodoxy. Today, they have assimilated to form an ethnic group that transcends the initial differences in nationality. Not that Jews are a homogeneous group. Among them are the Reformed, the Conservative, and Orthodox denominations, listed in ascending order of adherence to traditional rituals.

Nonreligious Jews make up another group, probably as large as any one segment, and still look on themselves as Jewish.

Jewish identity is reaffirmed from within and outside the Jewish community; however, both sources of affirmation are less strong today. Identity is strengthened by the family, religion, and the vast network of national and community-based organizations. Anti-Semitism outside the Jewish community strengthens the in-group feeling and the perception that survival as a people is threatened.

Today, American Jews face a new challenge: they must maintain their identity in an overwhelmingly Christian society in which discrimination is fading and outbreaks of prejudice are sporadic. Yiddishkait may not so much have decreased as changed. Elements of the Jewish tradition have been shed in part because of modernization and social change. Some of this social change—a decline in anti-Semitic violence and restrictions—is certainly welcome. While kashrut observance has declined, the vast majority of Jews care deeply about Israel, and many engage in pro-Israel activities. Commitment has changed with the times, but it has not disappeared (S. Cohen, 1988).

Some members of the Jewish community view the apparent assimilation with alarm and warn against the grave likelihood of the total disappearance of a sizable and identifiable Jewish community in the United States. Others see the changes not as erosion but as an accommodation to a pluralistic, multicultural environment. We are witness to a progressive change in the substance and style of Jewish life. According to this view, Jewish identity, the Orthodox and Conservative traditions notwithstanding, has shed some of its traditional characteristics and has acquired others. The strength of this view comes with the knowledge that doomsayers have been present in the American Jewish community for at least two generations. Only the passage of time will divulge the nature of Jewish life in the United States (I. Finestein, 1988; N. Glazer, 1990).

Despite their successes, Jews experience discrimination and prejudice, as does any subordinate group. Michael Lerner (1993), editor of the liberal Jewish journal *Tikkun*, declares that "Jews can only be deemed 'white' if there is massive amnesia on the part of non-Jews about the monumental history of anti-Semitism" (p. 33). As we noted earlier, reports of episodes of anti-Semitism are on the increase in Europe and North America, even on the college campuses in the United States.

Although discrimination against the Jews has gone on for centuries, far more ancient than anti-Semitism and the experience of the diaspora is the subordinate role of women. Women were perhaps the first to be relegated to an inferior role and may be the last to work collectively to struggle for equal rights. Studying women as a subordinate group will reaffirm the themes in our study of racial and ethnic groups.

KEY TERMS

anti-Semitism Anti-Jewish prejudice or discrimination.

fringe-of-values theory Behavior which is on the border of conduct that a society regards as proper and which is often carried out by subordinate groups, subjecting those groups to negative sanctions.

halakha Jewish laws covering obligations and duties.

Holocaust revisionists Individuals who deny the Nazi effort to exterminate the Jews or who minimize the numbers killed.

in-group virtues Proper behavior by one's own group ("in-group virtues") becomes unacceptable when practiced by outsiders ("out-group vices").

Judaization The lessening importance of Judaism as a religion and the substitution of cultural traditions as the tie that binds Jews.

kashrut Laws pertaining to permissible (kosher) and forbidden foods and their preparation.

noshrim Immigrants who have discarded all traces of Jewish religious faith and commitment to the larger Jewish community.

out-group vices See *in-group virtues,* above.

peoplehood Milton Gordon's term for a group with a shared feeling.

Yiddishkait Jewishness.

Zionism Traditional Jewish religious yearning to return to the biblical homeland, now used to refer to support for the State of Israel.

FOR FURTHER INFORMATION

American Jewish Yearbook. New York: American Jewish Committee.

> Published annually since 1899, this is the best available reference book on Jewish Americans. Each edition contains different articles plus updated biographies and bibliographies.

M. Herbert Danzger. *Returning to Tradition.* New Haven: Yale University Press, 1989.

> A study of nonobservant Jewish families who have chosen to become practicing Orthodox Jews.

Leonard Dinnerstein. *Anti-Semitism in America.* New York: Oxford University Press, 1994.

> Historian Dinnerstein provides a comprehensive survey of anti-Semitism in the United States.

David G. Goodman and Masanori Miyazawa. *Jews in the Japanese Mind: The History and Uses of a Cultural Stereotype.* Champaign: University of Illinois Press, 1995.

> Demonstrates how Anti-Semitism exists throughout the world even in nations with virtually no Jews.

David M. Gordis and Yoan Ben-Horim, eds. *Jewish Identity in America.* Los Angeles: University of Judaism, 1991.

> A collection of conference papers on the topic of the elusive Jewish identity in a multicultural society.

Frederic Cople Jaher. *A Scapegoat in the New Wilderness.* Cambridge: Harvard University Press, 1994.

Traces U.S. intolerance of Jews, beginning with their arrival in 1654, and through the Civil War.

Charles S. Liebman and Steven M. Cohen. *Two Worlds of Judaism: The Israeli and American Experiences.* New Haven: Yale University Press, 1990.

The authors explore how Israeli and American Jews differ in how they conceptualize their Judaism.

Jack Nelson. *Terror in the Night: The Klan's Campaign Against the Jews.* New York: Simon & Schuster, 1993.

Journalist Nelson describes the efforts by the Ku Klux Klan against Jews in the South during the 1960s.

Marshall Sklare. *Observing America's Jews.* Hanover, NH: Brandeis University Press, 1993.

A collection of the famed sociologist's lifework on the Jewish community in the United States.

Periodicals

The Jewish community is served by many newspapers and periodicals, including the weekly *Commentary* (established in 1946), as well as *Tikkun* (1986). Journals include *Judaism* (1952), *The Jewish Journal of Sociology* (1958), the *Jewish Review* (1946), *Contemporary Jewry* (1975), and *Jewish Social Studies* (1938).

CRITICAL THINKING QUESTIONS

1. Why are the Jewish people most accurately characterized as an ethnic group?
2. How have the patterns of anti-Semitism changed or remained the same?
3. Why do African-American–Jewish-American relationships receive special scrutiny?
4. Why is maintaining Jewish identity so difficult in the United States?
5. Why does the family play such a critical role in Jewish identity?

OTHER PATTERNS OF DOMINANCE

Chapter *16*

Women: The Oppressed Majority

Chapter Outline

Highlights

Subordinate status means confinement to subordinate roles not justified by an individual's abilities. Society is increasingly aware that women are a subordinate group. There are biological differences between males and females even if not among races and nationalities; however, one must separate differences of gender from those produced by *sexism,* distinctions that results from socialization. The *feminist movement* did not begin with the women's movement of the 1960s but has a long history and, like protest efforts by other subordinate groups, has not been warmly received by society. A comparison of the socioeconomic position of men and women leaves little doubt that opportunities are unequal in employment and political power. Minority women occupy an especially difficult position, in that they experience subordinate status by virtue of their race or ethnicity as well as their gender.

Women are an oppressed group; they are a social minority in the United States and throughout Western society. Men dominate in influence, prestige, and wealth. Women do occupy positions of power, but those who do are the exception, as evidenced by newspaper accounts that declare "she is the first woman" or "the only female" to be in a particular position.

Many people, men and women, find it difficult to conceptualize women as a subordinate group. After all, women do not live in ghettos. They no longer have to attend inferior schools. They freely interact and live with their alleged oppressors, men. How, then, are they a subordinate group? Let us reexamine the five properties of a subordinate or minority group introduced in Chapter 1:

1. Women have physical and cultural characteristics that distinguish them from the dominant group (men).
2. Women do experience unequal treatment. Although they are not residentially segregated, they are victims of prejudice and discrimination.
3. Membership in the subordinate group is involuntary.
4. Through the rise of contemporary feminism, women have become increasingly aware of their subordinate status and have developed a greater sense of group solidarity.
5. Women are not forced to marry, yet many women feel that their subordinate status is most irrevocably defined within marriage.

In this chapter, the similarities between women and racial and ethnic groups will become apparent.

The most common analogy among minorities used in the social sciences is the similarity between the status of African Americans and that of women. Blacks are considered a minority group, but, one asks, how can women of all groups be so similar in condition? An entire generation has observed and participated in both the civil rights movement and the women's movement. A background of suffrage campaigns, demonstrations, sit-ins, lengthy court battles, and self-help groups are common to the movement for equal rights for both women and African Americans. But similarities were recognized long before the recent protests against inequality. In *An American Dilemma* (1944), the famous study of race described in Chapter 1, Gunnar Myrdal observed that a parallel to the Blacks' role in society was found among women. Others, like Helen Mayer Hacker (1951, 1974), later elaborated on the similarities.

What do these groups have in common besides recent protest movements? The negative stereotypes directed at the two groups are quite similar: both have been considered emotional, irresponsible, weak, or inferior. Their status is even rationalized by "Women's place is in the home." Both are thought to fight subtly against the system: women allegedly try to outwit men by feminine wiles, as Blacks allegedly outwit Whites by pretending to be deferential or respectful. To these stereotypes must be added another similarity: neither women nor African Americans are accepting a subordinate role in society any longer.

Nearly all Whites give lip service to, even if they do not wholeheartedly believe, the contention that African Americans are innately equal to Whites. They are inherently the same. But men and women are not the same, and they vary most dramatically in their roles in reproduction. Biological differences have contributed to sexism. *Sexism* refers to the ideology that one sex is superior to the other. Quite different is the view that there are few differences between the sexes. Such an idea is expressed in the concept of *androgyny*. An androgynous model of behavior permits people to see that persons can be both aggressive *and* expressive, depending on the requirements of the situation. People do not have to be locked into the labels *masculine* and *feminine*. In the United States, people disagree widely as to what implications, if any, the biological differences between the sexes have for social roles. We will begin our discussion of women as a subordinate group by treating this topic.

GENDER ROLES

Males and females are not biologically the same, nor are the sociocultural expectations and opportunities for men and women. How much do the biological differences of men and women contribute to their cultural differences? While research continues to unravel male–female differences, we already know the major distinctions: women can bear children, and men typically excel in physical strength. Even if these distinctions are clarified, their real meaning is dictated by the manner in which a society interprets and uses them (S. Bem, 1994).

Gender roles are society's expectations regarding the proper behavior, attitudes, and activities of males and females. "Toughness" has traditionally been seen in the United States as masculine—and desirable only in men—while "tenderness" has been viewed as feminine. A society may require that one sex or the other take the primary responsibility for the socialization of the children, economic support of the family, or religious leadership.

Without question, socialization has a powerful impact on the development of females and males in the United States. Indeed, the gender roles first encountered in early childhood are often a factor in defining a child's popularity. Sociologists Patricia and Peter Adler (1994) observed elementary-school children and found that boys typically achieved high status on the basis of their athletic ability, "coolness," toughness, social skills, and success in relationships with girls. By contrast, girls gained popularity based on their parents' economic background and their own physical appearance, social skills, and academic success.

Sociologist David Miller (1995) has studied the socialization of children by comparing the toys marketed to girls and boys in the United States. Toys created for girls tend to reinforce traditional female gender roles by focusing on familial relationships, nurturing and cooperative activity, fashion, style, and beauty. By contrast, toys created for boys are often action figures; these toys focus on command, control, aggression, and violence. There is even an entire category of assaultive toys for boys, ranging from plastic knives and grenades to multipurpose assault weapons.

It may be obvious how males and females are conditioned to assume certain roles, but the origin of gender roles as we know them is less clear. Many studies have been done on laboratory animals, for example injecting monkeys and rats with doses of male and female hormones. Primates in their natural surroundings have been closely observed for the presence and nature of gender roles. Animal studies do not point to instinctual gender differences similar to what humans are familiar with as masculinity and femininity. Historically, women's work came to be defined as a consequence of the birth process. Men, free of child care responsibilities, generally became the hunters and foragers for food. Even though women must bear children, men could have cared for the young. Exactly why women were assigned that role in some societies is not known. Women's role has not been the same cross-culturally. Furthermore, we know that definitions of masculinity and femininity change in a society. For example, the men in the royal courts of Europe in the late 1700s fulfilled present-day stereotypes of feminine behavior in their display of ornamental dress and personal vanity rather than resembling the men of a century later. The social roles of the sexes have no constants in time or space (J. Bernard, 1975; E. Kessler, 1976; Martin and Voorhies, 1975).

SOCIOLOGICAL PERSPECTIVES

Through socialization, people are labeled by virtue of their sex. Certain activities and behaviors are associated with men and others with women. Besides the labeling perspective, we can also employ functionalist and conflict perspectives to grasp more firmly how gender roles develop.

Functionalists maintain that sex differentiation has contributed to overall social stability. Sociologists Talcott Parsons and Robert Bales (1955) argued that, to function most efficiently, the family requires adults who will specialize in particular roles. They believed that the arrangement of gender roles with which they were familiar had arisen because marital partners needed a division of labor.

The functionalist view is initially persuasive in explaining the way in which women and men are typically brought up in U.S. society. It would lead us, however, to expect even girls and women with no interest in children to still become babysitters and mothers. Similarly, males with a caring feeling for children may be "programmed" into careers in the business world. Clearly, such a differentiation between the sexes can have harmful consequences for the individual who does not fit into specific roles, while depriving society of the optimal use of many talented individuals who are confined by sexual labeling. Consequently, the conflict perspective is increasingly convincing in its analysis of the development of gender roles.

Conflict theorists do not deny the presence of a differentiation by sex. In fact, they contend that the relationship between females and males has been one of unequal power, men being dominant over women. Men may have become powerful in preindustrial times because their size, physical strength, and freedom from childbearing duties allowed them to dominate women physically. In contemporary societies, such considerations are not as important; yet cultural beliefs about the sexes are now long-established.

Both functionalists and conflict theorists acknowledge that it is not possible to change gender roles drastically without dramatic revisions in a culture's social structure. Functionalists see potential social disorder, or at least unknown social consequences, if all aspects of traditional sex differentiation are disturbed. Yet, for conflict theorists, no social structure is ultimately desirable if it has to be maintained through the oppression of a majority of its citizens (Miller and Garrison, 1982; Schaefer and Lamm, 1995).

The labeling approach emphasizes how the media, even in the present, display traditional gender-role patterns. For example, the portrayal of women and men on television has tended to reinforce conventional gender roles. A cross-cultural content analysis of television advertising in the United States, Mexico, and Australia found that sexual stereotyping was common in all three countries. Australia was found to have the lowest level of stereotyping, but even in that country, feminist groups were working to eliminate the "use of the woman's body to sell products" (Courtney and Whipple, 1983; M. Gilly, 1988).

In the United States, women have traditionally been presented on prime-time television as homemakers, nurses, and household workers—positions that reflect stereotyped notions of women's work. However, by the late 1980s, women had achieved a better image on prime-time programs. A 1987 study found that 75 percent of the women portrayed on these shows were employed outside the home; only about 8 percent were full-time homemakers. Indeed, television seemed to be presenting an overly favorable picture of the types of jobs women held. In 1987, more than half the women characters on prime-time shows had professional careers, while only 25 percent worked in clerical or service jobs. Researchers noted that the real-life portrait was "almost exactly reversed": 47 percent of women held clerical or service jobs, while only 24 percent worked in professional or managerial jobs. Despite the improved media portrayal, by 1993 women still constituted only 37 percent of all prime-time television characters (D. Cabrera, 1989; D. Gable, 1993b, 1993c; Waters and Huck, 1989).

Women's roles have changed significantly since the early 1960s, when women were generally depicted in the media as mothers, as shown in the popular television series "Leave it to Beaver".

Knowledge about the similarity of the sexes and the establishment of equal opportunity for men and women are not the same. Feminists, both male and female, have struggled to allow the sexes to have the same options. It has not been an easy struggle, as documented in the next section.

THE FEMINIST MOVEMENT

Women's struggle for equality, like the struggles of other subordinate groups, has been long and multifaceted. From the very beginning, women activists and sympathetic men who spoke of equal rights were ridiculed and scorned.

In a formal sense, the American feminist movement was born in upstate New York, in a town called Seneca Falls, in the summer of 1848. On July 19, the first women's rights convention began, attended by Elizabeth Cady Stanton, Lucretia Mott, and other pioneers in the struggle for women's rights. This first wave of feminists, as they are currently known, battled ridicule and scorn as they fought for legal and political equality for women, but they were not afraid to risk controversy on behalf of their cause. In 1872, for example, Susan B. Anthony was arrested for attempting to vote in that year's presidential election.

All social movements—and feminism is no exception—have been marked by factionalism and personality conflicts. The civil rights movement and pan-Indianism have been hurt repeatedly by conflicts over what tactics to use and which reforms to push for first, not to mention personality conflicts. Despite similar divisiveness, the women's movement struggled on toward its major goal: to gain the right to vote (J. Sochen, 1982).

The Suffrage Movement

The *suffragists* worked for years to get women the right to vote. From the beginning, this reform was judged to be crucial. If women voted, it was felt, other reforms would quickly follow. The struggle took so long that many of the initial advocates of women's suffrage died before victory was reached. In 1879, an amendment to the Constitution was introduced that would have given women the right to vote. Not until 1919 was it finally passed, and not until the next year was it ratified as the Nineteenth Amendment to the Constitution.

The opposition to women voting came from all directions. Liquor interests and brewers correctly feared that women would assist in passing laws restricting or prohibiting the sale of their products. The South feared the influence more Black voters (that is, Black women) might have. Southerners had also not forgotten the pivotal role women had played in the abolitionist movement. Despite the opposition, the suffrage movement succeeded in gaining women the right to vote, a truly remarkable achievement because it had to rely on male legislators to do so (J. Sochen, 1982).

The Nineteenth Amendment did not automatically lead to other feminist reforms. Women did not vote as a bloc and have not themselves been elected to office in proportion to their numbers. The single-minded goal of suffrage was, in several respects, harmful to the cause of feminism. Many suffragists thought that any changes more drastic than granting the vote would destroy the home. They rarely questioned the subordinate role assigned to women. For the most part, agitation for equal rights ended when suffrage was gained. In the 1920s and 1930s, large numbers of college-educated women entered professions, but these individual achievements did little to enhance the rights of women as a group. The feminist movement as an organized effort that gained national attention faded, to regain prominence only in the 1960s (J. Freeman, 1975; W. O'Neill, 1969; A. Rossi, 1964).

Nevertheless, the women's movement did not die out completely in the first half of the century. Many women carried on the struggle in new areas. Margaret Sanger fought for legalized birth control. She opened birth control clinics because the medical profession refused to distribute birth control information. Sanger and Katherine Houghton Hepburn (mother of the actress Katharine Hepburn) lobbied Congress for reform throughout the 1920s and 1930s. Sanger's early clinics were closed by the police. Not until 1937 were nationwide restrictions on birth control devices lifted, and some state bans remained in force until 1965.

The Women's Liberation Movement

Ideologically, the women's movement of the 1960s had its roots in the continuing feminist movement that began with the first subordination of women in Western society, whenever that was. Psychologically, it grew in America's kitchens, as women felt unfulfilled and did not know why, and in the labor force, as women were made to feel guilty for no real reason. Demographically, by the 1960s, women had greater control over their reproductive capability by using contraception and hence had greater control over the size of the population (Heer and Grossbard-Shectman, 1981).

Sociologically, several events delayed progress in the mid-1960s. The civil rights movement and the antiwar movement were slow to embrace women's rights. The New Left seemed as sexist as the rest of society. Groups protesting the draft and demonstrating on college campuses generally rejected women as leaders and assigned them to preparing refreshments and publishing organization newsletters. The core of early feminists often knew each other from participating in other protest or reform groups that had initially been unwilling to accept women's rights as a legitimate goal. Beginning in about 1967, as Chapter 7 showed, the movement for Black equality was no longer as willing to accept help from sympathetic Whites. White men moved on to protest the draft, a cause not as crucial to women's lives. While somewhat involved in the antiwar movement, many White women began to struggle for their own rights, although at first they had to fight alone. Existing groups of women in nontraditional roles, like the 180,000-member Federation of Business and Professional Women, explicitly avoided embracing the feminist cause. Eventually, civil rights groups, the New Left, and most established women's groups endorsed the feminist movement with the zeal of new converts, but initially, they resisted the concerns of the growing number of feminists (J. Freeman, 1973, 1983).

A focal point of the feminist movement during the 1970s and early 1980s was the Equal Rights Amendment (ERA). First proposed to Congress in 1923, it was finally passed in 1972. The amendment declared that "Equality of rights under the law shall not be denied or abridged by the United States or by any State on account of sex." However, the ERA, like other constitutional amendments, requires approval of three-fourths, or 38, of the state legislatures. Ten years later, it had failed to meet this number by only three states. Clearly, the failure of the ERA effort was discouraging to the movement and its leaders. In many states, they had been outspent by their opponents, and in some states, they were outorganized by effective anti-ERA groups and insurance companies, which feared that their sex-differentiated insurance and pension plan payments would be threatened by the passage of an ERA. Ironically, these same insurance practices were overturned in the courts in 1983 (E. Langer, 1976; J. O'Reilly, 1982).

The movement has also brought about a reexamination of men's roles. Supporters of "male liberation" wished to free men from the constraints of the masculine value system. There is as much a masculine mystique as a feminine one. Boys are socialized to think that they should be invulnerable, fearless, decisive, and even emotionless in some situations. Men are expected to achieve physically and occupationally at some risk of their own values, not to mention those of others. Failure to take up these roles and attitudes can mean that a man will be considered less than a man. Male liberation is the logical counterpart of female liberation. If women are to redefine their gender role successfully, men must redefine theirs as workers, husbands, and fathers (Cicone and Ruble, 1978; W. Farrell, 1974; L. Richardson, 1981; J. Sawyer, 1972; Schaefer and Lamm, 1995).

Just as people have objected to the establishment of minority rights, they have had a negative response to the call for women's rights. Most recently, this view took hold after the 1994 election year. Some men saw themselves as victims whose power had been diminished by affirmative action, Title IX provisions upgrading women's sports, and unfair accusations of sexual harassment. Calling themselves *angry white men* (or AWM), these men hope to define a new political era. Feminists and others see the concern given to White males as deflecting attention from the "real issues" and as another example of blaming the victim. While the AWM contingent does not appear to be mobilizing into an organized social movement, its very presence in the national conversation confirms that women's rights are still an ideal and not a reality (E. Dionne, 1995; T. Edsall, 1995; K. Pollitt, 1995).

Amid the many changing concerns since the mid-1960s, the thinking in the feminist movement has undergone significant change. Betty Friedan, a founder of the National Organization for Women (NOW), argued in the early 1960s that women had to recognize the *feminine mystique,* which meant thinking of themselves only as their children's mother and their husband's wife. Later, in the 1980s, though not denying that women deserved to have the same options in life as men, she called for restructuring the "institution of home and wife." Friedan and others recognize that many young women are now frustrated when they are unable to do it all: career, marriage, and motherhood. Difficult issues remain, and there is much discussion and some debate among feminists over new concerns such as domestic violence and male bias in medical research (Ferree and Hess, 1994; B. Friedan, 1963, 1981, 1991; C. Somners, 1994)

WOMEN'S STATUS

Americans are constantly reminded of women's poor social status. The Commission on Civil Rights (1976b) concluded that the passage in the Declaration of Independence proclaiming that all men are created equal has been taken too literally for too long. Besides recognizing disparities in political and employment rights, the commission concluded that women are discriminated against in every facet of American society. The following section assesses the position of women in (1) employment, (2) education, (3) family life, and (4) political activity. The appropriateness of studying women as a social minority will become apparent in this evaluation of their status relative to men in these four areas.

Employment

Women experience all the problems in employment associated with other subordinate groups and several that are especially acute for women. Women's subordinate role in the occupational structure is largely the result of institutional discrimination, rather than individual discrimination. Women, more than any other group, are confined to certain occupations. Some sex-typed jobs for women pay well above the minimum wage and carry moderate prestige, like nursing and teaching. Nevertheless, they are far lower in pay and prestige than such stereotyped male

Women have begun to enter occupations formerly held exclusively by men, but full acceptance is developing slowly.

positions as physician, college president, or university professor. When they do enter nontraditional positions, women as a group receive lower wages or salary.

What about women aspiring to crack the "glass ceiling"? The phrase *glass ceiling,* as noted in Chapter 3, refers to the barrier blocking the promotion of a qualified worker because of gender or minority membership. Despite debate in the 1990s over affirmative action, the consensus is that there is little room at the top for women and minorities. The glass ceiling operates like a steel cage: all applicants may be welcomed by a firm, but when it comes to the powerful or more visible positions, there are limits on the number of women and nonwhites welcomed or even tolerated. Women are doing better in top management positions than minorities, but they still lag well behind men according to the 1995 report of the Federal Glass Ceiling Commission: only 5 percent of all senior managers are women because of a variety of barriers as listed in Table 16.1 (Department of Labor, 1995).

Women are still viewed differently in the world of management. In making hiring decisions, executives may assume that women are not serious about their commitment to the job and will be "distracted" by family and home. They assume that women are on a *mommy track*—a problematic career track for women who want to divide their attention between work and family. Not only is this assumption about all women false, but it also implies that corporate men are not interested in maintaining a balance between work and family (F. Schwartz, 1989).

Labor Force   The data in Table 16.2 present an overall view of the male dominance of high-paying occupations. Among the representative occupations chosen, men unquestionably dominate in high-paying professions and managerial occupations. Women dominate as secretaries, seamstresses, health service workers, and household workers. Trends show the proportions of women increasing slightly in the professions, indicating that women have advanced into better-paying positions, but these gains have not changed the overall picture.

How pervasive is segregation by gender in the workforce? To what degree are women and men concentrated in different occupations? Researchers have compiled a "segregation index" to estimate the percentage of women who would have to change their jobs to make the distribution of men and women in each occupation mirror the relative percentage of each sex in the adult working population. This study showed that 58 percent of women workers would need to switch jobs in order to create a labor force without sex segregation (J. Jacobs, 1990; Reskin and Blau, 1990). More recent studies indicate that there has been a decline in such segregation over the last 90 years, but its significance remains (B. Reskin, 1993).

While occupational segregation by gender continues, women have increased their participation in the labor force. A greater proportion of women seek and obtain paid employment than ever before in United States history. In 1890, fewer than one in seven workers was a woman, compared to almost one in two in 1992. The most dramatic rise in the female workforce has been among married women. In 1993, 58 percent of married women worked, compared to fewer than 5 percent

Table 16.1   MAJOR BARRIERS TO WOMEN'S EXECUTIVE ADVANCEMENT

Initial placement and clustering in relatively dead-end staff jobs or highly technical professional jobs.

Lack of mentoring.

Lack of management training.

Lack of opportunities for career development.

Lack of opportunities for training tailored to the individual.

Lack of rotation to line positions or job assignments that are revenue producing.

Little or no access to critical developmental assignments, including service on highly visible task forces and committees.

Different standards for performance evaluation.

Biased rating and testing systems.

Little or no access to informal networks of communication.

Counterproductive behavior and harassment by colleagues.

Source: Glass Ceiling Commission as found in Department of Labor (1995).

Table 16.2   EMPLOYMENT OF WOMEN IN SELECTED OCCUPATIONS, 1950 AND 1993

Most occupations are routinely filled by members of one sex.

Occupation	Women as a Percentage of All Workers in the Occupation	
	1950	1993
Professional workers	40	53
Engineers	1	9
Lawyers and judges	4	23
Physicians	7	22
Registered nurses	98	95
College teachers	23	43
Other teachers	75	75
Sales workers	35	48
Clerical workers	62	79
Machine operators	34	39
Transport operatives	1	9
Service workers	57	60

Sources: Bureau of the Census (1994, pp. 407–408); Department of Labor (1980, pp. 10–11).

in 1890. The proportions remain close to half regardless of whether the woman is single or married or a mother. Nearly 60 percent of married mothers with children under age 6 are working (see Table 16.3).

It is logical to assume that these proportions would be even higher if day care in the United States received more support. A number of European nations, including France, the Netherlands, Sweden, and the former Soviet Union, provide preschool care at minimal or no cost. However, in the United States, these costs are generally borne by the working parent. Recently, some employers have recognized the benefits of offering care and have begun to provide or subsidize this care, but they are the exception, not the rule (Schaefer and Lamm, 1995).

A primary goal of many feminists is to eliminate sex discrimination in the labor force and to equalize job opportunities for women. Without question, women earn less than men. As we noted earlier, in Table 3.1 and Figure 3.3, women earn less than men even when race and education are held constant; that is, college-educated women working full time make less than comparably educated men. Even when additional controls are introduced, like previous work experience, a substantial earnings gap remains. A detailed analysis of the wage gap, considering schooling, employment history, time with the current employer, and medical leaves of absence, found that all these factors can explain less than 42 percent of the wage differences between men and women (A. Wellington, 1994; also see D. Tomaskovic-Devey, 1993b).

Despite the analysis of a wage gap, there is still an illusion of progress. Women are earning more now, but so are men. Women are now more visible in primarily all-male occupations, but the wag gap persists. Women lawyers earn only 75 percent of their male counterparts' wages, and even female bus drivers earn 78 per-

Table 16.3   LABOR FORCE PARTICIPATION RATE

A growing number of women—married and single, with children and childless—participate in the nation's paid labor force.

	Percentage in Labor Force	
	1960	1993
Total		
Women	37.7	57.9
Men	83.3	75.2
Women by Marital Status		
Single	58.6	66.4
Married, husband present	31.9	59.4
Separated, divorced, widowed	41.6	47.1
Women, Presence of Children		
Married, children under 6	18.6	59.6
Married, any children under 17	27.6	67.5
Single, children under 6	40.0	47.4
Single, any children under 17	50.0	54.4

Source: Bureau of the Census (1993a, pp. 395, 401, 402). Data for 1960 for single women with children are the author's estimate based on 1980 data.

cent of what the male drivers earn. While longevity in an occupation may explain some of the disparity, it would be incorrect to conclude that women are fully accepted in the workplace (M. Mahar, 1993).

Sources of Discrimination   If we return to the definition of discrimination cited earlier, are not men better able to perform some tasks than women, and vice versa? If ability means performance, there certainly are differences. The typical woman can sew better than the typical man, but the latter can toss a ball farther than the former. These are group differences. Certainly many women outthrow many men, and many men outsew many women, but society expects women to excel at sewing and men to excel at throwing. The differences in those abilities are due to cultural conditioning. Women are usually taught to sew, and men are less likely to learn such a skill. Men are encouraged to participate in sports requiring the ability to throw a ball much more than are women. True, as a group, males have greater potential for the muscular development required to throw a ball, but U.S. society encourages men to realize their potential in this area more than it encourages women to pursue athletic skills.

Today's labor market involves much more than throwing a ball and using a needle and thread, but the analogy to these two skills is repeated time and again. Robert Tsuchigane and Norton Dodge (1974) identify three components of male-female earning differentials:

1. *Market discrimination.* Qualified women are underpaid or underemployed. This condition can be eliminated in a relatively short time by changes in hiring and promotion practices.

2. *Social and cultural conditioning.* There are not enough qualified women for certain high-paying, high-status jobs. This shortage could take longer to eliminate completely because it requires training women who are genuinely interested in pursuing what are now judged to be male careers.

3. *Physiological differences in capabilities.* Women suffer lost job experience and pay due to childbirth. Many feminists argue that employers should grant time for such absences and grant paid maternity leave. (pp. 97–99)

Removing barriers to equal opportunity would eliminate market discrimination and social and cultural conditioning. Theoretically, men and women would sew and perhaps even throw a ball with the same ability. We say "theoretically" because cultural conditioning would take generations to change. In some formerly male jobs, like being a gas station attendant, society seems quite willing to accept women. In other occupations (being president), it will take longer, and many years may pass before full acceptance can be expected in other fields (professional contact sports).

Many efforts have been made to eliminate what Tsuchigane and Dodge (1974) referred to as market discrimination. The 1964 Civil Rights Act and its enforcement arm, the Equal Employment Opportunity Commission, address cases of sex discrimination. As we saw in Chapter 3, the inclusion of sex bias along with prejudice based on race, color, creed, and national origin was an unexpected last-minute change in the provisions of the landmark 1964 act. Federal legislation has not removed all discrimination against women in employment. The same explanations presented in Chapter 3 for the lag between the laws and reality in race discrimination apply to sex discrimination: (1) lack of money, (2) weak enforcement powers, (3) occasionally weak commitment to using the laws available, and (4) most important, institutional and structural forces that perpetuate inequality. A fifth factor affects sex discrimination: the courts and enforcement agencies have been slower to mandate equal rights for women than for African Americans and other racial minorities.

Sexual Harassment A particularly damaging form of on-the-job discrimination experienced primarily by women is *sexual harassment,* which has been defined by U.S. Supreme Court Justice Sandra Day O'Connor and others as making one's environment "hostile and abusive" by imposing sexual requirements in a relationship of unequal power (L. Greenhouse, 1993c; C. MacKinnon, 1979). Sexual harassment can take a number of forms, including the direction of crude or suggestive remarks at a person, the solicitation of sexual activity by promising a reward, sexual coercion by threat of punishment, and sexual crimes and misdemeanors.

Although estimates and definitions vary, a study of the federal workplace released in 1988 found that 42 percent of the women had experienced some form of sexual harassment during the preceding two years. These figures remained constant during the 1980s. Not only is such harassment humiliating, but it is also costly. A 1992 estimate states that the problem cost $282 per employee per year in paying sick leave to employees who missed work, in replacing employees who left their jobs, and in reduced productivity (S. Webb, 1992).

Sexual harassment is pervasive. Pictured is Senator Robert Packwood apologizing at a 1992 news conference for "unwelcome and offensive" behavior toward female aides. He was ousted from the U.S. Senate in 1995 for this behavior, as well as for other questionable activities.

John Giustina/New York Times Pictures.

In 1986, in a unanimous decision (*Meritor Savings Bank v. Vinson*), the Supreme Court declared that sexual harassment by a supervisor violates the federal law against sex discrimination in the workplace as outlined in the 1964 Civil Rights Act. Harassment, if sufficiently severe, is a violation even if the unwelcomed sexual demands are not linked to concrete employment benefits such as a raise or promotion. Women's groups hailed the court's decisiveness in identifying harassment as a form of discrimination. In the fall of 1991, national attention was given to sexual harassment as Supreme Court nominee Clarence Thomas was accused by a former co-worker, law professor Anita Hill, of repeatedly harassing her over a period of years. While Thomas was eventually confirmed, the televised hearings encouraged women who had been harassed to come forward. A survey at the time found that 21 percent had been harassed at work, and 42 percent said that they knew someone who had been harassed (B. Kantrowitz, 1991).

Pay Equity What should be done to close the gap between the earnings of women and men? During the 1980s, pay equity, or comparable worth, was a controversial solution presented to alleviate the second-class status of working women. It directly attempted to secure equal pay when occupational segregation by gender was particularly pervasive. *Pay equity* calls for equal pay for different types of work that are judged to be comparable by measuring such factors as employee knowledge, skills, effort, responsibility, and working conditions.

This doctrine sounds straightforward, but it is not so simple to put into operation. How exactly does one determine the comparability of jobs in order to identify comparable worth? Should a zookeeper be paid more than a child care worker? Does our society pay zookeepers more because we value caretaking for children less than caretaking for animals? Or do zookeepers earn more than child care workers because the former tend to be male and the latter are generally female?

In the United States, women's work is undervalued and underpaid. Efforts to address the problem of wage discrimination have resulted in legislation and increased public awareness, yet women's salaries remain far lower than those of men. The federal Equal Pay Act of 1963, which mandates equal pay for equal work, applies to a relatively small proportion of female workers: those who perform the same job under the same roof as a male worker. Although these women's wages have increased as a result of the Equal Pay Act, most female workers, as we have seen, remain segregated in a few occupations in which no male workers do the same jobs. Therefore, these underpaid women cannot compare themselves with males.

As a society, have we begun to address adequately the problem of unequal wages for similar work? What are the potential solutions to this problem of wage discrimination? The courts have generally been reluctant to address this issue or to find wage discrimination in female-dominated occupations that pay less than male-dominated occupations requiring the same or fewer job skills. Some public employers have developed voluntary plans to put pay equity policies into effect, but such initiatives have been sporadic and are often short-lived.

Despite some local initiatives, pay equity has not received much support in the United States except from the women's movement. From a policy perspective, pay equity would have to be initiated at the federal level, and in the 1990s, the government is backing away from affirmative action, much less considering launching an initiative on pay equity (E. Sorensen, 1994).

Feminization of Poverty   Since World War II, an increasing proportion of the poor in the United States have been female—many of them divorced or never-married mothers. This alarming trend has come to be known as the *feminization of poverty.*

Poor women share many social characteristics with poor men: low educational attainment, lack of market-relevant job skills, and residence in economically deteriorating areas. Conflict theorists, however, feel that the higher rates of poverty among women can be traced to two distinct causes. Because of sex discrimination on the job and sexual harassment, women are at a clear disadvantage when seeking vertical social mobility. As mentioned in Chapter 3, year-round White female workers made only $22,423 in 1993, compared with $31,737 for White male workers.

The burden of supporting a family is especially difficult for single mothers, not only because of low salaries but because of inadequate child support as well. According to studies by the Bureau of the Census (1990), the average payment for child support in 1989 was a mere $2,995 per year, or about $58 per week. This level of support is clearly insufficient for rearing a child in the 1990s. Moreover, of the 4.9 million American women scheduled to receive child support payments from their former husbands in 1989, only 51 percent actually received all the money they were scheduled to get, while 24 percent received some of the money due and 25 percent did not receive any of the scheduled payments. In light of these data, federal and state officials have intensified efforts to track down delinquent spouses and ensure the payment of child support. Policymakers acknowledge that such enforcement efforts have led to substantial reductions in welfare expenditures (Bureau of the Census, 1994, pp. 387–388).

According to a study based on census data released in early 1994 by the advocacy group Women Work, single mothers and "displaced homemakers" are four times as likely to live in poverty as other households in the United States. *Displaced homemakers* were defined as women whose primary occupation had been homemaking but who did not find full-time employment after being divorced, separated, or widowed. Among the findings of the report were the following:

- The number of single mothers in the nation rose from 5.8 million in 1980 to 7.7 million in 1990. The number of displaced homemakers rose from 13.8 million in 1980 to 17.8 million in 1990.
- In 1990, 11 percent of all households in the United States lived in poverty. But the same was true of 44 percent of households headed by single mothers and 42 percent of households headed by displaced homemakers.

Gilda Nardone, president of Women Work, noted that single mothers and displaced homemakers tend to work in service jobs which offer low wages, few benefits, part-time work, and little job security. Moreover, single mothers and displaced homemakers tend to have an unstable housing situation, including a frequent change of residence (*New York Times,* 1994).

Many feminists feel that the continuing dominance of the political system by men contributes to government indifference to the problem of poor women. Patricia B. Reuss, a lobbyist for the Women's Equity Action League, has challenged male politicians who merely pay lip service to this issue: "I'm critical of the leaders of both parties who failed to take hold of the equity act and push the whole thing through. The things that have gotten through are nice beginnings, rather than real remedies" (S. Roberts, 1984, p. A18). As more and more women fall below the official poverty line, policymakers will face growing pressure to combat the feminization of poverty.

Education

The experience of women in education has been similar to their experience in the labor force: a long history of contribution but in traditionally defined terms. In 1833, Oberlin College became the first institution of higher learning to admit women, years after the first men's college began in this country. In 1837, Wellesley became the first women's college. But it would be a mistake to believe that these early experiments brought about equality for women in education: at Oberlin, the women were forbidden to speak in public. Furthermore,

> Washing the men's clothes, caring for their rooms, serving them at table, listening to their orations, but themselves remaining respectfully silent in public assemblages, the Oberlin "co-eds" were being prepared for intelligent motherhood and a properly subservient wifehood. (Flexner, 1959, p. 30)

The early graduates of these schools, despite the emphasis in the curriculum on traditional roles, became the founders of the feminist movement.

Today, research confirms that boys and girls are treated differently in school: teachers give boys more attention. In teaching students the values and customs of the larger society, schools in the United States have treated children as if men's education were more important than that of women. Professors of education Myra and David Sadker (1985) documented this persistence of classroom sexism: "Although many believe that classroom sexism disappeared in the early '70s, it hasn't" (p. 54). The researchers noted that boys receive more teacher attention than girls, mainly because they call out in class eight times more often. The Sadkers headed a three-year study in which field researchers observed students in more than 1,900 fourth-, sixth-, and eighth-grade classes in four states and the District of Columbia. The researchers found that teachers commonly engage in different treatment of students based on gender. Teachers praise boys more than girls and offer boys more academic assistance. In addition, they reward boys for academic assertiveness (for example, calling out answers without raising their hands) while reprimanding girls for similar behavior.

In addition, there are sexist aspects in the curriculum. Even brand-new history textbooks devote only 2 percent of their space to women. According to the researchers, the consequences of these inequities for young women are lowered achievement, lessened self-esteem, and limited career options. While girls' scores are equal to or even better than boys' on almost every standardized test given in the early grades, by high school girls score lower on the standardized exams that are crucial for college admission (Sadker and Sadker, 1994a, 1994b).

Besides receiving less attention, girls are more likely to be encouraged to take courses that will lead them to enter lower-paying fields of employment. This has been the experience of girls who are exposed to courses that prepare them to be housewives and who, even when showing the aptitude for "men's work," are advised to pursue "women's work." Researchers have documented sexism in education in the books used, the vocational counseling provided, and even the content of educational television programs. Perhaps the most apparent result of sexist practices and gender-role conditioning in education is staffing patterns. Administrators and university professors are primarily male, and public school teachers are female. Thus, at the college level, where women make up half the student body, they are 43 percent of the faculty. School systems grew more aware of sexism in the 1970s, just as they became suddenly aware of their racism during the 1960s.

At all levels of schooling, congressional amendments to the Education Act of 1972 and the Department of Health, Education, and Welfare guidelines developed in 1974 and 1975 made significant changes. Collectively referred to as *Title IX provisions*, the regulations are designed to eliminate sexist practices from almost all school systems. Schools must make these changes or risk the loss of all federal assistance:

1. Schools must eliminate all sex-segregated classes and extracurricular activities. This means an end to all-girl home economics and all-boy shop classes, although single-sex hygiene and physical education classes are permitted.
2. Schools cannot discriminate by sex in admissions or financial aid and cannot inquire into whether an applicant is married, pregnant, or a parent. Single-sex schools are exempted.
3. Schools must end sexist hiring and promotion practices among faculty members.
4. Although women do not have to be permitted to play on all-men's athletic teams, schools must provide more opportunities for women's sports, intramurally and extramurally. (*Federal Register,* June 4, 1975)

Title IX became one of the more controversial steps ever taken by the federal government to promote and ensure equality.

Efforts to bring gender equity to sports have been attacked as going too far, and they have fueled, as noted earlier, the "angry white men" perspective that men are the victims. Conflict theorists maintain that such criticism reflects an underlying desire to protect the privileged positions of males rather than any genuine feeling about federal control and education. Feminists opposed the government moves to soften some Title IX regulations, especially because Title IX fails to affect sex stereotyping in textbooks and curricula and exempts elementary schools and the military academies.

Its supporters feel that Title IX has played a major role in the growing involvement of U.S. women and girls in athletics. However, financial support has not kept pace. By 1993, one out of three college athletic scholarships went to a female, yet women make up half the college students. Similarly, in overall budgets, women's athletics grew from 2 percent in 1972 to 23 percent in 1993. There remain significant gaps in men's and women's athletics at almost all colleges. In 1995, the range of women's participation in intercollegiate sports in the Big Ten Conference ranged from 31 to 40 percent (A. Gottsman, 1995; K. Reith, 1992; K. Sharp, 1993).

Family Life

"Does your mother work?" "No, she's a housewife."

This familiar exchange suggests that a woman is married to both a husband and a house and that homemaking does not constitute work. Our society generally equates work with wages and holds work not done for pay in low esteem. Women, who, through household chores and volunteer work, do such work are given little status in our society. Furthermore, the demands traditionally placed on a mother and homemaker are so extensive as to make pursuing a career extremely difficult. For women, the family is, sociologists Lewis Coser and Rose Laub Coser (1974) say, a "greedy institution." They observed the overwhelming burden of the multiple social roles associated with being a mother and working outside the home.

Child Care A man, boy, or girl can act as a homemaker and caretaker for children, but in the United States, these roles are customarily performed by women. Rebelsky and Hanks (1973) examined interactions between fathers and babies and found that the longest time any father in the sample devoted to his infant was 10 minutes and 26 seconds. The average period of verbal interaction between father and baby was only 38 *seconds* a day. Psychologist Wade Mackey (1987) conducted a cross-cultural study of 17 societies—including Morocco, Hong Kong, Ireland, and Mexico—and found that the limited father–child interactions in the United States were also typical of all the societies surveyed.

American fathers currently find little time for the basic tasks of child rearing. Some men have reworked their job commitments to maximize the amount of time they can spend with their children. For example, a Connecticut sales representative comes home for lunch so that he can play with his 7-month-old daughter. On weekends, he rises at 6:00 A.M. so that he can spend time alone with her. Yet, while Bell Telephone has offered men the option of six-month paternity leave since 1969, there have been few takers. It remains difficult for men in two-parent households to deviate from their traditional occupational roles in order to become more involved in child rearing (L. Langway, 1981).

Housework If child rearing is still primarily women's work, even with most mothers in the labor force, what about housework?

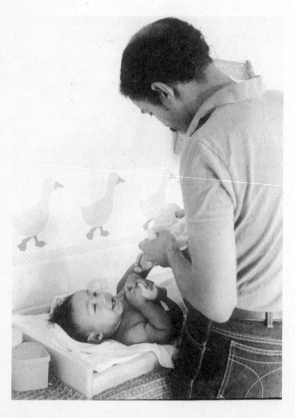

Changing gender roles, coupled with the increased presence of mothers in the labor force, have contributed to some men's taking on more responsibility for the care of their young children, but overall, women still perform most of the child care responsibilities.

The division of household and child care duties is far from trivial in defining power relations within the family. Heidi Hartmann (1981) argues that "time spent on housework, as well as other indicators of household labor, can be fruitfully used as a measure of power relationships in the home" (p. 377). Hartmann points out that, as women spend more hours per week working for wages, the amount of time they devote to housework decreases, yet their overall "work week" increases. However, men in dual-career marriages do not spend more time on housework chores than do husbands of full-time homemakers.

Despite public pronouncements about men taking on housework, in practice, there continues to be a clear gender gap. For example, a study by sociologists Scott South and Glenna Spitze (1994)—using data from a national sample of adults from 13,017 households, interviewed in 1987–1988—analyzed the differences in time spent on housework by men and women in six types of living situations: never married and living with parents, never married and living independently, cohabiting, married, divorced, and widowed. In *all* these living situations, women spent more time on housework than men: an overall average of 33 hours per week for women, compared with 18 hours per week for men. The gender gap in housework was widest among married couples: women devoted 37 hours per week, and men only 18 hours (see Figure 16.1).

Average Hours of Housework Performed Per Week

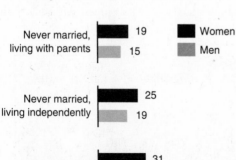

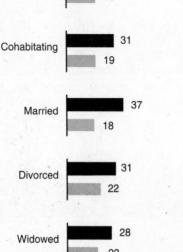

Figure 16.1 **Housework by Gender**
In all six living situations studied, there was a clear gender gap in the amount of time spent on housework. The gender gap was greatest among married couples, with women devoting 37 hours per week to housework and men only 18 hours.

Source: South and Spitze (1994).

Given the stresses of performing about two-thirds of all housework, why do married women accept this arrangement? Psychologist Mary Clare Lennon and sociologist Sarah Rosenfield (1994) studied this issue by using, as secondary data, interviews of adults from the same national sample discussed above. When questioned in that survey, almost 61 percent of the women and more than 67 percent of the men suggested that this uneven distribution of housework is fair to both spouses. According to the researchers, those married women with the fewest alternatives and financial prospects outside marriage are most likely to accept unequal household arrangements as fair. Apparently, the more dependent a particular wife is, the more she will do (and justify) to preserve the marital relationship. In a striking finding, Lennon and Rosenfield reported that women who *do* view unequal housework as unjust experience more symptoms of depression.

Sociologist Arlie Hochschild (1989, 1990) has used the term *second shift* to describe the double burden—work outside the home followed by child care and housework—that many women face and that few men share equitably. On the basis of interviews with and observations of 52 couples over an eight-year period, Hochschild reports that the wives (and not their husbands) drive home from the office while planning domestic schedules and play dates for children—and then begin their second shift. Drawing on national studies, she concludes that women spend 15 fewer hours in leisure activities each week than do their husbands. In a year, these women work an extra month of 24-hour days because of the second-shift phenomenon. Over a dozen years, they work an extra year of 24-hour days.

Hochschild found that the married couples she studied were fraying at the edges, and so were their careers and their marriages. The women she spoke with

Kirk Anderson, Ladysmith, WI.

hardly resembled the beautiful young businesswomen pictured in magazine advertisements, dressed in power suits but with frilled blouses, holding briefcases in one
hand and happy young children by the other. Instead, many of Hochschild's female
subjects talked about being overtired and emotionally drained by the demands of
their multiple roles. They were much more intensely torn by the conflicting
demands of work outside the home and family life than their husbands were.
Hochschild (1990) concludes that "if we as a culture come to see the urgent need
of meeting the new problems posed by the second shift, and if society and government begin to shape new policies that allow working parents more flexibility, then
we will be making some progress toward happier times at home and at work"
(p. 73). This view is shared by many feminists.

Abortion   A particularly controversial subject affecting family life in the United
States has been the call for women to have greater control over their bodies, especially their reproductive lives, through contraceptive devices and the increased
availability of abortions. Abortion law reform was one of the demands NOW made
in 1967, and the controversy continues despite many court rulings and the passage
of laws at every level of government.

On January 22, 1973, the feminist movement received unexpected assistance
from the 1973 U.S. Supreme Court decision in *Roe v. Wade.* The justices held, by
a 7–2 margin, that the "right to privacy . . . founded in the Fourteenth Amendment's concept of personal liberty . . . is broad enough to encompass a woman's
decision whether or not to terminate a pregnancy." However, the Court did set certain limits on a woman's right to abortion. During the last three months of pregnancy, the fetus was ruled capable of life outside the womb. Therefore, states were
granted the right to prohibit all abortions in the third trimester except those needed to preserve the life, physical health, or mental health of the mother. In subsequent decisions in the 1970s, the Court upheld the right of a woman to terminate
pregnancy without the consent of her husband or (in the case of younger, unmar-
ried women) her parents.

The Court's decision in *Roe v. Wade,* while generally applauded by "prochoice" groups, which support the right to legal abortions, was bitterly condemned
by those opposed to abortion. For people who call themselves "prolife," abortion is
a moral and often a religious issue. In their view, human life actually begins at the
moment of conception rather than at the moment of a baby's delivery. On the basis
of this belief, the fetus is a human life, not merely a potential life. Termination of
this life, even before it has left the womb, is viewed essentially as an act of murder.
Consequently, antiabortion activists were alarmed by the fact that, by 1992, over 24
million legal abortions had taken place in the United States in the years since the
Supreme Court decision of *Roe v. Wade* (Bureau of the Census, 1994; K. Luker,
1984).

In recent years, influenced by the vote of conservative justices appointed by
Ronald Reagan and George Bush, the Supreme Court has increasingly restricted
the right to an abortion. However, the election of Bill Clinton as president in 1992
delighted prochoice activists and led to an immediate and dramatic change in fed-

eral policies concerning abortion. In early 1993, only days after his inauguration and on the twentieth anniversary of the landmark *Roe v. Wade* ruling, President Clinton issued a series of memorandums which reversed the "prolife" policies of the Reagan and Bush administrations. The president lifted the ban on abortion counseling at federally funded clinics, eased government policy concerning abortions in military hospitals, and ended a prohibition on aid to international family-planning programs involved in abortion-related activities.

Recently, there has been an escalation of violent antiabortion protests. Five people working at abortion clinics were killed in 1993 and 1994. A 1994 federal law made it a crime to use force or threats, or to obstruct, injure, or interfere with anyone providing or receiving abortions and other reproductive health services. In signing the bill into law, President Clinton stated, "No person seeking medical care, no physician providing that care should have to endure harassments or threats or obstruction or intimidation or even murder from vigilantes who take the law into their own hands because they think they know what the law ought to be." A month later, the Supreme Court upheld most of a Florida state court injunction intended to prevent disruptive protestors from blocking access to abortion clinics. In a 6–3 ruling written by Chief Justice William Rehnquist, the Court's majority upheld the constitutionality of a 36-foot "buffer zone" that keeps antiabortion protestors away from a clinic's entrance and parking lot. Abortion remains a disputed issue both in society and in the courts (L. Greenhouse, 1994; G. Ifill, 1994).

Political Activity

Women in the United States constitute 53 percent of the voting population and 49 percent of the labor force, but only eight percent of high government position holders. In 1995, Congress included only 47 women (out of 435 members) in the House of Representatives and only eight women (out of 100 members) in the Senate. As shown in Table 16.4, while the number of women in state legislatures following the 1994 elections was more than five times larger than it was 25 years ago, only one state had a woman governor, New Jersey's Christine Todd Whitman. As of 1992, women had held no more than 18 percent of the available positions at any level of public office (Center for the American Woman and Politics [CAWP], 1992, 1995).

Table 16.4   WOMEN IN ELECTED OFFICE

Women have overcome tremendous barriers over the last few decades to make inroads into the male world of elective office.

	1969	1975	1981	1987	1995
House	10	19	21	23	47
Senate	1	0	2	2	8
Governors	0	1	1	2	1
State legislatures	301	604	908	1,170	1,532

Source: Center for the American Woman and Politics (1995).

Sexism has been the most serious barrier to women interested in holding office. Female candidates have had to overcome the prejudices of both men and women regarding women's fitness for leadership. Not until 1955 did a majority of people in the United States indicate that they would vote for a qualified woman for president. Moreover, women often encounter prejudice, discrimination, and abuse after they are elected. In 1979, a questionnaire was circulated among male Oregon legislators asking them to "categorize the lady legislators" with such labels as "mouth, face, chest, dress, and so forth" (Shreve and Clemans, 1980, p. 105).

The low number of women officeholders until recently has not been the result of women's not being active in politics. About the same proportion of eligible women and men vote in presidential elections. The League of Women Voters, founded in 1920, performs a valuable function in educating the electorate of both sexes, publishing newsletters describing candidates' positions and holding debates between candidates. Perhaps women's most visible role in politics until recently has been as unpaid workers for male candidates: doorbell ringers, telephone callers, newsletter printers, and petition carriers. In addition, wives of elected male politicians play significant supportive roles and have increasingly spoken out in their own right, the most recent and visible example being Hillary Rodham Clinton. Campaigns in the 1990s showed women overcoming one of their last barriers to electoral office: attracting campaign funds. Running for office is very expensive, and women candidates have begun to convince backers to invest in their political future. Their success as fund-raisers will also contribute to women's being more seriously considered as candidates in the future (Bledsoe and Herring, 1990; McCormick and Baruch, 1994).

Women have worked actively in both political parties, but successful women officeholders are more likely to be Democrats—although by a slight margin. A recent, effective force is the National Women's Political Caucus (NWPC), which works to get more women elected. The NWPC was founded in 1971 by Betty Friedan, Gloria Steinem (founder of *Ms.* magazine), Bella Abzug, and Shirley Chisholm (the last two have been Congresswomen from New York City). The NWPC oversees state caucuses that rally support for women's issues and works for the election of women. The caucus finds it difficult to represent all politically active women, because women now encompass a whole range of ideologies, and the NWPC includes women who are unmistakable antifeminists (CAWP, 1994; J. Freeman, 1975).

DOUBLE JEOPARDY: MINORITY WOMEN

We have seen the historical oppression of women that limits them by tradition and law to specific roles. Many women experience differential treatment not only because of sex but because of race and ethnicity as well. These citizens face a *double jeopardy*—that of subordinate status twice defined. A disproportionate share of this low-status group also is impoverished, so that the double jeopardy becomes a triple jeopardy. The litany of social ills continues for many as we add old age, ill-health, disabilities, and the like.

Only recently have women entered the highest judicial levels. U.S. Supreme Court Justice Sandra Day O'Connor (right) welcomes Justice Ruth Bader Ginsburg on her appointment to the Supreme Court.

Feminists have addressed themselves to the needs of minority women, but overshadowing the oppression of these women because of their sex is the subordinate status imposed by both White men and White women, because of their race or ethnicity. The question for the Chicana (Mexican-American woman), African-American woman, Asian-American woman, Native American woman, and so on appears to be whether she should unify with her brothers against racism or challenge them for their sexism. The answer is that society cannot afford to let up on the effort to eradicate both sexism and racism (E. Sutherland, 1970; E. Vasquez, 1970).

The discussion of gender roles among African Americans has always provoked controversy. Advocates of Black nationalism contend that feminism only distracts women from full participation in the African-American struggle. The existence of feminist groups among Blacks, in their view, simply divides the Black community and thereby serves the dominant White society. By contrast, Black feminists such as bell hooks (1994) argue that little is to be gained by accepting the gender-role divisions of the dominant society that place women in a separate, subservient position. African-American journalist Patricia Raybon (1989) has noted that the media commonly portray Black women in a negative light: as illiterate, as welfare mothers, as prostitutes, and so forth. Black feminists emphasize that it is not solely Whites and White-dominated media that focus on these negative images; Black men (most recently, Black male rap artists) have also been criticized for the way they portray African-American women (S. Fulwood, 1994a).

Native Americans standout as a historical exception to the North American patriarchal tradition. At the time of the arrival of the European settlers, gender roles varied greatly from tribe to tribe. Southern tribes, for reasons unclear to today's scholars, were usually matriarchal and traced descent through the mother. European missionaries sought to make the native peoples more like the Europeans and this aim included transforming women's role (E. Pleck, 1993). Some Native American women, like members of other groups, have resisted gender stereotypes. Menominee Carol Dodge was a leader in creating a community college to serve her people in Wisconsin and speaks of the importance of education in "Listen to Their Voices."

The plight of Chicanas is usually considered part of either the Mexican-American or women's movements, and the particular experience of Chicanas is ignored. In the past, they have been excluded from decision making in the two social institutions that most affect their daily lives: the family and the church. The family, especially in the lower class, feels the pervasive tradition of male domination called *machismo* discussed in Chapter 10. The Roman Catholic church relegates women to supportive roles, while reserving for men the leadership positions (Burciaga, Gonzales, and Hepburn, 1977; R. Rosaldo, 1985).

Activists among minority women do not agree on whether priority should be given to equalizing the sexes or to eliminating inequality among racial and ethnic groups. It is not solely a question of priorities, for, as Helen Hacker (1975) says, there are "conflicting interests of the beneficiaries of these movements" (p. 171). White women, encouraged to enter all occupations, may compete with minority males who are less educated and who are at a disadvantage in hiring that is free of sexism.

Chicana feminist Enriqueta Longauex y Vasquez, while acknowledging the importance of the Mexican-American movement, believes in stressing sexual equality: "When a man can look upon a woman as human, then, and only then, can he feel the true meaning of liberation and equality" (E. Vasquez, 1970, p. 384).

Perhaps it would be most accurate to conclude that neither component of inequality can be ignored. Helen Mayer Hacker (1973), who pioneered research on the role of being both Black and female, stated before the American Sociological Association that "as a partisan observer it is my fervent hope that in fighting the

Listen to Their Voices
Women of the Native Struggle

CAROL DODGE

Carol Dodge

When I was in school, if you made it through eighth grade, that was it. I think when we graduated from the eighth grade, there must have been at least thirty-five students in my class, and only six of us got through high school.

I was fortunate in that I had a really supportive father and he managed to get us through high school. There were eleven of us and we all made it. Eight of us got through college, and three who didn't want to go to college went through technical school.

One of the things that we try to instill in the children here on the reservation is that they should never be ashamed to learn about their own culture, their own ceremonies. We have quite a strong group of young people who have gone back to our traditional religion. I think a good portion of it is because we were instrumental in teaching them the language and the culture. As soon as we got our own school district started, we brought the language, culture, and history in right away. We have the traditional Menominee music, which gives them a good background on the importance of the songs and the drum. This has helped the children to understand who they are, and that if they choose not to be a Catholic or a Methodist, that there's nothing wrong with them.

Source: R. Farley (1993, p. 133).

twin battles of sexism and racism Black women and Black men together will [create] the outlines of the good society for all Americans" (p. 11). The recent history of the rights movements of women and racial minorities indicates some dispute over priorities, accompanied by a genuine recognition that social equality among all people is the ultimate goal.

CONCLUSION

Women and men are expected to perform, or at least to prefer to perform, specific tasks in society. The appropriateness to a sex of all but a very few of these tasks cannot be justified by the biological differences between females and males, any more than differential treatment based on race can be justified. Psychologists Sandra Bem and Daryl Bem (1970) make this analogy:

> Suppose that a white, male college student decided to room with a black, male friend. The typical white student would not blithely assume that his roommate was better suited

to handle all domestic chores. Nor should his conscience allow him to do so even in the unlikely event that his roommate would say, "No, that's okay. I like doing housework. I'd be happy to do it." We would suspect that the white student would still feel uncomfortable about taking advantage of the fact that his roommate has simply been socialized to be "happy with such an arrangement." But change this hypothetical black roommate to a female marriage partner and the student's conscience goes to sleep. (p. 99)

The feminist movement has awakened women *and* men to the assumptions based on sex and gender. New opportunities for the sexes require the same commitment from individuals and the government as they make to achieving equality among racial and ethnic groups.

Women are systematically disadvantaged in both employment and the family. Gender inequality is a serious problem, just as racial inequality continues to be a significant social challenge. Separate, socially defined roles for men and women are not limited to the United States. The United Nations declared 1975 International Women's Year (IWY), wishing to support women's rights in activities throughout the world that would culminate in an international woman's conference in Mexico City. Little changed directly as the result of the IWY, but the year did stress that women's subordinate status is worldwide. Chapter 17 concentrates on the inequality of racial and ethnic groups in societies other than the United States. Just as sexism is not unique to this nation, neither is racism nor religious intolerance.

KEY TERMS

androgyny The state of being both masculine and feminine, aggressive and gentle.

AWM (angry white men) Refers to the 1990s notion that men are a new victim group whose grievances need to be heard.

displaced homemakers Women whose primary occupation had been homemaking but who did not find full-time employment after being divorced, separated, or widowed.

double jeopardy The subordinate status twice defined, as experienced by women of color.

feminine mystique A woman's thinking of herself only as her children's mother and her husband's wife.

feminization of poverty The trend since 1970 that has women accounting for a growing proportion of those below the poverty line.

gender roles Expectations regarding the proper behavior, attitudes, and activities of males and females.

glass ceiling The barrier that blocks the promotion of a qualified worker because of gender or minority membership.

market discrimination The underpayment or underemployment of qualified women.

mommy track The problematic corporate career track for women who want to divide their attention between work and family.

pay equity The same wages for different types of work that are judged to be comparable by such measures as employee knowledge, skills, effort, responsibility, and working conditions; also called *comparable worth.*

second shift The double burden—work outside the home followed by child care and housework—that is faced by many women, and that few men share equitably.

sexism The ideology that one sex is superior to the other.

sexual harassment Creating a hostile or abusive environment by imposing sexual requirements in a relationship of unequal power.

suffragists Women and men who worked successfully to gain women the right to vote.

FOR FURTHER INFORMATION

Patricia Hill Collins. *Black Feminist Thought: Knowledge, Consciousness, and the Politics of Empowerment.* New York: Routledge, 1990.

> Considers such African-American feminists as Angela Davis, bell hooks, Alice Walker, and Audre Lorde.

Jane Condon. *A Half Step Behind: Japanese Women of the '80s.* New York: Dodd, Mead, 1985.

> Condon examines women's role in Japanese society within the family, in the educational system, and in the workforce.

Susan Faludi. *Backlash: The Undeclared War Against American Women.* New York: Crown, 1991.

> A Pulitzer Prize–winning journalist reviews the counterattack against the women's movement.

Myra Marx Ferree and Beth B. Hess. *Controversy and Coalition: The New Feminist Movement Across Three Decades of Change,* rev. ed. New York: Twayne, 1994.

> A sociological overview of the past and present of the women's movement.

Jo Freeman. *The Politics of Women's Liberation.* New York: David McKay, 1975.

> Freeman analyzes women's liberation as a social movement. Her coverage of the origins of the movement and of NOW is especially effective.

Betty Friedan. *The Feminine Mystique.* New York: Dell, 1963.

> Friedan explodes the myth that women's true fulfillment can come only through the home and motherhood. Still a classic despite the author's changed views in *The Second Stage,* published in 1981.

Arlie Russell Hochschild with Anne Machung. *The Second Shift: Working Parents and the Revolution at Home.* New York: Viking Penguin, 1989.

> A critical look at housework in dual-career families.

Robin Morgan, ed. *Sisterhood Is Powerful.* New York: Vintage Books, 1970.

> This is the most complete collection of writings from the beginning of the contemporary women's movement. It covers women in the professions, sexuality, sexism in advertising, lesbians, minority women, and much more.

Laurel Richardson and Verta Taylor, eds. *Feminist Frontiers III.* New York: McGraw-Hill, 1994.

> A collection of 53 articles covering such topics as socialization, work, the family, health, violence, and social movement.

Christina Hoff Somners. *Who Stole Feminism?* New York: Simon & Schuster, 1994.

> A philosophy professor looks critically at the directions being taken by feminism in the 1990s.

Elaine Sorensen. *Comparable Worth: Is It a Worthy Policy?* Princeton: Princeton University Press, 1994.

> Identifies the most and least successful strategies for combating inequality in wages.

Maxine Baca Zinn and Bonnie Thornton Dill, eds. *Women of Color in U.S. Society.* Philadelphia: Temple University Press, 1994.

Considers race, class, and gender, or interlocking systems of oppression.

Statistical Data

Almost all government-collected data (census, health statistics, crime data, labor figures, and so on) are broken down by sex.

Periodicals

Ms. (established in 1972) is a monthly mass-market publication that presents the feminist point of view. Other publications taking strong positions are the quarterly *Lilith* (1976), the monthly *Off Our Backs* (1970), and the monthly *Working Woman* (1976). The more traditional women's magazines have increasingly confronted the issues raised by the women's liberation movement. Journals devoted to women and men as social groups are the quarterly *Gender and Society* (1987), the quarterly *Masculinities* (1995), the bimonthly *Sex Roles: A Journal of Research* (1975), the quarterly *Signs: Journal of Women in Culture and Society* (1972), the quarterly *Women's Studies* (1972), and *Feminist Studies* (1972) published three times a year.

CRITICAL THINKING QUESTIONS

1. How is women's subordinate position different from that of oppressed racial and ethnic groups? How is it similar?
2. How has the focus of the women's movement changed during the twentieth century?
3. How do the patterns of women in the workplace differ from those of men?
4. How has the changing role of women in the United States affected the family?
5. What are the special challenges facing women of subordinate racial and ethnic groups?

Chapter *17*

Beyond the United States: The Comparative Perspective

Chapter Outline

Highlights

Subordinating people because of race, nationality, or religion is not a phenomenon unique to the United States; it occurs throughout the world. This chapter first explores patterns of domination in Brazil, where the descendants of slavery are still bound by second-class status. Despite its being viewed as a homogeneous nation like the United States, Canada faces racial, linguistic, and tribal peoples issues. Northern Ireland is a modern nation torn by religious strife. In Israel, Jews and Palestinians struggle over territory and the definition of each other's autonomy. The final example is the Republic of South Africa, where the legacy of apartheid dominates the future.

Ironically, modernization, by bringing more and more diverse groups of people into contact, has increased the opportunities for confrontation, both peaceful and violent, among culturally and physically different people. The decline in colonialism by European powers in the 1960s and the end of communist domination in eastern Europe during the 1990s has also allowed interethnic rivalries to resume. Throughout the world, groups defined by race, ethnicity, or religion confront other groups so defined. These confrontations, as Chapter 1 showed, can lead to extermination, expulsion, secession, segregation, fusion, assimilation, or pluralism. Confrontations among racial and ethnic groups have escalated in frequency and intensity in the twentieth century.

Indeed, racial, ethnic, and religious differences have also created new coalitions between nations termed the *kin country syndrome*. The old East–West Cold War alliances are being replaced by cooperation and coalitions based on ethnic, racial, and religious ties such as those among Arab, Christian, and Muslim fundamentalists, to name a few (S. Huntington, 1993).

As is true of intergroup relations in the United States, violent encounters have received the largest share of attention: the overturning of colonial regimes in developing countries, tribal warfare in Africa, and clashes in the Middle East. These conflicts remind us that the processes operating in the United States to deny racial and ethnic groups their rights and opportunities are at work throughout the world. The dissolution of the Union of Soviet Socialist Republics in 1991, for example, occurred along lines defined by ethnicity and language.

The sociological perspective on relations between dominant and subordinate groups treats race and ethnicity as social categories. As *social* concepts, they can be understood only in the context of the shared meanings attached to them by societies and their members. Dominant- and subordinate-group relationships vary greatly. Although these majority–minority pairings vary, there are similarities across societies. Racial and ethnic hostilities arise out of the economic needs and demands of people. These needs and demands may not always be realistic; that is, a group may seek out enemies where none exist or where victory will yield no rewards. Racial and ethnic conflicts are both the results and the precipitators of change in the economic and political sectors (Barclay, Kumar, and Simms, 1976; L. Coser, 1956).

Relations between dominant and subordinate groups differ from society to society, as this chapter will show. Conflict among racial, religious, and ethnic groups is not the same in Brazil, Canada, Northern Ireland, Israel, and South Africa. Differences such as the presence or absence of a history of slavery and the degree of central control of the movement of people within the country are evident. A study of these five societies, coupled with knowledge of subordinate groups in the United States, will provide the background from which to draw some conclusions about patterns of race and ethnic relations.

BRAZIL: NOT A RACIAL PARADISE

To someone knowledgeable about race and ethnic relations in the United States, Brazil seems familiar in a number of respects. Like the United States, Brazil was colonized by Europeans who overwhelmed the native people. Like the United States, Brazil imported Black Africans as slaves to meet the demand for laborers. Even today, Brazil is second only to the United States in the number of people of African descent, excluding nations on the African continent. Although the focus here is on Black and White people in Brazil, another continuing concern is the treatment of Brazil's native peoples, as this developing nation continues to modernize.

Legacy of Slavery

The present nature of Brazilian race relations is influenced by the legacy of slavery, as is true of Black–White relations in the United States. It is not necessary to repeat here a discussion of the brutality of the slave trade and slavery itself, or of the influence of slavery on the survival of African cultures and family life. Scholars agree that slavery was not the same in Brazil as it was in the United States, but they disagree on how different it was and how significant these differences are (S. Elkins, 1959; F. Tannenbaum, 1946).

Brazil depended much more than the United States on the slave trade. Franklin Knight (1974) estimated the total number of slaves imported to Brazil at 3.5 million, eight times the number brought to the United States. At the height of slavery, however, both nations had approximately the same slave population: 4 to 4.5 million. Brazil's reliance on African-born slaves meant that typical Brazilian slaves had closer ties to Africa than did their U.S. counterparts. Revolts and escapes were more common among slaves in Brazil. The most dramatic example was the slave *quilombo* (or hideaway) of Palmores, whose 20,000 inhabitants repeatedly fought off Portuguese assaults until 1698. It is easier to recognize the continuity of African cultures among Brazil's Blacks than among Black Americans. The contributions of the African people to Brazil's history have been kept alive by the attention given them in the schools. Whereas U.S. schools have just recently begun to teach about the Black role in history, the Brazilian schoolchild has typi-

By Mac Nelly for the *Chicago Tribune.* Reprinted by permission, Tribune Media Service.

cally become acquainted with the historical role of the Africans and their descendants. As in the United States, however, the surviving African culture is overwhelmed by dominant European traditions (G. Andrews, 1991; C. Degler, 1971; E. Frazier, 1942, 1943; M. Herskovits, 1941, 1943; R. Stan, 1985).

The most significant difference between slavery in the southern United States and in Brazil was the amount of *manumission,* the freeing of slaves. For every 1,000 slaves, 100 were freed annually in Brazil, compared to four per year in the U.S. South. It would be hasty to assume, however, as some have, that Brazilian masters were more benevolent. Quite the contrary. Brazil's slave economy was poorer than that of the U.S. South, and so slaveowners in Brazil freed slaves into poverty whenever they became crippled, sick, or old. But this custom does not completely explain the presence of the many freed slaves in Brazil. Again unlike in the United States, the majority of Brazil's population was composed of Africans and their descendants throughout the nineteenth century. Africans were needed as craftsworkers, shopkeepers, and boatmen, not just as agricultural workers. Freed slaves filled these needs.

In Brazil, race was not seen as a measure of innate inferiority, as it was in the United States. Rather, even during the period of slavery, Brazilians saw free Blacks as contributing to society, which was not the view of White U.S. southerners. In Brazil, you were inferior if you were a slave. In the United States, you were inferior if you were Black. Not that Brazilians were more enlightened than Americans. Quite the contrary, Brazil belonged to the European tradition of a hierarchical society that did not conceive of all people as equal. Unlike the English, who emphasized individual freedom, however, the Brazilian slave-owner had no need to develop a racist defense of slavery. These distinctions help explain why Whites in the United States felt compelled to dominate and simultaneously fear both the slave and the Black man and woman. Brazilians did not have these fears of free Blacks and thus felt it unnecessary to restrict manumission (D. Davis, 1966; C. Degler, 1971; M. Harris, 1964; M. Marger, 1985; P. Mason, 1970a; O. Patterson, 1982; R. Rose, 1988; T. Skidmore, 1972; I. Sundiata, 1987).

The "Mulatto Escape Hatch" Illusion

Carl Degler (1971) identifies the *mulatto escape hatch* as the key to the differences in Brazilian and American race relations. In Brazil, the mulatto is recognized as a group separate from either *brancos* (Whites) or *prêtos* (Blacks), whereas in the United States, mulattoes are classed with Blacks. Yet this escape hatch is an illusion because economically, mulattoes fare only marginally better than Blacks. In addition, mulattoes do not escape in the sense of mobility into the income and status enjoyed by White Brazilians. Labor market analyses demonstrate that Blacks with the highest levels of education and occupation experience the most discrimination in terms of jobs, mobility, and income (J. Fiola, 1989; R. Reichmann, 1995; H. Winant, 1989).

Today, the presence of approximately 40 racial groups along the lines of a color gradient (see Chapter 11) is obvious in Brazil because, unlike in the United States, mulattoes are viewed as an identifiable social group. The 1980 census in Brazil classified 55 percent White, 38 percent mulatto, 6 percent Black, and 1 percent other. Over the past 50 years, the mulatto group has grown, and the proportions of both Whites and Blacks declined (Brazil, 1981).

The presence of mulattoes does not mean that color is irrelevant in society or that miscegenation occurs randomly. The incidence of mixed marriages is greatest among the poor and among those similar in color. Marriages between partners from opposite ends of the color gradient are rare. The absence of direct racial confrontation and the presence of mixed marriages lead some writers to conclude that Brazil is a "racial paradise." The lack of racial tension does not, however, mean that prejudice does not exist, or that Blacks are fully accepted. For example, residential segregation is present in Brazil's urban areas.

In Brazil, today as in the past, light skin color enhances status, but the impact is often exaggerated. When Degler advanced the idea of the "mulatto escape hatch," he implied that it was a means to success. The most recent income data do show that mulattoes earn 42 percent more than Blacks. Given mulattoes' more extensive formal schooling, this difference is not particularly remarkable. Yet Whites earn another 98 percent more than mulattoes. Clearly, the major distinction is between Whites and all "people of color" rather than between mulattoes and Blacks (A. Dzidzienyo, 1987; N. Silva, 1985; E. Telles, 1992).

Brazilian Dilemma

The most startling phenomenon in Brazilian race relations since World War II has been the recognition that racial prejudice and discrimination exist. During the twentieth century, Brazil changed from a nation that prided itself on its freedom from racial intolerance to a country legally attacking discrimination against people of color. In 1951, the Afonso Arinos law was unanimously adopted, prohibiting racial discrimination in public places. Opinion is divided over the effectiveness of the law, which has been of no use in overturning subtle forms of discrimination. Even from the start, certain civilian careers, such as the diplomatic and military officers ranks, were virtually closed to Blacks. Curiously, the push for the law came from the United States, after a Black American dancer, Katherine Dunham, was denied a room at a São Paulo luxury hotel.

Despite legislative efforts which appear to ban all forms of discrimination, even racial-preference affirmative-action plans, fairly vivid reminders of racism remain. Employers still specify in job searches that only "Spanish" or "Portuguese" applicants need apply, which means Whites. In 1994, national attention was given to a shopping-mall Santa Claus who lost his job because he was too dark. He refused to file a complaint despite an offer of help from a Black rights group (L. Goering, 1994).

In 1988, Brazil marked as a national holiday the hundredth anniversary of the abolition of slavery, but for 40–50 percent of the Brazilian people of color, there was little rejoicing. Zézé Motta, Brazil's leading Black actress and a longtime campaigner for Black advancement, observed, "We have gone from the hold of the ship to the basements of society." Residential segregation exists between Whites and mulattoes and especially between Whites and Blacks. Of the 559 members of the Brazilian Congress, only seven are Black. Whites are seven times more likely to be college graduates. Even Black professionals such as physicians, teachers, and engineers earn 20–25 percent less than their White counterparts (L. Goering, 1994; M. Simons, 1988; E. Telles, 1992; Webster and Dwyer, 1988).

As in other multiracial societies, women of color fare particularly poorly in Brazil. White men, of course, have the highest incomes, while Black men have earning levels comparable to those of White women. Black women are the furthest behind: 68 percent earn less than the minimum salary, compared to 24 percent for White men (J. Fiola, 1989).

Groups working on behalf of people of color in Brazil are gradually becoming more visible. Geledes/SOS Racism, a Black rights group, filed a protest with a television network for depicting a Black gardener cowering before a White man falsely accusing him of theft (L. Goering, 1994).

The difficulty that Blacks have in becoming more organized is not that they fail to recognize the discrimination, but that the society tends to think the distinctions are based on social class. After all, if problems are based on poverty, they are easier to overcome than if problems are based on racism (L. Goering, 1994). For Black Brazilians, even professional status can achieve only so much in one's social standing. An individual's blackness does not suddenly become invisible simply because he or she has acquired some social standing. The fame achieved by the Black Brazilian soccer player Pelé is a token exception and does not mean that Blacks have it easy or even have a readily available "escape hatch" through professional sports (A. Dzidzienyo, 1979).

Is Brazilian society becoming more polarized, or are Brazilians as tolerant as they seem always to have been? There is no easy answer because Brazil has not

A Black Brazilian proudly displays his Malcom X T-shirt.

been the subject of the intensive research and opinion polling found in the United States. Several scholars of Brazilian society believe that race has become more important. This does not mean that a belief in racial inferiority and the practice of *de facto* segregation will become common in Brazil. Brazil does not have, nor is it likely to have, a Black middle-class society separate from White middle-class society. By suggesting that Brazil is becoming more conscious of race, these scholars mean that coming generations will have a heightened awareness of race in Brazil, similar to that witnessed in the United States in the 1960s, although not of the same magnitude.

Continued denial that racial inequality exists in Brazil means that there is little pressure to assist poor Blacks, because their subordinate status is perceived to reflect class, not differential racial treatment. As Philip Mason (1970b) summarized it, Brazil's great asset is public commitment to the idea that racial discrimination is wrong; its great weakness is its reluctance to admit that discrimination does take place. Even more than in the United States, class prejudice reinforces racial prejudice to the point of obscuring it. Lower-class Whites and Blacks do experience limited opportunities because of life-long poverty. For some Brazilians, though, skin color is an added disability, and even in Brazil, race makes a difference in a person's opportunities and way of life (G. Freyre, 1946, 1959, 1963; Webster and Dwyer, 1988).

CANADA

Multiculturalism is a relatively recent term in the United States used to refer to diversity. Yet, in Canada, it has been adopted as a state policy for over two decades. Still, many people in the United States, when they think of Canada, see it as a homogeneous nation with a smattering of Arctic-type people—merely a cross between the northern mainland United States and Alaska. This is not the social reality.

One of the continuing discussions among Canadians is the need for a cohesive national identity or a sense of common peoplehood. This need has been complicated by the immense size of the country, much of which is sparsely populated, and the diversity of its people.

In 1971, Canadian prime minister Pierre Trudeau presented to the House of Commons a policy of multiculturalism which sought to permit cultural groups to retain and foster their identity. Specifically, he declared that there should continue to be two official languages, French and English, but "no official culture" and no "ethnic group [taking] precedence over any other" (H. Labelle, 1989, p. 2). Yet it is not always possible to legislate a pluralistic society, as the case of Canada demonstrates.

The Aboriginal Peoples

Canada, like the United States, has had an adversarial relationship with its native people. Yet the Canadian experience has not been as violent. During all three stages of Canadian history—French colonialism, British colonialism, and Canadian nationhood—there has been, compared to the United States, little warfare between Canadian-Whites and Canadian Native Americans. Yet the legacy today is similar. Prodded by settlers, the colonial governments and later the Canadian governments drove the Native Americans from their lands. Already by the 1830s, Indian reserves were being established that were similar to the reservations in the United States. Tribal members were encouraged to renounce their status and become Canadian citizens. Assimilation was the explicit policy until relatively recently (C. Waldman, 1985).

The native peoples of Canada are collectively referred to by the government as the Aboriginal Peoples and represent about 4–6 percent of the population, depending on the definition used. This population is classified into the following groups:

1. *Status Indians:* The 604 tribes or bands officially recognized by the government, numbering about 533,000, of whom the majority live on Indian reserves (or reservations).

2. *Inuit:* The more than 30,000 people living in the northern part of the country who have been typically referred to as the Eskimos.
3. *Métis:* Canadians of mixed ancestry, officially numbering 213,000; depending on definitions, range in number from 100,000 to 850,000.
4. *Non-Status Indians:* Canadians of native ancestry who, because of voluntary decisions or government rulings have been denied registration status. The group numbers about 224,000.

The Métis and non-Status Indians have historically enjoyed no separate legal recognition, but efforts continue to secure them special rights under the law, such as designated health, education, and welfare programs. The general public does not understand these legal distinctions, so if a Métis or non-Status Indian "looks like an Indian," she or he is subjected to the same treatment, discriminatory or otherwise (Breton, Reitz, and Valentine, 1980; Statistics Canada, 1993).

The new Canadian Federal Constitution of 1982 included a Charter of Rights that "recognized and affirmed . . . the existing aboriginal and treaty rights" of the Canadian Native American, Inuit, and Métis peoples. This recognition received the most visibility through the efforts of the Mohawks. At issue were land rights involving some property areas in Quebec that were viewed by the Mohawks as having spiritual significance. Their protests and militant confrontations reawakened the Canadian people to the concerns of their diverse native peoples (Amnesty International, 1993).

Some of the contemporary issues facing the Aboriginal Peoples are very similar to those faced by Native Americans in the United States. The Canadian Human Rights Commission has ruled that some native Inuit had their rights violated when

Canadian tribal people participate in a land dispute demonstration in Alberta.

forcibly relocated from northern Quebec to isolated areas in the Arctic in 1953. In response, the Department of Indian Affairs and Northern Development indicated in 1992 that it would facilitate transportation but rejected the possibility of compensation.

Another setback, also in 1992, occurred when a national referendum, the Charlottetown Agreement, was defeated. This constitutional reform package embraced a number of issues, including greater recognition of the Aboriginal Peoples. Canadian Native American and Inuit leaders expressed anger over the defeat, and Ron George, the leader of the Native Council of Canada, accused those who rejected the agreement of "perpetuating apartheid in this country" (*Keesing's,* 1992, p. 39126). However, the federal government has declared its willingness to accept the right of the Inuit and the other aboriginal people of Northern Canada to self-govern.

The fate of urban Aboriginal Peoples is an equally difficult issue. Who is responsible for the hundreds of thousands of native peoples scattered across the country? In metropolitan Toronto alone, there are an estimated 65,000 Aboriginal People from 60 tribal groups. The frustration they face has led to the demand, not warmly greeted, for a House of Commons seat designated for Toronto's Aboriginal Peoples (E. Fulton, 1992).

The contemporary Aboriginal Peoples have an overall life expectancy that is ten years less than the national average. Infant mortality is twice as high, and violent deaths are three times greater in number. In education, only 20 percent complete high school, compared to a 75 percent national average. On the economic side, half of the Aboriginal Peoples are on public assistance. While many of these problems are blamed on their isolated living conditions, even Canadian native peoples who have attempted to enter the urban economy experience public assistance levels of 25–30 percent (C. Waldman, 1985).

The Quebecois

Assimilation and domination have been the plight of most minority groups. The French-speaking people of the province of Quebec–the Quebecois as they are known—represent a contrasting case. Since the mid-1960s, they have reasserted their identity and captured the attention of the entire nation.

Quebec amounts for about one-fourth of the nation's population and about one-fourth of Canada's wealth. Reflecting its early settlement by the French, fully 80 percent of the province population claims French as their first language, compared to only 25 percent in the nation as a whole (J. Fox, 1994).

The Quebecois have sought to put the French–Canadian culture on an equal footing with the English–Canadian culture and to dominate the province. At the very least, this effort has been seen as an irritant outside Quebec and has been viewed with great concern by the English-speaking minority in Quebec (D. Salée, 1994).

In the 1960s, the Quebecois expressed the feeling that bilingual status was not enough. To have French recognized as one of two official languages in a nation dominated by the English-speaking population gave the Quebecois second-class status in their view. With some leaders threatening to break completely with Canada and make Quebec an independent nation, Canada made French the official language of the province and the only acceptable language of commercial signs and public transactions. New residents are now required to send their children to French schools. The English-speaking residents felt as if they had been made aliens, even though many of them had roots extending back to the 1700s. These changes spurred them to migrate from Quebec, and some corporate headquarters to relocate to the neighboring English-speaking province of Ontario (J. Fox, 1994; D. Salée, 1994).

The long debate over how much independence Quebec should be permitted reached a stalemate with the Meech Lake Accords. In 1987, at Meech Lake, a group of constitutional amendments was developed which would recognize Quebec as a distinct society. Quickly, Quebec ratified the amendments, but two other provinces (Newfoundland and Manitoba) did not approve them within the three-year deadline. The accords died, but the effort did not.

In 1992, following a series of meetings and a new agreement, the Charlottetown Agreement, mentioned earlier as including provisions for the Aboriginal Peoples, was developed, but this time it was put to a national referendum following endorsement by all the provinces and territories. The proposal's rejection by a 55–45 percent margin has essentially closed the constitutional debate on the topic. It has not meant, however, the end of Quebec's seeking its unique role. There were many reasons for the referendum's defeat. For example, it was defeated even in Quebec, where many felt that the Charlottetown Agreement did not transfer sufficient powers to the province. Some Aboriginal Peoples were skeptical that their treatment at the hands of the Quebecois would improve, and some leaders even vowed they would secede if Quebec ever gained sovereignty (D. Farr, 1993; C. Trueheart, 1995a).

Through the decades of debate, the force both unifying and dividing the French-speaking people of Quebec has been the Parti Quebecois. Since its establishment in 1968, the Parti Quebecois has been a force in the politics of the provinces and gained majority control of the province's assembly in 1994. The national version, Bloc Quebecois, emerged second to the ruling party and therefore plays the role of the official opposition party within Canada's parliamentary form of government. The Bloc Quebecois has advocated separatism—the creation of an independent nation of Quebec. Separatists contend that Quebec has the confidence, the natural resources, and the economic structure to stand on its own. However, not all Quebecois who vote for the party favor this extreme position, although they are certainly sympathetic to preserving their language and culture.

In 1995, the people of Quebec were faced with a referendum question on whether they wished to separate from Canada and form a new nation. In a very close vote, 50.5 percent of the voters indicated a preference to remain united with Canada. The vote was particularly striking given the confusion over how separation would be accomplished and its significance economically. Discussion over the referendum was further complicated by calls from tribal people in Quebec that if secession was approved, the tribes themselves would secede from Quebec. There was little doubt that the majority of French-speaking people of Quebec favored secession with the remaining English-speaking Quebecois providing the margin of voters necessary to preserve a united Canada, at least for now. Separatists vowed to keep working for secession and called for another referendum in the new future. Canadians opposed to separation spoke of reconciliation following the bitter election debate, but it was unclear what further concessions they were prepared to make to the separatists (Trueheart, 1995b).

Canada is characterized by the presence of two linguistic communities: the Anglophone and the Francophone, the latter occurring in one province, Quebec. Outside Quebec, Canadians are opposed to separatism, and within this province, they are divided. Language, therefore, both unifies and divides a nation of 29 million people.

Immigration and Race

Immigration has also been a significant social force contributing to Canadian multiculturalism. In addition to Britain's France, and other European nations, the largest sources of ancestry in Canada, in descending order, are Ukrainie, the Aboriginal Peoples, China, and Southeast Asia. Each of these groups account for 1–2 percent of the population. Collectively, the "visible minorities," as they are referred to in government reports of Blacks and Asians account for up to 10 percent of the population, but 82 percent are in three provinces: Ontario (Toronto), British Columbia (Vancouver), and Quebec (Montreal) (I. McKenna, 1994; Statistics Canada, 1993).

People in the United States tend to view Canada in complementary terms with respect to race relations. In part, this view reflects Canada's role as the "promised land" to slaves escaping the U.S. South and crossing the free North to Canada, where they were unlikely to be recaptured. The social reality, past and present, is quite different. Africans came in 1689 as involuntary immigrants to be enslaved by French colonists. Slavery officially continued until 1833. It never really flourished because the Canadian economy did not require a large labor force, and therefore, most slaves worked as domestic servants. Blacks from the United States did flee to Canada before slavery ended, but some fugitive slaves returned following Lincoln's issuance of the Emancipation Proclamation in 1863. These early Black arrivals in Canada were greeted in a variety of ways, which varied over time and place. Often, they were warmly received as fugitives from slavery, but as their numbers grew in some areas, Canadians grew concerned that they would be overwhelmed (R. Winks, 1971).

The view of Canada as a land of positive intergroup relations is also fostered by Canadians' comparing themselves to the United States. They have long been willing to compare their best social institutions to the worst examples of racism in the United States and to pride themselves on being a bit more virtuous and high-minded (P. McClain, 1979).

The contemporary Black Canadian population consists of indigenous Afro-Canadians with several generations of roots in Canada, West Indian immigrants and their descendants, and a number of post–World War II immigrants from the United States. Each of these groups has been significant. For example, in 1987, there were 60,000 Jamaicans in Toronto alone (H. Denton, 1987).

Before 1966, Canada's immigration policy alternated between restrictive and more open, as necessary to assist the economy. As in the United States, there were some very exclusionary phases based on race. From 1884 to 1923, Canada levied a Chinese "head tax," which virtually brought to a halt immigration that had earlier been encouraged. Subsequent policies through 1947 were not much better. More recent immigration policy, while not explicitly racist, heavily favors White nationalities such as British, Australian, and New Zealander.

In 1967 favoritism by nationality was replaced by regulations that created a point system based on the prospective immigrant's education and occupational skill, in light of the occupational needs of Canada. These changes transformed the source of immigration to include greater numbers of Black immigrants from Jamaica and other Caribbean nations, as well as from Asia (P. McClain, 1979; Statistics Canada, 1993; R. Winks, 1971).

In 1977, in response to concerns about growing immigration and even outright racist calls to exclude non-Whites, Canada enacted Bill C-24, which allows immigration to be restricted to maintain the "safety and good order of Canadian society." While proponents argued that it was not race-specific, there was a definite increase in the number of non-Whites denied entry or deported. Overall immigration dropped to the lowest levels since the end of World War II (Simmons and Keohane, 1992).

An analysis of the 1986 Census of Canada found significant differences in income between Whites and others, including both Blacks and Aboriginal Peoples. The income gap tended to be around $2,400, or 14 percent. Research also documented another aspect of social inequality familiar in the United States: gender differences. In Canada, the gender gap is about $10,000; overall, White males earned twice what non-White females earned (P. Li, 1992).

Concerns over second-class status have led to organized protests, sometimes militant in nature. For example, after the initial verdict in the Rodney King case in Los Angeles, Black Canadians took to the streets of Toronto to protest police brutality in that city. The government and the courts have been far from silent on issues relevant to "the visible minorities" and the Aboriginal Peoples. Canadian courts have liberally interpreted their Charter of Rights and Freedoms to prevent systematic discrimination, and equal rights legislation has been passed. Yet institutional racism and continuing debates about immigration policy will remain a part of the Canadian agenda for the next century (I. McKenna, 1994).

It is difficult to escape the parallels with the United States. For example, the Ku Klux Klan spread into Canada in the 1920s and experienced a degree of resurgence in the 1980s. Its targets were Blacks, Asian immigrants, and Jewish Canadians. Similarly, in the 1990s, pressure increased to restrict the immigration of new arrivals from Central America seeking asylum. Agitation has been particularly intense when Latin Americans who have been denied permanent residence in the United States seek sanctuary in Canada (*Refugee Reports*, 1992; J. Sher, 1983).

In 1541, the Frenchman Jacque Cartier established the first European settlement along the St. Lawrence River, but within a year he withdrew because of confrontation with the Iroquois. Almost 500 years later, the descendants of the Europeans and Aboriginal Peoples are still trying to resolve Canada's identity as it is shaped by issues of ethnicity, race, and language.

NORTHERN IRELAND

Armed conflict between Protestants and Catholics is difficult for many in the United States to understand. Our recent history in racial and ethnic relations makes it relatively easy for us to recognize that societies may be torn apart by differences based on skin color or even language. But atrocities among fellow citizens who share the bond of the Christian faith, even if in name only, can strike us as incredible. Yet newspapers and television news regularly recount the horrors from Northern Ireland—a very troubled land of only 1.6 million people.

Partition

The roots of today's violence lie in the invasion of Ireland by the English (then the Anglo-Normans) in the twelfth century. England, however, preoccupied with European enemies and hampered by resistance from the Irish, never gained complete control of the island. The northernmost area, called Ulster, received a heavy influx of Protestant settlers from Scotland and England seventeenth century following Oliver Cromwell's defeat of the Irish supporters of Britain's Catholic monarch (refer to Figure 17.1).

Ireland was united with Great Britain (England, Scotland, and Wales) in 1801 to form the United Kingdom. Despite this union, Ireland was still governed as a colony. Most of the people of Ireland found it difficult to accept union and did not consider the government in London theirs. In secret, the native Irish continued to speak Irish (or Gaelic) and worship as Catholics in defiance of the Protestant British government. Protestant settlers continued to speak English and to pay homage to the British monarch after the Restoration. Unhappy with their colonial status, the Irish, as they had done for the previous seven centuries, again pushed for independence or at least *home rule* with a local Irish parliament. Protestants in Ireland and most people in Britain objected to such demands, derisively referring to them as "Rome rule." During the latter 1800s, as home rule bills were introduced, Irish Catholics marched in support, only to be confronted by angry Protestants.

A very limited home-rule bill was passed in 1914, only to have its implementation delayed by World War I. Tired of waiting, a small group of militant Irish nationalists declared they would accept no compromises and no more delays. What could have been an isolated incident, unsupported by the majority of Catholic and Protestant Irish alike, aroused an extremist reaction from England and escalated the Easter Rebellion of 1916 into the Anglo-Irish War of 1919–1921. In 1921, a

Figure 17.1 **United Kingdom**

Source: Department of State, *Background Notes,* July 1981.

treaty was signed that provided for establishing an independent sovereign nation in the south, which evolved into today's Republic of Ireland.

From 1921 through the present, the United Kingdom has retained its control over the counties of Ulster—today's Northern Ireland. The Republic of Ireland is 95 percent Roman Catholic, but Northern Ireland, with its population 57 percent Protestant and 43 percent Roman Catholic, is still a land divided. The partition had been completed, but peace was not established (D. Schmitt, 1974; Tuohy, 1994).

The Civil Rights Movement

The immediate post-partition period was fairly peaceful, with fewer than 20 deaths through the late 1960s related to the Protestant–Catholic conflict that had divided the island for centuries. Britain was relatively indifferent to Northern Ireland governance and looked the other way as the Protestants capitalized on their majority. Political districts were created that minimized the voting strength of Catholics in sending representatives to Stormont, Northern Ireland's Parliament, while Protestant areas were divided to maximize electoral power. In some local elections, the abuses were more blatant, tying voting to home ownership and thereby disenfranchising large numbers of Catholics, who were more likely to be renters or to be living with kin (R. Terchek, 1977).

These political problems faced by Roman Catholics were compounded by other social problems. Because they had historically worked for Protestant factory owners, the Catholics are more likely to be poor, to live in substandard housing, and to suffer from more and longer periods of unemployment. Residential segregation and separate schools further isolated the two groups from one another (Boal and Douglas, 1982; J. Conroy, 1981; J. Whyte, 1986).

The civil rights movement of Northern Ireland began with a march in Londonderry (see Figure 17.1) in 1969, with Catholics joined by some sympathetic Protestants, protesting the social ills described here. Marching in defiance of a police order, the demonstrators soon confronted the police, and violence broke out, leaving civilians injured. A year later, Belfast protests led to an escalation of violence, and ten demonstrators were killed. British troops were ordered into Northern Ireland the next day. Within two years, a well-organized guerilla movement, the Irish Republican Army (IRA), rose on behalf of militant Roman Catholics. Simultaneously, terrorist Unionists, paramilitary Protestant groups, surfaced. The violence continued to escalate amid futile efforts by civil rights workers to have the issues discussed. In 1971, Britain initiated the policy of internment, allowing Britain to hold suspected terrorists, mostly Roman Catholics, without making charges against them.

In late 1994, peace was made in Northern Ireland as both the militant Unionists and the IRA forces declared cease-fires. This development followed months of intense effort between Great Britain and the Republic of Ireland that pledged to involve the militant groups in negotiations that would bring a permanent end to the violence. The Irish Republic government also agreed to end its claim on Northern Ireland (J. Waite, 1993).

In contrast to its participation in the Middle Eastern and South African conflicts, which we discuss later, the United States has had no official role to play. Successive U.S. presidents since the mid-1960s have called for peace but have not presided over any negotiations. Indeed, the United States is regarded with suspicion by both Irish Protestants and Britains, who fear the influence of Irish-American Catholics. In 1995, President Bill Clinton welcomed Gerry Adams, leader of Sein Fein, the political arm of the Irish Republican Army, to the White House causing former British prime minister Margaret Thatcher to comment that the event was "equivalent to having the prime minister of England invite the Oklahoma City bombers to [London] to congratulate them on a job well-done" (Hevrdejs and Conklin, 1995, p. 21).

The Search for Solutions

A survey held in 1968 and probably still valid today found that three-quarters of the Catholics in Northern Ireland thought of themselves as "Irish." Protestants clearly rejected such a term and preferred *British* (39 percent) or *Ulster* (32 percent) as the appropriate labels. This mutually exclusive identification, coupled with violence, has defied a simple solution. Beyond continued hostilities with varying degrees of military and police control directed from London, what are the possible solutions? Any of them would be unpleasant or extremely difficult to achieve or both (R. Rose, 1971).

Maintaining the British Connection   The first solution, maintaining all ties with the United Kingdom, would restore, or some would say continue, dominance by the Protestants. Some Roman Catholics of Northern Ireland believe that Protestant rule would be solidified if political rule were left in the hands of either the British or the government of Northern Ireland. A compromise was proposed by the United Kingdom in 1995 that would create some joint Northern Ireland–Republic of Ireland decision making on cross-border issues such as fishing, tourism, roads, and health policy (W. Montalbano, 1995).

Federation with the South   The second alternative is the opposite of the first, that is, the unification of Ulster with the Republic of Ireland. Naturally, Protestants would be distressed by becoming a minority in a new federation. Objectively, the 5 percent of the Republic of Ireland's population that is Protestant seem to suffer little; yet the Protestants of the north are unlikely to surrender what they regard as their inalienable right to be a part of the United Kingdom. It is also reasonable to assume that even the Catholics of the south would not warmly welcome such a unification. Although they would applaud such a move on patriotic and ideological grounds, they certainly would worry about taking on the economic devastation of Northern Ireland. The people of Northern Ireland, whatever their attitudes toward London, are highly dependent on the United Kingdom, which employs 40 percent of the people in government jobs. The United Kingdom's current subsidy of Northern Ireland equals 16 percent of the Republic of Ireland's total economic output. There is no way the Republic could maintain that support on its own (J. Darnton, 1995; R. Stevenson, 1994).

Repartition   A third possibility is a further partition that would continue the "solution" first attempted in the 1920s. Boundaries would be redrawn between Northern Ireland (that is, the United Kingdom) and the Republic of Ireland. This repartition, coupled with a large-scale population migration could lead to a Northern Ireland without a Roman Catholic minority. To move people, especially the Roman Catholics of the north, who are tied to their land as farmers, would not be easy. Further, repartition would seem to end for Irish nationalists any prospects of a unified Ireland. Given the advances in negotiations during 1994 and 1995, this option seems unlikely given the cease-fire and the move to maintain the British connection.

The recent moves toward reconciliation with a cease-fire has been greeted with concern by all people in Northern Ireland, some of whom fear that too much violence has occurred to move forward. Yet a 1995 survey showed that 81 percent of the people do favor the continuation of talks by all parties, including the IRA and the Unionists (J. Clarity, 1995).

Skepticism remains within Northern Ireland and in outside observers that peace can be maintained. About a quarter surveyed feel that violence will resume. It is little wonder: During the years since that 1969 Londonderry march, over 3,200 people have been killed and over 200,000 injured. Keep in mind that this is a small area, a little larger than the state of Connecticut. Translated proportionally to the United States, it would be as if almost 4 million people had been killed or wounded. In light of the 1994 cease-fire agreements, divided people may now finally have a chance to accommodate one another in peace (J. Clarity, 1995).

ISRAEL AND THE PALESTINIANS

In 1991, when the Gulf War ended, hopes were high in many parts of the world that a comprehensive Middle East peace plan could be hammered out. The key element in any such plan was to resolve the conflict between Israel and its Arab neighbors and to resolve the challenge of the Palestinian refugees. While the issues are debated in the political arena, the origins of the conflict can be found in race, ethnicity, and religion.

Nearly 2,000 years ago, the Jews were exiled from Palestine in the *diaspora*. The exiled Jews settled throughout Europe and elsewhere in the Middle East. There, they often encountered hostility and the anti-Semitism described in Chapter 15. With the conversion of the Roman Empire to Christianity, Palestine became the site of many Christian pilgrimages. Beginning in the seventh century, Palestine gradually fell under the Muslim influence of the Arabs. By the beginning of the twentieth century, tourism had become established. In addition, some Jews had migrated from Russia and established settlements that were tolerated by the Ottoman Empire, which then controlled Palestine.

Great Britain expanded its colonial control from Egypt into Palestine during World War I, driving out the Turks. Britain ruled the land but endorsed the eventual establishment of a Jewish national homeland in Palestine. The spirit of *Zionism,* the yearning to restore a Jewish national existence in the biblical homeland, was well under way. From the Arab perspective Zionism meant the subjugation, if not the elimination, of the Palestinians.

Thousands of Jews came to settle from throughout the world; even so, in the 1920s, Palestine was only about 15 percent Jewish. Ethnic tension grew as the Arabs of Palestine were threatened by the Zionist fervor. Rioting grew to such a point that, in 1939, Britain yielded to Palestinian demands that Jewish immigration be stopped. This occurred at the same time as large numbers of Jews were fleeing the growing Naziism in Europe. Following World War II, Jews resumed their demand for a homeland despite Arab objections. Britain turned to the newly formed United Nations to settle the dispute. In May 1948, the British mandate over Palestine ended, and the State of Israel was founded (A. Lesch, 1983; Said et al., 1988).

The Palestinian people define themselves as the people who lived in this former British mandate along with their descendants on their fathers' side. They are viewed as an ethnic group, within the larger group of Arabs, who generally speak Arabic and most of whom are Muslim. With the rapid rate of natural increase, the Palestinians have grown in number from 1.4 million at the end of World War II to 6 million (N. Roudi, 1993).

Arab-Israeli Conflicts

No sooner had Israel been recognized than the Arab nations, particularly Egypt, Jordan, Iraq, Syria, and Lebanon, announced their intentions to restore control to the Palestinian Arabs, by force if necessary. As hostilities broke out, the Israeli military stepped in to preserve the borders, which no Arab nation agreed to recognize. Some 60 percent of the 1.3 million Arabs fled or were expelled from Israeli territory, becoming refugees in neighboring countries. An uneasy peace followed as Israel attempted to encourage massive new Jewish immigration. Israel also extended the same services, such as education and health care, to the Israeli as were available to Jews. The new Jewish population continued to grow under the country's Law of Return, which gave every Jew in the world the right to settle permanently as a citizen. The question of Jerusalem remained unsettled, and the city was divided into two separate sections—Israeli Jewish and Jordanian Arab—a division both sides refused to regard as permanent (A. Lesch, 1983).

In 1967, Egypt, followed by Syria, responded to Israel's military actions in what has come to be called the Six-Day War. In the course of defeating the Arab states' military, Israel occupied the Gaza Strip, the West Bank, the Golan Heights, and the entire Sinai of Egypt (see Figure 17.2). The defeat was all the more bitter for the Arabs as Israeli-held territory expanded.

The October 1973 war (called the Yom Kippur War by Jews and the Ramadan War by Arabs), launched against Israel by Egypt and Syria, did not change any boundaries, but it did lead to huge oil-price rises as Arab and other oil-rich nations retaliated for the European and U.S. backing of Israel. In 1979, Egypt, through the mediation of U.S. President Carter, recognized Israel's right to exist, for which Israel returned the Sinai, but there was no suggestion the other occupied territories would be returned to neighboring Arab states. This recognition by Egypt, following several unsuccessful Arab military attacks, signaled to the Palestinians that they were alone in their struggle against Israel (P. Seale, 1980).

While our primary attention here is on the Palestinians and the Jews, there is another significant ethnic issue present in Israel. The Law of Return has brought to Israel Jews of varying cultural backgrounds. European Jews have been the dominant force, but a significant migration of the so-called "Oriental" Jews from North Africa and other parts of the Middle East has created what sociologist Ernest Krausz (1973) termed "the two nations." Not only are the Oriental and European

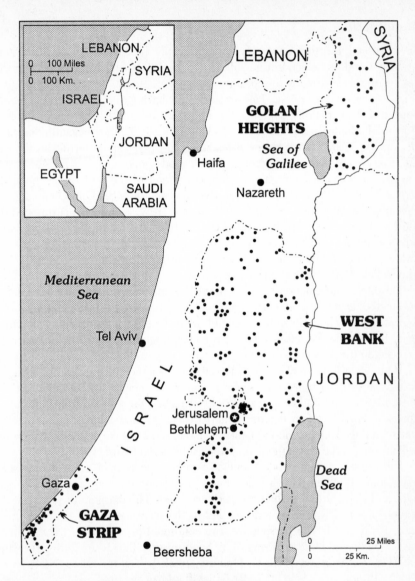

Figure 17.2 **Israeli Settlements and Palestinian Lands**
In 1994, the Gaza Strip and the West Bank became part of an autonomous territory under the Palestinian Liberation Organization. In this area, as well as the Golan Heights, are settlements built for Jews in areas that Israel captured in 1967 from Jordan, Egypt, and Syria.

Jews culturally diverse, but there are also significant socioeconomic differences, the Europeans generally being more prosperous, better represented in the Knesset (Israel's parliament), and better educated. The Oriental Jews are well aware of their subordinate status and even today are suspicious of efforts to ease the absorption of Russian Jews while their own problems seem to be unaddressed (Ben-Rafael and Sharot, 1991; Friendly and Silver, 1981).

The Intifada

The occupied territories were regarded initially by Israel as a security zone between it and its belligerent neighbors. By the 1980s, however, it was clear that they were also serving as the location of new settlements for Jews migrating to Israel, especially from Russia. Palestinians, while having the political and monetary support of Arab nations, saw little likelihood of yet another successful military effort to eliminate Israel. Therefore, in December 1987, they began the *intifada*, the uprising against Israel by the Palestinians in the occupied territories through attacks against soldiers, the boycott of Israeli goods, general strikes, resistance, and noncooperation with Israeli authorities. The target of the intifada has been the Israelis. It should be realized that for several years the intifada has been a grass-roots, popular movement whose growth in support was as much a surprise to the Palestine Liberation Organization (PLO) and the Arab nations as it was to Israel and its supporters. The broad range of participants in the intifada—students, workers, union members, professionals, and business leaders—showed the unambiguous Palestinian opposition to occupation.

Despite condemnation by the United Nations and the United States, Israel continued to expel suspected activists from the occupied territories into neighboring Arab states. The intifada began out of the frustration of the Palestinians within Israel, but the confrontations were later encouraged by the PLO, an umbrella organization for several Palestinian factions varying in their militancy.

With television news footage of Israeli soldiers appearing to attack defenseless youths, the intifada transformed world opinion, especially in the United States. Palestinians came to be viewed as people struggling for self-determination rather than as terrorists out to destroy Israel. Instead of Israel being viewed as the "David" and its Arab neighbors "Goliath," Israel came to take on the bully role and the Palestinians the sympathetic underdog role (A. Hubbard, 1993).

Palestinians now number 6 million, over 40 percent of them living under Israeli control. Of the Israeli Palestinians, about one-third are regarded as residents, and the rest live in the occupied territories. The diaspora of Jews that the creation of Israel was to remedy has led to the displacement of the Palestinian Arabs. From the Israeli perspective, the continued possession of these lands is vital, as evidenced by Iraq's firing of 39 Scud missiles into Israel during the 1991 Gulf War (G. Aronson, 1990; C. Doherty, 1992; J. Galtung, 1989; NBC News, 1992; N. Roudi, 1993; Said et al., 1988; Schiff and Ya'air, 1990).

Almost an entire generation of Israelis and Palestinians has been born since the 1967 Six-Day War. A declining number of Israelis personally recall the time when the Jews did not have a homeland. Yet the intifada and international reaction propelled Israel and the PLO to reach an agreement.

An Uncertain Future

In May 1994, Israeli prime minister Yitzhak Rabin and PLO chairman Yasser Arafat signed the Israel-Palestinian Accord. This and subsequent agreements ended the state of war and set in motion the creation of the first-ever self-govern-

President Bill Clinton brought the late Israeli prime minister Yitzhak Rabin and PLO chairman Yasser Arafat together for an historic handshake after the signing of the Israeli-PLO peace accord.

ing Palestinian territory in the Gaza Strip and the West Bank. The withdrawal of Israeli troops ended 27 years of military occupation.

Politically, the creation of a Palestinian Authority has been an unexpected achievement, but economically, the people are worse off. In the West Bank, the authority now operates education, health, welfare, and other services without the large Israeli subsidies of the past. In addition, many Palestinians—half in the Gaza Strip and nearly one-third in the West Bank—who commuted to work in Israel have lost their jobs. Occasional total closures of the Israel–Palestinian Accord border also create economic problems for the former occupied territories (B. Gellman, 1995a, 1995b).

The Israeli government must be constantly on guard against political attacks from within by those who feel that it sold out to the PLO. These right-wing Israelis also include residents in Jewish settlements who suddenly find themselves under Palestinian control. Indeed in 1995 prime minister Rabin was assassinated at a peace rally by an Israeli who felt the government had given up too much. Also, sporadic attacks and protests by militant Palestinians and extremist Israelis make the unsettled situation even more tense. Arafat, once despised by Israel (and the United States), is viewed desperately as the key to keeping the peace.

The Israeli and PLO leaders continue to be concerned about being able to control violence by those dissatisfied by the accord. Additional issues pending include:

- *The status of Jerusalem.* It is Israel's capital but is also viewed by Muslims as their third most holy city in the entire world.

- *The future of the Jewish settlements in the Palestinian territories.* Jews make up about 17 percent of the population in the West Bank and 2 percent in the Gaza Strip.
- *The creation of a truly independent Palestinian national state.*
- *The future of Palestinian refugees elsewhere.*

Added worries are the uneasy peace between Israel and its Arab neighbors and the sometimes interrelated events in Iraq and Iran (M. Parks, 1994; D. Perry, 1994).

The last 50 years have witnessed significant changes: Israel has gone from a land under siege to a nation whose borders are recognized by virtually everyone. The Palestinian people have gone from disenfranchisement to becoming a people with territory who can now welcome back those in exile. The current solution is fragile and temporary, as is any form of secession, but the foundation for accommodation is stronger than at any time in recent memory.

REPUBLIC OF SOUTH AFRICA

In every nation in the world, some racial, ethnic, or religious groups enjoy advantages denied other groups. Nations differ in the extent of this denial and in whether it is supported by law or by custom. In no other industrial society has the denial been so entrenched in law as in the Republic of South Africa.

The Republic of South Africa is different from the rest of Africa because the original African peoples of the area are no longer present. Today, the country is multiracial, as shown in Table 17.1. The largest group is the Black Africans, or Bantus, who migrated from the north in the eighteenth century. Cape Coloureds, the

SHAKY

By Locher for the *Chicago Tribune.* Reprinted by permission. Tribune Media Service.

product of mixed race, and Asians make up the remaining non-Whites. The small White community is made up of the English and the Afrikaners, the latter descended from Dutch and other European settlers. As in all the other multicultural nations we have considered, colonialism and immigration have left their mark.

The Legacy of Colonialism

The permanent settlement of South Africa by Europeans began in 1652, when the Dutch East India Company established a colony in Cape Town as a port of call for shipping vessels bound for India. The area was sparsely populated, and the original inhabitants of the Cape of Good Hope, the Hottentots and Bushmen, were pushed inland like the indigenous people of the New World. To fill the need for laborers, the Dutch imported slaves from areas of Africa farther north. Slavery was confined mostly to areas near towns and involved more limited numbers than in either the United States or Brazil. The Boers, seminomads descended from the Dutch, did not remain on the coast but trekked inland to establish vast sheep and cattle ranches. The trekkers, as they were known, regularly fought off the Black inhabitants of the interior regions. Sexual relations between Dutch men and slave and Hottentot women were quite common, giving rise to a mulatto group referred to today as Cape Coloureds.

The British entered the scene by acquiring South Africa in 1814, at the end of the Napoleonic Wars. The British introduced workers from India as indentured servants on sugar plantations. They had also freed the slaves by 1834, with little compensation to the Dutch slave owners, and had given the Blacks virtually all political and civil rights. The Boers were not happy with these developments and spent most of the nineteenth century in a violent struggle with the growing number of English colonists. In 1902, the British finally overwhelmed the Boers, leaving bitter memories on both sides. The British were victorious because of a successful alliance with the Black Africans. Once in control, however, they recognized

Table 17.1   RACIAL GROUPS IN THE REPUBLIC OF SOUTH AFRICA (PERCENTAGES)

Whites in South Africa are outnumbered by more than four to one, and their proportion of the population is declining. Yet they clearly represent the dominant economic and political force in this troubled nation.

	Whites	All Non-Whites	Black Africans	Coloureds	Asians
1904	22	78	67	9	2
1936	21	79	69	8	2
1951	21	79	68	9	3
1990	14	86	75	9	3
2010 (est.)	10	90	81	7	2

Notes: Data for 1990 include the Black homelands/"nations." Percentages do not add up to 100 because of rounding.

Sources: South African Institute of Race Relations (1992, pp. 2, 3); P. van den Berghe (1978, p. 102).

that the superior numbers of the non-Whites were a potential threat to their power, as they had been to the power of the Afrikaners.

The growing non-White population consisted of the Coloureds, or mixed population, and the Black tribal groups, collectively referred to as Bantus. The British gave both groups the vote but restricted the franchise with property qualifications. *Pass laws* were introduced, placing curfews on the Bantus and limiting their geographic movement. These laws, enforced through "reference books" until 1986, were intended to prevent urban areas from becoming overcrowded with job-seeking Black Africans, a familiar occurrence in colonial Africa (Barclay et al., 1976; G. Fredrickson, 1981; J. Treen, 1983; P. van den Berghe, 1965; W. Wilson, 1973).

Apartheid

In 1948, South Africa was granted its independence from the United Kingdom, and the National Party, dominated by the Afrikaners, assumed control of the government. Under the leadership of this party, the rule of White supremacy, already well under way in the colonial period as custom, became more and more formalized into law. To deal with the multiracial population, the Whites devised a policy called *apartheid* to ensure their dominance. Apartheid (in Afrikaans, the language of the Afrikaners, it means "separation" or "apartness") came to mean a policy of separate development, euphemistically now called *multinational development* by the government.

Multinational development reached its full evolution during the 1980s. Officially, multinational development called for "economic co-operation between Blacks and Whites coupled with the highest possible degree of political freedom"

A group of South Africans display their passbooks, which were used to regulate the movement of Black people under apartheid.

(South African Department of Foreign Affairs and Information, 1983, p. 195). Beginning in 1976, the most developed Bantustan area, the Transkei, was awarded "independence." Because of the close control that White South Africa exercised over the people of the Transkei, no other nation recognized this new state as having independent status.

The White ruling class was not homogeneous. The English and Afrikaners belonged to different political parties, lived apart, spoke different languages, and worshiped separately, but they shared the belief that some form of apartheid was necessary. Apartheid can perhaps be best understood as a twentieth-century effort to reestablish the paternalistic form of race relations typified by the master–slave relationship (J. Burns, 1978; J. Butler, 1974; W. Wilson, 1973).

Four independent republics and six "self-governing" states were identified by the Republic of South Africa through 1992 (see Figure 17.3), which for simplicity's sake we will refer to as *homelands,* or *Bantustans.* These changes were regarded outside South Africa and by most Black South Africans as cosmetic. Blacks and most foreign governments felt the changes were going too slowly.

The United States and other nations increasingly isolated South Africa economically, and politically, during the 1980s. Of special embarrassment to South Africa was its virtual elimination from international sports competition, such as the Olympics, because of its apartheid athletic practices.

A significant turn of events came in 1990, when South African prime minister F. W. De Klerk legalized 60 banned Black organizations and freed Nelson Mandela, leader of the African National Congress (ANC) after 27 years of imprisonment. Mandela's triumphant remarks following his release appear in "Listen to Their Voices." The following year, De Klerk and Black leaders signed a National Peace Accord, pledging themselves to the establishment of a multiparty democracy and an end to violence. Following a series of political defeats, De Klerk called for a referendum in 1992 to allow Whites to vote on ending apartheid. If he failed to receive popular support, he vowed to resign. A record high turnout gave a solid 68.6 percent vote favoring the continued dismantling of legal apartheid and the creation of a new constitution through negotiation. The process toward power-sharing ended symbolically when De Klerk and Mandela were jointly awarded the 1993 Nobel Peace Prize (Ottaway and Taylor, 1992).

The Mandela Era

In April 1994, South Africa held its first universal election. Nelson Mandela's ANC received 62 percent of the vote, giving him a five-year term as president. The National Party's F. W. De Klerk is serving as one of two executive deputy presidents. The ANC is faced with making the transition from a liberation movement that for 80 years used boycotts, protests, and occasional sabotage as political statements to a governing party that needs to practice political compromise (F. Clines, 1994; B. Nelan, 1994).

The political and economic agenda is very full. Local and area elections are still to come in a country where local politicians are often not respected. The Black population itself is hardly homogeneous, speaking nine languages, holding ethnic rivalries that stretch back for centuries, and having political disputes across gener-

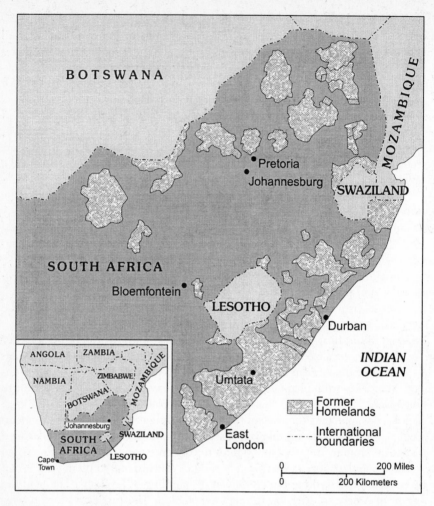

Figure 17.3 **Republic of South Africa**

Homeland	People	Homeland	People
1. Transkei°	Xhosa	6. Gazankulu	Shangaaan/Tsonga
2. Ciskei°	Xhosa	7. Bophuthatswana°	Tswaba
3. Kwazulu	Zulu	8. Basotho Qwaqwa	S. Sotho
4. Lebowa	Pedi/N. Ndebele	9. Swazi (KaNgwane)	Swazi
5. Venda°	Venda	10. S. Ndebele (KwaNdebele	S. Ndebele

°Indicates homelands declared to be independent by South Africa.

Source: From Roger J. Southall, *South Africa's Transkei.* Copyright © 1983 by Roger Southall. Reprinted by permission of Monthly Review Foundation.

ations. At best, one-fifth of the nation's Blacks can compete in the nation's economy, while the balance, reflecting apartheid, form a huge underclass. Two-thirds live in homes without electricity or running water, and nearly a fifth are actually squatters or backyard slum dwellers (P. Taylor, 1993).

Listen to Their Voices
"Africa, It Is Ours"

NELSON MANDELA

The following excerpts are from 71-year old Black nationalist leader Nelson Mandela's speech, delivered in front of the Cape Town City Hall following his being released from a 27-year imprisonment on February 12, 1990.

Amandla! Amandla! i-Afrika, mayibuye! [Power! Power! Africa, it is ours!]

Nelson Mandela

My friends, comrades and fellow South Africans, I greet you all in the name of peace, democracy and freedom for all. I stand here before you not as a prophet but as a humble servant of you, the people.

Your tireless and heroic sacrifices have made it possible for me to be here today. I therefore place the remaining years of my life in your hands.

On this day of my release, I extend my sincere and warmest gratitude to the millions of my compatriots and those in every corner of the globe who have campaigned tirelessly for my release.

Negotiations on the dismantling of apartheid will have to address the overwhelming demand of our people for a democratic nonracial and unitary South Africa. There must be an end to white monopoly on political power.

And a fundamental restructuring of our political and economic systems to insure that the inequalities of apartheid are addressed and our society thoroughly democratized. . . .

Our struggle has reached a decisive moment. We call on our people to seize this moment so that the process toward democracy is rapid and uninterrupted. We have waited too long for our freedom. We can no longer wait. Now is the time to intensify the struggle on all fronts.

To relax our efforts now would be a mistake which generations to come will not be able to forgive. The sight of freedom looming on the horizon should encourage us to redouble our efforts. It is only through disciplined mass action that our victory can be assured.

We call on our white compatriots to join us in the shaping of a new South Africa. The freedom movement is the political home for you, too. We call on the international community to continue the campaign to isolate the apartheid regime.

To lift sanctions now would be to run the risk of aborting the process toward the complete eradication of apartheid. Our march to freedom is irreversible. We must not allow fear to stand in our way.

Universal suffrage on a common voters' roll in a united democratic and nonracial South Africa is the only way to peace and racial harmony.

In conclusion, I wish to go to my own words during my trial in 1964. They are as true today as they were then. I wrote: I have fought against white domination, and I have fought against black domination. I have cherished the idea of a democratic and free society in which all persons live together in harmony and with equal opportunities.

It is an ideal which I hope to live for and to achieve. But if needs be, it is an ideal for which I am prepared to die.

With the emergence of the new multiracial government in South Africa, we see a country with enormous promise but many challenges that are similar to those of our own multiracial society (B. Keller, 1993). Some of the controversial issues facing the Mandela government are very familiar to citizens in the United States:

- *A Human Rights Commission?* Formed in 1994 to end discrimination, this commission also faced controversy about achieving its goals without intruding on individual rights.
- *Affirmative action.* Using this familiar program, name, race-based employment goals, and other preference programs are being discussed with cries that it constitutes reverse apartheid.
- *Illegal immigration.* Given the poverty of Africa and the civil upheavals in some nations, foreigners seek out the economic opportunity and political peace developing in South Africa. An estimated 5 percent of the population are illegal aliens, neighboring Mozambique and Zimbabwe being the leading sources.
- *Rights of Whites.* Amid the enthusiasm for recognition of the rights of Blacks, Coloureds, and Asians, some South Africans have expressed a concern that the culture of Whites is being set aside. For example, debate has centered on the decline in Afrikaans-language television programming.
- *Crime.* While government-initiated violence has ended, the generations of conflict and years of intertribal attacks have created a climate for crime, the ownership of illegal guns, and a disrespect for law enforcement.
- *Medical care.* The nation is trying to confront the duality of private care for the affluent (usually White) and government-subsidized care (usually for people of color).
- *School integration.* Multiracial schools are replacing the apartheid system, but for some, the change is occurring too fast or not fast enough.

The issues are to be addressed with minimal increases in government spending, as Mandela seeks to reverse deficit spending without an increase in taxes that would frighten away needed foreign investment. As difficult as all these challenges are, perhaps the most difficult is land reform (J. Frielinghaus, 1995; J. Kane-Berman, 1995; Randall, 1995; South African Institute of Race Relations, 1994, 1995).

The Mandela government has pledged itself to addressing the issue of land ownership. Between 1960 and 1990, the government forced 3.5 million Black South Africans from their land and frequently allowed Whites to settle on it. Under the 1994 Restitution of Land Rights Act, these displaced citizens can now file for a return of their land. The goal of redistributing 30 percent of the nation's agricultural land before the year 2000 has been uprooted.

The magnitude of this land reform issue cannot be minimized. While not all Blacks would return, an estimated 1 million may seek ownership. Many will face objections by settled White families, and a Land Claims Court has been created to resolve the inevitable land disputes that will occur, even with the promise of government compensation (P. Hawthorne, 1994; South African Institute of Race Relations, 1995).

By Horsey for the *Seattle Post-Intelligencer.*

Despite the major achievements by the ANC, the problems facing the new government are immense. Nelson Mandela does enjoy the advantage of wide personal support throughout the nation—a 90 percent approval rating as of mid-1995. He has publicly declared his intention to retire in 1999 when his term ends; he most likely will leave his successors much work still to be done in the next century because of the legacy of apartheid (B. Drogin, 1995).

CONCLUSION

Intergroup relations in Brazil, Canada, Northern Ireland, Israel, and South Africa are striking in their similarities and contrasts. The colonial experience has played a role in all cases, but particularly in South Africa. In Brazil and South Africa, where there are long histories of multiracial societies, mixed-race sexual relations have been widespread but with different results. Mulattoes in Brazil occupy a middle racial group and experience reduced tension, whereas in South Africa the Cape Coloureds had freedoms under apartheid almost as limited as those of the Bantus. South Africa enforced *de jure* segregation; Israeli communities seem to have *de facto* segregation; and Brazilian relations resemble some pattern of integration. Israel's and South Africa's intergroup conflicts involve the world community. Indigenous people figure prominently in Canada and Brazil. Complete assimilation is absent in all five societies and is unlikely to occur in the near future; the legal and informal barriers to assimilation and pluralism vary for those subordinate people choosing either option.

If we add the United States to these societies, the comparison becomes even more significant. The problems of racial and ethnic adjustment in the United

States have dominated our attention, but they parallel past and present experiences in other societies with racial, ethnic, or religious heterogeneity. The U.S. government has been involved in providing educational, financial, and legal support for programs intended to help particular racial or ethnic groups, and it continues to avoid interfering with religious freedom. Bilingual, bicultural programs in schools, autonomy for Native Americans on reservations, and increased participation in decision making by residents of ghettoes and barrios are all viewed as acceptable goals, although they are not pursued to the extent that many subordinate-group people would like.

While it promotes racial, ethnic, and religious diversity, the United States strives to impose universal criteria on employers, educators, and realtors, so subordinate racial and ethnic groups can participate fully in the larger society. In some instances, in order to bring about equality of results, not just equality of opportunity, programs have been developed to give competitive advantages to women and minority men. This latest answer to social inequality has provoked much controversy over how to achieve the admirable goal of a multiracial, multiethnic society, undifferentiated in opportunity and rewards.

Relations among racial, ethnic, or religious groups take two broad forms, as situations characterized by either consensus or conflict. Consensus prevails where assimilation or fusion among groups has been completed. Consensus also prevails in a pluralistic society in the sense that members have agreed to respect differences among groups and not to demand conformity. Pluralism tolerates disagreement, but relations among groups are harmonious. By eliminating the contending group, extermination and expulsion also lead to a consensus society. In the study of intergroup relations, it is often easy to ignore conflict where there is a high degree of consensus because it is assumed that an orderly society has no problems. In some instances, however, this assumption is misleading. Through long periods of history, misery inflicted on a racial, ethnic, or religious group was judged to be appropriate, if not actually divinely inspired (D. Grove, 1974; J. Horton, 1966; R. Schermerhorn, 1970).

In recent history, harmonious relations among all racial, ethnic, and religious groups have been widely accepted as a worthy goal. The struggle against oppression and inequality is not new. It dates back at least to the revolutions in England, France, and the American colonies in the seventeenth and eighteenth centuries. The twentieth century is unique in the extension of equality to the less privileged classes, generally racial and ethnic minorities. Conflict along racial and ethnic lines is especially bitter now because it evokes memories of slavery, colonial oppression, and overt discrimination. Today's African Americans are much more aware of slavery than contemporary poor people are of seventeenth-century debtors' prisons (P. Mason, 1970a).

Racial and ethnic equality implies the right of the individual to choose his or her own way of life. As Hunt and Walker (1979) observed, however, individual rights may conflict with the group consensus. This conflict makes the situation exceedingly complex; even if a society allows a group to select its own destiny, individual members of the group may then be unable to freely pursue their own course of action. If Native Americans as a group choose to emphasize their cultural distinctiveness, those individuals who wish to integrate into White society may be looked on by their peers as traitors to their tribe.

Unquestionably, the struggle for justice among racial and ethnic groups has not completely met its goals. Many people are still committed to repression, although they may see it only as the benign neglect of those less privileged. Such repression leads only to the dehumanization of both the subordinated individual and the oppressor. Growth in equal rights movements and self-determination for Third World countries largely populated by non-White people has moved the world onto a course that seems irreversible. The new ethnic battlelines in Bosnia, Serbia, Rwanda, and the former Soviet Union have only added to the tensions. Philip Mason (1970b) acknowledged that people are more willing to reject stability if preserving it means inequality.

Self-determination, whether for groups or individuals, is often impossible in societies as they are currently structured. Bringing about social equality will therefore require significant changes in existing institutions. Because such changes are not likely to come about with everyone's willing cooperation, the social costs will be quite high. If there is a trend in racial and ethnic relations in the world today, however, it is the growing belief that the social costs, however high, must be paid to achieve self-determination.

It is naive to foresee a world of societies in which one person equals one vote and all are accepted without regard to race, ethnicity, religion, or gender. It is equally unlikely to expect to see a society, let alone a world, that is without a privileged class or prestigious jobholders. Contact between different peoples, as we have seen numerous times, precedes conflict. Contact also may initiate mutual understanding and appreciation.

In a commencement address at American University in 1963, President John F. Kennedy declared, "If we cannot end now our differences, at least we can help make the world safe for diversity" (H. Cleveland, 1995, p. 23). In 1994, addressing the graduating class at the U.S. Naval Academy in Annapolis, President Bill Clinton (1994) observed about current wars that "the hardest cases involved the many ethnic and religious conflicts that have erupted in our era" (p. 1160). What may well emerge from contemporary and future unrest is the recognition by human beings that people are fundamentally alike and share the same abilities, weaknesses, and dreams.

KEY TERMS

apartheid The policy of the South African government intended to maintain separation of Blacks, Coloureds, and Asians from the dominant Whites.

diaspora The exile of Jews from Palestine several centuries before Christianity began.

home rule Britain's grant of a local parliament to Ireland.

intifada The Palestinian uprising against Israeli authorities in the occupied territories.

kin country syndrome Coalitions between nations based on ethnic, racial, or religious ties.

manumission The freeing of slaves by a master.

mulatto escape hatch In Brazil, social movement into a higher class based on gradation of skin color.

multinational development A South African government program promoting the creation of so-called homelands, or Bantustans, in desolate areas.

pass laws Laws that control internal movement by non-Whites in South Africa; now called *reference-book laws.*

quilombo A hideaway used by Brazilian slaves in the nineteenth century.

Zionism The traditional Jewish religious yearning to return to the biblical homeland, now used to refer to support for the State of Israel.

FOR FURTHER INFORMATION

Pierre-Michel Fontaine, ed. *Race, Class, and Power in Brazil.* Los Angeles: UCLA Center for Afro-American Studies, 1986.

A collection of essays examining the various aspects of Black Brazilians' changing situation.

Alfred McClung Lee. *Terrorism in Northern Ireland.* Bayside, NY: General Hall, 1983.

A sociohistorical analysis of the problems besetting the people of Northern Ireland.

Alan Paton. *Cry, the Beloved Country.* New York: Scribner, 1948.

Paton's widely acclaimed novel about an old Zulu parson who discovers that his sister is a prostitute and his son the murderer of a White industrialist.

Lynda Shorten. *Without Reserve: Stories from Urban Natives.* Edmonton, Alberta: NeWest Press, 1991.

A collection of autobiographical profiles of individual native people who live in a Western Canadian city.

Thomas Skidmore. *Black into White.* New York: Oxford University Press, 1974.

A perceptive analysis of the myth and reality of the "whitening" of Black people in Brazil.

Allister Sparks. *Tomorrow Is Another Country.* New York: Hill & Wang, 1995.

A journalistic account of the massive social change from apartheid to a multiracial shared governance.

Pierre L. van den Berghe. *Race and Racism: A Comparative Perspective,* 2d ed. New York: Wiley, 1978.

Besides presenting his typology of paternalistic and competitive race relations, van den Berghe incisively analyzes the patterns of race relations in Mexico, Great Britain, South Africa, and the United States.

Ronald Weitzer. *Transforming Settler States: Communal Conflict and Internal Security in Northern Ireland and Zimbabwe.* Berkeley: University of California Press, 1990.

A study of two settler groups, Protestants in Northern Ireland and Europeans in Zimbabwe, and the social change and political violence that followed.

William J. Wilson. *Power, Racism, and Privilege: Race Relations in Theoretical and Sociohistorical Perspective.* New York: Macmillan, 1973.

Wilson concentrates on relations between Blacks and Whites in South Africa and the United States, stressing the historical development of racial stratification and the emergence of institutional racism. The author revised some of his conclusions about the United States in his 1980 book, *The Declining Significance of Race.*

Periodicals

Journals that cover race and ethnic relations from a cross-national perspective include *Ethnic and Racial Studies* (established in 1978), *Race and Class* (1959), and *Race Today* (1968). A special issue on Blacks in Brazil appeared in *The Journal of Black Studies* (December 1980). Other journals relevant to this chapter include *Israel Social Science Research* (1983), *Israeli Studies* (1981), *Journal of South African Studies* (1974), and *Palestine Refugees Today* (1960).

CRITICAL THINKING QUESTIONS

1. What kind of information or additional data are necessary to clarify the relative importance of class and race in Brazil?
2. On what levels can one speak of an identity issue facing Canada as a nation?
3. What role has secession played in Canada, Northern Ireland, and Israel?
4. How have civil uprisings affected intergroup tensions in Northern Ireland and Israel?
5. To what extent are the problems facing Nelson Mandela a part of apartheid's legacy?

Glossary

Parenthetical numbers refer to the chapters in which the term is used.

abolitionists Whites and free Blacks who favored the end of slavery. (7)

absolute deprivation The minimum level of subsistence below which families or individuals should not be expected to exist. (3)

affirmative action Positive efforts to recruit subordinate group members or women for jobs, promotions, and educational opportunities. (3)

Afrocentricm perspective An emphasis on the customs of African cultures and how they have penetrated the history, culture, and behavior of Blacks in the United States and around the world. (1)

AJAs Americans of Japanese ancestry in Hawaii. (12)

amalgamation The process by which a dominant group and a subordinate group combine through intermarriage to form a new group. (1)

androgyny The state of being both masculine and feminine, aggressive and gentle. (16)

anti-Semitism Anti-Jewish prejudice or discrimination. (15)

apartheid The policy of the South African government intended to maintain separation of Blacks, Coloureds, and Asians from the dominant Whites. (17)

assimilation The process by which an individual forsakes his or her own cultural tradition to become part of a different culture. (1)

authoritarian personality A psychological construct of a personality type likely to be prejudiced and to use others as scapegoats. (2)

AWM (angry white men) Refers to the 1990s nation that men are a new victim group whose grievances need to be heard. (16)

barrios Segregated urban slums populated by Chicanos, Puerto Ricans, or other Hispanic groups. (10)

bilingual education A program designed to allow students to learn academic concepts in their native language while they learn a second language. (9)

bilingualism The use of two or more languages in places of work or education and the treatment of each language as legitimate. (1, 9)

biological race The mistaken notion of a genetically isolated human group. (1)

bipolar occupational structure Clustering at the higher- and lower-paying ends of the occupational scale, with relatively few in the middle—a situation in which Chinese Americans, and other Asian Americans, find themselves. (12)

Bogardus scale Technique to measure social distance towards different racial and ethnic groups. (2)

borderlands The area of a common culture along the United States–Mexican border. (10)

bracero Contracted Mexican laborers brought to the United States during World War II. (10)

brain drain Immigration to the United States of skilled workers, professionals, and technicians who are desperately needed by their home countries. (4, 9)

caste approach An approach that views race and social class as synonymous, with disadvantaged minorities occupying the lowest social class and having little, if any, opportunity to improve their social position. (2)

checklist approach Technique of presenting respondents with traits to be applied to ethnic groups. (2)

Chicanismo An ideology emphasizing pride and positive identity among Chicanos. (10)

civil disobedience A tactic promoted by Martin Luther King, Jr., based on the belief that individuals have the right to disobey unjust laws under certain circumstances. (7)

civil religion The religious dimension in American life that merges the state with sacred beliefs. (5)

class As defined by Max Weber, persons who share similar levels of wealth. (1, 8)

colonialism A foreign power's maintenance of political, social, economic, and cultural dominance over a people for an extended period. (1)

color gradient The placement of people on a continuum from light to dark skin color rather than in distinct racial groupings by skin color. (9, 11)

comparable worth See *pay equity.*

conflict perspective A sociological approach that assumes that social behavior is best understood in terms of conflict or tension among competing groups. (1)

contact hypothesis An interactionist perspective stating that interracial contact between people of equal status in noncompetitive circumstances will reduce prejudice. (2)

creationists People who support a literal interpretation of the Biblical book of Genesis on the origins of the universe and argue that evolution should not be presented as established scientific thought. (5)

crossover effect An effect that appears as previously high-scoring Native American children become "below average" in intelligence when tests are given in English rather than their native languages. (6)

culture of poverty According to its proponents, a way of life that involves no future planning, and no enduring commitment to marriage, no work ethic; this culture follows the poor even when they move out of the slums or the barrio. (11)

curanderismo Hispanic folk medicine. (10)

defensive insulation The framework of social structures for mutual help found in enclaves like Chinatowns. (13)

denomination A large, organized religion not officially linked with the state or government. (5)

diaspora The exile of Jews from Palestine several centuries before Christianity began. (17)

discrimination The denial of opportunities and equal rights to individuals and groups because of prejudice or for other arbitrary reasons. (2, 3)

displaced homemakers Women whose primary occupation had been homemaking but who did not find full-time employment after being divorced, separated, or widowed. (16)

double jeopardy The subordinate status twice defined, as experienced by women of color. (16)

dual labor market Division of the economy into two areas of employment, the secondary one of which is populated primarily by minorities working at menial jobs. (3)

dysfunction An element of society that may disrupt a social system or lead to a decrease in its stability. (1)

educational pipeline The process that begins when students passing through formal schooling and travel in an ever-narrowing funnel attaining professional degrees at the end. (10)

emigration Leaving a country to settle in another. (1)

English immersion Teaching in English by teachers who know the students' native language, but use it only when students do not understand the lessons. (9)

ethclass The merged ethnicity and class in a person's status. (5)

ethnic cleansing Policy of ethnic Serbs to eliminate Muslims from parts of Bosnia. (1)

ethnic group A group set apart from others because of its national origin or distinctive cultural patterns. (1)

ethnocentrism The tendency to assume that one's culture and way of life are superior to all others. (2)

ethnophaulism Ethnic or racial slurs, including derisive nicknames. (2)

evacuees Japanese Americans interned in camps for the duration of World War II. (14)

evangelical faiths Christian faiths that place great emphasis on a personal relationship between the individual and God and believe that each adherent must spread the faith and bear personal witness by openly declaring the religion to nonbelievers. (11)

exploitation theory A Marxist theory that views racial subordination in the United States as a manifestation of the class system inherent in capitalism. (2)

familism Pride and closeness in the family that result in placing family obligation and loyalty before individual needs. (10)

feminine mystique A woman's thinking of herself only as her children's mother and her husband's wife. (16)

feminization of poverty The trend since 1970 that has women accounting for a growing proportion of those below the poverty line. (16)

fiesta politics Blatant overtures by presidential candidates to Chicanos for their support. (10)

fish-ins Tribes' protests over government interference with their traditional rights to fish as they would like. (6)

fobs Recent immigrants from China, *fresh off the boat*. (13)

fringe-of-values theory Behavior which is on the border of conduct that a society regards as proper and which is often carried out by subordinate groups, subjecting those groups to negative sanctions. (15)

functionalist perspective A sociological approach emphasizing how parts of a society are structured in the interest of maintaining the system as a whole. (1)

fusion A minority and a majority group combining to form a new group. (1)

gender roles Expectations regarding the proper behavior, attitudes, and activities of males and females. (16)

genocide The deliberate, systematic killing of an entire people or nation. (1)

gerrymandering Redrawing districts bizarrely to create politically advantageous outcomes. (8)

glass ceiling The barrier that blocks the promotion of a qualified worker because of gender on minority membership. (3, 16)

glass wall A barrier to moving laterally in a business to positions that more likely to lead to upward mobility. (3)

gook syndrome David Riesman's phrase describing Americans' tendency to stereotype Asians and to regard them as all alike and undesirable. (12)

halakha Jewish laws covering obligations and duties. (15)

Haoles Hawaiian term for Caucasians. (12)

Holocaust revisionists Individuals who deny the Nazi effort to exterminate the Jews or who minimize the numbers killed. (15)

home rule Britain's grant of a local parliament to Ireland. (17)

hui kuan Chinese-American benevolent associations organized on the basis of the district of the immigrant's origin in China. (13)

ilchomose The 1.5 generation of Korean Americans—those who immigrated into the United States as children. (12)

immigration Coming into a new country as a permanent resident. (1)

inactivity rate Proportion of a population neither in school nor in the labor force. (12)

in-group virtues Proper behavior by one's own group ("in-group virtues") becomes unacceptable when practiced by outsiders ("out-group vices"). (15)

institutional discrimination A denial of opportunities and equal rights to individuals or groups resulting from the normal operations of a society. (3)

intelligence quotient (IQ) The ratio of an individual's mental age (as computed by an IQ test) divided by his or her chronological age and multiplied by 100. (1)

interactive effect Pettigrew's view that race and class act together to place an individual in a stratification system. (1)

internal colonialism The treatment of subordinate peoples like colonial subjects by those in power. (1)

intifada The Palestinian uprising against Israeli authorities in the occupied territories. (17)

irregular economy Transfer of money, goods, or services that are not reported to the government. Common in inner-city neighborhoods and poverty-stricken rural areas. (3)

Issei First-generation immigrants from Japan to the United States. (14)

Jim Crow Southern laws passed during the latter part of the nineteenth century that kept Blacks in their subordinate position. (7)

jook-sings Chinese Americans who fail to carry on the cultural traditions of China or to maintain a sense of identification with other Chinese Americans. (13)

Judaization The lessening importance of Judaism as a religion and the substitution of cultural traditions as the tie that binds Jews. (15)

kashrut Laws pertaining to permissible (*kosher*) and forbidden foods and their preparation. (15)

Kibei Japanese Americans of the Nisei generation sent back to Japan for schooling and to have marriages arranged. (14)

kickouts or pushouts Native American school dropouts, who leave behind an unhealthy academic environment. (6)

kin country syndrome Coalitions between nations based on ethnic, racial, or religious ties. (17)

kye Rotating credit system used by Korean Americans to subsidize the start of businesses. (12)

labeling theory An approach introduced by Howard Becker that attempts to explain why certain people are viewed as deviants and others engaging in the same behavior are not. (1)

La Raza "The People"—a term referring to the rich heritage of Chicanos, and hence used to denote a sense of pride among Chicanos today. (10)

life chances People's opportunities to provide themselves with material goods, positive living conditions, and favorable life experiences. (5, 10)

machismo A male's sense of virility, of personal worth, in his own eyes and in those of his peers. (10)

manumission The freeing of slaves by a master. (17)

marginality The status of being between two cultures at the same time, such as the status of Jewish immigrants in the United States. (1)

marianismo A female's acceptance of male's dominance and the placing of family needs first. (10)

Marielitos People who arrived from Cuba in the second wave of Cuban immigration, most specifically those forcibly deported via Mariel Harbor. The term is generally reserved for those refugees seen as especially undesirable. (9)

market discrimination The underpayment or underemployment of qualified women. (16)

melting pot Diverse racial or ethnic groups or both forming a new creation, a new cultural entity. (1)

middlemen minorities Groups such as Japanese Americans that typically occupy middle positions in the social and occupational stratification system. (12)

migration A general term that describes any transfer of population. (6)

millenarian movements Movements, such as the Ghost Dance, that prophesy a cataclysm in the immediate future, followed by collective salvation. (6)

minority group A subordinate group whose members have significantly less control or power over their own lives than that held by the members of a dominant or majority group. (1)

model or ideal minority A group that, despite past prejudice and discrimination, succeeds economically, socially, and educationally without resorting to political or violent confrontations with Whites. (12)

mojados "Wetbacks"; derisive slang for Mexicans who enter illegally, supposedly by swimming the Rio Grande. (10)

mommy track The problematic corporate career track for women who want to divide their attention between work and family. (16)

mulatto escape hatch In Brazil, social movement into a higher class based on gradation of skin color. (17)

multinational development A South African government program promoting the creation of so-called homelands, or Bantustans in desolate areas. (17)

nativism Beliefs and policies favoring native-born citizens over immigrants. (4)

Neoricans Puerto Ricans who return to the island to settle after living on the mainland of the United States (also *Nuyoricans*). (11)

Nisei Children born of immigrants from Japan. (14)

normative approach The view that prejudice is influenced by societal norms and situations that serve to encourage or discourage that tolerance of minorities. (2)

noshrim Immigrants who have discarded all traces of Jewish religious faith and commitment to the larger Jewish community. (15)

out-group vices See *in-group virtues*. (15)

panethnicity The development of solidarity among ethnic subgroups, as reflected in the terms *Hispanic* or *Asian American*. (1, 12)

pan-Indianism Intertribal social movements in which several tribes, joined by culture but not by kinship, unite, usually to confront an enemy such as the federal government. (6)

pass laws Laws that control internal movement by non-Whites in South Africa; now called *reference-book laws*. (17)

pay equity The same wages for different types of work that are judged to be comparable by such measures as employee knowledge, skills, effort, responsibility, and working conditions; also called *comparable worth*. (16)

pentecostal faiths Religious groups similar in many respects to evangelical faiths which, in addition, believe in the infusion of the Holy Spirit into services and in religious experiences such as faith healing. (11)

peoplehood Milton Gordon's term for a group with a shared feeling. (15)

pluralism Mutual respect between the various groups in a society for one another's cultures, allowing minorities to express their own culture without experiencing prejudice or hostility. (1)

politically correct A description of efforts on behalf of racial, ethnic, and religious minorities as well as women. The phrase is often used negatively, in criticism of such measures. (1)

powwow Native American gatherings of dancing, singing, music playing, and visiting, accompanied by competitions. (6)

prejudice A negative attitude toward an entire category of people, such as a racial, or ethnic minority. (2)

principle of third-generation interest Marcus Hansen's contention that ethnic interest and awareness increase in the third generation, among the grandchildren of immigrants. (5)

quilombo A hideaway used by Brazilian slaves in the nineteenth century. (17)

racial formation A sociohistorical process by which racial categories are created, inhibited, transformed, and destroyed. (1)

racial group A group that is socially set apart from others because of obvious physical differences. (1)

racism A doctrine that one race is superior. (1)

redlining The practice of financial lenders' refusing to grant home and commercial loans in minority and racially changing neighborhoods. (8)

refugees Persons living outside their country of citizenship for fear of political or religious persecution. (4)

relative deprivation The conscious experience of a negative discrepancy between legitimate expectations and present actualities. (1,3, 7)

repatriation The program of deporting Mexicans during the 1930s. (7, 10)

respectable bigotry Michael Lerner's term for the social acceptance of prejudice against White ethnics, when intolerance against non-White minorities is regarded as unacceptable. (5)

restrictive covenants Private contracts or agreements that discourage or prevent minority-group members from purchasing housing in a neighborhood. (7)

riff-raff theory Also called the *rotten-apple theory;* the belief that the riots of the 1960s were caused by discontented youths, rather than by social and economic problems facing all African Americans. (7)

Sansei The children of the Nisei, that is, the grandchildren of the original immigrants from Japan. (14)

scapegoat A person or group blamed irrationally for another person's or group's problems or difficulties. (2)

secessionist minority Groups such as the Amish, that reject assimilation as well as coexistence. (5)

second shift The double burden—work outside the home followed by child care and housework—that is faced by many women and that few men share equitably. (16)

segregation The act of physically separating two groups; often imposed on a subordinate group by the dominant group. (1)

self-fulfilling prophecy The tendency of individuals to respond to and act on the basis of stereotypes, a predisposition that can lead to validation of false definitions. (1)

set-asides Programs stipulating a minimum proportion of government contracts that must be awarded to minority-owned businesses. (8)

setoffs Deductions from U.S. money due in U.S. government settlements with

Native Americans, equal to the cost of federal services provided to the tribe. (6)

sexism The ideology that one sex is superior to the other. (16)

sexual harassment Creating a hostile or abusive environment by imposing sexual requirements in a relationship of unequal power. (16)

slave codes Laws that delineated the low position held by enslaved Blacks in the United States. (17)

states' rights The principle reinvoked in the late 1940s, that holds that each state is sovereign and has the right to order its own affairs without interference by the federal government. (3)

stereotypes Unreliable generalizations about all members of a group that do not take into account individual differences within the group. (1)

stratification A structured ranking of entire groups of people that perpetuates unequal rewards and power in a society. (1)

suffragists Women and men who worked successfully to gain women the right to vote. (16)

symbolic ethnicity Herbert Gans's term that describes emphasis on ethnic food and ethnically associated political issues rather than deeper ties to one's heritage. (5)

tongs Chinese American secret associations. (13)

total discrimination The combination of current discrimination with past discrimination created by poor schools and menial jobs. (3)

tracking The practice of placing students in specific curriculum groups on the basis of test scores and other criteria. (8, 11)

tsu Clans established along family lines and forming a basis for social organization by Chinese Americans. (13)

underclass Lower-class members who are not a part of the regular economy and whose situation is not changed by conventional assistance programs. (3)

underemployment Work at a job for which the worker is overqualified, involuntary part-time instead of full-time employment, or intermittent employment. (8)

victim discounting Society's viewing crimes as less socially significant if the victim is viewed as less worthy. (8)

victimization surveys Annual attempt to measure crime rates by interviewing ordinary citizens who may or may not have been crime victims. (8)

White backlash White resistance to further improvement in the status of Black people. (2)

White primary Legal provisions forbidding Black voting in election primaries, which in one-party areas of the South effectively denied Blacks their right to select elected officials. (7)

xenophobia The fear or hatred of strangers or foreigners. (4)

yellow peril A term denoting a generalized prejudice toward Asian people and their customs. (12, 13)

Yiddishkait Jewishness. (15)

Yonsei The fourth generation of Japanese Americans in the United States, the children of the Sansei. (14)

Zionism Traditional Jewish religious yearning to return to the biblical homeland, now used to refer to support for the state of Israel. (15, 17)

zoning laws Legal provisions stipulating land use and the architectural design of housing, often used to keep racial minorities and low-income persons out of suburban areas. (8)

zoot-suiters Chicano youth during the mid-1940s in southern California; a derisive term based on their dress. (10)

References

Aberbach, Joel D., and Walker, Jack L.
 1973   *Race in the City.* Boston: Little, Brown.

Abramson, Harold J.
 1973   *Ethnic Diversity in Catholic America.* New York: Wiley.

Abron, JoNina M.
 1986   The Legacy of the Black Panther Party. *The Black Scholar* 17 (November–December), pp. 33–37.

Acosta, Oscar Zeta
 1972   *The Autobiography of a Brown Buffalo.* San Francisco: Straight Arrow Books.

Acosta-Belén, Edna
 1986   *The Puerto Rican Women,* 2d ed. New York: Praeger.

Acuña, Rodolfo
 1981   *Occupied America: A History of Chicanos,* 2d ed. New York: Harper & Row.

Adams, David Wallace
 1988   Fundamental Considerations: The Deep Meaning of Native American Schooling, 1880–1900. *Harvard Educational Review* 58 (February), pp. 1–28.

Adams, Romanzo
 1969   The Unorthodox Race Doctrine of Hawaii. In Melvin M. Tumin, ed., *Comparative Perspectives on Race Relations,* pp. 81–90. Boston: Little, Brown and Co.

Adler, Patricia A., and Adler, Peter
 1994   Social Reproduction and the Corporate Order: The Institutionalization of Afterschool Activities. *Sociological Quarterly* 35 (2), pp. 309–328.

Adler, Patricia Rae
 1974   The 1943 Zoot-Suit Riots: Brief Episode in a Long Conflict. In Manuel P. Servin, ed., *An Awakened Minority: The Mexican Americans,* 2d ed., pp. 142–158. Beverly Hills, CA: Glencoe Press.

Adorno, T. W.; Frenkel-Brunswik, Else; Levinson, Daniel J.; and Sanford, R. Nevitt
 1950   *The Authoritarian Personality.* New York: Wiley.

Aguilar-San Juan, Karin, ed.
 1994   *The State of Asian America: Activism and Resistance in the 1990s.* Boston: South End Press.

Akwesasne Notes
 1972a   Columbus a Trader in Indian Slaves. 4 (Early Autumn), p. 22.

 1972b   Navajo Testimony Reveals Treatment at Hands of Traders. 4 (Early Autumn), p. 5.

 1988   Competing Sovereignties in North America and the Right-Wing and Anti-Indian Movements. 20 (Early Spring), pp. 12–13.

Alaracón, Odette; Erkut, Sumra; Coll,
Cynthia García; and García, Heidie A.
Vázquez
    1994   *An Approach to Engaging in
           Culturally-Sensitive Research
           on Puerto Rican Youth.*
           Wellesley, MA: Center for
           Research on Women.

Alba, Richard D.
    1990   *Ethnic Identity: The Transfor-
           mation of White America.*
           New Haven: Yale University
           Press.

    1985   *Italian Americans: Into the
           Twilight of Ethnicity.* Engle-
           wood Cliffs, NJ: Prentice-
           Hall.

Alba, Richard D., and Moore, Gwen
    1982   Ethnicity in the American
           Elite. *American Sociological
           Review* 47 (June) pp. 373–382.

Allen, Irving Lewis
    1990   *Unkind Words: Ethnic
           Labeling from Redskin to
           Wasp.* New York: Bergin &
           Garvey.

Allen, James Paul, and Turner, Eugene
James
    1988   *We the People: An Atlas of
           America's Ethnic Diversity.*
           New York: Macmillan.

Allport, Gordon W.
    1979   *The Nature of Prejudice,* 25th
           Anniversary Edition. Reading,
           MA: Addison-Wesley.

American Indian Policy Review
Commission
    1976a   *Indian Law Revision, Consoli-
           dation and Codification.* Task
           Force #9. Washington, DC:
           U.S. Government Printing
           Office.

    1976b   *Task Force on Alaskan Natural
           Issues.* Washington, DC: U.S.
           Government Printing Office.

    1976c   *Urban and Rural Non-Reser-
           vation Indians.* Task Force #8.
           Washington, DC: U.S. Gov-
           ernment Printing Office.

American Jewish Committee
    1965   *Mutual Savings Banks of New
           York City.* New York: Ameri-
           can Jewish Committee.

    1966a   *Mutual Savings Banks: A Fol-
           low-up Report.* New York:
           American Jewish Committee.

    1966b   *Patterns of Exclusion from the
           Executive Suite: Corporate
           Banking.* New York: American
           Jewish Committee.

    1987   Family Issues and Jewish Unity.
           Newsletter 6 (Fall), pp. 1–3.

Amnesty International
    1993   *Amnesty International Report
           1993.* New York: Amnesty
           International.

Andrews, George Reid
    1991   Blacks and Whites in São
           Paulo, Brazil, 1888–1988.
           Madison: University of Wis-
           consin Press.

Angier, Natalie
    1993   U.S. Opens the Door Just a
           Crack to Alternative Forms of
           Medicine. *New York Times*
           (January 10), pp. 1, 13.

Annin, Peter
    1994   Looking for a Piece of the
           Action. *Newsweek* 124 (June
           13), p. 44.

Anti-Defamation League of B'nai B'rith
    1993   *Young Nazi Killers: The Rising
           Skinhead Danger.* New York:
           Anti-Defamation League.

    1995   *Audit of Anti-Semitic Inci-
           dents: 1994.* New York: Anti-
           Defamation League.

Aponte, Robert
    1991   Urban Hispanic Poverty: Dis-
           aggregations and Explana-
           tions. *Social Problems* 38
           (November), pp. 516–528.

Aran, Kenneth; Arthur, Herman; Colon,
Ramon; and Goldenberg, Harvey
    1973   *Puerto Rican History and Cul-
           ture: A Study Guide and Cur-
           riculum Outline.* New York:
           United Federation of Teach-
           ers.

Arden, Harvey
1975   The Pious Ones. *National Geographic* 168 (August), pp. 276–298.

Aronson, Geoffrey
1990   *Israel, Palestinians and the Initifada.* London: Kegan Paul.

Asante, Molefi Kete
1987   *The Afrocentric Idea.* Philadelphia: Temple University Press.

1992   Afrocentric Systematics. *Black Issues in Higher Education* 9 (August 13), pp. 16–17, 21–22.

Ashe, Arthur R., Jr., with Branch, Kip; Chalk, Ocania; and Harris, Francis
1989   *A Hard Road to Glory: A History of the African-American Athlete.* New York: Amistad Books.

Asian American Journalists Association
1991   *Project Zinger: The Good, the Bad and the Ugly.* Seattle: Center for Integration and Improvement Association.

1993   *Project Zinger: A Critical Look at News Media Coverage of Asian Pacific Americans.* Los Angeles: Center for Integration and Improvement Association.

1994   *News Watch: A Critical Look at Coverage of People of Color.* San Francisco: Center for Integration and Improvement Association.

Asianweek
1994   FBI Releases Data on 1992 Hate Crimes. (April 1), p. 13.

Aspy, David N.
1970   Groping or Grouping for Teachability. *Contemporary Education* 41 (May), pp. 306–310.

Associated Press
1995   Resolving Civil Rights Claims Takes Years, Panel Asserts. *Chicago Tribune* (June 24), sect. 1, p. 16.

Ayaniun, John Z.
1994   Race, Class, and the Quality of Medical Care. *Journal of the American Medical Association* 271 (April 20), pp. 1207–1208.

Ayres, Ian
1991   Fair Driving: Gender and Race Discrimination in Retail Car Negotiations. *Harvard Law Review* 104 (February), pp. 817–872.

Bach, Robert L., and Bach, Jennifer B.
1980   Employment Patterns of Southeast Asian Refugees. *Monthly Labor Review* 103 (October), pp. 31–38.

Bachman, Ronet
1992   *Death and Violence on the Reservation: Homicide, Family Violence, and Suicide in American Indian Populations.* New York: Auburn House.

Bacon, John
1987   Court Ruling Hasn't Quieted School Prayer. *USA Today* (April 3), p. 3A.

Bagley, Christopher
1970   *Social Structure and Prejudice in Five English Boroughs.* London: Institute of Race Relations.

Bahr, Howard M.
1972   An End to Invisibility. In Howard M. Bahr, Bruce A. Chadwick, and Robert C. Day, *Native Americans Today: Sociological Perspectives*, pp. 404–412. New York: Harper and Row.

Baker, Bob
1992   Stereotype That Won't Go Away. *Los Angeles Times* (May 31), pp. A1, A18.

Baldwin, James
1967   Negroes Are Anti-Semitic Because They're Anti-White. *New York Times* (May 21), p. 114.

Ball, Harry V., and Yamamura, Douglas S.
  1960   Ethnic Discrimination and the
         Market Place. *American Soci-
         ological Review* 25 (October),
         pp. 687–694.

Baltzell, E. Digby
  1964   *The Protestant Establishment:
         Aristocracy and Caste in
         America.* New York: Vintage
         Books.

Balzar, John
  1994   Majority Support Steps to
         Diversity in the Workplace,
         Times Poll Finds. *Los Angeles
         Times* (November 28), p. A13.

Barbaro, Fred
  1974   Ethnic Resentment. *Society*
         11 (March–April), pp. 67–75.

Barclay, William; Kumar, Krishna; and
Simms, Ruth P.
  1976   *Racial Conflict, Discrimina-
         tion, and Power: Historical
         and Contemporary Studies.*
         New York: AMS Press.

Bardacke, Frank
  1993   Caesar's Ghost. *The Nation*
         251 (July 26), pp. 130–135.

Barrera, Mario; Munos, Carlos; Ornelas,
Charles
  1972   The Barrio as an Internal
         Colony. In Harlan Mahlan
         (ed.), *People and Politics in
         Urban Society*, pp. 465–549.
         Beverly Hills, CA: Sage Publi-
         cations.

Barrett, Wayne, and Cooper, Andrew
  1981   Koch's 99 Attacks Against the
         Other New York. *Village Voice*
         26 (April 15–21), pp. 22–31.

Barringer, Felicity
  1992   As American as Apple Pie,
         Dim Sum or Burritos. *New
         York Times* (May 31), p. E2.

Barta, Russell
  1974   *The Representation of Poles,
         Italians, Latins and Blacks in
         the Executive Suites of Chica-
         go's Largest Corporations.*
         Chicago: Institute of Urban
         Life.

  1984   *The Representation of Poles,
         Italians, Hispanics and Blacks
         in the Executive Suites of
         Chicago's Largest Corpora-
         tions.* Minority Report #2, pp.
         1–4. Chicago: Institute of
         Urban Life.

Bash, Harry M.
  1979   *Sociology, Race and Ethnicity.*
         New York: Gordon & Breach.

Baskin, Jane A.; Hartweg, Joyce K.;
Lewis, Ralph G.; and McCullough, Lester
W., Jr.
  1971   *Race Related Civil Disorders:
         1967–1969.* Waltham, MA:
         Lemberg Center for the Study
         of Violence, Brandeis Univer-
         sity.

Baskin, Jane A.; Lewis, Ralph G.; Mannis,
Joyce Hartweg; and McCullough, Lester
W., Jr.
  1972   The Long, Hot Summer. *Jus-
         tice Magazine* 1 (February),
         p. 8.

Bastian, Lisa D., and Taylor, Bruce M.
  1994   *Young Black Male Victims.*
         Washington, DC: U.S. Gov-
         ernment Printing Office.

Bauer, Raymond A., and Bauer, Alice H.
  1942   Day to Day Resistance to
         Slavery. *Journal of Negro His-
         tory* 27 (October), pp.
         388–419.

Baumann, Marty
  1992   Agreement on King, *USA
         Today* (May 11), p. 4A.

Beach, Walter G.
  1934   Some Considerations in
         Regard to Race Segregation in
         California. *Sociology and
         Social Research* 18 (March),
         pp. 340–350.

Becerra, José E., et al.
  1991   Infant Mortality Among His-
         panics: A Portrait of Hetero-
         geneity. *Journal of the Ameri-
         can Medical Association* 265
         (January 9), pp. 217–221.

Beck, Roy
1994   The Ordeal of Immigration in Wausau. *Atlantic Monthly* (April), pp. 84–90, 94–97.

Becker, Maki
1995   Keeping Alive Culinary Customs of Japan. *Los Angeles Times* (January 3), p. B3.

Bedell, Kenneth B., ed.
1995   *Yearbook of American and Canadian Churches 1995.* Nashville: Abingdon Press.

Belair, Felix, Jr.
1970   1965 Law Changes Ethnic Patterns of Immigration. *New York Times* (August 31), pp. 1, 37.

Bell, Daniel
1953   Crime as an American Way of Life. *Antioch Review* 13 (Summer), pp. 131–154.

Bell, David A.
1985   The Triumph of Asian-Americans. *The New Republic* 193 (July 15), pp. 24–26, 28–31.

Bell, Derrick
1994   The Freedom of Employment Act. *The Nation* 258 (May 23), pp. 708, 710–714.

Bell, Wendell
1991   Colonialism and Internal Colonialism. In Richard Lachmann, ed., *The Encyclopedic Dictionary of Sociology*, 4th ed., pp. 52–53. Guilford, CT: Dushkin Publishing Group.

Bellah, Robert
1967   Civil Religion in America. *Daedalus* 96 (Winter), pp. 1–21.

1968   Response to Commentaries on "Civil Religion in America." In Donald R. Cutler, ed., *The Religious Situation: 1968*, pp. 388–393. Boston: Beacon Press.

1970   *Beyond Belief: Essays on Religion in a Post-Traditional World.* New York: Harper & Row.

1989   Comment to Mathisen. *Sociological Analysis* 50 (Summer), p. 147.

Bem, Sandra Lipsitz
1994   In a Male-Centered World, Female Differences Are Transformed into Female Disadvantages. *Chronicle of Higher Education* 39 (August 17), pp. B1–B3.

Bem, Sandra L., and Bem, Daryl J.
1970   Case Study of a Nonconscious Ideology: Training the Woman to Know Her Place. In Daryl J. Bem, ed. *Beliefs, Attitudes, and Human Affairs*, pp. 89–99. Belmont, CA: Brooks/Cole.

Benedek, Emil
1993   No More War, Forever. *Newsweek* 121 (March 8), pp. 58–60.

Benjamin, Robert
1993   Illegal Chinese Immigrants Flood U.S. *Chicago Sun-Times* (February 28), p. 27.

Bennett, Claudette E.
1995   The Black Population in the United States: March 1994 and 1993. *Current Population Reports*, Series P-20, No. 480. Washington, DC: U.S. Government Printing Office.

Bennett, Lerone, Jr.
1965   *Confrontation: Black and White.* Chicago: Johnson.

1966   *Before the Mayflower,* rev. ed. Baltimore: Penguin.

Bennett, Phillip
1993   Ethnic Labels Fail to Keep Up with Reality. *The Cincinnati Enquirer* (November 18), p. A10.

Ben-Rafael, Eliezer, and Sharot, Stephen
1991   *Ethnicity, Religion and Class in Israel Society.* Cambridge: Cambridge University Press.

Berger, Joseph
1995   Two Classes of Students: Itha-
       ca High Joins Debate. *New
       York Times* (June 4), pp. 37,
       46.

Bergheim, Kim
1995   Why She's Not Leaving
       Home. *Hispanic Outlook* 5
       (January 15), pp. 8–9.

Bernard, Jessie
1975   *Women, Wives, Mothers: Val-
       ues and Options.* Chicago:
       Aldine.

Berndt, Ronald M., and Berndt,
Catherine
1951   *From Black to White in South
       Australia.* Melbourne: F. W.
       Chesire.

Bernstein, Richard
1990   In U.S. Schools a War of
       Words. *New York Times Mag-
       azine* (October 14), pp. 34–38,
       48, 50, 52.

Berreman, Gerald D.
1960   Caste in India and the United
       States. *American Journal of
       Sociology* 66 (September), pp.
       120–127.

1973   *Caste in the Modern World.*
       Morristown, NJ: General
       Learning Press.

Bettelheim, Bruno, and Janowitz, Morris
1964   *Social Change and Prejudice.*
       New York: Free Press.

Bielski, Vince
1994   American Indians Walk for
       Justice. *The Daily Citizen*
       (February 18), pp. 1, 13.

Bigelow, Rebecca
1992   Certain Inalienable Rights.
       Friends Journal 38 (Novem-
       ber), pp. 6–8.

Billingsley, C. Andrew
1992   *Climbing Jacob's Ladder: The
       Enduring Legacy of African-
       American Families.* New York:
       Simon & Schuster.

Billson, Janet Mancini
1988   No Owner of Soil: The Con-
       cept of Marginality Revisited
       on Its Sixtieth Birthday. *Inter-
       national Review of Modern
       Sociology* 18 (Autumn), pp.
       183–204.

Blackstock, Nelson
1976   *COINTELPRO: The FBI's
       Secret War on Political Free-
       dom.* New York: Vintage
       Press.

Blau, Peter M., and Duncan, Otis Dudley
1967   *The American Occupational
       Structure.* New York: Wiley.

Blauner, Robert
1969   Internal Colonialism and
       Ghetto Revolt. *Social Prob-
       lems* 16 (Spring), pp. 393–408.

1972   *Racial Oppression in America.*
       New York: Harper & Row.

Blawis, Patricia Bell
1971   *Tijerina and the Land Grants:
       Mexican Americans in Strug-
       gle for Their Heritage.* New
       York: International Publishers.

Blea, Irene I.
1988   *Toward a Chicano Social Sci-
       ence.* New York: Praeger.

Bledsoe, Timothy, and Mary Herring
1990   Victims of Circumstances:
       Women in Pursuit of Political
       Office. *American Political Sci-
       ence Review* 84 (March), pp.
       213–224.

Bloom, Leonard
1971   *The Social Psychology of Race
       Relations.* Cambridge, MA:
       Schenkman.

Boal, Frederick W.; Douglas, J.; and
Neville, H.
1982   *Integration and Division: Geo-
       graphical Perspectives on the
       Northern Ireland Problems.*
       New York: Academic Press.

Bogardus, Emory
1968   Comparing Racial Distance in
       Ethiopia, South Africa, and

the United States. *Sociology and Social Research* 52 (January), pp. 149–156.

Bohland, James R.
1982   Indian Residential Segregation in the Urban Southwest: 1970 and 1980. *Social Science Quarterly* 63 (December), pp. 749–761.

Bonacich, Edna
1972   A Theory of Ethnic Antagonism: The Split Labor Market. *American Sociological Review* 37 (October), pp. 547–559.

1976   Advanced Capitalism and Black/White Race Relations in the United States: A Split Labor Market Interpretation. *American Sociological Review* 41 (February), pp. 34–51.

1988   The Social Costs of Immigrant Entrepreneurship. *Amerasia* 14 (Spring), pp. 119–128.

1989   Inequality in America: The Failure of the American System for People of Color. *Sociological Spectrum* 9 (No. 1), pp. 71–101.

Bonacich, Edna, and Modell, John
1981   *The Economic Basis of Ethnic Solidarity.* Berkeley: University of California Press.

Booth, William
1993   Puerto Rico Rejects Statehood. *Washington Post* (November 15), pp. A1, A12.

Borjas, George
1990   *Friends or Strangers: The Impact of Immigrants on the U.S. Economy.* New York: Basic Books.

Boswell, Thomas D., and Curtis, James R.
1984   *The Cuban-American Experience.* Totowa, NJ: Rowman & Allanheld.

Bouvier, Leon F., and Gardner, Robert W.
1986   Immigration to the U.S: The Unfinished Story. *Population Bulletin* 41 (November).

Bracey, John H.; Meier, August; and Rudwick, Elliot, eds.
1970   *Black Nationalism in America.* Indianapolis: Bobbs-Merrill.

Bradley, Martin B.; Green, Norman M., Jr.; Jones, Dale E.; Lynn, Mac; and McNeil, Lou
1992   *Churches and Church Membership in the United States 1990.* Atlanta: Glenmary Research Center.

Braus, Patricia
1993   What Does "Hispanic" Mean? *American Demographics* 15 (June), pp. 46–49, 58.

Brazil
1981   *IX Recenseamento Geral do Brasil—1980, 1, P + .1.* Rio de Janeiro: Secretaria de Planejamento da Presidencia da República, Fundacão Instituto Brasilerio de Geografia e Estatistica.

Breasted, Mary
1977   3-Year Inquiry Threads Together Evidence on F.A.L.N. Terrorism. *New York Times* (April 17), pp. 1, 49.

Breton, Raymond; Reitz, Jeffrey G.; and Valentine, Victor
1980   *Cultural Boundaries and the Cohesion of Canada.* Montreal: Institute for Research on Public Policy.

Bridges, George S., and Crutchfield, Robert D.
1988   Law, Social Standing and Racial Disparities in Imprisonment. *Social Forces* 66 (March), pp. 699–724.

Briggs, Kenneth A.
1976   Churches Found Still Largely Segregated. *New York Times* (November 14), p. 26.

1978   Jewish Leader Urges a Program to Convert "Seekers" to Judaism. *New York Times* (December 3), pp. 1, 37.

1983   Among Hispanic Catholics, Another Pattern of Practice. *New York Times* (January 9), p. E10.

Briggs, Vernon M., Jr.
1975   Illegal Aliens: The Need for a More Restrictive Border Policy. *Social Science Quarterly* 56 (December), pp. 477–484.

Brooks, Andree
1987   Women in the Clergy: Struggle to Succeed. *New York Times* (February 16), p. 15.

Broom, Leonard
1965   *The Transformation of the American Negro.* New York: Harper & Row.

Brown, Christopher
1990   Discrimination and Immigration Law. *Focus* 18 (August), pp. 3–4, 8.

Brown, Dee
1971   *Bury My Heart at Wounded Knee.* New York: Holt, Rinehart & Winston.

Brown, Scott Shibuya
1994   Indonesian Culture Takes Root in Hollywood. *Los Angeles Times* (October 2), pp. B1, B4.

Bufalino, William E.
1971   Housing and Ethnicity. In Otto Feinstein, ed., *Ethnic Groups in the City,* pp. 277–279. Lexington, MA: Heath.

Bunzel, John H.
1992   *Race Relations on Campus: Stanford Students Speak.* Stanford, CA: Portable Stanford.

Burciaga, Cecilia Preciado de; Gonzales, Viola; and Hepburn, Ruth A.
1977   The Chicana as Feminist. In Alice G. Sargent, ed., *Beyond Sex Roles,* pp. 266–273. St. Paul: West.

Bureau of Indian Affairs
1970   *Answers to Your Questions About Indians.* Washington, DC: U.S. Government Printing Office.

1974   *American Indians: Answers to 101 Questions.* Washington, DC: U.S. Government Printing Office.

1981   *BIA Profile: The Bureau of Indian Affairs and American Indians.* Washington, DC: U.S. Government Printing Office.

1986   *American Indians Today: Answers to Your Questions.* Washington, DC: U.S. Government Printing Office.

1988   *Report of BIA Education: Excellence in Indian Education Through the Effective School Process.* Washington, DC: U.S. Government Printing Office.

Bureau of Labor Statistics
1986   *Employment and Earnings Characteristics of Families: Third Quarter, 1986.* Washington, DC: U.S. Government Printing Office.

Bureau of the Census
1960   *Historical Statistics of the United States, Colonial Times to 1957.* Washington, DC: U.S. Government Printing Office.

1982a   Ancestry and Language in the United States: November 1979. *Current Population Reports,* Series P-23, No. 116. Washington, DC: U.S. Government Printing Office.

1982b   *Statistical Abstract, 1982.* Washington, DC: U.S. Government Printing Office.

1988   *Statistical Abstract, 1989.* Washington, DC: U.S. Government Printing Office.

1989   Money Income of Households, Families, and Persons in the United States, 1987. *Current Population Reports,*

Series P-20, No. 162. Washington, DC: U.S. Government Printing Office.

1990   Child Support and Alimony, 1987. *Current Population Reports* Series P-23, No. 167. Washington, D.C: U.S. Government Printing Office.

1991a   *Statistical Abstract of the United States, 1991.* Washington, DC: U.S. Government Printing Office.

1991b   The Hispanic Population in the United States: March 1990. *Current Population Reports,* Series P-20, No. 449. Washington, DC: U.S. Government Printing Office.

1992   *Statistical Abstract of the United States, 1992.* Washington, DC: U.S. Government Printing Office.

1993a   *Statistical Abstracts of the United States, 1993.* Washington, DC: U.S. Government Printing Office.

1993b   *Population Projections of the United States, by Age, Sex, Race, and Hispanic Origin: 1995–2050,* Series P-25, No. 104. Washington, DC: U.S. Government Printing Office.

1993c   *Money Income of Households, Families, and Persons in the United States: 1992,* Series P-60, No. 184. Washington, DC: U.S. Government Printing Office.

1993d   *We the . . . First Americans.* Washington, DC: U.S. Government Printing Office.

1993e   *We the American . . . Asians.* Washington, DC: U.S. Government Printing Office.

1993f   *We the American . . . Hispanics.* Washington, DC: U.S. Government Printing Office.

1994   *Statistical Abstract of the United States, 1994.* Washington, DC: U.S. Government Printing Office.

1995   *Statistical Abstract, 1995.* Washington, DC: U.S. Government Printing Office.

Burgess, Mike
1992   American Indian Religious Freedom Act Hearings. *News from Indian Country* (Late December), pp. 8–9.

Burke, Tod W., and O'Rear, Charles E.
1990   Home Invaders: Asian Gangs in America. *Police Studies* 13 (Winter), pp. 154–156.

Burma, John H.
1953   Current Leadership Problems Among Japanese Americans. *Sociology and Social Research* 37 (January–February), pp. 157–163.

1970   *Mexican Americans in the United States.* Cambridge, MA: Schenkman Publishing.

Burnett, Myra N., and Sisson, Kimberly
1995   Doll Studies Revisited: A Question of Validity. *Journal of Black Psychology* 21 (February), pp. 19–29.

Burns, John F.
1978   How Rules of "Petty Apartheid" Are Whittled Away. *New York Times* (June 4), pp. 1–14.

Bustamante, Jorge A.
1972   The "Wetback" as Deviant: An Application of Labeling Theory. *American Journal of Sociology* 77 (January), pp. 706–718.

Butler, Jeffrey E.
1974   Social Status, Ethnic Divisions and Political Conflict in New Nations: Afrikaners and Englishmen in South Africa. In Wendell Bell and Walter E. Freeman, eds., *Ethnicity and Nation-Building: Comparative, International and Historical Perspectives,* pp. 147–169. Beverly Hills, CA: Sage.

Butterfield, Fox
1985   Chinese Organized Crime Said to Rise in U.S. *New York Times* (January 13), pp. 1, 10.

1986   Bostonians Debating Drive to Carve Out a Black City. *New York Times* (October 12), p. 26.

Cabrera, Denise
1989   Women on TV: More Than Just a Pretty Sight. *New York Post* (December 15), p. 113.

Cacas, Samuel R.
1995   Against the Wind. *Filipinas* 3 (January), pp. 18, 20.

Caine, T. Allen.
1972   Comparative Life-Styles of Anglos and Mexican Americans. In Arnold M. and Caroline B. Rose (eds.) *Minority Problems,* 2nd ed., pp. 290–306. New York: Harper & Row.

Calica, Perry
1995   Filipino Soldier: "We Were Abandoned." *Los Angeles Times* (February 4), p. B7.

Callanan, Tuss
1987   Coyote: A Town Without Pity. *Chicago Tribune* (April 12), sect. 10, pp. 8–11, 13–20, 27.

Camarillo, Albert
1993   Latin Americans: Mexican Americans and Central Americans. In Mary Kupiec Coyton, Elliot J. Gorn, and Peter W. Williams, eds., *Encyclopedia of American Social History,* pp. 855–872. New York: Scribners.

Campbell, Angus, and Schuman, Howard
1968   *Racial Attitudes in Fifteen American Cities.* Ann Arbor, MI: Institute for Social Research.

Campbell, Ben Nighthorse
1992   Funding for Tribal Colleges Getting Short Shrift? *USA Today* (December 15), p. 11A.

1995   The Foxwoods Myth. *New York Times* (March 29), p. A23.

Carnegie Foundation for the Advancement of Teaching
1990   Native Americans and Higher Education: New Mood of Optimism. *Change* (January–February), pp. 27–30.

Carroll, Raymond
1975   An "Infamous Act" at the U.N. *Newsweek* (November 24), pp. 51–54.

Carson, Clayborne, et al.
1991   *The Eyes on the Prize Civil Rights Reader.* New York: Penguin Books.

Carter, Deborah J., and Wilson, Reginald
1993   *Minorities in Higher Education.* Washington, DC: American Council on Education.

Carter, Stephen
1991   *Reflections of an Affirmative Action Baby.* New York: Basic Books.

Casavantes, Edward
1970   Pride and Prejudice: A Mexican American Dilemma. *Civil Rights Digest* 3 (Winter), pp. 22–27.

Center for the American Woman and Politics (CAWP)
1992   *Women in Elective Office, 1992.* New Brunswick, NJ: CAWP.

1994   Women State Legislators in 1995: A Tale of Two Parties. Press release.

1995   *Fact Sheet.* New Brunswick, NJ: CAWP.

Cerio, Gregory
1992   Playing a Losing Game. *Newsweek* 119 (May 4), p. 29.

Chan, Mei-Mei
1986   For Chinese in USA, All Is Not Happy. *USA Today* (February 7), p. 1A.

Chan, Sucheng, ed.
1994   *Hmong Means Free: Life in Laos and America.* Philadelphia: Temple University Press.

Chanes, Jerome A.
1994   Intergroup Relations. In
        David Singer, ed., *American
        Jewish Year Book, 1994,* pp.
        113–152. New York: American
        Jewish Committee.

Chávez, César E.
1973   The Mexican American and
        the Church. In O. I. Ramano,
        ed., *Readings from El Grito,*
        pp. 215–228. Berkeley, CA:
        Quinto Sol Publications.

Chavez, Linda
1994   Multilingualism Getting Out
        of Hand. *USA Today* (Decem-
        ber 14), p. 13A.

Chayat, Sherry
1987   JAP-Baiting on the College
        Scene. *Lilith* (Fall), pp. 6–7.

Chen, Pei-ngor
1970   The Chinese Community in
        Los Angeles. *Social Casework*
        51 (December), pp. 591–598.

Chicago Tribune
1993   Victors in Recall Plan to End
        School Busing. (December
        16), p. 4.

Chideya, Farai
1993   Endangered Family.
        Newsweek 122 (August 30),
        pp. 16–27.

Chin, Frank
1974   "Kung Fu" Is Unfair to Chi-
        nese. *New York Times* (March
        24), p. D19.

Chin, Rocky
1971   New York Chinatown Today:
        Community in Crisis. In Amy
        Tachiki, Eddie Wong,
        Franklin Odo, and Buck
        Wong, eds. *Roots: An Asian
        American Reader,* pp.
        282–295. Los Angeles: Asian
        American Studies Center,
        UCLA.

Ching, Frank
1973   Expansion of Asian-American
        Studies on U.S. Campuses
        Reflects Growth of Ethnic
        Consciousness. *New York
        Times* (July 26), p. 18.

Christopulos, Diana
1974   Puerto Rico in the Twentieth
        Century: A Historical Survey.
        In Adalberto Lopez and James
        Petras, eds., *Puerto Rico and
        Puerto Ricans: Studies in His-
        tory and Society,* pp. 123–163.
        New York: Wiley.

Chuman, Frank F.
1976   *The Bamboo People: The Law
        and Japanese Americans.* Del
        Mar, CA: Publishers, Inc.

Cicone, Michael V., and Ruble, Diane N.
1978   Beliefs about Males. *Journal
        of Social Issues* 34 (Winter),
        pp. 5–16.

Cinel, Dean
1969   Ethnicity: A Neglected
        Dimension of American His-
        tory. *International Migration
        Review* 3 (Summer), pp.
        58–63.

Cioe, Rob
1994   A Look at the Electorate. *Los
        Angeles Times* (November 10),
        p. B2.

Clarity, James F.
1995   Ulster Debates Its Future, but
        Prefers Talking to Violence.
        New York Times (February
        26), p. 3.

Clark, Kenneth B., and Clark, Mamie P.
1947   Racial Identification and Pref-
        erences in Negro Children. In
        Theodore M. Newcomb and
        Eugene L. Hartley, eds.,
        Readings in Social Psychology,
        pp. 169–178. New York: Holt,
        Rinehart and Winston.

Cleaver, Kathleen
1982   How TV Wrecked the Black
        Panthers. *Channels* (Novem-
        ber–December), pp. 98–99.

Cleveland, Harlan
    1995   The Limits to Cultural
            Diversity. *Futurist* 29
            (March–April), pp. 19,
            22–26, 43–44.

Clines, Francis X.
    1994   Dance for Joy! Come Dance a
            Toyi-Toyi! *New York Times*
            (May 11), pp, A1, A8.

Clinton, William J.
    1994   Remarks at the United States
            Naval Academy Commence-
            ment Ceremony in Annapolis,
            Maryland. *Weekly Compila-
            tion* (May 25), pp.
            1157–1162.

Clymer, Adam
    1993   Daughter of Slavery Hushes
            Senate. *New York Times* (July
            23), p. B6.

Coddington, Ron
    1991   Native American Health Cri-
            sis. *USA Today* (November
            12), p. 1A.

Cohen, Debra Nussbaum
    1994   Daughters of Lilith Come of
            Age. *Jewish World* 23
            (December 23), pp. 20–23.

Cohen, Steven M.
    1988   *American Assimilation or
            Jewish Revival?* Blooming-
            ton: Indiana University
            Press.

    1991   *Content or Continuity? Alter-
            native Bases for Commitment.*
            New York: American Jewish
            Committee.

Coleman, James S.; Campbell, Ernest Q.;
Hobson, Carol J.; McPartland, James;
Mood, Alexander M.; Weinfold, Frederic
D.; and Link, Robert L.
    1966   *Equality of Educational Oppor-
            tunity.* Washington, DC: U.S.
            Office of Education.

Collette, Lin
    1994   Encountering Holocaust
            Denial. *The Public Eye* 8
            (September), pp. 1–15.

Collins, Patricia Hill
    1990   *Black Feminist Thought:
            Knowledge, Consciousness,
            and the Politics of Empower-
            ment.* New York: Routledge.

Comer, James P., and Poussaint, Alvin F.
    1992   *Raising Black Children.* New
            York: Plume.

Commission on Civil Rights
    1972   *The Excluded Student: Educa-
            tional Practices Affecting Mex-
            ican Americans in the South-
            west.* Washington, DC: U.S.
            Government Printing Office.

    1974   *Toward Quality Education for
            Mexican Americans.* Washing-
            ton, DC: U.S. Government
            Printing Office.

    1975   *Twenty Years After Brown:
            Equality of Economic Oppor-
            tunity.* Washington, DC: U.S.
            Government Printing Office.

    1976a   *Fulfilling the Letter and Spirit
            of the Law: Desegregation of
            the Nation's Public Schools.*
            Washington, DC: U.S. Gov-
            ernment Printing Office.

    1976b   *A Guide to Federal Laws and
            Regulations Prohibiting Sex
            Discrimination.* Washington,
            DC: U.S. Government Print-
            ing Office.

    1976c   *Puerto Ricans in the Conti-
            nental United States: An
            Uncertain Future.* Washing-
            ton, DC: U.S. Government
            Printing Office.

    1977   *Window Dressing on the Set:
            Women and Minorities in
            Television.* Washington, DC:
            U.S. Government Printing
            Office.

    1980a   *Asian Americans: An Agenda
            for Action.* Washington, DC:
            U.S. Government Printing
            Office.

    1980b   *Characters in Textbooks: A
            Review of the Literature.*
            Washington, DC: U.S. Gov-
            ernment Printing Office.

1980c   *Success of Asian Americans:
Fact or Fiction?* Washington,
DC: U.S. Government Print-
ing Office.

1981   *Affirmative Action in the
1980s: Dismantling the
Process of Discrimination.*
Washington, DC: U.S. Gov-
ernment Printing Office.

1986   *Recent Activity Against Citi-
zens and Residents of Asian
Descent.* Washington, DC:
U.S. Government Printing
Office.

1992   *Civil Rights Issues Facing
Asian Americans in the 1990s.*
Washington, DC: U.S. Gov-
ernment Printing Office.

Commission on Wartime Relocation and
Internment of Civilians
1982a   *Report.* Washington, DC: U.S.
Government Printing Office.

1982b   *Recommendations.* Washington, DC: U.S. Government
Printing Office.

Condon, Jane
1985   *A Half-Step Behind, Japanese
Women of the '80s.* New York:
Dodd, Mead.

Conforti, Joseph M.
1974   WASP in the Woodpile:
Inequalities and Injustices of
Ethnic Ecology. Paper presented at American Sociological Association Annual Meeting, Montreal.

Congressional Hispanic Caucus
1994   *Fact and Fiction: Immigrants
in the U.S.* Washington, DC:
Congressional Hispanic Caucus.

Congressional Quarterly
1984   Democratic Party Rules,
Mondale Delegates Lead. 42
(June 23), pp. 1504–1505.

Conot, Robert
1967   *Rivers of Blood, Years of
Darkness.* New York: Bantam.

Conroy, John
1981   Ulster's Lost Generation. *New
York Times Magazine* (August
2), pp. 16–21, 70–72, 74–75.

Conver, Bill
1976   Group Chairman Lists Problems Endangering Jewish
Family. *Peoria Journal Star*
(December 4), p. A2.

Cooper, Kenneth J.
1994   Wrong Turns on the Map?
*Washington Post National
Weekly Edition* 11 (February
6), pp. 14, 15.

Cornacchia, Eugene J., and Nelson,
Dale C.
1992   Historical Differences in the
Political Experiences of American Blacks and White Ethnics: Revisiting an Unresolved
Controversy. *Ethnic and
Racial Studies* 15 (January),
pp. 102–124.

Cornell, Stephen
1984   Crisis and Response in Indian–
White Relations: 1960–1984.
Social Problems 32 (October),
pp. 44–59.

Cornell, Stephen, and Kalt, Joseph P.
1990   Pathways from Poverty: Economic Development and
Institution-Building on American Indian Reservations.
*American Indian Culture and
Research Journal* 14 (No. 1),
pp. 89–125.

Cortés, Carlos E.
1980   Mexicans. In Stephen Thernstrom, ed., *Harvard Encyclopedia of American Ethnic
Groups,* pp. 697–719. Cambridge: Harvard University
Press.

Cortés, Dharma E.
1995   Variations in Familism in Two
Generations of Puerto Ricans.
*Hispanic Journal of Behav-
ioral Sciences* 17 (May), pp.
249–255.

Cose, Ellis
    1989   Yellow-Peril Journalism. *Time* 139 (November 27), p. 79.

    1993   *The Rage of a Privileged Class.* New York: HarperCollins.

Coser, Lewis A.
    1956   *The Functions of Social Conflict.* New York: Free Press.

Coser, Lewis, and Coser, Rose Laub
    1974   *Greedy Institutions.* New York: Free Press.

Cosford, Bill
    1981   Charlie Chan Wit: Some High Proof. *The Miami Herald* (March 1), pt. L, pp. 1–2.

Council on Scientific Affairs
    1991   Hispanic Health in the United States. *Journal of the American Medical Association* 265 (January 9), pp. 248–252.

Courtney, Alice W., and Whipple, Thomas W.
    1983   *Sex Stereotyping in Advertising.* Lexington, MA: Lexington Books.

Cowley, Geoffrey
    1989   The Plunder of the Past. *Newsweek* 113 (June 26), pp. 58–60.

Cox, Oliver C.
    1942   The Modern Caste School of Race Relations. *Social Forces* 21 (December), pp. 218–226.

Cross, William E., Jr.
    1991   *Shades of Black: Diversity in African-American Identity.* Philadelphia: Temple University Press.

Crull, Sue R., and Bruton, Brent T.
    1985   Possible Decline in Tolerance Toward Minorities: Social Distance on a Midwest Campus. *Sociology and Social Research* 70 (October), pp. 57–62.

Cuellar, Alfredo
    1970   Perspectives on Politics. In Joan W. Moore with A. Cuel-

lar, eds., *Mexican Americans,* pp. 137–158. Englewood Cliffs, NJ: Prentice-Hall.

Daily Citizen
    1994   Anti-Asian Violence on the Rise in U.S. (April 27), p. 12.

Daniels, Roger
    1967   *The Politics of Prejudice: The Anti-Japanese Movement in California and the Struggle for Japanese Exclusion.* New York: Antheneum.

    1972   *Concentration Campus, USA.* New York: Holt, Rinehart & Winston.

    1988   *Asian America: Chinese and Japanese in the United States Since 1850.* Seattle: University of Washington Press.

    1990   *Coming to America.* New York: HarperCollins.

Danzger, M. Herbert
    1989   *Returning to Tradition.* New Haven: Yale University Press.

Darnton, John
    1995   Protestant and Paranoid in Northern Ireland. *New York Times Magazine* (January 15), pp. 32–35.

Davis, David Brion
    1966   *The Problem of Slavery in Western Culture.* Ithaca, NY: Cornell University Press.

Davis, Shelley
    1994a   Split in AIM Leads to Charges. *News from Indian Country* 8 (Mid-January), pp. 1, 2.

    1994b   "Welcome Home" Says Clinton. *News from Indian Country* 8 (Mid-May), p. 102.

Dawidowicz, Lucy S.
    1967   *The Golden Tradition: Jewish Life and Thought in Eastern Europe.* New York: Holt, Rinehart & Winston.

    1975   *The War Against the Jews, 1933–1945.* New York: Holt, Rinehart & Winston.

De Fleur, Melvin; D'Antonio, William; and De Fleur, Lois
1976 *Sociology: Human Society*, 2d ed. Glenview, IL: Scott, Foresman.

Degler, Carl N.
1969 The Negro in America— Where Myrdal Went Wrong. *New York Times Magazine* (December 7), p. 64.

1971 *Neither Black nor White: Slavery and Race Relations in Brazil and the United States.* New York: Macmillan.

de la Garza, Rodolfo O.; De Sipio, Louis; Garcia, F. Chris; Garcia, John; and Falcon, Angelo
1992 *Latino Voices: Mexican, Puerto Rican, and Cuban Perspectives on American Politics.* Boulder, CO: Westview Press.

Dellios, Hugh
1993 Peyote: Drug or Religious Ritual? *Chicago Tribune* (August 29), pp. 1, 9.

Deloria, Vine, Jr.
1969 *Custer Died for Your Sins: An Indian Manifesto.* New York: Avon.

1971 *Of Utmost Good Faith.* New York: Bantam.

1992 Secularism, Civil Religion, and the Religious Freedom of American Indians. *American Indian Culture and Research Journal* 16 (No. 2), pp. 9–20.

Deloria, Vine, Jr., and Lytle, Clifford M.
1983 *American Indians, American Justice.* Austin: University of Texas Press.

Denny, Ruth
1992 Indian Casinos Hit the Jackpot. *Utne Reader* (November–December), pp. 35–37.

Dent, David J.
1992 The New Black Suburbs. *New York Times Magazine* (June 14), pp. 18–25.

Denton, Herbert H.
1987 Canada's Jamaican Son. *Washington Post* (September 4), pp. A1, A28.

Denton, John
1985 The Underground Economy and Social Stratification. *Sociological Spectrum* 5 (Nos. 1–2), pp. 31–42.

DeParle, Jason
1991 New Rows to Hoe in the "Harvest of Shame." *New York Times* (July 28), p. E3.

Department of Health, Education, and Welfare
1974 *A Study of Selected Socio-Economic Characteristics of Ethnic Minorities Based on the 1970 Census: Vol. 2. Asian Americans.* Washington, DC: U.S. Government Printing Office.

Department of Justice
1994 *Crime in the United States, 1993.* Washington, DC: U.S. Government Printing Office.

1993 *Highlights From 20 Years of Surveying Crime Victims.* Washington, D.C.: U.S. Government Printing Office.

Department of Labor
1965 *The Negro Family: The Case for National Action.* Washington, DC: U.S. Government Printing Office.

1980 *Perspectives on Working Women: A Databook.* Washington, DC: U.S. Government Printing Office.

1993 *Breaking the Glass Ceiling.* Washington, DC: U.S. Government Printing Office.

1995 *Good for Business: Making Full Use of the Nation's Capital.* Washington, DC: U.S. Government Printing Office.

Deutscher, Irwin; Pestello, Fred P.; and Pestello, H. Frances
1993 *Sentiments and Acts.* New York: Aldine de Gruyter.

Dinnerstein, Leonard
1988 Antisemitism in the United States Today. *Patterns of Prejudice* 22 (Autumn), pp. 3–14.

1994 *Anti-Semitism in America.* New York: Oxford University Press.

Dinnerstein, Leonard, and Reimers, David M.
1975 *Ethnic Americans: A History of Immigration and Assimilation.* New York: Harper & Row.

Dionne, E. J., Jr.
1988 Jackson Share of Votes by Whites Triples in '88. *New York Times* (June 13), p. B7.

1994 Race and IQ: Stale Notions. *Washington Post National Weekly Edition* 11 (October 24), p. 24.

1995 Slandered White Men. *Washington Post National Weekly Edition* 12 (May 8), p. 28.

Doherty, Carroll J.
1992 Question of Ability to Repay Loans Shadows Israel's Guarantee Request. *Congressional Quarterly Weekly Report* (January 18), pp. 120–121.

Domestic Council Committee on Illegal Aliens
1976 *Preliminary Report of the Domestic Council.* Washington, DC: Immigration and Naturalization Service, Department of Justice.

Donovan, Robert J., and Levers, Susan
1993 Using Paid Advertising to Modify Racial Stereotype Beliefs. *Public Opinion Quarterly* 57 (Summer), pp. 205–218.

Dorris, Michael A.
1988 For the Indians, No Thanksgiving. *New York Times* (November 24), p. A23.

Dovidio, Jack
1994 Unpublished data on stereotyping. Hamilton, NY: Colgate University.

Drogin, Bob
1995 Mandela After One Year: Public Acclaim, Private Pain. *Los Angeles Times,* (May 9), pp. 1, 4.

Du Bois, W. E. B.
1903 *The Souls of Black Folks: Essays and Sketches.* Reprinted in 1961 by New York: Facade Publications.

1939 *Black Folk: Then and Now.* New York: Holt, Rinehart & Winston.

1952 *Battle for Peace; The Story of My 83rd Birthday.* New York: Masses and Mainstream.

1961 *The Souls of Black Folk.* New York: Fawcett.

1968 *Dusk of Dawn.* New York: Schocken.

1969a *An ABC of Color.* New York: International Publications.

1969b *The Suppression of the African Slave-Trade to the United States of America, 1638–1870.* New York: Schocken.

1970 *The Negro American Family.* Cambridge: MIT Press.

Du Brow, Rick
1994 Portrayals of Latinos on TV Regressing. *Los Angeles Times* (September 7), p. A5.

Duff, John B.
1971 *The Irish in the United States.* Belmont, CA: Wadsworth.

Duke, Lynne
1993 Blacks and Jews: The Great Divide. *Washington Post National Weekly Edition* (October 18), p. 11.

Duncan, Beverly, and Duncan, Otis Dudley
1968 Minorities and the Process of Stratification. *American Sociological Review* 33 (June), pp. 356–364.

Duncan, Otis Dudley; Featherman, David; and Duncan, Beverly
1972 *Socioeconomic Background and Achievement.* New York: Seminar Press.

Dunn, Ashley
1994   Southeast Asians Highly
        Dependent on Welfare in U.S.
        New York Times (May 19), pp.
        A1, A20.

Durant, Thomas J., Jr., and Louden,
Joyce S.
1986   The Black Middle Class in
        America: Historical and Con-
        temporary Perspectives. *Phy-
        lon* 47 (December), pp.
        253–263.

Dworkin, Anthony Gary
1965   Stereotypes and Self-Images
        Held by Native-Born and For-
        eign-Born Mexican Ameri-
        cans. *Sociology and Social
        Research* 49 (January), pp.
        214–224.

Dzidzienyo, Anani
1987   Brazil. In Jay A. Sigler, ed.,
        *International Handbook on
        Race and Race Relations.*
        New York: Greenwood
        Press.

Dzidzienyo, Anani, with Casai,
Lourdes
1979   *The Position of Blacks in
        Brazilian and Cuban Society.*
        New York: Minority Rights
        Group.

Early, Gerald
1994   Defining Afrocentrism. *Jour-
        nal of Blacks in Higher Educa-
        tion* 1 (Winter), p. 46.

Echo-Hawk, Walter
1992   Preface. *American Indian
        Culture and Research Journal*
        16 (No. 2), pp. 1–7.

Edmonds, Patricia
1992   Tribes Fight Desperation with
        Determination. *USA Today*
        (April 8), p. 8A.

Edsall, Thomas B.
1995   The U.S. Male, Caught in a
        Cultural Shift. *Washington
        Post National Weekly Edition*
        12 (May 8), p. 25.

Edwards, Harry
1970   *Black Students.* New York:
        Free Press.

Egerton, John
1971   Racism Differs in Puerto
        Rico. *Race Relations Reporter*
        2 (July 6), pp. 6–7.

El-Badry, Samia
1994   The Arab-American Market.
        American Demographics 16
        (January), pp. 22–31.

Elkins, Stanley
1959   *Slavery: A Problem in Ameri-
        can Institutional and Intellec-
        tual Life.* Chicago: University
        of Chicago Press.

Ellis, Richard N.
1972   *The Western American Indian:
        Case Studies in Tribal History.*
        Lincoln: University of Nebras-
        ka Press.

El Nasser, Haya
1991a   Melting Pot of Blacks, Kore-
        ans Boils Over. *USA Today*
        (September 18), p. 7A.

1991b   Japanese Americans Face
        Prejudice. *USA Today*
        (December 6), p. 8A.

1993   In Hawaii, an Identity Crisis.
        USA Today (January 18),
        p. 10A.

Epenshade, Thomas J.
1990   A Short History of U.S. Policy
        Toward Illegal Immigration.
        Population Today 18 (Febru-
        ary), pp. 6–9.

Epstein, Joseph
1972   Blue Collars in Cicero. *Dis-
        sent* 19 (Winter), pp. 118–127.

Esber, George S., Jr.
1987   Designing Apache Houses
        with Apaches. In Robert M.
        Wulff and Shirley J. Fiske
        (eds.) *Anthropological Praxis:
        Translating Knowledge into
        Action.* pp. 187–196. Boulder,
        CO: Westview.

Eschbach, Karl
1995   The Enduring and Vanishing
        American Indian: American

Indian Population Growth and Intermarriage in 1990. *Ethnic and Racial Studies* 18 (January), pp. 89–108.

Espinosa, Dula J.
1992   Affirmative Action: A Case Study of an Organization Effort. *Sociological Perspectives* 35 (No. 1), pp. 119–136.

Espiritu, Yen Le
1992   *Asian American Panethnicity: Bridging Institutions and Identities.* Philadelphia: Temple University Press.

Farber, Bernard; Mindel, Charles H.; and Lazerwitz, Bernard
1976   The Jewish American Family. In Charles H. Mindel and Robert W. Habenstein, eds., *Ethnic Families in America: Patterns and Variations*, pp. 347–378. New York: Elsevier.

Farber, M. A.
1975   Immigration Service Inquiry Ending; Results in Dispute. *New York Times* (April 27), p. 47.

Farley, Reynolds
1993   The Common Destiny of Blacks and Whites: Observations About the Social and Economic Status of the Races. In Herbert Hill and James E. Jones, Jr., eds., *Race in America: The Struggle for Equality*, pp. 197–233. Madison: University of Wisconsin Press.

Farley, Reynolds, and Allen, Walter R.
1987   *The Color Line and the Quality of Life in America.* New York: Sage.

Farley, Reynolds; Schuman, Howard; Bianchi, Suzanne; Colasanto, Diane; and Hatchett, Shirley
1978   Chocolate City, Vanilla Suburbs: Will the Trend Toward Racially Separate Communities Continue? *Social Science Research* 7 (December), pp. 319–344.

Farley, Reynolds; Steeh, Charlotte; Kryson, Maria; Jackson, Tara; and Reeves, Keith
1994   Stereotypes and Segregation: Neighborhoods in the Detroit Area. *American Journal of Sociology* 10 (November), pp. 750–780.

Farr, D. M. L.
1993   Canada. In *1993 Britannica Book of the Year*, pp. 463–465. Chicago: Encyclopedia Britannica.

Farrell, Warren T.
1974   *The Liberated Man.* New York: Random House.

Fayer, Joan M.
1985   Puerto Rican Identity: Themes That Unite and Divide. *Journal of American Culture* 8 (Winter), pp. 83–91.

Feldman, Paul, and McDonnell, Patrick J.
1994   Prop. 187 Backers Elated— Challenges Imminent. *Los Angeles Times* (November 9), pp. A1, A20.

Feng, Shih Tree
1988   Chinese Immigrants in the United States. Unpublished paper, Western Illinois University, Macomb.

Fermi, Laura
1971   *Illustrious Immigrants*, rev. ed. Chicago: University of Chicago Press.

Ferree, Myra Marx, and Hess, Beth B.
1994   *Controversy and Coalition: The New Feminist Movement Across Three Decades of Change*, rev. ed. New York: Twayne.

Finder, Alan
1994   Muslim Gave Racist Speech, Jackson Says. *New York Times* (January 23), p. 21.

1995   Despite Tough Laws, Sweatshops Flourish. *New York Times* (February 6), pp. A1, B4.

Finestein, Israel
1988 The Future of American Jewry. *The Jewish Journal of Sociology* 30 (December), pp. 121–125.

Fiola, Jan
1989 Race Relations in Brazil: A Reassessment of the "Racial Democracy" Thesis. Paper presented at the annual meeting of the Midwest Sociological Society, St. Louis.

Firmat, Gustavo Pérez
1994 *Life on the Hyphen: The Cuban-American Way.* Austin: University of Texas Press.

Fishman, Joshua A., ed.
1985 *The Rise and Fall of the Ethnic Revival.* Berlin: Mouton.

Fishman, Joshua A.; Hayden, Robert G.; and Warshaver, Mary E.
1966 The Non-English and the Ethnic Group Press, 1910–1960. In Joshua A. Fishman, ed., *Language Loyalty in the United States,* pp. 51–74. London and The Hague: Mouton.

Fiske, Edward B.
1988a Colleges Are Seeking to Remedy Lag in Their Hispanic Enrollment. *New York Times* (March 20), pp. 8, 16.

1988b The Undergraduate Hispanic Experience. *Change* (May–June), pp. 28–33.

Fitzhugh, George
1857 *Cannibals All! or Slaves Without Masters.* Richmond, VA: A. Morris.

Fitzpatrick, Joseph P.
1987 *Puerto Rican Americans: The Meaning of Migration to the Mainland,* 2d ed. Englewood Cliffs, NJ: Prentice-Hall.

1989 Puerto Ricans as a Social Minority on the Mainland. *International Journal of Group Tensions* 19 (Fall), pp. 195–208.

Fix, Michael, and Passel, Jeffrey S.
1991 *The Door Remains Open: Recent Immigration to the United States and a Preliminary Analysis of the Immigration Act of 1990.* Washington, DC: Urban Institute.

Fixico, Donald L.
1988 The Federal Policy of Termination and Relocation, 1945–1960. In Phillip Weeks, ed., *The American Indian Experience,* pp. 260–277. Arlington Heights, IL: Forum Press.

Flexner, Eleanor
1959 *Century of Struggle: The Women's Rights Movement in the United States.* Cambridge: Harvard University Press.

Flores, Juan
1985 Que Assimilated, Brother, Yo Soy Assimilado: The Structuring of Puerto Rican Identity in the U.S. *Journal of Ethnic Studies* 13 (Fall), pp. 1–16.

Foderaro, Lisa W.
1990 Japanese in New York Area Feel Sting of Prejudice. *New York Times* (July 22), p. 20.

Fong, Stanley L. M.
1965 Assimilation of Chinese in America: Changes in Orientation and Perception. *American Journal of Sociology* 71 (November), pp. 265–273.

1973 Assimilation and Changing Social Roles of Chinese Americans. *Journal of Social Issues* 29 (No. 2), pp. 115–127.

Fong, Timothy P.
1994 *The First Suburban Chinatown.* Philadelphia: Temple University Press.

Fong-Torres, Ben
1986 The China Syndrome. *Moviegoer* 5 (July), pp. 6–7.

Ford, W. Scott
1986 Favorable Intergroup Contact May Not Reduce Prejudice:

Inconclusive Journal Evidence, 1960–1984. *Sociology and Social Research* 70 (July), pp. 256–258.

Forni, Floreal
1971 *The Situation of the Puerto Rican Population in Chicago and Its Viewpoints About Racial Relations.* Chicago: Community and Family Study Center, University of Chicago.

Fox, Elaine
1992 Crossing the Bridge: Adaptive Strategies Among Navajo Health Care Workers. *Free Inquiry in Creative Sociology* 20 (May), pp. 25–34.

Fox, Jim
1994 Election Stirs Talk (in English and French) of Independence. *USA Today* (August 8), p. 4A.

1995 Tutsi, Hutu Alike Try to Rebuild Life. *USA Today* (January 6), p. 6A.

Fox, Stephen
1990 *The Unknown Internment.* Boston: Twayne.

Francis, Emerich K.
1976 *Interethnic Relations: An Essay in Sociological Theory.* New York: Elsevier.

Frankel, Bruce
1995a N.Y.'s "Jewish Rosa Parks" Wins Bus Battle, *USA Today* (March 17), p. 4A.

1995b D'Amato Owns Up to "Sorry Episode." *USA Today* (April 7), p. 2A.

Franklin, John Hope, and Moss, Alfred A., Jr.
1994 *From Slavery to Freedom,* 7th ed. New York: McGraw-Hill.

Frazier, E. Franklin
1942 The Negro Family in Bahia, Brazil. *American Sociological Review* 7 (August), pp. 465–478.

1943 Rejoinder: The Negro in Bahia, Brazil. *American Sociological Review* 8 (August), pp. 402–404.

1957 *Black Bourgeoisie: The Rise of a New Middle Class.* New York: Free Press.

1964 *The Negro Church in America.* New York: Schocken.

Fredrickson, George M.
1981 *White Supremacy: A Comparative Study in American and South African History.* New York: Oxford University Press.

Freeman, Jo
1973 The Origins of the Women's Liberation Movement. *American Journal of Sociology* 78 (January), pp. 792–811.

1975 *The Politics of Women's Liberation.* New York: David McKay.

1983 On the Origins of Social Movements, In Jo Freeman, ed., *Social Movements of the Sixties and Seventies,* pp. 1–30. New York: Longman.

Frey, William H., and Farley, Reynolds
1993 Latino, Asian, and Black Segregation in Multi-Ethnic Metro Areas: Findings From the 1990 Census. Paper presented at the Annual Meeting of the Population Association of America.

Freyre, Gilberto
1946 *The Masters and the Slaves: A Study in the Development of Brazilian Civilization.* New York: Knopf.

1959 *New World in the Tropics.* New York: Knopf.

1963 *The Mansions and the Shanties: The Making of Modern Brazil.* New York: Knopf.

Friedan, Betty
1963 *The Feminine Mystique.* New York: Dell.

1981 *The Second Stage.* New York: Summit Books.

1991   Back to the Feminine Mystique? *The Humanist* 51 (January–February), pp. 26–27.

Friedman, Georges
1967   *The End of the Jewish People?* Garden City, NY: Doubleday.

Frielinghaus, Julia
1995   The Seeds of Change. *Frontiers of Freedom* (January), pp. 11–23.

Friendly, Alfred, and Silver, Eric
1981   *Israel's Oriental Immigrants and Druzes.* London: Minority Rights Group.

Friends Committee on National Legislation
1993   American Indian Religious Freedom. *News from Indian Country* (Mid-February), p. 8.

Fuchs, Estelle, and Havighurst, Robert J.
1972   *To Live on This Earth: American Indian Education.* New York: Doubleday.

Fulton, E. Kaye
1992   Drumbeats of Rage. *Macleans* (March 16), pp. 14–17.

Fulwood, Sam, III
1994a   Views of Reality Differ, Split U.S. Blacks, Whites. *Chicago Sun-Times* (August 9), p. 8.
1994b   A Dilemma for Black Women. *Los Angeles Times* (August 27), pp. A1, A26.

Gable, Donna
1993a   In Search of Prime-Time Faith. *USA Today* (July 12), p. 3D.
1993b   On TV, Lifestyles of the Slim and Entertaining. *USA Today* (July 27), p. 3D.
1993c   Series Shortchange Working-Class and Minority Americans. *USA Today* (August 30), p. 3D.

Galarza, Ernesto
1964   *Merchants of Labor: The Mexican Bracero Story.* Santa Barbara, CA: McNally & Loften.

1971   *Barrio Boy.* Notre Dame, IN: University of Notre Dame Press.

Gallup, George H.
1972   *The Gallup Poll, Public Opinions 1935–1971.* New York: Random House.

Galtung, Johan
1989   *Nonviolence and Israel/Palestine.* Honolulu: University of Hawaii Institute for Peace.

Galvan, Manuel
1982   On the National Scene, Two Who Are Making Their Mark. *Chicago Tribune Magazine* (June 20), sect. 2, p. 2.

Gambino, Richard
1974a   *Blood of My Blood.* New York: Doubleday.
1974b   The Italian Americans. *Chicago Tribune Magazine* (May 5), pp. 56–58.

Gans, Herbert J.
1956   American Jewry: Present and Future. *Commentary* 21 (May), pp. 424–425.
1979   Symbolic Ethnicity: The Future of Ethnic Groups and Cultures in America. *Ethnic and Racial Studies* 2 (January), pp. 1–20.
1994   Letter. *New York Times Book Review* (November 13), p. 3.

Garbarino, Merwyn S.
1971   Life in the City: Chicago. In Jack O. Waddell and O. Michael Watson, eds., *The American Indian in Urban Society,* pp. 168–205. Boston: Little, Brown.

García, Mario T.
1989   *Mexican Americans: Leadership, Ideology, and Identity, 1930–1960.* New Haven: Yale University Press.

Gardner, Robert W.; Robe, Bryant; and Smith, Peter C.
1985   Asian Americans; Growth, Change, and Diversity. *Population Bulletin* 40 (October).

Garfinkel, Herbert
1959   *When Negroes March.* New York: Atheneum.

Garrison, Troy
1974   Another Oriental Treat from San Francisco. *Chicago Tribune* (February 3), sect. 4, pp. 6–7.

Gary, Lawrence E.; Beatty, Lula A.; Berry, Greta L.; and Price, Mary D.
1983   *Stable Black Families: Final Report.* Washington, DC: Institute for Urban Affairs and Research, Howard University.

Garza, Melita Marie
1995   Bilingual Bill Called Unconstitutional. *Chicago Tribune* (February 7), sect. 2, p. 4.

Gates, Henry Louis, Jr.
1992   Black Demagogues and Pseudo-Scholars. *New York Times* (July 20), p. A15.

Gates, Mireille Grangenois
1989   TV's Black World Turns—But Stays Unreal. *New York Times* (November 12), pp. H1, H40.

Gedicks, Al
1993   *The New Resource Wars.* Boston: South End Press.

Gellman, Barton
1995a The Honeymoon Is Over. *Washington Post National Weekly Edition* 12 (March 6), p. 28.

1995b Israelis Ponder a Final Split from the Palestinians. *Washington Post National Weekly Edition* 12 (April 17), p. 16.

Gerber, David A.
1993   *Nativism, Anti-Catholicism, and Anti-Semitism.* New York: Scribners.

Gerson, Walter
1969   Jews at Christmas Time: Role-Strain and Strain Reducing Mechanisms. In Walter Gerson, ed., *Social Problems in a Changing World,* pp. 65–76. New York: Crowell.

Gibbons, Tom
1985   Justice Not Equal for Poor Here, *Chicago Sun-Times* (February 24), pp. 1, 18.

Giles, Michael W.; Gatlin, Douglas S.; and Cataldo, Everette F.
1976   Racial and Class Prejudice: Their Relative Effects on Protest Against School Desegregation. *American Sociological Review* 41 (April), pp. 280–288.

Gilly, M. C.
1988   Sex Roles in Advertising: A Comparison of Television Advertisements in Australia, Mexico, and the United States. *Journal of Marketing* 52 (April), pp. 75–85.

Giovanni, Nikki
1994   *Racism 101.* New York: Morrow.

Girdner, Audrie, and Loftis, Anne
1969   *The Great Betrayal: The Evacuation of the Japanese Americans During World War II.* New York: Macmillan.

Gittler, Joseph B., ed.
1981   *Jewish Life in the United States: Perspectives from the Social Sciences.* New York: New York University Press.

Glassman, Bernard
1975   *Anti-Semitic Stereotypes Without Jews: Images of the Jews in England, 1290–1700.* Detroit: Wayne State University Press.

Glazer, Nathan
1971   The Issue of Cultural Pluralism in America Today. In *Pluralism Beyond Frontier: Report of the San Francisco Consultation on Ethnicity,* pp. 2–8. San Francisco: American Jewish Committee.

1990   American Jewry or American Judaism? *Society* ?5 (November–December), pp. 14–20.

Glazer, Nathan, and Moynihan, Daniel Patrick
1963   *Beyond the Melting Pot: The Negroes, Puerto Ricans, Jews, Italians, and Irish of New York City.* Cambridge: MIT Press.
1970   *Beyond the Melting Pot: The Negroes, Puerto Ricans, Jews, Italians, and Irish of New York City,* 2d ed. Cambridge: MIT Press.

Gleason, Philip
1980   American Identity and Americanization. In Stephen Therstromm, ed., *Harvard Encyclopedia of American Ethnic Groups,* pp. 31–58. Cambridge: Belknap Press of Harvard University Press.

Gledhill, Ruth
1992   Losing the Chosen Race. *The Times* (London) *Saturday Review* (November 14), pp. 10–12.

Glock, Charles Y., and Stark, Rodney
1965   Is There an American Protestantism? *Transaction* 3 (November–December), pp. 8–13, 48–49.

Glock, Charles Y.; Wuthnow, Robert; Piliavin, Jane Allyn; and Spencer, Metta
1975   *Adolescent Prejudice.* New York: Harper & Row.

Goering, John M.
1971   The Emergence of Ethnic Interests: A Case of Serendipity. *Social Forces* 48 (March), pp. 379–384.

Goering, Laurie
1994   Beneath Utopian Facade, Brazilians Uncover Racism. *Chicago Tribune* (December 20), pp. 1, 11.

Gold, Michael
1965   *Jews Without Money.* New York: Avon.

Gold, Steven J.
1988   New Immigrant Organizations and Old Country Links: The Case of Soviet Jews in the U.S. Paper presented at the annual meeting of the American Sociological Association, Atlanta.

Goldstein, Sidney
1981   Jews in the United States: Perspectives from Demography. In Joseph B. Gittler, ed., *Jewish Life in the United States,* pp. 31–102. New York: New York University Press.

Goldstein, Sidney, and Goldscheider, Calvin
1968   *Jewish Americans: Three Generations in a Jewish Community.* Englewood Cliffs, NJ: Prentice-Hall.

Goleman, Daniel
1990   As Bias Crime Seems to Rise, Scientists Study Roots of Racism. *New York Times* (May 29), p. C1.

Gomez, David F.
1971   Chicanos: Strangers in Their Own Land. *America* 124 (June 26), pp. 659–652.

Gompers, Samuel, and Gustadt, Herman
1908   *Meat vs. Rice: American Manhood Against Asiatic Coolieism: Which Shall Survive?* San Francisco: Asiatic Exclusion League.

Gonzalez, David
1992   What's the Problem with "Hispanic"? Just Ask a "Latino." *New York Times* (November 15), p. E6.

Gonzalez, Gilbert G.
1990   *Chicano Education in the Era of Segregation.* Philadelphia: Balch Institute Press.

Gonzales, Rodolfo
1972   *Yo Soy Joaquin (I Am Joaquin).* New York: Bantam Books.

Goodman, David G., and Miyazawa, Masanori
1995 *Jews in the Japanese Mind: The History and Uses of a Cultural Stereotype.* New York: Free Press.

Goodstein, Laurie
1990 New York's Racial Tinderbox. *Washington Post National Weekly Edition* 7 (May 21), p. 9.
1994 The Ethnic Evolution of Jesus Christ. *Washington Post National Weekly Edition* (April 4), p. 33.

Goozner, Merrill
1987 Age-old Tradition Bankrolls Koreans. *Chicago Tribune* (July 19), sect. 7, pp. 1–2.

Gordon, Leonard
1986 College Student Stereotypes on Blacks and Jews on Two Campuses: Four Studies Spanning 50 Years. *Sociology and Social Research* 70 (April), pp. 200–201.

Gordon, Milton M.
1964 *Assimilation in American Life: The Role of Race, Religion, and National Origins.* New York: Oxford University Press.
1978 *Human Nature, Class, and Ethnicity.* New York: Oxford University Press.

Gordon, Wendell
1975 A Case for a Less Restrictive Border Policy. *Social Science Quarterly* 56 (December), pp. 485–491.

Goren, Arthur A.
1980 Jews. In Stephen Thernstrom, ed., *Harvard Encyclopedia of American Ethnic Groups,* pp. 571–592. Cambridge, MA: Belknap Press of Harvard University Press.

Gottsman, Andrew
1995 Gender Equity Hit by Backlash. *Chicago Tribune* (May 7), sect. 3, p. 5.

Gould, Ketayun H.
1988 Asian and Pacific Islanders Myth and Reality. *Social Work* 43 (March–April), pp. 142–147.

Gould, Stephen Jay
1981 *The Mismeasure of Man.* New York: Norton.

Gouldner, Alvin
1970 *The Coming Crisis in Western Sociology.* New York: Basic Books.

Grant, Neil, and Middleton, Nick
1987 *Atlas of the World Today.* New York: Harper & Row.

Greeley, Andrew M.
1974a *Ethnicity in the United States: A Preliminary Reconnaissance.* New York: Wiley.
1974b Political Participation Among Ethnic Groups in the United States: A Preliminary Reconnaissance. *American Journal of Sociology* 80 (July), pp. 170–204.
1976 *Ethnicity, Denomination and Inequality.* Sage Research Paper No. 4. Beverly Hills, CA: Sage Publications.
1977 *The American Catholic.* New York: Basic Books.

Greeley, Andrew M., and Sheatsley, Paul B.
1971 Attitudes Toward Racial Integration. *Scientific American* 225 (December), pp. 13–19.

Greenberg, Blu
1992 Feminism Within Orthodoxy. *Lilith* 17 (Summer), pp. 11–17.

Greenberg, Simon
1970 Jewish Educational Institutions. In Louis Finkelstein, ed., *The Jews: Their Religion and Culture,* 4th ed., vol. 2, pp. 380–412. New York: Schocken.

Greene, Elizabeth
1987 Asian Americans Find U.S. Colleges Insensitive, Form Campus Organizations to

Fight Bias. *Chronicle of Higher Education* 34 (November 18), pp. A1, A38–A40.

Greenhouse, Linda
1989   Court Bars a Plan Set Up to Provide Jobs to Minorities, *New York Times* (January 24), pp. A1, A19.

1990   Use of Illegal Drugs as Part of Religion Can Be Prosecuted, High Court Says. *New York Times* (April 18), p. A10.

1993a   Court, Citing Religious Freedom, Voids a Ban on Animal Sacrifice. *New York Times* (June 12), pp. 1, 8.

1993b   High Court Backs Policy of Halting Haitian Refugees. *New York Times* (June 22), pp. 1, 8.

1993c   Court, 9–0, Makes Sex Harassment Easier to Prove. *New York Times* (November 10), pp. A1, A22.

1994   Court Rules Abortion Clinics Can Use Rackets Law to Sue. *New York Times* (January 25), pp. A1, A17.

Gremley, William
1952   Social Control in Cicero. *British Journal of Sociology* 3 (December), pp. 322–338.

Griggs, Anthony
1974   Chicago Gets a Third Chinatown. *Race Relations Reporter* 5 (March 25), pp. 6–7.

Grimshaw, Allen D., ed.
1969   *Racial Violence in the United States.* Chicago: Aldine.

Gross, Jane
1989   Diversity Hinders Asians' Power in U.S. *New York Times* (June 25), p. A22.

Grove, David John
1974   *The Race vs. Ethnic Debate: A Cross-National Analysis of Two Theoretical Approaches.* Denver: University of Denver Press.

Guerin-Gonzales, Camille
1994   *Mexican Workers and American Dreams.* New Brunswick, NJ: Rutgers University Press.

Guererro, Ed
1993   *Framing Blackness: The African American Image in Film.* Philadelphia: Temple University Press.

Gutiérrez, Armado, and Herbert Hirsch
1970   The Militant Challenge to the American Ethos: "Chicanos" and "Mexican Americans." *Social Science Quarterly* 53 (March), pp. 830–845.

Guzman, Pablo
1995   La Vida Para: A Lord of the Barrio. *Village Voice* 40 (March 21), pp. 24–31.

Gwertzman, Bernard
1985   The Debt to the Indochinese Is Becoming a Fiscal Drain. *New York Times* (March 3), p. E3.

Haak, Gerald O.
1970   Co-opting the Oppressors: The Case of the Japanese-Americans. *Society* 7 (October), pp. 23–31.

Hacker, Andrew
1994   White on White. *The New Republic* 211 (October 31), pp. 12–13.

1995   *Two Nations: Black and White, Separate, Hostile, and Unequal,* exp. and updated ed. New York: Ballantine.

Hacker, Helen Mayer
1951   Women as a Minority Group. *Social Forces* 30 (October), pp. 60–69.

1973   Sex Roles in Black Society: Caste Versus Caste. Paper presented at the annual meeting of the American Sociological Association, New York.

1974   Women as a Minority Group: Twenty Years Later. In Florence Denmark, ed., *Who*

*Discriminates Against
Women*, pp. 124–134. Beverly
Hills, CA: Sage.

1975   Class and Race Differences in
Gender Roles. In Lucille
Duberman, ed., *Gender and
Sex in Society*, pp. 138–184.
New York: Praeger

Hagan, William T.
1961   *American Indians.* Chicago:
University of Chicago Press.

Halpern, Ben
1974   America Is Different. In Marshall Sklare, ed., *The Jew in
American Society*, pp. 67–89.
New York: Behrman House.

Handlin, Oscar
1951   *The Uprooted: The Epic Story
of the Great Migrations That
Made the American People.*
New York: Grossett & Dunlap.

1957   *Race and Nationality in American Life.* Boston: Little,
Brown

Hansen, Kristen A., and Bachu, Amarv
1995   The Foreign-Born Population:
1994. *Current Population
Reports* Ser. P-20, no. 486.
Washington, DC: U.S. Gov-
ernment Printing Office.

Hansen, Marcus Lee
1937   Who Shall Inherit America?
Speech delivered at the
National Conference of Social
Work, Indianapolis.

1952   The Third Generation in
America. *Commentary* 14
(November), pp. 493–500.

1987   *The Problem of the Third
Generation Immigrant with
Introductions by Peter Kvisto
and Oscar Handlin.* Rock
Island, IL: Swenson Swedish
Immigration Research Center.

Harlan, Louis R.
1972   *Booker T. Washington: The
Making of a Black Leader.* New
York: Oxford University Press.

Harris, David
1992   An Analysis of the 1990 Census
Count of American Indians.
Paper presented at the annual
meeting of the American Sociological Association, Pittsburgh.

Harris, David A.
1987   Japan and the Jews. *Morning
Freiheit* (November 8), pp. 1, 3.

Harris, Marvin
1964   *Patterns of Race in the Americas.* New York: Norton.

Hartmann, Heidi
1981   The Family as the Locus of
Gender, Class, and Political
Struggle: The Example of
Housework. *Signs* 6 (Spring),
pp. 366–394.

Harvard Law Review
1993   Racial Violence Against Asian
Americans. 106 (June), pp.
1926–1943.

Hatchett, Shirley J.; Cochran, Donna L.;
and Jackson, James S.
1991   Family Life. In James S. Jackson, ed., *Life in Black America*, pp. 46–83. Newbury Park,
CA: Sage.

Hawaii
1994   *Vital Statistics Supplement
1991–1992.* Honolulu: Department of Health, State of Hawaii.

Hawkins, Hugh
1962   *Booker T. Washington and His
Critics: The Problem of Negro
Leadership.* Boston: Heath.

Hawthorne, Peter
1994   South Africa: Quiet Revolution. *Time* 144 (December
19), pp. 52–53.

Hays, Kristen L.
1994   Topeka Comes Full Circle.
Modern Maturity
(April–May), p. 34.

Hechinger, Fred M.
1987   Bilingual Programs. *New York
Times* (April 7), p. C10.

Heer, David M., and Grossbard-
Shectman, Amgra
1981   The Impact of the Female Mar-
        riage Squeeze and the Contra-
        ceptive Revolution on Sex Roles
        and the Women's Liberation
        Movement in the United States,
        1960 to 1975. *Journal of Mar-
        riage and the Family* 43 (Feb-
        ruary), pp. 49–76.

Heilman, Samuel C.
1982   The Sociology of American
        Jewry: The Last Ten Years. In
        Ralph H. Turner, ed., *Annual
        Review of Sociology, 1982,* pp.
        135–160. Palo Alto, CA:
        Annual Reviews.

Henry, William A., III
1994   Pride and Prejudice. *Time* 143
        (February 28), pp. 21–27.

Hentoff, Nicholas
1984   Dennis Banks and the Road
        Block to Indian Ground. *Vil-
        lage Voice* 29 (October), pp.
        19–23.

Herberg, Will
1983   *Protestant-Catholic-Jew: An
        Essay in American Religious
        Sociology,* rev. ed. Chicago:
        University of Chicago Press.

Hernandez, Luis F.
1969   *A Forgotten American: A
        Resource Unit for Teachers on
        the Mexican American.* New
        York: Anti-Defamation
        League of B'nai B'rith.

Herrmann, Andrew
1994   Survey Shows Increase in His-
        panic Catholics. *Chicago Sun-
        Times* (March 18), p. 4.

Herrnstein, Richard J., and Murray,
Charles
1994   *The Bell Curve: Intelligence
        and Class Structure in Ameri-
        can Life.* New York: Free
        Press.

Herskovits, Melville J.
1930   *The Anthropometry of the
        American Negro.* New York:
        Columbia University Press.

1941   *The Myth of the Negro Past.*
        New York: Harper.

1943   The Negro in Bahia, Brazil: A
        Problem in Method. *American
        Sociological Review* 8
        (August), p. 394–402.

Hevrdejs, Judy, and Conklin, Mike
1995   Bradley May Wish Top of the
        Mornin' to Sinn Fein Leader.
        Chicago Tribune (May 16),
        p. 22.

Heyck, Denis Lynn Daly
1994   *Barrios and Borderlands: Cul-
        tures of Latinos and Latinas in
        the United States.* New York:
        Routledge.

Higham, John
1966   American Anti-Semitism His-
        torically Reconsidered. In
        Charles Herbert Stember, ed.,
        Jews in the Mind of America,
        pp. 237–258. New York: Basic
        Books.

Hilkevitch, Jon
1995   Evanston High Admits Minor-
        ity Gap. *Chicago Tribune*
        (June 6), p. 5.

Hill, Herbert
1967   The Racial Practices of Orga-
        nized Labor—The Age of
        Gompers and After. In Arthur
        M. Ross and Herbert Hill,
        eds., *Employment, Race, and
        Poverty,* pp. 365–402. New
        York: Harcourt, Brace &
        World.

Hill, Robert B.
1972   *The Strengths of Black Fami-
        lies.* New York: Emerson
        Hall.

1987   The Future of Black Fami-
        lies. *Colloqui* (Spring), pp.
        22–28.

Himmelfarb, Harold S.
1982   Research on American Jewish
        Identity and Identification:
        Progress, Pitfalls, and
        Prospects. In Marshall Sklare,
        ed., *Understanding American*

Jewry, pp. 56–95. New Brunswick, NJ: Transaction Books.

Hing, Bill Ong
1993   *Making and Remaking Asian America Through Immigration Policy, 1859–1900.* Stanford, CA: Stanford University Press.

1994   Support the Chinese Boat People. *Asianweek* 14 (June 3), pp. 1, 19.

Hirschman, Charles
1983   America's Melting Pot Reconsidered. In Ralph H. Turner, ed., *Annual Review of Sociology,* pp. 397–423. Palo Alto, CA: Annual Reviews.

Hirschman, Charles, and Wong, Morrison G.
1986   The Extraordinary Educational Attainment of Asian Americans: A Search for Historical Evidence and Explanations. *Social Forces* 65 (September), pp. 1–27.

Hirsley, Michael
1991   Religious Display Needs Firm Court. *Chicago Tribune* (December 20), sect. 2, p. 10.

Hochschild, Arlie, with Machung, Anne
1989   *The Second Shift.* New York: Viking.

1990   The Second Shift: Employed Women Are Putting in Another Day of Work at Home. *Utne Reader* 38 (March–April), pp. 66–73.

Hochschild, Jennifer L.
1993   Middle-Class Blacks and the Ambiguities of Success. In Paul M. Sniderman, Philip E. Tetlock, and Edward A. Carmines, eds., *Prejudice, Politics, and the American Dilemma,* pp. 148–172. Stanford, CA: Stanford University Press.

Hofstadter, Richard
1992   *Social Darwinism in America Thought.* New York: George Braziller.

Holford, David M.
1975   The Subversion of the Indian Land Allotment System, 1887–1934. *Indian Historian* 8 (Spring), pp. 11–21.

Holmberg, David
1974   Pekin Isn't Ready to Give up "Chinks." *Chicago Tribune* (July 28), p. 24.

hooks, bell
1994   Black Students Who Reject Feminism. *Chronicle of Higher Education* 60 (July 13), p. A44.

Hormann, Bernhard L.
1972   Hawaii's Mixing People. In Noel P. Gist and Anthony Gary Dworkin, eds., *The Blending of Races,* pp. 213–236. New York: Wiley.

1982   The Mixing Process. *Social Process in Hawaii,* 29, pp. 116–129.

Horton, John
1966   Order and Conflict Theories of Social Problems as Competing Ideologies. *American Journal of Sociology* 71 (May), pp. 701–713.

Hosokawa, Bill
1969   *Nisei: The Quiet Americans.* New York: Morrow.

1982a *JACL in Quest of Justice.* New York: Morrow.

1982b Accentuating the American in Japanese American. *Civil Rights Perspectives* 14 (Fall), pp. 40–44.

Howe, Marvin
1989   Asians in New York Region: Poverty amid High Ambition. *New York Times* (April 17), p. B4.

Hsu, Francis L. K.
1971   *The Challenge of the American Dream: The Chinese in the United States.* Belmont, CA: Wadsworth.

Huang, Lucy Jen
1975   The "Banana" Syndrome: Alienation of Chinese Ameri-

cans and the Yellow Power Movement. Paper presented at the annual meeting of the American Sociological Association, San Francisco.

1976   The Chinese American Family. In Charles H. Mindel and Robert W. Habenstein, eds., *Ethnic Families in America; Patterns and Variations,* pp. 124–147. New York: Elsevier.

Hubbard, Amy S.
1993   U.S. Jewish Community Responses to the Changing Strategy of the Palestinian Nationalist Movement: A Pilot Study. Paper presented at the annual meeting of the Eastern Sociological Society, Boston.

Hudgins, John L.
1992   The Strengths of Black Families Revisited. *The Urban League Review* 15 (Winter), pp. 9–20.

Hufker, Brian, and Cavender, Gray
1990   From Freedom Flotilla to America's Burden: The Social Construction of the Mariel Immigrants. *Sociological Quarterly* 31 (No. 2), pp. 321–335.

Hughes, Michael, and Demo, David H.
1989   Self-Perceptions of Black Americans: Self-Esteem and Personal Efficacy. *American Journal of Sociology* 95 (July), pp. 132–159.

Huizinga, David, and Elliott, Delbert S.
1987   Juvenile Offenders: Prevalence, Offender Incidence, and Arrest Rates by Race. *Crime and Delinquency* 33 (April), pp. 206–223.

Hunt, Chester L., and Walker, Lewis
1979   *Ethnic Dynamics: Patterns of Intergroup Relations and Various Societies,* 2nd ed. Holmes Beach, FL: Learning Publications.

Huntington, Samuel P.
1993   The Clash of Civilizations? *Foreign Affairs* (Summer), pp. 22–49.

Hurh, Won Moo
1977a   *Assimilation of the Korean Minority in the United States.* Philip Jaisohn Memorial Papers, No. 1. Elkins Park, PA: Philip Jaisohn Memorial Foundation.

1977b   *Comparative Study of Korean Immigrants in the United States: A Typological Approach.* San Francisco: R & E Research Associates.

1990   The "1.5 Generation": A Paragon of Korean American Pluralism. *Korean Culture* 4 (Spring), pp. 21–31.

1994   Majority Americans' Perception of Koreans in the United States: Implications of Ethnic Images and Stereotypes. In H. Kwon, ed., *Korean Americans: Conflict and Harmony,* pp. 3–21. Chicago: Center for Korean Studies.

Hurh, Won Moo, and Kim, Kwang Chung
1982   Race Relations Paradigms and Korean American Research: A Sociology of Knowledge Perspective. In E. Yu, E. Phillips, and E. Yang, eds., *Koreans in Los Angeles,* pp. 219–255. Los Angeles: Center for Korean American and Korean Studies, California State University.

1984   *Korean Immigrants in America: A Structural Analysis of Ethnic Confinement and Adhesive Adaptation.* Cranbury, NJ: Farleigh Dickinson University Press.

1986   The Success Image of Asian Americans: Its Validity, Practical and Theoretical Implications. Paper presented at the annual meeting of the American Sociological Association, New York City.

1987   *Korean Immigrants in the Chicago Area: A Sociological*

Study of Migration and Mental Health. Interim Report to National Institute of Mental Health. Macomb IL: Western Illinois University.

1988 *Uprooting and Adjustment: A Sociological Study of Korean Immigrants' Mental Health.* Final Report submitted to National Institute of Mental Health. Macomb, IL: Western Illinois University.

1989 The "Success" Image of Asian Americans: Its Validity, and Its Practical and Theoretical Implications. *Ethnic and Racial Studies* 12 (October), pp. 512–538.

1990 Religious Participation of Korean Immigrants in the United States. *Journal for the Scientific Study of Religion* 29 (No. 1), pp. 19–34.

Hwang, David Henry
1985 Are Movies Ready for Real Orientals? *New York Times* (August 11), pp. H1, H21.

1994 Forward: Facing the Mirror. In Karin Aguillar-San Juan, ed., *The State of Asian America*, pp. ix–xii. Boston: South End Press.

Hyman, Herbert H., and Sheatsley, Paul B.
1964 Attitudes Toward Desegregation. *Scientific American* (July), pp. 16–23.

Ichioka, Yuji
1988 *The Issei.* New York: Free Press.

Ichiyama, Michael A.
1991 Anti-Asian Sentiment and Activities in the United States: Contributing Factors. Paper presented at the annual meeting of the American Psychological Association, San Francisco.

Ifill, Gwen
1994 Clinton Signs Bill Banning Blockades and Violent Acts at Abortion Clinics. *New York Times* (May 27), p. A18.

Ingrassia, Michele
1994 America's New Wave of Runaways. *Newsweek* 123 (April 4), pp. 64–65.

Inoue, Miyako
1989 Japanese Americans in St. Louis: From Internees to Professionals. *City and Society* 3 (December), pp. 142–152.

Irelan, Lola M; Moles, Oliver C., and O'Shea, Robert M.
1969 Ethnicity, Poverty and Selected Attitudes: A Test of the "Culture of Poverty" Hypothesis. *Social Forces* 47 (June), pp. 405–413.

Irwin, Victoria
1987 Puerto Ricans Register Voters to Gain Voice on Capitol Hill. *Christian Science Monitor* (June 10), p. 7.

Isikoff, Michael
1988 Bitterness on the "Taco Circuit." *Washington Post National Weekly Edition* 6 (November 27), p. 11.

Isonio, Stevan A., and Garza, T.
1987 Protestant Work Ethic Endorsement Among Anglo Americans, Chicanos, and Mexicans: A Comparison of Factor Structures. *Hispanic Journal of Behavioral Sciences* 9 (December), pp. 414–425.

Iverson, Peter
1993 American Indian of the West. In Mary Kupiec Clayton, Elliot J. Gorn, and Peter W. Williams, eds., *Encyclopedia of American Social History*, pp. 667–680. New York: Scribners.

Jacobs, Jerry A.
1990 *Revolving Doors: Sex Segregation in Women's Careers.* Palo Alto, CA: Stanford University Press.

Jaher, Frederic Caple
1994 *A Scapegoat in the New Wilderness.* Cambridge: Harvard University Press.

Jaimes, M. Annette
1992   *The State of Native America.* Boston: South End Press.

Jaschik, Scott
1990   U.S. Accuses UCLA of Bias Against Asian Americans. *Chronicle of Higher Education* 37 (October), pp. A1, A26.

Jehl, Douglas
1994   Clinton and Indians Meet to Underline New Stature. *New York Times* (April 30), p. 9.

Jennings, James, and Rivera, Monte (eds.)
1984   *Puerto Rican Politics in Urban America.* Westport, CT: Greenwood Press.

Jennings, Jerry T.
1993   Voting and Registration in the Election of November 1992. *Current Population Reports,* Series P-20, No. 466. Washington, DC: U.S. Government Printing Office.

Johnson, George
1987   The Infamous "Protocols of Zion" Endures. *New York Times* (July 26), p. E6.

1995   Some Indians Back a Stereotype. *New York Times* (April 25), p. E6.

Johnson, Kevin
1992   German Ancestry is Strong Beneath Milwaukee Surface. *USA Today* (August 4), p. 9A.

Johnson, Kirk
1994   An Indian Tribe's Wealth Leads to the Expansion of Tribal Law. *New York Times* (May 22), pp. 1, 16.

Joint Center for Political Studies
1995   *National Roster of Black Elected Officials, 1995.* Washington, DC: Joint Center for Political Studies.

Jolidon, Laurence
1991   Battle Builds over Indians' Fishing Rights. *USA Today* (March 21), pp. 1A, 2A.

Jones, Del
1995   Denny's Strives to Eliminate Racist Elements. *USA Today* (November 2), pp. 1A, 2A.

Jones, James M.
1972   *Prejudice and Racism.* Reading, MS: Addison-Wesley.

Journal of Blacks in Higher Education
1994a   The Continuing Shortfall in Black Ph.D. Awards. 1 (Winter), p. 17.

1994b   The Progress of African Americans in Medical School Education. 1 (Spring), p. 38.

1994c   Are Nonresident Asian Students Displacing Black Ph.D.'s in Science and Engineering. 1 (No. 2), p. 15.

Juarez, Alberto
1972   The Emergence of El Partido de La Raza Unida: California's New Chicano Party. *Aztlan* 3 (Fall), pp. 177–204.

Kagan, Jerome
1971   The Magical Aura of the IQ. *Saturday Review of Literature* 4 (December 4), pp. 92–93.

Kagiwada, George, and Fujimoto, Isao
1973   Asian American Studies: Implications for Education. *Personnel and Guidance Journal* 51 (January), pp. 400–405.

Kahn, Katherine L., et al.
1994   Health Care for Black and Poor Hospitalized Medicare Patients. *Journal of the American Medical Association* 271 (April 20), pp. 1169–1174.

Kalish, Susan
1992   Interracial Baby Boomlet in Progress. *Population Today* 20 (December), pp. 1–2, 9.

1995   Multiracial Births Increase as U.S. Ponders Racial Definitions. *Population Today* 24 (April), pp. 1–2.

Kallen, Horace M.
   1915a Democracy Versus the Melting Pot. *The Nation* 100 (February 18), pp. 190–194.

   1915b Democracy Versus the Melting Pot. *The Nation* 100 (February 25), pp. 217–221.

   1924 *Culture and Democracy in the United States.* New York: Boni & Liveright.

Kalmijn, Matthijs
   1994 Trends in Black/White Intermarriage. *Social Forces* 72 (September), pp. 119–146.

Kamakahi, Jeffrey J.
   1994 "Native Hawaiians" in Native-L: A Study of a Racial/Ethnic Category Within Discussions of Indigenous Peoples. Paper presented at the annual meeting of the American Sociological Association, Los Angeles.

Kanamine, Linda
   1992 Amid Crushing Poverty, Glimmers of Hope. *USA Today* (November 30), p. 7A.

   1994 Tribal Leaders Now Feel They "Can Be Heard." *USA Today* (April 28), pp. 1A, 2A.

Kanamine, Linda, and Hoversten, Paul
   1995 N.M. Tribe Says No Niskes. *USA Today* (February 2), p. 3A.

Kane-Berman, John
   1995 One Year On. *Frontiers of Freedom* (Second Quarter), p. 16.

Kanellos, Nicholás
   1994 *The Hispanic Almanac: From Columbus to Corporate America.* Detroit: Visible Ink Press.

Kantrowitz, Barbara
   1991 Striking a Nerve. *Newsweek* 118 (October 21), pp. 34–40.

Kantrowitz, Nathan
   1973 *Ethnic and Racial Segregation in the New York Metropolis: Residential Patterns Among White Ethnic Groups, Blacks, and Puerto Ricans.* New York: Praeger.

Kaplan, Dave
   1993 Constitutional Doubt Is Thrown on Bizarre-Shaped Districts. *Congressional Quarterly Weekly Report* (July 3), pp. 1761–1762.

Kaser, Tom
   1977 Hawaii's Schools: An Ethnic Survey. *Integrated Education* 15 (May–June), pp. 31–36.

Kass, Drora, and Lipset, Seymour Martin
   1980 America's New Wave of Jewish Immigrants. *New York Times Magazine* (December 7), pp. 44–45, 100, 102, 110, 112, 114, 116–118.

   1982 Jewish Immigration to the United States from 1967 to the Present: Israelis and Others. In Marshall Skalre, ed., *Understanding American Jewry*, pp. 272–294. New Brunswick, NJ: Transaction Books.

Katz, David, and Braly, Kenneth W.
   1933 Racial Stereotypes of One Hundred College Students. *Journal of Abnormal Sociology and Psychology* 28 (October–December), pp. 280–290.

Keesing's
   1992 Canada: Rejection of Charlottetown Constitutional Reform Package. *Keesing's Record of World Events* (October), p. 39126.

Keller, Bill
   1993 Is That Really South Africa? *New York Times* (October 10), sect. H., pp. 13, 24.

Kelly, Dennis
   1991 A Call for Better Native Education. *USA Today* (December 3), p. D4.

Kelly, Gail P.
   1986 Coping with America: Refugees from Vietnam, Cambodia, and Laos in the

1970s and 1980s. *Annals* 487 (September), pp. 138–149.

Kennedy, John F.
1964 *A Nation of Immigrants.* New York: Harper & Row.

Kephart, William M., and Zellner, William
1994 *Extraordinary Groups: The Sociology of Unconventional Life-Styles,* 5th ed. New York: St. Martin's Press.

Kessler, Evelyn S.
1976 *Women: An Anthropological View.* New York: Holt, Rinehart & Winston.

Kessner, Thomas, and Caroli, Betty Boyd
1981 *Today's Immigrants, Their Stories.* New York: Oxford University Press.

Killian, Lewis M.
1975 *The Impossible Revolution, Phase 2: Black Power and the American Dream.* New York: Random House.

Kim, Elaine H.
1994 Between Black and White: An Interview with Bong Hwan Kim. In Karin Aguilar-San Juan, ed., *The State of Asian America,* pp. 71–100. Boston: South End Press.

Kim, Hyung-chan
1980 Koreans. In Stephen Thernstrom, ed., *Harvard Encyclopedia of American Ethnic Groups,* pp. 601–606. Cambridge: Belknap Press of Harvard University Press.

Kim, Illsoo
1988 A New Theoretical Perspective on Asian Enterprises. *Amerasia* 14 (Spring), pp. xi–xiii.

Kim, Kwang Chung, and Hurh, Won Moo
1983 Korean Americans and the Success Image: A Critique. *Amerasia* 10 (No. 2), pp. 3–21.

1984 The Wives of Korean Small Businessmen in the U.S: Business Involvement and Family Roles. Paper presented at the annual meeting of the American Sociological Association, San Antonio.

1985a Immigration Experiences of Korean Wives in the U.S: The Burden of Double Roles. Paper presented at the annual meeting of the National Council on Family Relations, Dallas.

1985b The Wives of Korean Small Businessmen in the U.S.: Business Involvement and Family Roles. In Inn Sook Lee, ed., *Korean-American Women: Toward Self-Realization,* pp. 1–41. Mansfield, OH: Association of Korean Christian Scholars in North America.

Kimura, Yukiko
1988 *Issei: Japanese Immigrants in Hawaii.* Honolulu: University of Hawaii Press.

King, Martin Luther, Jr.
1958 *Stride Toward Freedom: The Montgomery Story.* New York: Harper.

1963 *Why We Can't Wait.* New York: Mentor.

1967 *Where Do We Go from Here: Chaos or Community?* New York: Harper & Row.

1971 I Have a Dream. In August Meier, Elliott Rudwick, and Francis L. Broderick, eds., *Black Protest Thought in the Twentieth Century,* pp. 346–351. Indianapolis: Bobbs-Merrill.

King, Patricia
1989 When Desegregation Backfires. *Newsweek* (July 31), p. 56.

Kinloch, Graham C.
1974 *The Dynamics of Race Relations: A Sociological Analysis.* New York: McGraw-Hill.

Kitagawa, Evelyn
  1972   Socioeconomic Differences in
          the United States and Some
          Implications for Population
          Policy. In Charles F. Westoff
          and Robert Parke, Jr., eds.,
          *Demographic and Social
          Aspects of Population Growth,*
          pp. 87–110. Washington, DC:
          U.S. Government Printing
          Office.

Kitano, Harry H. L.
  1971   An Interview. In Amy Tachiki,
          Eddie Wong, Franklin Odo,
          and Buck Wong, eds., *Roots:
          An Asian American Reader,*
          pp. 83–88. Los Angeles: Asian
          American Studies Center,
          UCLA.

  1976   *Japanese Americans: The Evo-
          lution of a Subculture,* 2nd ed.
          Englewood Cliffs, NJ: Pren-
          tice-Hall.

  1980   Japanese. In Stephen Thern-
          strom, ed., *Harvard Encyclo-
          pedia of American Ethnic
          Groups.* Cambridge: Belknap
          Press of Harvard University
          Press.

  1991   *Race Relations,* 4th ed. Engle-
          wood Cliffs, NJ: Prentice-
          Hall.

Kitano, Harry H. L., and Daniels, Roger
  1988   *Asian Americans: Emerging
          Minorities.* Englewood Cliffs,
          NJ: Prentice-Hall.

Kitano, Harry H. L., and Matsushima,
Noreen
  1981   Counseling Asian Americans.
          In P. Pederson, J. Draguns,
          W. Lonenr, and J. Trimble,
          eds., *Counseling Across Cul-
          tures,* rev. ed., pp. 163–180.
          Honolulu: University of
          Hawaii Press.

Kitsuse, John I., and Broom, Leonard
  1956   *The Managed Casualty: The
          Japanese American Family in
          World War II.* Berkeley: Uni-
          versity of California Press.

Klausner, Samuel Z.
  1988   Anti-Semitism in the Execu-
          tive Suite: Yesterday, Today,
          and Tomorrow. *Moment* 13
          (September), pp. 32–39, 55.

Klein, Stephen P.; Turner, Susan; and Petersilia, Joan
  1988   *Racial Equality in Sentencing.*
          Santa Monica, CA: Rand.

Kleinhuizen, Jeff
  1991a   Traditions Guard Hispanic
          Babies' Health. *USA Today*
          (February 4), p. 4D.

  1991b   Tribal Colleges Combine Aca-
          demics and Heritage. *USA
          Today* (May 7), p. 4D.

Kleinman, Dena
  1977   The Potential for Urban Ter-
          ror Is Always There. *New York
          Times* (March 13), p. E3.

Knight, Franklin W.
  1974   *The African Dimension in
          Latin American Societies.*
          New York: Macmillan.

Knowles, Louis L., and Prewitt, Kenneth
  1969   *Institutional Racism in Ameri-
          ca.* Englewood Cliffs, NJ:
          Prentice-Hall.

Knudson, Thomas J.
  1987   Zoning the Reservations for
          Enterprise. *New York Times*
          (January 25), p. E4.

Kornblum, William
  1991   Who Is the Underclass? *Dis-
          sent* 38 (Spring), pp. 202–211.

Kosmin, Barry A.
  1991   *The National Survey of Reli-
          gious Identification.* New York:
          City University of New York.

Kosmin, Barry, A., and Lachman,
Semour P.
  1993   *One Nation Under God.* New
          York: Harmony Books.

Kosmin, Barry A., and Scheckner, Jeffrey
  1994   Jewish Population in the Unit-
          ed States, 1993. In David
          Sanger, ed., *American Jewish*

Year Book, 1994, pp. 206–226. New York: American Jewish Committee.

Kosmin, Barry A., et al.
1991 *Highlights of the CJF 1990 National Jewish Population Survey.* New York: Council of Jewish Federations.

Kozol, Jonathon
1994 Romance of the Ghetto School. *The Nation* 258 (May 23), pp. 703–706.

Krausz, Ernest
1973 Israel's New Citizens. In *1973 Britannica Book of the Year,* pp. 385–387. Chicago: Encyclopedia Britannica.

Kruszewski, Z. Anthony; Hough, Richard L.; and Ornstein-Galicia, Jacob
1982 *Politics and Society in the Southwest: Ethnicity and Chicano Pluralism.* Boulder, CO: Westview Press.

Kuo, Wen H., and Lin, Nan
1977 Assimilation of Chinese-Americans in Washington, DC. *Social Forces* 18 (Summer), pp. 340–351.

Kwong, Peter
1994 The Wages of Fear. *Village Voice* 39 (April 26), pp. 25–29.

Labelle, Huguette
1989 Multiculturalism and Government. In James S. Frideres, ed., *Multiculturalism and Intergroup Relations,* pp. 1–7. New York: Greenwood Press.

Lacayo, Richard
1988 A Surging New Spirit. *Time* 132 (July 11), pp. 46–49.
1989 Between Two Worlds. *Time* 133 (March 13), pp. 58–68.

Lacy, Dan
1972 *The White Use of Blacks in America.* New York: McGraw-Hill.

Ladner, Joyce
1967 What "Black Power" Means to Negroes in Mississippi. *Transaction* 5 (November), pp. 6–15.

Lai, H. M.
1980 Chinese. In Stephen Thernstrom, ed., *Harvard Encyclopedia of American Ethnic Groups,* pp. 222–234. Cambridge: Belknap Press of Harvard University Press.

Landry, Bart
1987 *The New Black Middle Class.* Berkeley: University of California Press.

Langdon, Steve J.
1982 Alaskan Native Land Claims and Limited Entry: The Dawes Act Revisited. Paper presented at the annual meeting of the American Anthropology Association, Washington, DC.

Langer, Elinor
1976 Why Big Business Is Trying to Defeat the ERA. *Ms.* 4 (May), p. 64.

Langway, Lynn
1981 Women and the Executive Suite. *Time* (September 14), pp. 65–67.

LaPiere, Richard T.
1934 Attitudes vs. Actions. *Social Forces* 13 (October), pp. 230–237.
1969 Comment on Irwin Deutscher's Looking Backward. *American Sociologist* 4 (February), pp. 41–42.

Lauerman, Connie
1993 Tribal Wave. *Chicago Tribune* (April 5), sect. 2, pp. 1–2.

Laumann, Edward O.
1969 The Social Structure of Religious and Ethnoreligious Groups in a Metropolitan Community. *American Sociological Review* 34 (April), pp. 182–197.

Lauter, David
1995   Affirmative Action Poised to
        Become Political Divide, *Los
        Angeles Times,* (February 21),
        pp. A1, A15.

Lavender, Abraham D., ed.
1977   *A Coat of Many Colors: Jew-
        ish Subcommunities in the
        United States.* Westport, CT:
        Greenwood Press.

Lawson, Paul E., and Morris, C. Patrick
1991   The Native American Church
        and the New Court: The
        "Smith" Case and Indian Reli-
        gious Freedoms. *American
        Indian Culture and Research
        Journal* 15 (No. 1), pp. 79–91.

Laxson, Joan D.
1991   "We" See "Them" Tourism
        and Native Americans. *Annals
        of Tourism Research* 18 (No.
        3), pp. 365–391.

Lazerwitz, Bernard
1993   Correspondence to Richard T.
        Schaefer. Unpublished data
        from Jewish Survey.

Leatherman, Courtney
1994   Number of Blacks Earning
        Ph.D.'s Rose 15% in Year.
        *Chronicle of Higher Educa-
        tion* 61 (October 12), p. A16.

Lee, Calvin
1965   *Chinatown, U.S.A.* Garden
        City, NY: Doubleday.

Lee, Don
1992   A Sense of Identity. *Kansas
        City Star* (April 4), pp. E1,
        E7.

1995   Courting Workers They Once
        Shunned. *Los Angeles Times*
        (May 6), pp. A1, A22–A23.

Lee, Elisa
1993   Silicon Valley Study Finds
        Asian Americans Hitting the
        Glass Ceiling. *Asianweek*
        (October 8), p. 21.

1994   Wisconsin Asian Americans
        Battle School Segregation.
        Asianweek (January 14), pp. 1,
        20.

Lee, Felicia R.
1991   "Model Minority" Label Taxes
        Asian Youths. *New York Times*
        (March 30), pp. B1, B4.

Lee, Rose Hum
1960   *The Chinese in the United
        States of America.* Hong Kong:
        Hong Kong University Press.

Leebaw, Milton, and Heyman, Harriet
1976   Puerto Rico and Economics.
        New York Times (October 17),
        p. E5.

Leehotz, Robert
1995   Is Concept of Race a Relic?
        Los Angeles Times (April 15),
        pp. A1, A14.

Lem, Kim
1976   Asian American Employment.
        Civil Rights Digest 9 (Fall),
        pp. 12–21.

Lemann, Nicholas
1986a   The Origins of the Underclass.
        The Atlantic Monthly 258
        (June), pp. 31–43, 47–55.

1986b   The Origins of the Underclass.
        The Atlantic Monthly 258
        (July), pp. 54–68.

1991   The Other Underclass. *The
        Atlantic Monthly* 286
        (December), pp. 96–102, 104,
        107–108, 110.

1994   The Myth of Community
        Development. *New York
        Times Magazine* (January 9),
        pp. 26–31, 50, 54, 60.

LeMoyne, James
1990   Most Who Left Mariel Sailed
        to New Life, a Few to Limbo.
        New York Times (April 15),
        pp. 1, 12.

Lennon, Mary Clare, and Rosenfield,
Sarah
1994   Relative Fairness and the
        Division of Housework: The
        Importance of Options.
        *American Journal of Sociolo-
        gy* 100 (September), pp.
        506–531.

Lerner, Michael
  1969   Respectable Bigotry. *Ameri-can Scholar* 38 (August), pp. 606–617.

  1993   Jews Are Not White. *Village Voice* 38 (May 18), pp. 33–34.

Lesch, Ann M.
  1983   Palestine: Land and People. In Naseer H. Aruri, ed., *Occupation: Israel Over Palestine*, pp. 29–54. Belmont, MA: Association of Arab-American University Graduates.

Leslie, Connie
  1991   Classrooms of Babel. *Newsweek* 117 (February 11), pp. 56–57.

  1995   The Loving Generation. *Newsweek* (February 13), p. 72.

Levin, Jack, and Levin, William C.
  1982   *The Functions of Prejudice*, 2d ed. New York: Harper & Row.

Levine, Gene N., and Montero, Darrel M.
  1973   Socioeconomic Mobility Among Three Generations of Japanese Americans. *Journal of Social Issues* 29 (No. 2), pp. 33–48.

Levine, Irving M., and Herman, Judith
  1972   The Life of White Ethnics. *Dissent* 19 (Winter), pp. 286–294.

Levine, Naomi, and Hochbaum, Martin, eds.
  1974   *Poor Jews: An American Awakening.* New Brunswick, NJ: Transaction Books.

Levy, Jacques E.
  1975   *César Chávez: Autobiography of La Causa.* New York: Norton.

Lewinson, Paul
  1965   *Race, Class, and Party: A History of Negro Suffrage and White Politics in the South.* New York: Universal Library.

Lewis, Oscar
  1959   *Five Families: Mexican Case Studies in the Culture of Poverty.* New York: Basic Books.

  1965   *La Vida: A Puerto Rican Family in the Culture of Poverty—San Juan and New York.* New York: Random House.

  1966   The Culture of Poverty. *Scientific American* (October), pp. 19–25.

Li, Peter S.
  1992   Race and Gender as Bases of Class Fractions and Their Effects on Earnings. *Canadian Review of Sociology and Anthropology* 29 (No. 4), pp. 488–510.

Li, Wen Lang
  1976   Chinese Americans: Exclusion from the Melting Pot. In Anthony and Rosalind Dworkin, eds., *Minority Report,* pp. 297–324. New York: Praeger.

Lichtenstein, Eugene, and Denenberg, R. V.
  1975   The Army's Ethnic Policy. *New York Times* (July 20), p. E2.

Lichter, S. Robert, and Lichter, Linda S.
  1988   *Television's Impact in Ethnic and Racial Images.* New York: American Jewish Committee.

Liebman, Charles S.
  1973   *The Ambivalent American Jew.* Philadelphia: Jewish Publication Society of America.

Light, Ivan H.
  1973   *Ethnic Enterprise in America: Business and Welfare Among Chinese, Japanese, and Blacks.* Berkeley: University of California Press.

  1974   From Vice District to Tourist Attraction: The Moral Career of American Chinatowns, 1880–1940. *Pacific Historical Review* 43 (August), pp. 367–394.

Light, Ivan H., and Bonacich, Edna
1988   *Immigrant Entrepreneurs: Koreans in Los Angeles 1965–1982.* Berkeley: University of California Press.

Light, Ivan H.; Sabagh, Georges; Bozorgmehr, Mendi; and Der-Martirosian, Claudia
1994   Beyond the Ethnic Enclave Economy. *Social Problems* 41 (February), pp. 65–80.

Light, Ivan H., and Wong, Charles Choy
1975   Protest or Work: Dilemmas of the Tourist Industry in American Chinatowns. *American Journal of Sociology* 80 (May), pp. 1342–1368.

Lin, Clarice, and Arguelles, Dennis
1995   Focus On: The Filipino-American Community. *LEAP Connections* 8 (February), pp. 4, 7.

Lincoln, C. Eric
1994   *The Black Muslims in America,* 3d ed. Grand Rapids, MI: William B. Eerdmans.

Lind, Andrew W.
1946   *Hawaii's Japanese: An Experiment in Democracy.* Princeton: Princeton University Press.

1969   *Hawaii: The Last of the Magic Isles.* London: Oxford University Press.

Lindsey, Robert
1978   Latinos Have Numbers but Not Yet the Voters. *New York Times* (June 4), p. E5.

Linthicum, Leslie
1993   Navajo School Working to Revive Language. *News From Indian Country* (Late June), p. 5.

Lippmann, Walter
1922   *Public Opinion.* New York: Macmillan.

Llanes, José
1982   *Cuban Americans: Masters of Survival.* Cambridge, MA: Abt Books.

Lloyd, Sterling, and Miller, Russell L.
1989   Black Student Enrollment in U.S. Medical Schools. *Journal of the American Medical Association* 261 (January 13), pp. 272–274.

Logan, Rayford W.
1954   *The Negro in American Life and Thought: The Nadir, 1877–1901.* New York: Dial Press.

Lomax, Louis E.
1971   *The Negro Revolt,* rev. ed. New York: Harper & Row.

Lopez, David, and Espiritu, Yen
1990   Panethnicity in the United States: A Theoretical Framework. *Ethnic and Racial Studies* 13 (April), pp. 198–224.

López, Fred A., III
1992   Reflections on the Chicano Movement. *Latin American Perspectives* 19 (Fall), pp. 79–102.

Lopez, Julie Amparano
1992   Study Says Women Face Glass Walls as Well as Ceilings. *Wall Street Journal* (March 3), pp. B1, B2.

López-Rivera, Oscar, with Headley, Bernard
1989   Who Is the Terrorist? The Making of a Puerto Rican Freedom Fighter. *Social Justice* 16 (Winter), pp. 162–174.

Louw-Potgieter, J.
1988   The Authoritarian Personality: An Inadequate Explanation for Intergroup Conflict in South Africa. *Journal of Social Psychology* 128 (February), pp. 75–88.

Luce, Clare Booth
1975   Refugees and Guilt. *New York Times* (May 11), p. E19.

Luebben, Ralph A.
1964   Prejudice and Discrimination Against Navahos in a Mining Community, *The Kiva* 30 (October), pp. 1–17.

Luker, Kristin
  1984 *Abortion and the Politics of Motherhood.* Berkeley: University of California Press.

Lum, Joann, and Kwong, Peter
  1989 Surviving in America: The Trials of a Chinese Immigrant Woman. *Village Voice* 34 (October 31), pp. 39–41.

Lupsha, Peter A.
  1981 Individual Choice, Material Culture, and Organized Crime. *Criminology* 19 (May), pp. 3–24.

Lyman, Stanford M.
  1974 *Chinese Americans.* New York: Random House.
  1986 *Chinatown and Little Tokyo.* Milwood, NY: Associated Faculty Press.

Macias, Reynaldo Flores
  1973 Developing a Bilingual Culturally-Relevant Educational Program for Chicanos. *Aztlan* 4 (Spring), pp. 61–77.

Mackey, Wade C.
  1987 A Cross-Cultural Perspective on Perceptions of Paternalistic Deficiencies in the United States: The Myth of the Derelict Daddy. *Sex Roles,* 12 (March), pp. 509–534.

MacKinnon, Catherine A.
  1979 *Sexual Harassment of Working Women: A Case of Sex Discrimination.* New Haven: Yale University Press.

MacMurray, Val Dan, and Cunningham, Perry H.
  1973 Mormons and Gentiles: A Study of Conflict and Persistence. In Donald E. Gelfand and Russell D. Lee, eds., *Ethnic Conflicts and Power: A Cross-Nation Perspective,* pp. 205–218. New York: Wiley.

Maguire, Brendan, and Wozniak, John
  1987 Racial and Ethnic Stereotypes in Professional Wrestling. *Social Science Journal* 24 (No. 3), pp. 261–273.

Mahar, Maggie
  1993 The Truth About Women's Pay. *Working Women* (April), pp. 52–55, 100, 102.

Mahar, Adrian
  1995 Black Tradesmen Face a Daily Wall of Suspicion. *Los Angeles Times* (March 20), pp. A1, A20.

Malcolm X
  1964 *The Autobiography of Malcolm X.* New York: Grove Press.

Mallery, Paul
  1994 Riots or Revolts? UCLA Students' Attributions During the LA Unrest. Paper presented at the annual meeting of the American Psychological Association, Los Angeles.

Mandel, Michael J., and Farrell, Christopher
  1992 The Immigrants. *Business Week* (July 13), pp. 114–120.

Manigan, Katherine S.
  1991 Mexican Students, Including Commuters, Succeed at Texas Universities. *Chronicle of Higher Education* 38 (February 26), pp. A36–A37.

Mann, James
  1983 One-Parent Family: The Troubles—And the Joys. *U.S. News and World Report* 95 (November 28), pp. 57–58, 62.

Manzo, Kathleen Kennedy
  1994 Flaws in Fellowships. *Black Issues in Higher Education* 11 (July 14), pp. 46–47, 52.

Marger, Martin N.
  1985 *Race and Ethnic Relations: American and Global Perspectives.* Belmont, CA: Wadsworth.

Margolis, Richard J.
 1972 Lost Chance for Desegregation. *Dissent* 19 (Spring), pp.
   249–256.

Marquez, Benjamin
 1987 The Politics of Race and
   Class: The League of United
   Latin American Citizens in
   the Post–World II Period.
   Social Science Quarterly 68
   (March), pp. 84–101.

Martin, M. Kay, and Voorhies, Barbara
 1975 *Female of the Species.* New
   York: Columbia University
   Press.

Martin, Philip, and Midgley, Elizabeth
 1994 Immigration to the United
   States: Journey to an Uncertain Destination. *Population
   Bulletin* 49 (September).

Martinez, Angel R.
 1988 The Effects of Acculturation
   and Racial Identity on Self-
   Esteem and Psychological
   Well-Being Among Young
   Puerto Ricans. Unpub. Ph.D.
   City University of New York.

Martínez, Estella A.
 1988 Child Behavior in Mexican
   American/Chicano Families:
   Maternal Teaching and Child-
   Rearing Practices. *Family
   Relations* 37 (July), pp.
   275–280.

Martinez, Rubén, and Dukes, Richard L.
 1991 Ethnic and Gender Differences in Self-Esteem. *Youth
   and Society* 32 (March), pp.
   318–338.

Martinez, Thomas M.
 1973 Advertising and Racism: The
   Case of the Mexican-Ameri-
   can. In I. O. Romano, ed.,
   *Voices: Readings from El
   Grito*, rev. ed., pp. 521–531.
   Berkeley, CA: Quinto Sol
   Publications.

Martinez, Vilma S.
 1976 Illegal Immigration and the
   Labor Force. *American Behavioral Scientist* 19 (January–
   February), pp. 335–350.

Marty, Martin E.
 1976 *A Nation of Behaviors.* Chicago: University of Chicago
   Press.

 1985 Transpositions: American
   Religion in the 1980s. *Annals*
   480 (July), pp. 11–23.

Marx, Karl
 1967 *Capital: Vol. 1. A Critical
   Analysis of Capitalist Production.* New York: International
   Publishers.

Marx, Karl, and Engels, Frederick
 1955 *Selected Works in Two Vol-
   umes.* Moscow: Foreign Languages Publishing House.

Masayesva, Vernon
 1994 The Problem of American
   Indian Religious Freedom: A
   Hopi Perspective. *American
   Indian Religions: An Interdisciplinary Journal* 1 (Winter),
   pp. 93–96.

Mason, Philip
 1970a *Patterns of Dominance.* London: Oxford University Press.

 1970b *Race Relations.* London:
   Oxford University Press.

Massey, Douglas S.
 1986 The Social Organization of
   Mexican Migration to the
   United States. *Annals* 487
   (September), pp. 102–113.

Massey, Douglas S.; Alarcán, Rafael; Du-
rand, Jorge; and González, Humberto.
 1987 *Return to Atzlan.* Berkeley:
   University of California Press.

Massey, Douglas S., and Bitterman,
Brooks
 1985 Explaining the Paradox of
   Puerto Rican Segregation.
   Social Forces 64 (December),
   pp. 306–331.

Massey, Douglas S., and Denton, Nancy A.
1993   *American Apartheid: Segregation and the Making of the Underclass.* Cambridge: Harvard University Press.

Massey, Douglas S., and Gross, Andrew B.
1993   Black Migration, Segregation, and the Spatial Concentration of Poverty. Unpublished paper, Harris Graduate School of Public Policy Studies, University of Chicago.

Mathews, Jay
1992   Undercover Bias Busters. *Newsweek* 120 (November 23), p. 88.

Mathews, Tom
1990   The Long Shadow. *Newsweek* 115 (May 7), pp. 34–44.

Mathisen, James A.
1989   Twenty Years After Bellah: Whatever Happened to American Civil Rights? *Sociological Analysis* 50 (Summer), pp. 129–146.

Matthiessen, Peter
1983   *In the Spirit of Crazy Horse.* New York: Viking.

1993   Cesar Chavez. *New Yorker* 69 (May 17), pp. 62–63.

Matza, David
1964   *Delinquency and Drift.* New York: Wiley.

1971   Poverty and Disrepute. In Robert K. Merton and Robert Nisbet, eds., *Contemporary Social Problems*, 3d ed., pp. 601–656. New York: Harcourt, Brace & World.

Mauro, Tony
1993   Students "Taking Stand" for Prayer in Schools. *USA Today* (September 15), p. 4A.

Maykovich, Minako Kurokawa
1972a   *Japanese American Identity Dilemma.* Tokyo: Waseda University Press.

1972b   Reciprocity in Racial Stereotypes: White, Black and Yellow. *American Journal of Sociology* 77 (March), pp. 876–877.

McClain, Paula Denice
1979   *Alienation and Resistance: The Political Behavior of Afro-Canadians.* Palo Alto, CA: R & E Research Associates.

McCord, Colin, and Freeman, Harold P.
1990   Excess Mortality in Harlem. *New England Journal of Medicine* 322 (January 18), pp. 173–177.

McCormick, John
1992   Radical Chic: A Panther on the Hill. *Newsweek* 120 (November 2), p. 52.

McCormick, Katheryne, and Baruch, Lucy
1994   Women Show Strength as Campaign Fundraisers. *CAWP News and Notes* 10 (Winter), pp. 16–17.

McCully, Bruce T.
1940   *English Education and Origins of Indiana Nationalism.* New York: Columbia University.

McFadden, Robert D.
1983   F.A.L.N. Puerto Rican Terrorists Suspected in New Year Bombings. *New York Times* (January 2), pp. 1, 17.

McFate, Katherine
1994   The Grim Economics of Violence. *Focus* 22 (October), p. 4.

McIntosh, Shawn
1992   Survey of Those Arrested in the Riots. *USA Today* (May 11), p. 7A.

McKenna, Ian
1994   Legal Protection Against Racial Discrimination Law in Canada. *New Community* 20 (April), pp. 415–436.

McLeod, Beverly
1986   The Oriental Express. *Psychology Today* 20 (July), pp. 48–52.

McMillen, Liz
1991   American Indian College Fund seeks Recognition and $10-Million for Tribal Institutions. *Chronicle of Higher Education* (May 1), p. A25.

McNickle, D'Arcy
1973   *Native American Tribalism: Indian Survivals and Renewals.* New York: Oxford University Press.

McNulty, Timothy J.
1994   Conference on Violence Faces Reality. *Chicago Tribune* (January 9), p. 7.

McVeigh, Roy
1993   Creating Opportunities for Insurgency: The Case of the United Farm Workers Movement. Paper presented at the annual meeting of the American Sociological Association, Miami.

McWilliams, Carey
1968   *North from Mexico: The Spanish-Speaking People of the United States.* New York: Greenwood Press.

Meier, August, and Rudwick, Elliott
1966   *From Plantation to Ghetto: An Interpretive History of American Negroes.* New York: Hill & Wang.

Meier, Matt S., and Rivera, Feliciano
1972   *The Chicanos: A History of Mexican Americans.* New York: Hill & Wang.

Meléndez, Edwin
1994   Puerto Rico Migration and Occupational Selectivity, 1982–1981. *International Migration Review* 28 (Spring), pp. 49–67.

Meléndez, Edwin, and Meléndez, Edgardo, eds.
1993   *Colonial Dilemma: Critical Perspectives on Contemporary Puerto Rico.* Boston: South End Press.

Meléndez, Edwin; Rodriquez, Clara; and Figueroa, Janis Barry, eds.
1991   *Hispanics in the Labor Force: Issues and Policies.* Washington, DC: Plenum.

Melendy, Howard Brett
1972   *The Oriental Americans.* New York: Hippocreme.

1980   Filipinos. In Stephen Thernstrom, ed., *Harvard Encyclopedia of American Ethnic Groups,* pp. 354–362. Cambridge: Belknap Press of Harvard University Press.

Merton, Robert K.
1949   Discrimination and the American Creed. In Robert M. MacIver, ed., *Discrimination and National Welfare,* pp. 99–126. New York: Harper & Row.

1968   *Social Theory and Social Structure.* New York: Free Press.

1976   *Sociological Ambivalence and Other Essays.* New York: Free Press.

Meyers, Gustavus
1943   *History of Bigotry in the United States.* Rev. by Henry M. Christman, 1960. New York: Capricorn Books.

Miller, David L.
1995   Toys for Boys. In Richard T. Schaefer and Robert P. Lamm, *Sociology, 5th ed., Annotated Instructor's Edition,* pp. IM26–IM28. New York: McGraw-Hill.

Miller, Joanne, and Garrison, Howard H.
1982   Sex Roles: The Division of Labor at Home and in the Workplace. In Ralph Turner, ed., *Annual Review of Sociology, 1982,* pp. 237–262. Palo Alto, CA: Annual Reviews.

Miller, Margaret I., and Linker, Helene
1974   Equal Rights Amendment Campaigns in California and Utah. *Society* 11 (May–June), pp. 40–53.

Miller, Norman
1987   Hazards in the Translocation of Research into Remedial Interventions. *Journal of Social Issues* 43 (No. 1), pp. 119–126.

Miller, Stuart Creighton
1969   *The Unwelcome Immigrant: The American Image of the Chinese, 1785–1882.* Berkeley: University of California Press.

Miller, Walter
1977   The Rumble This Time. *Psychology Today* 10 (May), pp. 52–59, 88.

Mills, C. Wright
1943   The Sailor, Sex Market and Mexican: The New American Jitters. *The New Leader* (June 26), pp. 5–7.

Min, Pyong Gap
1987   Filipino and Korean Immigrants in Small Business: A Comparative Analysis. *Amerasia* 13 (Spring), pp. 53–71.

1995   *Asian Americans: Contemporary Trends and Issues.* Thousand Oaks, CA: Sage.

Mincy, Ronald B., ed.
1994   *Nurturing Young Black Males.* Washington, DC: Urban Institute Press.

Mindel, Charles H.; Habenstein, Robert W.; and Wright, Roosevelt, Jr., eds.
1988   *Ethnic Families in America: Patterns and Variations,* 3d ed. New York: Elsevier.

Mineta, Norman
1991   Pearl Harbor and Japanese Americans. *Asianweek* 13 (December 6), p. 14.

Miyamoto, S. Frank
1973   The Forced Evacuation of the Japanese Minority During World II. *Journal of Social Issues* 29 (No. 2), pp. 11–31.

Mizio, Emelica
1972   Puerto Rican Social Workers and Racism. *Social Casework* 53 (May), pp. 267–272.

Moffat, Susan
1995   Violent Acts Against U.S. Asians Climb. *Los Angeles Times* (August 1), p. A3.

Mohl, Raymond A.
1986   The Politics of Ethnicity in Contemporary Miami. *Migration World* 14 (No. 3), pp. 7–11.

Montagu, Ashley
1972   *Statement on Race.* New York: Oxford University Press.

1975   *Race and IQ.* London: Oxford University Press.

Montalbano, William D.
1995   Britain, Ireland, Unveil a Peace Plan for Ulster. *Los Angeles Times* (February 23), pp. A1, A6.

Montero, Darrel M.
1981   The Japanese Americans: Changing Patterns of Assimilation over Three Generations. *American Sociological Review* 46 (December), pp. 829–839.

Montgomery, Patricia A.
1994   The Hispanic Population in the United States: March 1993. *Current Population Reports,* Series P-20, No. 475. Washington, DC: U.S. Government Printing Office.

Moore, David W.
1993   Americans Feel Threatened by New Immigrants. *The Gallup Poll Monthly* 334 (July), pp. 2–16.

Moore, Helen A., and Iadicola, Peter
1981   Resegregation Processes in Desegregated Schools and Status Relationships for Hispanic Students. *Aztlan* 12 (September), pp. 39–58.

Moore, Joan W.
1970   Colonialism: The Case of the Mexican Americans. *Social Problems* 17 (Spring), pp. 463–472.

1989   Is There a Hispanic Under-
        class? *Social Science Quarter-
        ly* 70 (June), pp. 265–284.

Moore, Joan W., and Pachon, Harry
1985   *Hispanics in the United States.*
        Englewood Cliffs, NJ: Pren-
        tice-Hall.

Moore, Joan W., and Pinderhughes,
Raquel, eds.
1993   *In the Barrios: Latinos and
        the Underclass Debate.* New
        York: Sage.

Moquin, Wayne, and Van Doren, Charles,
eds.
1971   *A Documentary History of the
        Mexican Americans.* New
        York: Praeger.

Morales, Royal F.
1976   Philipino Americans: From
        Colony to Immigrant to Citi-
        zen. *Civil Rights Digest* 9
        (Fall), pp. 30–32.

Morgan, Joan
1991   All-Black Male Classrooms
        Run into Resistance. *Black
        Issues in Higher Education* 7
        (January 17), pp. 1, 21–22.

Morgan, Richard E.
1974   The Establishment Clause and
        Sectarian Schools: A Final
        Installment. In Philip B. Kur-
        land, ed., *1973, The Supreme
        Court Review,* pp. 57–97.
        Chicago: University of Chica-
        go Press.

Morganthau, Tom
1994   How Can We Say No?
        Newsweek 124 (September 5),
        pp. 28–29.

Morin, Richard
1983   What Miami Thinks. *Miami
        Herald* (December 18), pp.
        7M–8M.

1994   An Attitude Problem. *Wash-
        ington Post National Weekly
        Edition* 11 (June 20), p. 37.

Morris, Aldon D.
1984   *The Origins of the Civil Rights
        Movement: Black Communi-
        ties Organizing for Change.*
        New York: Free Press.

1993   Birmingham Confrontation
        Reconsidered: An Analysis of
        the Dynamics and Tactics of
        Mobilization. *American Socio-
        logical Review* 58 (October),
        pp. 621–636.

Morris, Milton D., and Rubin, Gary E.
1993   The Turbulent Friendship:
        Black–Jewish Relations in the
        1990s. *Annals* (November),
        pp. 42–60.

Morse, Samuel F. B.
1835   *Foreign Conspiracy Against
        the Liberties of United States.*
        New York: Leavitt, Lord.

Moskos, Charles
1966   Racial Integration in the
        Armed Forces. *American
        Journal of Sociology* 72 (Sep-
        tember), pp. 132–148.

Mosley, Leonard
1966   *Hirohito: Emperor of Japan.*
        Englewood Cliffs, NJ: Pren-
        tice-Hall.

Moss, Desda
1995   FOR Tribute Fuels Debate on
        Disability. *USA Today* (April
        13), p. 6A.

Muranaka, Gwen
1993   Despite Protests "Jap Road,"
        "Jap Lane" Remain in Texas
        Towns. *Asianweek* 14 (Febru-
        ary 12), pp. 1, 20.

Murray, Charles, and Herrnstein,
Richard J.
1994   Race, Genes, and I.Q.—An
        Apologia. *New Republic* 211
        (October 31), pp. 27–37.

Muschkin, Clara G.
1993   Consequences of Return
        Migrant Status for Employ-
        ment in Puerto Rico. *Interna-
        tional Migration Review* 27
        (Spring), pp. 79–102.

Muto, Sheila
    1991   Pearl Harbor Day Sparks
            Concern About Racism.
            Asianweek 13 (December 6),
            pp. 1, 14.

Mydans, Seth
    1992   A Target of Rioters, Korea-
            town Is Bitter, Armed, and
            Determined. *New York Times*
            (May 3), pp. 1, 16.

    1993   Giving Voice to the Hurt and
            Betrayal of Korean America.
            New York Times (May 2), p.
            E9.

Myrdal, Gunnar
    1944   *An American Dilemma: The
            Negro Problem and Modern
            Democracy.* With the assis-
            tance of Richard Steiner and
            Arnold Rose. New York:
            Harper.

NAACP
    1989   *The Unfinished Agenda on
            Race in America.* New York
            City: NAACP Legal Defense
            and Educational Fund.

Nabokov, Peter
    1970   *Tijerina and the Courthouse
            Raid,* 2d ed. Berkeley, CA:
            Ramparts Press.

Nagata, Donna K.
    1990   The Japanese American
            Internment: Exploring the
            Transgenerational Conse-
            quences of Traumatic Stress.
            Journal of Traumatic Stress 3,
            pp. 47–69.

    1991   The Impact of the World War
            II Internment Policies upon
            the Present-Day Japanese
            American Community. Paper
            presented at the annual meet-
            ing of the American Psycho-
            logical Association, San
            Francisco.

Nagel, Joane
    1988   The Roots of Red Power:
            Demographic and Organiza-
            tional Bases of American
            Indian Activism 1950–1990.
            Paper presented at the annual
            meeting of the American
            Sociological Association,
            Atlanta.

Nagel, Joane, and Johnson, Troy, eds.
    1994   Alcatraz. *American Indian
            Culture and Research Journal*
            18 (No. 4), pp. 1–301.

Nakanishi, Don T.
    1986   Asian American Politics: An
            Agenda for Research. *Amera-
            sia* 12 (Fall), pp. 1–27.

Nash, Manning
    1962   Race and the Ideology of
            Race, *Current Anthropology* 3
            (June), pp. 285–288.

The Nation
    1993   The Chavez Legacy. 257
            (November 22), pp. 606,
            635.

National Advisory Commission on Civil
Disorders
    1968   *Report.* With introduction by
            Tom Wicker. New York: Ban-
            tam.

National Clearinghouse for Bilingual
Education
    1994   Johnson O'Malley Act Pro-
            motes. *Native American Edu-
            cation* 17 (Winter), pp. 1, 3.

National Commission on Population
Growth and the American Future
    1972   *Population and the American
            Future.* Washington, DC:
            U.S. Government Printing
            Office.

National Conference of Christians and
Jews (NCCJ)
    1994   *Taking America's Pulse.* New
            York: NCCJ.

National Jewish Family Center
    1982   How the Family "Figures" in
            the 1980 Census. *Newsletter* 2
            (Fall).

National Opinion Research Center
    1995   *General Social Survey
            1972–1994: Cumulative Code-
            book.* Chicago: National Opin-
            ion Research Center.

National Public Radio
1992   Morning Edition (August 13).

1994   United Farm Workers March on Sacramento. Broadcast of "All Things Considered." April 22.

Navarro, Mireya
1995   Puerto Rico Reeling Under Scourge of Drugs and Rising Gang Violence. *New York Times* (July 23), p. 11.

NBC News
1992   *World Atlas and Almanac.* Chicago: Rand McNally.

Nee, Victor G., and DeBary, Brett, eds.
1973   *Longtime Californ': A Documentary Study of an American Chinatown.* New York: Pantheon.

Nee, Victor G., and Sanders, Jimmy
1985   The Road to Parity: Determinants of the Socioeconomic Achievements of Asian Americans. *Ethnic and Racial Studies* 8 (January), pp. 75–93.

Neier, Aryeh
1994   Watching Rights. *The Nation* 228 (February 14), p. 187.

Nelan, Bruce W.
1994   Time to Take Charge. *Time* (May 9), pp. 26–30, 34–35.

Nelson, Dale C.
1980   The Political Behavior of New York Puerto Ricans: Assimilation or Survival? In Clara E. Rodriquez, Virginia Sanchez Karrol, and Jose Oscar Alers, eds., *The Puerto Rican Struggle,* pp. 90–110. Maplewood, NJ: Waterfront Press.

Nelson, Jack
1993   *Terror in the Night: The Klan's Campaign Against the Jews.* New York: Simon & Schuster.

Newman, William M.
1973   *American Pluralism: A Study of Minority Groups and Social Theory.* New York: Harper & Row.

Newsweek
1971   Success Story: Outwhiting the White. 101 (June 21), pp. 24–25.

1979   A New Racial Poll. 109 (February 26), pp. 48, 53.

New York Daily News
1984   Overcrowding? Hispanics "Prefer" It, HUD Aide Says. (May 13), p. 19.

New York Times
1917a   Illiteracy Is Not All Alike. (February 8), p. 12.

1917b   The Immigration Bill Veto. (January 31), p. 210.

1979   Hispanic Pupils Held Hampered by Tests Tied to English Ability. (September 16), pp. 1, 66.

1982   Converts to Judaism. (August 29), p. 23.

1990   Health Data Show Wide Gap Between Whites and Blacks. (March 23), p. A17.

1991   For 2, an Answer to Years of Doubt on Use of Peyote in Religious Rite (July 9), p. A14.

1992   Bias-Incited Beating Death of a Vietnamese Stuns a Florida Town. (August 23), p. 16.

1994   Single Women and Poverty Strongly Linked. (February 20), p. 35.

1995a   Georgia Superintendent Battles a Subtle Racism. (February 14), p. A10.

1995b   Reverse Discrimination of Whites is Rare, Labor Study Reports. (March 31), p. A23.

1995c   California Governor Moves Quickly Against Affirmative Action (June 2), p. A15.

Ng, Johnny
1991   More Asian Children Living in Poverty. *Asianweek* 12 (June 14), pp. 1, 17.

Nickerson, Steve
1971   Alaska Natives Criticize Bill. *Race Relations Reporter* 2 (November 15), pp. 7–10.

Nie, Norman H.; Currie, Barbara; and Greeley, Andrew M.
1974   Political Attitudes Among American Ethnics: A Study of Perceptual Distortion. *Ethnicity* 1 (December), pp. 317–343.

Niebuhr, H. Richard
1929   *The Social Sources of Denominationalism.* New York: Holt.

Niebuhr, R. Gustav
1990   American Moslems: Islam Is Growing Fast in the U.S., Fighting Fear and Stereotypes. *Wall Street Journal* (October 15), sect. A, p.1.

Nishi, Setsuko Matsunga
1995   Japanese Americans. In Pyong Gap Min, ed., *Asian Americans: Contemporary Trends and Issues,* pp. 95–133. Thousand Oaks, CA: Sage.

Noel, Donald L.
1972   *The Origins of American Slavery and Racism.* Columbus, OH: Charles Merrill Publishing Co.

Nordheimer, Jon
1988   Older Migrants' Years of Toil in Sun End in Cold Twilight. *New York Times* (May 29), pp. 1, 9.

Novak, Michael
1973a   *The Rise of the Unmeltable Ethnics: Politics and Culture in the Seventies.* New York: Collier.

1973b   How American Are You If Your Grandparents Came from Serbia in 1888. In Sallie TeSelle, ed., *The Rediscovery of Ethnicity,* pp. 1–20. New York: Harper & Row.

Novello, Antonia C.; Wise, Paul H; and Kleinman, Dushanka V.
1991   Hispanic Health: Time for Data, Time for Action. *Journal of the American Medical Association* 265 (January 9), pp. 253–257.

Oakes, James
1993   Slavery. In Mary Kupiec Clayton, Elliot J. Gorn, and Peter W. Williams, eds., *Encyclopedia of American Social History,* pp. 1407–1419. New York: Scribners.

Oakes, Jeannie
1995   Two Cities' Tracking and Within-School Segregation. *Teachers College Record* 96 (Summer), pp. 681–706.

Oberschall, Anthony
1968   The Los Angeles Riot of August 1965. *Social Problems* 15 (Winter), pp. 322–341.

O'Dea, Thomas F.
1957   *The Mormons.* Chicago: University of Chicago Press.

Oehling, Richard A.
1980   The Yellow Menace: Asian Images in American Film. In Randall M. Miller, ed., *The Kaleidoscopic Lens,* pp. 182–206. Englewood, NJ: Jerome S. Ozer.

Ogletree, Earl J., and Ujlaki, Vilma E.
1985   American-Hispanics in a Pluralistic Society. *Migration Today* 13 (No. 3), pp. 30–34.

O'Hare, William P., and Curry-White, Brenda
1992   Is There a Rural Underclass? *Population Today* 20 (March), pp. 6–8.

O'Hare, William P., and Felt, Judy C.
1991   *Asian Americans: America's Fastest Growing Minority Group.* Washington, DC: Population Reference Bureau.

O'Hare, William P.; Pollard, Kelvin M.; Mann, Taynia L.; and Kent, Mary M.
1991   African Americans in the 1990s. *Population Bulletin* 46 (July).

Ohnuma, Keiko
1991   Study Finds Asians Unhappy at CSU. *Asian Week* 12 (August 8), p. 5.

O'Kane, James M.
1992   *The Crooked Ladder: Gangsters, Ethnicity, and the American Dream.* New Brunswick, NJ: Transaction.

Omi, Michael, and Winant, Howard
1994   *Racial Formation in the United States,* 2d ed. New York: Routledge.

O'Neill, William
1969   *Everyone Was Brave: The Rise and Fall of Feminism in America.* Chicago: Quadrangle.

Ong, Paul, ed.
1994   *The State of Asian Pacific America: Economic Diversity, Issues and Policies.* Los Angeles: Leadership Education for Asian Pacifics.

Ong, Paul, and Umemoto, Karen
1994   Diversity Within a Common Agenda. In Paul Ong, ed., *The State of Asian Pacific America,* pp. 271–276. Los Angeles: Leadership Education for Asian Pacific.

O'Reilly, Jane
1982   After the ERA: What Next? *Civil Rights Quarterly Perspectives* 14 (Fall), pp. 16–19.

Orfield, Gary
1987   *School Segregation in the 1980's.* Chicago: National School Desegregation Report.

1993   *The Growth of Segregation in American Schools: Changing Patterns of Segregation and Poverty Since 1986.* Alexandria, VA: National School Boards Association.

Orlov, Ann, and Ueda, Reed
1980   Central and South Americans. In Stephan Thernstrom, ed., *Harvard Encyclopedia of American Ethnic Groups,* pp.

210–217. Cambridge: Belknap Press of Harvard University Press.

Ostling, Richard N.
1992   The Second Reformation. *Time* 140 (November 23), pp. 52–58.

Ottaway, David S., and Taylor, Paul
1992   A Minority Decides to Stand Aside for Majority Rule. *Washington Post National Weekly Edition* 9 (April 5), p. 17.

Owen, Carolyn A.; Eisner, Howard C.; and McFaul, Thomas R.
1981   A Half-Century of Social Distance Research: National Replication of the Bogardus Studies. *Sociology and Social Research* 66 (October), pp. 80–97.

Padilla, Raymond V.
1973   A Critique of Pittian History. In O. I. Romano, ed., *Voices: Readings from El Grito,* rev. ed., pp. 65–106. Berkeley, CA: Quinto Sol Publications.

Paik, Irvin
1971   That Oriental Feeling: A Look at the Caricatures of the Asians as Sketched by American Movies. In Amy Tachiki, Eddie Wong, Franklin Odo, and Buck Wongs, eds., *Roots: An Asian American Reader,* pp. 30–36. Los Angeles: Asian American Studies Center, UCLA.

Parfit, Michael
1994   Powwows. *National Geographic* 185 (June), pp. 85–113.

Park, Robert E.
1928   Human Migration and the Marginal Man. *American Journal of Sociology* 33 (May), pp. 881–893.

1950   *Race and Culture: Essays in the Sociology of Contemporary Man.* News York: Free Press.

Park, Robert E., and Burgess, Ernest W.
1921   *Introduction to the Science of Sociology.* Chicago: University of Chicago Press.

Parker, Suzy
1992   Catholics in the U.S.A. *USA Today* (November 20), p. 1A.

Parks, Michael
1994   On Nobel Day, Reality Falls Short of Noble Hopes. *Los Angeles Times* (December 10), p. A2.

Parrish, Michael
1995   Betting on Hard Labour and a Plot of Land. *Los Angeles Times* (July 7), pp. A1, A20.

Parsons, Talcott, and Bales, Robert
1955   *Family, Socialization and Interaction Processes.* Glencoe, IL: Free Press.

Passalacqua, Juan M. Garcia
1994   The 1993 Plebiscite in Puerto Rico: A First Step to Decolonization? *Current History* 93 (March), pp. 103–107.

Patterson, Orlando
1982   *Slavery and Social Death.* Cambridge: Harvard University Press.

Pedder, Sophie
1991   Social Isolation and the Labour Market: Black Americans in Chicago. Paper presented at the Chicago Urban Poverty and Family Life Conference, Chicago.

Pederson, Daniel
1987   All These Guys Owe Willie. *Newsweek* 109 (March 16), pp. 30, 32.

Penalosa, Fernando
1968   Mexican Family Roles. *Journal of Marriage and the Family* 30 (November), pp. 680–689.

Pennock-Román, Maria
1986   New Directions for Research on Spanish-Language Tests and Test-Item Bias. In Michael A. Olivas, ed., *Latino College Students*, pp. 193–220. New York: Teachers College Press.

Perez, Miguel
1986   The Language of Discrimination. *New York Daily News* (November 13), p. 47.

1989   "English" Racism Is Now Out in the Open. *New York Daily News* (August 10), p. 42.

Pérez-Stable, Marifeli, and Uriarte, Miren
1993   Cubans and the Changing Economy of Miami. In Rebecca Morales and Frank Bonilla, eds., *Latinos in a Changing U.S. Economy*, pp. 133–159. Newbury Park, CA: Sage.

Perry, Dan
1994   Extremist Group Kach is Focus on Crackdown. *USA Today* (February 28), p. 7A.

Perusse, Roland I.
1990   *The United States and Puerto Rico: The Struggle for Equality.* Malabor, FL: Robert E. Krieger Publishing Company.

Petersen, William
1971   *Japanese Americans: Oppression and Success.* New York: Random House.

Petersilia, Joan
1983   Racial Disparities in the Criminal Justice System. Santa Monica, CA: Rand.

Peterson, Eric D.; Wright, Steven M.; Daley, Jennifer; and Thisault, George E.
1994   Racial Variation in Cardiac Procedure Use and Survival Following Acute Myocardial Infarction in the Department of Veterans Affairs. *Journal of the American Medical Association* 271 (April 20), pp. 1175–1207.

Pettigrew, Thomas F.
1958   Personality and Socio-Cultural Factors in Intergroup Attitudes: A Cross-National Comparison. *Journal of Conflict Resolution* 2 (March), pp. 29–42.

1959   Regional Differences in Anti-Negro Prejudice. *Journal of Abnormal and Social Psychology* 59 (July), pp. 28–36.

1981   Race and Class in the 1980s: An Interactive Brew. *Daedalus* 110 (Spring), pp. 233–255.

Pettigrew, Thomas F., and Martin, Joanne
1987   Shaping the Organizational Context for Black American Inclusion. *Journal of Social Issues* 43 (No. 1), pp. 41–78.

Pido, Antonio J. A.
1986   *The Filipinos in America.* New York: Center for Migration Studies.

Pileggi, Nicolas
1971   Risorgimento: The Red, White, and Greening of New York. *New York Magazine* (June 7), pp. 26–36.

Pinkney, Alphonso
1975   *Black Americans,* 2d ed. Englewood Cliffs, NJ: Prentice-Hall.

1984   *The Myth of Black Progress.* New York: Cambridge University Press.

1994   *Black Americans,* 4th ed. Englewood Cliffs, NJ: Prentice-Hall.

Pitt, Leonard
1966   *Decline of the Californios: A Social History of the Spanish-Speaking Californians, 1846–1890.* Berkeley: University of California Press.

Pleck, Elizabeth H.
1993   Gender Roles and Relations. In Mary Kupiec Clayton, Elliot J. Gorn, and Peter W. Williams, eds., *Encyclopedia of American Social History,* pp. 1945–1960. New York: Scribners.

Poe, Janita
1992   Blacks Finding Places to Call Their Own in Suburbs. *Chicago Tribune* (September 29), pp. 1, 11.

Pollitt, Katha
1995   Subject to Debate. *Nation* 260 (June 19), p. 76.

Porter, Jack Nusan
1970   Jewish Student Activism. *Jewish Currents* (May), pp. 28–34.

1981   *The Jew as Outsider.* Washington, DC: Washington University Press.

1985   Self-Hatred and Self-Esteem. *The Jewish Spectator* (Fall), pp. 51–55.

Portes, Alejandro
1974   Return of the Wetback. *Society* 11 (March–April), pp. 40–46.

Ports, Alejandro, and Stepick, Alex
1985   Unwelcome Immigrants: The Labor Market Experiences of 1980 (Mariel) Cuban and Haitian Refugees in South Florida. *American Sociological Review* 50 (August), pp. 493–514.

1993   *City on the Edge: The Transformation of Miami.* Berkeley: University of California Press.

Post, Tom
1994   Against the Wind. *Newsweek* 124 (September 5), pp. 22–27.

Potok, Mark
1994   Blacks Move into White Texas Project. *USA Today* (January 14), p. 3A.

Powell-Hopson, Darlene, and Hopson, Derek
1988   Implications of Doll Color Preferences Among Black Preschool Children and White Preschool Children. *Journal of Black Psychology* 14 (February), pp. 57–63.

Powers, Charles H.
1976 Two Forms of Ethnicity: A Brief Description of Japanese-American Organization. Paper presented at the annual meeting of the American Sociological Association, New York.

Preble, Edward
1968 The Puerto Rican-American Teenager in New York City. In Eugene B. Brody, ed., *Minority Group Adolescents in the United States,* pp. 48–72. Baltimore: Williams & Wilkins.

Presidential Commission on Indian Reservation Economics
1984 *Report and Recommendations to the President of the United States.* Washington, DC: U.S. Government Printing Office.

Price, John A.
1968 The Migration and Adaptation of Indians to Los Angeles. *Human Organization* 27 (Summer), pp. 168–175.

Princeton Religion Research Center
1986 Importance of God in Lives. *Emerging Trends* 8 (November–December), p. 5.

1993 Catholics Are Becoming the New Middle Class. *Emerging Trends* 15 (March), p. 5.

1994 Membership Trends—Mainline Churches. *Emerging Trends* 16 (February), p. 6.

1995 Both Students and Parents Approve of School Prayer. *Emerging Trends* 17 (March), p. 2.

Puente, Maria
1994 A Real Melting Pot. *USA Today* (August 1), p. 3A.

Pyle, Amy
1995 Pressure Grows to Reform Bilingual Education in State. *Los Angeles Times* (May 22), pp. A1, A12–A13.

Quan, Katie
1986 Chinese Garment Workers. *Migration World* 14 (No. 1–2), pp. 46–49.

Quintana, Frances Leon
1980 Spanish. In Stephen Thernstrom, ed., *Harvard Encyclopedia of American Ethnic Groups,* pp. 950–953. Cambridge: Belknap Press of Harvard University Press.

Rabaya, Violet
1971 Filipino Immigration: The Creation of a New Social Problem. In Amy Tachiki, Eddie Wong, Franklin Odo, and Buck Wong, eds., *Roots: An Asian American Reader,* pp. 188–200. Los Angeles: Asian American Studies Center, UCLA.

Rabinove, Samuel
1970 Private Club Discrimination and the Law. *Civil Rights Digest* 3 (Spring), pp. 28–33.

Rachlin, Carol
1970 Tight Shoe Night: Oklahoma Indians Today. In Stuart Levine and Nancy Oestreich Lurie, eds., *The American Indian Today,* pp. 160–183. Baltimore: Penguin.

Ramirez, Anthony
1986 America's Super Minority. *Fortune* 114 (November 24), pp. 148–149, 152, 156, 160.

Ramirez, J. David; Yuen, Sandra D.; and Ramey, Dena R.
1991 *Final Report: Longitudinal Study of Structured English Immersion Strategy, Early-Exit and Late-Exit Transitional Bilingual Education Programs for Language-Minority Children.* San Mateo, CA: Aguirre International.

Randall, Peter
1995 Integration, Even if Forced, Is Working. *Frontiers of Freedom* (Second Quarter), pp. 22–23.

Rapson, Richard L.
1980 *Fairly Lucky You Live in Hawaii! Cultural Pluralism in the Fiftieth State.* Landham, MD: University Press of America.

Rasmussen, Cecilia
1995 Where Latinos' March Toward Justice Began. *Los Angeles Times* (April 24), p. B3.

Raspberry, William
1991 Grim Reruns of the '60s. *Washington Post* (May 8), p. A3.

Rawick, George P.
1972 *From Sundown to Sunup: The Making of the Black Community.* Westport, CT: Greenwood Press.

Raybon, Patricia
1989 A Case of "Severe Bias." *Newsweek* 114 (October 2), p. 11.

Raymer, Patricia
1974 Wisconsin's Menominees: Indians on a Seesaw. *National Geographic* (August), pp. 228–251.

Raymond, Chris
1991 Cornell Scholar Attacks Key Psychological Studies Thought to Demonstrate Blacks' Self-hatred. *Chronicle of Higher Education* 37 (May 8), pp. A5, A8, A11.

Rebelsky, Freda, and Hanks, Cheryl
1973 Fathers' Verbal Interaction with Infants in the First Three Months of Life. In Freda Rebelsky and Lynn Dorman, eds., *Child Development and Behavior,* 2d ed., pp. 145–148. New York: Knopf.

Refugee Reports
1992 Canada Tightening Refugee Law, Takes Step Toward Turning Asylum Seekers Back to the United States. 13 (September 30), pp. 1–8.

Reich, Robert
1994 Two Million New Jobs Are Not Enough. *Focus* 22 (July), pp. 3–4.

Reichmann, Rebecca
1995 Brazil's Denial of Race. *Report of the Americas* 28 (May–June), pp. 35–42.

Reid, John
1982 Black America in the 1980s. *Population Bulletin* 37 (December).
1986 Immigration and the Future U.S. Black Population. *Population Today* 14 (February), pp. 6–8.

Reimers, David M.
1983 An Unintended Reform: The 1965 Immigration Act and Third World Immigration to the United States. *Journal of American Ethnic History* 3 (Fall), pp. 9–28.

Reinhold, Robert
1992 A Century After Queen's Overthrow, Talk of Sovereignty Shakes Hawaii. *New York Times* (November 8), p. 14.

Reith, Kathryn M.
1992 *Playing Fair: A Guide to Title IX in High School and College Sports.* New York: Women's Sports Foundation.

Religion Week
1995 Reform Synagogues Increasingly Adopting Orthodox Practices. 10 (March), p. 7.

Research Committee on the Study of Honolulu Residents
1986 *The Third Attitudinal Survey of Honolulu Residents, 1983.* Honolulu: University of Hawaii Press.

Reskin, Barbara
1993 Sex Segregation in the Workplace. In Judith Blake, ed., *Annual Review of Sociology 1993,* pp. 241–270. Palo Alto, CA: Annual Reviews.

Reskin, Barbara, and Blau, Francine
1990   *Job Queues, Gender Queues: Explaining Women's Inroads into Male Occupations.* Philadelphia: Temple University Press.

Rice, Berkeley
1977   The New Gangs of Chinatown. *American Sociological Review* 42 (May), pp. 60–69.

Richardson, Laurel Walum
1981   *The Dynamics of Sex and Gender,* 2d ed. Boston: Houghton Mifflin.

Richman, Ruth
1992   Glass Ceiling? Break It Yourselves, Federal Official Says. *Chicago Tribune* (August 16), sect. 6, pp. 1, 11.

Ridgeway, James
1986   Que Pasa, U.S. English? *Village Voice* 31 (December 2), pp. 32, 33.

Rieff, David
1993   *The Exile: Cuba in the Heart of Miami.* New York: Simon & Schuster.

Rivera, George, Jr.
1988   Hispanic Folk Medicine Utilization in Urban Colorado. *Sociology and Social Research* 72 (July), pp. 237–241.

Roberts, D. F.
1955   The Dynamics of Racial Intermixture in the American Negro—Some Anthropological Considerations. *American Journal of Human Genetics* 7 (December), pp. 361–367.

Roberts, Steven B.
1984   Congress Stages a Pre-emptive Strike on the Gender Gap. *New York Times* (May 23), p. A18.

Roche, John Patrick
1984   An Examination of the Resurgence of Ethnicity Literature. *Sociological Spectrum* 4, pp. 169–186.

Rodriquez, Clara E.
1989   *Puerto Ricans: Born in the USA.* Boston: Unwin Hyman.

Rodriquez, Richard
1982   *Hunger of Memory.* Boston: Godine.

Rodriquez, Roberto
1993   Ingles: Si o No? Debate Rages on in Puerto Rico. *Black Issues in Higher Education* 9 (February 11), p. 13.

Rodríquez, Robert
1994   Immigrant Bashing: Latinos Beseiged by Public Policy Bias. *Black Issues in Higher Education* 10 (February 24), pp. 31–34.

Rohter, Larry
1992   Miami Leaders Are Condemned by Rights Unit. *New York Times* (August 19), p. A18.
1993a Trade Pact Threatens Puerto Rico's Economic Rise. *New York Times* (January 3), pp. 1, 14.
1993b As Hispanic Presence Grows, So Does Black Anger. *New York Times* (June 20), pp. 1, 11.
1993c Rights Groups Fault Decision, As Do Haitians. *New York Times* (June 22), p. 18.
1993d Moderate Cuban Voices Rise in U.S. *New York Times* (June 27), p. 14.

Rolle, Andrew F.
1972   *The American Indians: Their History and Culture.* Belmont, CA: Wadsworth.

Roos, Philip D.; Smith, Dowell H.; Langley, Stephen; and McDonald, James
1977   The Impact of the American Indian Movement on the Pine

Ridge Indian Reservation. Paper presented at the annual meeting of the Society for the Study of Social Problems, Chicago.

Rosaldo, Renato
1985 Chicano Studies, 1970–1984. In Bernard J. Siegal, ed., *Annual Review of Anthropology, 1985*, pp. 405–427. Palo Alto, CA: Annual Reviews.

Rose, Arnold
1951 *The Roots of Prejudice.* Paris: UNESCO.

Rose, Peter I.
1981 *They and We,* 3d ed. New York: Random House.

Rose, R. S.
1988 Slavery in Brazil: Does It Still Exist Today? Paper presented at the annual meeting of the American Sociological Association, Atlanta.

Rose, Richard
1971 *Governing Without Consensus.* Boston: Beacon Press.

Rosen, Sanford Jay
1974 Letter: When the Look Is Latin. *New York Times Magazine* (April 7), pp. 21, 102.

Rosenbaum, James E., and Meaden, Patricia
1992 Harassment and Acceptance of Low-Income Black Youth in White Suburban Schools. Paper presented at the annual meeting of the American Sociological Association, Pittsburgh.

Rosenberg, Morris, and Simmons, Roberta G.
1971 *Black and White Self-Esteem: The Urban School Child.* Washington, DC: American Sociological Association.

Rossi, Alice S.
1964 Equality Between the Sexes: An Immodest Proposal. *Daedalus* 93 (Spring), pp. 607–652.

1988 Growing Up and Older in Sociology 1940–1990. In M. W. Riley, ed., *Sociological Lives,* pp. 43–64. Newbury Park, CA: Sage.

Roth, Elizabeth
1993 The Civil Rights History of "Sex." *Ms.* 3 (March–April), pp. 84–85.

Roudi, Nazy
1993 The Palestinians. *Population Today* 21 (January), p. 11.

Rubien, David
1989 For Asians in U.S., Hidden Strife. *New York Times* (January 11), p. C1.

Rudwick, Elliott
1957 The Niagara Movement. *Journal of Negro History* 42 (July), pp. 177–200.

Ryan, William
1976 *Blaming the Victim,* rev. ed. New York: Random House.

Saad, Lydia, and McAneny, Leslie
1994 Most Americans Think Religion Losing Clout in the 1990s. *Gallup Poll Monthly* (April), pp. 2–4.

Sadker, Myra, and Sadker, David
1985 Sexism in the Schoolroom of the '80s. *Psychology Today* 19 (March), pp. 54–57.

1994a Why Schools Must Tell Girls: "You're Smart, You Can Do It." *USA Weekend* (February 4), pp. 4–6.

1994b *Failing at Fairness: How America's Schools Cheat Girls.* New York: Scribners.

Said, Edward W., et al.
1988 A Profile of the Palestinian People. In Edward W. Said

and Christopher Hitchens, eds., *Blaming the Victims*, pp. 235–296. London: Verso.

Salée, Daniel
1994   Identity Politics and Multiculturalism in Quebec. *Cultural Survival Quarterly* (Summer–Fall), pp. 89–94.

Salgado, Sebastião
1995   War Without End: Twenty Years After the Fall of Saigon, Thousands of Vietnamese Are Still Trying to Find a Home. *New York Times Magazine* (July 30), pp. 24–33.

Samuels, Frederick
1969   Color Sensitivity Among Honolulu's Haoles and Japanese. *Race* 11 (October), pp. 203–212.

1970   *The Japanese and the Haoles of Honolulu: Durable Group Interaction.* New Haven, CT: College and University Press.

Sanchez, George I.
1934   Bilingualism and Mental Measures. *Journal of Applied Psychology* 18 (December), pp. 765–772.

Sanchez, Sandra
1991   Feelings of Frustration Boil Over. *USA Today* (May 8), p. 3A.

1995   Increasingly, Immigrants Pursuing Citizenship. *USA Today* (March 7), p. 3A.

Sanders, Irwin T., and Morawska, Ewa T.
1975   *Polish-American Community Life: A Survey of Research.* Boston: Community Sociology Training Program.

Sandmeyer, Elmer Clarence, with an introduction by Daniels, Roger
1973   *The Anti-Chinese Movement in California.* Urbana: University of Illinois Press.

Savage, David G.
1995a   Plan to Boost Firms Owned by Minorities Is Assailed. *Los Angeles Times* (April 2), p. A14.

1995b   Court Deals Blow to School Desegregation Rules. *Los Angeles Times* (June 13), p. A15.

Sawyer, Jack
1972   On Male Liberation. *Civil Rights Digest* 5 (Winter), pp. 37–38.

Schaefer, Richard T.
1969   *The Ku Klux Klan: Continuity and Change.* Working Paper, No. 138. Chicago: Center for Social Organization Studies, University of Chicago.

1971   The Ku Klux Klan: Continuity and Change. *Phylon* 32 (Summer), pp. 143–157.

1976   *The Extent and Content of Racial Prejudice in Great Britain.* San Francisco, CA: R & E Research Associates.

1980   The Management of Secrecy: The Ku Klux Klan's Successful Secret. In Stanton K. Tefft, ed., *Secrecy: A Cross-Cultural Perspective,* pp. 161–177. New York; Human Sciences Press.

1986   Racial Prejudice in a Capitalist State: What Has Happened to the American Creed? *Phylon* 47 (September), pp. 192–198.

1987   Social Distance of Black College Students at a Predominantly White University. *Sociology and Social Research,* 72 (October), pp. 30–32.

1992   People of Color: The "Kaleidoscope" May Be a Better Way to Describe America Than "The Melting Pot." *Peoria Journal Star* (January 19), p. A7.

1996   Education and Prejudice: Unraveling the Relationship. *Sociological Quarterly* 37 (Winter), Forthcoming.

Schaefer, Richard T., and Lamm, Robert P.
1995 *Sociology,* 5th ed. New York: McGraw-Hill.

Schaefer, Richard T., and Schaefer, Sandra L.
1975 Reluctant Welcome: U.S. Responses to the South Vietnamese Refugees. *New Community* 4 (Autumn), pp. 366–370.

Schemo, Diana Jean
1994 Suburban Taxes Are Higher for Blacks, Analysis Shows. *New York Times* (August 17), pp. A1, B5.

Schermerhorn, R. A.
1970 *Comparative Ethnic Relations: A Framework for Theory and Research.* New York: Random House.

Schiff, Ze'en, and Ya'air, Ehud
1990 *Intifada.* New York: Simon & Schuster.

Schmelz, U. O., and Della Pergola, Sergio
1994 World Jewish Population, 1992. In David Singer, ed., *American Jewish Year Book, 1994,* pp. 465–489. New York: American Jewish Committee.

Schmidt, Robert
1994 American Indian Beliefs Still Separate and Unequal. *The Daily Citizen* (July 12), pp. 6, 11.

Schmidt, William E.
1988 Religious Leaders Try to Heal Rift in Chicago. *New York Times* (November 27), p. 14.

Schmitt, David E.
1974 *Violence in Northern Ireland: Ethnic Conflict and Radicalization in an International Setting.* Morristown, NJ: General Learning Press.

Schoenfeld, Eugen
1976 Jewish Americans: A Religo-Ethnic Community. In Anthony Dworkin and Rosalind J. Dworkin, eds., *The Minority Report: An Introduction to*

Racial and Ethnic Minorities, pp. 325–352. New York: Praeger.

Schrieke, Bertram J.
1936 *Alien Americans.* New York: Viking.

Schultz, Ray
1974 The Call of the Ghetto. *New York Times Magazine* (November 10), p. 34.

Schwartz, Felice
1989 Management Women and the New Facts of Life. *Harvard Business Review* 67 (January–February), pp. 65–76.

Schwartz, John
1994 Preserving Endangered Speeches. *Washington Post National Weekly Edition* 11 (March 21), p. 38.

Schwartz, Mildred A.
1967 *Trends in White Attitudes Toward Negroes.* Chicago: National Opinion Research Center.

Scott, Robin Fitzgerald
1974 Wartime Labor Problems and Mexican Americans in the War. In Manuel Servin, ed., *An Awakened Minority: The Mexican Americans,* 2d ed., pp. 134–142. Beverly Hills, CA: Glencoe Press.

Seale, Patrick
1980 Two Peoples—One Land. In *1980 Britannica Book of the Year,* pp. 64–69. Chicago: Encyclopedia Britannica.

Sears, David O., and McConahay, J. B.
1969 Participation in the Los Angeles Riot. *Social Problems* 17 (Summer), pp. 3–20.

1970 Racial Socialization, Comparison Levels, and the Watts Riot. *Journal of Social Issues* 26 (Winter), pp. 121–140.

1973 *The Politics of Violence: The New Urban Blacks and the Watts Riots.* Boston: Houghton Mifflin.

Selzer, Michael
  1972   *"Kike"—Anti-Semitism in America.* New York: Meridian.

Sentinel (Orlando)
  1993   Puerto Rico Says "No" to Statehood. *Chicago Tribune* (November 15), pp. 1–2.

Servin, Manuel P.
  1974   The Beginnings of California's Anti-Mexican Prejudice. In Manuel P. Servin, ed., *An Awakened Minority: The Mexican Americans,* 2d ed., pp. 2–26. Beverly Hills, CA: Glencoe Press.

Serwatka, Thomas S.; Deering, Sharia; and Grant, Patrick
  1995   Disproportionate Representation of African Americans in Emotionally Handicapped Classes. *Journal of Black Studies* 25 (March), pp. 492–506.

Severo, Richard
  1970   New York's Italians: A Question of Identity. *New York Times* (November 9), pp. 43, 50.

  1974   The Flight of the Wetbacks. *New York Times Magazine* (March 10), p. 17.

Seward World
  1988   Gangs in Chinatown—Extortion, Prostitution, and Drugs. 31 (April), p. 2.

Shaffer, Gwen
  1994   Asian Americans Organize for Justice. *Environmental Action* 25 (Winter 1994), pp. 30–33.

Shah, Sonia
  1994   Presenting the Blue Goddess. In Karin Aguilar-San Juan, ed., *The State of Asian America,* pp. 147–158. Boston: South End Press.

Shannon, Lyle W.
  1979   The Changing World View of Minority Migrants in an Urban Setting. *Human Organization* 38 (Spring), pp. 52–62.

Shapiro, Laura
  1988   When Is a Joke Not a Joke? *Newsweek* (May 23), p. 79.

Sharp, Deborah
  1994   A Culture Clash Divides Florida County. *USA Today* (May 18), p. 11A.

Sharp, Kathleen
  1993   Foul Play. *Ms.* 4 (September–October), pp. 22–26.

Sheils, Merrill
  1977   Teaching in English—Plus. *Newsweek* (February 7), pp. 64–65.

Shenker, Israel
  1974   How Yiddish Survives at 2 New York City Schools. *New York Times* (January 16), p. 68.

  1979   With Them, It's Always Strictly Kosher. *New York Times Magazine* (April 15), pp. 32, 33, 36–38, 40, 42.

Sheppard, Nathaniel, Jr.
  1994   Desegregation Ruling May Hit at Black Colleges' Roots. *Chicago Tribune* (July 10), sect. 5, pp. 8–9.

Sher, Julian
  1983   *White Hoods: Canada's Ku Klux Klan.* Vancouver, British Columbia: New Star Books.

Sherif, Musafer, and Sherif, Carolyn
  1969   *Social Psychology.* New York: Harper & Row.

Sherman, C. Bezalel
  1974   Immigration and Emigration: The Jewish Case. In Marshall Sklare, ed., *The Jew in American Society,* pp. 51–55. New York: Behrman House.

Sherry, Linda
  1992   New President at Chinese Six Co. *Asianweek* (January 10), p. 3.

Shin, Linda
  1971   Koreans in America, 1903–1945. In Amy Tachiki, Eddie Wong, Franklin Odo,

and Buck Wong, eds., *Roots: An Asian American Reader,* pp. 200–206. Los Angeles: Asian American Studies Center, UCLA.

Shipler, David K.
1981   Soviet Jews Choosing U.S., Put Israelis in a Quandary. *New York Times* (August 13), p. E5.

Shorris, Earl
1992   Latino, Sí. Hispanic, No. *New York Times* (October 28), p. A21.

Shreve, Anita, and Clemans, John
1980   The New Wave of Women Politicians. *New York Times Magazine* (October 19), pp. 28–31, 105–109.

Shuit, Douglas P.
1995   Filling the Void. *Los Angeles Times* (July 27), p. B2.

Siddiqi, Mohammad
1993   The Portrayal of Muslims and Islam in the U.S. Media. Paper presented at the conference on the Expression of American Religion in the Popular Media, Indianapolis.

Silberman, Charles E.
1971   *Crisis in the Classroom: The Remaking of American Education.* New York: Random House.

1985   *A Certain People.* New York: Summit.

Silva, Helga
1985   *The Children of Mariel.* Miami: Cuban American National Foundation.

Silva, Nelson Do Valle
1985   Updating the Cost of Not Being White in Brazil. In Pierre-Michel Fontaine, ed., *Race, Class, and Power in Brazil,* pp. 42–55. Los Angeles: Center for Afro-American Studies, UCLA.

Simmons, Alan B., and Keohane, Kieran
1992   Canadian Immigration Policy: State Strategies and the Quest for Legitimacy. *Canadian Review of Sociology and Anthropology* 29 (No. 4), 427–451.

Simon, Rita J.
1993   Old Minorities, New Immigrants: Aspirations, Hopes, and Fears. *Annals* 530 (November), pp. 61–73.

Simon, Rita J., and Simon, Julian L.
1982   Some Aspects of the Sociocultural Adjustment of Recent Soviet Immigrants to the United States. *Ethnic and Racial Studies* 5 (October), pp. 535–541.

Simons, Marlise
1988   Brazil's Blacks Feel Prejudice 100 Years After Slavery's End. *New York Times* (May 14), pp. 1, 6.

Simpson, Jacqueline C.
1995   Pluralism: The Evolution of a Nebulous Concept. *American Behavioral Scientist* 38 (January), pp. 459–477.

Skidmore, Thomas E.
1972   Toward a Comparative Analysis of Race Relations Since Abolition in Brazil and the United States. *Journal of Latin American Studies* 4 (May), pp. 1–28.

1974   *Black into White.* New York: Oxford University Press.

Sklare, Marshall
1971   *America's Jews.* New York: Random House.

1993   *Observing America's Jews.* Bedford, NH: Brandeis University Press.

Skocpol, Theda
1988   An "Uppity Generation" and the Revitalization of Macroscopic Sociology. In M. W.

Riley, ed., *Sociological Lives,*
pp. 145–159. Newbury Park,
CA: Sage.

Skolnick, Jerome
1969 *The Politics of Protest.* New
York: Simon & Schuster.

Slavin, Robert E.
1985 Cooperative Learning: Applying Contact Theory in Desegregated Schools. *Journal of Social
Issues* 41 (No. 3), pp. 45–62.

Slavin, Stephen L., and Pradt, Mary A.
1979 Anti-Semitism in Banking.
Bankers Magazine 162
(July–August), pp. 19–21.

1982 *The Einstein Syndrome: Cor-
porate Anti-Semitism in
America Today.* Washington,
DC: University Press of
America.

Sloan, George
1980 30 Pekin High School Students Walk Out of Classes.
Peoria Journal Star (September 4), p. 4.

Smith, Erma R.
1991 *What Color Is the News?* San
Francisco: Center for Integration and Improvement Association, San Francisco State
University.

Smith, M. Estelli
1982 Tourism and Native Americans. *Cultural Survival Quarterly* 6 (Summer), pp. 10–12.

Smith, Tom W.
1990 *Jewish Attitudes Toward Blacks
and Race Relations.* New York:
American Jewish Committee.

1991 *What Do Americans Think
About Jews?* New York: American Jewish Committee.

1994 *Anti-Semitism in Contemporary America.* New York:
American Jewish Committee.

Smith, Tom W., and Sheatsley, Paul B.
1984 American Attitudes Toward
Race Relations. *Public Opinion* 7 (October–November),
pp. 14–15, 50–53.

Snipp, C. Matthew
1980 Determinants of Employment
in Wisconsin Native American
Communities. *Growth and
Change* 11 (No. 2), pp. 39–47.

1989 *American Indians: The First of
This Land.* New York: Sage.

Sochen, June
1982 *Herstory: A Woman's View of
American History,* 2d ed. Palo
Alto, CA: Mayfield.

Somners, Christina Hoff
1994 *Who Stole Feminism?* New
York: McGraw-Hill.

Son, In Soo; Model, Suzanne W.; and
Fisher, Gene A.
1989 Polarization and Progress in
the Black Community: Earnings and Status Gains for
Young Black Males in the Era
of Affirmative Action. *Sociological Forum* 4 (September),
pp. 309–327.

Sonenshein, Raphael J.
1993 *Politics in Black and White:
Race and Power in Los Angeles.* Princeton: Princeton University Press.

Song, Tae-Hyon
1991 Social Contact and Ethnic
Distance Between Koreans
and the U.S. Whites in the
United States. Unpublished
paper, Western Illinois University, Macomb.

Sontag, Deborah
1993 Émigrés in New York: Work
off the Books. *New York Times*
(June 13), pp. 1, 42.

Sorensen, Elaine
1994 *Comparable Worth. Is It a
Worthy Policy?* Princeton:
Princeton University Press.

Soto, Lourdes Diaz
1991 Understanding
Bilingual/Bicultural Young
Children. *Young Children* 46
(January), pp. 30–36.

South, Scott J., and Spitze, Glenna
1994 Housework in Marital and Nonmarital Households. *American Sociological Review* 59 (June), pp. 327–347.

South African Department of Foreign Affairs and Information
1983 *South Africa, 1983: Official Yearbook of the Republic of South Africa.* Johannesburg: Republic of South Africa.

South African Institute of Race Relations (SAIRR)
1992 *Race Relations Survey, 1991/92.* Johannesburg: SAIRR.
1994 *Race Relations Survey, 1993/94.* Johannesburg: SAIRR.
1995 *Race Relations Survey, 1994/95.* Johannesburg: SAIRR.

Southern, David W.
1987 *Gunnar Myrdal and Black-White Relations.* Baton Rouge: Louisiana State University.

Sparks, Allister
1995 *Tomorrow Is Another Country: The Inside Story of South Africa's Road to Change.* New York: Hill & Wang.

Spearman, Diana
1968 Enoch Powell's Postbag. *New Society* 11 (May 9), pp. 667–669.

Spector, Michael
1990 In New York's Chinatown, the Newest Frontier. *Washington Post National Weekly Edition* 8 (December 24), p. 22.

Spencer, Gary
1987 JAP-Baiting on a College Campus: An Example of Gender and Ethnic Stereotyping. Unpublished paper, Syracuse University.

Spicer, Edward
1980 American Indians. In Stephen Thernstrom, ed., *Harvard Encyclopedia of American Ethnic Groups*, pp. 58–122. Cambridge: Belknap Press of Harvard University Press.

Spiegel, Irving
1973a Jewish Official Fears a Backlash. *New York Times* (October 27), p. 9.
1973b Jews Are Warned of Oil Backlash. *New York Times* (November 16), p. 35.
1974 Rabbi Deplores Small Families. *New York Times* (January 24), p. 20.
1975 Educators Called Remiss About Bias. *New York Times* (November 9), p. 63.

Spillman, Susan
1995 New Hispanic Films Defy Clichés. *USA Today* (May 2), p. 4D.

Spindler, George, and Spindler, Louise
1984 *Dreamers with Power: The Menominee.* Prospect Heights, IL: Waveland Press.

Spirit of Crazy Horse
1994 *Chronology of the Case of Leonard Pettier.* (March–April), pp. 6–7.

Squitieri, Tom
1989 Many Await Restitution. *USA Today* (September 13), p. 3A.

Stains, Laurence R.
1994 The Latinization of Allentown, PA. *New York Times Magazine* (May 15), pp. 56–62.

Stampp, Kenneth M.
1956 *The Peculiar Institution: Slavery in the Ante-Bellum South.* New York: Random House.

Stan, Robert
1985 Samba, Candomble, Quilombo: Black Performance and Brazilian Cinema. *Journal of Ethnic Studies* 13 (Fall), pp. 55–84.

Staples, Brent
1994   *Parallel Times: Growing Up
        Black and White.* New York:
        Pantheon Books.

Staples, Robert, and Johnson, Leanor
Boulin
1993   *Black Families at the Cross-
        roads: Challenges and
        Prospects.* San Francisco:
        Jossey-Bass.

Stark, Rodney
1987   Correcting Church Mem-
        bership Rates: 1971 and
        1980. *Review of Religious
        Research* 29 (September),
        pp. 69–77.

Stark, Rodney, and Glock, Charles
1968   *American Piety: The Nature of
        Religious Commitment.*
        Berkeley: University of Cali-
        fornia Press.

Starr, Paul, and Roberts, Alden
1981   Attitudes Toward Indochi-
        nese Refugees: An Empirical
        Study. *Journal of Refugee
        Resettlement* 1 (August),
        pp. 51–61.

Statistics Canada
1993   *Canada Year Book 1994.*
        Ottawa, Ontario: Statistics
        Canada.

Stedman, Raymond William
1982   *Shadows of the Indian: Stereo-
        typing in American Culture.*
        Norman: University of Okla-
        homa Press.

Steinberg, Stephen
1977   *The Academic Melting Pot.*
        New Brunswick, NJ: Transac-
        tion Books.

Steiner, Stan
1968   *The New Indians.* New York:
        Harper & Row.

1974   *The Islands: The Worlds of the
        Puerto Ricans.* New York:
        Harper & Row.

1976   *The Vanishing White Man.*
        New York: Harper & Row.

Steinfels, Peter
1992   Debating Intermarriage, and
        Jewish Survival. *New York
        Times* (October 18), pp. 1, 16.

Stepick, Alex
1991   The Haitian Informal Sector
        in Miami. *City and Society* 5
        (June), pp. 10–22.

Stern, Kenneth S.
1991   *Crown Heights: A Case Study
        in Anti-Semitism and Commu-
        nity Relations.* New York:
        American Jewish Committee.

Stevens, Evelyn P.
1973   Machismo and Marianismo.
        Society 10 (September–Octo-
        ber), pp. 57–63.

Stevens-Arroyo, Antonio M., and
Díaz-Ramírez, Ana María
1982   Puerto Ricans in the States. In
        Anthony Dworkin and Ros-
        alind Dworkin (eds.) *The
        Minority Report,* 2d ed., pp.
        196–232. New York: Holt.

Stevensen, Richard W.
1994   Peace on Irish Horizon Doesn't
        Spell Prosperity. *New York
        Times* (September 4), p. E3.

Stoddard, Ellyn R.
1973   *Mexican Americans.* New
        York: Random House.

1976a   A Conceptual Analysis of the
        "Alien Invasion": Institutional-
        ized Support of Illegal Mexi-
        can Aliens in the U.S. *Interna-
        tional Migration Review* 10
        (Summer), pp. 157–189.

1976b   Illegal Mexican Labor in the
        Borderlands: Institutionalized
        Support of an Unlawful Prac-
        tice. *Pacific Sociological
        Review* 19 (April), pp.
        175–210.

Stone, Andrea
1992   No Simple Answers to
        Rebuilding a Community.
        USA Today (May 5), p. 4A.

Stonequist, Everett V.
1937   *The Marginal Man: A Study in Personality and Culture Conflict.* New York: Scribners.

Street, Richard Steven
1992   New Voices from Rural Communities. Portland, OR: NewSage Press and California Rural Legal Assistance.

Stuart, Reginald
1982   Judge Overturns Arkansas Law on Creationism. *New York Times* (January 6), pp. QA1, B7–B8.

1984   Protestants Stepping Up Puerto Rico Conversion. *New York Times* (February 14), p. 13.

Suarez, Manuel
1985   F.B.I. Discerns Big Gain on Puerto Rico Terror. *New York Times* (August 8), p. 10.

Sullivan, Cheryl
1986   Seeking Self-sufficiency. *Christian Science Monitor* (June 25), pp. 16–17.

Sun, Lena H.
1995   A Cultural Park and Trust. *Washington Post National Weekly Edition* 12 (February 27), p. 9.

Sundiata, Ibrahim K.
1987   Late Twentieth Century Patterns of Race Relations in Brazil and the United States. *Phylon* 48 (March), pp. 62–76.

Sung, Betty Lee
1967   *Mountains of Gold: The Story of the Chinese in America.* New York: Macmillan.

Suro, Roberto
1994   Different Strokes for Different Refugees. *Washington Post National Weekly Edition* 11 (July 4), p. 23.

Sutherland, Elizabeth
1970   Colonized Women: The Chicano. In Robin Morgan, ed.,

Sisterhood Is Powerful, pp. 376–379. New York: Random House.

Suttles, Gerald D.
1972   *The Social Construction of Communities.* Chicago: University of Chicago Press.

Svensson, Craig K.
1989   Representation of American Blacks in Clinical Trials of New Drugs. *Journal of the American Medical Association* 261 (January 13), pp. 263–265.

Swagerty, William R.
1983   Native Peoples and Early European Contacts. In Mary Kupiec Clayton, Elliot J. Gorn, and Peter W. Williams, eds., *Encyclopedia of American Social History,* pp. 15–16. New York: Scribners.

Swan, Yvonne
1993   The Light Within. In Ronnie Farley, ed., *Women of the Native Struggle,* p. 62. New York: Orion Books.

Sweet, Jill D.
1990   The Portals of Tradition: Tourism in the American Southwest. *Cultural Survival Quarterly* 14 (No. 2), pp. 6–8.

Tachibana, Judy
1990   Model Minority Myth Presents Unrepresentative Portrait of Asian Americans, Many Educators Say. *Black Issues in Higher Education* 6 (March 1), pp. 1, 11.

Takagi, Dana Y.
1992   *The Retreat from Race: Asian-American Admissions and Racial Politics.* New Brunswick, NJ: Rutgers University Press.

Takaki, Ronald
1989   *Strangers from a Different Shore: A History of Asian Americans.* Boston: Little, Brown.

Takezawa, Yasuko I.
1991   Children of Inmates:
        The Effects of the Redress
        Movement Among Third
        Generation Japanese
        Americas. *Qualitative
        Sociology* 14 (Spring), pp.
        39–56.

Talbot, Tony
1993   The Dream Is No Longer
        Havana. *New York Times*
        (September 12), Book Review
        Section, p. 12.

Tamir, Orit
1991   Relocation of Navajo
        from Hopi Partitioned
        Land in Pinon. *Human
        Organization* 50 (No. 2),
        pp. 173–187.

Tannenbaum, Frank
1946   *Slave and Citizen.* New York:
        Random House.

Taylor, Donald M., and Moghaddan,
Fathali
1994   *Theories of Intergroup Rela-
        tions: International Social
        Psychological Perspectives,*
        2d ed. Westport, CT:
        Praeger.

Taylor, Frank J.
1942   The People Nobody Wants.
        The Saturday Evening Post
        2, 142 (May 9), pp. 24–25,
        64, 66–67.

Taylor, Paul
1993   The Fault Line Between
        South Africa's Blacks. *Wash-
        ington Post National Weekly
        Edition* 10 (November 22),
        p. 18.

Taylor, Robert Joseph; Chatters, Linda
M.; Tucker, M. Belinda; and Lewis, Edith
1990   Developments in Research on
        Black Families: A Decade
        Review. *Journal of Marriage
        and the Family* 52 (Novem-
        ber), pp. 993–1014.

Taylor, Stuart, Jr.
1987   High Court Backs Basing Pro-
        motion on a Racial Quota.
        New York Times (February
        26), pp. 1, 14.

1988   Justices Back New York Law
        Ending Sex Bias by Big Clubs.
        New York Times (June 21), pp.
        A1, A18.

Telles, Edward E.
1992   Residential Segregation by
        Skin Color in Brazil. *American
        Sociological Review* 57 (April),
        pp. 186–197.

ten Brock, Jacobus; Barnhart, Edward N.;
and Matson, Floyd W.
1954   *Prejudice, War and the Con-
        stitution.* Berkeley: University
        of California Press.

Tenenbaum, Shelly
1993   The Jews. In Mary Kupiec
        Coyton, Elliot J. Gorn, and
        Peter W. William, eds., *Ency-
        clopedia of American Social
        History,* pp. 769–781. New
        York: Scribners.

Terchek, Ronald J.
1977   Conflict and Cleavage in
        Northern Ireland. *The Annals*
        (September), pp. 47–59.

Terry, Clifford
1975   Chicagoans—Pro Soccer.
        Chicago Tribune Magazine
        (May 5), p. 26.

Terry, Don
1994   Minister Farrakhan: Conserv-
        ative Militant. *New York
        Times* (March 3), pp. A1, A10.

Terry, Wallace
1984   *Bloods: An Oral History of the
        Vietnam War by Black Veter-
        ans.* New York: Random
        House.

Third World Journalists
1994   *Third World Guide 93/94.*
        Toronto: Garamond Press.

Thomas, Curlew O., and Thomas, Barbara Boston
1984   Blacks' Socioeconomic Status and the Civil Rights Movement's Decline, 1970–1979: An Examination of Some Hypotheses. *Phylon* 45 (March), pp. 40–51.

Thomas, Dorothy S.
1952   *The Salvage.* Berkeley: University of California Press.

Thomas, Dorothy S., and Nishimoto, Richard S.
1946   *The Spoilage: Japanese-American Evacuation and Resettlement.* Berkeley: University of California Press.

Thomas, Piri
1967   *Down These Mean Streets.* New York: Signet.

Thomas, William Isaac
1923   *The Unadjusted Girl.* Boston: Little, Brown.

Thornton, Russell
1981   Demographic Antecedents of the 1890 Ghost Dance. *American Sociological Review* 46 (February), pp. 88–96.

1991   North American Indians and the Demography of Contact. Paper presented at the annual meeting of the American Sociological Association, Cincinnati.

Tienda, Marta
1989   Puerto Ricans and the Underclass Debate. *Annals* 501 (January), pp. 105–119.

Time
1969   The Little Strike That Grew to La Causa. (July 4), pp. 16–22.

1972   What It Means to Be Jewish. (April 10), pp. 54–64.

1974a   Are You a Jew? (September 2), pp. 56, 59.

1974b   Brown's Bomb. (November 25), pp. 16, 19.

1975   The A.J.A.'s Fast Rising Sons (October 20), pp. 26, 31.

Tirado, Miguel David
1970   Mexican American Community Political Organization. *Aztlan* 1 (Spring), pp. 53–78.

Tomaskovic-Devey, Donald
1993a   *Gender and Racial Inequality at Work: The Sources and Consequences of Job Segregation.* Ithaca, NY: ILR Press.

1993b   The Gender and Race Composition of Jobs and the Male/Female, White/Black Pay Gaps. *Social Forces* 72 (September), pp. 45–76.

Tomlinson, T. M.
1969   The Development of a Riot Ideology Among Urban Negroes. In Allen D. Grimshaw, ed., *Racial Violence in the United States*, pp. 226–235. Chicago: Aldine.

Toner, Robin
1987   Bible Is Being Translated into a Southern Coastal Tongue Born of Slavery. *New York Times* (March 1), p. 18.

Torres, Andres, and Bonilla, Frank
1993   Decline Within Decline: The New York Perspective. In Rebecca Morales and Frank Bonilla, eds., *Latinos in a Changing U.S. Economy*, pp. 85–108. Newbury Park, NJ: Sage.

Trask, Haunami-Kay
1993   Hawaiian Sovereignty Drive Signals Trouble in Paradise. *USA Today* (November 3), p. 11A.

Treen, Joseph
1983   Apartheid's Harsh Grip. *Newsweek* (March 28), pp. 31–32, 37.

Trimble, Albert
1976   An Era of Great Change, A Single Decency Is Goal for Oglala Sioux. *Wassaja* 4 (May), p. 5.

Trottier, Richard W.
1981 Charters of Panethnic Identity: Indigenous American Indians and Immigrant Asian-Americans. In Charles F. Keyes, ed., *Ethnic Change*, pp. 272–305. Seattle: University of Washington Press.

Trueheart, Charles
1995a In Quebec, Separation from Separatists Is the Goal. *Washington Post National Weekly Edition* 12 (February 13), p. 19.

1995b An Issue Left Unresolved. *Washington Post National Weekly Edition* 13 (November 16), p. 16.

Tsuchigane, Robert, and Dodge, Norton
1974 *Economic Discrimination Against Women in the United States: Measures and Change.* Lexington, MA: Heath.

Tumin, Melvin M., with Feldman, Arnold
1961 *Social Class and Social Change in Puerto Rico.* Princeton: Princeton University Press.

Tuohy, William
1994 Many Protestants Skeptical About Ulster Peace. *Los Angeles Times* (October 23), p. A4.

Ture, Kwame, and Hamilton, Charles
1992 *Black Power: The Politics of Liberation.* New York: Vintage Books.

Turner, Margery; Struyck, Raymond J.; and Yinger, John
1991 *Housing Discrimination Study: Synthesis.* Washington, DC: Urban Institute.

Turner, Wallace
1972 New Hawaii Economy Stirs Minority Upset. *New York Times* (August 13), pp. 1, 46.

Turque, Bill
1993 Playing a Different Tune. *Newsweek* (June 28), pp. 30–31.

Twining, Mary Arnold
1985 Movement and Dance on the Sea Islands. *Journal of Black Studies* 15 (June), pp. 463–479.

Tyler, Gus
1972 White Worker/Blue Mood. *Dissent* 190 (Winter), pp. 190–196.

Tyler, S. Lyman
1973 *A History of Indian Policy.* Washington, DC: U.S. Government Printing Office.

Uchida, Yoshiko
1982 *Desert Exile.* Seattle: University of Washington Press.

USA Today
1994 Urban League Urges a "Marshall Plan," (January 21), p. 3A.

Usdansky, Margaret L.
1991 USA at Home: Streets Still Isolate Race. *USA Today* (November 11), pp. 1A, 2A.

1992a Old Ethnic Influences Still Play in Cities. *USA Today* (August 4), p. 9A.

1992b Asian Immigrants Changing Face of Rural USA. *USA Today* (September 10), p. 10A.

1993 Census: Languages Not Foreign at Home. *USA Today* (April 28), pp. A1, A2.

Valentine, Charles A.
1968 *Culture and Poverty: Critique and Counter-Proposals.* Chicago: University of Chicago Press.

Van Deburg, William L.
1992 *New Day in Babylon: The Black Power Movement and American Culture. 1965–1975.* Chicago: University of Chicago Press.

van den Berghe, Pierre L.
1965 *South Africa: A Study in Conflict.* Middletown, CT: Wesleyan University.

1978 *Race and Racism: A Comparative Perspective,* 2d ed. New York: Wiley.

Vasquez, Enriqueta Longauex y
1970 The Mexican-American Women. In Robin Morgan, ed., *Sisterhood Is Powerful,* pp. 379–384. New York: Random House.

Vaughan, Mary K.
1974 Tourism in Puerto Rico. In Adalberto Lopez and James Petra, eds., *Puerto Rico and Puerto Ricans: Studies in History and Society,* pp. 271–295. New York: Wiley.

Vecoli, Rudolph J.
1970 Ethnicity: A Neglected Dimension of American History. In Herbert J. Bass, ed., *The State of American History,* pp. 70–88. Chicago: Quadrangle Books.

1987 Hansen's Classic Essay Revisited. Presentation at Ethnic Mosaic of the Quad Cities Conference, Rock Island, IL.

Vega, William A., et al.
1986 Cohesion and Adaptability in Mexican-American and Anglo Families. *Journal of Marriage and Family* 48 (November), pp. 857–867.

Vidal, David
1977 Bilingual Instruction Is Thriving but Criticized. *New York Times* (January 30), p. E19.

Vigil, Maurilio
1990 The Ethnic Organization as an Instrument of Political and Social Change: MALDEF, a Case Study. *The Journal of Ethnic Studies* 18 (Spring), pp. 15–31.

Wacquant, Loïc J. D.
1993 Redrawing the Urban Color Line: The State of the Ghetto in the 1990s. In Craig Calhoun and George Ritzer, eds., *Social Problems,* pp. 663–690. New York: McGraw-Hill.

Wagley, Charles, and Harris, Marvin
1958 *Minorities in the New World: Six Case Studies.* New York: Columbia University Press.

Waite, Juan J.
1993 Since 1541, a Deep Grudge; Now, a Chance for Peace. *USA Today* (December 16), p. 5A.

Waitzkin, Howard
1986 *The Second Sickness: Contradictions of Capitalist Health Care.* Chicago: University of Chicago Press.

Waldman, Carl
1985 *Atlas of North American Indians.* New York: Facts on File.

Wallace, Steven P.
1989 The New Urban Latinos: Central Americans in a Mexican Immigrant Environment. *Urban Affairs Quarterly* 25 (December), pp. 239–264.

Walters, Pamela Barnhouse
1994 Education. In Craig Calhoun and George Ritzer, eds. *Introduction to Social Problems,* pp. 1017–1042. New York: McGraw-Hall.

Wang, L. Ling-Chi
1991 Roots and Changing Identity of the Chinese in the United States. *Daedalus* 120 (Spring), pp. 181–206.

Warner, Sam Bass, Jr.
1968 *The Private City: Philadelphia in Three Periods of Its Growth.* Philadelphia: University of Pennsylvania Press.

Warner, W. Lloyd, and Srole, Leo
1945 *The Social Systems of American Ethnic Groups.* New Haven: Yale University Press.

Warren, Robert
1994 Immigration's Share of U.S. Population Growth: How We Measure It Matters. *Population Today* (September), p. 3.

Warren, Robert, and Kraly, Ellen Percy
1985　*The Elusive Exodus: Emigration from the United States.*
Washington, DC: Population
Reference Bureau.

Washburn, Wilcomb E.
1984　A Fifty-Year Perspective on
the Indian Reorganization
Act. *American Anthropologist*
86 (June), pp. 279–289.

Washington, Booker T.
1900　*Up from Slavery: An Autobiography.* New York; A. L. Burt.

Watanabe, Colin
1973　Self-Expression and the Asian-
American Experience. *Personnel and Guidance Journal* 51
(February), pp. 392–396.

Waters, Harry F.
1994　Listening to Their Latin Beat.
Newsweek 123 (March 28),
pp. 42–43.

Waters, Harry F., and Huck, Janet
1989　Networking Women.
Newsweek 113 (March 13),
pp. 48–54.

Watson, Russell
1988　Your Jewishness Is Not Good
Enough. *Newsweek* 112
(November 28), p. 51.

Wax, Murray L.
1971　*Indian Americans: Unity and
Diversity.* Englewood Cliffs,
NJ: Prentice-Hall.

Wax, Murray L., and Buchanan, Robert W.
1975　*Solving "the Indian Problem":
The White Man's Burdensome
Business.* New York: New York
Times Book Company.

Wax, Rosalie H.
1967　The Warrior Dropouts. *Transaction* 4 (May), pp. 40–46.

Waxman, Chaim I.
1983　*America's Jews in Transition.*
Philadelphia: Temple University Press.

Webb, Susan L.
1992　*Step Forward: Sexual Harassment in the Workplace.* New
York: Master-Media.

Webster, Peggy Lovell, and Dwyer,
Jeffrey W.
1988　The Cost of Being Nonwhite
in Brazil. *Social Science
Research* (January), pp.
136–142.

Weglyn, Michi
1976　*Years of Infamy.* New York:
Quill Paperbacks.

Wei, William
1993　*The Asian America Movement.*
Philadelphia: Temple University Press.

Weiss, Melford S.
1974　*Valley City: A Chinese Community in America.* Cam-
bridge, MA: Schenkman.

Weitz, Rose
1992　College Students' Images of
African American, Mexican
American, and Jewish American Women. Paper presented
at the annual meeting of the
American Sociological Association, Pittsburgh.

Wellington, Alison J.
1994　Accounting for the
Male/Female Wage Gap
Among Whites: 1976 and 1985.
American Sociological Review
59 (December), pp. 839–848.

Wells, Robert N., Jr.
1989　Native Americans' Needs
Overlooked by Colleges.
Unpublished paper.

1991　Indian Education from the
Tribal Perspective: A Survey
of American Indian Tribal
Leaders. Unpublished paper.

Weppner, Robert S.
1971　Urban Economic Opportuni-
ties. In Jack O. Waddell and
O. Michael Watson, eds., *The
American Indian in Urban
Society,* pp. 44–273. Boston:
Little, Brown.

Wertheimer, Jack
1994   Family Values and the Jews. *Commentary* 97 (January), pp. 30–34.

Whitman, David
1987   For Latinos, a Growing Divide. *U.S. News and World Report* (August 10), pp. 47–49.

Whyte, John H.
1986   How Is the Boundary Maintained Between the Two Communities in Northern Ireland? *Ethnic and Racial Studies* 9 (April), pp. 219–234.

Wickham, DeWayne
1993   Subtle Racism Thrives. *USA Today* (October 25), p. 2A.

Wiley, Ed
1994   How Far Have We Come Since Brown? *Focus* 22 (June), pp. 5–6.

Wilkinson, Glen A.
1966   Indian Tribal Claims Before the Court of Claims. *Georgetown Law Journal* 55 (December), pp. 511–528.

Williams, Norma
1990   *The Mexican American Family: Tradition and Change.* Dix Hills, NY: General Hall.

Willie, Charles V.
1978   The Inclining Significance of Race. *Society* 15 (July–August), pp. 10, 12–13.
1979   *The Caste and Class Controversy.* Bayside, NY: General Hall.

Wilson, James Q., and Banfield, Edward C.
1964   Public Regardingness as a Value Premise in Voting Behavior. *American Political Science Review* 58 (December), pp. 876–887.

Wilson, William J.
1973   *Power, Racism and Privilege: Race Relations in Theoretical and Sociohistorical Perspectives.* New York: Macmillan.

1980   *The Declining Significance of Race: Blacks and Changing American Institutions,* 2d ed. Chicago: University of Chicago Press.
1987a   *The Truly Disadvantaged: The Inner City, The Underclass, and Public Policy.* Chicago: University of Chicago Press.
1987b   The Ghetto Underclass and the Social Transformation of the Inner City. Paper presented at the annual meeting of the American Association for the Advancement of Science, Chicago.
1988   The Ghetto Underclass and the Social Transformation of the Inner City. *The Black Scholar* 19 (May–June), pp. 10–17.
1991   Poverty, Joblessness, and Family Structure in the Inner City: A Comparative Perspective. Paper presented at the Chicago Urban Poverty and Family Life Conference.
1992   The Plight of Black Male Job-Seekers. *Focus* (September), pp. 7–8.

Winant, Howard
1989   The Other Side of the Process: Racial Formation in Contemporary Brazil. Paper presented at the annual meeting of the American Sociological Association, San Francisco.
1994   *Racial Conditions: Politics, Theory, Comparisons.* Minneapolis: University of Minnesota Press.

Winkler, Karen
1990a   Scholars Say Issues of Diversity Have "Revolutionized" Field of Chicano Studies. *Chronicle of Higher Education* 37 (September 26), pp. A1, A6, A8.
1990b   Researcher's Examination of California's Poor Latino Population Prompts Debate over the Traditional Definitions of the Underclass. *Chronicle of Higher Education* 37 (October 10), pp. A5, A8.

Winks, Robin W.
1971   *The Blacks in Canada: A History.* Montreal, Quebec: McGill-Queen's University Press.

Winsberg, Morton
1994   Specific Hispanics. *American Demographics* 16 (February), pp. 44–53.

Wirth, Louis
1928   *The Ghetto.* Chicago: University of Chicago Press.

Witt, Shirley Hill
1970   Nationalistic Trends Among American Indians. In Stuart Levine and Nancy Oestreich Lurie, eds., *The American Indian Today,* pp. 93–127. Baltimore: Penguin.

Wittstock, Laura Waterman, and Salinas, Elaine J.
1994   A Brief History of the American Indian Movement. *News from Indian Country* (Late August), pp. 6–7.

Wolf, Richard, and Benedetto, Richard
1992   Bush Moves "to Restore Hope." *USA Today* (May 13), p. 4A.

Wolfe, Ann G.
1972   The Invisible Jewish Poor. *Journal of Jewish Communal Sciences* 48 (No. 3), pp. 259–265.

Wolfe, Tom
1969   The New Yellow Peril. *Esquire* (December), p. 190.

Woll, Allen
1981   How Hollywood Has Portrayed Hispanics. *New York Times* (March 1), pp. D17, 22.

Wong, Bernard P.
1982   *Chinatown.* New York: Holt, Rinehart & Winston.

Wong, Eugene F.
1985   Asian American Middleman Minority Theory: The Framework of an American Myth. *The Journal of Ethnic Studies* 13 (Spring), pp. 51–88.

Wong, Morrison G.
1991   Rise in Anti-Asian Activities in the United States. Paper presented at the annual meeting of the American Sociological Association, Cincinnati.

1995   Chinese Americans. In Pyong Gap Min, ed., *Asian Americans: Contemporary Trends and Issues,* pp. 58–94. Thousand Oaks, CA: Sage.

Woodrum, Eric
1981   An Assessment of Japanese American Assimilation, Pluralism, and Subordination. *American Journal of Sociology* 87 (July), pp. 157–169.

Woodson, Carter G.
1968   *The African Background Outlined.* New York: Negro Universities Press.

Woodward, C. Vann
1974   *The Strange Career of Jim Crow,* 3d ed. New York: Oxford University Press.

Woodward, Kenneth L.
1991   The Intermarrying Kind. *Newsweek* 118 (July 22), pp. 48–49.

Worthington, Rogers
1993   School Desegregation Efforts Divide Town. *Chicago Tribune* (December 13), p. 3.

Wright, Mary Bowen
1980   Indochinese. In Stephen Thernstrom, ed., *Harvard Encyclopedia of American Ethnic Groups,* pp. 508–513. Cambridge: Belknap Press of Harvard University Press.

Wright, Paul, and Gardner, Robert W.
1983   *Ethnicity, Birthplace, and Achievement: The Changing Hawaii Mosaic.* Honolulu: East–West Population Institute.

Wright, Susan
1993   Blaming the Victim, Blaming Society, or Blaming the Discipline: Fixing Responsibility for Poverty and Homelessness. *Sociological Quarterly* 34 (No. 1), pp. 1–16.

Wrong, Dennis H.
1972   How Important Is Social Class? *Dissent* 19 (Winter), pp. 278–285.

Wu, Cheng-Tsu
1972   *Chink!* New York: Meridian.

Wuthnow, Robert
1982   Anti-Semitism and Stereotyping. In Arthur G. Miller, ed., *In the Eye of the Beholder,* pp. 137–187. New York: Praeger.

Yancey, William L.; Erickson, Eugene P.; and Juliani, Richard N.
1976   Emergent Ethnicity: A Review and Reformation. *American Sociological Review* 41 (June), pp. 391–403.

Yee, Albert H.
1973   Myopic Perceptions and Textbooks: Chinese Americans' Search for Identity. *Journal of Social Issues* 29 (No. 2), pp. 99–113.

Yee, Min S.
1972a   Busing Comes to Chinatown. *Race Relations Reporter* 3 (January), pp. 18–21.

1972b   Cracks in the Great Wall of Chinatown. *Ramparts* 7 (October), pp. 34–38.

Yinger, J. Milton
1976   Ethnicity in Complex Societies: Structural, Cultural, and Characterological Factors. In Lewis Coser and Otto Larsen, eds., *The Uses of Controversy in Sociology,* pp. 197–216. New York: Free Press.

Yoneda, Karl
1971   100 Years of Japanese Labor History in the USA. In Amy Tachiki, Eddie Wong, Franklin Odo, and Buck Wong, eds., *Roots: An Asian American Reader,* pp. 150–158. Los Angeles: Asian American Studies Center, UCLA.

Yu, Elena S. H.
1980   Filipino Migration and Community Organizations in the United States. *California Sociologist* 3 (Summer), pp. 76–102.

Yuan, D. Y.
1963   Voluntary Segregation: A Study of New York Chinatown. *Phylon* 24 (Fall), pp. 255–265.

Zenner, Walter P.
1991   *Minorities in the Middle: A Cross-Cultural Analysis.* Albany: State University of New York Press.

Zhou, Min, and Kamo, Yoshinori
1994   An Analysis of Earnings Patterns for Chinese, Japanese, and Non-Hispanic White Males in the United States. *Sociological Quarterly* 35 (No. 4), pp. 581–602.

Zhou, Min, and Logan, John R.
1989   Returns on Human Capital in Ethnic Enclaves. *American Sociological Review* 54 (October), pp. 809–833.

Zich, Arthur
1986   Japanese Americans, Home at Last. *National Geographic* 169 (April), pp. 512–539.

Ziegler, Dolores
1992   Family Associations: Role in a Racist American Society. *Asianweek* (August 28), pp. 17, 19.

Zinn, Maxine Baca, and Dill, Bonnie Thornton, eds.
1994   *Women of Color in U.S. Society.* Philadelphia: Temple University Press.

Zinsmeister, Karl
1988   Black Demographics. *Public Opinion* 10 (January–February), pp. 41–44.

Zorn, Eric
1995   American Justice Sees Black and White over Death Penalty. *Chicago Tribune* (May 4), sect. 2, p. 1.

Zweigenhaft, Richard L., and Domhoff, William G.
1982   *Jews in the Protestant Establishment.* New York: Praeger.

Credits

Index

Aaron, Henry, 4
Aberbach, Joel D., 212
abolitionists, 194–195, 217
Aboriginal Peoples, 467–469
abortion, 451–452
Abramson, Harold J., 126
Abron, JoNina M., 213
absolute deprivation, 72–73, 94
Abzug, Bella, 453
Acosta, Oscar Zeta, 298
Acosta-Belén, Edna, 321
Acuña, Rodolfo, 284, 301
Adams, David Wallace, 179
Adams, Gerry, 475
Adams, Romanzo, 340
Adarand Construction v. Pena, 89, 90
Adler, Patricia A., 432
Adler, Patricia Rae, 281
Adorno, T. W., 47–48, 49
affirmative action, 71, 87–92, 94, 231
Afonso Arinos law, 465
Africa, 193–194
African Americans, 4, 5, 16, 25–27, 28, 46, 50–51, 53, 55, 56, 57–59, 63, 75, 77, 79–87, 90, 102, 124–125, 126–127, 131, 133–134, 189–250, 259, 290, 329–331, 338, 407–409, 410, 430–431, 454–456
Afrikaners, 483–485
Afro-Canadians, 471–472
Afrocentric perspective, 32–33, 36, 127
Age discrimination, 11
Aguilar-San Juan, Karin, 352
AIDS, 11
AJA. *See* Americans of Japanese Ancestry
Alaracón, Odette, 312
Alaska Native Settlement Act of 1971, 171
Alaskan Federation of Natives (AFN), 171
Alba, Richard D., 79, 128, 135, 148, 401

Albanians, 5
Alcatraz occupation, 170–171
Alianza Federal de Mercedes, 284
Alien Act, 101
Alien Land Act, 376, 384–385
aliterate, 259
Allen, Irving Lewis, 68, 236
Allen, Richard, 336
Allen, Walter R., 248
Allotment Act, 154, 159
Allport, Gordon W., 21, 47, 62, 68, 401
Alvarez, María D., 321
Alvarez, Rodolfo, 301
amalgamation, 29, 36
Ambert, Alba N., 321
American Colonialization Society, 25–26
American Federation of Labor (AFL), 201
American Indian Movement (AIM), 156, 170, 171–174
American Indian Religious Freedom Act, 183
American Indians, 25, 27–28, 144, 153–188, 362, 455, 490
American Jewish Committee, 411, 417–418
American Jewish Congress, 411
Americans of Japanese Ancestry (AJAs), 339, 351
amhaaretz, 418
Amish, 144
amnesty, 112–113
Andrews, George Reid, 463
androgyny, 431, 457
Angier, Natalie, 182
Anglo, 255–256
Anglo-Irish Accord, 473
annexation, 22, 276
Annin, Peter, 177
Anthony, Susan B., 434
Anti-Defamation League (ADL), 405–407
anti-Semitism, 395, 400–409, 423–424

apartheid, 484–485, 491
apikoros, 418
Aponte, Robert, 293
Arab Americans, 59–61
Arafat, Yasser, 480–481
Aran, Kenneth, 304
Arden, Harvey, 414
Arguelles, Dennis, 333
Arias, Anna Maria, 34
Aronson, Geoffrey, 480
Asante, Molefi Kete, 32–33, 217
Ashe, Arthur R., Jr., 217
Asian American Journalists Association, 348–349
Asian Americans, 5, 34, 59, 323–393
Asian Americans for Fair Employment, 369
Asian Indians, 324, 342
Asian Law Collective, 349
Asians, 13
Asian Women United, 349
Aspira, 319
Aspy, David N., 257
assimilation, 4, 30–31, 36, 126, 139, 160, 270–271, 275, 325, 361, 386–390, 404, 420, 489
Associated Free State, 304
asylum, 117
attitude change, 53, 55
authoritarian personality, 47–48, 49, 67
AWM (angry white men), 457
Ayaniun, John Z., 244
Ayres, Ian, 79

Bach, Jennifer B., 334
Bach, Robert L., 334
Bachman, Ronet, 186
Bacon, John, 144
Bagley, Christopher, 62
Bahr, Howard M., 168
Baker, Bob, 235
Baldwin, James, 409
Bales, Robert F., 432
Ball, Harry V., 339

575